Angels
in the
Darkness

To Debra,
I hope you enjoy!
Kim Poppey Pola

Angels
in the
Darkness

A Family's Triumph over Hitler and
World War II Berlin: 1935–1949

Lisa Farringer Parker

Angels in the Darkness: A Family's Triumph over Hitler and World War II Berlin: 1935–1949

Published by
Success Publishing
Scottsdale, Arizona

ISBN: 978-0-615-52781-9
LCCN: 2010924412

For my mother, Jutta Bolle,
and my grandparents, Heti and Johannes Bolle

Contents

Acknowledgements

Thank you to my mother for the countless conversations and recorded interviews. I thank my mother and Fritz for tirelessly chauffeuring me around Berlin, showing me the sites and neighborhoods of their story. I am deeply grateful to my dear friend and former writing professor, Beth Luey, for her countless hours of advice, editing, and support. Thank you for your positive reaction to the manuscript and your constant encouragement. I thank my friend and fellow writer Len Sherman, for believing in me and pushing for publication. I thank my husband for his steady support and for insisting I publish this book. Finally, I thank my son for his adamance that the summary be catchy.

Preface

The Germany into which I was born in 1929 was a far cry from the Germany I would leave twenty years later in 1949. If my parents had known of the horrors that were to embrace Germany beginning just four short years after my birth, they might have rethought my conception. But in 1929 my parents knew nothing of the darkness that would wash over Hitler's Germany. Germany in 1929, for those who had the money, was a marvelous place to live. A place filled with intellectuals and artists, the finest symphony in the world, and fabulous art museums and every other type of conceivable museum—they lined the waters of Museum Island like grand old ladies, hoarding treasures from ancient Egypt and Troy and Rome. Berlin boasted two opera houses, as well as theaters that performed deep into the night. In 1929, Berlin was the center of Europe's film industry, offering numerous studios and attracting artists like Alfred Hitchcock, Billy Wilder, and Marlene Dietrich. And, in 1929, Berlin was the cultural and fashion epicenter of the world.

The Nazi takeover in 1933 changed everything. Almost overnight, my father would later say, it was as if a dark mantle fell over Germany, blocking even the most delicate ray of light. Initially, Hitler concentrated on his political power, which he secured with alacrity in 1933 when he banned any political party other than the Nazi Party and silenced the press. By 1935, artists had been banned, musicians silenced, films edited, and books and newspapers censored. The colors had already darkened, though it would take Kristallnacht and the outbreak of the war to blacken them. I would learn of these things only indirectly. My parents tried their best to protect me from the darker aspects of Nazi Germany. Only my curious nature and insistence on explanations led to a more direct knowledge of these events.

I really don't remember anything from before the age of six. What follows are my recollections from six on. Much of the time I have not recorded my thoughts with distinct dates and ages because, in most cases, I do not know these with any specificity. The great dividing line for me, as for most Germans, is the beginning of the war, by which I mean the actual day German troops marched into Poland. I do recall with a clarity beyond my years those events that occurred just before my tenth birthday—from September 1939 on.

Introduction

The House

I grew up in Dahlem, surrounded by the Grunewald Forest and a park filled with willow trees and a small lake. Dahlem, lush and green, wedged between Potsdam and Berlin, attracted my father because of its proximity to the Grunewald Forest with its lovely lake, the Grunewaldsee, and to the lakes and forests of nearby Wannsee and Potsdam. I spent many hours riding my bicycle and walking with my friends and family in the Grunewald Forest. Not the least of the Grunewald Forest's treasures was Forsthaus-Paulsborn, a quaint combination of stables, restaurant, and inn next to the ancient Kurfürst Joachim's hunting lodge. My mother kept her horse, Tasha, at Forsthaus-Paulsborn and rode in the forests with great regularity, stopping afterwards for lunch or cake at the beautiful restaurant with its garden terrace full of roses in the summer.

In 1935 Dahlem had an untouched freshness to it that the other wealthy suburbs lacked. The village still held on to its medieval look, having once been primarily farmland, in the center of which stood a medieval village that grew up around the manor house and the church, St. Annen Kirche. The manor house and church remained surrounded by the tiny village, and it was the quaintness of this setting that inspired my father, even though by 1935 the farmlands of Dahlem were dotted with sumptuous homes designed by the best architects of the time. To design our home, my father hired the most famous of these, Egon Eiermann, a prominent member of the Bauhaus movement. I was very impressed that such a famous architect designed our house, and later, when Hitler banned the Bauhaus movement, I was even more impressed!

Our house, number twelve Föhrenweg, directly faced the Grunewald Forest, unobstructed by the homes that would later be built across the street. Only the lovely wide lanes of the Kronprinzenallee that ran all the way out to Potsdam separated us from the Grunewald Forest. Built in two stories, our house had two bathrooms and four bedrooms upstairs, each bedroom with its own built-in closets—unheard of at the time, Mutti would say proudly—and cubbies built into the walls for the beds. I felt so protected in my bed surrounded by walls; it was like my own miniature, elegant cave. My room was directly above the kitchen, with a long, double-doored picture window that ran from the floor to ceiling. It let in huge splashes of light and overlooked the front garden and the street beyond. My parents' room also had built-in beds with closets on each side, one for Vati by the bathroom, and one for Mutti by the garden side of the room. A sitting area next to tall French doors opened onto a balcony and offered a view of the back garden. From the other side of the room, you could stand at the enormous picture window and look out to the side garden, where in the summertime we kept goldfish in a rectangular pond with a fountain of water that spilled out of the wall from a copper pipe onto lily pads with pink and white flowers. A combination of pines, spruce, fir, and kiefer trees lined the back fence and blocked our views of the houses behind us. From the landing that separated the other bedrooms from my parents' room, a staircase with a looping iron design and a wood-topped railing descended sharply and dramatically to the living room.

The downstairs masterfully combined the living room, dining room, and music room into one flowing space. A fireplace, open on three sides and made of brown brick, separated the rooms, and the living room ceiling opened two stories high and slanted to the roof line, creating a dramatic mood. Windows lined the entire wall of one side of the living room and opened onto the side garden, where in the spring and summer, rhododendrons and peonies resided under the protection of a row of fir trees. Flagstone floors ran throughout the downstairs and the job of keeping them clean and polished was a big one—left to Luise, my mother's housekeeper.

The music room stands out in my memory because I was not allowed in there very often. It was a warm room with walls that held tiny little pebbles shoved into the stucco, giving the wall an interesting texture, enhanced by my mother's having it painted a cream color. The furniture was big and comfortable and floral, and many small tables held books and flowers and interesting bowls of glass or wood. An enormous window, stretching almost to the floor, looked out to the back garden and let the sun in on those few days when we had some. It was my parents' sanctuary. This was where they went for wine after dinner or to listen to music and talk late into the evening.

A long row of modern-looking wooden shelves, covered with a shiny beige paint with maroon trim, held glasses and records and a phonograph and radio, and they ran the full length of the wall that backed onto the living room; only the space for the back side of the fireplace was left open. My mother's baby grand piano, a Bechstein, dominated the opposite side of the room next to the window. Off the music room was my mother's private room for reading or talking quietly to friends, and next to it my father's library and study housed his enormous collection of books.

The kitchen was at the front of the house, with the dining room sandwiched between it and the living room. Mutti insisted the window in the kitchen be large and face out to the front garden so she could watch me play with my friends and see who was coming and going. The bathroom, next to the kitchen by the back stairs that curved down to the basement and also up to my room, served me well, especially after school. But my favorite room of all was the garden room next to the front entrance. It brought a touch of summer to the long, drab Berlin winters by housing my mother's numerous plants, including a lemon tree and exotic herbs, as well as begonias, orchids, and hydrangeas. I would sit out there in one of the lounge chairs from the garden and read, pretending I was on an exotic island off the coast of Africa. My father once bought dozens of African finches in bright shades of green and yellow and put them in cages in the garden room. The tiny birds were too small for the cages and fit through the bars. We slipped and slid on the polished flagstone floors as we dashed about trying to catch the little things before they crashed into windows and doors!

The Neighborhood

Between 1935 and 1938, Dahlem changed. More and more people built homes, and soon houses sprouted up all along our street, blocking the views of the Kronprinzenallee. Many of the new arrivals were *Nazibonzen* (Nazi bigwigs). Some bought their own homes, but some, I learned from whispers between my parents I was not meant to hear, took the homes of wealthy Jewish people. I knew my parents were not pleased when Heinrich Himmler and his daughter Gudrun moved behind a high white wall into an estate on the Vogelsang Way. In fact, they were not pleased that our neighborhood sported a veritable who's who of Nazi Germany, as Vati put it, including Baldur von Schirach, the head of the Hitler Youth Program who lived a few streets over. Even worse, Field Marshal Wilhelm von Keitel, the head of the German Army, lived two houses down in what we called "the Max Schmeling house." Max Schmeling lived in that house until 1938 and then mysteriously fled Berlin with his actress wife, Anni Ondra. The children in the neighborhood were sad to see him leave, for he often played ball with us and his wife was so beautiful. The Keitels were grouchy and boring and old, and we had strict instructions to stay away from their house. Bernhard Rust, the Reich Minister of Education, also lived in Dahlem, but thankfully not that close to us. His presence meant the public schools in Dahlem were certain to follow all Nazi education guidelines very carefully. And one of the most ostentatious homes belonged to Foreign Minister Joachim von Ribbentrop, whose Dahlem home was the scene of an elaborate party during the Berlin Olympics. Nobody talked about this sudden and strange transition. Instead they spoke of the latest play or book or symphony or opera—anything other than the changes taking place in their neighborhoods.

But I did not understand all of this at the time. In 1935 I was six years old, and I looked at the world through that prism. To me it was just my wonderful, warm home that looked out onto the green finery of the Grunewald Forest. Ours was a house without sin, as it had been built on a vacant piece of property bought by my grandfather many years before. Onkel Kurt, my father's brother, and his wife, Tante Hilde, also built a house in Dahlem, a bit closer to town than ours and on a more developed street. This meant that my cousins Peti and Ingrid, who were close to my age, went to school with me. My cousin Dieter attended the boys' school down the street. What really impressed me about the other Bolles' house was the fact that Leni Riefenstahl lived next door to them. For me, Frau Riefenstahl was glamorous and talented and fascinatingly exotic. Her exploits as an actress and a director of films had already become legendary by 1935. Frankly, she could have been far less than she was and I still would have been impressed, simply by virtue of her connection to the film industry. She was far more interesting to me than the Nazi officials who lived in my neighborhood, and my cousin Peti and I regularly spied on her through the giant rhododendron hedge that marked the property line between the other Bolles' house and Frau Riefenstahl's house.

The Family

Carl Bolle

A rumble on the cobblestones alerted me that a truck had arrived. I peered out the window of my bedroom. The name "Bolle," spelled out on the side of the white truck in the distinctive logo of my great-grandfather, told me it was the milk truck. A man emerged; he shouted a greeting to a neighbor, Frau Wolleck perhaps, before carrying the heavy glass milk jugs resting in the metal crate up the flagstone walk. They clinked together, a sound so familiar now I had come to expect this ritual every Monday morning. I watched as he set them down by the basement door, the bald spot on his head turned pink from the early fall morning. Luise greeted him. They laughed. I smiled.

I realized from a very young age that ours was an unusual family. Thanks to the entrepreneurial skills and eccentricities of my great-grandfather, Carl Bolle, our name was recognized by everyone in Berlin. Indeed, even if one did not know the history of Carl Bolle, it would have been difficult not to know the Bolle name. It appeared first on the hundreds of milk wagons, and now on the hundreds of milk trucks that traveled virtually every street in Berlin. The name, with the *O* in the center, the *B* as a head, and the *Ls* and *E* as the legs and arms of a little man, smiled at the world, friendly and warm, from the front of the numerous grocery stores that graced key intersections in suburbs and throughout the city.

Carl Bolle was born in Millow, a small farming town in Prussia, the son of a Lutheran pastor. He began his life with very little hope or thought of the grand fortune that was to come his way. His parents both died when he was young, and as the oldest he suddenly found himself responsible for his younger brothers and sisters. Originally a master bricklayer, he would eventually make and lose several fortunes before he settled on the milk business that would be his and our legacy.

In 1889, Carl Bolle came up with the idea of delivering fresh milk from the country to every household in Berlin. He believed children needed fresh, purified milk from the country to grow strong—not the awful, gray-blue colored milk that was sold in Berlin at the time and often went bad shortly after it was bought. Being a bit of a scientist herself, Mutti made sure I knew that he sponsored a woman scientist to figure out the best temperature to purify milk and kill the typhoid bacteria.* Carl Bolle took this very simple concept and created a business empire the likes of which had not been seen in Berlin before or since. Eventually employing over two thousand people, he had the largest dairy in all of Europe and a milk delivery business unheard of anywhere. Bolle wagons traversed the city with "Bolle boys" who stood on the back and rang bells to let the women of Berlin know the milk truck was coming. He made a fortune and created a milk empire, eventually adding the Bolle grocery stores that stood on every corner of Berlin. In the process, through his active philanthropy and his eccentric stunts, he grabbed the hearts and minds of Berliners, to whom he was known as "Bimmel Bolle," or Crazy Bolle. Berlin's newspapers were replete with articles, songs, and cartoons about him, and he was even knighted by the kaiser.

To me he was larger than life! I had seen his portrait in my grandfather's home, with eyes that twinkled and spoke of kindness and humor. His hair, pure white, with a matching beard trimmed to immaculate perfection, reminded me of Saint Nicolas. I wanted to crawl into his lap and give him a hug, and I knew he would hug me back with those large arms and hands. The photo in Vati's study showed a kind old man sitting wrapped up in blankets. His wheelchair, pushed by a manservant, was surrounded by his grandchildren, all riding the new bikes he had just bought for them. My father, the smallest, maybe age five, on a tricycle, rode immediately next to his grandfather, engaging him in conversation as the old man leaned toward him, smiling. A fat dachshund ran along beside the wheelchair, tail wagging. The setting was the long drive on his estate, Marienhain, in Kopenick, just outside Berlin. Fruit trees lined the drive on either side, and lush green fields peeked out between them. I had also seen pictures of his yacht, complete with a captain in uniform, on which he loved to take his grandchildren to cruise the waters of the Dahme River out to the Müggelsee. And I so wished he were still alive to take me on that yacht.

I grew up hearing many Carl Bolle stories, mostly from strangers, sometimes from my mother, but never from my father. It was almost as if Vati was embarrassed by all the attention. But I loved it! Imagine a man so bold he is

---

* He financed the research of Lydia Rabinowitz Kemper, the Jewish protégé of Dr. Koch, to establish the best temperature to pasteurize milk to kill the typhoid bacteria. As early as 1900, long before any laws existed requiring it, Carl Bolle insisted that all of his milk be pasteurized. Beginning in 1889, he sold a special children's milk provided by cows fed a special vitamin-rich diet: green food.

said to have ridden down the Kurfürstendamm in a carriage drawn by six white horses, creating quite a stir as astonished Berliners watched him speed by. He set up milk carts at the Berlin Zoo to serve the thirsty zoo visitors, and is even said to have ridden one of the elephants.

Everybody in Berlin talked about Bimmel Bolle; the moment they heard my last name, the stories would start. Mutti said he appealed to Berliners' egalitarian sensibilities—that he could come from so little, accomplish so much, and yet remain a good, caring citizen of their beloved Berlin. The fact that he was a bit flamboyant and eccentric, uninhibited by the conventions of the time, only added to his appeal.

What impressed Mutti the most (I know because she always spoke of it) is that he provided free doctor and hospital visits, free medicine, and sick pay to his workers. He even built a children's home in the village of his birth, Milow, for the recovery of the children of his employees who suffered from grave illness. He also provided longtime workers with a pension and death benefits to their families. He built housing for his unmarried workers and even built a restaurant on the company grounds that served nutritious meals to the unmarried workers. I thought Vati would at least be impressed that his grandfather built a library that housed over six hundred books and regularly invited world-renowned lecturers to educate any workers interested in philosophy, religion, and geography, but Vati never mentioned it.

A man of deep religious convictions, he not only financed many missions to Africa to bring both Christian religious teachings and literacy to Africans, but he personally invited and financed top students from the mission schools to come to Berlin to further their studies. He welcomed these students into his home, even letting some of them live with him. They discovered a man of deep religious convictions and absolutely no racial preconceptions. Mutti said if ever there was a color-blind man, it was Carl Bolle—this to the consternation of some of his more narrow-minded fellow Berliners.

But the thing I liked best about him was his sense of justice. Mutti said that he believed in giving the young second chances. The standard joke among Berliners when they found out that someone's son had gotten a job with Bolle was: "So when did your son get out [of jail], and what did he do?" She would say this line with her arms crossed in front of her chest in a heavy Berlin dialect that made me laugh. She always emphasized that he believed we are all God's people.

Opa Bolle (Andreas Bolle)

Carl Bolle passed both his entrepreneurial skills and his spirituality on to his son, Andreas Bolle, my grandfather, whom I always called "Opa Bolle." Opa Bolle continued the family fortune by purchasing the well-established Berlin firm of Grieniesen. Grieniesen was in the business of making coffins, leading Berliners to quip, "*Von der Wiege bis zur Bahre, Bolle ist das einzig wahre.*" "From the cradle to the grave, go Bolle all the way." Perhaps Opa Bolle sensed the coming of war, or perhaps he simply decided that it was a good business. At any rate, he took over the firm and developed it into a very large business whose factory covered an entire city block and was several stories high. He had a fleet of trucks for delivering the coffins and his own gas station in the center courtyard of his factory—a factor that would later play a key role during and after the war. He eventually handed the company to his two sons, my father, Johannes Andreas Bolle, and my uncle, Kurt Bolle. My father ran the business and public relations side of the company, and Onkel Kurt ran the manufacturing side. Together they eventually opened twenty-three satellite shops all over Berlin.

This was the legacy into which I was born on November 14, 1929. For my father it was perhaps a burden to be Carl Bolle's grandson and Andreas Bolle's son, but for me the legacy had very little significance. Although I was aware that we were different from other families, I was largely oblivious to my family's significance. It really never occurred to me to wonder why everybody in Berlin knew our last name and knew about my great-grandfather. That our last name was on the local grocery store my mother visited every day in Dahlem for her shopping did not seem in the least bit unusual, just as it never fazed me when the Bolle trucks, with our name splashed across the side, raced by to deliver milk to a neighborhood. That was just the way it was.

Vati (Johannes Bolle)

My father was always slightly embarrassed by this business his father had thrust upon him. An intellectual man who loved philosophy and the arts, he had in fact studied law at the University of Leipzig, but if he had followed his heart, he would have become a director of theater. He took my mother to the opera, the theater, and the symphony, as well as art exhibitions and popular clubs. The Nazi years, with their snuffing out of anything remotely cultured and artistic so that all "art" smacked of the same conventional norms, were very difficult for my father.

A handsome man, and meticulous about his appearance, Vati always wore a jacket with the white of his freshly pressed handkerchief peeking out of his lapel pocket; I often needed those beautifully pressed handkerchiefs. "Casual" for my father was a dress shirt with the sleeves rolled up and his tie loosened. He combed his thick black hair neatly back from his forehead, and the smell of 4711 aftershave followed him everywhere, like sprigs of citrus blossoms in the spring. But the thing I associate most with my father is reading.

My father read everything in sight, as far as I could tell. He had a favorite bookstore downtown, Geselius, where he spent hours browsing. He was a man of broad interests—a philosopher, or so my mother would say. He would sit in his library in the large brown leather chair, draped with Turkish blankets, reading all evening, or in the music room, in the corner chair, with his feet on the inlaid walnut table my mother treasured. On Saturday and Sunday he would do the same. In nice weather, he read out on the terrace. He read a lot about

God. I never understood what all there could be to read about God. Once you learned that he existed, wasn't that the end of the story? My father thought this was absolutely brilliant of me and made me repeat this to my mother and Opa Bolle and anyone else who would listen. I think he thought I was a lot smarter than I really was.

Vati never saw a bookstore that he could pass up. If we passed by a bookstore, I only had to point it out to him and he would take my hand and say, "Now let's not tell Mutti, *ja*, Jutta." I don't really think my mother minded his buying me every children's book ever printed, but by saying this, it made it our own secret.

I spent many hours carefully arranging my books so that I had space in between for my other treasures, like my porcelain figures and silver boxes from Opa Bolle. Opa Bolle gave me lovely boxes with flowers on the top made out of porcelain. "For treasures," he would say. Once, when I had the whooping cough, he brought over a beautiful silver box filled with candy engraved: "To Jutta from Opa Bolle in honor of the whooping cough!" My mother was not sure that the inscription was appropriate, but she laughed anyway.

Mutti (Heti Muller Bolle)

Mine was a warm and idyllic childhood. If I had any problem in my life, it was that I wanted to be with my mother more. She was a good, kind mother, but like many women of her station, she employed a governess to deal with the mundane aspects of my daily life. On very special occasions, she took me into Berlin for shopping, followed by cake at either Café Möhring or Café Kranzler.

I rarely spent time with my mother in the morning after the day I turned six, because I had to get up for school, and she would still be in bed. My parents often went out during the week, so there were times I did not see her after dinner, either. I did not think anything of this, really, because many of my friends in Dahlem lived the same way. Besides, Luise, our cook and housekeeper, adored me and was like an indulgent aunt, constantly feeding me. Sisi, my governess from 1936 to1943, was nice enough, but because she had to enforce the rules, I did not adore her like I adored Luise. They were a study in contrasts. Luise was chubby and cheerful with bright red cheeks that never faded; Sisi was well educated, tall and thin and pale, her hair always set in an elaborate chignon.

In the summer, Gustav, our gardener and handyman, let me help him pick the fruit from our cherry and plum trees. He was a friendly old man with a twinkle in his eyes and the most enormous hands I have ever seen. A cleaning lady came to the house three days a week to help Luise with the laundry and heavy cleaning. She always had to leave before Vati came home because he said, "I'll be damned if I have to watch what I'm saying in my own house." So only Luise and Sisi lived with us—Sisi had a room next to mine upstairs, and Luise had a room in the basement. Sasha, my beautiful, elegant, long-haired dachshund who ruled the house, and Harold, the turtle given to me by Opa Bolle, which resided in the fishpond during warm weather and the basement during cold, completed our household.

———

My first memories are of my mother playing the piano in the music room. If I was very good and very quiet, I was allowed to sit and listen to her play. After she finished, she would turn around and with outstretched arms say simply, "*Komm, Liebling,*" and I would run to her, snuggling into her arms. She always smelled so wonderful, and her hair would fall in my face. We would walk hand-in-hand to the garden, and Luise would bring us a *himbeeresaft* or *apfelsaft.* I cherished these moments with my mother. When she played, she sat perfectly straight, the beautiful instrument stretched out before her,glistening in the light. She played from memory, her eyes closed, her body outlined against the garden that peeked through the window behind her. The light reflected all around her, forming a halo where strands of her fine golden hair stood up. She played beautifully; my father always said she could have been a concert pianist. When she played Chopin, I knew she was in a cheerful mood, her fingers flitting rapidly across the keys, punctuating the air with his lighthearted melodies. Mozart also meant a bright mood; Beethoven, a more serious, contemplative mood. She played Mendelssohn's "Lieder Ohne Worte" when I couldn't sleep at night, the music drifting up to my room, soothing and caressing me. And she insisted that one day she would perfect Bach's Goldberg variations. She loved Mozart the most, though, and she never stopped reminding me that Mozart was German and Hitler was Austrian.

———

Every morning, Luise arrived punctually at eight by my mother's bedside with a soft-boiled egg and toast on a tray that she placed carefully on the bed next to my mother. After she ate, Mutti began her morning with her bath and then two phone calls, one to Vati at the office and the other to Tante Hilde. The second always took much longer than the first, and she would often talk to Tante Hilde for a good thirty minutes. After her phone calls, she rode her horse, Tasha, almost every day, usually around midmorning at Forsthaus-Paulsborn in the Grunewald Forest. Nestled between the forest and the Grunewaldsee, Forsthaus-Paulsborn had a wonderful garden in the front where they served lunch and afternoon cake in the spring and summer. In the winter, the restaurant served lunch and dinner indoors on elegant, dark wood tables with white linen tablecloths, surrounded by moss green walls that held enormous elk and deer heads, their huge, dark eyes reflecting the light from chandeliers that once held hundreds of candles.

Mutti always wore an elegant riding habit with soft calfskin boots that came up to her knees. She had the boots made in Italy on one of my parents' holiday trips to Florence. A chocolate brown, velvet riding jacket that fit her perfectly and a matching velvet riding hat completed her outfit. I thought she looked amazing in this attire, and I regretted, after I started school, only seeing her in it on weekends. On the weekends she rode with my father, but during the week she rode with different friends. Some kept horses at Forsthaus-Paulsborn, and others would simply ride my father's horse. Sometimes she rode with one of the Hohenzolleren princes, giving her legendary status among my friends.

On weekends during the summer, I was allowed to join them for lunch. Sisi would take me swimming in the Grunewaldsee in my wool Jantzen bathing suit while my parents rode their horses. Oh, how I hated the way that swimsuit smelled when it got wet! I would swim out into the dark waters of the lake, Sisi calling from behind not to go any farther. After my swim, sheltered behind a tree, Sisi would brush the bits of grass and leaves off me with a towel; then, spreading the towel on the ground, she would fuss at me to stay on the towel until she got my shoes on. She did her best to change me into my dress so I could join my parents for lunch. My hair, wet but combed, always took on the smell of the lake.

———

My mother wore beautiful printed dresses of silk and chiffon, the latest styles from Paris. They were all hand-sewn by Frau Schultz, who had a shop in Berlin off the Kurfürstendamm. Sometimes Mutti wore tight-fitting knits that clung to her body, also the element of fashion. She joked to Frau Schultz that she had to ride Tasha twice as long or walk twice as far before she could wear them. My favorite dress was made of black lace overlaid on tulle, with a low-cut neck and a tight-fitting bodice that overlapped and was held at her waist by hooks. She always wore the thick gold chain Vati had bought her with that dress. I thought she was more elegant than any model in my magazines.

The latest fashion magazines from Paris were flung across tables and Frau Schultz's desk, and she and my mother studied them at great length to select dress and suit styles for every occasion. Frau Schultz had a huge drawing tablet on which she could sketch a dress in a matter of seconds; she was an artist as well as a very skilled seamstress, Mutti said. Sometimes, Mutti let me come with her. I loved the fabrics that lined the walls from floor to ceiling wrapped around long bolts: silks and chiffons and georgette, and, in the winter, wool and cashmere—the colors bright and bold, reminding me of pencils lined up in a pencil box. I ran my hand along the fabrics, feeling their textures and folds. To complement her dresses, Mutti selected purses from Gold Pfeil and shoes from Bally. Sometimes she went with Tante Hilde to Horn. Tante Hilde loved Horn, on the Kurfürstendamm and Uhlandstrasse, with its distinctive cursive script in gold above the entrance. Whenever Tante Hilde sported a new purse, Mutti joked, "You must have been mad at Kurt again," because Onkel Kurt always bought Tante Hilde a new purse from Horn to make up for a disagreement.

I thought my mother was the loveliest woman in Berlin, and I know Vati thought the same. She always looked impeccable, but she wasn't consumed by fashion. She thought it was important to look your best, but she also read the paper, read books, and could quote passages from Shakespeare as if she had just read them. And in the afternoons she always played the piano, the music drifting out to me as I did my homework with Sisi.

The Early Years: 1935–1939

1

A Child with Imagination

My story begins in 1936, when we moved into our home in Dahlem. By 1936, Hitler had already been in power for three years. So from the time I was cognizant, I had no understanding of anything different. As far as I knew, in 1936, we led the perfect life. My early childhood was full of fun-filled holiday trips to Berchtesgaden and the North Sea and lovely parties. I was not aware of the dark undercurrents that were a part of my world and that my parents lived with daily.

This idyllic life changed abruptly when I turned six and had to begin school. I could hardly wait to get my *Schultüte*, but otherwise, I was not excited about the idea that I had to leave my comfortable home every day for the gray, bleak atmosphere of the Dahlem *Volksschule*. We called it the *Lansschule* because it stood on Lansstrasse between Taku and Iltiss. Mutti refused to call it by its Nazi-sanctioned name. Whatever name we attached to it, I knew all that awaited me were hard benches and stern teachers. The ugly gray stucco walls depressed me, and I hated the idea that I would spend half my day inside those walls. Mutti was furious because she had signed me up to attend the private girls' school in our area, but suddenly, and without warning, Hitler banned all private education, and I was forced to attend the public school.

Opa Bolle and Tante Ebi had come over the night before, for the "last supper" as Vati put it. Officially, Tante Ebi was Opa Bolle's housekeeper. Oma Bolle had died when my father was only eight years old, and at some point Tante Ebi had become Opa Bolle's constant companion. I loved her, with her straight, elegant nose and her brown hair swept up high above her forehead. She was tall and thin and had a dark complexion. She was a good fifteen years younger than Opa Bolle, but she always said he was harder to keep up with than any twenty-year-old.

Opa brought an enormous box of chocolates for me; a different color marzipan flower decorated the top of each chocolate, which Mutti immediately confiscated to be "doled out appropriately." She let me have two, only because Opa insisted that I have a little something sweet to see me through the night.

The morning of the first day of school, I clattered noisily down the stairs. As I came around the corner, I spotted my *Schultüte* leaning against the front door.

Luise anticipating my arrival shooed me into the kitchen, "No! No! Mutti wants you to eat breakfast first!" she commanded taking my hand and leading me to the kitchen table where she presented me with a soft-boiled egg and *Brötchen*. Mutti came in just as I finished eating and sat next to me at the small table in front of the kitchen window, placing my *Schultüte* before me, and together, we explored its wonders.

Packed with oil crayons and bright colored pencils, the beautiful colors stacked together in the box looked like a rainbow. I screamed with delight as I pulled out a pencil sharpener in the shape of a bright red mushroom with a little frog sitting on top. I thought it was the prettiest thing I had ever seen! I had admired it when we had gone to Duhr to shop for art supplies in the Nicoli Platz. My mother had told me it was not practical—the little frog will break off, she said—and I thought that was the end of it. But now, here it was staring back at me in my *Schultüte*! I placed it gently next to my pencils and grinned up at my mother. "I can't believe you bought it, Mutti!"

"Well, you said you liked it, but my goodness, I had a time distracting you from it—I tried to show you the colored paper and the pastel paints—but no, you would not leave that sharpener alone!"

I laughed, remembering.

"Finally," continued Mutti, hugging me as she spoke, "I had the saleslady set it aside and asked Vati to pick it up the next day!"

I dug further into the *Tüte* and found a beautiful pad of paper with little angels all over the front. The paper was a pale pink. This could never be desecrated with my poor scribbles, I thought. I looked further, and there at the bottom were chocolates, very special ones, covered in pink, purple, and red foil paper in the shapes of flowers: pansies, roses, and tulips. I had never seen anything so beautiful. I knew Erica, my best friend and neighbor across the street, would beg me for one, but I would let no one destroy these beautifully shaped flowers. Ripping off the delicate foil, only to discard it and consume the pressed and creased chocolate flower inside, never again to see the beauty of the colors and the shape of the intricate petals—I could never participate in such an act of violence directed against beauty.

Sisi came to the door. "It is time for us to leave, Frau Bolle."

"Oh dear!" Mutti looked up at the blue clock above the stove. "We've lost track of the time, *mein Herz!*"

I threw my arms around her and hugged her, thanking her for the wonderful *Schultüte*.

I stood up. Luise grabbed me, hugging me to her, her arms sweaty and warm from the heat of cooking. With her face so close, I saw that her eyes swam in tears. She turned quickly back to the stove, wiping her face on her apron.

Mutti said, "Well, Miss School Girl, we had better go!"

Sisi waited patiently at the door as I skipped past her to grab my brand-new red and blue book bag from Opa Bolle. Mutti walked us to the gate. Hugging me, she squatted down so that our eyes were on the same level. She sighed. "Listen: you have a wonderful day, and pay attention to the teacher."

I nodded. "Mutti, I don't want to go to school. Why can't I stay here and have Sisi teach me?"

Sisi smiled.

"Listen, Jutta. Life is full of changes, and this is one of many we must adjust to." She looked out to the garden and pointed to a tall stand of grass bending in the wind. "See? Change is constant, and we must bend and adjust and never stand rigid, or it will snap us in two!"

"But I don't want to change."

"Sure you do. Just like you used to not be able to walk, and now you can. That is change, right?"

I nodded, not sure what this had to do with going to school.

"Well, you can't read and write or do numbers, so now it is time to go to school and learn all these things."

I shrugged.

She stood up, kissed me on top of my head and said, "You will see. It is for the best, and soon it will seem like you have always gone to school."

Sisi nudged me forward, and I reluctantly left our garden to head out into the street. I looked back. My mother waved, and behind her Luise stood at the kitchen window, still wiping her eyes.

Sitting on the streetcar, secure between Erica and Sisi, I regained my confidence. After today, Erica and I would have to walk to school: through the park, then along the tiny neighborhood streets, and down Königin Luise Strasse. But today, my first day, Sisi came with me on the streetcar.

"I could do this every day!" Erica said, licking the chocolate off her fingers.

"Do you think we get more candy tomorrow?"

"No. Our parents would lose all their money if they gave us this much each school day, and we would get as fat as Luise." We both giggled.

Sisi shook her head to hush us up.

We both held our hands to our mouths to smother our giggles, but it made things worse. Turning red, a giggle escaped as I tried to speak. When I regained my composure I said, "Well, I bet we get something, but maybe not this much. They have to give us something since they are sending us away from home, don't you think?"

"Yes, I suppose you're right. We'll just have to wait and see. Maybe it's a surprise every day, like opening the Advent calendar," Erica said hopefully.

We soon learned there were no more treats and that school was a very serious business. We had to sit up straight at our wooden desks with their hard backs, and worst of all, we could not talk until recess. It was awful, because I had so much to tell Erica! I was terrified of Frau Eberhadt, my first grade teacher. She was very strict. I guess they thought they would break us in with the strictest teacher in the whole school. We even had to wait until recess to go to the bathroom! This presented a real problem for me, because Luise's hot cocoa usually ran through me by about the time I got to school. If the line was too long or I forgot to go, I sometimes had to cross my legs very tight and hope I did not giggle or laugh until recess.

Frau Eberhadt was very pale, with a huge nose that reminded me of our ski slope in the park, and she had an enormous bun of brownish blond hair perched right on the center of her head. I found myself staring at it, thinking what a lovely nest it would make for *Vögelein*, the red robin that lived in the spruce tree outside my bedroom window. Every morning and night I opened the French doors in my bedroom, leaned out against the tiny iron balcony, and spoke to *Vögelein*, leaving her bread crumbs or dessert crumbs if I had them. Why should *Vögelein* struggle so to find grass and paper to make a nest, when they could so easily snuggle into Frau Eberhadt's hair? I pictured *Vögelein* with her eggs on top of Frau's head, safe from that awful Max, the cat next door. Just as I was imagining the father robin coming to the nest with a worm, I realized that the entire class was staring at me in silence.

"Fräulein Bolle, have you suddenly lost your hearing, or are you always in the habit of not answering when adults speak to you?"

"I am very sorry, Frau Eberhadt," I said as the other girls giggled.

"I asked you to tell me what we call the smallest form of rock?"

I stared at her, terrified. I had no idea

"It is found at the bottom of a river or a stream," she continued. "We have been talking about it all week."

I remember it reminded me of my mother's face powder that came in big round boxes, but I could not think of the name, so I mumbled, "Face powder." Hearing the giggles from my friends, I added for effect, "I think Chanel makes it." For that comment, Frau Eberhadt sent me to the time-out corner with tape over my mouth and placed a horrid black pointed hat that looked like a witch's hat on my head for the rest of the class. I had to write "silt" on the board fifty times while the other children were at recess. But worst of all, Frau Eberhadt put a note in my backpack; she said I had to return it to her the next day with my mother's signature. As we walked home through the park, I plotted with Erica how I could lose the note.

"I could let it blow away in the wind and land at the bottom of the lake."

"Or you could just put it under your bed or in your underwear drawer," suggested Erica helpfully.

"No, because Sisi always takes my book bag first thing and looks to see what I have for homework. I'll never get past her! She stands at the front door waiting for me."

"Besides," said Erica, "what are you going to tell Frau Eberhadt when you don't return with the note?"

"Maybe she won't remember," I said hopefully.

"Don't be daft! Teachers never forget things like that; they have memories like elephants!"

In the end I decided to take my chances with my mother rather than face the awful prospect of explaining to Frau Eberhadt what happened to my note. So I arrived at Erica's house and spent a good five minutes chatting with her about anything I could think of until her mother called out from the front door, " Erica, come in. Go on, Jutta. Sisi will wonder what happened to you."

I saw Sisi standing on the front step waiting for me. She waved, but I pretended I did not see her. I took my time walking the short distance across the street, popping as many white berries as I could and kicking stones as I *bummeled* along to my gate. I opened the gate and saw Sisi's hand had gone from waving to me to resting on her hip. I carefully latched the iron gate in place and bent to pick up a bright orange leaf that had drifted down from one of the acacia trees—the beginnings of fall. I balanced it on my nose and walked in a circle several times with my nose sticking up in the air.

"*Jutta! Komm doch—hör auf mit diesem bummeln. Ich hab nicht den ganzen Tag*," called Sisi.

I could not think of anything else to do to delay my arrival, so I slowly walked up the garden path, hopping on one foot from one flagstone paver to the next, making sure I did not land on the lovely green moss between each one. By this time, Sisi's expression had turned to one of mild irritation, but I knew a kiss and a smile from me would soften her. When I reached the front steps, I ran up quickly and flashed one of my sweetest smiles at her while giving her a big peck on the cheek. I ran past her as fast as I could and headed for the stairs to my room.

"Jutta! Wait! Come here and give me your book bag. What is the matter with you, child? You are positively crazy today!"

I tossed her the book bag and ran up the stairs, announcing loudly, "*Ich muss aufs clo!*" And that was no lie! I hadn't been to the bathroom since I left the house.

She shook her head and said, "Don't forget to wash your hands before you come to the dining room."

After a few minutes I resigned myself; I could no longer put off the inevitable, and I came back down the stairs. I heard my mother and Sisi talking in the dining room. I took a deep breath and walked in. They both stopped talking and looked at me. Sisi excused herself to see if Luise had lunch ready. My mother studied me for a few seconds; I studied the tablecloth. It seemed like an eternity.

"Come. Sit here by me, Jutta," she said finally. "I read here that you have been disrespectful to your teacher?" She unfolded the note as she spoke.

I looked down in my lap, where I had folded my hands and was twiddling my thumbs.

"She writes that 'such disrespect for authority will not be tolerated and is troublesome in one so young.' What did you say to her, Jutta?"

"Mutti, I couldn't help it. I didn't hear her asking me questions because ..."

"Yes? Because why? Can you not hear? Do we need to take you to see the doctor?"

"No, no." And then I told her about Frau Eberhardt's hair and how it looked like a bird's nest and how I pictured *Vögelein* and her family on top of her head.

Mutti laughed. "You're right, Jutta. I couldn't put my finger on what her hair looks like, but you're right. It would be perfect for *Vögelein*." Sisi came out of the kitchen frowning—she obviously thought my mother was not taking this matter seriously enough. I told Mutti the question the teacher had asked and how, when the class laughed at my answer, I had added the Chanel bit. My mother tried to look serious, but I could tell she also found this amusing. "What should you have done when you got the wrong answer and the other children laughed?"

"Said I didn't know?" I asked meekly.

"Yes." She took my hand in hers and added, looking at me without a smile now, "Jutta, don't go along with what the crowd wants you to do. Who got in trouble today? Did they?"

I shook my head.

"No. Only you did. So for that moment of glory, when they all gave you attention for being clever and funny, what happened? You got in trouble and had to miss recess. Next time, what will you do?"

"Say I'm sorry, but I don't know the answer."

"*Ja,*" said my mother. She let go of my hand and grabbed the pen that lay on the table. "*Ja,* I will sign this and we will speak no more of it. But I do not want to get any more notes like this from Frau Eberhadt, Jutta. Do you understand?"

"Yes, Mutti. But she is so mean! And her nose is big."

"Jutta! She can't help her nose, and you just have to adjust to her." She looked to the heavens. "And it is only the first month of school, child!"

"I'll try," I reached over to hug her.

She stroked my hair. "I would rather have a child with an imagination than one that knows all the answers." I smiled, my face hidden in Mutti's sleeve.

Erica couldn't believe it when I told her I did not get in trouble. She said she would have been sent to her room without dinner for such an offense.

Music and Life

The drab gray days of Berlin's winter depressed me, and we had a lot of those days. I loved it when it poured rain or when the sun shone brightly. But when the heavens could not make up their minds and only dingy gray drizzle came down, as so often happened in Berlin, I hated it.

My mother knew about this propensity of mine, and from the time I was very small she would find special activities for me on such days. One of my favorites was when she allowed me to dance to music in the music room. We would waltz to Johann Strauss's "Blue Danube" or the "Happy Life Waltz," or I would play by her side while she practiced some fast-paced Mozart melody or one of Chopin's cheerful polkas—music to bring the spirits up, she would say. Occasionally, she would let me pick an album from Vati's cabinet filled with record albums. He had swing and jazz and all the other popular music. He loved the classics as well, but he lived for jazz! My mother, on the other hand, only tolerated jazz. In fact, I heard when she was pregnant with me, the sound of a jazz saxophone drove her mad! My father, of course, specialized in playing every jazz saxophone piece in his library just to tease her. She would come tearing out of whatever room she had been in, rush to the gramophone, and yank the record off. This always delighted my father, who would profess that he had not realized the sound bothered her so much. He would then complacently put a piece of classical music on the phonograph, until the next time, when he would pick a new record and the process would repeat itself until he worked his way through his entire library. Well, you had to know my father. He was not malicious, just playful. He said he was just trying to give her some much-needed exercise.

I, like my father, loved jazz and swing. To my mother's dismay, I preferred jazz and swing over any other type of music. I tried, rather unsuccessfully, to convince my mother that one could hear strong elements of a Strauss waltz in certain jazz pieces like "I'm in the Mood for Love," or that Duke Ellington's "Creole Rhapsody" had Stravinsky-like qualities, an idea I parroted from my father. As I grew older, I noticed her enthusiasm for jazz grew concomitant to the Nazi enforcement of their bans against it. By the time they banned even the word "jazz" in 1943, she had become an ardent admirer—especially if the musicians and composers were either black or Jewish. This was a wonderful development for me, because suddenly Louis Armstrong, Duke Ellington, and Benny Goodman regularly graced the airwaves of our home. Their sound was no longer confined to special occasions or my moody days.

Cab Calloway, Paul Whiteman, Ella Fitzgerald, Benny Goodman, Artie Shaw, Louis Armstrong, and Duke Ellington all found refuge in my father's cabinet. But without a doubt, it was Ellington and Armstrong who stood alone as my father's favorites and also mine. I knew every song on those albums by heart. It would delight him to see me puff up my cheeks and in a gravely voice sing "I'm in the Mood for Love" or "Solitude." He especially liked my rendition of the line, "Mama, I'm afraid." He would roar with laughter to see his little redheaded, freckle-faced German daughter with her upper-crust German accent pretending to be Louis Armstrong. So, of course, I did it as often as possible in front of Mutti or Tante Hilde. He never let me down; he always rewarded me for my efforts with that laugh.

My parents both liked gypsy music, as well as what was called gypsy jazz, delighting in the work of the gypsy jazz guitarist Django Reinhardt. Both styles of music were equally hard to find in Germany in 1937, as both gypsies and jazz were unwelcome. So instead, Mutti and Vati traveled to Budapest for long weekends to eat goulash and hear gypsy jazz in one of the many stylish clubs in Budapest. Budapest in the 1930s was an exciting city filled with restaurants and music, and a direct train line ran from Berlin, so it was relatively easy to get to. They would go with Tante Hilde and Onkel Kurt, or with our next-door neighbors, Werner and Greta Kittel. Herr Kittel owned a wholesale bakery supply company. It was Herr Kittel who in 1939 would provide the lard to Mutti so she could make hundreds of bars of soap that she scented with rose oil. When soap became scarce, we and the other Bolles were still able to wash clothes and bathe, thanks to Mutti and Herr Kittel. He loved to travel, and his wife, a beautiful but lonely lady, happily went anywhere he would take her.

Mutti especially loved to go on these mini vacations. She had a special fascination with gypsies ever since her days as a pharmacist in Halberstadt. She loved the rich, spicy flavors of their food and found their music moving—she even tolerated their version of jazz. She thought they were exquisitely beautiful, "as if chiseled from bronze," their black eyes, dark hair, and dark skin a welcome relief from the homogeneity of the blond-haired, blue-eyed nation Hitler wanted to create.

The gypsy practice of palm reading fascinated her too, and she occasionally thrilled me and my friends by trying it on us. She would tell us how many children we were going to have—three in my case, and two in Erica's—and whether we had strong life lines. She had had her palm read by an old gypsy woman who came into the pharmacy in Halberstadt for medicine for her granddaughter. She had no money; instead, my mother accepted her offer of a palm reading as payment. The old lady surprised my mother by agilely hoisting herself up on the countertop, where she professed to have the best lighting for reading my mother's palm. The woman had to be at least seventy years old, but she moved like a twenty-year-old, my mother would say with admiration each time she told the story. The gypsy told her that she would soon marry a very wealthy man and live near a beautiful forest by many lakes. About six months later, my mother married my father and moved to Berlin. Eventually they bought our house in Dahlem that faced the Grunewald Forest—a forest filled with many small lakes. She also told my mother that while her life would start out easy and carefree, in the middle of her life she would face enormous hardships, hardships that were out of her control. She said it would take all my mother's courage and strength to pull through these hardships. This tiny old woman made an impression on my mother, but to Nazi Germany, gypsies were an unwelcome element.

I did not know at the time that we were listening to contraband. Indeed, I never thought about it; in my parent's house, it was just the music we listened to the same way we listened to Beethoven, Strauss, Chopin, or Mozart. I could not understand why they did not play this wonderful music on the German radio. The BBC played it all the time. They had a special jazz hour that my father and I loved. The German radio professed to be playing jazz, but it was very mediocre, boring band music called "*Neue Deutsche Tanzmusik.*" Even I, with my untrained ear, could tell that the German music was no match for the intricate sounds coming out of America. When I asked my father why the German station did not play real jazz, he would simply say, "Because they are ignorant." The truth is, Hitler had banned what he termed degenerate "Negro-Jewish" music from German radio. Vati said, "Beware of laws meant to protect the public. They are tools to control the public—especially those who are powerless, who are different, or who express their individualism." My father was full of such sayings, and the words stuck with me, even though at the time the content went over my head. Later in life they would pop up and haunt me.

———

When my parents traveled, I moved into the domain of Opa Bolle and Tante Ebi over in Lichterfelder, in Opa Bolle's enormous house on the corner of Weddigenweg and Paulinen Strasse. The house actually faced Weddigenweg, but the huge garden took up the entire block all the way to the corner of Paulinen Strasse. The garden was a child's paradise with its many different paths, each with a boxwood hedge along it, and at the end of each stood a surprise—a fountain, or a small gazebo. It was a wonderful place to explore. Opa Bolle had every type of fruit tree imaginable: cherry, plum, apple, and peach, as well as berries and a huge vegetable garden. Wilhelm, the gardener, indulged me, letting me pick whatever I wanted, so long as I ate it then and there. That was the only rule, unless Tante Ebi wanted something picked for the day's meals, then I would help her select the biggest and ripest.

I loved staying at Opa Bolle's. He spoiled me completely, and he had more help than my parents, and they always made a huge fuss over me. I think they were just glad to have a young person in the house. My room looked out over the back garden, next door to Opa Bolle's room. It was a gigantic room with two huge French doors that opened onto a balcony above the garden. I was allowed to take my breakfast on the terrace if the weather was nice.

Opa Bolle had almost no rules in his house—at least not as far as I was concerned. I could eat what I wanted, do what I wanted, and go to bed when I wanted. Tante Ebi tried to impose some sense of order when he was not watching, and as a result I usually did go to bed at a reasonable hour. Opa Bolle did expect me to be polite to adults and especially to the servants. Requests had to be accompanied by the appropriate tone, along with please and thank you. Occasionally I would forget this rule, and Opa Bolle would immediately say,

"Please ignore that request, unless Fräulein Bolle would care to repeat it with a please and thank you attached."

The only other rule was that all of us, including the help, had to gather around just after dinner to sit in the front room quietly listening to him read passages from the Bible. He sat in his high-backed leather chair, his tawny, thin hands wrapped around his Bible, his little gold-rimmed glasses slipping down his nose. Quickly taking a hand off the Bible, he would shove them back up. I sat at his feet with Tante Ebi to his right. Wilhelm always sat by the door on the hard chair, his hat in hand, twisting it again and again. The rest fell in where they could find space. For the most part, over the years, they had developed their favorite seats. Periodically I peeked up through pressed lashes to watch them, but all eyes were down, heads bent, and hands clasped. He would select new passages every evening—usually two or three, depending on the length—and read them to all of us in his magnificent deep voice. I often thought it was God himself reading those passages. After he read the new passages, he always read the same two: "For God so loved the world that He gave His only begotten Son, that whoever believes in Him should not perish but have everlasting life." (John 3:16) He would clear his throat while he flipped to the next familiar passage and continue: "There is neither Jew nor Greek, there is neither slave nor free, there is neither male nor female: for you are all one in Christ Jesus." (Galatians 3:28) And then he said a short prayer before he led us in the Lord's Prayer. The entire ritual took no more than twenty minutes, and I always enjoyed it because there was such a warm, sweet spirit in that room after he had finished.

Then all the help would say good night and retire upstairs to the top floor for bed. Only Opa Bolle, Tante Ebi, and I would remain. Opa Bolle would then ask, "What shall it be for tonight? Are we reading? Or playing checkers? What do you think?" We would take turns picking I always wanted Opa Bolle to read, for I loved his melodious voice, but Tante Ebi loved to play games, so one night we would play a game and the next we would listen to Opa read. No matter what we did, Tante Ebi always brought in warm chocolate milk and freshly baked cookies before we started. Eventually Opa Bolle would announce that he was tired. Rising, he would kiss me good night and tell me I could stay up as long as I liked with Tante Ebi. She waited for him to settle in upstairs, and then she ushered me up that grand staircase to my room. I suspect they had a routine going, those two. She made sure I bathed, washed my face and hands, and brushed my teeth before she tucked me into bed with a kiss on the forehead. Tante Ebi's room was across the landing from my room and from Opa Bolle's. I could hear her footsteps retreating across the landing to her room and then the soft click of the door closing behind her. I never wondered why Tante Ebi lived on the same floor as us, rather than up on the top floor of the house with the others. It had always been like that.

Berlin Olympics

My first memory of official Berlin was of the 1936 Olympics. I was too young to go, but I heard about the elaborate preparations in school. The Nazis erected enormous statues of athletes in various powerful poses all along the main street to the Olympic Stadium. My mother's aunt, Tante Ite, lived on the Kaiserdamm only a few blocks from the stadium. One Sunday a few weeks before the Olympics were to start, we visited Tante Ite so we could go see the stadium. Tante Ite, her bulk cumbersome as she lumbered up the street, her black dress almost touching the cement of the sidewalk, shook her head in disbelief over the many statues of muscled and naked athletes. They looked large and awkward to me, not at all the way I pictured an athlete.

As we passed through the entrance to the stadium, I glanced up to the top of the columns of gray block that towered above us, squinting because of the sun. The five Olympic rings hung suspended between them on a thin wire. My head swam, dizzy from the height, and I moved quickly out of the way, fearful the wire might snap.

The adults discussed Hitler's remodeling of the stadium and its cost and inconvenience because of all the street closings. Vati said Hitler was determined his stadium would be the largest in the world, and he would spare no expense. Tante Ite almost fell off the sidewalk when Vati told her it could seat over one hundred thousand people!

As we walked back from the stadium, flags fluttered in the wind, their crisp canvas making snapping sounds. They hung from every available place along the main routes to the stadium and anywhere else tourists might wander. It seemed every inch of Berlin had been covered by the red and black of the flags. In between, the Olympic rings peeked through occasionally. My father joked that it was a shame my mother had not invested in red canvas cloth, rather than all that silk she bought from Frau Schultz!

Tante Ite said the Nazis had spruced up the streets and painted buildings all around her apartment. Restaurants and hotels were told to make sure they made a good impression. She said a block captain even came to her apartments and ordered the owners to trim the bushes and paint the windows and doors. It was great, she said—it was the only way to get her landlord to do anything around the place! Hitler wanted the world to see Germany as a grand modern nation populated by educated and sophisticated people. At least that is what my parents said. I had no idea what they were talking about. As far as I was concerned, we were just Germans, some polite like me and Erica, and some obnoxious like Hannelore and Liesel.

Mutti muttered that despite all the clean-up efforts, Hitler would still have to shove a lot of dirt under the carpet. I was not quite sure whether they were talking about Hitler's own house, or whether they were talking about the dirt on German streets. But I thought it was very odd for him to be thinking about housekeeping when he surely must have more important things to do.

———

"Can you believe the hypocrisy, Hans? They don't even have the courage to stand up for their views in front of the rest of the world! They must know that it's wrong! In their hearts, they must know! Don't you think?" Mutti had been shopping all afternoon with Tante Hilde along the Kurfürstendamm. She announced to my father over drinks in the music room that all of the "Don't shop here—Jewish owned" signs had mysteriously come down from the stores. That was the first I had heard about such signs, but I didn't have a chance to ask what this all meant because she continued, her agitation obvious. "It's so ridiculous! The whole thing is just ridiculous!" She rose suddenly from her chair to turn the radio down. "They know, Hans. They know they are wrong!" she said again, spinning around. "Why else would they take the signs down?"

"No. They know it is not popular. They have convinced themselves of the truth of their views. Otherwise they could not believe in them," said my father, putting down his paper.

"Does that mean you believe that Jews are bad?" I asked, puzzled. This seemed to contradict all that I knew of my parents' teaching. Weren't they best friends with Tante Anne and Onkel Ludwig?

"No!" I had my father's full attention now. "I said *they* believe it is true. That does not make it true." I was confused and must have looked it, for he continued, "There are real truths—God's truths, natural truths—and then there are truths that people convince themselves of because it suits their purpose. Do you understand?"

"I think so. Like when I have one more chocolate before dinner. Mutti won't know, so it's all right, even though in my heart I know that Mutti told me no more chocolate before dinner." My mother cocked her head and looked at me with interest. "Not that I would ever take chocolate without permission," I added quickly.

"Good example! Yes, exactly!" beamed my father, obviously pleased at my logic. "All people are equal, Jutta. There are some good and some bad in every group."

I smiled. "Right! Jutta and Erica good, and Hannelore and Liesel bad," I quipped.

"Jutta, don't talk about other children that way," said Mutti, frowning her disapproval.

"Yes, well. The point is, Jutta, there is natural law, if you will, that says we should treat people as individuals. We should not decide before we even know people that they are bad or good just because they belong to a certain group or race or religion or they come from a certain country. Do you understand me?" I nodded my head. He continued, "You should never say a Jewish person is bad just because he or she is Jewish. Maybe they are bad, maybe they are good. Who knows until you get to know them? Tante Anne and Onkel Ludwig are two of the best people I know."

"*Ja*, and Herr Goldfarb is one of the worst!" I said.

"Oh, Jutta! Stop!" Mutti's irritation was clear.

"Who in God's name is Herr Goldfarb?" asked my father.

"He is Jutta's piano teacher. He comes to the house on Mondays. He is perfectly nice."

"He is not!" I said vehemently. "His nose is always dripping, and he stinks."

"Jutta!" said my mother sharply. "He may not have soap to wash. Even if that is true, which I have never noticed, just because he stinks and his nose drips does not make him a bad person."

"But he says that I have no talent. That he wishes I had just one-quarter of the talent of my mother!" I wailed. I knew if I seized the moment I could maybe get rid of Herr Goldfarb and maybe piano lessons entirely. My father believed that people should enjoy the arts and literature, and if it became a chore, then they were perhaps not meant for it. My ploy worked. My father looked horrified.

"If that is true, Heti, then I want him out of this house immediately!" railed my father. "But if it is not true, then, Jutta, you will be confined to your room for a long time for hurting another person with lies."

I held my ground, for he had in fact told me I had no talent, unlike my lovely mother.

"Besides, he scares me to death because he shouts 'No! No!' at me whenever I miss my notes." I added, to make sure my father had the complete picture.

"We will discuss this later," said my mother, looking at me pointedly, irritated at this deviation from the conversation. "Well, anyway, Hilde and I have decided we are going to round up all our friends and shop and shop for the next two weeks at all the Jewish stores people like Mannie won't go to because of the hecklers outside. What an opportunity!" She laughed. "And if Hitler only knew how many of my friends are going to spend their marks at the Jewish shops, he would slap the signs back up in a hurry."

The gong sound of the BBC interrupted our conversation, and Vati raised his finger to his lips for silence so he could hear the BBC's international news. My parents refused to listen to the official German news broadcasts—political theater, Vati called it.

The BBC broadcaster spoke only of the Berlin Olympics and the American Jesse Owens, who they were predicting would win the hundred meters. They spoke of elaborate preparations in the German capital, Berlin. How strange to hear them speak of Berlin as if it were a far-off place, and yet I lived right here in the middle of it.

"Mutti, Vati, are you going to see the Olympic races where they run in a circle? We are supposed to win all the races!" I announced with authority.

"They run on a track, Jutta, not a circle, and I think the Americans will probably win most of the races, not the Germans."

"That is not what Frau Eberhardt told us!"

"Well, anyway, yes. Mutti and I have tickets to see the big races, like the one with Jesse Owens, and the women's and men's relay teams."

"Frau Eberhadt says that Jesse Owens is one of the *Untermensch* because he is black, and that even in America, where he is from, they understand this, because he can't sit on the bus with the other people and he can't eat in the same restaurants. So we will probably beat him."

"Has Frau Eberhadt ever met Jesse Owens?" asked my father.

"I doubt it!" I laughed. "He lives in America!"

"Well then, what does she really know about Jesse Owens?"

I smiled, remembering his earlier point. "Nothing."

"Exactly. And we shall see who wins the race. All I can tell you is that all the reports outside of Germany are that Jesse Owens will win, as you just heard."

"But how can he be an *Untermensch* and win?"

"Exactly! Something to think about, isn't it? I tell you what: I will rush home and report the outcome to you." Then, after a pause, he added, "Better yet, I will show Fräulein Sisi how to tune in the radio, and you can hear the races on the radio as they are happening!" My mother raised her eyebrows but said nothing.

"Oh would you, Vati? That is so exciting!" I jumped up and ran to him and practically knocked his wine out of his hand.

"Calm down, calm down! Such exuberance. My goodness!"

True to his word, Vati checked the schedule the next evening and gave me a list of the times for each of the races. If it was an important race, he even let me miss school.

Vati viewed the Olympic Games as an opportunity for learning about the world outside the confines of Dahlem. Anything that would expand my perspective was, in his view, worthwhile. For me, it was the first lesson in understanding that what they taught us at school was not necessarily the truth. My father wanted me to learn the lesson first-hand, hearing for myself who won the races. He made sure I listened to the BBC version of the broadcast of the games, and he gave me a list of English words and their translation. Sisi spoke English fairly well, and he asked her to translate those parts I could not understand.

The radio in the music room was much more powerful than my little radio upstairs, and Vati said I could sit on his favorite chair and eat and drink whatever I wanted. Sisi raised her eyebrows but knew better than to say anything. Luise brought me a plate of my favorite raspberry-filled cookies, *Himbeertaschen*, with a glass of milk. I usually managed to consume all the cookies and milk before the races ever started. I waited anxiously for the Olympic music to begin, hardly containing my excitement when the broadcast began. Mostly I loved the excitement of the announcer's voice and the sound of the crowd's roar when a race was close. It seemed to echo and vibrate inside the metal confines of the radio. I half expected the thing to explode from the waves of roars that ripped through it, but it never did.

When Jesse Owens ran the hundred meters, it sounded like all of Germany was in that stadium. I closed my eyes, and I was there! The announcer's voice began softly and quietly as he announced the lineup in the blocks. Then the gun went off and his voice quickened, conveying the urgency—Owens in the lead, Owens still in the lead—the crowd roared like the ocean when the tide comes in—and then—Owens wins with a new world record of 10.3 seconds! He stretched the words "new world record" out as long as possible. And then only the sound of the crowd, the announcer silent for a moment, letting the crowd's excitement seep through the radio to those of us listening before he finally spoke again, slowly and deliberately, in a deep, resonant voice. "What an upset! Owens is the fastest man in the world!" I had leaped up, unaware that my plate had fallen from my lap to the carpet, crumbs scattering all about Vati's chair as I jumped up and down shrieking "Yes!" and "Go!" and "Faster!" until the end, when I collapsed in a heap of excitement.

Sisi looked at me sternly. "*Gott im Himmel!* Child! Look at the mess you've made!" I ignored her as she retrieved the plate, now licked clean by Sasha. She shook her head in disapproval but said nothing more.

I couldn't believe it! Jesse Owens won the gold medal! I bounced up again and grabbed Sisi's hand, twirling her around with me, singing, "Jesse! Jesse! Jesse!" She rolled her eyes, but a smile crept across her mouth. I was thrilled that the American had won. For me, it proved my father's view of the world was right. It comforted me because I didn't want Frau Eberhadt to be right. Jesse Owens was no *Untermensch*—according to my father, such a person did not exist. And now I knew I didn't have to believe anything that Frau Eberhadt told me—things that bothered me in my stomach when she said them.

When my parents returned from the Olympic Stadium I ran to my father, "Vati, 10.3 seconds! Can you believe it? Did you see it?"

"Yes, I know. I saw it! It was spectacular!" he beamed. "How did it sound on the radio?"

"Like an ocean of voices, Vati. The stadium must have had all of Germany in it."

"It was packed, completely full—and the excitement was unbelievable!"

"I thought we were going to be crushed." Mutti took off her hat and jacket, handing them to Luise. "And leaving the stadium, my God! What a nightmare!"

"But it was spectacular, Heti."

"Yes, yes. I just can't handle the crowds—all raising their arm when Hitler walked in—disgusting."

"Well, we didn't raise ours, and I saw others who did not, so forget about it—the events were amazing."

My mother looked at him for a moment with a look I could not quite read, and then turned and walked up the stairs. My father shrugged his shoulders and handed me an Olympic flag he had saved for me.

"Wow! Thanks, Vati!" I ran around the living room, waving the flag and shouting, "Go, Jesse. Run, Jesse. And Owens wins it! " My father cheered as if I were the real Jesse Owens winning the race. From that day on, my father brought me everything he could find on Jesse Owens—every foreign magazine or newspaper that ran articles about him, and if the BBC aired an interview of him, Vati would run and get me. I could only understand a bit of what he said, so we recruited Mutti, who spoke the best English, to translate for me. I thought his voice sounded magical—the voice of a kind man, an honest man. He became my hero, and even more than a hero. He became a symbol for me, and I determined from that point forward that I would learn to speak English well, and I would visit America one day and meet Jesse Owens.

During the Olympics, many tourists and foreign dignitaries traveled through Dahlem on their way to Potsdam or Wannsee, where they attended parties and met with wealthy Germans. Their fancy limousines careened down the Kronprinzenallee at high speeds, flags flapping carelessly in the wind from shiny front fenders. One day Erica and I snuck out to the Kronprinzenallee to meet Christa to watch these limousines and fancy cars swish by us in the bright summer sun. To do so meant we were violating rules. We were allowed to go to the park at the end of our street, but the Kronprinzenallee was strictly off-limits. The park was at the end of our street to the left, but if you turned to the right and walked one block, you ran smack into Kronprinzenallee, one of the main arteries connecting downtown Berlin to Dahlem, Potsdam, and the Wannsee. If you took Kronprinzenallee toward Berlin, its wide lanes fed right into the Kurfürstendamm at the Roseneck. I only knew this because my mother's friend, Anna Muller, or Tante Anna as I called her, lived on Kronprinzenallee near the Roseneck. I loved to go with my mother to pick her up during the summer when the roses were in full bloom, brilliant dabs of pink, red, and orange glistening in the bright summer sun. There must have been two hundred roses standing in the center of those converging streets, a lone, beautiful holdout against the asphalt and cement that surrounded them.

My chest swelled with pride that these visitors to my gracious city, Berlin, were driving on this magnificent boulevard, leaving the grandeur of downtown Berlin behind them, heading past the Roseneck and the Grunewald Forest and past all our beautiful homes with their spectacular summer gardens in full bloom. I imagined the Americans telling their friends at home about the glorious homes and scenery in Berlin. Further down the road, they would come to the calm blue waters of the Krumme Lanke and the Schlachtensee, and even further down, the broad expanse of the Wannsee, its waters flat from the summer heat.

Erica, Christa, and I stood on the corner of Auf dem Grat and Kronprinzenallee, waiting to see if we could spot one of the fancy cars. We were not disappointed. They came in huge, shiny black limousines with drivers in uniform; they came in smart sports cars in pale yellow and bright blue with chrome fenders all around, and in convertibles with the tops down. They were filled with elegant ladies and sporty-looking men, their hair blowing in the wind, smiles fixed to their faces. Their laughter spilled out of the cars and hung on the wind as they passed by us—three little fresh-faced German girls, waving. Perhaps they thought we were part of the official welcoming committee, for they pointed and waved and smiled at us. When we spotted a car up the road, a dot of color that grew larger and larger, we grabbed each other's hands, jumping up and down, and when it came close enough we all shouted out, "Welcome to Berlin," waving frantically until the car blew past us, sending wisps of hair into my eyes and mouth. If American flags graced the front of the car, I shouted especially loudly, and I even blew a kiss at one of the cars. The driver tooted a greeting back, much to our delight.

By the time the sun had dropped behind the pines of the Grunewald Forest, casting purple shadows across the sky, we had counted thirty-five foreign cars. Erica and Christa were ready to go, but I spotted one last car coming very quickly toward us. "Let's stay for this last one!" I begged, grabbing Erica's arm. We waved and screamed our usual greeting. The driver slammed on the brakes and turned into our little side street at an alarming speed—tires squealed, and the passengers, shocked and not prepared for the driver's sudden turn, grabbed the window casings to stay upright. Puzzled and a little frightened, we retreated to the edge of the trees that hugged the center median of our little road. The driver made a U-turn down by the park and pulled up horizontal to us, calling out, "Well hello, ladies!"

I was the only one who spoke some English, so I responded with the greeting they had taught us in my first English class. "Good day, sir!" I knew the "sir" from the BBC. The driver laughed, but in a friendly way. I could tell the driver was American by the way he was dressed and the slow way he spoke. I knew from the BBC that English people spoke much faster, more clipped, and they were much harder to understand. He waved for us to come over to the car. Erica and Christa pushed me forward. I knew my mother and Sisi would have a heart attack if I approached a stranger's car, but the man looked so pleasant and friendly. One of the women said, "You're frightening them, Billy." The man stuck his hand out the window and tossed a pale green packet at us, saying, "I just want to give you ladies a candy from America." At least that is my interpretation of what he said, with my seven-year-old expertise in English.

Smiling, I ran over to pick it up and said, "*Danke, sehr.*"

This seemed to delight the car's occupants, and they began singing, "*Danke sehr, danke sehr,"* and then, *"aufwiedersehn,"* except that the way they said it, it came out *arfwiedersan.*

We all laughed and waved and said, *"Aufwiedersehn."*

"Bye!" called the driver and took off, waving and making a left back onto Kronprinzenallee without even looking for traffic. The ladies screamed as the car tipped to the side from the speed with which the driver took the turn.

We all stared at the bright green package in my hand. It was long and thin, and I could not imagine what sort of candy could possibly be inside. The wrapper read WRIGLEY'S SPEARMINT GUM. We tried to pronounce it, but it came out *Vrigl* and *Guhm.* Only I attempted spearmint: *schparment.* We giggled at these strange-sounding names. I carefully opened the package so the name remained intact and I could save it. Beneath the bright green wrapping were five separate pieces, each one individually wrapped in foil. I handed one to Christa and one to Erica. We each meticulously unfolded the foil, taking care not to tear it. A long, thin, pale piece of what looked like cookie dough fell onto my palm. "It's gum!" cried Christa, delighted. "Americans are famous for their gum. They all chew it, all the time, even at balls and parties, even at church and school! They smack it with their mouths wide open! My mother thinks it's disgusting!"

We turned the gum over, examining the cuts that crisscrossed the dough in a pattern, and then we all simultaneously popped it in our mouths, giggling as we did so. The sugar immediately hit my tongue, and then the mint flavor. It tasted like the tiny green plant Mutti grew in the garden room and put in my lemonade, only much stronger. We chewed for a moment in silence before pronouncing it *wunderbar!*

"If I had this stuff around, I would chew it all the time, too!" I announced.

We tore the two remaining pieces in thirds, giving each of us a second helping. With big smiles and our mouths full of gum, we said goodbye to Christa at the corner. Erica and I skipped arm in arm all the way down the Föhrenweg.

———

All week, Mutti spoke about the party our neighbors to the right, the Kittels, were having in honor of the Olympics. Men dressed in green uniforms spent the afternoon of the party arranging tables and draping tiny firefly lights on all the trees in the back garden. They covered every tree, except the giant apple tree in the back of the garden that bloomed profusely every year but never bore any fruit. Frau Kittel did not want the blossoms disturbed, Mutti explained when I asked her. I watched from the upstairs bathroom window as Gretel, the Kittel's housekeeper, helped Frau Kittel arrange the flowers and the centerpieces. An area had been cleared for the band and for dancing, and to me it seemed like the grandest affair I could ever imagine.

Mutti decided to have a pre-party cocktail party: a small group of friends as well as the Kittels, and of course Onkel Kurt and Tante Hilde. I spent the entire afternoon in the kitchen, singing and watching and "helping" my mother and Luise prepare the appetizers for the party. Mutti was an excellent cook. She especially loved to make appetizers. Luise was the sous-chef, and I was the designated prep cook, chopping and dicing and mixing as best I could. Mutti stood over a huge iron skillet in which she carefully made tiny pancakes out of powdered Parmesan cheese and a small bit of flour. After they cooled, Luise placed a spoonful of goat cheese mixed with chives and basil in between two of them. We made paté on toast wedges with asparagus spears on top, stuffed mushrooms with Parmesan cheese and, my least favorite of all foods, smoked eel on toast and herring salad. I tried to talk Mutti out of these last two, but she said the guests would like them even if I did not. When the food was ready, Mutti and I went upstairs to dress, leaving Luise to clean up. Mutti laid out my best blue dress with pink flowers and smocking—all hand-sewn by Oma Muller, my grandmother. I put tiny blue violets from the garden in my hair, and I felt very grown up because Mutti had said I could stay up for the entire party. I ran downstairs and waited with Vati. I held my wineglass, filled with apple juice, as I imagined Mutti would hold it.

She came down the stairs slowly while my father and I waited at the bottom. She was always late for her own parties. All the guests were assembled in the living room when she descended our long living room staircase. I had never seen my mother look so beautiful. Her dress clung to her body perfectly. The top fit snugly to her upper body, coming in at the waist to accentuate its tiny proportions, while the bottom draped in perfect waves over her hips. It closed tightly at the neck, held by a single large pearl. The fabric, made from lace with large embroidered flowers and leaves interspersed with beads, flashed and danced in the light of the chandelier, cascading a rainbow of colors about the room. Under the lace was a pale beige chiffon fabric that so closely matched her skin, at first I thought she had nothing on underneath. A long slit up the front of her skirt freed her legs to move gracefully down the stairs, and in the process provided the spectator with an ample view. Her face was radiant, her hair perfect in waves of golden color. I noticed that she was wearing the pearls my father had bought her for her birthday in May. My father beamed with pride and he held her in his gaze.

When the adults left to go next door, I lay awake late into the evening, listening to the sounds of the Kittels' party, waiting for Mutti and Vati to return. Bursts of laughter would erupt, and music echoed off the walls, eventually fading and merging with my imagination—and the next thing I knew, it was morning.

I waited as long as possible before I ran to her bedroom. Vati had long since left for work, but I knew Mutti would sleep in. I stood in the kitchen, watching

Luise prepare Mutti's breakfast tray, and then tagged behind her to deliver it. My mother was awake and sitting up in her bed, reading.

"*Guten Morgen*, Frau Bolle."

"Good morning, Luise. Thank you."

"I trust you slept well despite the late hour of your arrival?" Luise always spoke very formally to my mother.

"Yes, thank you. Perhaps not enough, is all," responded my mother. Then, peeking around Luise's rather ample figure, she said, "Well, hello, little Jutta. I suppose you came to get the report!" She laughed.

I nodded my head, smiling, my eyes bright with expectation.

"Come here and sit with me," she said, patting the bed, the pink of her nail polish bright against the soft white sheet.

I ran over to the bed and bounced onto the side of it, giving my mother a peck on the check after I settled into the folds of the bedcover.

"No bouncing, Fräulein," said Luise firmly as she set the breakfast tray across my mother's lap. The tray held coffee, an egg, and a roll.

"No. No, Jutta promises to be the picture of elegance, don't you?"

"Naturally, Mutti," I said, crossing my hands in my lap as if any other thought were ridiculous.

Luise smiled and asked if there was anything else before she turned to go. Mutti stopped her before she reached the door. "Luise, please bring Jutta a sweet roll." I grinned and licked my lips in mock hunger. I could not believe my good fortune. Not only did I get to hear about the party, but I was allowed to eat sticky sweet rolls on my mother's bed while doing so. Luise raised her eyebrow but said, "Certainly, Frau Bolle."

I sighed. How perfect, to sit on my mother's bed with its delicate floral pattern, light from the late summer morning spilling across the covers, illuminating the contrast of the white sheets with the pale beige and white flowers of the bedcover, as I talked with the woman I loved more than any other.

"Tell me about it," I prompted.

"Is that why you came to see me so early?" she teased.

"Oh, come on, Mutti! What were they wearing? What did you eat? I want to know!" I begged.

So my mother told me about the hundreds of guests, all of whom ate and danced under the beautifully lit marquee in the garden. She seemed particularly impressed by the thousands and thousands of tiny lights that outlined the tree, and the marquee. It was as if an army of fireflies had invaded the garden, she said. She told me how she loved the glorious bouquets of roses and delphiniums, and the long sprays of lavender that graced every table and every corner of the party. She told of lobster, caviar, champagne, and hundreds of desserts. She described the ice sculptures of Olympic athletes and the perfectly stacked fruit pyramids. She described the ladies, their dresses made of silk and chiffon that clung in layers, and their hair all done up in fancy arrangements on top of their heads. When she was all done, I realized that I had been eating my sweet roll, but had no idea when Luise had brought it to me.

"Oh, I almost forgot," she said climbing out of bed. She retrieved a small box from her dresser and brought it back to the bed. Handing it to me, she said, "For you."

I opened it with great expectation. What had she brought me from this grand affair? I cracked the lid up, peeked inside, and then threw the lid off. "Thank you, Mutti!" In the box were the most perfect marzipan figures of Olympic athletes: a javelin thrower, a female track runner, and a gymnast, all of them perfectly proportioned with muscles bulging.

"These are so real!"

"Aren't they?"

"The only problem is I never want to eat them."

"Well, that is entirely up to you."

Mutti and the Hitler Youth

The birds woke me—hundreds of them in the spruce tree. I stared dreamily at the floral pattern of the wallpaper that decorated my walls, the soft pastels—pink and blue and moss green—contrasting perfectly with the darker blue of the baseboards and the molding around the ceiling. A tree branch scraped my window, jolting me back to reality. Today is Monday! Sisi's day off! I bounced out of bed, suddenly excited about the day. I loved Mondays! I saw Mutti first thing in the morning, and Mutti saw me off to school on Monday, not Sisi. Not only that, but Monday was our outing day.

My mother's door was open. I suspected she was already downstairs with Luise. "Mutti," I called quietly. No response. I turned and headed down the stairs, taking them two at a time.

Luise's voice from the dining room startled me. "Jutta Bolle! I have told you not to do that! You're going to break your neck!"

"Oh, sorry. Where is Mutti?"

"How about, '*Guten Morgen*, Luise?'"

"*Guten Morgen*, Luise," I said sweetly.

"That's better. Your mother is in the kitchen, dear."

I ran past Luise and pushed the kitchen doors open. Mutti was at the sink, her back to me, washing an enormous basket of berries. Great pots stood on the stove with steam drifting up to the ceiling. She turned as I walked in and smiled. "Good morning, *mein Herz*."

"Good morning, Mutti! Why are you up so early?"

"Is it so unusual to see me up in the morning?" she chuckled, splashing water across the bright red and black skins of the berries.

"Actually, yes!"

We both laughed.

"I decided to make jam. I went out to pick raspberries and blackberries before the sun grew too strong and the bees got busy."

I peeked around her waist, wrapping my arms around her at the same time. The berries' color, deepened from the water, made the tiny brown hairs on their skins stand out. "I wanted to help! Why didn't you wake me?" I was disappointed.

"Because you needed your sleep, so you will be rested for when we go to town today."

"Yes!" I jumped up, clapping my hands. "Where are we going?"

"To Duhrs for some art supplies, and then I thought you girls might like to go get cake at either Café Kranzler or Café Möhring. Which would you like?"

"You *girls*?"

"Yes. Tante Hilde and Peti are joining us."

"Hurrah!" I shouted. "Café Möhring, I think. And can we please buy chocolate?"

"Did I say anything about chocolate, Jutta?" asked my mother in mock surprise. "Café Möhring it is, but we will see about the chocolate." She knew I loved chocolate from Fassbender & Rausch more than any other treat in the world. She usually said no, but sometimes she would acquiesce if it was not too late by the time we finished shopping.

The grinding of the bread truck's brakes caught her attention; she looked out the kitchen window. "Oh! Our *Brötchen!* Jutta, be a dear and run out and get them, please."

I was out the kitchen door before she finished her request. I delighted in collecting the *Brötchen* they deposited in a large, sturdy brown bag in our mailbox at the end of the drive. I pulled the mailbox open; the wonderful rich smell of the hot rolls escaped through the paper and hit my nostrils with astonishing speed. I peeked inside the bag and let the steam curl out onto my face, breathing in the smell of the golden brown rolls, their crusts hard and crisp.

"*Mensch haben wir es gut!*" Life could not be any better! I skipped happily back up the flagstone path, Sasha following at my heels. The sun peeked over the kiefer trees in the back garden, trying to wake the day. I deposited the bag of *Brötchen* in the dining room. Orange dahlias stood in a crystal vase on the table, their stems thick in the clear water like the stalks of a wild plant. Luise had set the table and placed a soft-boiled egg at each place setting, as well as a glass of juice. Mutti joined me at the table. "Tomorrow we will have raspberry or blackberry jam to eat with our *Brötchen*," she announced. I smiled—such a perfect morning.

I rushed home from school to make sure I ate my lunch and finished my homework quickly, so I would be ready when Mutti arrived. As I hurried into the music room calling for Mutti, I was a little disappointed to find she was not home. She went riding that morning, explained Luise, who was a little surprised herself that she had not yet returned. Mutti had told her she would be back for lunch. By two o'clock my mother had still not returned, and I begged Luise to phone Vati at the office, but she did not want to disturb him. My concern growing, I sat in the garden talking to Harold, the turtle we kept in the small pond by the house. Harold's head bobbed in and out of the lily pads, looking for algae. At three o'clock the phone rang, and Luise answered it. I rushed in and heard her say, "Bolle residence, Luise speaking." And then, after a pause, "Oh, Herr Bolle, Frau Bolle is not yet here, and I am so worried. She went riding this morning and said she would be back for lunch." Another pause, "No, I don't think so, because she said she was going to take the children to town this afternoon. *Ja, gut.*" She hung up and turned to find me staring at her from the doorway. "Jutta Bolle! You're the nosiest little thing!"

"Well, what did Vati say?"

"He said he was going to call the stables, and also call Tante Hilde."

"Luise, you don't think anything happened to Mutti, do you?"

"No. No, we would have heard about it, my dear. But your Vati's coming home after he makes his phone calls. Now you go wash your hands and let's have cake here, since you did not get to go to town." Luise's answer for everything was food.

"What would you like, my dear? I have some *Pflaumenkuchen*, or *Apfelstrudle*, or some cookies I baked this morning."

"*Pflaumenkuchen* and cookies, please. And milk."

"*Ja.* The order is in, although I am not sure your mother would like you to have cookies as well as *Pflaumenkuchen.*" She winked at me. "But since she is not here, she can't say anything."

I grinned at our conspiracy and turned to go up the stairs, stopping in my tracks when the phone rang again. Luise answered, "Oh, hello, Frau Bolle." I stood still, anticipating news of Mutti, but when Luise continued, "No. I have not heard from her since this morning when she went riding," I knew it was only Tante Hilde asking about Mutti. I continued up the stairs, disappointed and very worried.

———

Sasha's bark echoing off the walls alerted me to a car in our driveway. I ran to the window. Vati's little silver BMW sports car, the top down and doors flung open, was parked at an odd angle, and he had stopped at the walk rather than pulling it into the garage as he usually did. To my relief, Mutti sat in the passenger seat. Vati reached in the backseat and pulled out what looked like two long sticks. Then he came over to Mutti's side of the car and helped her out. As she stepped out of the car, I saw she had a large bandage on her arm from her hand to her elbow, and it was tied in a sling around her neck. "What on earth?" I turned from the window and raced down the stairs, Sasha at my heels. Luise's hand was on the door, ready to open it for them. "Good God above! Slow down! Your father does not need all his ladies injured," she said before she pulled the door open.

"*Gott im Himmel!* Frau Bolle, what on earth happened to you?"

Mutti laughed and said, "I fell off Tasha."

Luise mumbled, "*Gott sei dank* you are not dead!" My mother ignored her. Luise disapproved of mother's riding.

"Mutti!" I shouted at the same time and ran to her. My father blocked my assault for fear I would knock her over. "Slow down! Don't charge your mother! She is an invalid with broken bones."

"Oh, Hans! It's okay. Come here, Jutta. I am so sorry about this afternoon; I know you are so disappointed!"

"It doesn't matter, Mutti. But tell us what happened."

"Sasha, go! Out of the way!" Vati scowled at Sasha, who was trying to greet Mutti by jumping on her. "Jutta, get Sasha out of the way!"

"Sasha, *komm!*" I called, dropping on my knees on the other side of the carpet. She came running, ears flapping and collar jingling. "Mutti, what happened?" I asked again as I held Sasha in my lap.

"Not here in the doorway, if you don't mind!" said my father irritably. "Let's go in the music room and let your mother sit down. Luise, Frau Bolle is famished. She has not eaten since breakfast."

"Yes, of course. Shall I bring *Abendessen* to the music room?"

"No, please. I am not so crippled I can't sit at the table. The dining room will be fine, Luise."

Luise hurried off to the kitchen, and I followed my parents to the music room.

"I am going to have to learn how to use these idiotic sticks. I can't depend on your help for every step I take," complained my mother.

"You, completely dependent on me? What a lovely thought!" chuckled my father.

Vati placed Mutti in his reading chair with the overstuffed arms. He carefully lifted her foot onto the ottoman and gently placed a pillow behind her back. I came over and sat on the arm of the chair.

"So what happened?" I asked impatiently for the third time.

"No, first things first, Jutta. Heidchen, would you like a schnapps or wine?" She nodded her head. "I think this is a schnapps day, don't you?"

Vati nodded and went to retrieve her schnapps. She put her hand on my arm and motioned for me to sit on the ottoman.

"I was riding along with Wilhelm, the air was fresh and the sun was shining, and the horses were excited and ready to run. All of a sudden, we heard the most god-awful racket coming from the path ahead of us. We were at a full gallop at that point, and as we turned the bend we came upon a group of Hitler Youth making a terrible noise, singing and shouting and playing their trumpets and banging on their drums. You know, one of those silly marching songs they sing. Well, I tried to stop and pulled in on the reins as hard as I could. I was just thinking it would be all right and I would miss them when one of the dummies starts on his trumpet again. Well, Tasha shied, bucking up in the air. All I could see were her hooves flailing in the air in front of me, and behind me was the ground."

"Oh, just like in the movies!" I interjected excitedly.

"Yes, just like in the movies!" she laughed.

"Except in the movies people manage to stay on the horse," joked my father as he handed Mutti her schnapps.

"Anyway," said my mother giving my father a look. "She knocked me off and ran off at full speed into the forest. Wilhelm was so worried about me he let her go, and leaped off his horse to help me up. In his haste, he forgot to hold on to his horse, and she took off running after Tasha!" My mother laughed. "I wanted him to get the horses under control, so I said I was fine, but when I tried to get up I had such pain in my ankle and wrist that I collapsed back down. Those poor boys felt really terrible; they all rushed over, and Wilhelm cursed them out good and sound." She laughed again.

Vati rolled his eyes and mumbled, "*Idioten! Verdammte Nazi Programme!* Making children run around in the forest singing idiotic marching songs!"

"They can't help it, Hans! That's what they are made to do."

Vati didn't respond.

"Well, the older ones helped me back to the stables. They took turns supporting me, one on each side, because we were several kilometers from the lodge. It took us forever to hobble back."

"Why didn't Wilhelm take you on his horse?" asked my father.

"At first he was trying to find the horses, and then, frankly, I was afraid if I got on his horse he might shy again, and then I would really be in trouble.

"We finally got to the lodge, and of course Wilhelm's driver was not there waiting for us as he should have been. Wilhelm was furious. We waited over an hour for him. My arm hurt so bad I could not eat, but I did manage some hot tea. By the time the driver got there it was nearly one o'clock. So we went straight to Dr. Tölle."

"Why you did not call me is beyond my comprehension!" Vati threw his hands in the air.

"I knew you were very busy today, Hans."

"Well, that is idiotic! I am never too busy for something like this."

"Anyway, it turns out that I broke my wrist and twisted my ankle." I glanced at the ottoman and Mutti's poor ankle, swollen to twice its normal size.

"Finally, I was ready at three o'clock and thought we might still have time for town ..."

"Oh yes, in your condition," said my father sarcastically.

"...But your father had found out where I was somehow, and called the doctor to say that I was not to leave. He was coming to get me. And that is the end of my saga." She sipped her schnapps and shook her head.

I patted her good hand. "Poor Mutti!"

She smiled at me. "And you, my poor Juttalein. So looking forward to our time together!" She shook her head again. "I'm so sorry, *mein Herz*. Next week we will try it again."

I nodded enthusiastically. "If you think you can manage."

"Oh, I think I'll have the hang of these silly sticks by then." She shrugged. "Who knows? Maybe I won't need them by next Monday." She hooked her arm through mine. "Or, if I do, maybe we can borrow Heinz for the afternoon—*nicht*, Hans?"

"Of course." He pointed at Mutti. "But no more riding until Dr. Tölle says so!"

Mutti smiled but didn't answer. Luise bustled in with our food: freshly sliced bread, ham, cheese, cucumber salad, and fruit. I glanced at Mutti, realizing Luise had ignored Mutti's request to eat in the dining room, but she smiled serenely, basking in the attention we were showering on her. Luise set the tray down and lifted Sasha to banish her to the kitchen. "Oh, Frau Bolle called earlier, wondering what happened to you."

"Oh my God! Hilde! Hans, call her, please!"

2

Anna Muller and Judenfreunde

1937

I opened my window, letting the crisp, early afternoon air embrace me. The sun sent rays through the clouds that streaked the sky, casting thin shadows across the lawn below. I sniffed. It was one of those April days, no longer cold enough for a heavy coat, but too cold for a simple sweater. I threw my heavy school skirt onto the bed and pulled on my lightweight tan pants. My beige sweater hung on a hanger at the end of my closet. I reached for it and pulled it over my head, leaving my blouse on beneath so the wool fibers would not scratch my skin. Returning to the window, I leaned out to test the temperature. A taxi pulled up in front of our house, the door flew open, and the tiny figure of Anna Muller came charging up the walk to our door.

"Tante Anna is certainly in a hurry!" I thought. She was one of my mother's closest friends, a member of her *Kaffee Klatsch*. I called her Tante Anna, even though she was no relation. My mother had known her since I was a baby, and she had always been Tante Anna, never Frau Muller. But this did not look like a social visit to me. I watched as she passed by the eave of the house, heading for the front door. In another month, the leaves of the wisteria would pop out of their curled buds, blocking my view of the corner of the house.

I could hear my mother say, "Anna, what a nice surprise! Come in."

I ran through Sisi's room to the landing above the living room stairs. Sisi had taken the day off, or I would never have been so bold as to run through her room uninvited. I heard Mutti ask Luise to bring coffee to the music room.

"*Ja*, Anna. What brings you here?"

There was a pause as she waited for Luise to leave the room. "Heti, I had to see you." Her voice resonated urgency. "Ludwig says things will become more and more difficult for us. Remember, I made several trips last fall and this winter to take as many of our valuables as I could to Ludwig's sister in Amsterdam, but this last time the authorities stopped me and asked why I was taking so many trips to Holland."

"Oh, no!" exclaimed my mother.

"Yes! *Gott,* Heti! Just the sight of them scares me to death in their uniforms, coming on the train with that band around their arm with that broken cross.

They came towards me and then stopped and pointed, 'You! Come with us and bring your luggage!' I thought my heart would stop!"

I heard my mother gasp.

"Heti, I tell you my stomach fell to my feet."

"What did you do?"

"Well, I had to go with them, of course, so I said, 'Of course, sir,' and they took me to a small room in the back of the station. And can you believe all I could think about were the special flower seeds I was bringing Ludwig's sister. I didn't want them to take them! Isn't that stupid?" They paused and cups clattered—Luise must have brought the coffee in—and after a few moments, Anna continued. "They asked me question after question: Where was I going? Why did I need so many clothes? Why was I taking so many trips out of Germany? Why did I need a mink coat in the middle of spring?"

"What did you say?" asked my mother.

"I tell you my mind has never worked so fast! I said that my sister was sick with cancer and that I had to come for long periods of time to help take care of her when she has a lapse, and I said I walk in the early morning when she is asleep and it is very cold!"

"Good for you, Anna!" said my mother with obvious admiration.

"My God, Heti! They checked every seam in every one of my dresses and coats, and they even took the heels off my shoes!"

"What were they looking for?" asked my mother.

"They look for money or jewelry or gold—anything valuable, because you can't take anything valuable out of the country. It's illegal, Heti!"

"They didn't find anything, did they?"

"No, of course not! I'm such a chicken, I would never be brave enough to smuggle something like that out of here. Ludwig made the first trip with those things."

Luise came in and asked if they had everything they needed.

"Yes. Thank you, Luise. Could you see if Jutta would like anything, please?"

"Certainly, Frau Bolle." I heard Luise walk through the dining room to come up the stairs by the kitchen. I raced through Sisi's room and across the hall to my room. I jumped on my bed, crossed my legs, and opened my book just as Luise knocked on my door.

"Jutta, would you like some tea or juice?" she asked.

"No thank you, Luise. I'm in a good part of my book."

Luise frowned at me and came over to feel my forehead, "Are you sick, child? You look flushed, and you're hot and sweaty."

"Oh, I was just dancing before I settled down to read. I feel great," I added, smiling back at her.

My enthusiasm must have convinced her, for she nodded and said, "If you change your mind, come down to the kitchen."

I nodded, pretending I couldn't take my eyes off my book. As soon as she left, I rushed across the hall through Sisi's room and had my hand on the door handle ready to open it when I heard my mother's and Tante Anna's voices. They walked past the door and into my mother's bedroom. I listened for my mother's bedroom door to close and carefully opened Sisi's door before crossing the landing on tiptoes to crouch beside my mother's bedroom door.

"Orders are down. There's no money because many people won't buy from us anymore. The big government contracts have all gone to the non-Jewish firms. Ludwig is up at night drinking schnapps. He thinks I don't know, but I hear him get up. Heti, we have to leave right away!"

There was silence, broken only by the breeze outside in the trees, rustling the new spring leaves and sprinkling flower buds on the terrace below. The birds sang; I presumed *Vögelein* was among them, unaware of the anguish inside my mother's bedroom.

I heard my mother rummaging around in a closet and then a minute later say, "Take this."

Tante Anna gasped. "No, Heti. I couldn't possibly."

"Just take it. It's all I have. Here."

"Heti, I can't. Ludwig would not allow it, and my God, if they caught me with this much U.S. currency they would shoot me on the spot."

"Well, Ludwig doesn't need to know, does he? You know perfectly well you can't get a penny for your property or your business right now. You take this bill and sew it into the bottom of your shoe—on the inside. Here..." My mother must have taken off one of her shoes. "... just lift the leather like this, and then glue it back down. Because it is a single bill, they will never notice it."

"Heti, how did you get this bill?"

"Before things became difficult, Hans thought the German mark was going to go down, so he began to buy U.S. dollars, but only in large denominations."

"He plans well, your Hans!"

Mutti did not respond. Then she said, "What about your diamond solitaire? You must take it; you can't leave it behind. And your emerald earrings you wore last month to the opera?"

"But they are so big. They will take them, and they check everything if they even remotely suspect you."

Silence hung in the air for what seemed like an eternity.

"I have an idea!" said Mutti suddenly. "I have a hairpiece I had made for the evening when I put my hair up. You take it and we'll pin the jewelry inside and cover it with the hairpiece. They will never see them, and they will never think to ask you to take down your hair."

She must have gone to get it because it was a few seconds before they spoke again.

"But Heti, this is your own hair. It took you forever to grow this."

"Anna, it is just hair! I can grow some more. She paused, and I imagined her holding the hairpiece up to Tante Anna. "Don't even argue with me. We'll have Frau Schmidt dye your hair to match," she said after a moment.

Tante Anna sobbed, and I could tell my mother was holding her and whispering comfort just like she did when I was sad. "Heti, I can't bear it. I can't bear leaving you and Dahlem—this beautiful place, Berlin, my beautiful Berlin."

A lump formed in my throat. Why did Tante Anna have to leave? I didn't understand any of this.

"Anna, it's not the same as it once was; he has seen to that. Don't mourn leaving this place. Be glad you have a way out. I will see you again when this is all over. I know I will."

And then Tante Anna's voice said between sobs, "I came only to ask if I could leave our Meissen and silver and a few of my special pieces of furniture with you, because I have no way to take them out of here. You can keep them and use them—but I would rather die than know that one of those pigs got their hands on my beautiful things."

"Of course, and I will mail them to you as soon as that is possible."

"No. That will place you at too much risk."

"I will mail it to you as soon as possible!" my mother repeated. "Heinz can drive one of the factory trucks to pick them up."

"No. No, Ludwig will send a driver." Herr Muller owned a large manufacturing plant that produced fine furniture made from cherry, walnut, and exotic woods from Asia. His trucks tore through the city delivering tables and chairs to the wealthy in Dahlem, Grunewald, and Wannsee. It would be natural for one to stop at our house.

Silence filled the air, and again the birds sang. A bee flew through the open window, surveyed the house, and flew back out. My mother said, "Tomorrow we will see Frau Schmidt, and then we will come here and I will fix your hairpiece."

Silence again fell, and I decided to tiptoe as quietly as I could back to my room. I came down the stairs on the other side of the house and was greeted by Luise. "*Ja*, Jutta. Are you ready for some juice now?"

"Yes, please."

I heard my mother and Tante Anna come downstairs. I turned abruptly. I had to say goodbye to Tante Anna.

"Ah, Jutta, come here and hug me, dear," said Tante Anna, her eyes rimmed in red. "Honestly, these allergies of mine!" she added, blowing her nose to hide her crying. I hugged her extra long and planted a kiss on her cheek. She was not much bigger than I, and she felt so small and vulnerable. "I love you, Tante Anna," I whispered. She hugged me back, long and hard, and then quickly turned away to the door and said goodbye to my mother. I ran into the kitchen as if I had intended all along to come down only for juice.

Mutti came to the door and frowned at me. "You are not usually so demonstrative with Tante Anna." She studied me carefully. "Why such a demonstration of love today?" she asked, her eyes firmly planted on my face.

I didn't dare look up; I knew if I made eye contact, my mother would know—she always did. "I don't know. I am just in a loving mood." A lump sprang to my throat again, and I feared the tears would give me away; I leaped up suddenly and ran to my mother, practically knocking her over with my hug. I snuggled my face in her chest as she gently hugged me back and ran her fingers through my hair. After a few seconds she disengaged me and, holding my face with both hands, she kissed me gently on the forehead. "Let's go on the terrace for a moment." She led me through the living room and out onto the terrace. I stopped and looked at the goldfish pond, orange streaks in the dark water rushing back and forth, excited by our presence, but she pulled me over to where two wicker chairs with white and red canvas cushions stood on the sunny part of the flagstone terrace. Pots of pansies and hyacinths sat all about the terrace, spewing bits of color out over their edges. She placed me gently but firmly in a chair and then pulled another very close to mine so that we were face-to-face.

Taking my hand in hers, she said, "Jutta, listen to me very carefully." She waited until I looked up and our eyes met. "When you overhear something that Vati and I say to each other—or that a friend and I say to each other—about how things are right now in Germany and what they are doing to Germany, you must not repeat it to anyone. Do you understand? Not to Erica, not to Sisi, and especially not to anyone at school. Do you understand?"

"Yes," I said gravely.

My eyes had wandered back to the goldfish pond, and she shook my hand to get my attention. She continued, "This is very important, Jutta, because it could harm us or someone else very seriously if you do repeat things. We live in a time when we are not free to speak our minds and say what we think. Terrible things have happened to very good people simply for speaking their minds."

"Are you sure, Mutti?" I asked seriously. "Because at school they say that the Führer only sends away people who are doing very bad things—trying to destroy Germany."

Mutti stiffened and looked at me intensely, her eyes deepening to a sapphire color. "Don't you ever call him the Führer in this house again! He is no Führer for this family, or any other decent German." I looked down, stung by her words. She said nothing for a moment. Then she softened. "This is difficult to explain to you at your age, but those are lies they are telling you." I looked up sharply. Mutti had never openly disagreed with my teachers before. "Hitler has sent away very good people—people who have done nothing more than disagree with him. I know I have always taught you to be honest and to speak your mind, but in these times…" She hesitated a moment. "Well, we have to be careful, Jutta." She looked away before she said, "Say anything you like at home, with us—but not in public. Not with them in power… in the government, I

Lisa Farringer Parker

mean. It is too dangerous. We will keep all of our opinions to ourselves. Do you understand?"

I nodded.

She stood, pulling me up with her, and walked to the edge of the terrace; she looked up, studying the sky, the clouds stretched now to thin wisps. "Since it is not raining, perhaps we should walk to the Grunewaldsee and check on Tasha."

The idea did not excite me as it normally would have; Tante Anna's red-rimmed eyes inserted themselves into my memory. Why did she have to leave? It made no sense. I loved Tante Anna with her sparkle and enthusiasm and ready hugs, and now she would be gone—out of my life, maybe forever.

"Why don't you run to the kitchen and have Luise give you a bag of carrots and whatever else she has for Tasha. But no kohlrabi! It gave her the worst gas last time." Chuckling, she added, "No one would ride behind me after she ate it."

I smiled.

"Good. A smile. An eight-year-old should not wear such a worried face," she said, kissing me gently on the forehead.

I stopped at the pond. Harold's head stuck up like a tiny periscope among the lily pads where he hid from the fish twice his size. I fished him out and set him on the ledge, his head retracting as he tried to look like a tiny flat stone. "I'll bring you something, too," I said, stroking his shell before I ran to the kitchen.

The bell rang, and I sprinted out of the room. "Walking, not running, is appropriate, Fräulein Bolle," called Frau Dütz. I slowed my pace until I was out of her sight. I grabbed my jacket and book bag off the peg in the hall, shoving my books into the bag as I walked. Erica ran after me, stopping to pick up the mushroom pencil sharpener that had fallen out. She handed it to me. "What is the big rush? You drop *this* and don't even notice?"

"Oh, nothing," I replied casually. "I just want to see how fast I can get home. It's sort of a race against myself that I thought I would try." I took off at a sprint. I ran past the sweet's pavilion and only waved to Christa and Magda, already in line.

A taxi stood waiting in front of our gate. I hurried, half running down the street. The driver sat reading a newspaper and chewing on a blade of grass. I flung open our gate and ran up the path toward our front door, tripping on the uneven flagstones in my haste. I dropped my book bag and fell, landing on my knees. Not bothering to pick up my bag, I brushed off my knee, covered now with blood and bits of moss, and hobbled up the path, arriving on the front step just as my mother opened the door for Tante Anna. She looked at me with a start. "Jutta, I wasn't expecting you for another fifteen minutes." Her eyes lowered to my knee and my disheveled appearance. "Good heavens!

What happened to you? Are you hurt?" She bent to study my knee more carefully.

"Oh, I fell on the path is all," I said, waving it off as nothing. Mutti turned her head toward our front gate, and I knew she saw my book bag and jacket where I had left them on the path.

"Tante Anna, I want to say goodbye."

Tante Anna's eyes filled with tears as she hugged me to her. "You sweet, dear child."

Her hair, piled on top of her head, looked natural, as if she had always worn it that way. I knew it must have taken many hours to achieve such a nonchalant elegance, one that would not raise much curiosity. "Your hair looks lovely!"

"Thank you." She touched my mother's hairpiece self-consciously.

My mother tilted her head to one side and looked at me quizzically, but she did not betray her thoughts. Instead she crossed her arms and said, "Jutta, say your goodbyes and run on into Luise for lunch."

I hugged Tante Anna again and whispered, "I love you." My eyes filled with tears. I pulled away quickly and ran inside so as not to give myself away.

"What an extraordinary child she is!" I heard Tante Anna say as I entered the house.

"She is that," my mother replied.

I ran to the kitchen window to watch them walk arm in arm slowly toward the waiting taxi.

"What are you up to now, child?" asked Luise, her arms covered with soap suds from the dishes.

I could hold them back no more, and my eyes filled with tears. Without answering, I turned abruptly and ran from the kitchen up to my room, hurling myself on the bed. I cried for Tante Anna. It was so unfair. Why did she have to leave? Why would we never see her again? Outside I heard the taxi door slam and the engine start. I hurried to the window to catch one last glimpse of her. My hand raised, I waved, but she did not see me. Her gaze fixed straight ahead. Mutti turned, and with her head down she walked slowly up the path. I could not tell if she was crying. She stopped to pick up my things and looked up to my window as she straightened up. I ducked down. The front door closed. "She is acting very strange! Shall I bring her down, Frau Bolle?" I heard Luise ask.

"No. I will go to her," my mother responded.

Her footsteps echoed on the landing outside my door, and then she came quietly in my room and sat on the bed. I did not move or look up. She grabbed me to her, smoothed my hair, and kissed my face. We both began to cry as she held me close. "*Ja, Püppchen*. We'll both miss her."

"But it's not fair," I wailed.

"I know, I know," she whispered.

The bright, sunny day defied the mood in my bedroom. For once I longed for it to rain, for the gray, cold darkness to fill my room with a day that spoke to my loss, our loss. How could God allow this to happen in the first place, and then let the sunshine out to mock us with its brightness? I covered my ears to block the sound of the birds calling to each other, a call that today sounded of unspeakable loneliness.

I never saw Tante Anna again. I was grateful my mother never asked what I knew or how I knew it. She just let me grieve.

Always the Reminders

By the time the Mullers left Berlin, there were no more Jewish friends or colleagues to invite over. If they could get out, they had all done so by 1938. The only Jewish people left in Berlin were those who were married to Germans, or those who were too poor, or too old and sick, to get out. At least that is what Vati said when I asked him. How many my parents helped, I never knew. I did not dare ask. To talk about it was far too dangerous, and I knew not to raise the subject. But I was certain if they could help, they would.

I sat on my bed, extending my legs up and down, lost in thought. For as long as I could remember, my parents had Jewish friends: close friends like Tante Anna, as well as business colleagues from the factory. We attended the same parties and events. I played with their children. It never occurred to me they were Jewish until Hitler made it an issue to be Jewish. They were just German girls like me. They read the same books, played with the same toys, loved the same fashion magazines, and longed to be movie stars, just like the rest of us. We never discussed religion. I honestly did not remember if they celebrated Christmas or not. It never occurred to me they might not. I presumed everyone was Lutheran like we were. I do remember sometimes on Saturdays the Jewish girls could not play, but they could on Sunday, which always struck me as a bit odd.

My father had many Jewish business colleagues, both at the Grieneisen factory and at the various business organizations he belonged to. His chief financial officer at Grieneisen was Jewish. Vati was devastated when he decided to emigrate to England in 1936 after Hitler banned interracial marriages between Aryans and Jews. Herr Bernstein's wife was German, and they decided the Germany of Hitler was not an environment in which to raise their children. I was only six years old at the time, and I did not understand all of this. I just knew that Vati came home one night in a terrible mood. Over drinks in the music room, while I played quietly on the floor with my dolls, he told my mother he would never be able to replace Herr Bernstein. "They are causing some of the best German minds to flee Germany!" My parents, like all parents of small children, thought I was not listening. But I was, and it stuck with me that my father had said "German minds," that we would lose "the best German minds." I had not understood that it was German-Jewish minds that were forced to leave, until now. I stretched my arms over my head. Sasha stirred in her basket. I guess Hitler would just call them Jewish minds. But that made no sense to me.

They looked like us, dressed like us, ate like us, and they even spoke German like us. Take Elfriede, a girl in my class. Her family had lived in Dahlem since Bismarck's time! She was every bit as much German as I was! None of it made sense, and Mutti and Vati had no answers for me. Why did they leave? Where were they going?

———

The day after Tante Anna left, we went to the pharmacy on Königin Luise Strasse in Dahlem to buy some arnica cream for my bruised and cut knee. Mutti was worried the cuts would develop into scars. A young mother, much younger than Mutti, I noted, came in with her son, a boy of maybe five. We heard her tell the pharmacist that he had a chronic cough.

"I'm sorry. I couldn't help but overhear," said Mutti, placing her hand on the woman's arm. The woman turned and looked at Mutti, a blank expression on her face. Mutti smiled and continued. "The only cure that really works is a remedy I learned from an old gypsy lady when I lived in Halberstadt. Have your child eat the peel of a lemon dipped in honey." She patted the boy's head. "It works like a dream, and I have used it many times on Jutta here," she added, pointing to me.

The woman's expression turned to horror. Her cheeks flushed and her eyes grew large. "I would never take advice from a gypsy."

My mother shrugged her shoulders and calmly said, "Then I guess your child must suffer the cough. Eventually it will go away on its own." She grabbed my hand and turned and walked out.

We walked up Königin Luise Strasse in the sun, and I noted the propaganda all about us. The kiosks outside the U-Bahn station sported posters that screamed at us: "The Jews of the whole world want to destroy Germany. German *Volk*! Defend yourselves! Do not buy from Jews!"

"Mutti, why did Herr Schmeling leave?" I asked suddenly. It occurred to me he might be Jewish.

For a moment Mutti didn't answer, and at first I thought she was going to ignore me. She took my hand as we walked. "Because he lost his fight to the American, and Hitler didn't like that very much."

"Why didn't he like it? Didn't Herr Schmeling try to fight?"

"Of course he did. He just didn't fight as well."

I frowned. It didn't seem like a reason to have to leave, especially not the way he left, all hushed and quiet. One day they were there and the next they were gone. "Well, I don't understand."

Mutti smiled. "Good. Because if you did, I would be worried!"

"No, Mutti. Really, I don't understand."

"He ruined Hitler's program, Jutta. Germans are supposed to be superior, especially to people like this American, what was his name?" She looked up to the sky, remembering. "Well, I don't pay any attention to sports, but anyway, he was a black man and, according to Hitler, Germans shouldn't lose to black men."

"Well, that's ridiculous! Maybe he was a better boxer?"

"*Genau!*" Mutti nodded her head. "Now is not a good time to discuss these things." We had come up to the subway station and people were coming home from downtown, spilling out into the wide Dahlem streets. "Maybe we have time for a slice of cake? Would you like that?"

"Yes!"

We crossed the Thielallee and headed back along Kuckusweg, the golden wheat fields dancing in the breeze on one side, a contrast to the neat houses with moss-covered, crossed-wood fences along the other. At Musausstrasse we turned and headed through the park. A stately white stucco house, its red tile roof and copper dome glistening in the sunlight, guarded the corner of the street. Whenever I walked by, I studied that house, hoping when I was older I would remember it and tell my children about the beautiful house on the corner just before the park. The sounds of the park were pleasant in the early afternoon. Children called to each other, and a breeze rustled the new buds of the willow trees that swept paths of ripples on the water of the lake.

Instead of turning right at Auf dem Grat to head home, we continued straight to Kronprinzenallee and turned left to the little *Konditorei* run by Herr Michael at the corner of Meissen Strasse. As we turned the corner a black limousine passed us. Its tires splashed huge sheets of muddy water high into the air from the puddles along the road. I turned to see the driver accelerate much too fast for our tiny street, and I knew it was one of Field Marshal Keitel's cars. Since he had moved into Herr Schmeling's house, our street was often filled with big black limousines, the Nazi flags on their hoods jutting out and flapping violently in the wind. "Mutti, isn't it strange how Herr Keitel moved into the Schmelings' house so quickly?"

Mutti smirked slightly. "It is indeed, Jutta."

"I miss them. He was so nice, and she was so beautiful!" I thought of his wife, Anni Ondra. I had never seen her movies; I was too young. I didn't mind, though, because, even better, I had seen her in person in my own neighborhood. She came to the window sometimes and watched him play with us. I was very impressed that we had a movie star in our neighborhood. "And so glamorous! I loved all those long, sleek dresses. And the hats she wore! Mutti, you should have seen all of her hats! She had this one with feathers in it—purple, I think—with white and brown pheasant feathers and a little veil that she wore just so, to the side." I demonstrated for Mutti.

She laughed. "Jutta, you had better become a fashion designer, as much as you pay attention to these things." She grabbed my arm suddenly and yanked me out of the street before a second limousine could hit me. "Slow down!" she shouted to the blackened windows that shut us out. "Damn those things! This is a neighborhood with children." She shook her head. "Are they having a convention or something at Keitel's house?"

I sighed. "I would much rather have movie stars and athletes in our neighborhood than *Nazibonzen*."

"I couldn't agree more!"

We turned the corner at Kronprinzenallee. But my mind lingered on the Föhrenweg, still seeing Herr Schmeling and his beautiful wife in front of their beige stucco house with the purple and blue hydrangea hedge. It seemed so strange, everybody leaving mysteriously. One day they were here and the next they were gone. First Tante Anna, and then Herr Cohen from the shoe store—gone, the store closed, boarded up—and then Herr Schmeling. I remembered how we would play soccer in front of his house hoping he would come out and play with us. I would play with Erica and Hannelore and Jürgen, the boy from across the street. One time, just as I was winding up to take what I hoped would be an amazing kick for the goal, I looked up and saw him coming toward us. We all stopped and ran to him, shouting, "Herr Schmeling, play with us! Play *fuss ball* with us."

He said, "Well, what do you think I came out here for? To admire your skills?"

We laughed at this. "What would the Führer say about missing these shots?" He asked jokingly. How ironic that comment seemed now. Maybe he already knew.

We all laughed, except for Hannelore, who furrowed her brow and began playing as if her life depended on it!

"What is up with her?" whispered Erica.

"Hey, you! Hannelore," yelled Jürgen. "Do you think you'll be playing for Hertha or something?"

After the game, I said to Hannelore, "*Was war denn mit dir loss?*" "What was that all about?"

She shrugged. "I just thought about the Führer's desire that we do our best at all times, and I wanted to win."

We had reached my gate, and as I traced the number twelve, I waved to Hannelore and watched her continue down the street, her braids swinging with each step. The sun was setting, leaving only slivers of light through the trees of the Grunewald. I turned to Erica. "Do you ever dream of traveling? Seeing another country? Like maybe America or China?" I asked.

"No," she said. "Why, do you?"

"Oh, yes. I want to travel to the American West and see the cowboys and Indians like Karl May describes."

"Jutta, you're crazy! Nobody even speaks German there! How would you ask for the bathroom?" We giggled.

"Toilet," I said. "They would understand; it's the same word in English.

Besides, I am doing very well in English, thank you very much! One more year and I will be able to talk to anyone I want in America."

"Well, what would you eat? They only eat snakes and cactus."

"No they don't," I said. "And besides, Frau Dietrich appears to do just fine in the American West!"

"She lives in Hollywood, and the Führer says that they live like gypsies there."

"Oh, the Führer this and the Führer that! You really drive me crazy with this stuff."

"Shhh!" she whispered violently. "Honestly, Jutta, you and your crazy mother will get us all into trouble one day."

"Well, if your Führer loves you so much, why are you afraid of him?"

"I'm not! He is like a father—he just wants us to behave our best and act our best at all times."

"Well, I have dreams. Places I want to see," I said stubbornly.

"You can't leave, because you can't leave me here alone to face Hannelore!" We laughed. "Wasn't that strange today? How she played soccer like her life depended on it?"

I nodded.

It had grown dark, so we hugged and went up our separate driveways. The light glowed warmly in my mother's kitchen. As I entered, I could smell the schnitzel Luise had prepared for dinner. It all seemed so long ago, and now his house was teeming with Nazis, he and his wife erased from our street as if they had never lived there.

"You are so quiet, *mein Schatz*," said Mutti, still holding my hand.

"I was just remembering Herr Schmeling playing ball with us."

"Oh, I see." She held the door to the *Konditorei* for me.

"Mutti, Erica says you're crazy!"

"Well, so does your father." She laughed. And seeing my face, she added, "Oh, stop it, Jutta! What does Erica know of me! Don't worry about what she thinks." She smiled at Herr Michael. "*Guten Tag*, Herr Michael. Can we still get some cake and coffee?"

"But of course, Frau Bolle," said Herr Michael, his stomach seeming to move ahead of the rest of his body as he offered my mother a chair. "Would you like the seat by the window?"

"Yes. Perfect! Jutta, you go pick from the case for both of us." And that was the end of the conversation. Was Erica right? Would Mutti get in trouble with *them*? I worried about Mutti and her outspokenness, and I decided I would bring it up again, but not now. Maybe in private, in her bedroom, one day in the morning before I went to school. But for now I would forget these thoughts. I examined the plates of cake in the case, choosing hazelnut cream for me and sour cream cheesecake for Mutti. We sat in the late afternoon light, watching the cars speed past on the Kronprinzenallee. Across its broad lanes, the forest of the Grunewald hugged its edge like a picket fence. I savored my cake and my time with my mother; in the background, the buzz of café talk added comfort, blocking the sounds of the world outside. Mutti squeezed my hand and smiled at me, and for that moment I could forget.

I hated physical education! No other class in school worried me or caused me to lose sleep like physical education. Unfortunately for me, they subjected us to it every school day, deeming it an important and necessary part of our development into fit German adults. Every other one of our "extra" classes, as Vati called them, like music or art, met only twice a week, but not physical education. Oh no, in Hitler's Germany, in order to build good, strong bodies and mold us into the perfection of German womanhood, we had physical education every single day. How I dreaded it! How most of us dreaded it! Only a handful—the athletic ones, like Hannelore Bergman—embraced it with zeal. I was fairly good at running and jumping, but I was horrible at every other sport.

Völkerball was one of my least favorite—you were made to run in a line in front of the other team while one member of the team threw a large, hard, white ball at you and tried to tag you out. Some of the more zealous of my classmates threw the ball as hard as possible. Large bruises on my thighs and bottom were testimony to my habit of turning my back to shield my front. Eventually I developed the strategy of running as slowly as possible in front of the line so as to be hit by the ball and thus expelled from the game as soon as possible. I could then spend the remainder of the period sitting on the sidelines, cheering on my more competitive friends.

In the winter we had gymnastics. I hated gymnastics even more than *Völkerball!* We trained for rallies and marches, prancing around and doing tumbling routines while waving flags and hoops over our heads. Sometimes they would send the class to line the street for a parade, or they would send out notices through the Hitler Youth that they wanted us, the "bright flowers of German womanhood," to create mass displays of athletic beauty for some rally or another. Frau Berringer actually used that phrase one day in class: "the flowers of German womanhood." Erica had to pinch me to keep me from laughing out loud. I did raise my hand and ask if we weren't more like buds. She stared blankly at me for a moment, and then continued to show us the proper technique for ribbon waving, wrist position and all. To my relief, my parents never allowed me to participate in the rallies. I was always inexplicably ill on the day of such events. I found the entire exercise tiresome. My arms ached from holding rings over my head, and I could never keep the flags from touching the ground. Not to mention the fact that I unintentionally messed up the marching routines, never remembering if the next step was to the right or to the left, causing Frau

Berringer to shout in frustration. I think she was actually relieved I never came to the Nazi events, her fear that I would make her look bad overtaking the desire to insist on my participation.

I was no better at the double rings, which hung menacingly from long metal poles seemingly miles above the ground, than I was at ribbon and flag waving. I seemed to be completely devoid of upper body strength and could not master the simplest routine, and I had such a fear of falling that my hands sweated so profusely I could not hold on to the rings. But my true nemesis was the horse. The horse terrified me! I was convinced I would not clear it, and if I did clear it, I would land on my bottom on the other side. I always had to follow Hannelore Bergman, since she came alphabetically before me—they did everything in alphabetical order, the Nazis, and Hannelore could have been the poster child for Nazi Germany. A superb athlete, she also looked the part with her thick golden braids and rosy cheeks, and she enthusiastically embraced all Nazi activities. After Hannelore's turn, Frau Berringer always beamed. Then she frowned and called out, "Bolle, Jutta Bolle." With a lump in my throat, I took my place before the horse. It stood waiting for me, cold and impersonal at the end of the long blue mat. My eyes darted around nervously—anything to avoid looking at the horse—always coming to rest on the enormous posters that hung on the back of the gym wall directly in front of me. Huge propaganda signs plastered the otherwise stark walls of the gymnasium with slogans: "*Fur dem Vaterland!*" and "*Alle Sagen Ja!*" But the one on the back wall always held my attention: a blond boy, about my age, staring mystically into the distance, superimposed over Hitler's face in muted colors; Hitler's eyes, those blue eyes, cold, intense, and focused. On the bottom it read: "*Alle Zehnjährigen in die H.J.*" (All ten-year-olds in the Hitler Youth.)

"Jutta, Bolle! You're next!" called the instructor again, irritation creeping into her voice. Unable to avoid it any longer, I took a final deep breath and began the long run down the blue mat to the horse at the end.

———

Just as propaganda posters were never far away, Nazi instruction in alleged patriotism was a constant companion. I grew weary of hearing about Hitler's life; every year on his birthday, the same stories. It was like your mother telling you to sit up at the table: the same thing again and again! And it did not end there! In history class, we learned about Hitler's struggle for National Socialism against the evils of communism. We learned what was done to Germans after World War I—how they took our land, how they took our industry, how they took our people—and always we heard about the Jews: the Jewish bankers who stole from honest Germans and the Jewish shopkeepers who overcharged hardworking Germans. They drilled into us that the Führer loved the young people of Germany—and they burdened us with the hideous belief that it was up to us to save Germany. Erica and I did not take these things very seriously, but some of the girls, Hannelore and Liesel especially, took it all to heart.

Each time Hitler gave a radio address they would herd us into the auditorium to listen to the live broadcast. His voice, angry and harsh, assaulted us from huge loudspeakers set out all around the auditorium, the sound echoing off the walls and ceiling. On special occasions like his birthday or the anniversary of the Nazi takeover, they decorated the auditorium with enormous flags—deep red, draped from ceiling to floor, with huge black swastikas in the center. The flags terrified me. In between the flags they placed enormous posters with Hitler's face on them saying things like *"Ganz Deutschland Hört den Führer"* (all Germans hear the Führer) or pictures of the Hitler Youth with *"Führer wir folgen!"* (Führer command we will follow.)

They made us line up alphabetically for these events, which meant I always ended up in the front row and had to pay attention, since the school authorities sat in front of us. Each event began the same way: you held your right arm out and up by your ear in the Nazi salute and sang both *"Deutschland über Alles"* and the Horst Wessel song. The songs were long and tiresome, and my arm would drift lower and lower until I finally had to prop it up with my left hand. My friends blessed with names later in the alphabet could rest their arms on the shoulders of the students in front of them, but I had no one in front of me, and I longed for a name like Zimmer.

Their propaganda was not limited to the schools. All over the city, propaganda posters hugged the walls of buildings and the cylindrical poles that stood on every street corner for announcements: there, next to an announcement for the symphony, a warning in thick black print to "be wary of the Jews." There were constant reminders of the presence of the Nazis. Even in the quiet streets of Dahlem and peaceful Lichterfelde, where Opa Bolle lived, you could not escape it. Posters were plastered everywhere, and periodically the Hitler Youth organized a parade and marched through these suburbs. The hearty singing seemed innocent until you listened to the words and read the banners that screamed their messages. Liesel often led the girls, in crisp and clean BDM uniforms, proudly marching along, flags held high, synchronized ribbons dancing in the air. Christa and I giggled as we watched them march by in their ugly "aa" colored uniforms. I did not care that Mutti thought it rude to call their brownish, mustard-colored uniforms dog-pooh-colored; it was the truth.

Reichskristallnacht

November 10, 1938

November 10, 1938, began like any other day for me, except that I was in a big hurry for lunchtime to come. My birthday was only four days away, and Mutti had promised we could shop for a birthday dress on the Kurfürstendamm.

First we were going to go to *KadeWe* for a light lunch and a look around for a dress. If we did not find one there, Mutti said we would go to Mignon, and then finish the afternoon at Café Möhring for cake and *Eis Kaffee*. I loved these outings into the city. I could hardly contain myself as I ran to my mother's bedroom to let her know that I was ready to go. She was putting the final touches on her hair. Looking up from the mirror, she said, "*Ja*. Juttalein, are you ready, my darling?"

"I've been ready for an hour, Mutti!"

"Well, bring me the phone. I'll call to see if Heinz can drive us. If not, we will take the subway into town." I ran over to lift the elegant cream-colored telephone off its usual stand by her bed and brought it to her at her dressing table. It was extremely heavy, and I always wondered how she held it up to her ear for those lengthy morning conversations with Tante Hilde. An extra-long cord ran from its base to the wall, so my mother could talk on the phone either from her bed or from one of the sitting chairs she favored by the large bay window that looked out over the garden. She dialed my father's office from memory, and I heard her exchanging greetings and polite conversation with Frau Schiller, his secretary, before asking for Heinz. After some small talk, she said, " Jutta and I would like to go shopping today, and I was wondering if you were free to drive us to the Kurfürstendamm?"

After a brief pause, she said, "Why is that?"

Then she fell silent for a moment until I heard her say, "*Gott*! No!" Then another pause. And then, "I don't believe it! I had no idea! I haven't had the radio on today." And then finally, after another brief pause, "Oh, of course not. No; we will go another day."

My heart sank as I heard these last words. She looked pale and worried. She said goodbye to Heinz and then slowly put the receiver back in the cradle. She stared out the window until I broke into her thoughts.

"We aren't going?" I asked.

"No. We can't"

"But why not? You promised, Mutti!"

She turned to look at me. I could see tears forming in her eyes. "Last night they smashed all of the Jewish-owned shops along the Kurfürstendamm! The entire downtown is in chaos! Heinz says glass, bricks, and debris are everywhere, and they have looted and destroyed the shops."

"But what about *KadeWe*? They didn't destroy that, I'm sure!"

She gave me a look that shot straight to my conscience. "It's too dangerous, Jutta, and we are not going." With that, she picked up the phone again and called my father.

"Hans, why didn't you call me? I had no idea!" Then a pause. "Well, I only found out from Heinz because Jutta and I were planning to go shopping today!" She nodded her head at something my father said, as if he could see her. "It is too awful! What does it mean?" She frowned. "But I thought after last summer they were done with this ridiculous behavior—they called out the police to stop it. Remember?"

Another pause. "*Ja,* we'll talk when you get home." She turned and looked at me. "Vati is coming home early. He does not want to talk on the phone about it."

I stared out into the garden. Why would they destroy shops? My mother's voice came from behind me. "Jutta, I know you are disappointed, but we will go another time. You must understand that something terrible has happened."

I did not respond. I studied the wisteria vine that climbed from the ground all the way up to my mother's bedroom window. Brown and hard, it wrapped around the iron grill of her window in small, tight, knobby clusters, its leaves long lost to the season.

"I don't understand! Why?" I turned and searched her face. "Why would they do this?"

She did not respond. She stood staring out to the garden with me. With the goldfish and furniture long since put up for the winter, the terrace looked bleak and uninviting. I sank into the chair by the window. "Can we, just for once, talk about it all? Can I hear all about it when Vati comes home?" I said, sinking further back into the comfort of the chair with my head in my hands.

"Yes. You can sit with us and listen to the news, and then we will ask Vati together about what happened today." She came over to me and stroked my hair. "I don't know why, Jutta. Honestly, I have no explanation for you."

We sat, staring at nothing. In the distance I heard a horn on Kronprinzenallee, and then she sighed. "Let's go for a walk." I rose slowly from the chair. I quietly left the room to go change into my walking clothes.

———

Vati came home late that night. I had eaten and already had my bath before I heard the crunch of the tires on the drive. I ran downstairs to tell Mutti that Vati was home. She sat at the piano, her head bent over in concentration and her body moving fluidly to the music. I recognized the Beethoven sonata; she played it often. The melody was hauntingly beautiful. After a moment, she sensed my presence and stopped. "Vati is home, I take it?"

I nodded.

She continued to play. Vati walked through the archway and stopped in surprise when he saw me sitting there. "I thought you would be in bed, Jutta."

"I told her she could stay up and listen to the news with us, Hans," said Mutti, stopping her playing to greet Vati.

Vati looked at my mother and raised his eyebrows but said only, "I see. Well, then, come here and give your tired Vati a hug." I sprang up from my seat and ran to him.

Mutti glanced at her watch, and for a moment it caught a glint of light and flashed a single second of brightness in the soft light of the room. "The BBC will be on any second. Should I have Luise bring your supper in here?"

My father did not respond. Mutti shrugged and left to speak to Luise.

I watched Vati carefully, as if his face would give me a clue to the strange events of the night before. He ran his hands through his hair, sweeping it straight back, and stared at the carpet. We sat in silence, neither of us feeling like making any small talk. After a moment, Vati turned the radio on just as the distinctive sound of the gong that marked the beginning of the BBC newscast came on. Luise had, in the meantime, brought a tray full of food, and my mother had retrieved a bottle of wine from the wine cellar.

The reporter's voice was hurried and dramatic as he spilled forth the day's news. By far the biggest story was the news coming out of Germany. I had to concentrate to understand him. Periodically my mother translated words she knew I did not understand. We sat trying to absorb what he was saying. Vati did not touch his food as the reporter continued to recount the horrors of the night before. He told of the destruction of hundreds of synagogues and thousands of Jewish-owned businesses all over Germany. He told of families thrown out of their apartments—their belongings either looted or destroyed, their apartment buildings ransacked. He spoke of the millions of shards of glass that littered the main shopping street of Berlin, the Kurfürstendamm.

Mutti sucked in her breath. "Thank God Anna and Ludwig got out!"

My father stared straight ahead.

The BBC reporter said that countless Jewish men had been rounded up or had disappeared. The police stood by, he said, and did nothing to intervene and stop the mob violence. He said packs of young men who instigated the violence, and those that joined in, roamed the streets freely. Eventually, he spoke of the outrage expressed by many Germans at the senseless destruction of property and the mob violence. I clung to these statements—the fact that many of my fellow Germans did not condone these acts of barbarism. The sharp criticism by many Germans, he noted, has caused Hitler to back away from responsibility for the actions. He said the German media has portrayed the attacks of the night before as a spontaneous outrage against the Jewish population, sparked by the assassination of Ernst vom Rath in Paris by a young Jewish dissident. Finally, he spoke of the horrified reaction of citizens all over the world. When the announcer finished the international report and began relating the local news about England, Vati turned off the radio. The music room was unnaturally quiet after the noise of the radio. Only the ticking of the clock and the sounds of Luise cleaning up the kitchen interrupted the silence.

"I hate it! Why can't we get rid of them? The entire world will think this is what Germans are like. That we are animals that kill and loot!" The words burst out of me.

"What the world thinks of us is the least important thing. It is what we think of ourselves that matters," said my father.

I threw my hands in the air. I didn't understand what he meant. I didn't understand any of it. I thought about Eva and Magda from school. I had walked home with them on occasion and sat with them during morning break. I knew they were Jewish; girls like Liesel whispered about it. How must they feel to-night? They must be terrified!

"But why? I just don't understand why." I searched my parents' faces for a clue.

Vati cleared his throat and reached for my hand. "Do you remember when you were so upset when one of the boys at the end of the street shot a bird with his slingshot?"

I did not respond.

"And then he kicked the little bird, and it was still alive…"

"Vati, please!" I held up my hand, the memory too awful—the bird's tiny neck broken, hanging limp, and the expression of cruel pleasure on the boy's face too much for me to bear.

Vati continued. "And you asked me then, why? And I had no explanation, because there is no explanation for such an act." He paused, letting the words sink in. "And it is the same now. There is no explanation."

I removed my hand from his. I knew he was right, but it wasn't enough. I needed them to say something else, something to fix it.

"What has become of Germany?" Mutti said it more to herself than to us. She stood up and began to pace the room. "Those poor people!" My mother shook her head.

I will help Eva and Magda, I decided. I will be friendlier than ever to them.

Mutti sat down next to me. "These are things that no nine-year-old should have to know about." She hugged me, her cheek grazing mine, and I smelled her makeup and perfume.

"I would rather know than grow up thinking that the world is one way and then find out how wrong I was," I said firmly.

My parents' eyes met, and then we again sat in silence. Finally, Vati stood and walked to the window, his back to us, arms clasped behind his back. He looked out into the dark. At what? There were no lights on in the garden, and the window looked as if it had been painted black. After a moment Mutti said, "Jutta, eat your dessert. It is time for bed."

But I had lost my appetite, "No thank you, Mutti. I am finished." I got up to go upstairs, for I was suddenly very tired.

"I will be up in a moment," said Mutti.

I walked slowly out of the room and up the stairs; when I got to the top of the stairs I heard their voices again. I stood on the landing for a moment, listening.

"It's even worse than the reports," said my father quietly. "Kurt heard word that they have rounded up almost thirty thousand Jews and sent them to who knows where. We hid Herr Burger in the factory basement. We arranged for his wife and children to leave the country tonight. That's why I was so late.

In fact," he said, "they should be on a train for the Netherlands right now. And then we hope to get them to England."

"What about him? He must leave," said my mother.

"He will leave tomorrow, as soon as his family is safe. A Jewish man traveling with his family attracts too much attention. He wanted his family safe first."

"What else can we do, Hans? There must be something."

"The business council held an emergency meeting today. Kurt and I and others wanted to send a letter of protest from the council to Goebbels and Göring, but we lost by two votes. So we are, instead, sending individual letters."

"But will they really send them, and sign them?" the skepticism in her voice betrayed her view.

"Some yes. Some will say they have but won't do it." After a moment he added, "Most will couch it in language objecting to the economic waste at a time when resources are scarce." My mother said something, and I heard my father respond, "They are afraid, Heti. Afraid of being called *Judenfreunde* and risking a visit from Herr Himmler's people." Then they were silent for a moment before my father spoke again.

"I haven't even spoken to my father. I must see him tomorrow and see if he can help some of the others at the factory. We will lose some of our best workmen." I knew that Herr Burger was an exceptionally talented woodworker. He and his division produced the elaborate coffins used for state funerals. My father often spoke of his work as if he were a famous artist. I wondered how my father could possibly replace him. I turned to go into my room; I did not want to hear any more. It was all too depressing.

I went through the motions of getting ready for bed, unaware that I was doing it. All I could think about was poor Eva and poor Magda. I thought about Tante Anna and Frau Schultz, my mother's dressmaker. I had seen the Star of David around her neck once. My mother, seeing it too, had pointed to it silently, and Frau Schultz had quickly tucked it back into her dress. Had they destroyed her shop, too? It was all just too horrible to imagine. The senselessness overwhelmed me. I climbed into bed and pulled the covers high up to my neck. I stared at the ceiling, trying to think of what I could do to put it all right. My mother came in and sat on my bed. She stroked my hair and kissed my forehead.

"Mutti, if there is a God, why does he allow such things?"

"Well, you have asked *the question*, haven't you? All I can say is that man does these terrible things and man must put them right again."

"So there is no God?"

"No. I did not say that. Man, with God's help, will put things right again. Good will win, Jutta. It always does, sometimes not on our schedule, but in the end, good will win." I clung to her words for comfort. I needed certainty. I needed to believe that good would win. She hugged me and stood to leave.

"I love you, Mutti."

"And I love you, Jutta."

She left my room, closing the door softly behind her. I heard her footsteps go down the hall and become more distant as she headed down the stairs to rejoin Vati in the music room. I knew they would talk until late into the night.

I sat up suddenly and threw my covers off. I had forgotten to say good night to *Vögelein*. The floor was cold on my bare feet. The window stuck a bit as I pushed it open. A cold breeze blew back the curtains and prickled my skin, chilling me. *Vögelein* lifted her head in surprise. I smiled at her and held out my hand. But she did not leave her nest. "*Ja. Vögelein*. You are always there. You are not aware of all these awful things, are you?" I clucked at her. "You are lucky."

———

I rose early; the pale, gray lavender light that slipped through my curtains told me the sun would have to fight to break through the clouds that hung from the sky. I needed to see my mother before I went to school. I dressed quickly and tiptoed down the stairs by my room and then back up the stairs on the other side by the living room. As I stepped onto the landing I could hear my mother's voice sounding unusually loud and agitated. She must have gotten up early, too, I thought. But to whom could she be talking at this hour? Certainly not Tante Hilde! I opened the door to her room and stepped in, closing it softly behind me. She was sitting, her back to me, in one of the chairs by the window. She was still in her robe and nightgown, talking on the phone. Engrossed in her conversation, she did not hear me. I stood quietly by the door, wondering if I should stay or leave. Suddenly she leaped up out of the chair and walked to the window, shouting into the phone, "Of course it was planned and organized, Vati! How can you possibly think this was just a spontaneous uprising? What, all the hoodlums in Berlin suddenly decided to run down to the Kurfürstendamm and smash shop windows—but only Jewish ones? You can't really believe that! How did they even know which ones were Jewish? Of course the party organized it from start to finish ... Well, fine! You believe what you want, but your head is in the sand about these people! ... Fine. Let me speak to Mutti." She turned to sit back down and spotted me by the door. "Oh, good morning, Jutta. I didn't see you there. How long have you been there?"

But before I could answer, her mother had gotten on the phone. "Mutti, you don't believe this rubbish that Vati is spouting, do you? Well, thank God for some sanity in the family ... No, I won't bring it up. I'm sorry; I don't mean to increase his blood pressure, but his thinking is the reason they get away with so much ... I know, but he doesn't want to see. Ja, ja. I'm sorry. Listen. I called because I would like to come with Jutta for a visit this weekend. I need to get away from this town … No, I already promised I won't bring it up. But if he brings it up, I can't promise … Now don't go to any trouble. Don't run around baking like crazy like you do. Ja, we will see you on Saturday, Mutti. I love you. Tell Vati I love him, too. Bye-bye." She hung up the phone and looked up at me expectantly.

"I just came to say good morning to you, Mutti. I didn't mean to listen in."

"Oh, it's all right, Jutta. That was just me and your grandfather having one of our discussions." Then she paused. "Can you believe he thinks that yesterday's destruction was not organized by Hitler and his gang?" She shook her head in disbelief.

I had never heard my mother speak so angrily to my grandfather. I knew they did not get along as well as they should, but for my mother to be so agitated was unusual. I felt uncomfortable discussing it, so instead, I said, "Are we going to visit Oma on Saturday?"

"Yes, if I can get Heinz to drive us. I will call this morning to see." She rubbed her forehead and smoothed her brow. "I need to get away from this chaos. Halberstadt will do us good."

I clapped my hands and smiled an enthusiastic yes. I loved to visit Oma Muller; she, like *Vögelein*, was always there to count on. She was never exciting or fun or full of surprises like Opa Bolle, but she was always there with a ready smile, a hug, a new embroidery stitch to show me, or a freshly baked plum cake or my favorite, *Marmorkuchen*.

"Let me see you," said my mother, frowning. I came over to her. She tucked my shirt into my skirt and, looking at my long legs and knobby knees, she noted that we would soon need to get all new school clothes, for I was growing in leaps and bounds.

"Have you had your breakfast, Jutta?"

"No, I came to say good morning to you first."

She nodded. "You better get downstairs or Sisi will wonder what has happened to you." She kissed me on the cheek. I bent down and hugged her around the neck, letting my cheek linger on her pale pink satin robe. It felt so wonderful and cool. I could hear her heart beating through the fabric. We hugged for a few moments. Then she turned my face up to her. "I don't want you worrying about these things today. It will all work out somehow. *Ja?*"

I nodded my head.

Wooden Clowns

I searched for Magda and Eva at morning recess, but they were not at school. I began to worry. What if they too had been taken away? I had to find out what happened to them. After school I searched the hallway, looking for them again. But they were not to be found. Erica ran up to me and said, "Jutta, why do you always get out on the first round in *Völkerball*? I saw you today. That was pathetic! "

"I hate *Völkerball,*" I responded, still looking around.

"Who are you looking for?" asked Erica

"Eva and Magda. Have you seen them today?"

"As a matter of fact, no. They must not be here. Come on. We have to go or our mothers will worry. Well, at any rate, Sisi will worry about you." I looked at her and rolled my eyes. She was always trying to say that my mother was not a good German mother like hers because sometimes she was not at home when I came home from school. I knew this was Erica's mother talking. Soon Hannelore, Liesel, and the others joined us on the walk home down the Kuckusweg to Musäusstrasse and then through the park, past the wheat fields and the gardens now brown and gold in the fall light.

"I really wanted to talk to Eva and Magda," I said. It was a test to see if anyone would discuss the events of the day before.

"I doubt that they would show their faces today," snorted Liesel.

"Why shouldn't they? They are just girls like you and me. They have no part in any of this," I said fiercely.

"I just meant that after the other night's events, I doubt that they will show their faces," she said defiantly.

"What happened? Did they get in trouble?" asked Erica innocently.

My God! She really does not know! Liesel, of course, lost no time in relaying the facts of the night of November ninth to her. She took great pleasure in recounting the details.

I walked quickly ahead so I did not have to listen. As I turned in to my gate, it struck me that nobody at school had mentioned what happened: not the teachers, not the administrators, not any of us. It was as if it had never happened.

For the next few days I searched for Magda and Eva at school, and as the days turned into weeks, I realized with a sinking heart I would never see them again.

———

Germans had developed a dual personality, Vati said. We were like the wooden clown puppet Opa Bolle bought me—when I pulled the string, new pieces fell into place and the clown became a dancing monkey. They said "Heil Hitler" to each other; they hung their flags outside the house on Hitler's birthday and national holidays to avoid being reported by their block captains. They signed their children up for the Hitler Youth program to avoid imprisonment. They placed their pictures of Hitler strategically in their homes, so visitors would see it. They claimed to listen only to the official Nazi radio programs and to read only the official papers. They had learned to embrace silence. By 1938, resisting openly was suicidal. The examples were impossible to ignore: friends who had disappeared, or acquaintances, or shopkeepers, or teachers, or more famous advocates like Martin Niemoeller or Father Josef Spieker—all had spoken out, and all had disappeared.

Many Germans loved the system, especially those who had never fit in before, whose sense of self-worth was enhanced by belonging. But many hated the propaganda, the mind control, the authoritarian policies, and the violence with which the Nazis imposed their will. They shared these thoughts with their spouses and close relatives, and perhaps close friends, but not their children—lest the children speak out at school or at Hitler Youth meetings.

My parents were the exception. They spoke candidly in front of me, at least enough to let me know they did not approve of Hitler and his party. We had no picture of Hitler in our house, no flag out front on special occasions, and both Mutti and Vati refused to greet anyone with "Heil Hitler."

———

Herr Stimple was old, which is why in 1940 he was still in Berlin rather than at the front. He had been the headmaster of the *Lansschule* forever—at least twenty years. He was a nice old man with gray hair and kind blue eyes. Whenever he saw me at school he would wink at me and say, "Greetings to you and your family, Fräulein Bolle." I sensed Herr Stimple did not fully embrace the Nazi education program, nor did he approve of all of their propaganda. I don't know what gave me this idea. He, of course, never said anything, nor did he do anything specific to give me this impression. With Gudrun Himmler as one of his students and Herr Rust, the minister of education, living only a mile from the school, it would have been suicidal to do so. He just did not display the same zeal for all the Nazi symbols that so many of his teaching staff displayed.

Our teachers, for the most part, went along with the Nazi curriculum; they had to, I suppose, for self-preservation. But some of them tried, in subtle ways, to show us another way. I remember Herr Obermann, who taught us history He taught the propaganda, but he also taught endlessly of the Renaissance, with its emphasis on creativity and nonconformity, and of the search for freedom of thought that led the pilgrims to journey to America.

Hitler knew the well-educated teachers of the Reich could weaken his propaganda machine, so, he turned to the Hitler Youth program. In 1936 the Nazis made joining the Hitler Youth compulsory for all children ten and over so they could feed their hate more steadily to the young. In speech after speech, Hitler told us our parents did not understand—they were too old—but we, the young of Germany, would save Germany. We understand. When parents told their children not to participate in a rally or in a special program of the Hitler Youth, children ignored them, and there was nothing the parents could do—not wanting to risk the horror of their own children denouncing them.

The Nazis fed us their propaganda subtly—in small pieces, day after day—so that it became so familiar that it was almost second nature. And always there was something about the Jews. Some of my friends thought they were helping to save Germany from the Jews or from the English and the French. Others, like Erica, joined in the rallies and camping programs for the fun, the adventure of traveling to other cities, and the thrill of performing at rallies with music and excitement echoing around them. Erica participated in their programs, free from the worry of what they really stood for. My parents, on the other hand, would not allow me this luxury.

I was not allowed to participate in the Hitler Youth. I did not turn ten until 1939, so, for the moment, the issue did not face us. But my parents had already forbidden me from attending the May Day Hitler Youth rally in Berlin last spring. Many of my friends had gone. Erica attended, along with her older sister, who was active in the *Bund Deutscher Mädchen* (BDM), the section of the Hitler Youth for older girls. Liesel, who was fourteen and lived at the corner of our street, had risen through the ranks of the BDM to achieve the power and authority she craved. A true believer, Liesel did not miss any of the major rallies. She regaled us with detailed descriptions. She told of the glories of the Führer. How he had spoken. How his words moved her. It was like a religious experience for her. Her eyes would moisten as she described the flags, the music, the floats, and the Führer. "Liesel is living testament that the Nazis excel at political theater," said Vati when I told my parents at dinner of Liesel's enthusiastic descriptions of the events—like a Wagner opera with symbols blaring and kettle drums thundering.

As for me, Mutti made it clear I was never to attend any sort of Nazi rally, no matter how small, and no matter if my class was recruited to participate. "You'll just have to be sick that day. I will not allow my child to be cannon fodder for their propaganda." I had attended a few meetings of the *Jungmädel* with Erica, who was a year older than I was. The JM, as we called it, was the section of the Hitler Youth for girls ten to fourteen. My mother surprised me when she said I could go with Erica to the meeting. She was a smart woman; she knew I would hate it.

And I did. I hated the singing and the marching! I didn't sing well, and the marching hurt my feet and made my knees ache. I looked at Erica and wondered what on earth my friend, who in so many other ways was like me, found appealing about all of this. She was working on getting her next button so she could be one of the directors of the group. She said, "Oh, Jutta, it will be so great when I am in charge because I can pick you to lead the group. Won't that be fun?" I just looked at her, and before I could respond, the group leader had started another song. By the time I got home at five o'clock, I vowed never to attend another meeting.

I went straight to my room to rest my feet and read. My mother came in before dinner and sat on my bed. I had just started reading *Max und Moritz* to lighten my mood and try and forget about my afternoon.

Max und Moritz diese Beiden

Wolten sich die Zeit Vertreiben,
Doch da war die Witwe Bolte
Die das nicht so gerne wolte.

"So how was the meeting?" she asked softly.

"I hated it," I said without looking up.

"Oh."

The clock sounded loud in the quiet room. I could hear a breeze moving the branches of the pine tree against the house.

"So I guess you don't want to go again?"

"Nope."

"Well, enjoy your book."

I nodded my head.

"Luise is making spaghetti for dinner."

"Yes!" I said enthusiastically, setting the book down.

As she walked toward the door I saw a slight smile on her face. "Come down in fifteen minutes and join us in the kitchen."

From then on, whenever I strayed too far out of line, she would threaten me with the *Jungmädel,* saying, "You know, Jutta, by law I am supposed to be sending you. If you don't behave, I may have to start sending you—maybe they can shape you up!" It was a very effective weapon in her disciplinary arsenal. I don't suppose Hitler or Baldur von Shirach would find it very funny. But use it she did.

The War Years: 1939—1945

3

September 1939

Sisi dried my hair with a towel and combed it to the side. "So. Now you look presentable. All the zoo dirt, gone." She snapped her fingers. "Washed away!"

I grinned. "The penguins are the best! Oh, Sisi, you should have seen them waddling to the water and then slipping in all sleek and quiet."

She smiled. "They are interesting creatures. Now I hope your Opa has no more surprise zoo visits in mind—throwing off our schedule like that!" she said in mock irritation.

Unplanned, Opa Bolle and Tante Ebi had taken me to the zoo that afternoon. I had eaten pretzels with mustard rather than dinner and loved every minute of it. Sisi did not approve. But Mutti had simply kissed me, unconcerned. "Have fun with your Opa," she called after us. Opa had said there were two new baby lions, and we were on a mission to find them. Passing under the great Chinese gates that marked the entrance to the Berlin Zoo, I thought of Carl Bolle, selling his milk in the shade to zoo visitors so many years ago.

"Opa, did *Grossvater* Bolle really ride an elephant through the zoo?"

Opa chuckled. "I don't think so, but there's no telling what my father did!"

"But he did ride white stallions down the Kurfürstendamm?"

"He drove a carriage pulled by six white stallions," corrected my grandfather.

"How fantastic! Can you imagine?"

"No. And neither could the rest of Berlin!"

The crowd in front of the organ grinder laughed as he made faces at the children while a tiny monkey dressed in a red suit danced on his shoulder. I stared, mesmerized by the monkey's human movements.

Opa tapped me on the shoulder. "Come! Let's get you an ice cream in honor of your great-grandfather."

"Has Jutta had any lunch?" asked Tante Ebi.

"Ice cream makes a great lunch, huh, Jutta?" answered Opa Bolle.

I grinned.

Tante Ebi raised her eyebrows but let it go.

After we ate our ice cream, we searched for and found the lion cubs. Opa insisted I take a picture with them—one on each side of my lap, their paws as big as the palm of my hand. Tante Ebi shook her head with relief when the photo session ended and I had no scratch or bite marks from the playful little balls of fur snuggled on my lap.

"Those lions are so cute! " I said to Sisi.

"And full of fleas, no doubt!"

"Their eyes! Oh, you should have seen their eyes, so big and beautiful, and they just lay on my lap, licking their paws and washing their faces."

"Well, no matter. I think we have you de-fleaed! And I'm glad you had a good time."

"I had a wonderful time," I said, twirling in front of the mirror.

Sisi laughed, "Now go join your parents—they are in the music room." She glanced at her watch. "But hurry. The news will start soon, and your father will want quiet!"

I put my finger to my lips, imitating Vati's gesture of silence. She laughed again and sent me down to my parents. I hurried down the stairs, my hand caressing the wooden rail of the iron banister that hugged the stairs to the living room. As I reached the last steps, I slowed my pace. An unnatural quiet had settled over the house. I should have heard my parents' voices, but all I heard was the clipped sound of the radio announcer. The door to the music room stood open, and I waited there a moment, looking in on my parents. They sat together on the sofa, staring intently at the radio across the room on the bookshelf. My father's face was pale and drawn, the muscles in his temples working. Something was very wrong, and I turned and studied the radio as if I would find the answer in its smooth, beige curves. Then I heard the announcement: The German Army has entered Poland.

I glanced over to my parents. A single tear slid down Vati's cheek. He grabbed Mutti's hand and held it so hard it turned white, and then another tear fell. "They will destroy us," he said quietly, almost to himself. "That's the end for Germany." My stomach fell. I didn't think I should hear this. This was private, between my parents. I turned quickly, accidentally knocking the door as I ran upstairs, my heart racing with each step.

I hid my face in my pillow and pulled the covers over my head. It was only a matter of moments before I heard her come in, Sasha behind her. The jingle of Sasha's collar seemed miles away. Mutti sat on my bed and hugged me through the covers without saying a word. I heard Sasha settle into her basket as Mutti's even breathing calmed me.

"Why is Vati crying?" I asked, my voice muffled through the covers.

I felt her sigh. "Because there will be war."

I pushed her up, abruptly uncovering my head.

"Will Vati have to fight?" I asked urgently with tears welling in my eyes.

"No, no," said my mother. "Vati is thankfully too old, and so is Onkel Kurt. But many young German men will have to fight."

"Then why is Vati crying?" I asked.

"Because he knows ..." She paused. "Because he knows that war is difficult;

Vati and I have lived through war before. We were very young—only a little older than you—just fourteen years old when the last war started, and only eighteen when it ended." She stroked my forehead and kissed me. "We had so hoped to spare you the experience of war."

"But he said they will destroy us. Who will?"

"Jutta, don't worry. Your father was just upset by the news."

"Destroy what?" I insisted.

She looked away, "Germany."

I frowned. "How could that be?"

She did not respond. Instead she stared out the window into the black of night.

"But surely he's wrong! Isn't he, Mutti?"

"Let us hope. Now I want no more discussion." She switched off my light and lay down with me. Curving her body to mine, she held me.

"Please stay with me, Mutti."

"I will." She stroked my hair. "Shhh. Go to sleep, my love, and don't worry about anything."

But Vati's tear-stained face haunted me. "I've never seen Vati cry," I said into the darkness of my room.

"I know." And she held me tight until finally I drifted off on the river of sleep, my bed a ship with me and Mutti on it, twirling down the river's long, curved expanse.

In the morning, everything was just as it was every other day of the week, and when nothing happened over the next few weeks, I began to think my father was mistaken and pushed the scene from that evening out of my mind. But still his face stayed with me, and life was never again quite so simple.

4

And Now You Are Ten

November 14, 1939

It was my birthday on Wednesday, November 14, 1939. My mother had promised me a big party for my tenth birthday. We had discussed it for weeks, and now I could hardly believe the day was finally here. Mutti let me plan the menu: *Wiener Würstchen, Möhrenkopfe,* a *Bolle Eisbombe* of chocolate ice cream, and *Apfelsaft* with slices of apple floating around on top. Luise had set everything out on the table, except for my favorite, the *Bolle Eisbombe*, which took up an entire shelf in the freezer. The truck with our name splashed across it had delivered it only minutes ago. It came in big metal tins, and you could choose from vanilla, chocolate, or strawberry. My favorite was chocolate.

Luise had set the table in the winter garden room, and we sat in the beautiful room with green plants surrounding us as if we were in the middle of a great jungle. A white tablecloth covered the tables Gustav had brought in from the garden. Luise had decorated each place setting with the Meissen dessert plates I loved. At mine, she had placed my favorite—a pale lilac blue graced its outer edges, and delicate pink roses embraced its center. My mother's best silver lay next to each plate. Some mothers might have objected to such an unconventional contrast between *Wiener Würstchen* and fine dinner china, but Mutti thought it inspired and delightful. My friends brought beautiful packages that Sisi took and placed on a table in the corner. I had selected the music for the occasion: the "Blue Danube" and the "Happy Life Waltz" by Strauss, played by the Berlin Philharmonic. Mutti took me by the hand and demonstrated the basic steps to a waltz. We glided across the polished flagstone floor, the room spinning around, and my mother calling to each girl to grab a partner and follow behind us. We spun around the room, forming circles of color around the table; Sisi looked on, shaking her head and smiling in amusement. We tripped over each other, giggling with hysterics as my mother kept time, calling out, "And one, two, three—now turn. And again: one, two, three, turn…" After two waltzes we collapsed, exhausted from the physical effort of giggling.

I sat at the head of the table with Erica to my right and Peti to my left. Christa sat next to Peti. The rest of the girls ran to grab the seats closest to their own friends. There was an awkward moment when everyone avoided sitting next to Gudrun Himmler. We were all cautious around her. I had invited my entire class, twenty-four of us total, so she was included with the rest of the girls.

My mother had placed a napkin on top of each plate. The napkin hid a marzipan candy in the shape of a daisy flower. We squealed with delight, popping the delicious, soft, almond-flavored sweets into our mouths, just as Vati walked through the door. He had come home early from work to experience the festivities. I glanced up from my plate and waved to him as he walked into the garden room. He winked at me and chuckled in amusement over the spectacle. He only stayed for a few minutes, as the noise was too much for him to tolerate. He soon retreated upstairs with a Campari. My mother, on the other hand, was in her element helping Luise and Sisi serve us, a group of loud, boisterous girls. Vati did stay long enough to give the toast. He grabbed a spoon and clicked it against a glass. We fell silent, all eyes turned toward him.

"To Fräulein Jutta Bolle, who on this very day was born ten years ago to the loveliest woman on earth. A healthy, bouncy, redheaded, freckle-faced delight of a girl. We wish her the most joyous of birthdays. *Prost.*" Everyone raised their glasses and screamed out "*prost.*" When Christa missed her mouth and sent a good portion of her apple juice down her dress, we burst out laughing, spraying apple juice mist from our mouths.

Christa stood up and did a perfect imitation of Frau Eberhardt, now our vice principal, complete with her hands on her hips and right foot deliberately tapping the ground to punctuate every word as she spoke. With eyebrows at full arch, she said, "Now, girls, do you really think that is an appropriate way to behave at Fräulein Bolle's very elegant and sophisticated birthday party? Because if you do, I would be happy to speak to Herr Schultz about it."

We doubled over, shrieking with laughter until we could barely breathe, and then Luise appeared through the open French doors with her tray of *Wiener Würstchen.* She had dressed up as a wurst vendor on the Kurfürstendamm, complete with apron and hat. She carried a large metal pan with a lid on it, held by a thick leather strap around her neck, just like the vendors in Berlin. As we lined up in a straight row with me heading the line, she lifted the lid and let us select our *Wiener Wurst.* We carried them back to our places and heaped every conceivable type of fixing on them. My mother had set out four different spinning trays with pickles, mustard, onions, grated cheese, and tomatoes. For a moment there was silence in the room as we took our first bites. Noticing the silence, we stopped chewing and looked at each other. I burst out laughing, which once again started the chorus of giggling, bits of food splattering onto our plates

By the time the *Möhrenköpfe* arrived, their chocolate icing glistening and melting under the lights, we were quite out of control. Sisi looked disapproving, but my mother beamed. And then Mutti carried in the *Bolle Eisbombe* and, with much fanfare, served each of us a huge scoop of the soft ice cream. My mother knew how to give a party! She made every occasion special, and I ran over to her and hugged her, whispering, "Thank you! This is the best party ever!"

She bent down and kissed me. "You're welcome, Jutta. You deserve it; you're a very special girl."

That night I went to bed exhausted and happy, the look on my father's face in the music room a distant memory. I opened my window and described the party to *Vögelein* in great detail. *Vögelein* cocked her head and flapped her wings. I reached out and carefully placed a crumb of my *Möhrenkopfe* on the branch by her nest and shut the window to watch. She cautiously inched her way along the branch, looking around and twitching her head. Then she quickly grabbed the crumb and hopped back to her nest, where she devoured it in a matter of seconds. I grinned at her. "I knew you would like *Möhrenkopfe!*"

On the way to school the next day, Erica and Christa carried on about how fabulous my party was. Was I having a party next year? No, I said, probably not. They looked disappointed. We waited at the Thielallee to cross the street. Liesel waited at the same light. Why was she waiting there when she had to cross the Königin Luise Strasse to go the opposite way to the high school? As we approached, Liesel turned toward us. I didn't like the look on her face.

"You're ten now, right, Jutta?" asked Liesel suddenly.

"Yes," I said proudly.

"Well, you know you will have to sign up for the JM now." I looked puzzled. She rolled her eyes. "The Jungmädel, Jutta. Perhaps you've heard of it."

"Only if I want to," I said, ignoring her sarcasm.

"No! It's compulsory!" she said, scoffing at my ignorance. "By law, everyone has to sign up for the Hitler Youth or their parents go to prison—even a Bolle!"

"Leave her alone!" shouted Erica. "Come on, Jutta!" She grabbed my hand and pulled me out into the street. "Don't worry about what Liesel says."

"Is that true? Will I have to go to JM?"

"I don't know, but if you do, it will be fun. You can be in my troop. Since I am one of the leaders, I will pick you for everything!"

I looked at her doubtfully, remembering the last meeting I had attended with her. She had thought it was great, and I had thought it was dull and tedious.

I worried all day about the JM. Would I really have to join and march around in those ugly *aa*-colored uniforms, singing stupid Nazi hymns? I had to talk to my parents about this! Perhaps they did not realize that I was supposed to sign up. Would they be arrested? In my mind, I saw the SS officers at my house right now, arresting my mother. Or perhaps they would go to my father's office and interrogate him right there! I broke out in a sweat. Frau Schmidt said, "Jutta, are you all right?" I shook my head. "Why don't you go to the office and lie down for a bit. If you don't feel better, Frau Gertrude can call your mother."

After five minutes on the nurse's cot, I asked Frau Gertrude, the school's secretary and nurse, to call my mother. There was no answer. So I spent the rest of the morning with Frau Gertrude in the front office.

After school I ran home, not even waiting for Erica. I slammed the gate and ran up the drive, stopping momentarily to listen for the piano. Chopin! Thank goodness, she was home! I hurried up the drive and rushed to the front door, but Sisi had spotted me from the kitchen. "Well, Jutta, you are here early."

"Yes. I have to talk to Mutti."

"Wait a minute. Slow down. What happened to, 'Good afternoon, Sisi?'"

"I'm sorry. Good afternoon, Sisi. But I have to talk to Mutti!" I said, bouncing up and down with impatience. Sisi crossed her arms in front of her chest. I knew this meant trouble.

"Your mother is playing. Whatever you have to talk about can wait until she is finished and you have washed your hands and eaten." I could tell by her raised eyebrows and crossed arms that arguing would be pointless. So I handed her my book bag and washed my hands in the guest bathroom. When I emerged, she was standing there ready to escort me to the dining room. I hung my head, moping as I went into the dining room. My mother had reached the crescendo of Chopin's "*Grande Valse*," and the music soared through the house. I closed my eyes to listen a moment in amazement as her hands flew over the keys. Her hands were too small, she always explained, when I asked why she had never played with the symphony. "Jutta, the difference is small to an untrained ear, but to a trained ear it is huge." Finally, the piano stopped. For the moment, the music room was silent. Then I heard her shuffling her music around and replacing it in the wooden inlaid box that held all of her music. She laid the piano cover down with a gentle click and scooted her chair out. I could hear her heels tapping on the flagstone as she came toward the dining room.

"Hello, Jutta, my dear. How are you?"

Before I could answer, Sisi announced, "How is she? She is practically bursting with the need to tell you something. I had to barricade the room to keep her from running in while you were playing."

"Really?" Mutti said with interest, as she pulled out a chair to join me at the table. "What is it my love?"

Luise bustled in with a tray covered with slices of *Leberkäse*, potato salad, and sliced tomatoes. Setting the tray down, she said, "Well, hello, Jutta. I saw you racing up the driveway—were the boys chasing you again?"

"No!" I said with embarrassment. I wanted them to leave. I wanted to speak to my mother alone. Sensing this, my mother turned to Sisi and Luise: "Would you mind terribly leaving us for a moment?"

"Of course, Frau Bolle," they said in unison. But I could tell Sisi was irritated. She considered it her role to know about all aspects of my life.

When they had left and we could hear them chatting in the kitchen, she said, "Now, Juttalein, why don't you tell me what is bothering you."

"Liesel said that now that I am ten, you have to sign me up for the *Jung-mädel* and that if you don't, you will go to prison, and that there is nothing you can do about it. Not even a Bolle can do anything!" I blurted out.

"Oh, I see," she said. "And you don't want to go to the *Jungmädel*, I take it?"

I looked at her in astonishment, "Mutti! You know I hate those meetings!"

This pleased her. "Well, when your father comes home we will discuss it with him and see what we can do. In the meantime, I want you to ignore Liesel. Tell her that your parents are taking care of it. Don't suggest that you will not be going. It's nobody's business what you do with your spare time—certainly not Liesel's." With that she rose from the table and told me to join her in her study to do my homework as soon as I was finished with lunch.

"Thank you, Mutti!" I said, pleased I was allowed to join her rather than having to do my homework in my room with Sisi.

That evening after dinner I wandered down to the music room to see if my mother had spoken to my father. They had had their usual light supper in the dining room and then retired to the music room for wine and cheese. Vati looked up. "Oh, good, Jutta. I was just going to come and get you." I came over and sat next to him on the sofa without saying anything. He put his arm around me and pulled me close. "I understand that you do not want to attend the JM meetings." I nodded my head and played with the tassels on my shirt. "So you do not have the same calling as your friend Erica?"

"What does calling mean?" I asked looking up at him.

"Enthusiasm. The same enthusiasm."

"No!" I said with emphasis.

Vati laughed. "Well, in that case, no one will make you go!"

"But Vati," I said turning to face him, "you don't understand! They will put you in prison!"

"No they won't!" He looked over to my mother. "I do not want her to sign up." My mother nodded in agreement.

"But…"

"Jutta!" My father stopped me rather sharply, and then, taking my hand in his right hand and using his left hand to smooth away my frown, he said more gently, "Jutta, I do not want you to worry about this. Do you understand? I will take care of it. If Liesel or any other girl says anything to you, ignore them, or tell them they can come speak to me. *Ja*, if they are in the business of enforcing Hitler's orders, they can come speak to me. I can assure you nothing will happen to me or your mother. So you must not worry. In fact, it causes *me* worry when you worry! So do me a favor and be a happy, carefree little girl."

I hugged him.

"Why does Hitler make children go to these meetings?"

"Control. He wants to convince you that all that he does is right so you will follow and never question him. Children are much easier to convince than we old people."

"But I know lots of girls that hate those meetings just like me. So he must not be convincing everyone."

"No. But he convinces enough. For every girl like you, there is a Liesel."

"I better talk to Erica. She may not realize what he is doing."

My mother looked alarmed. "You let Erica and her parents worry about what Erica does. You just worry about Jutta."

"But maybe she does not realize what he is doing!"

"Jutta, you must be very careful what you say to Erica or any of your friends." I didn't like the intense way both my parents were looking at me. "We share our views with you in private, because we want you to understand. But it is dangerous to talk to others."

I frowned.

"Look, Jutta. The Gestapo has the power to put people in prison for criticizing the government."

My eyebrows shot up. "Really?"

"Yes. And if you tell Erica something, maybe she will tell her parents or a teacher or another friend, and who knows who they will tell! Do you understand?"

I nodded gravely.

Mutti grabbed my hand. "So what we share in this room stays between us!"

I nodded again.

"Good," said Mutti, dismissing the topic. "Now go find Sisi and get ready for bed."

"First she has time for a chocolate!" Vati stood and walked over to the cabinet that held his special chocolate box. I was never to open this box on my own. I always obeyed this rule, fearing if I did not, the box would be empty one day. The box was silver, with his initials elaborately embossed on its lid: JBA, with the B twice as large as the other two letters. He opened the lid and held the box in front of me. The chocolates glistened in the light, their tops dusted with bits of nuts, sugar, and white chocolate. Some had darker chocolate swirls, and their rich smells leaped out of the box and caressed my nostrils. I knew they came from Fassbender & Rausch because my father bought all of his chocolates from Fassbender & Rausch. I selected a light-colored one that was round and tall. I hoped that it held either a hazelnut or marzipan in its mysterious center. I was not to be disappointed; the marzipan oozed out of the sides from between the chocolate layers into my mouth, and I grinned at my father, who winked back at me and whispered, so my mother couldn't hear, "Take another." Hiding the second chocolate behind my back, I said good night to both of them and ran up the stairs to Sisi. I stopped on the landing for a moment and listened.

"But Hans, how can we not sign her up?" asked my mother.

"I will speak to that boy, von Schirach, myself if I have to."

"But you don't know him. How can you get in to see him? You know how exclusive they are!"

"I see him at Schlichter's sometimes when he is not running around with his parade of zoo animals!"

"He goes to Schlichter's for lunch? I thought his type would only go to Horch."

"I don't see many of them, but every once in a while, one crawls in," answered my father.

"I think you will still have to sign her up," I heard my mother say.

"Well, if I do, I will face that then, but for now we will not sign her up. And if we end up having to, we will not permit her to attend."

"Oh, I agree with that—you leave that to me."

"I know you are very innovative, Heidchen, my love."

I pictured my mother smiling. Sisi broke my thoughts as she stepped out of her room. "Jutta, come! You must get ready for bed."

I ran to her and gave her a bear hug. She laughed. "What was that for?"

I shrugged and ran to my room.

That night, I lay in bed worrying. I was not convinced my father could do anything about all this business, and I did not want him to get into trouble. I began to feel guilty. Perhaps I should just go, and that way avoid all the trouble. I would speak to my mother about this tomorrow.

After breakfast, I ran up the stairs and knocked gently on her bedroom door before I entered. She had not heard me knock; she was sitting up in bed reading a book. "Good morning, Mutti," I whispered, peeking around the door.

She looked up over her reading glasses and smiled. "Well, what a nice early morning surprise!" Glancing at her watch, she added, "Shouldn't you be out the door on your way to school?"

"Well, yes, but I just came to say that it is all right. I will go to the JM meetings. I really don't mind. Tell Vati not to worry about it."

She studied me without speaking for several seconds. "Jutta, come here." I walked over to the bed and sat down on the plush down comforter. I traced the pale green orchids, their vines laced intricately around the blossoms, decorating the bed with hints of exotic lands. "Listen to me. Your father and I do not want you to go to the JM. This is not just you. *We* do not want you filled with their propaganda. Do you understand? I will not allow them to use my child! So don't think this is just all your choice. *Ja?*"

I nodded.

"Now, I am very serious when I say you are not to worry about this anymore! You are to worry about doing well in school and what you want for Christmas! But not this! *Alles klar?* Everything clear?"

I nodded again.

"Good. Now give me a kiss and run along to school so I don't hear from them because you are tardy."

I leaped up and kissed her on the cheek, taking in a faint scent of rose soap that I would hold in my mind throughout the day. I turned and ran out the door, shouting, "Bye, Mutti!" from the landing. I practically danced down the stairs, a great weight lifted off my shoulders.

As I opened the front door, I saw Erica at the end of my drive, waiting for me. The others had all gone on ahead. I skipped down the drive to join her.

"Well, you are certainly happy today." She laughed. "And late!"

"I'll race you to the park!" I said, taking off before she had a chance to react. I always needed a good head start, because Erica was much taller and had much longer legs than I. She almost always beat me, but not today. I managed to hold on to my lead all the way to the park, though just by a nose.

After the discussion with my parents, I put the JM and the Hitler Youth out of my mind. I didn't worry about it until one day in January 1940 when we received a visit from two Hitler Youth officials in our area. I had just come home from ice skating in the park. Flushed with the excitement of the fresh snow and ice, I burst into the kitchen to find Luise sitting at the table with two strangers in uniforms whom I had never seen before. In Nazi Germany, people in uniforms sitting in your kitchen was never a good thing. My heart stopped at the sight of them.

A Visit from the Hitler Youth

The snow was fresh and cold and crisp, and Erica and I decided to spend the afternoon skating on the lake. I walked to her house looking like a snowman, bundled up in two layers of clothes and my boots, scarf, and hat. My ice skates, slung jauntily over my shoulder, stabbed me in the back and the chest with their blades as I walked, but my clothing was so thick and my excitement so great, I barely noticed. The ice formed a silvery sheen over the cobblestones of our street. I stepped gingerly to avoid falling, making it to Erica's gate before gravity and the stealth of the ice pulled me to the ground. She was ready. Waiting impatiently by her door, she had spotted me the moment I left my gate and came slowly down her front steps, slipping and sliding between the rows of snow her father had shoveled that morning. On the branch above her gate a lone sparrow sat, forlorn, shaking snow and water from his feathers. "Poor little *Vogel*. Where is your home?" I asked. "Fly away from this cold to your warm home."

Erica rolled her eyes.

"Well, how would you like to be out here sitting on a branch in the cold with only your feathers to protect you?"

"It's a bird, Jutta! Besides, let's go. We're wasting time. It will be dark in two hours."

"I'll race you!" I said, lurching into a fast shuffle. We giggled as we slipped, slid, and fell down the street to the park. The shouts of other children echoing in the cold air greeted us as we neared the park. In winter, voices seemed always to pierce the air—with the trees stripped of leaves, there was no buffer as in summer.

"Hannelore and the others must be there already!"

"Darn! They beat us!"

"I know they will skate on the part right by the *Hexenhütte*."

"So? We can skate there, too. They don't own the lake!"

"But I don't skate as well as they do, and I don't want to make a fool of myself right there in front of Hannelore."

"Jutta! That's ridiculous! Just go out and have fun."

"But I can't relax if I'm falling and they're cruising about the ice looking like they're dancing a Strauss waltz."

Erica rolled her eyes. "You skate just fine."

"I still want to skate at the other end."

"Okay, okay. But we'll have to take the brooms to sweep the snow away at that end. I'm sure it's still covered with snow."

We turned the corner from our street to enter the park. Ahead of us were at least ten children, already skating and sledding in front of the *Hexenhütte*. Of course Hannelore was out with her friends, showing off, spinning and leaping and turning. Her blond braids wrapped around her neck as she leaped in the air, gracefully executing a perfect turn, her leg extended behind her on the landing. As we entered the *Hexenhütte* to collect our brooms, she called out, "Hello, Jutta. Hello, Erica." Erica smiled and waved back; I simply nodded my head.

"Why are you so unfriendly?" asked Erica.

"She irritates me," I said. "With her perfect everything and those stupid *Milch Madchen* braids. Why doesn't she cut her hair like the rest of us?"

Erica laughed.

"Oh, Erica, speaking of hair, I have to show you in my latest fashion magazine the way the American movie stars are wearing their hair all wavy and with perms. I saw pictures of Greta Garbo and Marlene Dietrich and some young actress named Elizabeth Taylor."

"Really? They just get a perm without curling it?"

"Yes! It looks too fantastic. I am going to beg my mother to have Frau Schmidt do my hair like that."

"She'll never let you."

"Well, if I start now, by the time I'm thirteen she might agree."

We laughed and both grabbed a snow broom made of long twigs that had been tied together at the base of a handle with a long reed. They were there to brush the snow off the benches and off the lake as well. Authentic-looking and right out of "Hansel and Gretel," I could imagine a witch sitting on their knobby exteriors, bent over, hook nose almost touching the broom handle as she zoomed off to wreak death and destruction on the innocent. They were stored in a little hut with a reed roof called the *Hexenhütte*, or witch's hut. We emerged from the *Hexenhütte* riding our witch's brooms, loping along to the other side of the lake, away from the other skaters. It was less crowded, but we had our work cut out for us clearing the snow off. The willow trees that framed the lake with their elegant green branches now stood lifeless, their thin branches crisscrossed like barbed wire. The evergreens alone stood tall and stately, the only remaining barricade against the gray of winter, their emerald green branches hanging gracefully in long, looping shapes, the snow clinging to each branch to form a perfect white skeleton on the tree. I did not like winter. Normally, I hated being out in the cold, and I found the gray and brown colors of winter dismal, but today I was excited to be out on the lake with the cold, crisp air brushing my face.

We sat down gingerly on a bench near the lake to change into our skates. The bench was cold and hard. In a matter of seconds I could feel the cold penetrate my snow pants. Behind me a willow tree scraped its branch on the back of the bench as the wind pushed it back and forth. It bothered me. I changed quickly to get away from the sound. We laced our skates and hurried out onto the lake, screaming our excitement in high-pitched voices. We may not have been any good, but we had enthusiasm. Erica and I joined hands and spun around in a circle, our version of a fancy skating move. I even got up the courage to try a simple jump. To my amazement, I landed upright with my skate pointing in the intended direction. After a bit more practice we were brave enough to join the other children at the large end of the lake. I skated to perfection that day! It was as if the god of ice skating had answered all my prayers. I not only skated fast and well, I jumped and I spun. Erica looked at me with eyes bulging. "What happened to you?" she asked. Hannelore, for the most part, ignored me. Every once in a while she would glance my way. I pretended not to notice her. After about an hour I decided that the god of ice skating would probably not stay with me forever, and I should quit while I was ahead. So I took one more turn around the lake and skated back to our bench.

Erica shouted, "Hey, Jutta, where are you going?"

"I'm freezing." I sat down on the bench without another word and began to take off my skates. I could see she was disappointed, so I said, "Let's go see if Luise will make us hot chocolate and cookies."

A smile creased her pale face. "You were really good out there!"

"Oh, thanks," I responded, as if my performance in no way surprised me.

We banged our skates against the bench to get the ice and bits of snow off. I tied mine together and waited for Erica. The Kohn boys had just arrived at the lake. I was relieved we were leaving; those boys could skate like professionals. They tore around the lake at a hundred kilometers per hour and everything and everyone in their way was expected to move over. I was always terrified they would run me over or, worse yet, that I would already be down on the ice and they would slice off a body part as they zoomed by. I pointed to the lake.

Erica looked up. "Oh boy!" Her disappointment about leaving now entirely vanished, and we headed happily for the warmth and safety of Luise's kitchen. The sun hung low behind the spruce trees, sending winter shadows across the houses and the street, and already the chill had increased by several degrees. The gate to my house stuck from the ice, and we could barely fit through the small opening. We avoided the flagstone path and walked up the frozen grass to keep from falling. The grass crunched under our boots like dry twigs. We steadied ourselves on the iron banister that ran up our steps to the front door; Gustav, apparently unable to keep up with the ice, had spread gravel and sand on the steps.

After hanging up our coats and taking off our boots, we ran to the kitchen. "Luise? Luise, we're hungry!" I called out as I pushed open the door. I stopped dead in my tracks; at the table sat two strangers drinking coffee and talking to Luise. I could not see their faces, but the swastikas on their shirts told me all I needed to know. My stomach fell to the ground. I knew whoever they were, this was not on a social visit.

"Hello, Jutta, Erica," said Luise cautiously. "This is Herr Schumann and Frau Becker."

"Hello," we both said politely.

"Oh, you have been playing in the snow!" said Herr Schumann with a friendly smile.

"Skating," I corrected.

"Yes of course, skating. You are far too old for playing in the snow, aren't you?"

I nodded my head. Erica stared, her mouth hanging open.

Luise had gotten up from the table. "What would you girls like to eat?"

"Well, actually, I must be going home," said Erica quickly.

"Oh no," I said firmly. "Luise, we would like a cup of hot chocolate with whipped cream and some of your delicious butter cookies, please."

"You must have worked up an appetite out there!" commented Herr Schumann.

Luise busied herself with our hot chocolate, relieved to have something to do.

The woman next to Herr Schumann said nothing. Her face was pinched up into a frown, and her hair pulled so tight into the braid that wrapped around the crown of her head I thought it might cut of her blood supply. She studied me with hard brown eyes and then, turning to Luise, she pointed at me and said, "I take it this one is Fräulein Bolle?"

Looking over her shoulder, Luise said, "Yes."

My stomach tightened into a knot. I did not like this woman, and I could tell that she did not like me. "I figured she was," she said with an almost imperceptible sneer.

I didn't want her to see my fear—Mutti said they loved fear. "I am standing right here. Why didn't you ask me who I was?"

Frau Becker narrowed her eyes at me and started to say something but changed her mind. Luise stopped fixing our hot chocolate, her mixing spoon held in mid-air, and said, "Why don't you girls wait in the dining room and chat while I finish your hot chocolate? Herr Schumann and Frau Becker are waiting for your mother."

I shrugged. "Well, they will wait a long time; she is having lunch and shopping with Tante Hilde." I said this much more casually than I actually felt. Herr Schumann's mouth lifted slightly at the corners.

Luise dropped her spoon down in the hot chocolate and hustled us out of the kitchen. Once out of earshot, Luise grabbed me by the shoulders and said, "What are you doing? You behave with these people or you will cause your mother a mountain of trouble."

I jerked my shoulders free and said, "When is Mutti coming?"

Luise shook her finger at me, but only for a moment. "She called over an hour ago and said she was on her way. Now go up and tell Sisi you are here and do not come back in this kitchen," she commanded, shaking a finger in front of my nose again.

"They are from the Hitler Youth," whispered Erica.

"How do you know?" I asked.

"I can tell by their uniforms."

I excused myself and ran upstairs to Sisi. "Sisi, don't you know we have two Hitler people in our kitchen with Luise?"

"Yes, I know."

"My God, have they been here over an hour!"

"The word is my 'goodness,' and yes, they have. You stay up here with me."

"I can't. Erica is downstairs and Luise is preparing hot chocolate and cookies for us."

Sisi nodded. "Well, come back up as soon as you are finished."

My hot chocolate had arrived, and I noticed that Erica had not waited for me to begin on the cookies. The hot chocolate looked so beautiful, steam struggling to escape through the mountain of white cream that capped the cup. Luise had placed six cookies on the flowered porcelain plate, of which five remained. Erica looked guilty with crumbs framing her mouth. I had no appetite. Erica reached for another cookie. I shot her a glance. My mother was about to be hauled off by these Nazis and she was happily eating cookies! Why did they have to come today and spoil my day? I sat down heavily, placing my head between my hands and resting my elbows on the table. A part of me hoped my mother would arrive soon, but another part of me did not want her to come home at all; I feared she would be arrested on sight. I sipped my hot chocolate and sat staring at the tablecloth. Erica said nothing, but I could hear her crunching on one cookie after another. We sat in silence, the only sound the muffled voices from the kitchen and Erica's crunching. The next time I looked up, all six cookies were gone.

Finally, I heard the car door slam and the sound of my mother's voice mixing with Tante Hilde's laughter. I ran to the door and walked carefully onto the icy steps; my mother chatted happily and waited for Tante Hilde to get back in the car. Heinz stood patiently next to the door, his breath steaming in the cold air. She waved casually, as if she had no care in the world, as if she had never heard of Nazis—as if we did not have two of them sitting in our kitchen. Our kitchen! Our warm, wonderful, friendly kitchen, the source of my comfort, where Luise prepared delicious cookies and food to calm and nurture me. Didn't she know who had invaded this space? I thought Luise had said she called. She continued to smile as she walked up the path to the front door, waving at me. She must have read my face, for as soon as she walked into the house she bent down and whispered, "I know they are here. But we will not let them intimidate us. Do you understand?"

I nodded.

She meticulously hung her coat and hat in the entry. She walked into the bathroom and took her time about arranging her hair and applying her lipstick. Then we walked together into the dining room.

"Why, hello, Erica. What a pleasant surprise," she said cheerfully, and a little loudly, I thought.

Erica said hello a bit nervously, and my mother was about to engage in more chitchat when Luise popped her head out of the kitchen. With a desperate look she said, "Excuse me, Frau Bolle, but you have visitors in the kitchen."

"Oh, how nice. Show them to the living room, please."

I looked at my mother as if she had lost her mind. Then she added, "That hot chocolate looks wonderful. I will take one too, please, Luise. And see if the visitors would like one. Jutta, you and Erica stay here and finish your hot chocolate, and then I think Erica's mother is probably wondering where she is—don't you think, Erica?"

"*Ja*, Frau Bolle." Erica licked the crumbs off her fingers before wiping her mouth with her napkin.

Smiling, she turned and walked into the living room, followed a moment later by the visitors.

I heard Frau Becker say, "Frau Bolle, this is not a social visit, if you don't mind. You have kept us waiting for over an hour as it is."

"I am terribly sorry. The traffic was unbelievable coming out of Berlin! I am so glad you are joining me in a little hot chocolate, Herr Schumann! It is so cold outside today. Are you sure I can't interest you, Frau Becker?"

"No, thank you." The thank you did not sound like a thank you, it sounded like a threat, the way Frau Becker said it. Then she added, "I would like to get to the point if we could."

Herr Schumann cleared his throat and began. "Frau Bolle, we understand that your daughter, Jutta, turned ten on ..." I heard papers shuffling. "November fourteenth of last year. Perhaps you are unaware that by order of the Führer, all children who turn ten must be registered with the Hitler Youth."

"Oh dear! Is that right? I really did not know. I thought we had until November 1940 to register her."

"No! They must be registered within the year that they turn ten."

"So if a child turns ten on December thirty-first, they still must be registered within that year?"

"That is not the case with your daughter, is it?" interjected Frau Becker.

"Well no, but it just doesn't make sense that a child who turns ten on January first has an entire year to register, and one that turns ten on December thirty-first has not even twenty-four hours." My mother's puzzlement seemed genuine. She should have been a lawyer, or so Vati said whenever they argued.

"Frau Bolle, we are not here to argue hypotheticals with you," said Frau Becker crisply. "We are here to discuss the fact that you have not registered your daughter, who turned ten two months ago."

"I understand, Frau Becker, but surely you can see my confusion over the law. It just doesn't make sense to me that I would have to register her before the end of 1939."

"I understand how Frau Bolle could have been confused by the registration requirements," I heard Herr Schumann say.

"Tell me, Frau Becker. I am puzzled. I was wondering why the need for such a law? I thought the Hitler Youth was very popular with Germany's young—at least the pictures of the rallies seem to suggest as much. I would not think the authorities would need such a law? I mean a law forcing parents to register their children!" The question was put innocently, but the moment of silence that followed told me Frau Becker understood my mother's purpose, and I prayed that Mutti would stop.

"Frau Bolle, I am not here to discuss the reasons behind the Führer's policies. It is not our place to question them. But while most German parents are enlightened about the educational and fitness merits of the Hitler Youth program, there are still a few, like yourself, who don't seem to comprehend the importance of the program. It is for that reason that we must enforce the policy of the Führer, so the children of less responsible parents do not miss out on this important aspect of their development."

"Well, I am sure Frau Bolle was simply not aware of the timing of the law. I am sure she and Herr Bolle had every intention of signing Fräulein Bolle up," offered Herr Schumann.

"I will consider signing her up, but I fear she will not be able to participate in many of the activities. She is absolutely terrified of loud noises, so she should not participate if loud music is involved. Drums especially set her off. And she suffers from anxiety attacks when surrounded by a crowd."

Erica and I looked at each other, our eyes growing bigger by the minute.

"Frau Bolle, this is by command of the Führer—there is no 'considering.'"
Frau Becker's fury was apparent now.

Luise wrestled with the kitchen door, and we both leaped quickly to our
seats, our hands folded politely in front of us. She stopped at the sight of us and
raised her eyebrows. "Perhaps I should be sitting here with you two," she said
before knocking lightly on the door.

"Come in," called my mother sweetly. Luise pushed open the door with her
shoulder and we strained our necks to look into the living room. But we could
not see anything. "Can I bring you anything else, Frau Bolle?" she asked.

"No thank you, Luise. We are almost finished here."

"Very good, Frau Bolle," said Luise as she closed the door. Turning abruptly,
she announced it was time for Fräulein Erica to run home. With that she ushered Erica out of the dining room to the front door while she sent me upstairs
to Sisi. I hurried up the stairs. After a few moments I heard the front door open,
and voices echoed in the entryway. I pushed the curtains aside and looked down
from my bedroom window. It was almost dark now; the streetlights had come
on, creating umbrellas of light along the Föhrenweg. They emerged from under
the eaves of the house and continued walking down the path to the gate. Frau
Becker appeared unhappy. She spoke rapidly, using her hands for emphasis. I
hoped for Herr Schumann's sake he outranked her, or he would be in big trouble. I wondered how they were going to get to their homes. Did people like Frau
Becker have homes? Did they have husbands? What about children? Poor things
if she did—oh, my heart went out to those poor children—but Herr Schumann
seemed pretty nice, for a Nazi anyway. I liked him. He had a nice face; he was
not supposed to have a nice face—he was one of them. I waited a few moments,
watching them as they turned right at our gate and walked down the Föhrenweg. As soon as they were out of sight, I spun around and quietly opened the
door, tiptoeing to the landing, not wanting Sisi to hear me and stop me. I raced
down the stairs, searching the living room for my mother. I heard voices coming
from the kitchen. She was in the kitchen with Luise, discussing dinner. I burst
through the kitchen door and startled them. "Mutti, what happened?"

"One moment, Jutta." She held up her hand and continued discussing dinner. Then, turning to me she said, "Come, let's go upstairs." She took my hand
and we walked side by side up the stairs to her bedroom. We sat down in my
favorite spot, her sitting area by the window. She let out a big breath of air. "Oh,
thank God that is over!" She stretched her legs out in front of her in relief.

I said nothing. It upset me to see my mother distressed. These people had
upset her!

Seeing my face, she rubbed my cheek. "Oh, it is fine, Jutta! Don't worry! It's
all taken care of, and Herr Schumann will not cause trouble."

"But what about Frau Becker?" I asked quickly.

"Awful woman! What a perfectly awful woman. She is like so many of them,
angry about her lot in life!"

"But won't she cause trouble, Mutti?"

"Oh, he outranks her, so I'm not worried about her."

I nodded with relief. "Do you think she has children?"

"*Gott im Himmel!* I hope not!" laughed my mother.

"So … do I have to go or not?" I asked impatiently.

"I signed you up, but you are not going. I will have Dr. Braun write out a note about your anxiety attacks."

I frowned. She had always taught me never to lie.

"Jutta, sometimes the rules must be bent. I know it is hard for you to understand why it is all right in this context but not others." She shrugged. "Perhaps it is not all right here either, but I just don't know what else to do," she said wearily. "I know I am right about not sending my child to that propaganda circus." This she said firmly. Then, looking me in the eye, she added, "You will not attend these programs or meetings. You get enough of their garbage at school!"

I nodded.

She smiled and winked, "Unless of course you irritate me, and then I may have to send you a few times as punishment." We both chuckled at this. "I don't want to tell your father about this right now. He has had enough troubles at the office today, and I know he has been meaning to talk to von Schirach but has not run into him at Schlichter's. He will only feel guilty about not talking to him."

And that was the end of it. I never did attend the *Jungmädel*. Every once in a while, my mother would receive a call about it, but whatever she told them seemed to work. The other girls were curious about why I did not attend. Some of them were jealous—they hated it as much as I did. Erica would inform them very seriously that I suffered from anxiety attacks. They never seemed to wonder why I didn't suffer from these same attacks at school. Well, nobody except for Liesel, of course, who would say, "Well, she seems fine during assemblies."

And then Vati managed a miracle—a letter arrived from von Schirach's office exempting me from the Hitler Youth due to my medical condition!

———

As winter turned to spring and the tiny bulbs peeked out from behind their dirt barricades, my worries faded, and I forgot about the *Jungmädel* and the Hitler Youth. And then new worries presented themselves, and soon my small problem seemed vague and insignificant.

For the War Effort

Mutti paced back and forth in the living room, between her chair and the window, her riding habit still on. Her legs swished as the leather breeches rubbed together. "How can they do this?"

Vati did not answer.

She turned on him, her velvet hat and jacket in her hand. "How?"

"They just can!" He studied the papers she had handed him, with the enormous official seal across the top.

"But isn't there something we can do?"

Vati shook his head. "They can do whatever they want, it seems. This is from the high command, and there is no place to go and dispute it."

I sat down on the sofa; they didn't seem to notice me.

"But my horse! My beautiful Tasha!" She threw her hands in the air. "I just don't understand!"

I sat up straight. "What has happened to Tasha?" I asked urgently.

They both turned to me at the same time, surprised by my presence. "They took Tasha," said Vati.

"Who?"

"The authorities." He waved his hand vaguely. "For the war effort, supposedly."

"But that's horrible!" I ran to Mutti, tears welling up in my eyes. She hugged me to her but said nothing.

Mutti had arrived at Forsthaus-Paulsborn in the Grunewald Forest to ride with a friend, only to find Tasha had been locked into a huge horse trailer along with the other horses that were boarded there. She had no warning. A young officer rudely handed her the papers when pressed, and that was the end of it. They drove off with her horse and left her standing there in her riding habit, reduced to tears and without an explanation.

And then reports of imminent bombings made even this atrocity pale. As my father began to speak about evacuating us to Berchtesgaden, I worried I would not see Opa Bolle or Erica or Luise or Sasha or Harold or *Vögelein* again, and it seemed nothing would be the same.

5

Berchtesgaden

1940

The intense blues and greens of Berchtesgaden will mark my memory forever: the crystal blue waters of the Königssee set against the dusty purple blues of the mountains that dominate the scenery from every vantage point; the pale green of the meadows surrounding the village and our house, outlined in the distance by the deep, rich greens of the spruce and pine forests. Our first visit was in the spring, with the vivid newness of the greens that spring brings. Dew sat in tiny droplets on the new grasses, and the newly budded leaves of the trees fluttered translucent in the breeze. This is the palette of Berchtesgaden, and these are the shades I will hold dear—but always in the background will be a more somber palette—a palette for Berlin, for the war.

We traveled to Berchtesgaden sometime before Easter of 1940. I know this because I recall attending a Catholic Easter service at the local church, a beautiful baroque building with pale pink walls and gold angels. The service seemed to go on forever and was much more formal than the services we occasionally attended at the Lutheran Church in Dahlem. Ever since Reverend Neimoller had been arrested, my parents attended only to celebrate important occasions.

Rumors of imminent bombings swirled around Berlin during the winter of 1939–40, so my father decided to evacuate us to Berchtesgaden. Tante Hilde and my cousins Peti, Dieter, and Ingrid came as well, and my father and Onkel Kurt came down for holidays and long weekends. A train ran directly from Berlin to Munich, so the trip was relatively easy, even though we had to spend the night in Munich before taking a smaller train to Salzburg and then Berchtesgaden. We were by no means the only Berliners to evacuate the city. Many families left town during that spring of 1940, leaving it a virtual bachelor town—it seemed only men were left. At the time, most Germans believed it would be a short war and that peace could be achieved quickly, so most did not see a trip to the South as anything other than an early summer vacation. My parents were less optimistic about the war's length.

I was excited about going to Berchtesgaden. I waited impatiently for the day to arrive when Opa Bolle and Tante Ebi would deliver us to the train for our great adventure. I must admit my excitement stemmed in part from the prospect of no school, no singing with our arms held up in salute, no gym with its horse to tremble before, no music class to humiliate me, and no learning about Hitler's life! I knew my mother had arranged for a tutor to teach us when we arrived, but this would be a vacation compared to the rigors of my school life. Overshadowing my excitement, however, was the persistent fear that a bomb really would hit Berlin and our neighborhood, and I would never see Opa Bolle or Erica or *Vögelein* or Harold again. Mutti dismissed my fears, saying they would never target our neighborhood, which led me to wonder why we were leaving for Berchtesgaden, but I didn't ask.

Opa Bolle promised he would keep Harold for me, and he said he would check on *Vögelein* at least once a week, but that still left Erica. The evening before our departure, Erica and I said a tearful goodbye. We promised each other we would write at least once a week. I said I would start, since we were not sure where we were staying. Vati had reserved rooms in the local hotel, but we planned to move from there to a house as soon as my mother and Tante Hilde could find a suitable one to rent.

The day we departed, Opa Bolle and Tante Ebi came with Opa's car. We needed two vehicles to carry all of us and the luggage. My mother and father rode in one vehicle with the luggage; I followed behind, riding with Tante Ebi and Opa Bolle. We did not speak as Opa's chauffer raised the windows of the Daimler, sealing out the sounds of the city before he put the car in reverse and backed out of our driveway. I searched the front of our house, bathed in the bright spring sun, desperate to remember every detail. I gave one last goodbye to my bedroom window. I studied the fir tree, hoping to spot *Vögelein's* nest, but I could not see it from this distance. My parents would not let me say goodbye again, as I had already said goodbye to *Vögelein* twice. Luise and Gustav stood awkwardly on the front stoop, shoulders touching and hands laced in front. They seemed glum. Luise was especially distraught—very odd, as we had gone on vacation before and she had never fussed over me. She hugged me extra hard and long this time, quickly wiping away a tear and thinking I had not noticed.

"Why is Luise crying?" I asked Opa Bolle when the house was no longer in sight.

After a moment he said quietly, "Perhaps she will miss you."

I turned to look at his face, but he was looking out the window. The silence was uncomfortable; only the soft purr of the engine and the persistent swish of the oncoming cars passing by us on Kronprinzenallee could be heard. Nobody said anything until we reached the Roseneck, when I said, "Will we be able to swim, Opa?"

He chuckled. "Not now. It won't be warm enough. But maybe by the end of June or July."

"You think we will be there until the end of June or July?" I asked in amazement. Three months seemed like a lifetime.

He nodded.

"No school until August! *Wunderbar!*" I grinned.

Tante Ebi laughed and shook her head. "But you will have to learn your lessons with the tutor, Jutta. I expect you to come back here a very smart young lady!"

"Oh, don't worry. I will!"

"And I want you to do lots and lots of reading," said Opa Bolle, pulling a package out of his jacket pocket. It was wrapped in brown tissue with a purple geometric pattern on it and tied up with an elaborate purple ribbon. Three little crocuses were tucked into the ribbon, two purple and one white. He handed it to me, and I noticed his hand shook.

"Now don't open these until you get on the train. And promise me that when you look at them you will think of your Opa Bolle. *Ja?*"

"Of course I will, Opa. I always think of you." I leaned across the seat and gave him a big hug and kiss. "And," I said with adultlike emphasis, "you promise me you will come down for a visit soon."

"I will try, my dear. But your Opa's bones are getting too old for long train trips."

"No they aren't. You take the night train and then, poof, you are there in no time. You don't even know you've left Berlin!"

"Fräulein Jutta, you have all the answers, don't you?"

"Oh, I almost forgot!" He reached into his pants pockets and pulled out another package—a silver box with my name engraved on the top and tied with a white satin ribbon. "This is in case you get sick and I am not there to give you your medicine," he said with a twinkle in his eye. I knew he had filled the box with the anise candies he always brought when I was sick. My mother would roll her eyes when he arrived with the candies and he would say, "But it is healthy, Heti! Anise is very good for you."

I suddenly remembered the special farewell card I had designed for him. I reached into my bag and pulled out the masterpiece I had worked on all evening. "And this is for you, Opa, so you will remember me!"

He smiled. "I don't need a reminder of you, Jutta. I always think of you." He looked at the card and read what I had written. "This is beautiful, truly beautiful." I could tell he was touched. I had made it look like one of the Chagalls I knew he admired so. Giving myself far more credit than I deserved, I told him, "It looks like one of your favorite Chagalls, Opa Bolle."

"Why yes, it does! It is beautiful. I can't believe you remember the Chagalls, Jutta. That was almost four years ago!"

"I remember all of the paintings," I said proudly. "I often sketch them in my sketch pad." My grandfather looked at me in wonder.

Tante Ebi fixed her gaze on the passing buildings, the silence again embracing us as we watched the Daimler turn onto the Wilhelmstrasse to deliver us to the Excelsior Hotel, only a short distance ahead now. A small, dark-haired girl walked her dog along the sidewalk in front of an apartment building. It seemed so simple, to be in front of one's home, walking one's dog. I envied her. When would I see Opa Bolle again, or Tante Ebi, or my father for that matter? Suddenly, I didn't want to go. I longed to be like the girl—in my home, surrounded by familiar certainty. I watched as she ran up the steps to her apartment, where a woman waited for her and the dog. Why do we need to leave? I searched Opa's face, hoping to find a clue, but he only looked out the window, observing the same scene. Berlin seemed so calm that afternoon. People walked with purpose but without concern, and I began to wonder if my parents weren't overreacting just a bit. Nobody else seemed to be worried about bombs hitting Berlin. My thoughts were interrupted by Opa Bolle saying, "Now take in everything you see and tell me about it in nice long letters."

"Yes, Opa."

"Why so sad? This will be a grand adventure—something you will remember all your life. Before you know it, we will be back together and you will say, 'Life is so boring here in Berlin with Opa Bolle. I wish I were back climbing the mountains and swimming the streams of Berchtesgaden!'"

I shrugged. "Maybe," I said, not very convinced.

As we pulled up to the grand hotel, a surge of excitement thrilled me, suppressing my fears and discomforts of a moment ago. The bell captain ran to open our doors. "Welcome, Herr Bolle," he said to my grandfather as he reached past him to help Tante Ebi out first. I followed after her, and my grandfather emerged last. My parents' car had arrived a moment earlier. I pinched myself, unable to believe we were going to spend the night in this famous hotel. Flower boxes hung from every window and flags decorated the entrance. Ladies in elaborate hats and dresses and men in elegant suits milled about everywhere. Roman columns decorated the facade and at the top, just below the roofline, sat two robustly carved women—surely Roman goddesses, I thought. The windows came out in half-pentagon shapes with carved cornices above them.

My father called, "Come, Jutta. Hurry up! They are holding the door for you."

I ran to catch up with the rest of my family. As we walked into the lobby, Opa Bolle chuckled at me. My mouth gaped as the sheer size of the place took my breath away: the lobby was three times the size of my entire house, palm trees were set in pots bigger than my bathtub, and plants and flowers spilled out in huge clusters everywhere. This must be what the homes of the great European royal families were like! The carpet, with its lovely floral patterns, seemed too beautiful to step on, and I couldn't take my eyes off the elegant ladies talking and laughing. They were scattered about the room, draped in beautiful silk and chiffon patterns, adding to the bouquet of color. My father stood before an enormous white marble counter that seemed to go on forever. A man with his nose permanently up in the air called to someone, and we were quickly ushered to our suite of rooms upstairs. I ran to the farthest bed in what my mother designated as the children's room, flopping down and laying claim to the one nearest the window, so I could watch the activities below all night long—that is, if Sisi fell asleep early enough. I organized my clothes for the morning, and Sisi arranged my luggage. She combed my hair and made me wash up before I was allowed to explore the hotel with her.

That evening Opa Bolle took us for a lovely supper at the hotel's restaurant, where I partook heavily of pasta and schnitzel and a red beet salad followed by lemon cheesecake. Sooner than I wanted it was time for bed. We had to be up by 5:30 AM so we would not miss our train at 7:00. My mother had never been up before 7:00 AM as far as I could tell, and I wondered how she would manage. Mutti looked tense, and Vati looked very serious; a crease ran down his forehead that was not normally there. Again I wondered why we were leaving, especially since nothing threatening seemed to be going on in Berlin as far as I could tell.

We finished dinner and suddenly the moment we all had been avoiding— saying our final goodbye to Opa Bolle—had arrived. He rose quickly after we finished dessert and said he was too tired for small talk, since he single-handedly had to keep Berlin intact while we were gone so it would look exactly the same when we returned. With that sparkle in his eye, he winked at me while hugging Mutti, and then gave me an extra-long hug and kiss on top of my head before he turned so quickly on his heels that Tante Ebi had to rush to catch up with him. My mother immediately called up to the room for Sisi to come and usher me upstairs to our room and to bed, while she and my father remained downstairs "to dance dinner off." I crossed my fingers that Sisi would fall asleep first so I could look out onto my lovely Berlin all night long from my bed. I wanted to memorize all of it, just in case a bomb really did hit this city I loved. Instead, I fell asleep almost immediately.

"Jutta! Wake up!" Sisi shook me roughly.

"Is it time?"

"Yes, and hurry. We mustn't be late!"

I stretched and yawned, wanting to stay in the luxury of the down comforter a little bit longer. There was a knock on the door and I heard someone say, "Room service for Fräulein Bolle."

"I'm coming," called Sisi. She went to the door and an older man, his dark hair dotted with gray, pushed a silver cart covered with a white linen tablecloth and flowers into the room. Sitting on top was the most extravagant display of breads, rolls, and sweets I had ever seen. They sat on a two-tiered silver platter—some twenty different choices. There was juice in a cut crystal pitcher, and hot tea, and milk, and, best of all, a glorious bowl of fruit: oranges and apples, the last of the season, in perfect slices, neatly layered and covered with sugar.

"Well, come on, Jutta. Get up and let's eat!" Sisi said as soon as the man left. She handed me a plate with delicate pink roses against dark blue trimmed in gold.

I was still debating all the choices when Mutti came in from the adjoining suite. Seeing I still wore my nightgown, she raised her eyebrows. "Jutta, hurry up and eat something. We need to leave for the train in thirty minutes. There will be plenty to eat on the train, so don't think this is your last meal until Berchtesgaden. Sisi, make sure she wears a nice dress for the train, please."

"Yes, ma'am. Of course."

Sisi echoed my mother. "Jutta, just make up your mind."

"*Ja,* I'm trying, but there are so many choices."

After much deliberation that earned me several eye rolls from Sisi, I finally selected a raspberry roll and a *Salzstange* accompanied by ample strawberry jam and fresh butter. I heaped orange slices on my plate. No breakfast I have ever eaten tasted as good as the one that morning in the Excelsior Hotel!

When the porters arrived to take our luggage, Sisi took charge, telling them which train we were taking and that we were in first class. They added our luggage onto the cart that was already full from what I recognized as my mother's numerous bags. My parents appeared in the doorway together, and Vati smiled at me. "Let's go."

I swallowed the last bit of my sweet roll, licked my fingers, and ran past my parents to see where our luggage was heading. "Fräulein Jutta! What have you forgotten?" called Sisi. Rolling my eyes, I ran back to the table, wiped my face and hands as fast as I could, and charged past her once again.

I ran ahead of my parents, who were walking far too slowly for my liking. The tunnel connecting the Excelsior Hotel and the Anhalter Bahnhof was a hundred meters long and underground. The shiny floor and the clean tile walls sparkled in the light, and the sound of voices and shoes tapping out hurried footsteps echoed everywhere. Only my ears told me we were really underground. Berlin must be the most magnificently modern city in the world to have a tunnel like this one! I pondered how they would build such a thing without the roof collapsing on them. I couldn't understand it. My parents didn't have any more of an idea than I did.

How could so many people be up at this hour? Hundreds of them, hurrying in both directions, ladies with their hair fixed and their makeup perfect, men in business suits. Nobody strolled. Nobody stopped to chat. They all seemed to have some secret, very important purpose. I was astonished. My father was always out of the house by 7:30; but women, I just presumed, lay in bed having their breakfast like my mother.

I heard Mutti say, "This is wonderful! We don't have to walk outside and get wet in the drizzle."

I could hear the trains in the distance: whistles blew, wheels shrieked on the metal track, and up ahead I caught a glimpse of polished black metal. Modern, sleek in design with rounded curves, Vati said these trains could go up to one hundred kilometers per hour. My mouth gaped!

On the train platform, people crowded into the train cars. Some were hanging out of the windows saying goodbye to loved ones. Some were just looking around at the people on the platform. Some looked happy; some looked sad. It all looked a bit crowded and uncomfortable for my liking. My face must have expressed this, for my father said, "Jutta. We go this way, to the right." I turned toward where he was pointing. I saw an elegant steward in a blue suit with brass buttons helping my mother through a door. My father ushered me over to the door and helped me up. He followed behind. The compartment was spacious and almost empty, except for one elderly gentleman reading his paper and sipping coffee from a gold and blue porcelain cup. He glanced up and smiled at me as we entered.

"*Guten Morgen, mein Herr,*" said my father.

"*Guten Morgen,*" nodded the gentleman. I noted they both used the traditional greeting.

My father had arranged a large private compartment for us in first class. We had plenty of room to stretch and walk around. We stored our luggage in the elegantly appointed compartment with paneling in a rich brown color, maybe walnut or mahogany. The carpet was a subtle pattern of beige circles on a brown background, complemented by the pale brown seats with chocolate trim. Everything folded up, even the beds and the tables; I was fascinated by this economy of space. Every corner, every inch, had a purpose. It seemed so practical. I looked out the window and saw the many people still trying to shove their way onto the cars behind us.

"Vati, why are all the people back there? Don't they know there is much more room up here?"

"Jutta, this is first class. You have to pay more to sit up here."

"Oh. Well, why wouldn't they do that? Instead of sitting back there boxed in like chickens?"

"Not everybody has the money, my dear. Now let's get you settled, and then I must say goodbye."

Goodbye! This jolted me! I remembered why we were leaving! Suddenly it was not fun anymore and I tensed up, anxious from thoughts of bombs flashing through my mind. What if a bomb hit our house or the factory and I never saw my father again?

"Vati, why can't you come with us?" I asked quietly.

"I have to work to pay for first class!" He meant it as a joke, but it was the wrong thing to say.

"But I don't mind going to the back train!" I wailed. "Just so long as you come with us!"

His smile faded, replaced by tenderness. "Jutta, I was just joking about first class. I can't come. I have to look after everything here. But I will visit you in a few weeks, and then also for Easter."

"I want you to come with us now," I insisted.

"The time will fly. You will have so much fun hiking around and picking flowers and berries, before you know it two weeks will pass and you will say,

'What? Vati is already here?'" I crossed my arms over my chest and threw my-self in the seat, refusing to look at him. He stroked my cheek and said quietly, "Don't make this more difficult for me, Jutta." A single tear spilled onto my cheek. When he sat down next to me to hold me, the tears fell without the pretense of control.

"What if I never see you again?" I asked between sobs.

"That will not happen. You will see me again," he said firmly, and with such certainty that I stopped crying.

"I promise." Just then Sisi popped her head in to collect me, but Vati shook his head.

His certainty and the confidence with which he held me comforted me. I tried to convince myself this was simply one more vacation. I pushed my anxiety over bombs killing my father, or Opa Bolle, or destroying our house, to the recesses of my mind, determined to be brave.

"Two weeks?" I said.

"Two weeks!"

I stood up to let him know I was better. Without a word I opened the door to the compartment and went to my mother in the compartment directly oppo-site ours. She was busy arranging our things—books, handbags, coloring books, and the fruit that Luise would not let her leave the house without. "They never have enough fresh things on those trains," Luise announced to my mother as she handed her a large bag.

Vati followed me. Mutti studied my face as I came in but said nothing. I went to the window and stuck my head out to see if all those people had made it onto the train. The platform was less crowded, but there were still plenty of trav-elers wandering about. I heard my father saying goodbye to my mother, then there was a silence. I knew they were embracing. I gave them privacy, remaining at the window. I did not turn around. After a moment, Vati called, "Jutta!" I turned. He held up two fingers and then, kissing them, he blew me a kiss. I did the same, and we smiled at our secret gesture—two weeks.

The train ride took no time at all. Mutti and Sisi played games with me, read to me, and helped me draw. The best was that Mutti was constantly with me. For ten hours I had her undivided attention! I sat for most of the time in the main sitting area of first class. It was more fun to be with the other passengers rather than cloistered in our private compartments.

I spent hours talking to my mother about my friends, about school, about what I wanted to do in Berchtesgaden, and about what sort of fashion designer I would be when I grew up. And she listened patiently, adding a comment now and then when appropriate. We were treated like royalty on that train! The por-ters ran up and down the aisles in their white coats with brass buttons deliver-ing the most amazing *Brötchen*, with slices of ham that positively drooped over the sides of the bun. I must have had at least four of them before we arrived in Berchtesgaden.

The train stopped several times, and some passengers got off and new ones on. About halfway between Berlin and Munchin, several Nazi officials came through our compartment. They stopped for a moment, studied Sisi, and then moved on. Their black armbands always made my stomach knot up. Mutti was suddenly very pale, and she began tapping her foot nervously until they left the compartment.

"What do they want?" I asked my mother.

"Checking for travel papers, most likely." My mother shrugged.

I went back to my book. Fifteen minutes later the compartment door opened again, letting in the noise of the train station. I looked up, and my stomach tightened. They were back. They looked at Sisi again, and this time they stopped in front of her seat and demanded to see her papers. They had the mannerisms of officials: businesslike and cold. My mother stood up. "Can I help you?"

"No. We are talking to this lady, not to you," snapped the younger one with perfectly groomed blond hair and steely blue eyes. He kept his eyes on Sisi as he spoke.

"But she is my governess," said my mother.

"Are you responsible for her?"

"Yes, I am."

"We need to check her papers." The younger one turned and focused on my mother. He spoke with a chill meant to intimidate.

"May I ask why?"

My stomach tightened. Why can't she just hand over the papers?

"Ma'am, we are required to check for travel papers," said the older one, who was less forceful than the younger one.

"But why hers and not all the people up front here?"

By this time the old gentleman who had been sitting several rows ahead of us had turned around, as had several other people in the front rows.

"What is your name?" asked the younger officer, his irritation at my mother threatening to dominate his chilly demeanor.

"Bolle, Frau Bolle."

He frowned in vague recognition. "Frau Bolle, we are required to check the papers of suspicious-looking people."

"But there is nothing suspicious about this young lady!"

He looked at my mother for a long moment, debating, it seemed, whether he would compromise the inner thinking of the SS on such matters and tell this very impertinent woman why he had decided to ask for Sisi's papers and only Sisi's papers. Finally he stuck his jaw out, coming very close to my mother's face—too close for my liking. "She looks foreign," he said through clenched teeth.

"Well, she is not," said my mother, as if that should satisfy them. She turned to sit back down.

The older officer stepped in front of the younger one and said, "Frau Bolle, if you don't mind, we still need to see her papers. Just for a routine check."

His eyes were gentle, and he looked like he could be a grandfather. I wondered why he was with them. He did not seem the type. Mutti responded much better to him than to his rude companion.

"Oh, well. If you must." To my relief, she reached in her bag for Sisi's papers. Sisi too heaved a sigh of relief. She took a handkerchief out and wiped away the sweat beads that had formed on her forehead. The young officer snatched the papers from my mother and, after studying them for a moment, handed them back to her with a grunt of satisfaction. He turned and walked away. The other officer nodded his head to my mother and said, "We are sorry for bothering you, Frau Bolle. Enjoy the rest of your trip."

The fact is, Sisi did not look very German, with her dark hair and olive skin. Her nose was large and curved, and her eyes were deeply set.

The elderly gentleman rose from his seat and came over to my mother. "Well done, Frau Bolle," he whispered. "But you must be careful with them."

"Well, how dare they ask for her papers and only hers! And so rude and impertinent!" fumed my mother.

"They thought she was Jewish," whispered the old man. "They thought you were probably helping her. On all the trains heading south, they are always looking out for foreigners and Jews."

"How awful!"

He nodded in agreement. "It is, but that is the type we have allowed to take over our Germany." Mutti said nothing. Then he added, "Stand up to them, yes!" And then, pointing to me, added, "But for the sake of your child, be careful, Frau Bolle!" He smiled at me, and then he returned to his seat and buried his nose back in his paper. My mother continued to look at the back of his newspaper. For a long time she just stared, as if she was puzzling through something.

"What do they do to the Jews if they find some?"

"I don't know." She saw I was about to ask another question, so she added, "Read your book, Jutta."

The subject was closed, so I did as I was told, but the words on the page had no meaning for me. All I could think about was Tante Anna. What would they do if they found her on the train?

———

The late-evening sun beat down on the newly green trees, casting shadows across the meadows that flew past my window with each rhythmic clank of the train as it crossed over the thick wooden ties and curves in the track. The mountains, cold and blue, loomed ahead, and I knew we were almost to the tiny train station in Berchtesgaden.

Suddenly, the porter announced that we would be arriving in Berchtesgaden in fifteen minutes. My mother and Sisi quickly packed up our belongings, and

Mutti told me to go straighten up my hair and wash my hands and face. I could hardly sit still, I was so excited about finally arriving. I had been looking out the window for a good hour, astonished by the beauty of the mountain scenery. The train began to slow, and I pressed my face against the glass to search the station platform just ahead for Tante Hilde's imposing figure.

Tante Hilde had arrived the day before with her three children, so she had already organized our hotel room for us. And there she was, her cigarette holder in one hand and the leash for the two schnauzers in the other. I grinned. The train came to a complete stop. Tante Hilde leaped up, shouting out orders to porters and her children simultaneously. She paused briefly as my mother descended from the train to say, "My darling Heti, I am so glad you are here. It has been most dreadfully boring without you!"

"Hilde, you have only been here a day, and you are already bored?"

"My God, these people have no idea how to live down here! Their idea of a good meal is spatzle and schnitzel!"

Mutti laughed.

"I love schnitzel and spatzle!" I said, frowning.

"Well of course you do!" said Tante Hilde, hugging me. "All children do. That is my point." Pirouetting on her heels she said, "Come!" Without a word, we all followed her out of the station while two porters struggled with our luggage.

The hotel was positively plain after the extravagance of the Excelsior. But it was clean and pretty in the traditional Bavarian style, with wood shutters and window boxes of flowers, crocuses and daffodils primarily. Tante Hilde fumed about the need to be discrete about one's views on the current regime, as they were everywhere and had even taken over the neighboring village of Obersalzberg. She carried on about the horrible fate of the proprietor of the Hotel zum Turk, an establishment my mother seemed to know. Herr Schuster had made disparaging remarks about Hitler and the Nazis, so they arrested him and confiscated his hotel. It was now a headquarters for the Gestapo! "That horrid Bormann is behind all of it," added Tante Hilde in a whisper.

"How awful," whispered my mother for the second time this trip. "There is just no escaping them, is there?"

"No. But can one imagine anything so barbaric? One would think we lived in Bolivia or some such uncivilized place."

Mutti agreed.

The owners of our establishment, Hotel zur Post, were typical jolly, portly Bavarians. They were husband and wife, and it was not too likely that they were outspoken about much of anything, commented Hilde. Tante Hilde was not one to mince words. She clearly thought that the Bavarian intelligence was far below that of the Northern German. They had, after all, embraced Hitler, "Giving that lot their start," as she put it.

The wife did the cooking and, at least to my childish palate, it was very

good, but I could see that it was not fancy food. Luise would not be pleased at
the lack of fresh things on our plates, however. We only stayed there a week, for
my mother and Tante Hilde immediately set about looking for a house to rent.
Unfortunately, they could not find houses next door to each other. So we stayed
in Schönau and they stayed in the neighboring village of Bad Reichenhall. But
everything was so close together it did not matter.

I loved the little village of Berchtesgaden with its old, narrow, curving streets
lined with Bavarian buildings with their traditional pastel-colored stucco, the
pale shades of pink that contrasted so beautifully with the deep blue of the sky.
Window boxes hung from every available window or doorway; soon they would
burst with color. I wandered the streets of the town during the week we stayed
at the *Gasthaus*, with Sisi by my side, reminding me to look down occasionally
to prevent me from falling off curbs or running into people.

My mother rented the top half of a farmhouse built in the typical Bavarian style, with stucco and wood and big rocks on the roof to hold it down.
The house sat in the middle of a huge meadow of wildflowers, with our closest
neighbor a kilometer away. It had a private bath and three bedrooms. Mutti's
room had a beautiful view of the mountains in the distance, with meadow and
forest in the foreground. Nothing obstructed her view, and it was for this reason
she had rented the house. French doors opened onto a balcony that ran the full
length of the front of the house, allowing both sets of doors from her bedroom
to open onto the balcony. The balcony was just wide enough for the hand-
painted table and chairs that Frau Lindner, our proprietor, had placed there. I
thought they were delightful with their pink and orange flowers painted on a
blue background. The balcony's edge held a flower box full of bulbs: tulips, daffodils, crocuses, and hyacinths. Later, as soon as the weather warmed, I helped
Frau Lindner plant huge, vine-like geraniums in pinks and reds that hung over
the edges of the boxes. They became bigger and bigger as the summer wore on.
She added nasturtiums, and their orange and yellow flowers contrasted beautifully with the pinks and reds of the geraniums. The nasturtiums were like weeds,
with tentacles that hung over the edges of the boxes and climbed up the walls
and anything else available.

Sisi's room was less spectacular, as it looked out on the barn and ten piles of
boxes stacked on top of each other. These did not interest me until I discovered
that they were beehives, and that Herr Lindner made some of the finest clover
honey sold in Germany. Checking on the bees with Herr Lindner became part
of my routine. We would suit up in white canvas pants and jackets and our bee
helmets, which looked like something out of an African safari movie. They were
just like safari helmets, except made out of metal with netting that hung down
and snapped onto the inside collar of the jackets. I walked like a stick man,
the pants and jacket not allowing for very much mobility. My mother was not
thrilled about me playing at bee keeping; she would watch from the house to
make sure nothing happened. She said if she saw a black cloud around my head,

she would come running with her bottle of lavender water. Luckily, we never had to find out whether or not lavender water is as effective against bees as it is against garden bugs. We were too early for the honey harvest, but Frau Lindner promised me if we were not there in August, she would send me as many bottles as she could.

Frau Lindner cooked for us, and she cleaned the upstairs every morning as well. She brought our breakfast, which we ate on the balcony if it was warm enough outside. After breakfast, Frau Lindner would appear again to tidy up. As we came down for our morning lessons, she usually came up the stairs, her hair tied in a scarf, carrying her bucket full of mops and dust rags. She loved to strip our beds the moment our bottoms left them, or so it seemed to me. I could swear the sheets were still warm when she would march in very efficiently and remove our bedding. When it was not raining, she hung the bedding over the balcony for at least one hour. She said it took one hour for the fresh air to seep in. During this time, the windows would be left wide open to allow fresh air into the house as well. We learned not to order our breakfast until we were fully dressed and ready for the day. I think my mother suffered a bit because she was accustomed to her leisurely morning baths.

After breakfast I had lessons downstairs at the large, farm-style table with the tutor from the neighboring village who sat waiting, her coffee in hand, for me and the other Bolle children. Her name was Innes, but Mutti insisted we called her Fräulein Innes. Ingrid, Peti, and Dieter would eventually troop in, late by fifteen minutes or so. They walked over by themselves from Bad Reichenhall and never seemed to manage to make it by eight o'clock. Fräulein Innes taught us math, grammar, geography, and a bit of science. She was young and pretty and had a degree from the University of Munich, which impressed us very much. She worked with us until about 11:30, at which time we were handed over to my mother, who took it upon herself to teach us literature and history. My mother had found out that Fräulein Innes was active in the Hitler Youth program, and she and Tante Hilde did not want her indoctrinating us. If my mother had plans for the day, she would leave lessons for Sisi to teach us. By 12:30 we were completely done with our education, and we had the afternoon to play or explore. We often played tag in the meadow with the neighbor's little girl, Romy, or hide-and-go-seek in the forest. I was very impressed that Romy was the daughter of the well-known actress, Magda Schneider. We often saw Frau Schneider walking or riding her bicycle.

Sometimes we went on hikes with Sisi, or with Mutti and Tante Hilde, depending on their schedules. Not that my mother had a hectic schedule in Berchtesgaden, but she did sometimes go with Tante Hilde for a spa day, either at the salt spa in Berchtesgaden, or to Bad Reichenhall. She especially loved going to Bad Reichenhall, using the slightest stuffiness of the nose as an excuse to breathe in the saline spa waters that she believed aided many different respiratory disorders. She often took me as well, primarily to show me the spectacular scenery on the road between Berchtesgaden and Bad Reichenhall, where the Watzmann towered over the landscape with its 8,900 feet of majestic beauty.

Mutti frequently went to have lunch with Tante Hilde and new friends like Magda Schneider. Berchtesgaden was full of famous and wealthy people. Sometimes Mutti and Tante Hilde and their friends would go off on day trips to explore other parts of Bavaria or Austria. They often crossed the border for the day and went to Salzburg when the country life became too much for them and they needed a bit of city life. I longed to join them, sitting in the cafes and having coffee and cake until late in the day before taking the train back to Berchtesgaden. Other times they explored the surrounding countryside, or they targeted one of the many baroque churches in the area. If they deemed one of these magnificent examples of baroque architecture worthwhile, they would bring us the next day.

The Königssee

Mutti's favorite view of the surrounding mountains was from the Königssee. We often went on boat rides or walked around this example of God's ability to create perfection on earth—Mutti's words. Nothing could be more calming than to sit on the pristine glacial waters of the Königssee and look around at beauty that goes beyond any human description, she told me. The best views were from the *Malerwinkel* (artist's corner), or from the sanctuary of St. Bartholomä, about halfway around the lake. My mother would always exclaim, "Let anyone who does not believe in God come see this!"

One afternoon, Mutti packed a picnic lunch and took me and Peti boating on the lake's clear, glacial waters. Dieter and Ingrid had gone hiking with Tante Hilde, leaving behind Peti, whose ankle hurt, so it was just the three of us. We ate our lunch out on the lake, throwing bits of bread over the side to feed the fish. It was an incredible day, the sun brilliant and the lake still, its water smooth and flat, surrounded by the mountains of Berchtesgaden, their shadows reflected on the lake's surface. The birds, out in full force, sang to us from the pine trees that lined the shore, and the air held that freshness that only comes with spring air. It was a weekday, and we were the only ones on the lake. Mutti wrapped up what remained of our picnic in napkins and snapped the basket's sturdy leather strap in place. Grabbing the oars, her arms sporting brown freckles and reddening from the sun, she began to row us back to the small wooden dock where the boats were kept. As we reached the shallowest part of the lake, Peti and I hung over the edge of the boat, dragging our hands in the lake while we looked at the fish and plants on its bed, shouting out with excitement whenever we spotted something of interest. Peti had been playing with a gold bracelet that Opa Bolle had given her for her birthday, opening and closing it, pushing it up and down on her arm, and admiring how the sun reflected off it. She did this one time too many and the bracelet popped off her wrist, falling with a splash over the side of the boat and into the water.

Peti cried out, "No! I lost my bracelet! Tante Heti! I lost my bracelet!"

"Oh, no!" exclaimed my mother, jumping up and almost dropping the oars. Peti began crying hysterically. The bracelet was her first piece of adult jewelry.

"Mutti, do something!" I pleaded.

I needn't have bothered. She already had her dress over her head, and I watched in amazement as she stripped down to her slip and bra and dove over the side of the boat into the icy waters of the lake to fish the bracelet from the bottom of the shallows, where we could all see it had lodged itself between two rocks. Her first dive was unsuccessful. She came back up for air, her makeup running and her hair matted to her forehead. By this time Peti had stopped crying, astonished that my mother had hurled herself half-naked into the water in pursuit of the bracelet. She searched the lakebed carefully, and then took a deep breath and went down for a second time. We watched, fascinated, holding our breath along with her as she went under. It seemed to take her forever underwater, and all we could see was a constant flow of bubbles and foam as she kicked her feet to try and stay upside down in the water. Suddenly she emerged, triumphantly holding the bracelet up high above her head and grinning from ear to ear.

"I have it!" she shouted.

Peti clapped her hands and sang out, "Hurrah! Hurrah!"

Mutti swam quickly back to the boat and struggled over the side. She almost tipped all of us into the water as she straddled the side of the boat and her weight bore down on it. She was pink from the cold of the water, and her lips had already gone blue. A slight breeze caused goose bumps to jump out all over her skin as it hit her wet body. I had been holding her dress for her. I handed it to Peti to hold so I could grab the checkered cloth napkins out of our picnic basket. I handed them to Mutti to use as a towel.

"Oh! Wonderful idea!" she exclaimed, gasping for breath.

She crouched down in the bottom of the boat, removing her soaked slip. I looked around nervously. She rubbed herself with the napkins and then quickly pulled her dress over her head. She gave up the idea of putting her stockings back on, and instead simply slipped into her shoes.

"That was refreshing!" she said, grinning and running her fingers through her hair to try to tame it. "Now we have something to tell Vati! Mutti went skinny-dipping in the Königssee."

Peti laughed and clapped her hands in delight.

"Mutti, I think you're crazy!" I blurted out.

"Well, I think she is very brave and wonderful," said Peti, hugging her aunt. "Thank you! Thank you, Tante Heti!"

"Well, if you hadn't been messing around, she wouldn't have had to jump in there to begin with. Now she has to walk all the way home with her hair like that," I said, scrunching up my nose to indicate that I, for one, would be walking as far behind her as possible.

"Jutta, that's enough. Don't be embarrassed; no one we know will see us. And besides, who cares if they do?"

"I'm not embarrassed," I lied. I had rowed us to the dock by this time. We clambered out of the boat and my mother retrieved the picnic basket, almost falling in a second time. She caught her balance, and we all laughed. She tried to arrange her hair with her comb, but her fine hair simply hung limp and flat around her face. She reminded me of the sad pictures of Thumbelina in my fairy tale books. She didn't act pathetic, however. Indeed, she was positively jubilant. I noticed that two wet spots had begun to form around her breasts and a rather large one across her bottom where her underwear met her dress.

"Well, shall we?" she said enthusiastically "The three most elegant ladies in all of Berchtesgaden?" And then, with a twinkle in her eye, she asked me to grab the other handle of the picnic basket so that we could carry it together.

We had only walked about a half mile when Herr von Platen drove by in his fancy Mercedes sports car with the roof down. The von Platens lived down the road from us in a large house, their second home. He owned hotels and department stores, Mutti told me. He drove past us and looked surprised. We all waved. He slammed on the brakes and reversed. As his car came parallel to us he shouted, "Frau Bolle, could you use a ride?"

"Hello, Herr von Platen! You're a savior!" she called out as if she looked as charming as she always did. She always told me, "No matter how you feel, if you think you're beautiful, you will look it." I guess she really believed those words.

"What on earth happened to you?" he asked, reaching across the front seat and opening the door for my mother.

"I went for a little swim." She laughed.

"What, in that freezing water? You must have a death wish!"

Peti, of course, could not let it go at that, but revealed the entire story to him with full details—slip and all. I rolled my eyes and tried to interrupt, but Mutti shushed me to let Peti finish. Mutti, obviously, found the entire story entertaining, and my discomfort seemed to amuse her, too.

"Frau Bolle, I had no idea what a dedicated aunt you are. She will stop at nothing for the happiness of a child," he said, bowing with great dramatic flair. They both laughed as she lifted the picnic basket. He stood up and grabbed it from her, setting it on the backseat with its front facing his seat, leaving just enough room for Peti and me to fit next to it.

"It's a good thing you two are so thin!" he said, grinning. Taking my mother's hand as he helped her into the seat next to him, he kissed it as if she were the most elegant lady at the ball. Well, that beats all! I thought. Mutti looks like a drowned cat and she still has men hanging all over her. He slammed the door shut, ran to the other side, and we roared down the road. The wind blew her hair towards the backseat where I was sitting, and I had to fight it to keep it out of my face. By the time we reached our meadow it was completely dry and, though not stylish, she looked very pretty in an unkempt sort of way. I watched Herr von Platen steal glances at my mother the way Herr Kittel sometimes did and wondered what that must feel like. I doubted that I would ever know, with my freckles and red hair! They always seemed to go for blondes with perfect, small noses like my mother's. I didn't like Herr von Platen looking at my mother, and I was relieved Vati was coming this weekend.

The roar of the engine could be heard a half a mile away, echoing off the mountains and penetrating the stillness of the meadow. So before we arrived, Frau Lindner and Sisi were out front to see who was coming up the quiet road in the middle of the afternoon.

"Oh, Frau Bolle, you will catch your death of cold!" admonished Frau Lindner on seeing my mother. She made a big fuss over my mother, drawing a hot bath for her and fixing hot tea.

I Miss Them

I missed Vati and Opa Bolle terribly, but I thought it was marvelous to be away from the bad weather of Berlin, the drudgery of school, and, of course, the thing we never spoke about: the fear of bomb attacks. Here the war seemed so distant. There were no reminders—no teachers talking about race science, no propaganda reports, no speeches by Hitler to listen to, and no gossip about what was going to happen next. Indeed, the mountains blocked even the powerful BBC. On a very clear day, when it occasionally would come through, we had to keep it so low, because of Frau and Herr Lindner, that I could barely catch every other word. I often did not even make the attempt. Sometimes we listened to Swiss Radio Beromunster as it came in better than the BBC, but the news was not as complete.

Vati called Mutti once a week at an appointed time at the *Gasthaus*; the Lindners did not have a telephone. He kept her posted about the news from both Berlin and the rest of the world, but only in vague terms in case the censors were listening. We were in Bavaria, "the cradle of *his* birth," as my mother termed it. And, although nobody really paid much attention to all the Nazi propaganda and carrying on, they certainly would have noticed someone overtly antagonistic to the regime. At least much more so than in a populated area like Berlin, where one could hide better.

Before I went to sleep each night, the possibility of the bombs in Berlin still weighed on my mind. Despite the lack of conversation about the war, I could not get the image out of my mind of a bomb dropped directly on our house and then one on Opa Bolle's house. I watched as bits of dirt and branches of trees from the garden flew everywhere. My arms flung up and wrapped around my head to protect my eyes, and when I opened them, I saw nothing but a skeleton—our house black and smoking, the walls and all that had been between them destroyed. I prayed every night for my father and Opa Bolle, as well as for *Vögelein* and Harold and all the goldfish in the pond. It was easy enough during the day to forget about these worries in the bright warm Bavarian sun, but at night they were not so easily submerged.

———

We spent our afternoons wandering the wild meadows of the area, making crowns of wildflowers and picking bouquets to decorate our rustic but comfortable rooms. Mutti would find four-leaf clovers. I have never known anyone who could so consistently find four-leaf clovers. In later years, I have wondered if she pasted an extra leaf onto the three-pronged variety. But I prefer to believe in her miraculous powers of observation. She would tell me they were good luck, that the war would soon be over, and that we would soon return to our life in Berlin.

Mutti was very lonely without my father. She never said anything, but she smiled less and laughed less. She missed her friends in Berlin and the theater and the symphony, and she missed her piano. There was a piano at the *Gasthaus* she occasionally played, but it was the upright variety and not the baby grand Bechstein whose sound was so pure you thought you were in the *Philharmonie* concert hall. She also missed the telephone, and her weekly calls from the *Gasthaus* to Vati were small comfort. Occasionally, she would go on her own while we took our lessons and talk to Vati. I only learned about these calls after the fact, when she would say things like, "I spoke to Vati today, and he says that Harold is fat and happy." This was meant to cheer me, but I always wished she had allowed me to come along and talk to Vati myself.

We spent many hours that summer wandering through the forests and meadows of Berchtesgaden. I shared with her my dreams, my longing to be a fashion designer, and my desire to live in America. I asked her about her life, her childhood, and how she met Vati. It was all so peaceful that none of us—not even my mother—could have imagined what lay ahead for us.

———

Two days after our lake outing, we decided to take a long walk in the forest. Vati was scheduled to arrive late that evening, and I knew I would not be allowed to walk with Mutti after he arrived, for he would want to be alone with her. I would be relegated to long afternoon outings with Sisi. Not that I minded Sisi. I actually enjoyed her company, but I would have preferred to be with my parents. My father was like that; he would schedule time with my mother to be alone, and then he would schedule times for the three of us to be together. I did not question him. At least, it had been years since I had done so.

After lunch Mutti and I set out across the meadow, heading for the path that led through the forest and ended up by a small brook, beside which grew delicate wildflowers in purple and pink hues and small patches of bright green clover. We had been walking for quite some time when I decided to tell my mother how relieved I was to be freed from school and the burden of their propaganda campaign to encourage girls to serve Germany by having children—many of them. I knew this would bother my mother. It was not that I wanted to upset her, but I wanted to know what she thought. I wanted to be a fashion designer, and I wasn't sure if this desire was a selfish desire—a desire against nature, as my teachers told me.

Mutti pointed to the sun and said, "Just remember it is *die Sonne* and *der Mond*. In German, the sun is feminine and the moon is masculine! It is different from any other language because for hundreds of years, Germans have understood that women are strong. We are the foundation, the rock. Now all of a sudden they want us to believe we are no better than cows. Our only purpose is breeding. Ridiculous! No, little Juttalein, you be a fashion designer one day, if that is what you desire." Then she added, "If you choose to also give me grandchildren, that will also make me happy."

"Did you enjoy school, Mutti?"

"Yes, very much. But back then it was different. They simply tried to educate you; they didn't try to fill your mind with the government's way of thinking." She paused for a moment as we watched two robins chase each other in the sky and then dart to the top branches of a spruce tree. "You must remember when I was a girl, most girls did not go to school after they were fourteen or so. All my friends went to finishing school to learn to sew and cook and be a great hostess. I was not interested in these things. I liked literature and history and science. I had to plead with my parents to let me attend the *Gymnasium*." She laughed, remembering. "My parents had to plead with the head of the school to let me in! And when they finally agreed, I was so far behind the boys in my education!" She shook her head. "The girls' school did not prepare you for higher learning."

"Were you the only girl?"

"Yes, I was the only girl in a school of five hundred boys!"

"What did you do?" I was astonished at how one could survive in the midst of five hundred boys.

"I worked twice as hard, and my parents hired a tutor for me to catch up."

"Did the boys make fun of you?"

"At first, but then your father and I became friends, and then I had an ally!"

"You knew Vati way back then?" I said, surprised.

"Yes. We were both fourteen years old when we met. Can you imagine? Only three years older than you."

Indeed, I could not imagine! All the boys I knew were real idiots, and I doubted that three years would change that much.

"I wanted to be a pharmacist, and nothing was going to stop me. I knew I had to get better grades than any of the boys or I wouldn't have a chance." We walked on for a few minutes in silence.

"Mutti," I said, "Why did you not remain in the pharmacy?"

"I did it for four years, and then your father and I decided to get married. I was ready for a change. It is the same job over and over again once you have learned the basics about the human body and which drugs and herbs do what. It is not a new project each time or a new challenge. I was ready for a change, so I chose to have you. But the point is, I chose to do it. No one has the right to stifle a desire for learning. If you choose to have children and stop working, then that is your choice. But the government, or society, or your family should not force that on you."

"But Eric Hummer says that school is wasted on girls because they just go and have babies."

"Well, someone has to talk to those babies and teach them, don't they?"

"I guess."

"So who would make a better mother? Someone who could not think for herself? Or someone who can think and quote Shakespeare to them?"

I laughed. Mutti was always quoting Shakespeare to me.

"Next time Eric Hummer says that to you, ask him that. Besides, some women are better at thinking and creating than they are at being mothers. God gave us all talents as individuals. He did not say, okay, you're a woman, so no brains for math or science! You only get 'nurturing.' Isn't that the word they use? And sewing and cooking. And you're a boy, so you get a brain full of math and analytical thinking."

"That's for sure! Peti is smarter in math than any boy I know!"

"Yes, and Vati couldn't do a math problem if his life depended on it!"

I giggled.

"And I can't sew, despite your Omi's best efforts, and Tante Hilde can't cook! Lord, she cannot cook!"

I giggled again, thinking of Tante Hilde's efforts in the kitchen.

"Look around our neighborhood. Do you think you are smarter than Jürgen?"

I shrugged. Jürgen lived across the street; he was a pain, spying on my friends and me, but he seemed pretty smart.

"What about Eric Himmer?"

"Yes, of course!" I said, horrified.

"Well, then. Why should you not have the same choices to find what suits you best and make the most of your talents as he has? That is what God expects of us. To use those talents he has given us."

"Do you miss it?"

"Miss what?"

"Being a pharmacist."

"I miss helping people, but I have no regrets about quitting and having you." And then, after a pause, she added wistfully, "I do wish that I had pursued my music more." We walked on in silence for a moment before she added,

"Your father always says, 'If God gives you a talent, it is a sin to waste it.' In a way he is right, I think."

"But you play, Mutti; you play every day at home."

"Yes, but I still say 'What if?' What if I had focused on it? Could I have played professionally? I doubt I had that much talent, but you never know."

"You play beautifully, Mutti. Better than anyone!"

She laughed and hugged me. "I don't think that is true, but you are the only audience I need."

We walked on, listening to the breeze sing through the pine trees. Suddenly, she stopped and turned to me, grabbing me by both shoulders; she looked me in the eye and said, "Listen to me Jutta. I want you to always live your life so that you never say 'What if?' Do you promise me?"

I was startled by her sudden change in tone. "Yes, of course, Mutti."

"You do whatever it is that your heart tells you to do. Then you will be a happy person."

I nodded.

She let go of me, and we continued walking. Our feet slipped and slid on the ground, moist from a light rain that morning and the dew that hung on the blades of grass and tiny wildflowers that crossed our trail. We came around a bend, surprised by a couple walking their two German shepherds; we stood aside to let them pass. Their dogs came bounding toward us; one sniffed eagerly at our legs and shoes, while the other chased birds across the meadow.

"Bernard, *komm!*" commanded the woman sternly.

"*Grüss Gott,*" said my mother pleasantly.

The woman frowned. "Heil Hitler," she responded, looking back and forth between me and my mother as if to say what kind of an example for the child. Her husband looked away. My mother, oblivious to the woman, strolled on, looking up at the trees, a smile on her face. I turned around and noticed the woman continuing to stare at us after we had passed.

Mutti never once uttered the words "Heil Hitler." To replace "*Grüss Gott*" with "Heil Hitler" seemed to her farcical beyond anything Bertolt Brecht could have come up with. And she never used the word Führer; she always called him "Hitler." These were the little beachheads of defiance she clung to in a world gone crazy with the need for homogenization (that was Vati's word). I only realized much later how brave she was.

We arrived back at the house about five o'clock, hungry and invigorated. Mutti thought Vati might be there already, but he had not arrived. Instead, a telegraph arrived from him saying he would not be coming and to call him at seven o'clock that evening.

"I'm sorry, Frau Lindner; we are eating at the *Gasthaus* tonight. I hope you have not prepared dinner."

"No problem, Frau Bolle. I have not even started." She looked at my mother with concern, "I hope everything is all right."

"Yes. Yes, I am sure it is." I could see, though, that my mother was not certain. She hurried me up to the bathroom to clean up.

"Jutta, don't take too long. I am going to ask Herr Lindner to take us by Hilde's first on our way to the *Gasthaus*." Mutti was sure Hilde had received a similar telegraph from Onkel Kurt. I had just come out of the bathroom and was brushing my hair in Mutti's room when I heard a car pull up, tires spinning in the gravel drive. I stepped out onto the balcony through the French doors just in time to see the top of Tante Hilde's head passing out of view as she headed to the front door. Clattering down the stairs at breakneck speed to greet her, I yanked open the front door before she could reach it.

"Well, good God! A little more grace, child! I could hear you halfway down the drive!"

"*Guten Abend*, Tante Hilde," I said kissing her.

"Hello, *Püppchen*." She kissed me on both cheeks, unintentionally offering me a full view of her ample cleavage as she did so, the smell of Chanel No. 5 and cigarette smoke floating around her.

"Where is your mother?"

"Upstairs, getting ready to go to the *Gasthaus* for dinner."

"Did she get the telegram?"

"Yes. Vati is not coming, and we are to call at seven o'clock."

Tante Hilde nodded her head.

"Tell Mutti I am on my way to the *Gasthaus* now. Kurt wants me to call at six thirty." There was only one phone, so they had to take turns. "After the phone calls we can all have dinner together. *Ja?* So be a good girl and run and tell your Mutti."

I nodded. She kissed me again and, with a wave of her hand, did that special pirouette only Tante Hilde could do on a pair of high heels without falling over. She hurried out to the waiting car. I waved to Peti, who was peeking out through the back window. I closed the door quickly; the evening chill had already set in, reminding me to bring a sweater. I ran upstairs to report to my mother.

We arrived at the *Gasthaus* at six forty-five, delivered by Herr Lindner. Tante Hilde would drive us back—it was always an exciting experience to drive with Hilde. Hilde had rented a house that came with a car, so she was much more mobile than my mother. But my mother had not learned to drive, so it would have been pointless to rent a car. My father always joked that Hilde had not learned either, so perhaps she should do without a car as well.

As we walked in, Ingrid and Peti were sitting at a long wooden table drinking *Himbeersaft* and drawing pictures. Dieter played solitaire by the fire. Peti looked up. Both she and Ingrid were happy to see me, for other than each other, I was the only other child they had seen all day. My mother told me to order whatever I wanted before she hurried to join Tante Hilde at the only telephone in the lounge.

"It must be very bad news from Berlin," Peti said, as if she had some kind of inside information.

"Why do you say that?" I asked.

"Well, first of all, when we spoke to Vati, he would not say anything other than that everything was fine. You know what it means when they start with that stuff!"

"Maybe everything is fine," I said hopefully.

Ingrid looked at me, cocked her head, and rolled her eyes. "Please, Jutta! We are at war! How can everything be fine?" She continued her drawing of the inside of the *Gasthaus*. Ingrid was a very talented artist, and her impression was actually very realistic. "Besides, Mutti keeps saying, '*Gott im Himmel*! Kurt, no!' And then, 'No *Gott*, it will be a long war.' You know how Mutti's voice carries; half the *Gasthaus* can hear her."

I glanced over to Dieter, but he was completely engrossed in his game and adroitly blocking out the prattle of his sisters. His brow was furrowed in concentration, and with his blond hair combed straight back and perfectly groomed, he looked like any typical German boy of eight. I could not help but think that of all of us, he had the most to worry about, being a boy and all. The Nazis were talking about lowering the age for the draft to eighteen! It seemed so odd to think that the boy sitting across the room from me might have to kill other boys in the name of Germany. How awful! He would have no say as to whether he went to war or not, and once there, he would have to fight and kill. But he seemed completely oblivious to the perils that potentially lay ahead of him as he happily played solitaire in front of the fire.

Ingrid handed me a piece of paper and colored pencils. "Here, design one of your fancy ball dresses. Or maybe a *dirndl*. We certainly can't use a ball dress down here!" She and Peti giggled.

"Well, I will design something for our return to Berlin!" I said with great self-assurance.

"Good, Jutta. You do that. You'll have a long time to work on it."

"Don't be so pessimistic, Ingrid," said Peti.

The innkeeper brought my *Himbeersaft* and asked if we would like a little wurst plate to tide us over. We agreed enthusiastically. We usually ate around six o'clock, and it was already seven. Tante Hilde popped her head in from the arched doorway and called me to come and talk to Vati. I ran to the back of the room and out the door to the hallway. Near the entrance to the lounge were two chairs and a table with a single black telephone. Mutti was already talking to Vati. She stopped as I walked in and said, "Here she is, Hans. I will talk to you in a moment." With that, she handed me the telephone.

"Hi, Vati. How are you?" I asked, anxious to hear his voice.

"I am fine, my darling. How are you?" my father's voice sounded so far away.

"Okay, except that I miss Harold, and *Vögelein,* and you, and Opa Bolle."

"All in that order?" teased my father.

"No! Of course not! You are at the top of the list. But how is *Vögelein?*"

"Still there, chirping away happily, not a care in the world. It is much better to be a bird, don't you think?"

"Yes. Is Opa Bolle remembering to feed Harold?"

My father chuckled. He knew I always had to have the report on all of my friends before we could move to other topics.

"I spoke to him yesterday in anticipation of this call, and he wanted me to report that Harold is growing fat and lazy under his supervision," he said gravely

"Oh, good!"

"Now tell me, what have you been doing down there with your mother?"

"Well, today we took a long walk, and I learned all about how you and Mutti met and how Mutti had to fight to go to the *Gymnasium.*"

"Really! And did she tell you she was the smartest student in English class?"

"No!"

"Well, she could run circles around any of the boys, quoting Shakespeare and Schiller and explaining their meaning."

"Really! She never told me."

We spent a few more minutes talking about their school days and about our lake outing. My father was quite amused, though not surprised, to hear that my mother had stripped to her slip and jumped in the lake. I tried to ask him what happened that was so terrible, but he only said, "Nothing 'so terrible' happened, but you can talk to your mother about it. I don't want to spoil our few minutes together talking about unpleasant things." So we chatted about what he had been doing, where he went for dinner, and what books he had read. Then my mother came back to retrieve the telephone from me. We said goodbye and I love you, and I ran back to the table.

Mutti spoke to him for a long time, and Tante Hilde was nowhere in sight. I presumed that she was outside smoking a cigarette. So we ate our wurst plate and kept ourselves entertained, drawing and chatting. Finally, Mutti and Tante Hilde came back to the table. Before they could even sit down, we all said, seconds apart, so that it sounded like a harmonized chorus, "What happened?"

"Nothing of great importance," said Tante Hilde.

"Well then, why did we hear you carrying on about the war lasting a long time?" asked Peti.

"For God's sake," snapped Tante Hilde. "Can we order dinner first? Then we will tell you."

Mutti nodded, and they both sat down and took their time studying the menu.

"Jutta, I presume you want *Wiener schnitzel?*" asked my mother.

I nodded my head.

"Excuse me?" her eyebrows rose, letting me know my mistake.

"*Ja bitte,* Mutti."

"That's better. No potatoes?"

I nodded my head.

"Do you want spatzle instead?"

"Yes, please." My dislike of potatoes was a constant source of amusement. How could it be that a German child did not like potatoes?

"She must be part Italian, the way she loves pasta," announced Tante Hilde, amused.

"I think all the children want *Wiener schnitzel, nicht*?"

"Yes, please," called all three of hers.

Once we ordered, Tante Hilde and Mutti began to talk about their day. My mother carried on about our walk, and Hilde carried on about the lunch she had with Frau Schneider. Ingrid and I looked at each other in disbelief. She made her eyes very large and looked at her mother turning her head to the side.

"What on earth is the matter with you?" asked her mother, stopping mid-sentence when she noticed her daughter's odd expression.

"What happened? You promised you would tell us!"

To my amazement, Tante Hilde simply looked at her oldest daughter for a moment and then announced, "Your father and Onkel Johannes told us the very sad news that Hitler invaded Denmark and Norway yesterday."

"They are both very depressed about it. All of Berlin is depressed. At every meeting they go to, it is the only topic of conversation, and everyone is very worried," added my mother.

"Oh yes, and Kurt said nobody is in the mood for parties or dinner—Berlin is a complete ghost town."

"But why are they worried? We invaded Poland and it was no problem," said Ingrid.

"This is different," responded my mother. "It means the war will be long."

"We all hoped for a short war, but it doesn't look like that will be the case."

"Why invade Denmark and Norway?" asked Ingrid.

"Onkel Hans says it is because they don't want England to be able to block-ade the North Sea like they did during World War I," responded my mother. "Oh, how we starved in Germany! Remember, Hilde?"

"How could any of us forget? *Ach,* my mother lost thirty pounds, and she was not fat to begin with!" said Hilde, grabbing a roll. "But Kurt says it's also for the Swedish iron ore. I am sure Hitler has his reasons—he always seems to. If it makes sense to start a war, then it makes sense to capture the North Sea, I guess."

"Damn this war!" My mother's vehemence startled everyone. We all looked at her.

"Well, enough," said Tante Hilde, changing the subject by asking how our lessons were going, and what my mother was doing tomorrow, and was she going to take the waters in Bad Reichenhall?

Peti and I swapped stories about our afternoon, and I tried to enjoy my schnitzel, but my mood was forced and a heaviness poked at me. Like the sound of traffic, I could talk over it and ignore it, but it remained in the background. The news about the war and my mother's reaction bothered me.

After dinner we were allowed to go outside to run around on the lawn behind the *Gasthaus*, where a small pond attracted ducks and a swan. The azaleas bloomed a brilliant pink. It looked so peaceful, so far removed from war and trouble. We played tag, the crisp spring evening refreshing after the stuffiness of the *Gasthaus*. Mutti and Tante Hilde, inside having coffee, looked grave. I could see them through the window. I knew they were discussing the war. They were bent forward toward each other, and Tante Hilde's hand movements were less dramatic than usual.

Peti interrupted my thoughts. "Jutta, come. Look at the fish; they look just like the ones at your house."

I ran over and looked down. Suddenly I saw my mother's pond along the side of our house. I could feel the flagstone under my bare feet, and I saw how it came up to the edge of the pond. I saw myself and my mother bending down to examine and feed the fish. I saw their bright colors and felt the sun of a warm Berlin summer day on my back. I began to cry. Peti put her arm around me.

"I miss them," I said. I sat down in the grass; Peti sat next to me.

"I know, but we will see them soon. We will be back soon."

"No we won't! Didn't you hear Mutti and Tante Hilde? It will take years and years." Peti said nothing. Instead, she held me, her little arms reaching up to wrap around my shoulders. Ingrid had been squatting down, chasing a goldfish with a stick. She glanced over toward us, concerned. Seeing that I was not going to stop crying, she took off for the dining room to get my mother. After a minute I heard my mother come up behind me.

"Jutta, what is the matter?" she whispered, putting her arms around me from behind.

"I miss the goldfish," I wailed in between sobs. Mutti sat me down next to the little pond's edge and with a movement of her head gently told Peti to leave us. She stroked my hair and kissed the top of my head.

"You will see Vati soon. He promised to come in two weeks."

"But I don't want him to come here! I want to go home," I said, wiping my nose with the back of my hand. Mutti reached in her pocket and handed me her handkerchief, beautifully embroidered with white roses and lace and smelling of lilac. I recognized the work of Oma Muller, and it made me cry harder. I missed all of them: Oma Muller, Opa Bolle, and Vati.

"*Ja.* You have a good cry, and then we will talk." Mutti held me and rocked me and stroked my hair. I heard the birds chirp their final good night sounds as they settled down for the evening—content, oblivious to what the world around them was about to do.

"Why can't everything be like it was before this stupid Hitler?"

"*Ja.* That is a good question."

"I wish he would just die. Have a heart attack or something."

"I often wish the same, but I always add a few of his friends to that list."

"You do? I thought you would think it was terrible to wish someone dead."

"Well, he is doing terrible things to Germany, so I make an exception."

"Vati says we should not judge others—God will do that."

"I am sure Vati is right. But I am certain I know how God will judge Hitler." For some reason it gave me great comfort to hear that my mother harbored these thoughts, just like I did. "But Jutta, there is nothing you or I can do about this war, or any of the rest of it. So we must try to live through it as best we can. What is your Vati's favorite saying?"

"This too shall pass," I said without hesitation.

"Exactly! It will pass, and we will make it through, even though we wish it never had to be like this. I want so much to protect you from all of this, but I realize it will be impossible. You will hear things, and you are at an age where you will want to know."

I nodded my head.

"Now listen to me. I need to tell you something that will be difficult for you." She hesitated. I turned to face her, my eyes stinging from my tears. She looked at me with a frown line marking the bridge of her nose. I had not noticed it before.

"I am going to Italy tomorrow."

"No, Mutti! I don't want you to go," I cried.

"I don't want to go, but I cannot tell you why I am going until I return. I am going down to visit the Pagnis in Florence. That is all you need to know. Tante Hilde will stay here with you children, and of course Sisi is here."

"But what if something happens to you, Mutti?"

"Nothing will happen to me. It's quite safe in Italy for Germans. It is one of the few places they still like us." She laughed.

"How long will you be gone?"

"No more than a week."

"A week!" I moaned. "First I have no father, and now no mother."

"Jutta, please. I need you to be strong. I am doing this for the family. You will see when I return."

"But I will miss you, Mutti!"

"I know, and I will miss you." She grabbed my hand and squeezed it. "Tante Hilde will plan all sorts of activities. Your days will be so busy you won't even know I am gone."

I looked at her skeptically.

She took my face in her hands and kissed my forehead. Just then, Tante Hilde called from the *Gasthaus*, "Heti, we must go! It is getting late."

"*Ja*, we're coming," replied my mother. But she kept on hugging me for a long time. Finally she said, "Now we are going to be strong, right?"

"I'll try," I said without enthusiasm. "But can you make it five days, not a week?"

"I'll try," she said, echoing my phrase. We both chuckled as she pulled me to her. "I need you to help me, Jutta. Do you think you can do that?" she asked in a low voice.

"Sure," I said.

"The only reason I am going to Italy is to see the Pagnis. That is all you know, if anyone asks." She looked at me intensely. "Do you understand?"

I nodded my head. "You already told me."

"Good! Now we had better go. Tante Hilde is growing impatient." Mutti stood up and reached down to help me.

Italian Riches

The next morning I woke to bright sunshine and the sound of Herr Lindner chopping wood for the stove. I studied the knots in the wood ceiling above my head as I listened to the birds. I could hear my mother moving about in her room. Suddenly, I remembered she was leaving today. I threw off the duvet, shoved my feet into my slippers, and ran to my mother's room. The door was open, so I went in without knocking. She was busy laying out different outfits. Mutti turned and said, "Jutta, help me decide. The beige shoes with this dress, or the pink shoes?" She had laid out one of my favorite dresses. It was in a pale chiffon with large pink and beige flowers all over it.

"What else are you taking?" I asked with authority.

She showed me three or four different outfits, all in different fabrics and colors. She would have to take a different pair of shoes for each outfit if she packed like that, I thought.

"Take the beige shoes, and take two more outfits that you can wear them with, like that Chanel suit you have and the pretty navy dress. Beige looks great with navy, especially if you take a scarf with navy and beige." With that, I grabbed the two outfits I had in mind from her closet.

"What would I do without my fashion consultant? You are brilliant!"

"Now you only need one more dress or suit. Wait—what are you wearing on the train?"

She pointed to her charcoal gray knitted dress.

"Perfect. It's comfortable but elegant, and it is a dark color."

"Yes. One gets so dirty traveling!"

I nodded.

I watched her laying out the rest of the clothes we had picked and placing the ones I had rejected back in the cupboard. My latest copy of *Vogue* came to mind. They had just done an article on the growing fashion industry of Italy. Of course, one of the points of the article was how Mussolini had tried to kill the fashion industry by mandating that Italian women free themselves from the angular, unfeminine foreign styles—meaning American, French, and English—that my mother and I found so elegant. Women were to return to the styles that highlighted the feminine physique. I told my mother about all of this.

"Ridiculous! Their government is as crazy as ours."

"Do you think the Italian women actually buy those awful styles?"

"I doubt it. One thing Italian women know how to do is dress! I don't think they will let some stodgy government officials tell them how to dress. At any rate, I will report back to you."

I was silent again for a moment, thinking of what else my magazine had said. Then I suddenly remembered. "Mutti, I hear they have absolutely the best shoes in Florence, and you must stop in Milan at some of the fashion houses if you have a chance."

"Where do you learn all of this fashion knowledge?" she inquired, amused.

"From my magazines. But will you buy me a pair of shoes if you have time?" I pleaded.

Ignoring me, she snapped the lid to the suitcase shut and locked it. Turning, she said, "Are you ready for some breakfast?"

I remained standing by my mother's closet.

"Come on, Jutta."

"I'm not hungry." I pretended to study the pattern on her suitcase.

"Come and keep me company," she said, taking my hand and leading me to the stairs.

The welcome clatter of chairs being pulled out and plates being set down comforted me. Frau Lindner greeted us with her smile that stretched from one side of her face to the other. She had prepared a huge breakfast, complete with delicate, thin pancakes topped with the first berries of the season and a dab of whipped cream. She knew I loved her pancakes. Despite the temptation, my stomach felt queasy. I worried about Mutti leaving and traveling to Italy by herself. I knew she must have a good reason; I just didn't like the thought of her going. Even her promise to telegraph me from Florence when she arrived gave me small comfort.

Tante Hilde was scheduled to arrive just after breakfast to collect Mutti while I stayed with Fräulein Innes and Sisi to do my schoolwork for the day. I was not pleased by this arrangement, but I didn't want to argue with her. My tepid stab at asking if I could come to the train station had already been rejected, so I left it at that. I knew she thought it would be harder for us to say goodbye at the train station.

A car pulled up; the cuckoo clock above the sink said it was 9:00. Tante

Hilde was always punctual. Mutti opened the door before Hilde had a chance to knock.

"Goodness! You must be anxious!" exclaimed Hilde, almost falling over the threshold. The sun shone brightly behind her, spilling into the hallway so that my mother shaded her eyes from it.

"No. I just thought I would save you the knock."

"Hello, Tante Hilde!" I called from the kitchen

"Hello, my darling! Peti is so excited about you spending the night she will hardly be able to concentrate on her work this morning." They came into the kitchen, Peti, beside her mother, grinning excitedly. I heard Ingrid and Dieter in the front hall greeting Herr Lindner.

"Hilde, don't let them spend the night every night, or they will get no school work done!" admonished my mother.

"Now, Heti, you just run off to Italy and let me run the show!"

My mother sighed and shook her head.

"Oh, Jutta," added Tante Hilde, turning her back on Mutti. "I have talked to Magda Schneider, and she's letting that dear daughter of hers, Romy, come spend the night also, so you both will be with us." Smiling and clapping her hands, she added, "We'll have such a party!"

Despite my mood, a grin escaped me. My eyes met Mutti's, her eyebrows now raised. I had never had friends spend the night. Mutti was dead set against it. But she knew that Hilde would only ignore her if she complained, so she saved her breath.

"*Ja.* Heti, let's go. Jutta and Peti, you get all your work done. And where are the rest of you?" She spun around. "Ingrid, Dieter, get in here! I have a big afternoon planned for us. So I don't want to hear from Sisi and Innes that someone can't go because they haven't finished their work!"

Innes smiled, grateful for the reinforcement.

Tante Hilde pirouetted toward me again. She clapped her hands on both sides of my face, giving me a kiss on each cheek, practically yanking me off my feet in the process.

Herr Lindner brought Mutti's suitcases down, and in a matter of minutes she was ready to go. She lingered only a moment, examining my face carefully, as if she wanted to memorize how I looked. I kissed her on the cheek, and we hugged. With that, Hilde whisked her off, shouting out several more commands to us. Laughing and saying she would not tolerate any tears, she waved her cigarette holder like a baton over her head. We all laughed and waved. Tante Hilde always raised my spirits! I ran into the kitchen to get started on my work. I was not going to be left behind. Whatever Tante Hilde had in mind, I knew it would be a lot of fun.

Although I missed my mother very much, especially at night, I had a wonderful time with Tante Hilde, who took us hiking, boating, biking, and generally spoiled us rotten with cakes, cookies, and candy. She let us spend the night, twice at her house and twice at our house. My mother was gone for five nights and six days, and only on the last night did Hilde make me stay at my house with Sisi. She said she wanted me to look rested when my mother came back. I was so busy during those six days I hardly had time to think about my mother. In the morning we did our work with Fräulein Innes, and then in the afternoon the car would arrive to fetch us to explore some wonderful new part of Berchtesgaden, with Tante Hilde talking a mile a minute about everything in sight.

The morning of the day my mother arrived, I took special care to make sure her room looked perfect. I went deep into the meadow, the grasses and wildflowers tickling my legs, to collect two huge bouquets of wildflowers—blue bells, buttercups, Queen Anne's Lace, and my favorite, wild sweet peas—one for her bed stand and one for her writing table. I made a special card, decorated with drawings of bees, flowers, and hearts, and wrote, "Welcome home, Mutti! I missed you! Love, Jutta." Carefully, I pasted a violet I had pressed at the beginning of the week by my name. I leaned the card against the flower vase on her bed stand. Satisfied with the effect, I went downstairs to join Sisi, who was out front waiting for Tante Hilde to take us to the train station. Herr Lindner had already left with his car to pick up the luggage. I didn't see the need; Mutti had only left with one trunk. But Tante Hilde smiled at me and said she would be returning with far more. Tante Hilde even recruited Herr von Platen and his Mercedes sports car, which, other than transporting a few passengers, was really too small to do any good.

Mutti's train arrived on time. This was Germany, after all. But I thought the Italian end might slow things down a bit. Apparently, Mussolini had at least accomplished punctuality in train schedules. Mutti stepped off the train, and I noticed immediately how tan and healthy she looked. Indeed, she seemed to radiate good health making me wonder if she had missed me at all. She had bought a new navy blue suit with pale pink piping along the lapel; a hat, held in place with a pearl pin, sat on her head with an elegant tilt. She waved, and we ran to her. I arrived before the others. With my arms stretched wide, I shouted, "Mutti!"

She wrapped me in her arms. Then, pulling back, she said, "Well, I can see you did not spend much time inside, judging by the number of new freckles I see on your face." I grinned guiltily. "If I know Hilde, she had you going from one activity to the next." I nodded, hugging my face to her chest again. Tante Hilde had taken charge of the porter, and he and Herr Lindner both struggled to remove the luggage. "How many bags, Heti?" she called to my mother.

"Three luggage crates in addition to my bag!" she called back.

My eyes went wide.

"My goodness, Mutti, you must have really shopped. Did you go to all of the fabric stores in Milan?"

"Nothing so exciting, my dear. I will show you when we get home." She grinned mysteriously and went over to help Tante Hilde. But there was no need. Tante Hilde, with military precision, had everything under control. As we walked out arm in arm, Herr von Platen leaped out of the Mercedes and waved. Mutti looked surprised, but smiled and waved back. Tante Hilde told us to go ahead with Herr von Platen. She would follow with Sisi and the children and the leftover luggage. And so we set off for the house, with Herr von Platen taking the lead in the tiny Mercedes. He had the top down again, and my eyes stung from the wind that snapped at them. Mutti held her hat in place with one hand and with the other she gripped the door handle. Herr von Platen glanced over at my mother periodically, giving her that look I did not care for.

By the time we arrived home we had heard about the beautiful weather in Florence, the wonderful churches, the glorious cafes, and how the war seemed to have touched Italy very little so far. But not a word about what she had in her trunks following directly behind us with Tante Hilde and Herr Lindner. Herr von Platen pulled the car up to the front door with a squeal of tires and a cloud of dust.

Frau Lindner ran out of the house, wiping her hands on her apron. "I am so glad you are back in one piece, Frau Bolle!"

"Well, hello, Frau Lindner. Of course I am!" said Mutti, smiling as she let Herr von Platen help her out of the car.

"One hears all about the Italian men!" Frau Lindner threw her hands in the air. "And there you were traveling alone and all! Thank God nothing happened, or Herr Bolle would have been most unhappy with us."

"With you?" smiled Mutti, genuinely puzzled.

"Well, at any rate, you're home!" said Frau Lindner quickly. She swatted at the dust billowing around us as Tante Hilde pulled up immediately behind us, wheels spinning and gravel flying, followed moments later by Herr Lindner's car. The door flew open and Tante Hilde jumped out, Peti and Dieter at her heels and Ingrid following more leisurely. She popped open the trunk, shook her head and called, "*Gott im Himmel!* Heti, you've brought half of Italy with you!" Herr Lindner walked over to Tante Hilde's car and tried to lift one of the heavy trunks from the back. Herr von Platen, seeing Herr Lindner struggling with the large travel trunk, excused himself and ran over to help.

"My God, what do you have in here, bricks?" he shouted.

"No, just hams," called my mother, laughing.

"Maybe a whole pig!" he shot back, joking.

The trunks tipped and scraped the walls as the two men struggled to carry them up the narrow stairs to my mother's room. But they managed. I could hardly wait until everyone left so she would let me see what splendors lay within the trunks. Tante Hilde followed the men upstairs, instructing them to stack the trunks on top of each other in the far corner of the room, which made no sense to me. How were we to get them down to examine all of Mutti's purchases?

"Don't you want to spread them out?" I asked hopefully.

"Heavens no, child! They'll take up the entire room!"

I grew impatient as the adults drank wine outdoors in the late afternoon breeze, sitting around a table anchored by wild grass and flowers in a side yard of the Lindners' home. I listened only with half an ear to my mother's descriptions of Italy, running back and forth to the table, dividing my time between playing in the meadow with my cousins and listening to Mutti's conversation. "Anti-British posters everywhere! Plastered all over Florence!" I heard her say as I ran back out to Peti. I couldn't hear what Herr von Platen asked, but I heard Mutti respond, "The Italian people are totally uninterested! Indeed, one would not even think that a war was going on in Europe to judge by their calm and blasé manner. They have their cappuccinos and espressos and worry about style, and as far as I can tell they suffer from no shortages."

"No food rationing?" asked Tante Hilde, a hint of admiration in her voice.

"Not that I could see."

"Oh, to be Italian!" sang out Tante Hilde.

"No ability to plan ahead, these Italians!" commented Herr von Platen.

Tante Hilde didn't give Mutti a chance to respond to him as she launched into the raptures of Italian opera. "And does the opera still play?"

"Yes," said Mutti. "I saw the posters, but I did not have time to attend."

Finally Herr von Platen left, saying he had to meet his wife for dinner in Salzburg. Mutti led us upstairs, hooking arms with Tante Hilde as she whispered that in Italy, too, the same black-shirted militia marched around everywhere looking for trouble, just like the idiots that marched around Germany—a stiff, dark contrast to the ochre walls and relaxed attitude that normally permeated Italy.

"Look, Mutti. They stacked them so we can only look at the top one!"

"It doesn't matter. They're all identical."

I screwed up my face, and she laughed at my confusion. Finally, she undid the combination lock on the top trunk and threw open the lid, her arms spread proudly. I ran over and stopped dead in my tracks. My mouth twisted, and my eyes nearly popped out of my head.

"Well, come here, Jutta. This is far more precious than any suit by the finest Milanese tailor. This will save our lives." I looked at my mother and at Tante Hilde, both beaming at what one would have thought was a suitcase full of precious jewels. All I saw was a suitcase full of pasta, olives, and prosciutto hams.

"Mutti, I like pasta, but did you say the other two cases have exactly the same thing?" I asked, incredulous.

My mother nodded.

"Heti, this is amazing! You really did it." Tante Hilde clapped her hands, did a little dance, and hugged my mother.

"Well, it wasn't hard; it was just a matter of having the cash on hand. I had to go to several different stores because no one store had enough."

"Did they think you were crazy, buying so much pasta?"

"You know the Italians. They don't care! They were just glad of the business."

"But you didn't buy any tomato sauce!"

They both turned and looked at me.

"We'll make tomato sauce, of course!" said my mother. "I have already told Vati to tell Gustav to begin the garden. I will grow tomatoes and can them, my dear." And that is exactly what she did. From 1940 on, every summer she planted a glorious garden with at least a third of it dedicated to tomatoes. She and Luise spent all of August and September harvesting tomatoes and canning them. Gustave built wooden shelves in the basement along one entire wall dedicated to her canned vegetables; eventually, we had jars and jars of tomatoes, beets, green beans, and peas. Prior to 1940, I had never seen my mother grow a vegetable, let alone can one.

———

We ended up with over two hundred boxes of pasta, numerous jars of olives, and four huge prosciutto hams, as well as a variety of dried herbs, all stacked up in our basements in preparation for the shortages to come. We shared everything with the other Bolles, and both households would be grateful to Mutti for her foresight. At the time, I had no idea what precious cargo lay in those trunks. It saved our lives, took us through the worst years of the war, and even lasted until after, when we would need it most.

My father, of course, knew absolutely nothing about my mother's foraging mission in Italy. She had left the day after they had spoken on the phone about the invasion of Denmark and Norway, and she had returned the day before their next phone call. So by the time he heard about it, he could do nothing. He was horrified! Food rationing was a serious issue in Germany, and hoarding was a crime, and his wife's traveling alone to a foreign country did not thrill him, either. He insisted that he and Onkel Kurt take the food home to Berlin on their next visit. If the authorities were to stop them, he didn't want my mother and Tante Hilde to be the ones to face them. But my mother informed him that the risk was minimal. She had already checked, and neither pasta nor prosciutto ham were rationed in Germany, so the authorities could say nothing about cases and cases of pasta and four hams. My father was dumbfounded, but informed her he would still take the cargo home with him. He and Kurt would divide the trunks between them to arouse less suspicion. The authorities were very adroit at uncovering new regulations and laws to be used when convenient, and he was sure they could develop some sort of general anti-hoarding law to confiscate the pasta for their own use. My mother countered, insisting they rarely arrested women, and especially not ladies traveling in first class, whereas men were much more likely to be targeted. But my father would have none of it, and eventually he won this argument. Once my father decided to put his foot down, a thing he rarely did, especially with my mother, there was no moving him. And so it was that Vati and Kurt arrived the following week with only hand luggage so they could return with two trunks apiece and not look too suspicious.

———

May became June, and the crocuses and daffodils were replaced by delphiniums, marigolds, geraniums, and dahlias in Frau Lindner's garden. She had planted row upon row of dahlias in pinks and brilliant orange. They swayed in the breeze like big puffballs on the ends of their long green stems. Fields and fields of sunflowers sprang up, it seemed out of nowhere, their brilliant yellow flowers contrasting magnificently with the deep green forest. Wildflowers popped up all over the meadows. Our once-green meadow became a sea of buttercups that formed giant yellow clumps, followed in June and July by white, pink, and purple from the wild sweet peas. We enjoyed these summer days in the warm Bavarian sun with the fresh mountain air combing through our hair. Hundreds of freckles dotted my skin, turning it a lovely copper tone as the sun baked my arms and legs on our daily walks.

———

By mid-summer, few bombs had fallen on Berlin, and by August, my father and mother decided we should all return to Berlin. My mother grew bored in Berchtesgaden, and she missed Vati terribly. Furthermore, my father thought my education was suffering under the tutelage of Fräulein Innes. So in early August we returned to Berlin to find everything basically as we had left it.

We went back and forth between Berlin and Berchtesgaden three more times during 1940–41. My parents would suddenly decide it was time to vacate Berlin, having heard the rumors that spread like fire throughout the city that the English were serious this time. We would rush off to Bavaria, only to find no bombs were dropped after all. As the war progressed, travel became increasingly restricted, and we could only take the train at night for fear of bomb attacks. Eventually, it became more dangerous to take the train than to simply stay in Berlin. Ironically, we ended up in Berlin for all of 1943–45, when it was truly terrible to be there.

6

Berlin: 1940–1941

August 1940

It was late in August, warm and beautiful, the acacias still green in the garden and Mutti's dahlias in full bloom, when for the first time I heard the dreadful sound of the air raid sirens as they began their desperate lonely howls. My parents were out that evening, and my mind conjured up horrible images of Mutti and Vati hit in their car—metal flying everywhere, the roof crushed by the force of the bomb. We had no bomb shelter, not yet. Instead we ran around the house turning out lights, Sisi calm and Luise anxious as they closed curtains before grabbing me and descending to the basement.

On Sunday they came again. It was another warm August night, and Mutti had left the windows open to let in the breeze. The lace curtain that guarded against mosquitoes billowed in, pushed by the breeze that touched my skin with pulsing kisses. I was in bed, unable to sleep and fantasizing about travels to America, China, Madagascar, and other places I had read about, when in the distance a hideous buzzing sound began. Barely audible at first, I thought perhaps a fly had been caught in the curtain, but it grew louder and louder. Panic seized my heart, and I knew what it was. I leaped out of bed and shut off my night-light. Running across the hall, I jumped on Sisi's bed and began to shake her as hard as I could to wake her up. She woke with a start and, seeing the panic in my eyes, said nothing as in one motion she threw off her covers and rose from her bed. The air raid sirens began their horrid whine, and my parents, who had been at the Kittels' for dinner, came shouting through the front door, their voices carrying up the stairs. I stood at the top of the landing, frozen in terror. Tears fell from my eyes and ran down my cheeks, landing on the wooden floor in great wet drops; a chill ran down my side.

Vati shouted, "Come, Jutta!" I couldn't move. I stood glued to the landing. He threw the torch to Mutti and told her to go ahead with Sisi. Climbing the stairs two at a time and then bending to pick me up, he swung me around; in that single move, the entire living room swung around before me, a kaleidoscope of color. Mutti flashed the light for him as he ran down the stairs as best he could, with me a cumbersome burden. As we turned the corner at the entrance hall to go down the second flight of stairs to the basement, my foot caught on the umbrella holder by the door, and it crashed to the floor, shattering into hundreds of pieces, startling us as the sound burst through the room. I flinched. Mutti's beautiful porcelain umbrella holder, carried all the way back from a trip to Yugoslavia, gone—suddenly shattered in one movement. We burst into the basement just as Luise, her back to us, pulled a sheet up and tucked the ends crisply under the mattress of the garden lounge Mutti had had Gustav bring down to the basement. She turned as we clattered down the stairs and motioned to Vati to put me on the cot. Luise held my hand and brushed my forehead for a moment, but still the tears came spilling down my cheeks. Mutti squeezed herself onto the narrow cot with me, hugging me and whispering softly. Slowly my crying began to subside, and then it stopped.

Vati remained standing, periodically pacing the room. We could hear them flying overhead—hundreds of them. They flew so low I envisioned them scraping the tops of the trees in the Grunewald. I shuddered with terror, worrying about my poor *Vögelein* and Harold out in the pond. I began to cry again, quietly. Mutti stroked my hair and muttered, "Shhh. We are safe."

The vibrations shook the foundation of the house, and I thought the ceiling would crash in on us. The constant thud of the bombs was like the sound of thunder, but without the pauses of nature, just one after the other, hundreds and hundreds of them crashing down on us—the vibrations powerful, rocking the walls of the house, even though their target was central Berlin. After an hour, the all-clear sounded. Vati stood still and then headed cautiously up the stairs to inspect the damage. He motioned for us to remain in the basement. Despite my protests, Mutti followed him. She put her finger to her lips. "Hush, Juttalein, it is over. Wait here with Luise and Sisi." Luise sat by my bed and stroked my hand. Soon Vati came back downstairs.

"Where is Mutti?" I asked, panicked.

"She is out front talking to the Kittels."

Before he could utter another word, I tore up the stairs and out the front door. I saw her at the end of the drive, pointing to the sky and talking.

She turned, motioning me to come. "*Ja,* Jutta. God is watching over us. No fires, no damage!"

"Mutti, I must check on Harold," I said, running to the other side of the house to the pond. I peered into the dark green water, looking for him. He wasn't there! Panicking, I searched the pond, and then a dark object caught the corner of my eye. Turning, I saw him slowly lumbering along on top of the flagstone walkway, heading first one way and then another. Amazed I hadn't stepped on him, I hurried over and picked him up just as my mother came around the house. "Jutta, you must go back to bed now."

"Mutti, look! The poor thing is so scared he's completely disoriented. I found him on the sidewalk, almost ten feet from the pond!" I said, gently stroking his shell; he tucked his head and neck into his shell so far he looked like a textured pebble in the dull light.

"My goodness! But he is so lucky he has you to look after him!" Mutti watched me stroke his shell. She touched my head lightly with her hand. "Now put him back in his home, and let us go in."

I carefully tucked him in under the leafy ledge that was his haven. "Goodnight, Harold. All is safe," I whispered.

Taking my hand, Mutti gently pulled me up and walked me into the house. We took the living room stairs rather than the back stairs to avoid the only legacy of the bomb raid in our house—her broken umbrella holder. Vati stood waiting for us on the landing, a vacant look on his face. I knew he was troubled. I hugged him around the waist. "God looked after us, Vati." It was more a question than a statement.

"*Ja*. Let us hope he can keep man from destroying us," responded my father.

"Well of course he can! He is God!" I said confidently.

Vati only nodded. Sometimes he said such strange things. He grabbed me to him again and, reaching for my mother with the other hand, we stood there in the dark light, arms wrapped around each other, a family lost in the middle of this war we had not wanted and were powerless to stop.

———

The next morning we learned that the British had dropped twenty-two tons of bombs on Berlin, sending eighty bombers to do the job. Vati telephoned Mutti from the office to let her know. I walked into Mutti's bedroom rubbing my eyes, trying to ignore the gray day outside; I saw her shocked expression as she held the phone to her ear. Mutti had let me sleep, and after breakfast she walked me to school. As a result, I was late—a serious violation of the school rules. Good German children did not arrive late for school, but Mutti was not one to shrink before rules. I walked into Herr Schuster's music class, and all heads turned.

"Thank you for deciding to join us, Fräulein Bolle! We thought perhaps a bomber had lost its way last night and hit only your house here in Dahlem. No other houses, just the Bolle house!"

The children giggled at the teacher's attempt at wit. I simply looked at him and stood in the doorway.

"Well, come in. Come in. Sit down! You've disrupted class enough, haven't you?"

August 28, 1940

The next night, another air raid sounded. It was short, only thirty minutes—but then, two days later, another. This time we were still outdoors dining when we heard them—the persistent buzz of bombers, followed by a distant air raid siren. But they were far away this time. I climbed to my bedroom and watched in horrified fascination as green and red lights dropped from the sky in the distance.

Throughout the month of September, almost every other night an air raid warning sounded and the bombers came. I slept through some; they were late at night and on the other side of the city, so that sometimes I did not hear anything in my sleep, although Mutti would tell me in the morning she had heard them. But sometimes they were so close the house shook from the invisible force of the bombs. The noise deafening, I lay on the makeshift bed in the basement, terror climbing up my skin, my pillow over my head to block the hideous sounds of the sirens and the explosions that ripped through the night. With each crash of the bombs, my body jumped. I would doze off between assaults and wake up sporadically, the sound of the bombs drifting into my sleep. Often I woke to find my thumb in my mouth.

Throughout the fall, the air raids became a common occurrence. In November they suddenly stopped, and by the week of my birthday it had been almost two weeks since the last raid. We were beginning to feel normal, the luxury of uninterrupted sleep embracing us once again. And in my childish way I believed that perhaps the bombing was over. My parents had promised that for my eleventh birthday I could go to lunch at Schlichter's, my father's favorite restaurant. Mutti had said we could go shopping beforehand, but this was all agreed to in early August while we were still in Berchtesgaden, before all the bombings. I begged and pleaded with my parents. After all, the bombs only hit at night; it's safe during the day, I argued. In the end, Mutti decided *they* should not be allowed to destroy all of life's pleasures with their idiotic war. So she reluctantly agreed, so long as no air raid took place between now and my birthday. My father sent Heinz ahead to scout out the best route into the city, so we could avoid the skeletons that had once been buildings. I was touched by their effort to hide the damage from me, but I overheard Heinz talking about it to Luise in the kitchen.

I could hardly wait! I loved Berlin! I loved the cafés full of people laughing and talking. I loved the hurried way that people walked and ran to catch the subway and buses. I imagined they were going to very important jobs—jobs like my father's. It all seemed so much more alive than the suburbs.

The graceful old trees that lined Berlin's main arteries provided a beautiful contrast to the buildings they hugged. Like the pictures I had seen of canyons in the West of the United States, the trees wedged between the walls of the canyon and their lifeline, the river at the bottom. I loved the sound of the horns honking and traffic whirling by— a policeman at the corner of Kurfürstendamm and Martin Luther Strasse stopped all traffic when Vati drove by and let us through. I laughed when Vati told me it was because every Christmas he gave him a very nice tip.

I longed to be like the beautiful ladies in their elegant dresses and coats. They all seemed so thin and tall and elegant compared to the ladies one saw in Dahlem village. I tried to imagine where they were going—everybody seemed in such a hurry, like my music box wound up too tightly, the music and dancers suddenly performing at a frantic pace. Even the shopkeepers with their irreverent jokes, wry sense of humor, and rough manner fascinated me. They were sarcastic, and with their incredible accents I needed my mother to translate for me, as if I were hard of hearing.

I only ventured into this exciting haven a few times a year, usually for a birthday or a special occasion. Often it was with my mother, to go shopping on the Kurfürstendamm, or it was with Opa Bolle, to go to the museums or the zoo, or sometimes to see Shirley Temple movies at the UFA Palace. No matter what we were doing downtown, we always finished with coffee and cake, or lunch, depending on what time of day we wandered down the Kurfürstendamm.

—————

I tapped my foot impatiently, waiting at the top of the stairs for the car. It was a Thursday, and Mutti was picking me up from school a few minutes early, much to the consternation of Frau Schröder, who did not approve of children missing school unless they were half-dead from scarlet fever or some equally horrid ailment. I glanced up and down Im Gehege several times before I spotted them making their way slowly down the narrow cobblestone street, the black Daimler nosing its way gingerly to avoid parked cars and trees that jutted out into the street. I ran down the steps, only too happy to be free of the bricked confines of the *Gertrauden Schule* with its hard benches and rigid rules and Frau Schröder, our principal. I had graduated from the *Lansschule* and had eight long years of *Lyceum* ahead of me, eight long years of Frau Schröder and her stern face. The good part was that the school was housed in an attractive brick building, set back from the Königin Luise Strasse in a residential neighborhood; the other good thing was that the walk was much shorter—down the Föhrenweg, past the boys' school at the end, and then a shortcut across Königin Luise Strasse. Sadly, the sweets kiosk we walked by every day coming from the grade school was no longer part of my routine.

Heinz greeted me, shaking my hand as he opened the door for me. "*Frohlichen Geburstag*, Fräulein Bolle."

"*Danke, Herr Heinz. Ich bin aber sehr froh!*" I said, beaming. I practically leaped into the backseat, where my mother was waiting.

"Well, you do not look too sad about missing school!" She laughed, giving me a hug with her free arm.

"I'm not! I am so excited, Mutti, I could just bust!"

Mutti laughed again. "*Komm*, Heinz. We better get going before Jutta explodes from excitement." Heinz maneuvered the huge car around the grassy center median that set the school off from the homes on the street. He turned onto Königin Luise Strasse, heading for the Kronprinzenallee and its wide lanes that spilled into the Kurfürstendamm. Fall came late this year, and the trees still held their beauty. Leaves fluttered in the breeze, hues of honey and butter; occasionally a particularly spectacular tree stood alone in vibrant shades of red or orange. Stately homes lined the boulevard, beautiful with their beds of chrysanthemums and well-manicured lawns, the lawns still green but covered with that deep hue just before the winter cold turns their rugged blades a light brown. It was a bright, sunny day, the blue sky a stark contrast to the orange and burned hues of the trees. I pressed my face against the glass, not wanting to miss anything. I tried to take a picture in my mind of every home and building to savor for later.

We rounded the Roseneck with its roses trimmed back, ready for winter. A double-decker bus blocked our view. Heinz deftly swung the car around it.

"Mutti, this is a spectacular day!"

"Ordered special for Jutta. Now, where shall we find you a new dress? We can't take you to Schlichter's in your school clothes!" Raising her voice over the traffic so Heinz could hear, she said, "Please take us to *KadeWe* first, Heinz." He tipped his hat in the mirror.

"Yes, yes!" I shouted with excitement, hopping up and down in my seat. KadeWe was my favorite store. My mother thought it was too big and too impersonal. She preferred the private boutiques found on the Kurfürstendamm, or Frau Schultz's exclusive dressmaking boutique. But I loved the grand gold doors of the *KadeWe* and the heavy gilt escalator ascending to the top of the world, allowing me to fly without wings and from which I could view the entire store. I loved the fabrics and the colors, and the elegance of the women's section, and the sights and smells of the food court, where you could find pomegranates and oranges from Spain, and lavender from France, and all sorts of exotic mushrooms and fish, and cheeses that filled three cases. But with the war on, I knew we would not visit that floor; its shelves would be empty and free of goods from other nations.

We made our way up to the third floor to the children's section, making many stops along the way. I made a foray into the scarf section and found a brilliant purple Chanel silk scarf. In the hat section, I tried on hats until my mother insisted we go on. But first I had to stop in the shoe section, where I marveled over a pair of Prada shoes in lavender and purple with delicate hand stitching and a lovely purple rosebud on the top. "Oh, I wish I were old enough, Mutti!"

"You will be, all too soon," replied my mother. "*Komm*, Jutta. We must get to your section or we will never be able to meet Vati in time."

"But my section is so boring, and I really want to see the new styles for the ladies' dresses."

"If we have time afterwards, we can stop in the women's dresses. My goodness, I have never seen a child so in love with fashion." I did not respond. I was too busy drinking in all the colors and textures as I looked over the side of the escalator and down on to the women's section below. We arrived on the third floor, greeted by hundreds of Steiff stuffed animals. My favorite was the old green turtle with his head hanging to one side. "Oh look, Mutti. Just like Harold!"

We slowly made our way through the toy section to the dress section, where a supercilious salesclerk, with honestly the biggest nose I have ever seen on a female, clasped her hands together and pronounced everything I tried on as "*reizend!*" (darling). Even when I looked like an elf, because the skirt was so big that I nearly drowned in it, she grabbed my face and said, "Frau Bolle, she has the face of a princess with those darling blue eyes and that hair, what a color. Oh my goodness, you can tell what family she comes from! Such a darling girl, and so pretty." I rolled my eyes; a princess I was not. With my large Bolle nose, covered with freckles, and auburn hair, I had known for many years there was no way around the fact that mine was a face with features of "character," as they said—but never the delicate features of a princess or a movie star.

My mother smiled. "Thank you. Yes, we are very blessed."

"Frau Bolle, she will be a great beauty!"

I screwed up my nose and mouth at my mother, catching Mutti off guard for a moment. She burst out laughing. The sales lady thought she was laughing at the idea that I would be a great beauty and looked at Mutti in horror. Recovering quickly, Mutti said, "Oh yes, she will indeed."

I wore my new outfit out of the store, much to the astonishment of the sales lady—in Germany, one just did not do such a thing. "*Das macht man aber nicht!*" But my mother said the purpose of our shopping trip was to outfit me properly for an elegant lunch with my father. Why buy the outfit and not wear it? So wear it I did. And my new shoes and matching purse.

Heinz waited patiently across the street for us by the Wittenbergplatz U-Bahn station, where the road was wide. He saw us immediately and expertly brought the car around. Heinz stood sentry, watching like a hawk so as to always be ready for us at a moment's notice. As he opened the door, my mother said "Well, Heinz, I think we can go to Schlichter's in style now."

He nodded his head and, looking at me, said, "Yes. I see the shopping was a success. You look very elegant, Fräulein Jutta."

"*Danke sehr*, Herr Heinz!" I said in my best movie star imitation.

The car pulled up to the restaurant with its blue canopy jutting to the street, a grand, elongated umbrella protecting its special clients from the rain and snow. As I walked up the stairs side by side with my mother, feeling very important, I admired the beige-colored cut blocks that formed an arch around the windows and door. We passed through elegant doors of dark wood and glass, out of the hustle and bustle of Berlin's streets and into another world. It was a world of elegance and calm, filled with delicacies few could imagine, a world that most Berliners only dreamed about in 1940, when shortages were the norm. Somehow, Schlichter's managed to provide many of the same delicacies for their customers as before the war.

I was vaguely aware that not everyone spent their birthdays eating at Schlichter's or, if they did, they certainly weren't eleven years old. My friend Erica had never eaten there at all, nor had her mother and father. As the *maître d'* escorted us to our table, I took in the beauty of the place. Schlichter's stood for simplicity, minimalism at its most elegant. A small place, its size added to its simplicity and sense of exclusiveness. The polished dark wood panels reflected the light of the brass lamps, forming a cocoon of warmth. White tablecloths, starched and crisp and hanging almost to the floor, covered each table. At each place setting stood delicate Meissen china, in a floral pattern with butterflies and bees, flanked by heavy silver tableware with the letter *S* inscribed. Full bouquets of fresh flowers decorated every table in brilliant reds and blues. My father must have called ahead, for the flowers on our table were completely different from those at the other tables—beautiful, pale pink roses with the edges a darker pink.

I sucked in my breath as I sat down in the chair the *maître d'* held out for me. "My goodness, Mutti. They are exquisite! How sweet of Vati!"

"Hans Bolle! Where on earth did you find such flowers at this time of year and during a war?" my mother muttered to herself in amusement.

Mutti ordered a white wine, and I ordered a Shirley Temple, named after the famous American child star. I had read they were the rage in America. After some discussion among my mother, the waiter, and the bartender, a red beverage arrived at my table, looking beautiful with its red fruit interior. Having no grenadine available, the bartender used raspberry syrup mixed with soda water and completed the concoction with a strawberry, a slice of orange, and three wonderful, sweet red cherries. Whether it was authentic or not, I did not know. I only knew it was delicious. I happily sipped my "Shirley Temple" and admired my fellow diners. The tables held mostly men my father's age in business suits, engrossed in serious discussions. An occasional table dotted the landscape where a few ladies sat together having lunch, breaking the monotony of the suits with a spark of color from a scarf or dress. They looked like they were having much more fun, laughing and talking conspiratorially amongst each other, than were the men.

My father hurried into the restaurant, handsome in his suit and tie, his thick black hair parted and waved to one side. He handed his coat to the *maître d'*, who greeted Vati enthusiastically. My father hated all the fuss they made over him—"*Grussmaxe,*" he called them. I looked around and noted all the ladies who turned in their chairs to stare at my father. I stood and waved to him. Several men at different tables nodded a greeting to him and stood up. He held up one finger to them, to say just a moment, and came directly over to our table. I leaped from my chair and hugged him. "Thank you, Vati! Thank so much for the beautiful surprise!"

"Happy birthday, Juttalein, and thank you for being my guest today."

"Are you joking, Vati? I wouldn't miss this for the world!"

With a chuckle, he kissed my mother hello and said, "Just give me one moment. I will be right back." I watched him greet the various men and women who knew him around the room. I thought my father was the most important man in Berlin, and it flashed through my mind that maybe Vati could do something to stop this Hitler. He could stop this man. He could stop the war. Vati must not realize how many people like him! I would raise this with him later.

"Well, how are the most beautiful ladies in all of Berlin?" asked Vati, joining us again.

"Only Berlin, Hans? Usually you say the world," teased my mother.

"Of course, I meant all the world! Now what shall it be for the birthday girl today? Schnitzel? Venison? Or how about spaghetti?"

"Vati, they don't have spaghetti at Schlichter's!" I admonished.

"Oh, you don't think so?" he asked with a twinkle in his eyes.

"I would like the pork schnitzel and a salad with white asparagus, please," I announced in what I intended to be a very grown-up tone.

"Excellent choice, my dear. And you, Heidchen?"

"I will try the sole, but first let's look at the appetizer trolley."

"Anything your hearts desire." My father caught the waiter's eye and ordered food like I had never seen before. He ordered prosciutto and melon, a salad of artichoke hearts, pork schnitzel, oysters baked on the half shell, and "A secret surprise dish from the heart of Italy," he said. He had them bring everything all at once so we could sample and taste from each plate.

The plates of food spread across the table, their vibrant colors contrasting with each other: the pink prosciutto against the orange melon, the golden fried schnitzel surrounded by brilliant yellow lemon slices against the bright greens of the salad, all set off by a huge platter of steaming, bright red spaghetti Bolognese covered with Parmesan cheese—my *lieblings* dish. Our table, the white tablecloth peeking through now and then as background, looked magnificent. Ladies in knit dress that clung to their figures and dark hats with pheasant feathers in them craned their necks to see the food display on our table. They smiled at us: an indulgent father always evoked a soft spot.

As we left, Vati nodded a farewell to several men who sat in the corner as he held the door for Mutti and me.

Once on the street, Vati bent, kissed me, and said, "Happy Birthday, Juttalein." I wrapped my arms around his neck, the citrus smell of his 4711 aftershave familiar and comforting. "Thank you, Vati, for everything. This is the best day of my life," I whispered.

"You are more than welcome, *mein Herz*." Letting go, I turned to my mother and thanked her as well.

"I will see you two later this evening," said my father as he kissed my mother on the cheek.

Vati waved and walked to his car. The shiny blue BMW looked silver in the late afternoon light. He put the tiny sports car's roof down, probably for the last time this season, and roared off to his office on Belziger Strasse in Schöneberg.

I had no idea this would be my last visit to Schlichter's until after the war ended almost seven years later. None of us knew what was to come so soon after those calm November days of 1940.

A Birthday Invite

1941

The banging on the door startled us—it was not the knock of a social caller; it was the knock of an official. My eyes shot up from my homework; I hadn't seen anyone come up the driveway. Luise had just turned from the stove with a plate of my favorite sugar cookies and almost dropped them on the table. My mother looked at her; their eyes locked. I looked from one to the other. Luise looked terrified.

"Please go see who it is. It's probably a tradesman," my mother said with a forced calm. But I could tell she was nervous. Tradesmen always knocked on the kitchen door, not the front door. No. This was the sort of knock that, in Nazi Germany, brought the fear of unwelcome news. What if someone had denounced my mother for not saying Heil Hitler? I thought, panic rising in my throat. Or for not having our obligatory picture of Hitler in the front hall? Or for all the times we didn't put the swastika flag out on ceremonial days? Or maybe it had to do with me not going to the Hitler Youth program. My mind raced through a hundred different scenarios in a matter of seconds. My mother sensed my concern. "I am sure it is nothing."

Luise came back into the kitchen, the color drained from her face.

"It's two SS officers asking to speak to you, ma'am."

Mutti stood up quickly. Straightening herself to her full height, she left the room without a word. My heart in my throat, I could not suppress my curiosity. I ran to the door and cracked it just enough to peek through to the hallway. Two men stood just outside the door, dressed in the uniform of the SS. I prayed Mutti would for once be careful about what she said. One of the men held out an envelope to my mother and said that it had been sent at *Reichsführer* Himmler's personal request. My stomach dropped to my knees. Mutti took the envelope and thanked them.

I noticed how young they both were! It seemed to me they should be older. Tall and fit, they stood in the doorway with their thick-soled black boots laced up to their knees; leather straps hooked into buckles just below their knees held them firmly in place. My God, there must be fifty silver hooks running up and down each side, through which the laces intertwined. The effect was terrifying. Never have I seen such frightening-looking boots in all my life. Their pants, tucked into the boots, billowed out slightly on the sides and were belted at the waist with thick black leather belts held together by another large buckle of silver. The shirts were the same color as the pants and, of course, on their arms, as if they were tourniquets, were the black armbands—the black swastikas placed prominently on a white background. The combination of the black armbands, and what they stood for, with those black boots made my skin crawl. My mother thanked them again and closed the door as quickly as possible without being rude. She leaned against the door and held the envelope to her chest with her eyes closed, breathing heavily. I pushed the door to the kitchen open and ran to her.

"What is it, Mutti?" I asked urgently.

Without answering, she tore open the letter and let the envelope fall to the ground unnoticed. I stooped to pick it up for her. Mutti suddenly burst out laughing. I straightened up quickly and looked at my mother as if she had lost her mind. Luise rushed in from the kitchen, and we stared at my mother as she shook her head and chuckled! Then, seeing our perplexed faces, she read, "Fräulein Gudrun Himmler requests the presence of Fräulein Jutta Bolle at the celebration of her twelfth birthday, this Saturday at 2:00 PM."

Luise let her breath out in a huff. "*Gott seit Dank*! I thought you were heading to Ravensburg for sure, Frau Bolle!"

I breathed a sigh of relief, although I did not find it anywhere near as amusing as my mother seemed to find it. I would have to attend this event and stand in the presence of Gudrun's father and possibly many others like him. "I don't see what is so funny. I will have to go to that man's house!"

Recovering my mother said, "I'm sorry, Jutta. I was just so relieved that it was not anything serious. And then it just struck me as so funny. We were, all of us, terrified of those officers, and all they were doing was inviting my daughter to a birthday party."

"*Ja*, but look whose party it is, and look where it is being held!"

"You're right. In another way, it is not funny at all, is it? It's actually terribly sad, isn't it?" she said wistfully as she ushered us back to the dining room.

"Mutti, did you see those boots?"

"Absolutely terrifying!"

"I can't go to that party; a lot of those boots will be there."

"Well, I bet it will be a wonderful party," offered Luise. "I'll bet they have a clown and presents for everyone. I'm sure all the Bolle girls got an invitation; you can go with Peti and Ingrid."

"No." Mutti held up her hand to Luise and me. "I will discuss whether you are going or not with your father when he comes home. Now, let's stop talking about it and finish your homework, and when Sisi returns you need to practice piano with her." She tapped her forehead with the letter.

I stared at my math paper, unable to concentrate; I would ask for Sisi's help later. What was it like to walk around and instill terror in everyone you met simply by virtue of your uniform? I wondered if they enjoyed it. Or did they feel bad when they came to people's homes and so obviously scared them? Of course not! Not those men; they weren't the type to feel pity. I saw it in the line of their jaws and the pitch of their temples. Stripped of their uniforms, would they have been frightening? I imagined them in swim trunks and could not help but smile. Was that the point, I thought? Was that why they wore the uniform? To say we belong and you do not, like Hannelore and Liesel and their ugly BDM uniforms and all the sashes and badges they were so proud to wear?

My mother had been watching me while she drank her coffee. "Mutti, it's all about the uniform, isn't it?" Mutti looked at me thoughtfully, waiting for me to go on. "To be able to say, 'We are the ones who belong.'" I looked into her eyes and added, "If you behave and are good, we might let you join."

A sadness covered her face as I spoke, but all she said was, "You are much older than your years, Jutta."

"That's it, isn't it?" I said, more to myself than to her. "To make us feel like we all belong—we are part of the crowd—and the others: gypsies, Jews, and foreigners, are not."

My mother nodded her head and added, "And to control. Nothing terrifies people more than to not belong to the crowd."

"Well, I don't want to belong," I said forcefully. "I knew there was a reason I hated the Hitler Youth, I just never could express it before."

Mutti squeezed the bridge of her nose, her eyes closed. "I know, my dear. Now please, let's not think about our visitors anymore. Just finish your homework."

"But Mutti, you never want to talk about…"

"No, I don't," interrupted my mother quickly. "I never wanted you to know about any of this. Not at your age, not ever. Now go on upstairs, Jutta." I was astonished to see tears forming in the corners of her eyes. She hurried out of the dining room into the music room. Moments later, the delicate sound of Mendelssohn drifted to me as her fingers ran across the keys of the piano, softly, lightly, trying to block out the harsh and cold world.

That evening, my parents debated at great length whether I should attend the birthday party or not. My mother was firmly of the view I should not; to set foot in that house was somehow endorsing the evil that Herr Himmler represented. And besides, she said, Jutta doesn't want to go. My father, on the other hand, said it was not the child's fault. She could not help what her father was, and she was entitled to a happy birthday party just like any other child. Didn't she, after all, come to my party? This argument made some sense to me. From what I knew of her, Gudrun appeared to be a nice girl, though she always seemed a bit sad to me. We all knew her mother was very ill; some even said she was dead. At any rate, she was never around to comfort Gudrun or take care of her. How awful it must be not to have your mother around. Suddenly I felt sorry for her: surrounded only by men dressed in uniforms, black boots smacking the floor of the house, the sound echoing in the night. Poor Gudrun. Everybody avoided her because of her father. No one invited her over to play because she had to go everywhere with those SS bodyguards. She had no mother to comfort her. And she had to live in that house surrounded by a big white wall. I shuddered.

"If she doesn't go, they may read a meaning into it, Heti," suggested my father.

"I want to go!" I shouted suddenly. My parents, startled by my sudden outburst, stopped talking and looked at me. "I want to go, Mutti. Vati is right; it is not her fault. I will go, and I will look right through the booted men. I will pretend they do not exist."

"Welcome to Germany!" said my father wryly. My mother frowned at him.

After a long silence, she said softly and with a hint of sadness, "Well, fine. You may go."

I went to Gudrun Himmler's birthday party. Sisi made sure I was well scrubbed and had on just the right dress. Mutti did not want me wearing my best dress, implying that it was an honor to be invited to Himmler's house, so we chose a simpler blue cotton dress with a Peter Pan collar and a belted waist. I wore my hair pulled back and pinned on each side by barrettes. My mother refused to make me sport the braids and pigtails favored by the current regime for a young German girl.

Saturday afternoon arrived too soon. I carried a present for Gudrun. I had bought her a special pencil set with stationery from Duhr's. The Himmlers lived a few streets over, so Sisi accompanied me up to the gate. She said she would return at five o'clock sharp. I stood there, my heart racing, the huge white wall looming before me—at least twenty feet tall, it surrounded their entire property. At the end of the drive, by the street, a guardhouse anchored one side of the enormous black iron gate that reached the full height of the wall. It was like a prison. Butterflies danced in my stomach. Suddenly I thought I was going to be sick just as a booted man stepped out of the guardhouse and came toward me. I took in the armband and the boots, and my instinct was to flee, but I couldn't move.

"Fräulein Bolle, I presume?" said the guard pleasantly as he opened the gate for me. It swung inward toward the house, two doors like the mouth of a huge fish opening to take me in. How did he know who I was? My mind raced through a thousand bizarre scenarios. As the gate closed behind me with a loud clank, my heart sank. I looked up the long driveway and gulped. I began walking, my eyes fixed on the enormous white house that stood at the end. It was an ugly house—big, cumbersome, and ungraceful—without the beautiful garden that softened the front of ours. The door, like the wall and gate, must have been fifteen feet tall. Poor Gudrun! How could anyone live here? And without a mother! I reached out to press the doorbell, but it was unnecessary. The door opened before I could ring the bell—I had been watched. Two more booted men stood there. One of them looked at me and chuckled. He ushered me into the sitting room, calling me Fräulein Bolle. How eerie to already be known before one introduced oneself! Gudrun jumped up with delight upon seeing me and ran over to hug me. Her warmth eased my fears a bit, and I let her lead me over to the other girls. Erica was already there with her sister. "Why didn't you let me walk with you?" I whispered.

"My mother wanted us to come separate," she said, rolling her eyes.

"Why?"

Erica shrugged, but I knew why.

I tried to relax, joining in the games that had been organized by Frau Braun, Gudrun's governess. Gudrun said her father would also be there soon. Fear shot through me. I could not concentrate on anything other than the fact that Himmler himself would walk through the double doors across the room at any moment. I tried to think of an excuse for leaving: stomachache, headache—anything. But then it occurred to me these men were experts at ferreting out the truth. They will probably know you are faking, Jutta Bolle, and then they will arrest you and God knows what could happen to you.

The room suddenly fell silent. Gudrun looked up and smiled with delight. "Papi, you're here!" She leaped up and ran to him. He hugged her and kissed the top of her head. This man gave kisses? I found myself astonished. Somehow I had thought that a man responsible for so much misery would not kiss his daughter. But there he stood, looking perfectly normal—a little small perhaps, but then my own father was not a large man, either. He was very pale, and his dark hair made him seem even paler, for it contrasted starkly with his skin. He had a rather small face with cheeks that were disproportionately large and a chin that seemed too small. He looked like a bookkeeper or school administrator to me. But it was his eyes that bothered me: small and deeply set, with a slant to them. They were dark and beady, lacking all expression, and without depth, as if there were nothing behind them. There were no laugh lines around them that told of kindness and warmth and good humor. Those lines surrounded my father's eyes and my grandfather's eyes, and I had seen them in the pictures of my great-grandfather. No, these eyes were hard and cold. When he looked at Gudrun they seemed to soften almost imperceptibly, but when he looked at the rest of us they instantly lost that warmth—as if a veil had come down over them. This man scared me to death. I sucked in my breath and my hands grew sweaty; perspiration broke out on my forehead. I took a deep breath to keep my heart from racing. I looked from him to Gudrun, her blond braids swinging as she hopped around and smiled and looked lovingly into those hard, dark eyes, and I felt so, so sorry for her.

He seemed pleased to be at the party and greeted all of us individually. We all shook his hand and said our names. I wanted so badly to tell him what I thought of him. To tell him that I loved Tante Anna, and that he had no business making her flee, or Herr Bernstein or Herr Burger or Herr Cohen, either; to tell him what I thought of his arresting Pastor Niemoller; to tell him that he had ruined my friends Magda and Eva's lives for no reason at all. To tell him that he was nothing but a cruel bully. But I could say nothing; I was too terrified. My hands were so sweaty that I wiped them on my dress, and a tremor ran up my arm before I shook his hand. I could swear he lingered for an extra moment when I said my name, a slight pause as if he were going to say something and then changed his mind.

He did not stay at the party very long, maybe fifteen minutes or so. When he left the room, everyone's mood seemed to lift. A lightheartedness took over again where there had been silence and tension. I wondered if Gudrun noticed. How extraordinary, I thought, that one person could so completely change the atmosphere in a room full of children. At five o'clock, mothers and governesses began to arrive, escorted in by the booted men to take their children home. To my horror, Sisi was ten minutes late. Gudrun came up to me. "Thank you for coming, Jutta."

"Thank you for inviting me. I will ask Mutti if you can come over sometime," I added.

She smiled brightly. "That would be wonderful!"

"Bye. See you at school."

"Bye." She walked with us to the front door and then stood waving to us as we walked down the drive. I turned and saw her outlined in the door. She looked so small with her blond braids and her hand held up to wave. The huge door towered over her, and the light from the entrance hall spilled out past her into the yard. Behind her I could see the outline of one of the booted men.

"Well, she seems like a nice girl," said Sisi, once we were safely out of the gate and walking down the street.

"She is very nice. Do you think Mutti will let me have her over sometime?"

"Well, maybe," she said doubtfully. "Now tell me all about the party."

I did invite Gudrun over, but only once, because Luise objected to the two SS officers that accompanied her. They sat in the kitchen eating and drinking coffee the entire time Gudrun was over. Luise was such a nervous wreck she had to go down to her room for the rest of the afternoon and evening.

7

Evacuation

1942–1943

In December, Mutti began to talk about sending me away, but she didn't know where. Bombs were dropping all over Germany—Nurmberg, Dusseldorf, Hamburg, and the Ruhr. Even Bavaria was no longer safe, and with travel increasingly difficult, it was too far away. A few months before, a letter had arrived from a former governess now living in Saxony. She wrote that Saxony was unscathed by bombs and suggested to Mutti that if she needed a place for me to stay, a farm in Saxony would be the safest. Mutti studied the possibility. Then the bombs stopped, and she forgot about it until March first, when Berlin was hit with the biggest attack yet—fires burned for three days, and thirty thousand were left homeless. Destruction was ten times that which had occurred in all the previous bombings combined. Nine hundred tons of bombs fell in thirty minutes, and the fires could be seen one hundred fifty miles from Berlin. After this attack, Mutti leaped into action, and I was ready within two weeks.

January 1943

I could always feel my mood drop in winter, almost in unison with the thermometer, it seemed. From the time of my birthday, when the leaves began to fall, until January, my mood would plummet with the temperature. The only exception would be the short reprieve that the Christmas season provided. My excitement over Christmas would divert my attention from the cold gloom that was a Berlin winter. After Christmas I always looked forward to the New Year's party my parents held, and then the final event of the holiday season, Epiphany, when we would go from door to door singing Christmas carols, collecting candy and cookies for our efforts. Festivities such as these helped me make it through the dreary palette of Berlin's winter months. But this year, nobody sang Christmas carols, and nobody had any candy to give out. For the first time that I could remember, my parents did not have their New Year's Eve party. Gray and black replaced the gold and red of Christmas, and the trees screamed at me from the garden and along the walkways, their gnarled bark lifeless and dull in grayish shades of brown.

The realization that nothing green would sprout on the trees for another two months filled me with despair. I did not notice the deep green of the spruce trees that lined our garden and dominated the Grunewald Forest. Instead, I only noticed the dead look of the birch trees, the black bark of the acacias, denuded of all of their color, and the spindly twigs of the weeping willows that hung down to the edge of the lake in the park. All was bleak, cold, and gray, and the dark clouds that blanketed the sky told of an ominous future.

Surely it is colder than it has ever been in Berlin, I thought, shivering in my bed at night. My mother had Luise put extra duvets on my bed. I wore a double layer of socks and an extra T-shirt, as well as a sweater under my school blouse, but nothing seemed to take away the winter chill. My thirteen-year-old ego did not even mind being teased at school for looking like I had gained ten pounds. And always there were the bombs, disturbing my sleep and filling me with fresh fear each time they dominated the night.

"Ah, you're up," called my mother, looking up from the bottom of the stairs. "I was just coming to wake you. Come on down and have some breakfast."

"I'm not hungry," I said.

"Well, come down anyway, and we will see. Try and eat something, Jutta. I need to talk to you."

I tried. But I could only manage a few bites of the pancakes Luise had prepared. In my mind I knew they were delicious, but I could not even taste them. Mutti saw that it was pointless to force me to eat; she called Luise to take the plate away. "Luise, our little girl is not hungry today. But let her keep her hot chocolate. I want her to drink that if she can." Luise looked surprised at the unfinished pancakes but did not let forth with her usual comments about food left on plates. I knew the food would not go to waste. Luise would cut the pancakes into strips and fry them up for Gustav for lunch.

When she left, my mother began to talk rapidly. "Jutta, listen." She grabbed my hand and rubbed it. "Vati and I are worried about the bombs. They are causing all of us to worry, but you are especially anxious. We want you safe, away from all of this."

I frowned but said nothing. I stared at my hot chocolate, noting the swirls the liquid made as I stirred it with my spoon: dark, deep swirls in a symmetrical shape that formed a funnel the more I stirred the chocolate. I imagined being sucked into the funnel of some dark filthy river water—it reminded me of my dream from several nights before. I shuddered and looked up.

"Your father and I have begun to think about where we can send you." She paused again as Luise popped back in and asked if she could bring anything else. My mother shook her head.

"Why can't we go to Berchtesgaden again?" I asked.

My mother shook her head no. "It's too far away, and we worry because Hitler spends so much time there. Vati is afraid it may become a target."

"Why can't I go to Omi Muller's?"

"Well, you could, except that Opa Muller has just had another attack of gout, and Omi had to see the doctor again about her heart. I am worried that having you there would be too much for them."

"Oh," I said without expression.

"So," she began slowly, "I have written Elfriede, your old governess." She paused.

I said nothing.

"The one who is from Saxony."

I said nothing.

"Do you remember Elfriede?"

I nodded to indicate yes, and then said, "Vaguely. Rather plump, with a fat face and braids."

Mutti laughed and said, "Yes, that is the one. Well, she wrote a while ago to say that if we needed to send you away from Berlin because of the bombs, you could come and stay with her. So I have written to her."

I lifted my lip doubtfully.

She hurried on. "Saxony will be very safe. The English can't fly that far, and nothing in that region has been bombed, so you will be completely free from these awful bomb raids. She lives somewhere out in the country, in a pretty little town called Grosshartmansdorf. Even if they bomb Dresden—God forbid, such a beautiful city—or Leipzig, that wouldn't matter so much; they would never bomb a little town like Grosshartmansdorf."

Mutti prattled on breathlessly, most unusual for her. She was normally so calm and steady. Suddenly her eyes welled up with tears and she looked away. "Jutta, please say something."

I looked up in surprise and used all my energy to say, "Mutti, I'll be fine. I promise."

Her hand fluttered to her forehead and then to her cheek, brushing the tears away before she set it back down in her lap and clasped it around the wrist of her other hand as if to anchor it. "You can't imagine how awful this is. To be a mother and to have no control over these horrible events—and you watch them destroy your child, but you can't do anything about it." By this time the tears were streaming down her face.

I reached over and grabbed her hand. "Mutti, I will be fine. I just don't want to leave you."

She squeezed my hand and forced a smile, "Yes, I know." She tried to control her tears. "I'm sorry," she whispered as they defeated her again.

After a moment I said, "When would I go?"

She was once again calm. The breakdown had lasted only a moment. She took a deep breath. "As soon as I can arrange everything."

I nodded my head. "Mutti, will you play something for me?"

She looked at me in surprise. "Yes, of course!"

I settled myself on the large soft pillows of the sofa in the music room while she looked for her music. "Let's see. I think we need something cheerful. How about some Mozart?"

Grosshartmansdorf

And so it was that ten days later I found myself, along with my cousin Peti, on a train heading for Dresden. Tante Hilde decided Peti should join me, both for her own safety and to keep me company. Elfriede had received the letter from my mother within days and somehow found a phone and called her. It was all arranged, she said; she had found a lovely farmhouse with private quarters for us and a separate room for her. She also arranged that Peti and I would go to the *Gymnasium* in Freiberg. She told my mother that the countryside was lovely and the fresh air would do us good. She would meet us in Dresden and then escort us to Grosshartmansdorf herself.

I will never forget the trip from the train station to the farm. I don't know what I had expected, but there waiting for us was a hay wagon with a huge horse attached to the front of it and an equally huge man sitting on top of it, chewing on a blade of grass. What stands out in my mind is how bad he smelled. He was bald on top and wore a hat to cover it, which he removed upon meeting us. The sides of his head were covered with hair, but it stuck together and looked like he had smeared butter on it to hold it down. His shirt was soiled with dark stains, and his pants had holes where the knees peeked out from behind his knee patches. He introduced himself to us as Herr Scherz before he threw our bags onto the wagon and helped us sit on top of them, which might have been fun but for the freezing cold rain drizzling all about us. So we drove through the country in an open cart on top of our baggage. Elfriede sat next to him up front on the wooden seat. Well, more power to her, I thought. If she can handle that odor, she is a pretty tough lady. She did not seem to mind.

"What is that odor?" I whispered to Peti.

"Which one, the onion one or the other?"

"The other."

"I think it's cow manure."

"Oh my God! Are you serious?"

We bumped along the road, and everywhere I looked all I saw were flat fields of mud. "So when do we get to the pretty part?" I called to Elfriede.

She and Herr Scherz looked at each other and began to laugh.

"You have to go back to Dresden for that!" he called back to me. "If you're looking for pretty, you are in the wrong place, my dear. We don't have time for pretty here. Pretty gets in the way of farming and that is what we have here—farming."

I glanced around again. My eyes met only brown—no green, no pine or spruce trees to take away the monotony of winter, only brown: light brown where the sun hit the mounds of the plowed fields lying fallow for winter, and dark brown in the trenches.

"She told Mutti it was beautiful here!" I hissed to Peti. Peti screwed up her mouth to indicate how ugly she thought this place was.

After several miles with the wagon swaying from side to side, we pulled into a drive, more like a well-worn path, that was set off by two fence posts. At the end of the drive sat an old farmhouse. From stalls along one side of the first floor, cows poked their heads out, enjoying the feeble late-afternoon sun. My heart began to sink. Surely this was not where we were intended to spend the rest of the winter and spring! To my horror, Herr Scherz pulled up to the front of this barn-house and said, "Well, here we are!"

Elfriede got down as if nothing were wrong and said, "Come, girls. Our rooms are in the back, up the stairs." We followed Elfriede to the back of the house while Herr Scherz brought in our luggage. Elfriede had to practically kick open the door to our rooms, the hinges were so rusty. Everywhere I turned, the smell of cows and hay overpowered me. The rooms were dark and cold. The heater was a small, coal-operated affair in the corner and served to keep all the rooms warm. There was a sitting area and two bedrooms—one for us and one for Elfriede. She had already helped herself to the larger of the two. It was also the one that had the only view of anything; in this case, open fields. Ours had a view of another barn immediately next door, and of the tractor parts that were propped against the barn. I waited for Herr Scherz to leave, and then I turned on Elfriede.

"You told Mutti this was a lovely place!"

"What were you expecting, Berchtesgaden?" she responded.

"Frankly, yes!" I said, my eyes large with emphasis.

"Well this is Saxony, my dears, not Berchtesgaden."

"And country fresh air? You call cow manure fresh air?"

She bristled. "Listen. It is what it is, so just get used to it. And I will not tolerate that tone from you, do you understand me?"

I backed off, but I decided I would write to Mutti as soon as Elfriede left us alone. We simply couldn't stay here!

"Now you unpack your things, and then come downstairs to the kitchen for a snack and something to drink. It's the door directly below the stairs." She turned, unsmiling, to join Herr Scherz downstairs.

"This is too awful!" I said out loud, sitting on one of the rickety metal cots that served as beds. "How could Mutti have sent us here without checking it out first?" I grabbed my head with both hands and held it between my knees.

"I told Mutti I did not trust that Elfriede!" said Peti to the back of my head. "Remember when we were little and we came over to your house to make Christmas presents? She broke that Hummel figurine dusting in your room, and she lied and said I did it!" I had absolutely no recollection of the incident, but to make Peti feel good I acted like I did. "I guess Mutti thought anything was better than Berlin and air raids," Peti continued.

I looked out the window at the dismal gray sky and the brown-filled horizon—nothing but flat mud fields for as far as one could see! I could feel the tears begin to well up in my eyes. I stopped them quickly and tried to remind myself that I was older and had to be the leader. I sighed. "There is nothing we can do right now. Let's just make the best of it, and we'll send her a letter first thing in the morning."

Peti agreed and shrugged her shoulders. "Tante Heti didn't know, Jutta. She relied on what Elfriede told her."

I nodded and stood up to open my suitcase. I found a package and a note on top of my clothes. It was from Mutti:

> *Dear Jutta,*
>
> *By the time you read this, know that I already miss you. My heart aches for you girls to be home with me and with your mother, Peti, but we live in a time when things are not as they should be. We will get through this together, for you are always with me. Everywhere I look I see you, and I feel you with me in all that I do. I know that it seems hard now, but soon you will make friends, and you always have each other. Be good to each other. Before you know it, we will be together again and all will be happy and at peace as it should be. Be polite to Elfriede and your hosts and do well at school.*
>
> *Much love always,*
> *Your Mutti*

I collapsed back down on the bed and began to cry. I couldn't hold back the tears. Peti too started to cry after reading her own letter from her mother. She ran over and we hugged each other, letting out our frustration.

"Jutta, we each have a package!" said Peti, standing suddenly. She brought them over to the bed. We untied the pale purple ribbon that my mother must have saved from Christmas. As I folded back the brown paper, I saw the most wonderful assortment of treats. "Luise's sugar cookies! And chocolates!"

"And *gummi* bears! Where on earth did Tante Heti find *gummi* bears?"

I held up two bars of soap; Peti also had two bars. "Oh, thank God, she sent soap! Judging by Herr Scherz, I don't think they have seen much of this around here in a long time." We giggled.

"He smells like Luise's onion basket in the basement!" laughed Peti.

"Oh, and a heart book!" I held it up. She had made one for me in purple and one for Peti in pink. All the pages folded out into hearts like an accordion, four of them at each opening. A velvet ribbon held them together.

"It's beautiful. And look, she glued a four-leaf clover on the first page!"

"Your mother always adds these little touches. My mother ..." She stopped wistfully.

"Is a lot of fun!" I finished for her. "Your mother is a character, Peti, and you know it!"

She laughed. "She is that!" She hugged her package to her. "I guess they both have their benefits."

"And look! Mutti sent stationery and envelopes with the stamps already on them!"

"Oh, good! We won't even have to bother Elfriede for stamps."

After opening our packages, our spirits were lifted, and we quickly set about unpacking the rest of our things. There was no closet, only a small wardrobe in the corner of the room, so I took the top shelf, being taller, and gave Peti the bottom shelf. At the bottom of our suitcase were two more packages, one marked for Elfriede and one marked for the Scherzes. Armed with these, we went downstairs to meet Frau Scherz, leaving one last suitcase to unpack.

The stairs were sturdy but narrow, and a cold wind snapped about us as we descended to the kitchen. The kitchen door, like the doors to the bedrooms, needed a strong push to open, and as we walked in I had the distinct impression they had been talking about us.

"So here are the little misses," said Elfriede. I didn't like her tone; I knew she did not mean it as a compliment.

"Frau Scherz, this is Jutta Bolle," she said, nodding her head in my direction without bothering to get up. "And the little one is Peti Bolle."

"Well, it is good to have you girls here. Welcome!" said Frau Scherz, smiling and wiping her hand on her apron before she held it out to us. We smiled back and curtsied as we took her hand and greeted her. She had a broad, warm face, uncomplicated and honest, with brown eyes that twinkled in the kitchen light. I liked her immediately.

"Such nice manners you girls have! Well, well, you will have a lot of adjusting to do here," she added, looking down at our feet, still clad in our fancy travel shoes.

"The first thing you need to do is change your shoes! I hope you brought some boots with you!"

"I don't know. We haven't finished unpacking yet," I said.

"The little misses don't do their own packing," said Elfriede with sarcasm.

I did not respond. Instead, I handed Frau Scherz her package. Peti handed Elfriede hers at the same time. "Well, thank you. How kind of your mother!" said Frau Scherz, sitting at the table to open hers.

Elfriede opened hers a bit too quickly, I thought, tearing the paper and barely glancing at the note my mother had written. Her eyes lit up at the treats my mother had sent her: chocolates and coffee and soap.

"*Gott seit Dank*," cried Frau Scherz with delight. "Gert, she has sent real coffee! And look! Tea and jam, and here is some butter! And some real soap." She pressed the soap to her nose. "Oh, it smells lovely, like roses!" She was so excited that she forgot we barely knew each other, and she ran over to me and hugged me hard to her ample bosom. The pungent smell of onions and hair that had not been washed in a long time hit me hard. Elfriede's package was the same, except that my mother had included some of Luise's ginger snaps, I presumed because she had remembered they were her favorite. I was pleased that a bit of the wind was taken out of Elfriede's sails.

We joined them at the table, and there was an embarrassing silence as Frau Scherz served us bread with some sort of paste I could not identify. My mother had told us not to ask for the things that she was sending for the Scherzes or Elfriede. So we did not.

"What interesting bread," I said between mouthfuls. "It has a very unique flavor. What is it made from?"

"Rhubarb!" they all said in unison.

"Oh!" I said. I ate it because I was starving. Peti took a bite and made a face. I kicked her under the table.

"Do you not like regular bread?" I asked.

Frau Scherz looked amused, but Elfriede turned on me. "No, actually we love it, but we aren't all spoiled Bolle girls who can get anything they want, even in times of war! You do realize there is a war going on, don't you? Normal people have to endure shortages. Are you aware of that?" Her face was right up to mine, and she had turned all red. I felt tears spring to my eyes, and my face went hot and flushed. I leaped up from the table, sending my chair crashing to the floor, and ran out of the room. I ran up the stairs, taking them two at a time. The tears flowed down the side of my face, the wind freezing them to my cheeks. I grabbed the handle to the door and pushed, but it was stuck. I pushed again, panicking. I kicked the door in frustration and pushed again. Finally, it opened. I ran into our room and threw myself down on the bed.

As I sat alone in the room, Elfriede's personality began to come back to me. I remembered she and Luise fought because Luise thought she was too hard on me, but I was so small at the time, I couldn't remember too much. She was not warm and snuggly like my other early governesses. Why couldn't she be like Tante Rea? Or even Sisi? I thought of Sisi and hoped she would be happy. Mutti had found her a job with a family on the other side of Berlin, at least until I came back home. Hard shoes echoed on the wooden stairs outside; I turned my head toward the sound. There were two sets of footsteps, one heavy and one light.

I could hear Peti talking about Berlin and the bombs. I quickly wiped my tears, grabbed a book, and buried my nose in it. The door opened and Peti came in, followed by Frau Scherz, her size requiring her to turn sideways to maneuver through the narrow door.

"Look what we brought you, Jutta," said Peti cheerfully, showing me a tray with milk and my half-eaten bread, as well as one of the cookies my mother had sent.

"I'm not hungry," I said looking away. Frau Scherz sat down on the bed.

Her smell filled the room. Instinctively, I moved a few inches away to try and avoid it. She was trying to be kind, so I made an effort to look at her. She was a large woman—not fat; nobody was fat these days, and if they were, people stared at them, wondering if they bought on the black market. Well, nobody was fat except Göring. Frau Scherz took my hand. Her face round and friendly, she smiled from cheeks that looked like she had stuffed walnuts in them—one on each side, like knobs jutting out from the rest of her face. She was flushed from the climb up the stairs. I could not see how; it was freezing in the room, maybe fifty degrees at the most. She did not seem to notice the cold as she sat there in her short-sleeved dress with her apron cinched around her waist. Her bosom knocked up tight against her blouse and eased around the side of her bibbed apron, trying desperately to find some room. She squeezed my hand. "Don't pay attention to Elfriede. She is just under stress from this war," she said kindly. I brushed my hair out of my eyes with my free hand and waited. I looked at her hand covering mine: large and red with big bony knuckles—much larger than my mother's delicate hands. Hands that knew how to work hard, but kind hands, hands that caressed and held on firmly as they were doing now. After a bit she spoke. "You know her husband died on the Eastern Front." I looked up in surprise. "She has not been the same since. And she has had a hard time during this time of shortage getting all that she needs."

"When did her husband die?" I asked with interest. I didn't even know she had husband.

"I think it has been three months ago now." She said, thinking back.

I began to put things together. That was probably when she first wrote my mother, I thought. She needs money now that her husband is gone. It all began to make sense to me. She doesn't want us here any more than we want to be here. She just wanted my parents' money. "Well, I am sorry about that, but she doesn't need to be rude to me."

"No. You are right. She should not be rude to you. But let's forget about it and have something to eat. Oh, come on," she said encouragingly. Her smile, though engaging, revealed she only had half her teeth. I put her age at maybe ten years older than my mother. Forcing myself to smile, I thanked her for the tray and promised to eat.

"Good. Now I must go, and you girls make yourselves at home. If you need anything, just come to me." She patted my hand and rose to go.

"Oh, yes. Where is the bathroom?" I asked.

She looked amused. "We don't have a bathroom. We have a washroom downstairs, and if you need to use the toilet you have to go outside to the outhouse."

My eyes grew twice their normal size.

"What?" shrieked Peti. "We have to go to the bathroom outside?"

Frau Scherz laughed. "Welcome to farm life, girls." Seeing our horrified looks, she added, "It's not so bad, so long as you don't go in there after Herr

Scherz!" She found this very funny and had another good laugh. Stopping herself, she said, "*Komm*, don't look so unhappy." She pointed to the bowls on the dresser. "Those are for washing up in your room. I'll bring you hot water every night for a little scrub, and then once a week we take turns and fill the tub downstairs."

I thought my ears had not heard right. "Once a week we take a bath?"

"If you want to, but you don't have to take one that often."

Was she serious? I couldn't tell if she was making fun of me or if she was serious. "Frau Scherz, I wash my hair at least twice a week, and I bathe every night," I said, in a tone that indicated I intended to continue to do just that.

She looked at me for a moment and then smiled. "Well, you are welcome to do that in this bowl." She pointed to the bowl on the dresser. "But we are not heating water up and filling a tub for you every night." This last was said in such a way that there was no doubt left in my mind who would win this battle.

"You don't have running water, do you?" said Peti, looking like she had just made a great discovery.

"That's right!" she said with a wink. "Now, I must go about my chores. I will see you girls at dinner. Dinner is at six o'clock." She opened the door, and we heard her make her way down the stairs.

"Six o'clock! That's so early," I said. "I won't even be hungry at six o'clock."

"I guess they get up around here at the crack of dawn, so they eat early and go to bed early. Don't you think?" said Peti, more to herself than to me.

I shook my head and looked out the window. "I just can't believe Mutti sent us to a house that has no heat and no running water."

Peti agreed, despite her earlier support of my mother. "I read about this sort of thing in my social studies book. Hitler is making a big effort to bring water and electricity to all the farms," she said very authoritatively.

"Well, he is not working fast enough!" I muttered. "Why would Mutti send us to such a house? Why wouldn't she check?"

"She believed Elfriede and just assumed it was like a regular house with heat and water and toilets. Just like we did."

"Well, I am going to write her all about this—we can't stay here!"

"No." Peti agreed.

"Surely she can find a better place for us than this."

I rummaged through my bag until I found the paper and the stamped envelopes she had sent with us. Grabbing these, I walked over to the desk and sat down. I began to write. As I did so, I read what I was writing out loud so Peti could help me compose.

Dear Mutti,

We have arrived safely at the farm with Elfriede. We hope all is well at home. But we are very unhappy here. The house is very small and ugly and sits above a cow barn!

"Don't forget to tell her we can smell the cows all the time," whispered Peti helpfully.

"Okay. I'll add that."

The cows smell all the time. The food is awful.

"No, say horrible," said Peti.

"Okay."

The food is horrible, but the worst is they have no running water in the house and we have to go outside to use the toilet! Elfriede is awful as well. She is mean and became very angry with me this afternoon just because I asked why they didn't have regular bread. I am sure you did not realize what this place was like. We really want to come home as soon as possible. Say hello to Vati.

  Love

  Jutta

"Jutta, I have to go to the bathroom!" said Peti, as if she had never done it before.

I turned around from the desk. "Well, then go."

"No. You have to come with me. I don't want to go out there by myself." I rolled my eyes but decided I may as well go also.

"*Ja.* Let's go now, before Elfriede comes upstairs." I carefully folded over our letter. We opened the door and made our way down the back stairs. We peeked into the kitchen door and saw Elfriede talking to Frau Scherz. She must have seen our shadows, for she looked up and stopped talking for a moment. We quickly ducked down and made our way along the gravel path to the outhouse. Many years ago it had been painted a pale blue. The paint was mostly chipped off now, and only in a few places could you see the original color. Peti grabbed the door, and the hinges squeaked as she opened it. She stepped gingerly inside.

"Oh my God, it stinks! Jutta, hold the door so it can stay cracked. I think I will die if you close me in here." I obliged, considering what an effective weapon this could be if she became a pest. I could hear her going to the bathroom with a force that suggested she really did need to go. She flung the door wide open and stepped out quickly, practically knocking me off my feet as she ran past me down the path.

"Hey. Give me some warning!" I shouted. "Wait a minute. I need to go, too."

Peti came back reluctantly, making gagging sounds as she came.

"Oh, stop it. It can't be that bad," I said.

"You'll see!"

I stepped inside as she positioned herself to stand sentry the way I did.

"*Gott im Himmel!*" I cried. "How disgusting!" My urine didn't sound like it had to fall very far. "I think this hole is almost full, " I called mid-stream.

"Well, thank God it's dark out and we can't see."

"Coming out!" I shouted. Peti leaped back as I flung the door open. We both ran down the path, giggling and making retching noises, composing ourselves when we got back to the kitchen door. We quietly snuck upstairs. Elfriede was already upstairs in her room. She must have come upstairs while we were out using the outhouse.

I had carelessly left the letter to Mutti sitting out on the desk. Echoing my thoughts, Peti whispered, "I hope she did not read the letter." I went to the desk, and as I put the letter into an envelope, Elfriede came in, wiping her hands on a towel. She held my gaze for a moment, looking at me very hard. I knew she had read the letter.

But she just said, "Wash your hands, girls. Supper will be ready soon." She turned and walked back to her room. We took turns pouring water over each other's hands, trying our best not to spill water on the floor or the dresser as we did so. My hands turned bright red from the freezing water, and I thought my skin would crack. I quickly dried my hands on the towel that hung by the pitcher, the rough threads hurt my hands even more. We descended the stairs together in silence.

Dinner was no better than the snack we had that afternoon. But Herr and Frau Scherz did their best to make us feel welcome, asking about Berlin and our home and our parents. Frau Scherz told us they had no children. They had tried and tried, but had never been able to have children of their own. Herr Scherz looked up from his plate and frowned at her, obviously not comfortable with the conversation. He changed the subject by saying he had a nephew who was fighting on the Eastern Front. They said he wrote about once a month, and things did not sound good from his letters. But they blamed the stupidity of the German generals rather than Hitler. This was a different perspective from the one I usually got at home. I was always told that Hitler made all the decisions.

"But doesn't Herr Hitler know about all of the military decisions before they happen?" I asked.

"Oh, no! His generals keep him in the dark. They don't want him to know about all of their mistakes." Herr Scherz wiped his mouth with his napkin. "If he knew, he would put a stop to it," he said with great conviction.

Frau Scherz nodded her head in agreement.

"Well the news we listen to, the B ..." I kicked Peti under the table and glared at her.

"Ouch!" She cried.

"Sorry. My foot must have slipped," I muttered.

"Yes, Peti? The news you listen to?" said Elfriede with interest.

"On the radio they say that is true. What Herr Scherz just said, I mean. You know, that Hitler doesn't know," fumbled Peti.

"What radio station do your parents listen to that begins with a B?" persisted Elfriede.

"Radio Bavaria," I said quickly.

"Is there such a station?"

"Well, that is what we call it," I ad-libbed.

"You can get that station in Berlin?" Elfriede asked, astonished.

"Well, no. In Berchtesgaden."

Elfriede frowned at me and looked from me to Peti. But we both concentrated on our dinner as if it were the last food on earth. She let it go, and the conversation turned to the weather. A storm was on the horizon, apparently, and they were talking about lashing down the window shutters.

That night in bed I whispered, "It is a criminal offense to listen to the BBC, you idiot. Don't you remember we are not to tell anyone?"

"I forgot."

"Well, don't forget, or you'll land Mutti and Vati and your parents in jail. Elfriede is just the type to inform on them."

After a moment she said, "Do you think she bought your story about Radio Bavaria?"

"No. But I think the Scherzes did, so they will back us up if she tries something."

"*Gott*! What will tomorrow be like? I am not looking forward to school, are you?"

"Yes. Anything is better than staying here and smelling cows all day!" We fell silent, and after a moment I could tell that she had fallen asleep. I envied her. I wished I could put today behind me as quickly. I began calculating how long it would take a letter to reach Berlin—normally a few days, but with the bombing it may take longer. Vati said that many trains and roads have been disrupted, so maybe a week, I guessed. And then Mutti would have to organize a train ride down here to get us. I sighed. We would have to put up with this for at least ten days or maybe two weeks—an eternity. No heating and plumbing for two weeks. The thought totally depressed me. Maybe I will meet a nice girl at school, and school at least will have heat in the building. I actually began to look forward to school tomorrow, except that we would have to take the train with Elfriede. She was coming with us the first day to show us the way and make sure we were registered at the school.

Peti's even breathing distracted me, and I tried to block my thoughts so I could sleep.

Freiberg

I heard water splash and fall, water landing on water. Peti stood at the wash stand washing her face. She heard me stir and looked over. "Wake up, sleepy head. We have to go to the train in thirty minutes. It's six o'clock already." She showed me her watch.

I sat up, and the smell of cows assaulted my nostrils. I moaned.

She fluffed her hair and admired herself in the tiny mirror nailed to the wall above the wash stand. "What are you moaning about? I have been up since five, along with the Scherzes and the cows! My goodness, these people rise before the sun rises, and the cows start at it even earlier."

"Yuck," I said. "I couldn't sleep last night."

"I'm sorry. Well, you better learn to go to bed early, because believe me, we won't be sleeping in around here."

Elfriede came—in fully dressed, I noticed, and with her hair all done. She looked at me with disapproval. "Jutta, hurry up. We are leaving in twenty-five minutes, and you need to eat before we go." We heard her steps echoing down the stairs.

"What happened to a friendly '*Guten Morgen*?'" I asked sarcastically.

We giggled. "I don't think Elfriede does '*Guten Morgen*,'" said Peti, laughing. "Would you, if you had the name Elfreide and looked unhappy all the time like she does?"

"Shhh," I giggled. "She'll hear us." I got out of bed and stood by the stove exhaust pipe that ran from the kitchen stove through our room to the roof. It was the only warmth available while I dressed, but still goose bumps popped out all over my skin and my teeth began to chatter. "*Gott*! It could only be forty degrees in here!"

"It's freezing, isn't it?" acknowledged Peti.

Through the pipe I could hear Frau Scherz and Elfriede discussing their day. I hadn't been listening to their conversation, but suddenly I realized that Elfriede was complaining about having to take us all the way to Freiberg in this awful weather. Frau Scherz was comforting her, saying, "It's only for this one day, Elfriede, and then they can go themselves."

"Peti, she is such a pig! Can you believe she is complaining about taking us to Freiberg? All that money Mutti and Vati are paying her, and she complains." I sighed and buttoned my shirt to the neck to keep the cold out. "I figured out last night we will have to stay here at least ten days. Maybe two weeks."

Peti looked crestfallen. "You really think we have to stay that long?"

"Yes. With the bombs and everything, I don't think Mutti will get our letter for a week or so." I grabbed the letter and put it on top of my backpack. "I mustn't forget to give the letter to Frau Scherz before we leave." Peti was still brushing her hair in front of the mirror. I jokingly bumped her out of the way. "You look great! Now let me use the mirror for a moment." I looked in the water bowl. "Oh, no! I'm not going to wash my face in your dirty water!"

"Well, maybe you'll get up first tomorrow."

"No. Come here and pour the water over my hands. I'll wash that way."

"*Gott im Himmel*, that's freezing!" I jerked my hands back, flexing my fingers to keep them from going numb.

"Refreshing, isn't it?" she giggled.

"This will be a quick wash," I said, bracing myself for the cold once more. I managed to splash a bit of water on my face—just enough to get rid of the sleep in my eyes. I quickly brushed my teeth; the water was so cold it hurt.

"What are we supposed to do with this gunk?" I asked, indicating the dirty water.

"Just leave it, and I guess Frau Scherz will dump it." She shrugged. "I don't know, but hurry up. I'm hungry."

I quickly brushed my hair and finished up. I bent down, grabbed my backpack and letter, and headed for the door. "Well, come on," I said to Peti, now standing by the window, examining its edges.

She turned and came towards me. "You can feel the wind coming through the window!"

"Just wait until we go use the bathroom and you feel the wind on your bottom!" I said, giggling.

"Maybe we can hold it until we get to school."

"No. We better go here! After breakfast, though, or we won't be able to keep breakfast down." I opened the door, and the air stung my face. I ran down the steps as fast as I could to get into the kitchen. Peti clattered down right behind me. We burst into the kitchen, startling Frau Scherz and Elfriede, who almost dropped her coffee cup. Herr Scherz must be off with the blessed cows, I guessed, as he was not in the kitchen. The warmth of the kitchen enveloped me like a shawl. It was a startling contrast to the cold outside and in our rooms.

"My God! Slow down, and don't make such a racket coming in here!" cried Elfriede.

"*Guten Morgen*," I said with mock politeness, looking her directly in the eye.

Elfriede looked back at me, but Frau Scherz bustled over to the stove with a friendly, "*Guten Morgen,* girls." Followed by, "How did you sleep?"

"Very well, until the cows woke me," responded Peti.

I noticed Frau Scherz smelled of rose soap, and her hair was clean. She had put on a clean dress and apron, and I was thankful the onion smell had left the kitchen.

"Oh, you get used to them quickly. Soon you won't even notice them," said Frau Scherz cheerfully. She handed us bowls full of a watery beige cereal. It was cream of wheat, I deduced, but certainly not like Luise makes it—thick and hot with a beautiful ring of raspberry syrup around the edge. I began to long for Luise's cooking and my Brötchen in the mailbox in the morning. Peti wrinkled her nose as she sniffed the contents of her bowl.

"Cream of wheat," I whispered. She raised her eyebrows in recognition.

"What? Surely you children have had cream of wheat before!" said Elfriede. "Of course, I remember you had it at night when you were little. Didn't that … Luise? Yes, that was her name. Didn't Luise make it for you?"

I put a spoonful of the cereal in my mouth, its texture like soup, and it slid down, tasteless.

"You better eat. You will not have lunch until you get home, which will be nearly two o'clock by the time you take the train and the bus back."

"Oh, I have packed them a little snack. Two o'clock is much too long for them to wait for food." With a kindly smile, Frau Scherz handed us both a bag.

"Thank you," we both said politely. I peeked inside and saw more of the rhubarb bread and a hunk of white stuff that I guessed must be homemade cheese from the cows who shared the house with us. I put it in my backpack and grabbed the letter to our mother.

"Frau Scherz, would you mind giving this to the mailman when he comes today?"

"Oh, the mailman doesn't come anymore. They are all off fighting, so we have to go to town for mail. But I don't mind if you …"

"I'll mail your letter to your mother from town for you." Elfriede snatched the letter out of my hand, cutting Frau Scherz off in mid-sentence.

I looked at her in surprise. "That would be so nice of you. I just want to let Mutti know we arrived safely."

"Such a sweet daughter you are. So thoughtful," said Frau Scherz, smiling from the other side of the kitchen. "Now finish your breakfast and make sure you bundle up; it is freezing out there today."

We made a valiant effort to eat the cereal, but it was difficult to get down. I made it through half of mine, but Peti could only manage about a third.

"Come on. It's time to go." Elfriede stood by the door, tying a scarf around her head.

"Wait! I need to use the bathroom," announced Peti. We both pushed our chairs back at the same time and ran out of the kitchen to the battered house outside.

———

The walk to the bus was dreadful. Elfriede did not talk to us, and the cold seeped through the seams of my coat and stockings. My feet felt numb before we had walked even halfway, and by the time we got to the bus station, I thought my nose and ears were going to fall off like I had read happened to Cortez's men crossing the Andes. My eyes began to water, and I imagined them freezing to my face like pictures of Thumbelina. I looked around as we walked down the long, straight farm lane, posts for fences on each side. It struck me again how flat everything was in this part of Saxony—miles and miles of empty, flat, straight horizon, with only the occasional barn and farmhouse to break the landscape, and everywhere a blanket of silence. No traffic, streetcars, or people moving about to break the silence—just an empty stillness broken only by the wind rushing across the fields.

"Is it always this cold here?" I asked.

"Not always. This is unusually cold because of the wind," Elfriede mumbled in response, her voice muffled by her scarf.

Periodically, an ambitious farmer had planted a stand of pine trees to break the wind. The wind rustled their needles, the sound sending chills down my spine. Such a lonely sound. I longed for my warm, beautiful room, for my mother playing the piano, and for the comfort of my father, sitting in his chair, reading the paper and sipping his Campari.

Grosshartmansdorf, the town, consisted of houses one row deep on each side of the street. At one end, in the distance, I could see the church—the usual sort of German church with a spire reaching up to the heavens. The bus station was nothing more than a bench with a roof over it. Several people stood around, already waiting for the bus. They stared at us as we approached. I tried to produce a smile, but my lips were half frozen, so it came out more like a grimace. Nobody even attempted to smile back at us; they just stared. I noticed they stared the way children do, without embarrassment and without looking away.

"Good. We haven't missed it," mumbled Elfriede to herself. As she approached the people standing bundled up against the cold waiting for the bus, she said, "Heil Hitler!" They nodded at her. Elfriede was from the neighboring town. Apparently, they considered her an outsider. We stood in silence, all of us, for a long time. I listened to the sound of the wind on the open plain, blocked only by the small homes that lined both sides of the street. It whistled through the streets, ceasing for a moment only to kick back up with fresh vigor, sending clouds of snow swirling through the air. I was glad Peti was with me and I hugged her to me, both for warmth and to dispel the loneliness.

"So are these the girls from Berlin?" an old lady among the bunch startled us with this blast of human interest through the stillness of the cold. She was either friendlier or nosier than the rest of the group. I could not help but notice the huge mole on her cheek, out of which sprouted a tuft of exceptionally long gray hair. I found myself wondering why she did not cut it.

"Yes, they are," I heard Elfriede say with much more charm in her voice than she ever used with us. "From the Bolle family—the milk king!" said Elfriede, as if she had something to do with the Bolle family.

"Oh, my goodness! Really? Bimmel Bolle, the milk king?"

"Yes. That is the one." Everyone at the station stared at us again.

"Well, you must be doing well, having them stay with you!"

Elfriede simply nodded.

"What, too many bombs in Berlin for you?" asked an old man.

I nodded. Why else would I be in this godforsaken place? Before they could ask more questions, the bus came rumbling around the corner and pulled up in front of us. The driver drove very slowly so as not to skid on the ice. We all climbed in, Peti and I sitting in the back, away from everyone else, while Elfriede sat with her new friends up front and chatted away. I thought the bus would be warm, but apparently the heater did not work. But at least we were protected from the aggressive wind. Peti and I snuggled next to each other in silence. Elfriede said it was only five miles to the next town, where we would catch the train. It took forever because the bus drove so slowly on the icy roads. The landscape was exactly like that of Grosshartmansdorf.

Peti whispered, "I'm going to have to write the editors of my book on German geography and clarify that some parts of Saxony are not only without hills and rivers, they are downright ugly!"

I laughed.

The train station was not much bigger than the bus station. It was outdoors, of course, with no protection from the wind. It howled through the station. I looked up at the little town's name, written on a black lacquered wood plaque with gold lettering that hung above our heads: Langenau. It was written in the old German style that Hitler had banned from the classrooms of my generation. I could read it because Opa Bolle had taught us to read the old script. He would get down *Grimm's Fairy Tales*, a beautiful illustrated edition written entirely in the old German script. I loved the shapes the Gothic-looking lettering made on the page.

I hoped it would be warm on the train. We stood together, shivering. And for about the hundredth time I thought, "Why am I here instead of in my nice home? Why did Hitler start this damn war?" I looked around quickly, fearing that someone had just read my thoughts.

Elfriede made us come with her to get the tickets so we would know how to do it ourselves the next time. I didn't really blame her for not wanting to come with us—but still, I hoped that Mutti and Vati were not paying her much, as she certainly was not exactly giving it her all.

After what seemed an eternity, the train chugged up, spewing smoke from its front engine. It blasted its horn to warn us. I welcomed the engine's warmth as the train passed. My eyes focused on the river of steam flowing out behind it. The train came to a stop, and the engine master stuck his head out of the window and waved at the conductor, who stepped onto the platform. He helped us up the steps. Nobody smiled. We took a seat about four rows from the front. The train was crowded, and there were no places with three seats together. So Elfriede went to the back of the train car to find a seat. We did not mind. We settled into our seats, and the conductor came by to take our tickets.

Across from us was an old woman, her coat worn and torn at the sleeve. She had two scarves around her neck and an old green one tied under her chin to protect her head. Her wool gloves had holes in the fingers. She sat with her head leaning against the window, propped up by her hand. Her eyes were closed, and I thought she was sleeping, but she must have felt me staring at her, for she opened her eyes and looked at me without blinking. Coughing, she straightened her head and wiped her nose with the back of her hand. I guessed she had no teeth, for she ground her gums the way old people do who have no teeth. She looked out of the window without seeing. I tried to imagine what her life must be like. A life so bleak you look out but see nothing? Perhaps she had lost all of her sons to the war. And maybe her husband? No, she was too old to lose a husband. But maybe her husband had died and she had to work long, hard hours just to stay alive.

Peti nudged me. "Look. It's getting a little more interesting."

The woman turned from the window and focused on us for the first time. I peered out the window. My eyes found fields interspersed with hills and covered with pine forests. What a blessed relief from the flat brown terrain of Grosshartmansdorf.

"Do you think Mutti simply picked the ugliest place in Germany, the most godforsaken place, to deposit us?" I asked.

The woman shifted in her seat. Her movement roused the man next to her from his sleep. He had been snoring, completely oblivious to our arrival. Now he took us in with one quick glance from head to toe and raised an eyebrow to indicate his conclusion that we did not come from these parts. I noticed the soles of his shoes were separating. He had on only a thin coat. In this weather, the wind must go straight through that thing, I thought. I shivered as if I could feel the cold. Next to him sat a young woman. She was perhaps twenty-five, probably Elfriede's age. She nervously turned her wedding band around and around, and then she would cross her arms, tucking her hands by the side of her chest and then pulling them out, only to begin the whole dance again. Her clothes, though not torn, did not look much better than the old woman's and old man's. They were shabby and dingy in color, as if they had been washed a hundred times and worn over and over again. For the first time in my life I began to wish my clothes and shoes did not look quite so new. I decided I would smile at her if she made eye contact, but she never looked in my direction. I turned and looked around the train car. No smiles. And no conversation! Nobody was chatting about the weather, about the town gossip, or about their families. They just sat there, waiting for the train ride to end, unaware of all around them. Not that anyone really smiled in Berlin these days.

Peti and I chatted about what we guessed our new school would be like, and about being nervous since it was our first day, and about our hope that our teachers would be the nice type, and so on. Everybody looked at us as if we were in church, interrupting the minister during a particularly important part of his sermon.

Peti leaned close and whispered, "I don't think talking is allowed."

I shrugged my shoulders.

Finally, the train stopped and Elfriede came forward, giving us our signal that this was our stop. I was curious to see this Freiberg. Elfriede had spoken of earlier as if it were a second Dresden or Berlin! I doubted that it was very grand at all, but it must certainly be bigger than Grosshartmansdorf—not a great challenge. We rushed to catch up with Elfriede, who marched ahead of us and was already halfway out of the train station. She did not look behind to see if we were following. She led us up a narrow old street with two-story renaissance mansions. They looked like the pictures I had seen of Florence. Their facades were stuccoed in shades of terracotta and okra and accented with arches and carved cherubs and garlands. My spirits lifted and I decided, in the future, minus Elfriede, we would take our time walking to the train station.

"Elfriede, you were right. This is a beautiful town," said Peti.

"Yes. It was a very rich town in the old days because of the mining. They mined silver—some of the best silver in the world."

"Really?"

"Yes. People came from all over Europe, Italy, Czechoslovakia, and Poland just to mine here. It was a free mountain, thus the name of the town, which meant that anyone could stake a claim and mine here." I hadn't heard Elfriede say this much to us since we had arrived, and she said it with enthusiasm.

"Well, it is very beautiful," I said.

She nodded her head in agreement. "The Italians in particular came to this city and influenced the architecture." She waved her hand around and looked up at the old houses we passed by.

We turned a corner and came upon an old building several stories tall, also with a wonderful facade in earth tones. Children hurried up the steps. To go to school in such a building would make up for the bleakness of Grosshartmansdorf. They stared at us as we walked up the long set of steps that led to the grandest door I had ever seen. It was enormous, a good ten feet tall, with huge handles—silver, I presumed. It stood open to allow the free flow of children in and out of the building. I stepped inside and hurried to catch up with Elfriede and Peti. I passed by an enormous grandfather clock that stood in the front portico, right next to the largest picture of Hitler I had ever seen. He looked sternly at us from above that "odd little mustache of his," as Mutti always put it. The Nazi flag stood on one side of him, and some other flag was on the other side. I guessed it must be for the town of Freiberg, or perhaps Saxony.

Elfriede marched down the hall as if she knew where she was going. I guess she did, for a few moments later we were ushered into the principal's office and told to take a seat in hard leather chairs opposite a huge wooden desk in the middle of the large and otherwise empty room. It struck me as an odd place to put one's desk. It looked like an island that had broken off from the mainland and was stranded out at sea. On each side, a Nazi flag grounded the desk so it would not float away. The desk was absolutely spotless, a container with pencils and a pen the only thing visible on its surface.

I could hear a woman's voice issuing orders from a room to the right of us.

After a moment, the voice entered the room. It belonged to a very tall, thin woman in her forties, more or less my mother's age, with very blond hair pulled back severely in a braided bun at the back of her head. Her features were very regular, and her eyes were blue. She would have been pretty but for the scowl on her face and the downward turn of her pencil-thin lips. It was a face without joy. As she entered, Elfriede nudged me to stand up.

"Frau Dienz, these are the Bolle girls, Jutta and Peti." She pointed to each of us as she said our names.

"*Guten Morgen,* girls. Welcome to our school." No smile. "Sit down," she said, indicating the chairs.

She was not one for small talk; she did not ask about our new home or where we had come from. Instead, she immediately went over a few rules with us, stressing the importance of following these rules and being the best students we could possibly be for our new school's sake, our country's sake, and our Führer's sake. I found myself studying her and only vaguely listening. She wore a very large Nazi cross pinned to her breast lapel. I wondered if she wore it voluntarily, or if she felt she had to wear it. Definitely voluntarily, I thought. They probably pulled her from some dead-end job and molded her to their liking, giving her a little power. As Vati always said, "A small mind handed power is a most destructive combination."

Jolted out of my thoughts by Elfriede and Peti rising to their feet, I suddenly realized I was the only one left sitting. I stood up hurriedly, losing my balance and falling back onto the sofa. Elfriede looked at me with irritation, Frau Dienz looked at me without expression, and Peti tried unsuccessfully to stifle a giggle. I could feel the heat rise to my face. I managed to hoist myself back up and smooth out the front of my jacket and skirt before Frau Dienz asked, "Are we ready?"

"Yes, ma'am," I said politely. She escorted us out of the room and down a long hall. The hall had very high ceilings with lovely dome shapes every ten feet or so. All the children were in their classrooms by now, and our footsteps rang out into the stillness of the hallway. Each door was made of a reddish-colored wood with a window about three-quarters of the way up so only tall children and adults could peer into the classrooms. On each side of the doors, large silver hooks jutted out from the wall, practically invisible under the array of coats, hats, and scarves that decorated them. About ten doors down, Frau Dienz knocked on a door and opened it.

Thirty faces turned to stare; suddenly, upon seeing Frau Dienz, the bodies attached to the faces leaped up from their chairs and threw their arms up at an angle in the Nazi salute. Surprised, I observed the bizarre ritual, thinking we never saluted Frau Schöder, the headmistress at the *Gertrauden Schule,* or Herr Stimple at the *Lans Schule* for that matter. This looked more like a Hitler Youth meeting rather than a classroom. I realized this must be my class, for all the students looked about my age. After a moment, Frau Dienz must have signaled them to sit down, for they all did so in almost perfect unison. But still, nobody said a word, and not a giggle leaked out from anywhere. They simply stared at us.

Frau Dienz pointed to me and said, "This is Jutta Bolle. She will be in your class from now on. Fräulein Bolle, this is Frau Kaufman. She will be your teacher. I am sure you will comport yourself in the manner in which we discussed in my office."

I nodded my head and shook Frau Kaufman's hand. She took it and smiled at me. Nodding to Elfriede and Frau Dienz, she said, "We will get her organized and comfortable in no time at all."

Frau Dienz nodded and formed her lips into what I decided was her version of a smile. It was stiff and looked more like her lips hurt her from a bad sunburn than like a smile. "You and your cousin should meet outside my office after school so you can find each other. *Ja?*"

Peti and I nodded.

Frau Dienz turned to escort Peti and Elfriede out of the room. All the students leaped up, once again giving her the Nazi salute. They all stared at me, and I realized too late that I was the only one not saluting. After she left, they all sat back down, and the room visibly relaxed.

"Let's see, Fräulein Bolle. We have a desk for you in the back of the room," said Frau Kaufman, directing me to an empty desk that stood in the last row in the corner of the room. "I think you will find all your books on the chair. You will have to leave them at school, except for the ones you need for your homework. Now, first take off your coat and hang it outside the classroom, please. There are hooks to the right of the door, and each one has a name on it. I made one for you already."

Once in the hallway, I shut the door quietly and leaned against it with my eyes closed, trying to calm my nerves. I shook my head and began to search for my coat hook. There it was, with my name written in all capital letters above it: BOLLE. My stomach fell. Somehow, seeing my name above the hook made it all sink in—I really am not going to school in Dahlem. I really am in this strange town called Freiberg, in this strange school, with these strange people, living in a strange house that was actually half house and half barn. I don't know how long I stared at that hook. It must have been a good minute. Finally, I took off my coat and scarf and hung them on the hook. I looked again at "Bolle" written above that hook. It seemed to belong to some other girl, not me. I turned back to the door and, taking a deep breath, I braced myself for the return walk down the rows of desks to my desk in the most distant corner.

Frau Kaufman had already returned to the lesson she had been teaching as we entered the room. She had algebra scribbled all over the board, and apparently the particular problem they were working on was complicated enough that all eyes were focused, thankfully, on the board rather than me. I sat down and pulled out my tablet and struggled to focus on what she was saying. I was not terribly good at math to begin with, and arriving in the middle of the problem made matters worse. After a bit I gave up, figuring I could unravel it tonight. I looked around the room. I noticed that the obligatory Hitler picture hung at the front of the classroom was displayed prominently—not tucked discretely into the back like at the *Lans Schule* or the *Gertrauden Schule*. Here, he stared at you all day long from the front of the room, and there was no avoiding him.

Everyone ignored me in between classes. Although this was to my liking, I found it very strange that nobody had any curiosity at all about the new girl. The day seemed to take forever. At 1:00, school finally ended. Why I was glad it was over, I don't know, for it simply meant that I had to return to the farm with its drafty walls and smelly rooms. As I gathered up my homework books to put in my backpack, I reflected that fitting in at *Freiberg Schule* would be more difficult than I had anticipated. I once again began to wish I had a hole or two in my clothes and my shoes were a bit more worn. Maybe I could walk about the farm when we got back and get some mud and snow to crack them a bit, I thought to myself as I made my way to Frau Dienz's office in search of Peti. As I approached the office I saw Peti out in front already. She looked happy and was talking away merrily to another girl her age. They giggled about something. Peti caught sight of me and waved. "Jutta, this is Sabine."

"Nice to meet you," I said hurriedly.

"Hello," said Sabine, holding out her hand to me. She seemed like a very sweet girl. She had dark brown hair in two perfect braids and blue eyes that set off her pale skin.

"Nice to meet you," I said again, and then turned to Peti. "We better get going or we will miss our train."

"*Ja.* I'll see you tomorrow," said Peti cheerfully.

We walked down the hall, through the huge doors, and down the steps to the street. Peti had to run to keep up with me. "Slow down," she cried. "What is the matter with you?"

I slowed and took a deep breath. "Thank God I am away from that place!"

"Why? What happened?" asked Peti anxiously.

As we walked to the train station I told her about my day, beginning with my first embarrassing moments in the classroom and my trouble with the algebra problem.

Once we got on the train and took off for Langenau, I immediately fell asleep and did not wake up until Peti gently pushed my shoulder. "We're here, Jutta," she said. "And I finished your math problem for you," she added proudly, waving a paper in front of my nose.

"Great. Now you'll have to explain it to me."

"Sure!" she said with relish. She loved to explain math to me. "Now when we get to the house, I will write another problem for you to do so that we can make sure you understand."

I looked at her and rolled my eyes.

"I'm starving!" said Peti suddenly, rummaging through her backpack for the snack from Frau Scherz. "We better eat this stuff or she will feel bad."

"It was thoughtful of her to pack us a snack," I agreed. To my surprise, the cheese actually tasted good. The bread would take a little more getting used to, however. But it took away the hunger pangs.

The week passed by slowly. We took the long bus and train ride to Freiberg every day to go to school. Frau Scherz tried her best, packing us what she could spare as little treats to take with us to school. But the food continued to be pretty bad. I sensed that even without the war and all of its shortages, Frau Scherz's cooking was pretty awful.

School was the same, except that I had to suffer the humiliation of Peti being moved up to my math class. Everybody in my class thought it was obnoxious to have this perky little eleven-year-old in our algebra class. But Frau Kaufman, of course, loved Peti and made matters worse by calling on her all the time. The only good part was that we always worked together on the problems on the train ride home, and I could rely on her to catch what I missed in class because my mind was wandering back to Berlin and Mutti and Vati, Opa Bolle, Erica, *Vögelein*, and Harold.

By the time we returned from Freiberg to the Scherzes' it was always around three o'clock, depending on how long we took meandering our way to the train station. We were never in a rush to get back to the farm, so we began to take the longest possible route to the train station. Elfriede didn't seem to care when we arrived; she actually preferred us to come back as late as possible. It was less time she had to spend with us. Frau Scherz would have our main meal prepared. Every day it would consist of some form of meat combined with potatoes and cabbage. Unfortunately for me, I detest both potatoes and cabbage. Occasionally she would open a jar of carrots or peas and add them. They were usually cooked to mush by the time they arrived on our plates. I ate what I could and thought of my mother, who would eat one of Tante Hilde's perfectly awful meals with a smile and her face. She would always say, "Thank you, Hilde. As always, your hospitality goes above and beyond," never actually commenting on the food so she didn't have to lie. I once asked her if she really liked Tante Hilda's cooking. "Oh heavens no, Jutta, but we can't let her know that; it would hurt her feelings." I valiantly tried to follow my mother's example and accept Frau Scherz's meals with grace, a difficult assignment.

After our midday meal we helped clear up the dishes, and then Elfriede would sit with us while we did our homework. One thing I will say for Elfriede: she was not stupid. She certainly knew her math and she knew her grammar. She was a very good teacher. And the thought occurred to me that perhaps she was frustrated that she had missed her true calling in life.

By the time we were done with all of this, it was usually about five o'clock and already dark outside, so we would go upstairs and talk, write, or draw together until seven, when Elfriede would call us back downstairs for our evening snack. We only ate so late because we had our midday meal so late. The Scherzes and Elfriede usually ate their evening meal around six, when Herr Scherz came in from bedding down the cows for the night. We could hear them downstairs, scraping their chairs as they took their seats at the huge kitchen table. We heard the clinking of their silverware and the sound of their muted voices as they talked quietly. Herr Scherz would stay for a bit while we ate, listening to the radio or reading the newspaper, and then he would say good night and go off to bed.

Frau Scherz stayed in the kitchen with us until we went upstairs to bed. She genuinely seemed to like us and loved to tell us stories about the history of the area. Elfriede would sit there yawning until Frau Scherz would say, "Go on, Elfriede. Go upstairs and have some private time."

Elfriede would make a big show of acting like she really didn't want to go. "Are you sure, Frau Scherz?"

And Frau Scherz would respond, "Of course. You go on. I'll see that they get to bed." Every night, in exactly the same way, they engaged in this ritual. I began to realize this was the case with so many things in Grosshartmannsdorf. Nothing seemed to change—everything happened exactly the same way every day, every night, every month, and every year. How could people live like this year after year? No wonder our arrival was the big news of the town! Frau Scherz said the certainty of it all gave them comfort. That was the beauty of farm life—the certainty that the cows would calf in the spring, and that their mothers would give milk, and that the crops would pop up suddenly, as if from nowhere, out of the dead brown soil, the land suddenly transforming itself from brown to green. All this struck her as nothing short of miraculous. She worshiped the certainty of the change of the seasons. She could count on the cold of winter, the freshness of spring, the warmth of summer, and the crispness of fall. These were the only changes that she needed in her life, she said. I looked at her and longed to be like her. Taking such enormous pleasure from such a simple life, she was truly blessed with, as Vati would say, "that rare asset, contentment."

It was during those evenings sitting in the Scherzes' kitchen that I learned Hitler had condemned the "satanic rage of destruction" rained on Germany by the British. The Scherzes did not listen to the BBC like my parents. Instead, we listened to his speeches and to the news on the Nazi-sanctioned station on the Scherzes' primitive radio. Every German had a radio, no matter how simple. Hitler made sure of that, so his messages could be heard all over Germany, even in the smallest villages like Grosshartmansdorf. The British were worse than the devil, Hitler said in this same speech, killing innocent women and children with their hateful bomb attacks. I found myself agreeing with him, and this worried me. I knew that agreeing with Hitler on anything would upset Mutti and Vati. I needed to talk to them about this war. They would know how to explain everything. But it did seem more than barbaric to bomb cities—killing small children, mothers, and old people like the Scherzes.

We listened as the announcer detailed the latest bombing of Berlin. "Thousands of tons of bombs were dropped on Berlin last night." Peti and I stopped eating and stared at our plates. He continued. "Thousands are homeless, and fires raged all over the city overnight."

Frau Scherz stood quickly to turn off the radio. "I am sure your parents are fine. They drop the bombs on the center of town, not the residential areas." But before she could reach the radio, the announcer added, "This was the single biggest attack on Berlin since the beginning of the war. Authorities estimate that the destruction is ten times that of all previous raids."

"Yes, yes. Your parents are fine," agreed Herr Scherz as Frau Scherz finally managed to get to the radio dial. But still we worried, waiting in anguish for a letter to arrive from my mother, trying not to think about it, trying to block all thoughts of Berlin and the bombs out of our minds. I often awoke in the middle of the night to Peti's sobs. I would try my best to comfort her.

Mutti and Tante Hilde always sent word within a few days to let us know all was well. After the Berlin announcement in March, the Scherzes tried to screen the news by listening to it earlier in the day, before we came home. If a particularly bad bombing raid hit Berlin, they would not turn the radio on. We would always ask, "No radio tonight?"

"No, let's just talk tonight," Frau Scherz would say, making small talk about the weather or neighbors. But it was a struggle, and we soon learned why the radio was not on.

My mother wrote about the attacks and the discontent that stirred in Berlin over the war. She wrote carefully but honestly, without fear of reprisal. But that was my mother. She did not seem to fear what other people feared.

———

About two weeks after I started school, I made a friend. Her name was Gretchen Heissman. She was very plain looking: her tiny, heart-shaped face held a small nose and small brown eyes, and she had very pale skin that was covered with freckles. Her hands and arms were completely covered with freckles as well. "Sun fairy kisses," my mother would tell me when I complained about all the freckles on my nose. The combination made her look very sad and vulnerable. She rarely smiled, but when she did, her smile lit up her face. When she first introduced herself to me, she presented me with that smile, and it drew me in.

Gretchen came from a large family, and I had the impression that they did not have much money. Her clothes always looked a bit more rumpled and worn than the clothes of the others in my class. She never brought a snack to school to eat during the break, so I began to share Frau Scherz's cheese with her. One day, a few weeks after I met her, she suddenly offered to walk with us to the train station. After that, she would walk with us every day. She showed us all the "complicated routes," as she called them, to the train station—routes that took us past incredible entryways of arched stone and carved marble.

We ambled along Burgstrasse, past monumental stone homes built in the

Renaissance and Baroque periods, when Freiberg was an extremely wealthy city. Some had rooflines that looked like staircases. The snow lay packed on each stair, its white color contrasting with the orange and red brick of the building. Ice hung from the corners of the mansions, or from the mouth or ear of a statue or gargoyle, adding to it a grotesque look. The grandeur of these old buildings from the Renaissance impressed me, but they were cold and lonely. The stone had no warmth to it, and the carved figures always looked somewhat evil and menacing to me.

By the beginning of April the snow had begun to melt and it was not quite so cold, but the light was still pale and dull—never seeming able to give birth to the day, as if a curtain had been pulled across the sun. On those rare days when the sun managed to peek out from behind the constant gray cloud curtain that hid it, the streets would glisten so brilliantly from the running snowmelt that my eyes hurt. By the end of April, what snow remained was black with dirt and lay piled in corners where the sun never hit it, and soon even these piles were gone.

Alone

The weather warmed up significantly, and I began to notice that I was too warm with my hat and scarf on. Our walk across the flat, barren land to the bus stop from the farm was less bone-chilling. My teeth no longer chattered, and I could actually feel my toes as we walked. But the sky hung low and heavy, oppressing all below it, the cloud cover so thick and monotonous there was no finding the sun—no sunrise, no sunset; just the same steady light accented by nothing. Spring tried to break through, ever so subtly appearing now and then along the road. A few brave blades of grass peeked through the mud and the snow; a few ambitious buds began to appear on the trees, and every once in a while an impatient housewife set out a pot of crocuses, their delicate little heads barely visible over the top of the pot in pale lavenders and whites that brought a smile to my lips. "Once the crocus pops its head out, spring is not far behind," Mutti would say. The wind still howled, but a little of its bite had been removed, a degree of its harshness lessened.

The war and its uncertainty bothered Frau Scherz. She told us she hoped the war would soon end; far too many mothers had lost sons and husbands because of it. Nobody was enthusiastic about the war. At school, most of the girls had lost an older brother or father to the war already. Others had lost cousins and uncles; nobody was immune from the heartbreak. Every week somebody would be absent from school for days because they had lost a family member and their mothers needed them at home for comfort. Then they would return to class and everyone would pretend nothing had happened. Some of them would bury their pain deep inside, while others would periodically well up with tears during the day over seemingly nothing. The teacher would simply excuse the girl and continue the lesson without comment after she had left the room. Nobody said anything. Nobody comforted and nobody taunted; it touched everybody, and the horror was so great that nobody knew what to say.

Some girls would draw cards with flowers and hearts and birds and little sayings, giving these tokens in silent comfort to a grieving friend. I did one for Gretchen. She was out for a week at the beginning of April, and I learned that two of her older brothers had been killed on the Eastern Front. Because her father was also at the front, her mother lived in terror that he too would be killed. Gretchen told me her mother was in such a depression she was refusing to get out of bed and take care of the younger children, so poor Gretchen had to be mother to four younger siblings. She came to school with big, dark circles under her eyes, looking like she had not slept all night. She told me she could not walk around town with us any more, at least not until her mother was better.

My heart went out to her. At least we had plenty of food, unappealing as it was, and we had friendly old Frau Scherz to look after us, even if Elfriede was the meanest pig I had ever encountered. And we had parents at home in Berlin who worried about us, even if they did not respond to our complaints. I put my arm around her shoulder and gave her a small hug. She looked at me in surprise, but for the first time in weeks I caught a glimpse of a small smile that played across her lips. A tear welled up in her eye, and she said softly, "I hate this war. I hate what he has done to Germany and to my family."

I nodded my head. "I do, too."

The loss of Gretchen's companionship after school affected me more than I realized. My loneliness grew, and I missed my parents more and more each day. I ate little. Frau Scherz would bend down and look at me with a frown on her face. "You must eat, *mein Herz.*" Then she would say, "Elfriede, the child is not eating enough."

"She will eat when she gets hungry enough, I venture," Elfriede would respond without interest.

"Well, she needs to eat more now!" replied Frau Scherz. To stop her from worrying, I tried to eat a little more, but I really had very little desire for food. My mind wandered as people talked to me, and they often had to repeat what they said. I prayed every night for a swift end to this terrible war so I could be with my parents again, back in Berlin. I stared at the black ceiling every night, seeing nothing. I prayed: "Dear Lord, please make this war end quickly so I can go home, and so Peti can go home, and so Gretchen's father can go home, and please stop all the killing and bombing everywhere. And please, Lord, give Hitler a heart attack, or let him die in a car crash, or something. Forgive me for that last, but I can't help it. Amen."

My homesickness increased even more when Peti began to go home with Sabine after school on Saturday, only returning to Grosshartmannsdorf with me on Monday afternoon after school. This meant two nights alone in Grosshartmannsdorf. She surprised me with this news one Friday. I had noticed a bit of extra exuberance as we walked to the train; she seemed overly happy, skipping and twirling instead of walking down the street. As we left Freiberg station, she said, "Jutta, Sabine has asked me to spend the night tomorrow night." Her eyes sparkled, and she grinned from ear to ear.

"Wonderful."

"Her mother said I could stay until Monday and then go to school with Sabine."

I did not respond.

"I have to check with Elfriede if it is okay, of course."

"Of course it will be okay with Elfriede," I said, looking toward heaven. "It will mean one less mouth to feed, one less responsibility. She'll love it."

"And Sabine's mother says..." she hesitated a moment... "if it works out, I can stay every weekend if I want."

"I see," I said, feeling my stomach hit my feet. The thought of being left in Grosshartmannsdorf to face Elfriede, the cows, and the outhouse alone was overwhelming. Tears welled up in my eyes.

"I won't go if you don't want me to," said Peti quickly, seeing my distress.

"Oh, don't be silly!" I said, shrugging. "Of course you must go to get away from the *mist* heap in Grosshartmannsdorf. Why should two of us suffer?"

"Jutta, you shouldn't say *mist!*"

"Well, what else is it other than *mist?*"

We were silent for a moment, watching the factories and little towns flash by us as the train moved south.

"Maybe you will find a friend to invite you over. Maybe Gretchen will invite you," she said hopefully.

I did not respond. I continued to watch as the pine-studded hills flattened into fields, endlessly flashing past my window. I knew there was no possibility that I could stay with Gretchen; her mother couldn't even handle her own children, let alone another one. I looked down at my hands, intertwined on my lap, and wondered again why Mutti had not responded my letters. My mother wrote us every week, but her letters gave me little comfort; it was as if she never received out letters. She always ended her letters with *Please write to us. Love, Mutti and Vati.*

"But we have written!" I said to Peti.

"Well, maybe she means write again."

Tante Hilde also wrote, and her letters spoke of everything other than our discomfort, even though Peti had written her in no uncertain terms. A letter arrived from her in late March, and I was horrified to learn that Berlin had again been heavily bombed. She wrote:

Meine Lieben,

I am so happy that you are safe and away from the madness of Berlin. Last night Berlin was bombed again, but this time it was very, very bad. They say it was the heaviest bombing ever. The city was in flames this morning when Vati tried to go to the office—it was chaos everywhere. They say the flames could be seen from miles away. So you see, my darlings, no matter how hard it is for us both to be separated, and for you living in a strange environment, it is best that you are safe.

Peti looked up, "I guess she is receiving our letters."

"Seems like it. She just thinks it's best for us to be away from the bombs. But I would rather be with them."

I looked over and saw that tears were running down Peti's face. I put my arms around her. "It will be fine."

"What if they are hit? What if a bomb hits the house?"

"They will be fine in the basement."

"But what if they don't make it there, or what if the basement collapses?"

"They don't collapse."

She jerked herself away from me and turned to face me on the bed. "Yes they do!" she said adamantly. "Sabine told me about a family in Hamburg that was in their basement, and they died of suffocation because it collapsed."

"Sabine doesn't know what she is talking about. Those are just stories that get bigger and bigger."

"But lots of people talk about such things. Another group died because the water pipes burst and they got locked into the shelter and couldn't get out. They drowned."

"Well, that is not going to happen."

"But what if it did? And then nobody would know whose children we were and where we belong."

"Peti, please."

"We could end up war orphans," she sobbed dramatically.

"Peti, everything will be fine. And anyway, there's nothing we can do."

"Oh yes there is, Jutta! Don't you see? We must get back to Berlin, so if anything happens we are all together."

"What good is that going to do? If something like that happens, you would be dead, too."

"Wouldn't you rather be dead with your parents than alive here?" she asked me incredulously.

I honestly was not sure. The bombs so completely unnerved me, I wasn't sure if I could survive in Berlin even with my parents there to protect us.

"I will write to her again, and I will insist that she at least respond to us. *Ja?*" Peti nodded gratefully. "Now stop crying, or your eyes will be puffy tomorrow."

I wrote my mother again about how awful it was in Grosshartmannsdorf, but she never responded. Instead, she told us about two more bombing raids on

Berlin. Each time we would get one of these letters, Peti would go into a tailspin of worry again.

No one was hurt from our family or friends, although a number of the workers at the factory have lost their homes. They attack in broad daylight now! Most embarrassing for Göring, whose speech had to be canceled several times on the tenth-anniversary celebration! They do not drop the bombs out here in Dahlem, so do not worry about us. Luise says hello and misses her little girl. Harold has come out from the basement and is back in the goldfish pond, and Gustav has uncovered the azaleas and rhododendrons to ready the garden for spring. Study hard at school. Please write soon.

Alles Liebe, Diene Mutti

I folded the letter carefully and put it back in its envelope. It was very strange for my mother not to even acknowledge my letter with its complaints. It dawned on me that Elfriede was reading our letters and censoring them. The thought made my skin crawl. The more I thought about it, the more it made sense to me. My mother had never gotten the letters we wrote with our complaints. I did not share my thoughts with Peti until I could come up with a plan.

On Saturday, Peti and I walked quietly to the bus to head for Freiberg. The weather was warm enough that we only needed sweaters. Peti seemed excited about spending the night with Sabine, but she didn't want to make me feel bad, so she tried to hide it, the only sign an occasional, uncontrolled skip that escaped from her as we headed down the long, straight dirt road. As we walked along, I mulled over in my mind the letters and my mother's failure to respond. The more I thought about it, the more convinced I was that Elfriede had confiscated our letters. When we were comfortably seated on the train to Freiberg, I leaned over to Peti. "Let's write to Mutti one last time, and you can have Sabine's mother mail it for us."

"Sure, but why?"

"It will get to them faster if we mail it from Freiberg." I didn't tell her my suspicions.

Peti agreed enthusiastically. So we wrote a long letter that day—in very messy handwriting, for the train was bumpy. We poured our hearts out to Mutti and begged her to respond. I added the line that we had written her over and over about the conditions. Why hadn't she responded? I wanted her to know that Elfriede was taking our letters, but I didn't want to accuse Elfriede outright.

By the end of May, Peti had spent three weekends with Sabine's family. Her absences began to weigh heavily on me. It was Saturday and I decided to stay after school, lingering around the fountains and small streets of Freiberg—anything not to have to go back to the farm. I had gotten lost, and it was now late and I worried I might miss the six o'clock train.

I walked quickly in to the station and had to run to catch the train. As I raced through the door between the station house and the platform, I heard the whistle blow its warning. The train was about to depart. The conductor must have seen me when he looked down the station platform from behind his enormous black engine, for he slowed down enough for me to leap onto the steps. A puff of air on my back propelled me forward as the doors closed behind me. Several people looked up. Some shook their heads in disapproval.

I sat down quickly at the back of the compartment and scooted over to the window. It was growing dark, and I could see the lights of Freiberg as the train pulled out of the station. They twinkled like stars in the early night sky, warm and friendly; no one would ever guess what kind of lives people led behind those bright, cheery lights. I gazed unseeing into the blackness sweeping past my window. Tears threatened to come. I could not stop them because suddenly, more than anything in the world, I wanted my mother. Where was she? Why couldn't we be together? Why didn't she answer my letters? I ached for her—for her warmth, for her kind voice, for the way she always made my life so comfortable. I thought of the birthday parties that she made so special. I longed for the peace that seemed to envelope her and all that she did. I longed for her calm, steady, thoughtful speech. She always knew just what to say to comfort me. With her, I always feel whole. I never feel scattered, like I do now. The train began to slow as we approached Langenau. I braced myself for the cold that would greet me outside the station. The train slowed even more, and I could see the lights of the station house. The howl of the whistle startled me, its sound so empty in the night.

I took a deep breath and stood up, struggling to find my balance as the train came to a standstill. I was in the back row, the last one out of the door. I climbed down the steps slowly and deliberately. I sighed with relief to be standing on firm ground after hurling through the night on the train. My eyes scanned the platform, but it was empty. Everyone had hurried out of the station except a woman standing on the far side of the platform. She looked out of place with her brown hat and long fur coat. A city dweller, I thought, her clothes too elegant to be from here. Her back was to me as she searched each train car, looking for someone. And then, suddenly, I knew who it was.

"Mutti!" I screamed. I threw my book bag to the ground and ran. She whirled around so swiftly her coat seemed suspended as it floated in the air, forming an arc around her like a dancer, the dark colors contrasting with the white cement of the station platform. Her face lit up, and she too began to run. We met each other halfway, twirling around and around as we hugged and kissed. Tears ran down my face as she pressed it to her shoulder. She had come! She had finally come! It was a miracle! For a moment we said nothing. She just held my face between her hands and kissed me on the forehead, on the nose, on the eyes, on the cheeks. She was making up for all the kisses she had missed while we were apart. Her hands were soft and warm, and she smelled like heaven.

Finally she said, "Thank God, Jutta. I was so worried about you. Thank God you're all right!" Tears had formed in the corners of her eyes, rimming them in red, and I saw the worry in the lines around them.

"Mutti, you came! You finally came! I thought you would never come. I thought you forgot about us."

"Never! I thought of you every day, but I didn't know you were so unhappy until I got your last letter."

"So it is true—Elfriede was not mailing our letters?"

"Apparently, but let's not talk about her right now. I will deal with her later. Now, where have you been? I arrived this afternoon expecting you to come back around three o'clock. They said you usually got back then, and when you didn't come by five I began to worry. So I took the bus here, and if you hadn't been on this train, I was going to take the next train to Freiberg. What happened to you?"

I hugged her and whispered, "I am fine now."

She took my hand. "Let's get your book bag and go."

Relief washed over me as we walked to the end of the platform, stopping for a moment to pick up my book bag. Her hand still in mine, we walked through the double doors of the station house, the bright lights hurting my eyes after the dark train.

"I see you found her," said the stationmaster kindly. He knew me from my daily journey on the train. He was old, slightly stooped at the shoulders, and his hair was silver gray. His eyes crinkled up with laugh lines when he smiled. He would say, "Good morning, Fräulein," as I entered the station. And no matter how bad the weather was, he would always add, "And a beautiful morning it is. I feel certain we shall have a beautiful day." I would respond, "Good morning, sir. And I hope you are right." I liked our ritual; he brought me a certain comfort, and he reminded me so much of Opa Bolle: always positive, always certain that God will provide us with a wonderful day. Lately I had noticed he was there in the afternoon as well as the morning. The middle-aged man that was always there in the afternoon was suddenly gone.

"Fräulein, you had us all very worried!" he said, the concern obvious in his voice.

My mother answered for me. "Thank you for your help."

He nodded. "Have a good evening, ma'am."

"And you too."

Within minutes the bus came, spewing its filthy black slush all about us. Once we sat down, I began to talk, my thoughts pouring out of me. I told my mother about Elfriede and how much she disliked us; I told her about the conditions at the farm—especially the outhouse and the bathing arrangements. I told her about Peti staying at Sabine's house and how lonely I was without Peti. My mother raised her eyebrows, and her expression made it obvious she had no idea Peti had been staying somewhere else. I told her how awful school was, how unfriendly the girls were, and what a huge Nazi Frau Dienz was. I told her about the awful cold we had endured walking to the bus and then waiting for the bus and the train. I told her about all the fathers and brothers who had died and how sad it was at school when someone came to school with the black armband on.

"And this afternoon, what happened?"

"I stayed in town. I just couldn't come back to the farm."

Before I could stop them, the tears came again. Down my cheeks they rolled, and my nose began to run with determination. Mutti searched in her purse and handed me an embroidered handkerchief. Traces of Chanel No. 5 lingered in the folds, and a flood of memories from a better time engulfed me. I breathed deeply to make them last, but they passed quickly. The bus had stopped, and we disembarked slowly so as not to slip on the steps in the dark. The sky was black, lit only by a sliver of the moon, just enough light to cause the trees to form long, eerie shadows that jutted out into the road. They looked like those long, hideous faces Edvard Munch painted that so terrified me when Opa Bolle took me to the art museum. I thanked God my mother was with me.

I woke to sun streaming through the curtains—the brightest sun I had seen since moving to Grossharmansdorf—shedding a warm glow about the room. I glanced over to Peti's bed and sat straight up. It was empty! For a brief moment I thought I had dreamed it all—that my mother's arrival was a trick of my imagination. I stood up and sighed with relief when I saw her bag still sitting on the chair where it had been the night before. She must already be downstairs, I thought, as I hurried over to the window. Her voice came up through the cracks in the floor and the old stovepipe along the wall. How strange to hear my mother's voice in this house, in this setting. I smiled, flung open the curtains, and let the sun sting my eyes, forcing me to squint for the first time in many, many months. What a wonderful feeling, to squint. In the bright sunlight, the room looked almost welcoming. I walked to my mother's bed and picked up her pillow, hugging it hard, taking in her smell. With both hands, I carefully replaced the pillow on the bed, as if it truly were my mother's head, and turned to the mirror. My hand flew to my mouth as I took in my eyes, swollen as big as walnuts and as wrinkled! I splashed icy water on them as long as I could stand it before my hands and fingers grew numb from the cold. The effect was minimal. I gave up and quickly brushed my hair and dressed.

The Scherzes sat with Mutti, talking earnestly over coffee, the remains of breakfast on the table. Elfriede was nowhere to be found.

"*Guten Morgen, mein Schatz,*" said Frau Scherz, facing me as I came in the door.

Mutti turned to me, smiling, but upon seeing my eyes frowned slightly despite herself.

"How did you sleep, Juttalein?"

"*Wunderbar!* What time is it?"

"Nearly nine thirty," replied Frau Scherz, looking at the old-fashioned clock that hung over the sink.

"Oh my gosh!" I said, my eyes wide with surprise.

"Well, sit down. Let's get you some breakfast." Frau Scherz jumped up and flapped her hands at the chair next to my mother. I bent to kiss Mutti before I sat. Frau Scherz cut two thick slices of rye bread. Her sturdy arms made the knife slide through with ease. She put the loaf on the cutting board, the open side facedown to prevent the air from getting in. A plate sat on the counter for me with real butter and real strawberry jam. She added the bread to it and set it down before me.

"Your mother brought it for us. Now eat it, and stop looking so surprised." She smiled at me as I spread butter and jam on a thick slice of bread. I closed my eyes and let my teeth slowly sink in, the butter and jam spreading out onto my lips; I licked my lips and murmured appreciatively. Mutti laughed at me. I opened my eyes slowly and tried not to devour the entire slice in one second, chewing as slowly as possible and letting the flavor linger on my tongue for a moment. I had never remembered bread tasting so good. It was fresh, and the smell reminded me of cold winter days when I came home from school and smelled Luise's bread as soon as I opened the gate to our garden—a smell that drew me quickly up the walk and through the front door, my backpack dumped in the entrance hall as I headed immediately for the kitchen.

The adults continued to talk while I ate. They spoke of the weather and how it would affect the harvest. They spoke of how difficult it would be to harvest the rhubarb and potatoes with all the men at war. Herr Scherz said the government was offering free day laborers, prisoners of war, to the big farmers, but small farmers like him had to find labor where they could. He said they used to have a group of Jewish and foreign women, but that ended. Nobody said anything for a moment, and I was certain they could hear me chew across the table.

Finally, Mutti turned to me and said, "Jutta, I think we had better get going." I looked around the table. Herr Scherz looked down at his hands and fiddled with the sleeve of his old gray shirt, tattered and fraying at the sleeve. I noticed his hair was freshly washed, and he smelled faintly of rose soap. Frau Scherz smiled at my mother. "Oh yes, and we need to find my niece!" Mutti said.

"I'm so sorry, Frau Bolle! I would never have let her go if I had known you did not know."

My mother waved her hand and said simply, "I know."

"Where is Elfriede?" I asked, looking around the room as if I would find her.

"Gone. Packed up and gone. And you, my dear, slept through the entire thing."

"Oh, thank God. I hated that woman!" I said with passion.

"Jutta!"

"I'm sorry, but I did."

Herr Scherz chuckled.

It suddenly dawned on me: I had not asked if Peti and I were going home with Mutti, or if we were to stay on in Grosshartmansdorf. "Mutti, are we going home?"

"Of course. As soon as we take care of everything here, we will leave."

"Yes!" I said, pumping my arm in the air. I saw Frau Scherz's face fall. I quickly added, "But I will miss you both very much."

She looked relieved. "I know how difficult it has been for you, Jutta. It's always difficult to be away from one's home and family."

"But you always made me feel welcome here." Herr Scherz looked up and raised his eyebrows. "And, Herr Scherz, too," I added quickly.

He laughed and patted my hand. "Even with the cows?"

"I think I may actually miss the cows," I said, wondering at my own fickle nature, but it was true. There was something comforting about their sounds and their big brown eyes, and one even got used to their smell. They were so innocent, so uncomplicated, wanting only food and warmth and to be milked every day. I suddenly realized that Frau Scherz had been right after all.

I leaned forward as the train left the station in Dresden. I wanted to take in all the beautiful buildings. I looked at each one and tried to sear it into my memory. I nestled back in my seat and looked across to my mother, who sat opposite me with Peti snuggled in next to her. She smiled at me and reached over and patted my hand. I smiled back and looked out the window again, running through the events of the past few days in my mind. I watched the city turn to fields, and then to river and villages. Even in early spring, the Elbe River was beautiful, punctuated at each turn with tiny little villages still covered with a thin layer of snow.

A woman pushed a cart filled with firewood along the steep dirt road that ran the length of the river. How heavy that must be for her. Where is her husband or son ... I stopped, knowing the answer.

"Jutta, are you here?"

"I'm sorry, Mutti. What did you say?"

"I need to tell you something."

I said nothing.

"Your Opa Bolle is very sick," she said simply. "It is good you are coming home. He has been asking about both of you."

I nodded my head. I did not let it sink in. "He'll be fine," I whispered.

I turned to the window again. The river wound around in seemingly endless twists and turns, the villages nestled in its wider curves all drawing their purpose from the river. Why had they sprung up in those exact locations, I wondered? I supposed there were reasons for it. Just like Freiberg had its mines, I was sure these tiny villages had reasons for existing where they did. Maybe one man, like my great grandfather Bolle, had started a farm there and had found it easy to use the river water for his cattle, and then another farmer had come, and so on and so on. How odd that one man could begin a chain of events. All it took was one person with a strong will. Such a man was Carl Bolle, certainly. But so too was my mother; she could change the world with her will.

As the train traveled slowly, meandering toward Berlin, I reflected that I had arrived in Grosshatmannsdorf focused only on my own world and my own needs. Maybe Opa Bolle was right when he said, "God always has a purpose for everything. Even the things we think are terrible and we think we can't bear." I watched the small villages pass by with their ordered streets and fields and wondered about the lives they held hidden in their seeming peace.

He's Gone

Tante Ebi greeted us at the front door with cries of delight, hugging us to her bosom. When she finally let us go, I looked at her and noticed gray where there had been none, and deep lines around her mouth. We had stood there a good minute waiting for someone to answer the imposing oak door with its heavy lion-head knocker. I began to wonder if anybody lived there, and then Tante Ebi called, "I'm coming."

"How is he doing?" asked Mutti. The urgency of her tone struck me, and I knew that Opa Bolle would not live. I pulled away from Tante Ebi and ran up the broad, imposing staircase with its Persian-carpeted steps. I took them two at a time, and for the first time wished the staircase was not so grand. I rushed to Opa Bolle's bedroom door. I burst through the door. Two women stood over the bed and looked up in shock at my sudden arrival. I vaguely realized that one of them was Gretel, one of Opa Bolle's housekeepers. The other one appeared to be some type of nurse. I walked over to the bed as if in a dream. Opa Bolle lay propped up on several pillows. His eyes were open, but it appeared that he could not move. He was thin and gaunt and looked like he had not been out of bed for months—gone was the elegant, dapper grandfather I had known. His skin was so thin and pale I could see all of his veins, and his mouth hung open, struggling to let the air pass in and out. As I came into his line of vision, his eyes twinkled—they still held that same sparkle—and he patted the bed next to him. I sat down and put my head on his chest. He could not raise his arm, but he did manage to cover my hand with his as it lay on the bed by his side.

"Opa, I missed you so much," I moaned.

He patted my hand.

"Jutta, he can't talk," said Gretel gently. I glanced at her and saw that her eyes were brimming with tears. She wiped them away quickly and added, "He can understand you, but he can't respond."

I nodded and put my head back down. I heard my mother and Tante Ebi come in with Peti. Peti stood back. I heard my mother urge her to sit on the other side of the bed. After a long pause, she did so, and immediately began to tell Opa Bolle everything that had happened to her over the past several months—just as she used to do when she would climb in his lap and he would say, "So, *mein Herz*, tell me everything that has happened since we last met." Opa reached for her hand while he continued to pat mine.

Tante Ebi gently pulled me off his chest. "He can't breathe, Jutta." But he patted my hand more rapidly, and a slight frown on his face made me put my head back down—although I was conscious not to put my full weight on his chest. Tante Ebi said nothing.

After that first visit, I visited every day, bringing books from Vati's library, or selecting some from Opa Bolle's library. I would give him the choices I had selected and he would squeeze my hand when I came to one he liked. I read Schiller and Goethe. For some reason he especially liked it when I read to him in English, so I read Shakespeare and Hemingway and Steinbeck. I had never thought about whether Opa Bolle could speak or read in English, for I had never actually heard him do so. But I supposed he could; he was well educated and had an extensive library. Perhaps it was a last gesture of defiance. Frankly, it was difficult for me to understand some parts of what I read, but it didn't matter. I liked the flow of English; it had a melody to it German lacked.

So I spent the long summer days reading to my grandfather. Every day we ended our visit with a passage from the Bible. Tante Ebi would read him the different chapters of the Bible, and he would tap his hand at the one he wanted. And then she would list the verses within that chapter, and he would again tap his hand. But always, he insisted that she read Galatians 3:28. She sat with her half-glasses on her nose, reading from Opa Bolle's Bible, and he patted my hand as she read, and the clock ticked quietly in the background, and I knew he wanted me to understand that God was with me, even though it may not seem so. When she read, "What man intended for evil God intended for good," he stroked my hand more rapidly.

And then one day I came and he was gone. He had died an hour before, they told me, and they had not had time to call my mother. I had hurried over after school. Helga answered the door, and I knew instantly, before I ever set foot in the house. The house was still, empty, as if the life had been sucked out of it. I slowly walked up the stairs, dreading what I would find. I could hear her weeping before I ever even opened the door. I knocked on the door and waited. Gretel opened the door, and her tear-stained face contorted as she saw me. She grabbed me and hugged me and said over and over again, "He is gone. He is gone. What will we do? He is gone!"

I pushed free from her and saw Tante Ebi crumpled in the chair by his bed, sobbing. She still held his hand. I walked over and reached for his other hand. I recoiled in horror. I had not expected the cold hardness of what had once been warm and loving. "Why didn't you wait to say goodbye?" And the tears began to stream down my cheeks.

Tante Ebi looked up and stopped crying for moment. "He said goodbye to you every day this summer, Jutta," she said quietly.

I made no sound, tears running down my cheeks, spilling silently onto his cold marble hand. My mind raced through all the wonderful times we had together. I looked at this shell of a man and could not believe this had been my loving grandfather, with his abundant boxes of candy that drove my mother crazy, and his twinkling eyes. I pictured his gold watch with the gold chain that hung across his chest, just so. I could feel the touch of his winter blanket he used in the car whenever he drove anywhere, with the mink fur on the inside. "No need to show off," he would say. I heard his loving, melodious voice as he asked me about my day, my life, as if everything that happened to me was of greatest importance to him. And mostly I thought about those eyes, always twinkling, always laughing, with the hundreds of creases around them, now staring life-lessly at the ceiling.

"Close his eyes, please," I begged.

Gretel nodded and reached down to do so. Eventually, I felt a hand on my shoulder, and I knew without turning it was my father. He turned me toward him and hugged me for a long time.

"Go now, Jutta. Remember him as he was—not like this. Gretel, take Jutta downstairs to Frau Bolle. She is waiting for her."

I let Gretel lead me out of the room and down the grand staircase for the last time, without really being aware of my movements. My mother stood at the bottom of the curved banister as Gretel handed me off. She held me in her arms and stroked my hair, and then the sound came and I moaned and cried and gasped for air.

———

I can't say that I ever adjusted to the loss of Opa Bolle, but as time went by, and the events of the fall took over my life, I adjusted to the pain. It became a part of me. I stopped crying, but I no longer sang out or happily skipped down the stairs in the morning. My mother was right: time does numb the pain. The pain never leaves you, but it stops prickling toward the surface of your con-sciousness every day, as it does at first. It remains buried deep within, gradually becoming more and more muted. And so my life went on, as if he had never been here. It was this that frightened and depressed me. What was the point of it all? I watched the ants on our terrace, wondering: "Is that us? Do we wander about busily all day gathering food and water, and then one day a giant foot comes along and crushes us, and it is as if we were never here?" My mother tried to comfort me by saying, "You still have all the memories of Opa Bolle." But it struck me as so odd that the sun rose, the sun set, the rain came and went, and we just carried on with our day without him. And then, all of a sudden, my thoughts were diverted by circumstances out of my control and out of my parents' control—indeed, out of the Nazi government's control. I no longer had time to feel sorry for myself about Opa Bolle's death; I now worried about whether my parents and I would survive.

Opa Bolle had been dead for only six weeks when the news hit Berlin of the impending English bombing.

We Have No Choice

I leaned out the window of my bedroom taking in deep gulps of summer air, admiring how beautiful the front garden looked with its huge stands of pink and blue hydrangeas, set off by the emerald green of the lawn. The shadows of the trees formed long patterns across the large expanse of grass as the sun danced in between their stately boughs. We had not had a bomb raid in months, and the birds chirped away happily while the squirrels ran back and forth from tree to tree. I was lost in the thought that my life had returned to normal when something caught my eye. It fluttered to a halt in the plum tree not far from *Vögelein's* abandoned nest. I leaned out of the open window to see if I could grab it. I frowned, trying to see it through the tree's branches. It was a pamphlet of some sort, but how on earth could it have fallen out of the sky? I looked up and saw no sign of a plane. I had heard planes over Berlin earlier in the morning, before dawn. We had all gone down to the basement but the all clear had sounded almost immediately.

The wind stirred the trees; a warm comforting breeze swept all around the garden, causing acacia leaves to flutter to the ground. A spot of white danced in the sunlight, and another piece of paper come fluttering down. This time it floated all the way to the ground, landing next to a stand of wildflowers left uncut at Mutti's insistence. I clattered down the stairs and ran into the garden, hopping from one flagstone step to the next. As I approached the paper, I slowed my pace and circled it as if it were a landmine. Before I picked it up, I glanced to the sky again. This time I saw a cluster of white papers caught in the deep green arms of the elegant spruce trees that lined our side garden. The needles acted like a file sorter, holding the papers in until enough of a breeze came along to disrupt them. From my bedroom window, I had not been at the correct angle to notice them. I stared at my feet, wiggling my toes in the cool, wet grass closer and closer to the mystery paper. Sasha had followed me into the garden, and I heard her chasing squirrels in the bushes. Finally, in one quick motion, I picked it up. The message, in bold letters read: "Citizens of Berlin Beware." I unfolded it and read the warning from the British high command. My heart caught in my throat. I turned toward the house to find Mutti, but she was already heading my way, having seen me from the kitchen window. Silently, I handed the notice to her.

"Oh my God!" whispered my mother, her hand to her heart. "Oh my God," she said again as tears clung to the edges of her blue eyes. I fought to hold my own tears back. Mutti looked up and tried to regain her composure. "Now, Jutta, it will be all right," she said hugging me to her shoulder. "We will figure something out. Don't worry; we will figure something out." But I knew her bravado hid a fear she did not want me to feel. Then she quickly turned toward the house, saying, "I must call your father. I must speak to him. I must make plans." And she left me in the garden without looking back.

I stood staring up at the spruce trees until my neck ached. I called to Sasha; she ran to join me, shaking the leaves and twigs off her fur. "Come." I bent to pet her long, soft fur. "Let's go see Erica."

I ran across the street to Erica's house, Sasha at my heels. Erica was in her room, making a sign for her door with her name in big elaborate letters surrounded by flowers and hearts. It read "Erica's Room!"

"We all know this is your room, Erica!" I said, rolling my eyes.

"Well, when I am at the Baltic Sea, I want to make sure I still lay claim to this room, just in case my parents decide that some of our relatives from Hamburg should come and live here." She added matter-of-factly, "They lost their home in one of the bombing raids."

"What do you mean, when you go to the Baltic Sea?" I asked.

"Silly! Haven't you heard?" She looked up at me, surprised. "They have ordered all the schools to evacuate Berlin. The entire *Gertrauden Schule* will be moved to the Baltic Sea, maybe even next week; it just depends on how fast they can organize it all!" She looked at my shocked face and put her pencil down. Cocking her head to the side in amazement, she said, "Jutta! You really didn't know, did you? " I shook my head, still not sure whether to believe her or not. Sasha ran over to her and jumped into her lap. She rubbed Sasha's chin. "See? That's what she gets for not attending the BDM!" She glanced up at me. I walked over to the window and crossed my arms in front of my chest. Frowning, I looked at my house, nestled behind a protective wall of spruce and acacia trees.

I turned sharply, "But when was this decided?"

She shrugged. "They told us on Friday. I'm sure the school will make an announcement on Monday. Jutta, it will be fun, really. We can all live together in these huge rooms with bunk beds, and we'll be up at the Baltic Sea. It's so lovely there ..."

"Erica, it's freezing in the fall and winter up there!" I interrupted.

"And no parents to tell us what to do every five minutes," she continued, ignoring me. "And we can talk late into the night."

"But how will they divide us? They can't just put us all together. I will probably have to be with my class and you with yours."

Erica frowned for a moment. "I hadn't thought about that. I guess you're probably right, but we'll still see each other at free time and during meals."

I didn't say anything. Instead I turned back to the window and my house.

"Oh come on, Jutta! Why the gloom and doom? It will be a grand adventure—our first trip together."

I turned abruptly from the window, walked over to her, and with my fists clenched pounded the desk where she sat, causing all of her colored pencils to jump up down in unison. She leaned away from me in shock. "Erica! Do you understand that they are sending us away because the British plan to flatten Berlin with their horrid bombs?" I screamed. She looked at me in silence.

"Yes, but I don't believe they will succeed. The Führer's shield will protect us. Besides, this is just an extra precaution because he wants to make sure that nothing happens to us." She said it as if she had been made to practice the line.

I rolled my eyes and shook my head. Her bed stood only a few feet back from her desk. With my eyes still locked on her face, I took a step backwards and fell onto the bed. "And you really believe that, don't you?" I said quietly.

"Of course I do. I don't want to be all doom and gloom like you. I believe in this country. I believe in the Führer. He will look after us."

We eyed each other for several seconds, feeling the gulf between us widen. I debated pointing out that her relatives would not have to move into her home if the Führer had looked after Hamburg a little better. My thoughts were broken by the sound in the distance of a car door slamming. I ran to the window. Vati stepped out of the factory car. He waved to Heinz and walked quickly up the driveway. I turned on my heels, saying, "I must go. Vati is home."

"Jutta, come back tomorrow so you can help me pack. We can't bring very much, so we should coordinate."

I pushed past her, and before she could object, I was out the door and down the stairs. I walked quickly out the front door and then ran as fast as I could across the street and up my driveway. Sasha ran ahead, thinking I was playing, her tail wagging happily. I burst through the front door, banging it against the wall, practically knocking Vati's hat off its peg. Luise came rushing out of the kitchen shaking her head. "Slow down, young lady. This is not an asylum!"

"Sorry, but where is Vati?"

"In the music room, I think." Then, grabbing my arm, she whispered, "Give them a moment, Jutta. You come in the kitchen and calm down before you go barging in there." I pretended to follow her to the kitchen, but instead of going to the left, I veered suddenly right and hurried to the music room. I vaguely heard Luise sighing behind me.

My parents were sitting together on the sofa. Mutti's back was to me as I entered the room. She sat on the edge of the sofa, her body turned so she almost faced the back of the sofa. She was talking in a low but intense voice to my father, who sat with his back against the sofa facing her, his left arm stretched across the top of the sofa. He listened carefully as my mother spoke. He looked up as I walked in but did not say anything. Nor did he stop my mother, who had not heard me enter, from talking. "We don't have a choice, Hans! What else can we do?" Then, suddenly aware my father was focused on something elsewhere in the room, she turned. Her eyes landed on me, and her expression immediately changing from concern and worry to that slight smile she used more and more frequently to mask her face.

"Hello, Jutta," said my father.

"Have you heard?"

"Have I heard what?" he asked slowly.

"All the schools have to move to the Baltic. Does this mean I have to go, too?"

"Your mother and I were just talking about it, as a matter of fact."

Mutti turned her body to face me and smoothed out her dress. "And about this," she said, holding up the paper I had found in the garden.

I nodded my head and sat down in the armchair across from them.

Vati smiled as he fixed his eyes on my face. He looked at me carefully, as if he were weighing something in his mind, then he cleared his throat and said slowly and carefully, "Jutta, I think you will need to go away with your class."

"No!" I shook my head. "It's too cold up there, and I can't handle sleeping in the same room with a bunch of girls." Indeed, the very idea filled me with terror.

My parents exchanged looks. Then my mother spoke. "Jutta, you also can't handle the bombs."

"But maybe there won't be any. Maybe this is just to scare us. Maybe they just…"

My mother interrupted me. "Jutta, they are going to bomb Berlin like it has never been bombed before!" I opened my mouth to talk, but she shook her head to silence me. "We know what they have done to Hamburg. The same thing will happen here. You must go."

"I don't want to go! I want to stay together as a family." I sobbed. "Why can't I just live with my family? In my own house?" I was on the edge of my seat, and the tears fell down my cheeks and slid to my neck. Sasha whined as she put her head on my feet. Mutti looked away and bit her lip.

Vati reached across the table and grabbed my hands. "Juttalein, you must go. It will not work to have you stay."

"But why? Why can't I stay?" I yanked my hands away.

"It's for the best. Besides, there will be no school for you to go to here, and you are at a point in your studies where you can't be interrupted all the time. Even though you will be up north, it will be the same school, with the same teachers."

"What about the other Bolles?" I demanded.

"I have not yet spoken to Kurt or Hilde about this, but I am sure they will be going as well."

My stomach fell to the floor. I got up quickly, heading for the staircase. I ran up the stairs and only vaguely heard my mother pleading, "Jutta, please. We are only doing what we think is best." I ignored her. I knew I was going to be sick, so I headed for the bathroom with all the dignity I could muster.

For the next few days, as we prepared for my departure, my mother used every opportunity to tell me how much she loved me. I deemed her words sorry attempts at placating me. I looked at her blankly every time she said it. She was troubled; I could tell. But I also knew my mother had decided I would go with my class, and nothing I did was going to change her mind. I wasn't going to make it easy for her, though. I wanted her to feel the same rejection I felt from her decision Most appalling to me was the fact that my parents had made their decision in a matter of minutes—without even bothering to ask my opinion.

On the morning of my departure, Mutti came to my room early. I knew she would. It was her way. She came before the alarm went off to wake me herself. Sasha rustled in her basket. "Hello, my beautiful," whispered Mutti to Sasha. Sasha's tail thumped on the basket. I was already up. I knew she would come to have a quiet moment with me before the rest of the house awoke and we rushed around to get to the Anhalter Bahnhof in time for the train. I decided I would maintain my cold composure and not show her any warmth. I was leaning out the window in my nightgown, taking in the warm, late-summer morning, staring at each corner of the garden, trying to take a mental photograph in case it was not here when I returned. I could hear her walk toward me, and I braced myself for her touch. But it did not happen. I turned around. She was on the other side of my room by my dresser, looking at my photographs in their silver frames, photographs of me and Peti at the zoo with Opa Bolle and of Mutti holding me as a small child at Christmas. She touched each photograph as she looked at them. I turned back around so she would not see me watching her. After a moment I heard her walk to my bed. The sheets rustled when she sat down.

"Jutta, come here," she said in a voice I knew I should not ignore. I walked to the bed without looking at her and sat down. She held two packages in her hands. She handed me the larger one. "Here. Vati stopped at the bookstore yesterday and searched until he found the last of the English books for you." I took the package without opening it. "That's fine. You can open it on the train and think of your father." Then she handed me the other package. "Open this one now."

I took the package from her and meticulously unwrapped it without tearing the paper and ribbon. I let paper and ribbon fall to the floor. It held a beautiful walnut box with intricate inlaid wheat-colored pieces interlaced with tiny black wood pieces. I recognized it as Opa Bolle's candy box. I could see it sitting on his dresser in his upstairs bedroom, the light from the window hitting it, highlighting the contrasts of the inlaid pieces. I fought a lump in my throat. I lifted the lid and saw that my mother had made one of her heart-shaped books decorated on the top with pressed violets, wild sweet peas, and daisies. It was trimmed and tied closed with a pale green satin ribbon. It was the loveliest thing I had ever seen, and I knew immediately how much care and time she had taken to make it. I slowly untied the ribbon. Unable to see clearly, the tears blinding me and threatening to spill over onto my cheeks, I opened my eyes as wide as I could to prevent them from falling. On the first page of the book, through the curtain of my tears, I saw that she had pasted a picture of the two of us. Underneath she had written: *No matter where you are, I will always love you and you are always in my heart. With all my love. Your Mutti."* And there, directly under her name, one of her four-leaf clovers decorated the page. How she always found them, I don't know, but it was too much for me. I threw the book on the bed and burst into tears. I buried my face in her shoulder, hanging on to her with all my life. She rocked me and held me and whispered to me and kissed my head until I was finished. I slowly pulled away and said, "I'm so sorry, Mutti."

"Shhh. I know," she said simply, and hugged me to her again. We needed no words, and I knew I could go in peace now.

The Cold

I spent less than six weeks on the Baltic Sea. Mutti and Vati drove me to the train station. We hugged and kissed goodbye, none of us saying much. They watched silently as I joined my class on the train platform; Vati with his hands clasped behind his back, his face a mask, and Mutti with that half-smile she used to hide her feelings, her right arm crossed in front, the hand clasping her left elbow. I turned to wave to them from the top of the steps just before I entered the train car; they waved back quietly, and I entered and took my assigned seat on the train.

From that point on, that was how it was—assigned seats, assigned beds with assigned sheets, and an assigned box under the bed for your belongings with your name pasted to it. We ate on a schedule; we got up on schedule; we even had scheduled bathroom times. And we did all of this as a class, together. I hated it! Just looking at the long row of metal beds in our dormitory room caused tears to spring to my eyes. One night I looked down the long row of sinks in the bathroom where punctually, every night at nine o'clock, we were told to get ready for bed. Everyone was brushing their teeth in unison. I stared at their feet, and my mind flashed on the boots, the boots of many marches, hundreds and hundreds of them, rising in perfect unison, black, shiny—no longer belonging to individuals, but one solid mass. I turned back to the mirror and brushed my teeth as hard as I could.

I don't remember much about those six weeks, other than thinking that I had died and surely gone to hell. I do remember that every morning at 6:30 I held my breath listening to the hollow, efficient sound of Frau Schröder's sturdy leather shoes as she walked slowly down the long row of beds, making sure we had made them properly and placed all of our personal belongings in our chests. Every once in a while she would stop, and without looking I knew she had issued a citation to some poor girl. I imagined her frown and her finger pointing silently to a deviant crease in the bed covers. When she got to the end of the row, she would clap her hands and we would be allowed to file out quietly to the dining room for breakfast, where we stood saluting the flag, our hands held out in front of us, our elbows in line with our ears, while *"Deutschland Über Alles"* and the Horst Wessel song played. As always, my arm sagged to shoulder level, eliciting frowns from my teacher as well as Frau Schröder.

I was unable to sleep: the cold kept me up all night. We each had been allotted a fairly thick blanket, but it did no good. I put extra socks on, and an extra undershirt under my nightgown, but still the cold woke me every night as I lay listening to the other girls snoring and talking in their sleep. I felt so alone. I was in a room filled with at least thirty-five girls, and yet I felt totally and completely alone. I rarely saw Erica; her dormitory was at the other end of the building, and they scheduled things so that the classes would not overlap in the dining room or during class time. I rarely saw Peti, for she was two years younger. And not only did I not see my good friend or my cousin, but I was constantly paired up with Liesel Yanke. She hated me, and the feeling was mutual. I was an object of disgust to her—the essence of what was wrong with some Germans. I was a wealthy girl who did not appreciate the great things the Führer was doing for us, like providing for our safety and well-being. She would roll her eyes whenever I said it was cold, or when I said I missed my family. Liesel had no tolerance for weakness. She became our group leader, the one who reported all deviant behavior to Frau Schröder. Embracing this role with zeal, she complained that I did not participate in team sports with enthusiasm, and that I let the team down. She reported me to Frau Schröder for staring out the window during study hall. After about two weeks of this life, I came down with a high fever and had to be sent to the infirmary. This was only a slight improvement over living in the dormitory; at least I did not have to see Liesel every day, and I followed no routine. After about a week I improved enough to be sent back to join the rest of the girls, but after a few days, the fever returned, and I was again sent to the infirmary.

It was during my third visit to the infirmary that my fever returned with a vengeance, climbing as high as 104 degrees, frightening Frau Meyers, the nurse who took care of me. She called in Frau Schröder. I drifted in and out of consciousness. I heard them talking about calling my parents. Frau Schröder said to wait a few more days before we bother Frau Bolle, but Frau Meyers wanted to call immediately. They called my mother, and I heard through whispers that she wanted a doctor sent immediately.

A golden light flew back and forth across my eyes, and a woman's voice chanted in the night. I struggled to open my eyes. Frau Meyers sang as she sponged me down, her voice rich and deep, and I wondered why she was a nurse. Why hadn't she become an opera singer? I asked her, barely able to get the words out.

"I don't know, Jutta," she said, shrugging her shoulders.

"Did you ever sing in public?"

"Oh yes! I sang every Sunday in my church choir."

"Do you still sing at church?" I whispered.

"No."

"Why not?"

She just shrugged her shoulders.

"Now let's see if you can sit up, Fräulein Jutta," she said, to change the subject.

———

There was a small nightstand with a drawer by the side of the bed. On it always sat a light, a glass of water, and Frau Meyers' reading glasses. I watched Frau Meyers at the other end of the infirmary, busy with another patient who had somehow contracted food poisoning. I leaned up in bed on my elbow. A glitter of light caught my eye. The drawer of the nightstand was slightly ajar, and something inside caught the light of the pale sun that had for once decided to fight its way through the clouds. Frau Meyers had thrown the curtains open, announcing it was a beautiful day, and I would surely feel great with such glorious weather to comfort me! Curious, I leaned over farther. I remembered the distant sound of the drawer scraping open and closed when I was weak with fever. Funny, I thought the sound had come from somewhere far away. But I realized now that it had been the drawer of the nightstand. I assumed that Frau Meyers kept my medicine in the drawer. I reached over and pulled on the handle; it opened reluctantly, sticking a bit. The drawer was empty except for what looked like a long string of beads with a crucifix at the end. The light hit the crucifix and bounced off it, hitting my eye. I vaguely remembered Vati talking about Goebbels closing down hundreds of Catholic churches all over Germany, pronouncing them dens of homosexuality and debauchery. The golden light passing over me was her rosary. She had prayed for me, holding the crucifix over me. I gently closed the drawer and smiled. I knew I liked Frau Meyers.

———

We did several more cycles of me feeling better and going back to the dormitory, only to come back down with the fever within a few days and ending up back in the comfortable environs of Frau Meyers. The doctors could find nothing wrong with me. They tested me for everything they could think of and found nothing. I had lost so much weight, they began to worry that I would starve to death. I overheard Frau Meyers telling the doctor, "She is homesick. It's just that simple. And I think we should send her home because she can't keep losing weight, and the fever is eventually going to affect her brain." I heard the doctor respond, but I could not make out his words. His voice did not carry the way Frau Meyers' did—hers resonated with clarity. The doctor left, and Frau Meyers came to my bedside. "Jutta, we're sending you home."

They released me the next day, and by nightfall I was in Berlin. I did not see my classmates again until after the war, and some I never saw again at all, for they never returned to Berlin. I never saw Frau Meyers again, but as I left the infirmary I told her I would pray that she would one day be able to sing again in the choir.

"Thank you, Jutta." She smiled and nodded her head.

Vati stood on the busy platform of the Anhalter train station waiting for me, his hands laced together behind his back. He looked up and down the length of the train terminal to try and catch sight of me. I ducked back into the window and grabbed my case from under the seat, but it was too heavy for me to lift. Instead, I bent over and pushed it out into the aisle. People stepped around me, hurrying to get off the train. A young girl accidentally hit me on the head with her bag. She didn't even notice as she hurried past me. The corner of my case hit the edge of the seats, sticking and making my progress down the aisle slow. I could feel myself growing warm from embarrassment. A young officer pushed past the passengers who were clogging the aisle behind me. They parted quickly and without a word. He wore the gray green uniform of the army.

"Let me help you with that, Fräulein," he said with a smile. His even, white teeth flashed at me. It disturbed me that he seemed so nice, so normal, and I found myself feeling guilty that I thought he was attractive. He hoisted the case to his shoulder by swinging it above the seats. By carrying the bulky case on his shoulder, he avoided hitting the seats, and in single file we slowly made our way to the front of the train, I with my eyes trained on the back of his head. His hair was immaculately groomed, and the collar of his jacket met the base of his skull in a perfect symmetrical line. He could not turn around because he would have decapitated both me and the passenger in front of him with my large case, so conversation was impossible until we reached the doorway of the train. He lowered the case to the ground and turned to give me his hand to help me down the steps. Glancing at my name on the case, he said, "Fräulein Bolle, I am glad I could be of service to you. Is someone meeting you here?"

"Yes, my father," I said, trying to look over the hundreds of heads that crowded the platform. Then I added quickly, "Thank you very much. I don't know how I would have made it off the train without your help!"

"Oh, no problem." Glancing at my case again, he looked up. "Bolle … as in Bimmel Bolle? Are you part of that family?" he asked curiously.

"Yes. He was my great-grandfather." I smiled.

"Well, I am honored to meet someone from the Bolle family." He bowed slightly as a lock of brown hair fell casually across his forehead. He quickly swept it back in place with his right hand and looked down the platform. "Why don't you go look for your father while I watch your case here?"

"Oh, thank you!" I said without hesitation. As I headed to the area where I had seen my father standing, I wondered at my trust of this stranger. By now the crowd had cleared out a little. People called to one another, and the train master shouted orders to the conductor and the engineer as they climbed around on the train trying to fix something. I scanned the platform, looking for a dark-haired man in a gray coat. Every man on the platform seemed to fit that description.

"Jutta!"

I spun around and spotted him rushing toward me.

"Jutta, thank goodness!" Vati called with relief. "I thought maybe I had the wrong train, or maybe they decided to keep you up there." He hugged me quickly and pulled back, frowning at my thin shape hidden under my jacket. "We need to put Luise to work on you!" he said, studying my face.

"Vati! I can't believe I'm here!" I hugged him to me again. "I missed you so much."

Vati spun around. "Where is your case?" He asked, puzzled.

"Oh, it's back there. An officer helped me get it off the train; he's watching it for me."

Without responding, Vati's gaze followed my pointing finger. I could tell he was not comfortable, but he said nothing as he followed me back to where the officer stood.

"Herr Bolle, Lieutenant Hans Albrecht, at your service," said the young man, holding out his hand to Vati.

My father held out his hand, though a subtle concern creased his eyes. "Nice to meet you. Thank you very much for helping my daughter."

"I am proud to have helped a Bolle."

My father chuckled as if to dismiss this comment.

"No. Really, I am a great admirer of your family. My father was a Bolle boy, and he still talks about what a good man Bimmel Bolle was..." He looked embarrassed. "I'm sorry; Carl Bolle." He laughed, shaking his head at the silliness of the name.

My father, obviously embarrassed, said quickly, "Thank you again."

Lieutenant Albrecht reached down and picked up my case. "Let me get this for you. Young ladies don't travel lightly, I guess," he said with a wink in my direction.

"No, really. I can manage."

But Lieutenant Albrecht was already heading toward the main entrance to the station, his back to my father. Once outside, he set the case down by the curb.

"Many thanks," said my father. Then, seeing that the young man was not inclined to leave, he cocked his head and added, "Where do you work?"

"I work for Herr Rust at the Ministry of Education. I have a weak heart, so I cannot fight," he added with only the barest trace of embarrassment. Shifting his gaze to me, he said with mock authority, "Find Fräulein Bolle a good tutor."

"Oh, we most certainly will!" said my father, frowning slightly. I followed his gaze out across the Askanischer Platz. Heinz stood by the factory limousine, waving to us. Vati hurriedly shook the young man's hand and thanked him again. He turned his back and guided me out across the broad boulevard, unusually silent and empty and without traffic. I looked back over my shoulder and smiled and waved to Lieutenant Albrecht. He smiled back, tipping his hat to me.

"No, truly the thanks is for me to give," he called out. Vati stopped and turned back for a moment. "Carl Bolle saved my father's life. He had a rough childhood, my father, and Herr Bolle gave him a second chance." He repeated the words slowly, as if he had been reciting them since childhood.

My father paused. He studied the man for a moment, and then reached in his pocket, walked back the few steps to him, and handed him a business card. "If you ever need anything, give me a call." And then once again he turned his back. The young man stared at the card in his hand and then, grinning, he crossed the broad avenues that formed a triangle in the Askanischer Platz. Heinz passed him, their shoulders almost touching as he rushed to help with my heavy case. He greeted me with a warm hug before he lifted my case and headed back to the car that waited on the other side of the Askanisher Platz. Vati glanced uneasily toward the retreating figure of Lieutenant Albrecht. He had stopped and turned to watch us. His eyes followed Heinz to the car. The lieutenant did nothing; instead he simply stared for a moment and then, smiling, waved a final goodbye.

Heinz set the case down and greeted me again. "Welcome home, Fräulein Jutta!"

I smiled and thanked him as I stepped through the car door he held open for me. My father stepped in behind me and sat next to me on the wide leather seat. He reached over and cradled my hand in his. I smiled. Heinz put the car in gear and eased it out into the broad avenue; I could hardly wait to get home.

I looked out in the dim evening light, and it struck me again there was almost no traffic. Heinz maneuvered the car out of the Askanischer Platz and turned down Wilhelmstrasse. I sucked my breath in and covered my mouth with my hand, an unconscious act, as the utter devastation spread itself before me. Vati squeezed my hand but said nothing. Where only a few weeks before there had been beautiful buildings and streets teeming with people, there now stood great mountains of rubble with pale streams of smoke still escaping from their midst. How could this happen in only a few short weeks? I stared, my face pasted to the window, condensation forming from my breath. My father said nothing as I took in the immensity of the destruction. They had diverted streets around buildings that had crashed into their centers and spilled out into the street—too many to clean up.

The silence hung like fog, blanketing the streets. For me, the silence of the streets was the worst. The gigantic Excelsior Hotel, where we had stayed before leaving for Berchtesgaden, was now empty but for a few official-looking vehicles parked in front of it at odd angles to avoid the debris in the street. Nobody was on the street walking to a café, or out for dinner, or taking in a movie, or heading to the theaters or art galleries of Berlin. It was a city without life.

"Nobody is on the streets."

My father said softly, "There is nothing to be on the streets for." He followed my gaze out across Schöneberger Strasse. "Things have changed, Jutta. I'm sorry you must see this," he said, his voice heavy.

I did not respond. I simply could not process what had happened in the short time I was gone. I pressed my face against the glass of the window again and studied the scene before me, trying to remember what had once been where rubble now stood. We turned down the Kurfürstendamm; the faces of the tall buildings looked surprised as the headlights of our car illuminated them, but as my eyes adjusted, I saw that most of the grand apartment buildings had their top floors missing. They looked so vulnerable and naked, like a bald man without his toupee. I shook my head in disbelief and prayed none of their residents were hurt. Then suddenly I was thrown forward; my father extended his left arm across my chest to keep me from hitting my head on the seat in front as Heinz slammed on the brakes. My head snapped backward, and I rubbed the back of my neck to prevent the muscles from tightening.

"What is it?" asked Vati, urgently trying to peer out the front window. But there were no streetlights on anywhere, and the dark covered us like the silence.

"Police," said Heinz simply. My heart began to pound, and I wasn't sure if it was my hand or my father's that began to sweat as he pressed my hand in his.

"Good evening," said Heinz politely to a dark figure that appeared next to the car.

"Good evening. Why are you out driving? Are you not aware of the curfew?" asked the policeman in that abrupt way they all have.

"I have Herr Johannes Bolle in the car, and he had special business to attend to."

The officer stuck his head in the window and looked in the back at my father. Then his gaze drifted to me, where it lingered for a moment. "Good evening," said the officer, tipping his hat, and I breathed easier. He paused for a moment, not sure if he should continue with his interrogation. He seemed about to pull his head back out and let us go, but then he added, "What sort of business?"

"I had business meetings downtown, and then I had to pick my daughter up from the train station," interjected my father before Heinz had a chance to say anything.

"Do you have a permit?" asked the officer.

"No. I'm sorry. I was in such a hurry, I forgot to get one."

The officer stood up for a moment, uncertain what to do now that he had asked the question. "Wait a moment, please," he said. I heard him walk away, his heels clicking on the asphalt, to confer with another officer. I could see nothing because of the dark outside, but I heard men's voices, maybe twenty feet or so from our car, talking in the way officials talk when they are trying to figure out what to do with someone who has broken the rules. The silence inside the car vibrated all around us, the purr of the engine amplified. Shut off by the dark, we sat waiting. Finally he returned. "Go on!" He jerked his head in the direction we were going. "But remember to get a permit next time. You cannot travel without a permit. They are expecting an attack tonight, so hurry home and don't go anywhere else."

Heinz nodded. "Thank you, sir."

"Put your lights on dim; they want as little light as possible. Drive carefully." Then, turning to us, he tipped his hat and said, "Good evening, Herr Bolle." And to me he added, "Fräulein."

I nodded my head, too terrified to speak, but my father responded, "Thank you, sir. Next time I will remember to get the permit."

The officer nodded, and then he once again pulled his head back into to the night and disappeared. Heinz put the window up and let out his breath. "They are really becoming strict, Herr Bolle."

"Is it hard to get a permit?" I asked.

"Now, yes. They don't want anyone driving at night because of the headlights. But I don't plan to do this again. It was only because your train was so late that we ended up out at night." Then he added, "Jutta! Your hands are ice-cold!"

I didn't respond.

"We were all right," said Vati, trying to soothe me.

But I knew we weren't. We were lucky, that's all. Lucky the policeman was not one to stick by the book. Scared that we had to depend on such thin threads, I hated the uncertainty of it all.

Verdammte Nazis

The winter grasses stood tall in the soft light of the early morning, the fields broken here and there by islands of trees, the green of their pine needles contrasting sharply with the brown fields and the muted light of early winter. Mutti had allowed me to stay for my birthday, a small celebration with Mutti and Vati only. All my friends were gone, of course, and even my cousins. But Luise baked apple strudel with apples from Opa Bolle's tree and served it on my beautiful cake plate with the pale blue trim and pink roses. Now, the day after, November 15, Mutti wasted no time; she booked a 7:30 AM train to Halberstadt. Vati couldn't get a permit to take the factory car because the authorities had become impossible about rationing and using vehicles for private business. The week before they had even confiscated Vati's BMW sports car for the "war effort," orders from the Reichsmarschall himself, they said. Vati fumed all week. "For the war effort! What are they going to do with a BMW sports car? I bet the Reichsmarschall wants it for his wife! He can't use it! His ass is too big!"

"Hans Bolle," reprimanded Mutti. "Watch your language!"

But Vati ignored her and kept at it all through dinner. "*Verdammte* Nazis! Like taking Tasha for the cavalry! What are they going to use that horse for? Nothing but their own pleasure! They're criminals. It's legalized crime—an excuse to steal."

"Hans! Please! Jutta!" she nodded her head in my direction and then, turning to me she said, "Jutta, don't repeat these things to anyone, or they will not only have our car and horse, but our Vati also."

I nodded gravely and continued to eat.

"*Verdammte* Nazis!" he muttered again.

———

"Mutti," I said, turning from the window. "It looks so different in the winter, doesn't it?"

"Yes, the colors are so much duller."

I nodded. "And there are no orange and red poppies dotting the fields, and no sunflowers." I turned back to the window and pressed my face against the glass, feeling the cool morning against my cheek. The peach and apple trees had let go to flat fields of dark rich soil that held beets and potatoes in their upturned furrows.

Mutti reached over and grabbed my hand, patting the top of it with her other hand. "I will miss you," she said simply.

Tears filled my eyes. "I will miss you, too." I looked away. I didn't want to cry on the train. "Mutti," I turned back suddenly, "can I come home for Christmas? Or maybe you and Vati can come to Halberstadt?"

"Yes, I think Omi would like it if we came to Halberstadt. Don't you?"

"Yes! That would be better, just in case ..." I stopped.

She patted my hand again, and we watched the flat dark fields pass in checked patterns before us.

———

Mutti kept her promise; she and Vati came for Christmas. And then the bombs rained down on Berlin and every major city in Germany, and I didn't see them again until the summer.

8

Halberstadt: Omi's House

A scream broke the silence, shattering the warm comfort of my room. Each time it was the same: the eerie hoot and then, seconds later, the scream. The owl kept me awake at night hooting in the silence from somewhere in the group of trees in the middle of the field behind Omi's house. I knew it waited, scanning the field, looking for movement below, signs of life, before it lifted itself in silence, wings outspread, long claws stretched below its taut body, ready to kill. It was the one thing I didn't like about Omi's house.

Omi lived in a beautiful old apartment house on the southwest side of Halberstadt in an area called Spiegelsbergen. We were, in fact, only a mile from the center of Halberstadt, but it had the feel of the country about it. The town ended at my grandparents' apartment house, where fields replaced houses and ran in perfect geometric patterns up to the Spiegelsbergen Hills. These rolling hills spread out like waves before the magnificent Harz Mountains in the distance. For me, the carpet of golden wheat that spread from our doorstep across the fields and hills for as far as the eye could see held the promise of eternity. How many millions of kernels of wheat lay between us and those mountains, I wondered. Only God knew.

The apartment house was a few blocks up from a railroad crossing on the Spiegelsbergenweg, a broad road lined with chestnut trees on each side. It was an unusual road, eventually leading out to the hill country, consisting of two separate stretches that ran side by side. One side, covered with asphalt, was for vehicles; the other, immediately adjacent and equally wide, covered with sand, was a path for horses. Pedestrians and bicycles used the sandy path primarily now—ever since the Nazis had confiscated every horse in the land for their war. The sand-covered path drove my grandfather crazy because my friends and I preferred to walk along it, and somehow we always managed to track sand into the apartment. I never understood how he could notice the minute granules of sand when he never seemed to notice much of anything else—not to mention his eyesight was not very good any more. Yet he would call for me from the entrance hall, peering down at the floor over his bifocals like a doctor studying a specimen. "Jutta," I heard his big voice rattling its way down the hall to my room. "You've tracked sand in here again! Come sweep it up!"

I loved my grandmother's house. It was a refuge from the darkness of Berlin. Her loving presence and the smells—chicken roasting, potatoes boiling, and bread baking—filled me with comfort. On Sundays, when she could find the ingredients (rarely now), she baked my favorite cake, *Marmorkuchen*. The swirls of chocolate set in the yellow batter in perfect circles invited me to sniff their rich flavors. I loved to help her turn the cake and sprinkle it with powdered sugar. Her lavender scent, combined with the soft smell of the rose soap my mother supplied her, drifted to me between the aroma of chocolate cake baking in the oven. Such moments eased the pain of not seeing Mutti and Vati, and they eased the pain of living with uncertainty and chaos. Sitting in the kitchen watching the quiet, steady movements of my Omi, I could forget about the war.

I was fortunate living here with my grandparents. There were no air raid sirens, sounding with the certainty that many would die and much of the town would be destroyed by morning. These were the staples of life in Berlin, but not in Halberstadt, where life rolled on with relative regularity, except for the occasional display of Nazi pomp and circumstance that we all quietly tolerated. Luxuries like soap and shampoo were in short supply, but food was plentiful, surrounded as we were by the dark brown fields that in summer would fill with strawberries and asparagus. Yet a feeling of emptiness, of unstoppable despair, hung in the air all around us. It clung to us like moist summer air. None of us spoke about it. It combined with fear of what awaited us at the end of this war. It was at its worst at school when the teachers began with their lessons of German victories against the Russians, lessons that were getting shorter and shorter as German victories became harder and harder for even the best propagandists to fabricate. It clung to the frenzied way they spoke now of the Führer. How he loves Germany like a husband loves a wife. How they repeated his own shrill words that Germany will be saved by the young—they represent the true strength and greatness of the German people. It hung all about the boys standing in the middle of the *Holzmarkt*, leaning against the ancient fountain dressed in their Hitler Youth uniforms, their scarves and badges proudly attached to their uniforms.

One boy in particular stood out. I had seen his face many times around Café Deesen, my grandmother's sister's *Konditorei*. He was maybe a year younger than I; he wore his thick, golden blond hair neatly combed back from his forehead like a helmet, from beneath which he looked out on the world with large, innocent, blue eyes. On cold days the color rose to his cheeks, and somehow that face spoke of all of the innocence of the German youth, so taken in by Hitler's flattering, so ready to die for a doomed cause, a cause unworthy of their zeal. He seemed a kind boy, a boy who held the door for old ladies as they tried to enter the café with their shopping bags.

His face haunted me, that innocent face, the face of a child really; a face that I knew would not live past eighteen years of age. His face inserted itself at odd times in my mind, rosy-cheeked and smiling; it would appear suddenly while I was in mathematics, trying to figure out the relevance of algebra to my life. And then, just as suddenly, it twisted perversely into a ghostly, pale face with a bullet hole bursting out of its side just above the ear, blood oozing out of the blond mat onto a field of golden grass that turned darker and darker with the constant flow of his blood. He lay there, his mouth, once smiling, open slightly with a thick, deep red dribble of blood running from it, soiling his once-starched and crisp scarf as his friends marched on ahead, leaving him lonely and forgotten. I shuddered and tried to think of him as he was in front of Café Deesen, just a child like me trying to live in this crazy world our parents and grandparents had handed us.

We heard rumors the Nazi propaganda was wrong; we were losing this war, and what sort of terror would be unleashed upon us was anyone's guess. Everybody prayed that if we lost, the English or Americans would defeat us first, not the Russians. I had heard the stories, through the grapevine, of Russian atrocities in the East. Reports occasionally made it past the censors from the soldiers on the Eastern front—reports of vast Russian armies crushing our poorly equipped troops in distant parts of East Prussia, like Nemmersdorf, their numbers overwhelming and steadily heading our way.

I knew in my heart it would not end well for Germany, but I tried not to think about it. I pressed this knowledge deep down inside, and only at night, with the waking of the owl, did it rise up and leave me tired and empty.

The building that housed my grandparents' apartment had actually been a mansion, built in the late nineteenth century and converted after World War I into three apartments, presumably because the owner had lost his fortune like so many after the first war. Ours was the middle apartment, on the second floor; this allowed us the advantage of being closer to the street level so that my grandparents did not become winded going up the stairs, but high enough to take advantage of the spectacular view out of our living room window. The dining room took in the same view, as there was no partition between the living room and the dining room. The kitchen looked out onto the landing and the garden below with its stately old plum tree, whose leaves turned a glorious maroon color each fall, only to float off, covering the ground with a deep, rich mat of color.

Down the tiny hall, off the living room, on the opposite side from the kitchen, were two very large bedrooms. I monopolized one bedroom and my grandparents shared the other. My bedroom faced the street, and I would sit happily for hours by my window, watching the activity below, daydreaming. I shared the only bathroom in the apartment with my grandparents. I longed for my own bathroom in Berlin—though Grosshartmansdorf had taught me to be grateful for any indoor bathroom. Fortunately, Omi and Opa were early risers, much earlier than I, and they usually were completely finished in the bathroom by the time I got up. But still, I would rather have lingered in my own bathroom, like I did at home, practicing various looks in the mirror I copied from American movie stars. Sometimes I would take a pencil and imitate the way the ladies in *Vogue* magazine held their cigarettes. I would pout at myself with the pencil casually draped between the fingers of my right hand, wrist bent, with my left arm supporting my right arm at the elbow. Inevitably, if I stayed too long, I would hear my grandfather say in a loud, hoarse whisper, "What on earth could she possibly find to do in there?"

"She's a girl. Remember, Heidchen?" responded Omi patiently. I would wait until I heard the floorboards crack under Opa's weight as he moved off down the hall, and then quietly exit the bathroom, closing the door softly behind me, tiptoeing to my room so that it would look like I had been in my bedroom all along.

The rooms in the apartment were large and protected by ceilings that hung high in the air, like all the rooms built in the great mansions of that century, with elaborate moldings that always appeared to me to glue the ceiling and walls to each other. The windows in all the main rooms reached from about three feet off the floor all the way to the ceiling. The windows themselves must have been ten feet tall, of the double-sashed variety that you could unlatch and push up to open to half their full height.

The floors in the apartment were an elaborate parquet design in deep cherry-colored wood that every once in a while peeked out from under the numerous thick blue and red Persian carpets strewn about on top of them. Most of the carpets had been given to Omi by Mutti and Vati; others were antiques she had inherited from her parents. The apartment was beautiful, but I did not care for the dark wood furniture that my grandmother favored. It seemed so dreadfully old-fashioned to me. I tried to ignore the furniture and focus instead on the bright sunlight let through by the grand windows and the beautiful view of the mountains that more than made up for these somber drawbacks.

My friend Carla dropped into my life one day in the middle of January. I had been at the high school just down the street from Omi's house since November, and I found it difficult to fit in with the girls, all of whom had known each other since first grade. To them I was an outsider—another one of the many refugees fleeing from Berlin—except in my case they thought of me as a spoiled, rich one, even though I had never really spoken a word to them other than what was necessary for class. I could not escape my last name. They taunted me with Bolle songs. "Bimmel Bolle, Bimm Bimm," they would sing after me, or shout out lines from the newspaper cartoons of Carl Bolle.

Carla was different; she made no judgments about me. She suddenly appeared at school after Christmas. With her heavy Berlin accent, it was no secret that she too was a refugee from that careworn city. She knew about my family but she never said a word about them. She treated me the way she treated everybody, with an endearing roughness that hid a surprisingly warm heart.

One day after school, Carla came up to me as we exited the elaborate gold gates that towered above our heads and said, "Hello, Jutta Bolle. May I walk with you?"

I looked up in surprise to find the owner of the friendly voice smiling at me. "Well, yes. I mean sure," I said, startled.

"Great. I live near you, closer to town."

"Oh, really? How do you know where I live?" I asked, surprised.

"Because I walk this way every day, and you are always ahead of me because you blast out of school as fast as you can," she said, laughing at me.

"I guess I do. I'm not a huge fan of school," I acknowledged.

She smiled at me again and looked behind us. It struck me how oddly she moved, stiffly turning her entire body at once, rather than just her head, as if a single metal rod ran the full length of her body from her skull to her tailbone. "That makes two of us. I could take school or leave it—all that memorizing and repeating back to them. What they are trying to stuff into our heads gives me a headache." She paused for a moment. "Well, except for Frau Grabber's class. I love her class."

"Me, too!" I exclaimed, and that sealed it. We walked on, talking and laughing until we came to my grandmother's gate. From that day on we walked home together.

My life was very simple; I went to school, and I came home to Omi for lunch and did my homework. Some days I walked into Halberstadt to visit Tante Lieschen, my grandmother's sister, who owned Café Deesen.

The high school Carla and I attended was simply called the *Lyzeum*; it was an imposing old building with windows that ran the full length of its three stories. It had a red tile roof and a clock in the center of the top floor surrounded by carved stone. The school sat at the end of a rectangular park full of linden trees dating back to the 1800s. A wide horse path, lined on each side by trees, ran along both sides of the park. There was a large grass expanse in the middle where, before the war, the city workers planted bulbs in the spring, and in the summer daises grew in circular displays running down the center. On the right side of the school, sheltered behind an iron fence, an old manor house took up the full length of the park. Elegant mansions, their front yards filled with lilacs and rhododendrons in the spring and impatiens and dahlias in the summer, lined the park on the opposite side. It was a beautiful walk back and forth to school from Omi's house, especially once I turned off the Speigelsbergenweg onto Bernh-Thierschstrasse, the street that dead-ended into the park. Sheltered under the shade of the giant chestnut trees, I wandered along the cobblestone streets, kicking nuts and stones as I went past Tante Lieschen's house. I always looked up at the grand old house my aunt lived in, but I never stopped; she was never home during the day. "The *Konditorei* is a jealous lover," she would say.

The only complication to this simple life was that I had to watch out for the occasional group of Hitler Youth that periodically patrolled the streets, especially on the days that the BDM held its meetings. All girls my age were supposed to attend the BDM meetings and activities. I was the only girl in the school who did not.

Most German parents were not able to get a letter exempting their children from the Hitler Youth. Well aware of this fact, I was careful not to draw attention to myself on those days when they held meetings. I felt a pang of guilt for not participating in the war relief projects. I knew they helped repair bombed or burned buildings in neighboring towns, and they were always there to hand out blankets and food after the bomb raids in those towns. Often they collected money for the men on the front, especially at Christmastime.

In Halberstadt, the boys had less to do than those living in the cities targeted by the Americans and British, like Berlin. Here, they acted more like gangs of bullies with their arrogant stance and tone, and I despised them. They would stand in groups of three or four, never alone, and look for "unusual activities." I didn't pay much attention to them. I scanned ahead as I walked the streets of the town, and if I saw them, I took a quick turn to avoid them. Too busy amusing themselves, telling jokes and gossiping, they did not notice me, until one day a group of three suddenly blocked my path.

"Hello, Fräulein," called the big one. I pivoted quickly, sprinting around the corner to avoid them. I heard them laugh; their footsteps echoing on the cobblestones behind me propelled me forward. I was only a block from Café Deesen. I rushed into the café flushed and sweaty, something obviously wrong. Tante Lieschen looked up from behind the counter as she gave a customer her change. A frown creased her brow, and her usual smile evaporated as she studied my face. I sat at a table by the window looking out over the plaza. I saw them on the opposite side. They waited for a bit, and then, growing bored, they left. Tante Lieschen slipped into the chair across from me and covered my hand with hers. I told her about the incident. I waited at the café with her until closing, and then we walked home together.

After a few months, I noticed the big one and his cohorts no longer patrolled the streets. They had been replaced by much younger and far less vigilant boys—boys who were more interested in throwing stones and kicking whatever it is boys find to kick in the street than in patrolling the streets of Halberstadt. The other group must have turned eighteen and been packed off to do their duty, fighting for country and Führer. My heart ached for them; they would surely die.

Always behind the pleasant veneer of Halberstadt was the nagging reminder that we were at war, and that my parents and relatives in Berlin faced death every day. The regular stream of bombers flying overhead on their way to Berlin made it difficult to forget this—huge *V* shapes cutting through the sky, casting dark and treacherous shadows on the quiet town below. I had been in Halberstadt maybe four months when the Americans began bombing Berlin by day—their planes flew higher, out of reach of the German air defense system—and the British bombed Berlin by night. They performed this duet over and over, sometimes for days, like hordes of bees flying in formation with a singular concentration to devour their target. The sound always sent shivers up my back and perspiration down my face and palms. Sometimes they stopped for days, maybe even weeks. Just as I grew complacent, dropping my guard, suddenly in the distance the vague sound of the deadly buzz traveled the airwaves, at first very softly, almost imperceptibly growing louder and louder as it approached determinedly, until it reached its crescendo overhead with deafening purpose, never allowing the possibility of peace.

Opa Muller

Opa Muller, born Gustav Muller, did not play a big role in my life in Halberstadt. He was one of those grumpy old men who had very little to say, and as long as no loud noises or activities interfered with his routine, he kept to himself. He had a prominent nose connected to an extremely large forehead on one end and to an equally large handlebar moustache at the other. He took great care grooming his moustache, proudly waxing it until the ends turned up in perfect points. It appeared to me not to really belong to him but to be another creature entirely, separate from his face. When he spoke, it moved up and down and sometimes sideways.

Opa had an enormous brown leather chair with a reclining back and a footrest that could be lifted. One Christmas my parents surprised him with this vessel from which he surveyed the world. It was made by the finest manufacturer in Berlin, from the highest grade leather, which rendered its deep brown texture soft and velvety smooth. He loved that chair, and no one else was allowed to sit in it.

As far as I could tell, other than his daily walk to the corner bakery for our morning *Brötchen* and his newspaper, he never left that chair except for meals. He had positioned it to face the grand window in the living room, and from there he had a perfect view of the Harz Mountains—a lovely view, especially in winter, when the mountains were covered with snow that shimmered in the sunlight against the purple blue hues of the rock. I always thought it a bit unfair that Opa Muller so thoroughly dominated that window, as it was the best view from the apartment. If I stood in front of it to look out, he would grumble, "Move out of the way, child. You're blocking my light."

One morning when he was sick with his arthritis and could not get out of bed, I snuck into the living room and tested his chair. I lowered myself quietly into its rich folds and silently raised the footrest. A smile crept across my face as I relaxed and looked out upon Opa Muller's world. It was indeed very comfortable, and one could see the whole world, it seemed, from its embracing contours. My grandmother had come in, and I heard her skirts as she passed through the living room. She said nothing to me, but I knew she was chuckling.

All day long, Opa sat reading his paper and doing crossword puzzles. About mid-morning, Opa would doze off with his head leaning back, and from his wide-open mouth a veritable symphony of sounds would emanate. My grandmother found this amusing, but I personally made a note that my husband would never be allowed to be so thoroughly boring. After lunch he would get up to demand his coffee and cake. After which, the crumbs carefully wiped from his mustache, he would return to the chair, turn on the radio that stood on the small side table next to it, and listen to his favorite news program with Herr Fritsch as the commentator.

He listened to every word Herr Fritsch had to say, nodding his head or grunting in agreement to the man's ranting against the enemies of Germany. Herr Fritsch appeared to me to be the stand-in for Göebbels. He approached his subjects with a zeal not always found in other commentators. He spoke of the horrible English or of the Jewish conspiracy to perpetuate the war, or of the greatness of the Führer and all that he did for Germany. My mother could not stand Herr Fritsch. To me his show was simply tedious, filled with pedantic lecturing and grandiose language of German victories in the battlefield. But to my mother he was offensive beyond just boredom; it bothered her beyond my teenage comprehension that her father listened to this man.

My mother would roll her eyes. "Vati, please! Why do you listen to that ridiculous propaganda?" Opa would sit up rigid in the chair, his mustache quivering, and they would engage in a spectacular argument about the Nazis, each one determined to bend the other.

I missed listening to the BBC, although my mother said it was just as well that I did not know what was really going on in the war. But the BBC had other news, not just about the war, news about movie stars, and music, and horse racing, and sports. The German radio was like the German schools: everything was a lesson, and it seemed to me they lectured the adults just as they lectured us at school. Everything was the great Führer this and the great Führer that, and thank goodness we have such a wonderful Führer who loves his people. I stopped listening after the first week with Omi and Opa Muller. I chose instead to glean my news from Tante Lieschen, and from my mother when she visited in person. On the telephone we spoke of school and friends and our health. We certainly never risked discussing the real news because we were never certain whether our calls were private.

Opa Muller rarely spoke to anyone, other than those rare occasions when my mother came to visit, when he would astonish me with the force and speed of his words. It was the only time I ever saw my mother lose her cool. I watched as she paced up and down in front of the leather chair, her color deepening as she argued with him. He responded in kind but never left the chair, so it looked as if my mother was having an argument with the chair itself.

It was the only time I heard my mother speak openly about the Nazis and the war. She was so focused on her father, she forgot about my presence. When it became too bad, Omi would pop her head around the corner from the kitchen and say, "Heidchen, calm down or you will give yourself and your father a heart attack." Sometimes I escaped to the kitchen, where I listened, alert to every word, pretending only to peel potatoes or carrots with my grandmother. I think Omi wanted me to hear the argument and to judge for myself the truth of the matters discussed. She never took sides. Indeed, Omi never really said anything about politics or the Nazis, but somehow I came to understand that she thought my mother raised some good points. In her quiet way she taught me the world turned on the matters of the heart. There were people who were good and helped others, and there were people who helped only themselves. The latter would receive their rewards on earth through force by taking what they wanted, said Omi, but the former would receive their rewards in eternity. "Where you came from does not matter; it is what you are now that counts. What you are now is what you are inside."

I tried to force her to acknowledge that Opa's views differed from her own. "Opa says the Nazis are right! It is the Jews and the English who are responsible for this war. They only look out for themselves, and we must guard against ..."

"Your Opa is entitled to his opinions," she interrupted. "I am not discussing his opinions with you. I am discussing mine."

"But Omi, don't you think Mutti is right to argue with Opa? Maybe he will hear some of what she says."

"No. She is entitled to her opinions, but she is not right to argue so strongly with her father." She paused for a moment and stopped to look at me. "You see, I think it is more about the fact that her father, whom she loves, holds views that she abhors."

I searched her face. She had used the word "abhor," but her face was the same serene mask I had always known. No hint of her own views escaped from those blue eyes surrounded by a map of tiny lines.

"But there is no changing him," she continued. "He believes what he wants, and he hears what he wants, and what your mother fails to realize is that in arguing with him, she only makes him more determined in his views."

"Is that why you never argue with him?"

She nodded her head. "I find that sometimes there is more to be accomplished through silence." Smiling, she reached out for my hand with her soft, warm hand. She jiggled our hands, entwined at the fingers. "Through my silence I can tell him more than your mother's eloquent and impassioned speeches." She laced her arm through mine and quietly changed the subject to my friends, my school, and my ideas for fashion.

Herr Süss's House

I longed to see the house where Vati grew up. Before I left Berlin, I had pressed him for details on how the house looked and what street it was on. He told me the street name was Harmoniestrasse, but claimed not to know the house number. "It was so long ago, Jutta. What does it matter?"

"You lived there for ten years! And I'm living in Halberstadt, so I want to see it."

I couldn't believe Opa Bolle sent Vati away for school after the death of his mother. Vati was only eight years old. He lived with Professor Süss, the headmaster of the boys' school in Halberstadt. I could not imagine being eight years old and moving away from my family. The memory of Grosshartmansdorf and my brief stay at the Baltic still fresh in my mind.

I had been searching for the house, so one day when Omi took me shopping in town after school, I decided to press her. I needed new shoes and a few toiletries that "young ladies need," as Omi put it. We had to walk into the center of Halberstadt to shop, as there were no shops out by our apartment. Omi stood in front of the school, dwarfed by the huge gate, wearing her "town dress" and holding an umbrella. We walked together into town, taking twice as long as I would have taken by myself. Omi, unable to exert herself because of her heart, stopped every once in a while to regain her breath. But I didn't mind the slow pace. I made use of our time alone to prattle on and on about school and my friends. Omi dutifully nodded her head, adding a comment every once in a while to show she was listening. We walked arm in arm along the dirt path that ran the length of the park, listening to the birds sing in the early afternoon sun, and then turned onto Harmoniestrasse to head into town.

"Omi, isn't this the street that Vati lived on with Professor Süss?" I said a bit disingenuously, as I knew perfectly well that it was.

My grandmother looked up from the ground, which she generally studied while walking to make sure she did not trip on any uneven pavement or cobblestones. "Why yes! I believe it is," she said.

I grabbed her hand. "Please, Omi. Show me the house!"

"I don't even know if the house is still there, Jutta. It was so long ago, and ..."

"Of course it's still there, Omi! You know nothing has changed in Halberstadt for a thousand years!"

She walked on. "*Ja*, let's see. It was next to a house with huge windows that bend out. What do you call those windows?"

"Bay windows?" I said helpfully. I was used to finding words for Omi.

"Yes. Thank you," she said, patting my hand. "And it was on the right-hand side of the street," she continued. "Oh, maybe halfway down, I would say."

I glanced ahead. Harmoniestrasse dead-ended into Spiegelstrasse, and I knew Vati had not lived on the other side of Spiegelstrasse. I studied the old houses for a clue that would give away who their previous occupants had been. My grandmother studied a house. "No." She shook her head. "Not this one." She chuckled quietly. "We should have brought your Opa down here with us. He certainly knew the house well enough!" She laughed outright this time. "Oh, how he would complain about having to come and pick your mother up from dinner at Professor Süss's house with 'that boy from Berlin.'"

"That's what he called Vati?"

"Yes! 'That boy from Berlin!' Then he would say, 'All she can talk about is that boy from Berlin! I don't feel like I have a daughter anymore. Does she ever eat dinner with us?' Oh, how he worried about that boy from Berlin taking his daughter away from him." She chuckled again, lost in her memories.

"Well, I guess he was right," I said, searching each house as we walked closer and closer to the end of the street, my concern growing that Omi's memory would fail her.

"Well, he didn't take her away from us, really. He just added to our small family, and now we have a glorious granddaughter as a result." She gave me a small hug. She stopped suddenly and looked across the street. Lifting her arm, she pointed to a medium-sized, two-story house in the medieval half-timber style that the entire block sported. It sat back slightly from the street. The large house next to it did, indeed, have a huge bay window on the second floor.

"But Omi, you said it was on the right!"

"I know I did," she said frowning. She looked up the street and nodded her head toward the opposite end of the street. "That is because we usually came from that end of the street, not the way you and I walked this morning."

I grinned. This was where my father had spent so many years away from his family. I carefully examined the facade of the building. It looked like every other building on the block; there were no clues to tell the stories of its previous inhabitants. Someone had put out boxes of deep red geraniums that hung from each of the upstairs windows.

"Nine in all," I said, counting them.

"Nine what?" asked Omi.

"Nine windows."

I imagined my father leaning out when he heard the doorbell to see his pretty friend standing at the doorstep. I pictured him clattering excitedly down the stairs to greet her, huge smiles on both their faces as their eyes met.

I knew my mother spent many hours studying at the Süss's house. Her girls' school having left her years behind the boys, and as the only girl at the all-boys high school, she was not about to be at the bottom of the class. My father was proud to tell how, in a very short time, my mother not only caught up with the rest of the boys, but surpassed them—thanks in large part to Professor Süss.

"He was a dear man," mused my grandmother.

"Professor Süss?" I asked.

"Yes, such a gentleman, and his wife was a very good cook—a gourmet cook! Oh, how your mother would rave about what fine food she ate at the Süsses'."

"Did that make you feel bad?"

"Yes, a little. But I was glad she was experiencing so many new things."

"What about Opa?"

She laughed. "No. You know your Opa doesn't handle change very well!"

"But doesn't that bother you?"

"We are all different, Jutta."

I shrugged.

"*Ja*. Professor Süss taught both your mother and your father to love classical music and literature. He was a very cultured man."

"Opa Bolle was a cultured man, too."

"Yes, but when your father was little, he was never around. He worked all the time at the factory."

"Is that why he sent Vati away after Oma Bolle died?"

"Yes. And also," she continued, looking at the windows on the second floor, "because your father resembled his mother so. The pain was too great for your Opa."

"Poor Vati!" I couldn't imagine kind, gentle Opa Bolle doing anything so cruel.

"Yes. Then when your Opa was over the pain, when your father was about ten, he wanted him to come home to Berlin, but your father would have none of it. He was happy at Professor Süss's house. It had become home."

"It was because of Professor Süss that Vati wanted to be a play writer and director, wasn't it, Omi?"

"Yes. But your Opa Bolle would have none of it! I remember when Herr Bolle came down for a visit and told his son that he would not provide money for his son to study theater at the university! He would go to law school in Leipzig, and that was the end of it. Your father was outraged and complained bitterly to your mother about his father. But there was nothing he could do about it. So off he went to study law after they graduated from the *Martineums Gymnasium*."

We fell silent, studying the house with its ubiquitous swastika flag hanging above the door. I knew Vati would object to that flag hanging over the threshold of his former home, and I suspected Professor Süss would feel the same.

Lost in our conversation, we had not noticed the woman who opened the front door. "Can I help you?"

"Oh, hello," said my grandmother softly.

The woman did not respond.

"My father used to live here; my grandmother was just showing me which room was his," I said, beaming.

The woman's stern face grew the slightest bit anxious. "Well, surely you have seen enough. Now move on!" she said coldly.

"Her father boarded here when he was a young man and went to the *Martineums Gymnasium*," offered my grandmother soothingly.

The woman softened a bit and nodded her head in understanding. "Oh, I see. Well, anyway, I can't let you in."

"Oh, heavens no! We don't want to come in. We'll be on our way, dear. Don't mind us." Omi smiled kindly at the woman. Omi grabbed my hand and said, "Let's be off, Juttalein." We walked slowly down the street. I turned. The woman remained rooted on her front porch, guarding it possessively with her arms crossed and her hands rubbing away unconsciously at her sleeves.

When we were out of earshot, I whispered, "What was that all about?"

"Oh, never mind, dear."

"She was so unfriendly!"

"Some people just are, dear. They hide things inside that they are unhappy about, things they are ashamed of, and then they take it out on the rest of the world."

Slowly we walked the rest of the way to town, taking our time in each store until Omi was satisfied that we had found all we needed. We gingerly maneuvered along the Hoherweg, the road behind the *Domplatz*, careful to avoid the pockets where cobblestones had come loose.

Omi suddenly turned to me. "Listen, dear. I want to take a moment in the *Dom*. Why don't you go visit Tante Lieschen and get yourself a treat? I'll meet you over there in a bit." She squeezed my hand and smiled.

Café Deesen

I sometimes accompanied Omi into town for her prayers, mostly because I loved to walk through the old town with its stately buildings and lovely formal squares, especially the *Domplatz* in front of the *Dom*, the cathedral. Omi and I would slowly walk up its curved steps and through the massive wood doors. Our shoes clicked quietly on the marble floor until we reached the tenth row and bowed to the altar before slipping into the pew. We always sat in the tenth row, but I never asked her why. I sat next to her, absorbing the beauty of the old gothic church built almost a thousand years ago, its arches perfectly formed above my head. I tried to imagine what it was like for the men who built this magnificent place. The organ soared into the ceiling, hundreds of pipes surrounded by intricately carved wooden angels, and the stained glass windows cast shadows of blue and green on us in the late afternoon light. The quiet, cool interior eased my spirits, and here inside this building I believed I was safe. I usually stayed for twenty minutes or so before I silently slipped out, leaving my grandmother to her prayers. Refreshed, I would skip down the steps and turn to the left, following the tiny old medieval street around the side of the church, back toward the *Martinikirche* and the *Fischmarkt*, where Café Deesen dominated the square.

"Are you sure you don't mind, Omi?" I asked, studying her face.

"No. No." She patted my arm. "You go on. Besides, you're too young to feel the need of prayer, dear," she added with a twinkle in her eye.

I kissed her on the cheek, turned, and headed for Café Deesen. I stopped before turning the corner, just in time to see my grandmother slowly maneuver up the steps at the front of the church in the manner of the old, letting both feet rest on each step. I worried about Omi. Lately she was going at least twice a week to the *Dom* to pray, and not just for a short time; she was usually there for thirty minutes to an hour. Always, she said, she was praying for Germany.

Opa Muller scoffed at this. "What is prayer going to do?"

Omi would just smile and say, "Well, Gustav, it can't hurt." And then she would bend down and kiss her cantankerous husband soundly on the forehead before she retrieved her umbrella from the coat closet for the walk to the cathedral. I noticed that about Omi. Behind the soft exterior, she had the strength of the thin willow branches that danced in the strong winds of Berlin—the wind never able to snap them. She rarely insisted on having her way, but if she made up her mind about something, there was no moving her.

———

Tante Lieschen was a small, friendly woman with an ample bosom and a welcome smile. She wore her hair tied neatly in a bun on top of her head, "so it never falls into anyone's cake," she said. I knew a long, warm hug, the kind that would crush the life out of me when I was smaller, accompanied by a loving smile and any treat I wanted, waited for me at Café Deesen. She wore glasses that hid intelligent, attentive eyes that could bore into you and read your thoughts, no matter how hard you tried to hide them. She had a small, perfectly straight nose, just like all the members of my mother's family, and not for the first time, I wished that that gene pool had had a little more dominance over my father's large-nosed family. Her chin was more pronounced than my grandmother's, and she often stuck it forward when trying to make a particularly controversial point, as if to say, "Go ahead, challenge me." She did not get along particularly well with my grandfather—neither was shy about expressing their views. But I adored her.

I ran through the *Holzmarkt*. Its giant fountain spouted water, wetting the cobblestones all around. I continued past the statue of Roland and into the *Fischmarkt* where, on the second floor of an old medieval building, I entered Café Deesen. Its windows supported by half-timbered beams and filled with huge flower baskets, the café ran the full length of the second floor. The windows wrapped around the side, allowing a view of the *Martinikirche* and, in the distance, the very top spire of the *Dom*.

Tante Lieschen and her husband established Café Deesen together, but the success of the business really rested on her capable, friendly shoulders. Everyone came to Café Deesen because of Tante Lieschen. People flocked to her because she made them feel comfortable, and a few moments with her could brighten your day. The fact that the cake was good helped, but customers would still have come, no matter how the cake tasted, just to chat with Tante Lieschen.

Café Deesen was, for me, like one of those salons in Paris in the nineteenth century, a place where I could talk about anything I wanted: politics, the arts, and what life was like in Halberstadt. No matter what I wanted to talk about, Tante Lieschen always bent an interested ear to me. She would talk to me about anything—the same way she talked to adults—never telling me I was too young for a topic. Her only precaution was to reserve a table in the corner, away from prying ears, where she leaned forward so that our faces were only inches apart.

I headed up the stairs to the second floor and opened the glass door to the café, waiting for the familiar tinkle of the bells that hung from the inside handle. Tante Lieschen was chatting with a customer across the room; she looked up at the sound and stopped midstream, announcing loudly, "Look! It's my favorite niece, Juttalein!" Turning back to the customer, she said with emphasis, "Isn't she a lovely girl?"

I grinned at her and waved. The customer nodded and smiled at me.

"Well, I'll talk to you later, Frau Schmidt. I have a very important customer to attend to!" She waved me to her with both arms outstretched, practically suffocating me in her embrace. Kissing me roundly on each cheek she said, "So, is the Omi praying again?"

"Yes. The second time this week," I said, chuckling.

"Good! We all need it!" She motioned me to a table and sat down across from me. "Now, first of all, what do you want? Your usual?"

I grinned. "Yes, please."

"Heidi!" she called to the waitress in the red dress, its seams vulnerable, stretching and pulling with her every step. I admired the craftsmanship that held the over-taxed dress together. "Please bring Fräulein Bolle her usual fare," announced Tante Lieschen. My usual fair was hot chocolate and a slice of the most delicious hazelnut cream cake ever made.

"And you, Frau Deesen?" asked Heidi, bending over as she placed forks and napkins on the table, giving me a full view of her ample bosom.

"Since you ask, maybe I will have a coffee, and add just a little touch of whipping cream," she said, winking at Heidi.

Heidi smiled and left with our order. She knew that a little touch meant a rather generous scoop to Tante Lieschen, who reached across the table and grabbed my hand, beaming at me. "Now, tell me what you and your Omi have been up to in the city today."

I showed her our purchases, and she was duly impressed. She listened attentively as I prattled on about the trivial things in my life, my friends at school, and the latest on Opa Muller and his addiction to crossword puzzles. After a few minutes I fell silent. I turned to study the activity in the *Fischmarkt* below; an old woman pushed a cart filled with vegetables. She struggled as she pushed it over the uneven cobblestones, the tire catching in the crevices.

Tante Lieschen cocked her head. "What is it? What are you thinking about, my dear?" I turned back to face her. She studied me, her kind blue eyes hidden behind glasses with dark brown frames.

"Oh, it's nothing, really." I stirred my hot chocolate. Her hand covered mine. Without looking up I said, "It's just that Omi showed me where Vati used to live."

"Oh! Excellent! You've wanted to see that house, haven't you?"

"Yes. And it was a beautiful old house, the half-timbered kind, just as I imagined it..." I trailed off, not entirely sure what was bothering me about the house. Tante Lieschen continued to look at me. I looked down at my napkin. "Well, it's just that while we were looking at the house, this woman came out and asked us if she could help us."

"Sour cream cheesecake with extra whipped cream on top," she interrupted.

"Excuse me?" I glanced around, startled, thinking she was calling out an order.

"The lady who owns the house. She comes in all the time, and that's what she orders, dear."

"Oh. Well, sour makes sense, because let me tell you, she was so unfriendly."

"Really?"

"Yes, especially after I told her Vati had lived there. She practically ran us off!"

"Oh well. That's because she probably thought that your Vati was part of the Süss family."

"What would be wrong with that?" I asked.

She bent forward and lowered her voice. "They were Jewish, dear." Sensing that I still wasn't quite getting it she said, "Your father lived with a Jewish family for ten years. She probably thought that you were Jewish."

My eyes widened, and my mouth fell open! "Oh!"

Tante Lieschen nodded her head and looked around before she continued, her voice barely audible now. "Yes, 'oh' is right. And not only that, they stole that house from Herr Süss, and she probably thought you were there to reclaim it!" Tante Lieschen sat back in her chair, chuckling.

"What do you mean, 'they stole the house?'" I whispered, my interest keen now.

She bent closer to me again. "The Nazis, of course. They stole all the houses of the Jews who fled, and then gave them to their party chiefs." She waved her hand vaguely in the air. "I forget what that woman's husband is, but he is something big in their network."

"When? When did this happen?"

She paused for a moment, and for the first time I thought that Tante Lieschen might not tell me something. But after a moment, she continued. "Well, let's see. It would have been 1938. Sometime after November ninth."

"You remember the exact date?" I said incredulously.

"Yes I do, because it was after *Kristallnacht*. I remember it like it was yesterday." She looked out the window. "I can still see your father walking across the square looking sadder than I have ever seen a man look." She shook her head, remembering. "My God, I thought something had happened to your mother—that maybe she left him or something. He came in for a little pick-me-up before he returned to Berlin, and he ..."

"Wait!" I held up my hand dramatically. Tante Lieschen blinked. "My father was here? Here in Halberstadt after *Kristallnacht*? But why?"

"To help Professor Süss and his family, of course," she said so quietly that I had to lean even closer to hear her. "But they had already left. The house was abandoned. Herr Süss was like a father to your Vati."

I nodded, every muscle taut as I leaned in so close that our noses almost touched.

"Your father didn't know if they had left on their own or been sent away. He needed the comfort of knowing they were safe. He was devastated."

My cake arrived on the plump arm of Heidi, and we waited in silence as Heidi arranged our plates. Reaching in her pocket, Tante Lieschen handed Heidi the ration card she always kept for me—where she got these extra cards, I have no idea, but I was glad she had them. Heidi punched the card and handed it back to Tante Lieschen. Heidi walked away, her shoes easing out air like the folds of an accordion.

I looked up at Tante Lieschen, who seemed to know what was going through my head. "Yes. He came alone. The one and only time he came to Halberstadt alone after he married your mother."

A chill ran through me as I thought of that flag hanging over what once was the Süss house. A house filled with learning and music and culture, and now filled with what? I couldn't imagine. My grandmother's words echoed in my ears: "Some people hide things inside that they are unhappy about, things they are ashamed of ..." It all made sense to me now. The horrified look on the woman's face, the anxiety in her eyes. Tante Lieschen stirred her coffee absentmindedly.

"Where did they go?"

She set the spoon down. "He never heard from them again."

"Now, listen. I told you, not a word to anyone—not your Omi, not your mother, and certainly not your father." She looked at me, her eyes drilling into my soul.

I held up my hand. "I promise," I said gravely.

"Good, because he would be unhappy if he knew I told you." She frowned at me over her glass. "And he is right. The less you know, the better."

A customer called out "Heil Hitler" as he left the café. The bells of the door jingled as it closed behind him. Tante Lieschen made a face of distaste. "He is a big Nazi, too," she said under her breath. I turned to look at him, but his back was to me as he descended the steps down to the *Fischmarkt*. He was tall and appeared to be fairly young—certainly younger than my parents. As he reached the bottom, just ahead of him, across the square, I saw my grandmother emerging from around the corner of the *Martinikirche*. I watched her make her way with slow, careful steps, a contrast to his crisp ones. They passed each other, and I knew by the nod of her head she had greeted him with her usual polite, "*Guten Nachmittag.*" I wondered how they each regarded the other: these two Germans from such different worlds, two different generations colliding in the square behind the *Martinikirche*.

Tante Lieschen saw my grandmother, too. "Let's lighten the mood a little, shall we, so your grandmother does not think we have been discussing anything too serious."

Omi continued up the steps, her hand balanced on the rail for support. She moved in sharp contrast to Tante Lieschen, whose gait was always at top speed. Only two years separated them in age, but it seemed much more as I watched Omi. I worried about Omi. I knew she had a heart condition, but today she seemed to move much slower than normal. I made a mental note to help her more around the house. Tante Lieschen pushed her chair back and scurried off to the kitchen; I knew a box of cakes would emerge with her. Omi saw me in the window and smiled at me. I waved back and hurried to finish my cake. She would not want to stay. It was almost five o'clock, and she would want to return home to prepare dinner for Opa. She entered through the tinkling glass door just as Tante Lieschen came from the kitchen. They greeted each other with the warmth of two sisters who have always been close. I stood up and put on my coat, buttoning it at the collar against the evening chill that I knew would descend on us as we walked slowly home.

"Did you pray for all of us?" asked Tante Lieschen cheerfully.

"I did!" answered Omi, smiling at her sister and kissing her on the cheek.

"Good! Now take these home to the Opa," said Tante Lieschen, handing me a small package when I was done with my coat.

"*Danke, Sehr! Lieschen!* But that is too much!" protested Omi. "You know he shouldn't have all these sweets!"

From behind my right ear I heard a man clear his throat. "I'm sure you asked for their card, Frau Deesen?"

We turned toward the voice; it belonged to a young man in full uniform, the armband a stark reminder of his power. "You just mind your business, young man," snapped Tante Lieschen, "and don't be telling an old lady how to do her job!"

He smirked but said nothing. A tense silence had fallen over the café. Turning her back on him, a clear statement that she intended to waste no more time on him, Tante Lieschen hooked her arm through mine and escorted us out the door. We stood outside on the top step. "You better be careful what you say, Lieschen!" whispered Omi.

Her sister scoffed, waving her hand. "My biggest customers are Nazis! Do you think they are going to shut me down because some young idiot says I didn't ask my sister for her ration card? Let him try it."

Omi smiled. "I wouldn't want to tangle with you!"

I giggled.

Tante Lieschen smiled and hugged me, wrinkling up her nose. "*Ja*, just let him try it! No more sour cream cheesecake because Frau Deesen has been denounced! I don't think that is in their interest. And we all know they only do that which is very much in their personal interest."

With a firm kiss for both of us, she said goodbye. We walked along in silence in the dwindling light of the day, the chilly air soaking through our clothes. I looked at my watch: almost 5:15. I hooked arms with Omi and held on to her for the walk home.

Carla

I came home from school to find a package for me waiting on the table by the front door. The postmark said Berlin. I ripped the brown paper off with great excitement, uncovering my father's small but distinct handwriting on his Grieneisen stationary. Underneath his note were three books: two by Carl May and, to my amazement, *Gone with the Wind* by Margaret Mitchell. Had my mother changed her mind? Or had my father not realized that my mother had specifically told me not to read that book? I had told my father I could not find any good books in Halberstadt. I marveled that with his hectic schedule at the factory, he took the time to send me books—books he knew I could not purchase in Halberstadt. Most bookstores, especially in a small town like Halberstadt, were carefully monitored, but not those in Berlin. I went to find Omi in the kitchen, where she was preparing my lunch.

"Omi, look what Vati sent me!"

"Show me, *Liebling*!" said Omi, wiping her hands on her apron.

I displayed the titles to her one by one, placing each one on the counter separately, giving her a moment to adjust her vision through her bifocals. She hugged me around the waist as she read their titles out loud. She nodded her head in approval. I waited for her say something about *Gone with the Wind*, but she did not seem to recognize the book.

"These are wonderful. You'll love *Winnetou*. It takes place in America!"

"Really?" I smiled. "I can hardly wait to start reading."

"Not until your homework is done, young lady," she said, hugging me to her. "First things first! Go wash up and come eat." She had made a plum tart for dessert, and I hurried, my mouth watering, the smell of the tart lingering in the air. I loved Omi's plum tarts filled with rich, tangy plums from the tree in the garden and surrounded by a fluffy crust that caressed my mouth, the purple color from the plums bleeding onto the corners. The crop had come early this year, and we had been picking them all week.

I ran out to the living room. "Opa!" I called. "Did you see what Vati sent me?"

He peeked out from behind his newspaper for a moment.

"Vati says it's hard to find good books because they use all the paper in Germany for their propaganda and there is none left for decent reading!"

Opa raised his eyebrows but only said, "Really? Does he say that?"

I nodded my head.

Opa grunted. "Well, go on child. Wash up. You'll starve a man taking so long." Popping back behind his newspaper, he snapped the fold and continued to read. I looked at Opa's distinctly round figure and thought it would take a lot to starve him.

Again and again, the sound. I cover my ears, pressing my fingers deep into them to block it, but the sound grows louder and with each second more distinct. I open my eyes, and the endless blackness of my bedroom assaults me. I shut them tight. Must be British; only the British fly at night. The sound draws closer—bombers flying high in the sky, heading for Berlin. The buzz low, barely perceptible, still several miles from Halberstadt—even so, they woke me. I glance at the clock, barely able to make out its outline on my bedside table, its face too dark for me to read. No light comes through the curtains, no moon. Of course not, they only fly when the moon is covered. Shivering in the cold, I pull the duvet up to my chin and cover my head with my pillow, but the sound, the horrible, omnipresent sound penetrates, the layers of cloth and goose feathers never enough to keep it from climbing through me, shaking my bed and windows until the vibrations make my head spin.

Like a pesky mosquito carrying a deadly disease, the buzz drills through my pillow and duvet, and it makes my stomach drop, for I know it will only be a matter of minutes before the first group hits Berlin. I pray and pray they will hit the center of Berlin and not the outskirts—please don't hit Dahlem—knowing that I am praying for someone else's death, some other family's misfortune. And after I pray for that, I pray for God to forgive my selfishness. "Please, God, forgive me, but it would be a lie for me not to admit that this is what I want... unless you can make them run out of gas or crash—but then forgive me for praying for their death... or make the bomb chutes not open." And then, just to be safe, I go back to my original prayer.

The buzzing sound comes in waves, sometimes fifteen minutes apart, sometimes thirty, and sometimes as much as an hour apart. It is always the same. I know there are hundreds of them in wave after wave. Will they come back this way? Sometimes they do. How do they live with themselves? Knowing they have killed hundreds of people: old women and men, young mothers and their children. In my mind I hear the sound of the bombs dropping and the crackling of fires, able to destroy in a matter of minutes buildings that have stood for hundreds of years. I hear screams rising in the night as mothers and wives and sisters try to account for loved ones lost in the fire, and I see them watching helplessly as their homes, hit by the deadly cargo, burn to the ground. It happened to our neighbors—not a direct hit, but portions of a bomb hit their home, catching it on fire. My father and the other men in the neighborhood did what they could to try and save the house, but the entire front half burned to the ground. I remember the sounds of the bombs dropping on Berlin, their explosions sounding like the kettledrums on my father's classical recordings, distinguished only by the terrible whining sound as they fall from the plane and then, after a few seconds, explode—massive, heavy, and without mercy. I shiver in the dark, remembering the whine of the bombs, the sound of certain death—the sound that means somebody will die. Perhaps somebody I knew, perhaps somebody I met on the street, or in the subway, or perhaps it would be a sales lady at *KadeWe*, or the policeman who directed traffic at the light at Potsdamer Platz. But one thing was certain: that sound meant that some of them would be dead.

I try to think of other things, anything: the buttercups dotting Mutti's lawn in the spring, the icy blue waters of Berchtesgaden, but always the images creep in, and then the sound—an endless buzzing—and then suddenly, abruptly, it stops. I wait, barely breathing, listening for the next group, but this time they don't come. I drift to sleep, the images and sounds penetrating my dreams. My eyes flutter open, and I realize they were not dreams. I hear the sound again, rousing me from my sleep, but with less force and from the opposite direction—fewer planes flying overhead. Had Goring's defense system caused a few casualties? Rumors swirled that no defense systems remained in northwestern Germany. I turn on the light: three o'clock in the morning; I would have to get up at six. I grab my book. I don't want to think about it. I don't want to imagine smoke drifting to the sky and smell the stench of broken sewer lines. I have to block Berlin out of my mind, but I can't. The images flash through my mind, and the words on the page disappear before the deadly, sickening images.

Opa had heard about it on the radio. Phosphorus bombs, he called them, bombs that left entire city blocks devastated by fire, needing only the slightest breath of wind to spread their destruction further. I read letters and not words, no meaning. I close my eyes and try again: buttercups, daisies, fields of yellow and white daisies spreading for as far as the eye can see; water, mountains, Sasha playing in the grass. No use. I get up and do jumping jacks and stretches, anything to keep my mind off Berlin.

My mother will call later to let us know that everything is all right—that they are safe. I tell myself this with certainty. If they hit the telephone lines, she may not call for a day or two, but she will call. I punch my palm with my fist. She will call. Opa's radio will shout out: "The Führer's air defense system has saved the majority of Berlin from the mass destruction that the evil acts of a savage enemy tried to level on us." And Opa will say, "See, my dear? Nothing to worry about. The great German *Luftwaffe* has protected your parents and Berlin." And I will pray it is the truth. But I know I will have to wait for the real numbers when my mother calls. Or maybe my father will call first from the office; they often repair the business lines first.

Carla looked startled that I was ready on time for the walk to school in the morning. I noted it was 7:20 am according to the large pewter clock Omi kept in the kitchen to make sure she had Opa's dinner on the table by 6:30 pm exactly. We didn't need to leave for another ten minutes. Usually Carla came ten minutes early. While I rushed to my room to finish my hair and collect my books, she would take my place at the table and Omi would offer her the rest of the bread and, if we had it, an egg. I don't think Carla's aunt had much money, and the ration cards from the government bought less and less. My grandparents had extra because my parents sent them money, so my grandmother fed Carla whenever she could.

They would go through the same dance each morning. My grandmother would offer Carla my chair and something to eat, and Carla would say, "No thank you, Frau Muller. I have eaten."

And then my grandmother would say, "But surely you have room for a little more. It will take Jutta a few minutes anyway, so come sit down."

And then Carla would say with feigned reluctance, "Well, if you insist. Thank you, Frau Muller." I always smiled, knowing she would eat everything placed in front of her, as if she had had no breakfast at all, and finish by picking up the crumbs on her plate with her fingers just as I walked back in the kitchen.

I pushed my chair back as soon as I heard her at the front door. Omi stopped me and told me to wait a moment. It had been a tense morning, with Omi trying her best to act unconcerned but unable to hide the worried look that creased the tiny folds around her eyes. I sat back down and waved to Carla through the window. She let herself in, and I heard her greet the back of Opa's chair as she passed through the dining room on her way to the kitchen.

He responded as usual, his head tilted up to the ceiling so he could be heard over the back of the chair. "Good morning, Fräulein Carla!" But this morning, it sounded the slightest bit forced.

Carla looked disappointed that I was dressed and my books were set out, ready to go. I got up and announced, "I'm ready to go. Aren't you surprised?"

"Very!" she said, her eyes wide. Her nostrils quivered as the smell of the rolls reheating in the oven swirled around us in the small kitchen.

My grandmother had anticipated Carla's disappointment and said, "Sit, dear. It's still early, and you don't need to rush off to school."

Carla smiled and did as she was told. We watched Omi place a roll with a touch of jam on a plate with tiny pink and blue flowers forming a border along the edge. She set the plate in front of Carla. "Oh, really, Frau Muller. You mustn't bother!"

"Heavens, it is no bother at all! Now hush up and eat."

I smiled. I needed the certainty of the exchange this morning, more than ever.

She ate with gusto, licking her fingers when she was finished. Omi chuckled and kissed me on the head. "Now go and have a wonderful day at school."

"Bye, Omi."

"Bye, Frau Muller, and thank you."

She waved to us as we bustled out the door. I called goodbye to Opa in the living room. He grunted a barely audible goodbye from the chair.

"Why are you so efficient this morning, Jutta?" asked Carla as we went out the door.

"Oh God, the bombers woke me last night, all night long. And then I couldn't go back to sleep, so I read, and then I just got up and decided to get ready for school."

"Yes. I heard them, too."

"Don't they terrify you?" I asked anxiously. She shrugged her shoulders as we descended the stairs to the street, but did not respond.

"It's horrible lying there listening to them, knowing they are heading toward your family and home." Tears sprang to my eyes. Carla did not notice; she was concentrating on the ground as we walked. Words poured out as I tried to explain. Still she said nothing. I stopped walking. She continued on for a few steps and then turned in that funny, stiff way of hers. Our eyes held each other's for a moment. "Why do you never say anything when I talk to you about this? Don't you care?"

Tiny muscles around her eyes and lips worked furiously, but she held my stare for what seemed like forever. Suddenly she stepped forward, grabbed my arm, and dragged me around the corner into a small alleyway. Too startled to say anything, I tripped and caught my book bag as we rounded the corner. She glanced quickly in both directions to make sure nobody was coming. "Carla, what are you doing?" I asked, alarm edging my voice. With a mixture of horror and fascination, I watched her set her books down and pull the ends of her shirt out of her skirt. She began to unbutton her shirt. I couldn't imagine what she might be doing. "Carla, what are you doing?" I asked again, sweat forming on my upper lip. I crossed my arms in front of my chest. She did not respond; instead she pulled her arm out of her shirt and held my eyes again, steadily and without embarrassment. And then I saw it, from the neck down, beginning at the shoulder: the skin on her arm, all the way to her wrist, was so scarred and pinched and discolored that I didn't at first recognize it as skin. It was raised and pinched into bright pink and abnormally white clusters, like spoiled milk disrupted by a spoon; the once-perfect, smooth white surface formed discolored folds of thick, yellowish white milk. This was Carla's skin.

"Oh my God, Carla!" I cried, my hand clapped over my mouth reflexively in horror. She pulled her camisole down so that I could see that the scarring continued down past her shoulder and breast, covering half of her body. My hand still over my mouth, I tore my eyes away from her abused skin and looked up at her face.

"This," she said, nodding downward with her head as a single tear spilled onto the scarred skin of her shoulder. "This is why I don't talk about it, Jutta."

My eyes traveled from her tear-stained face to her scarred body and back again.

"I lived in Berlin, Jutta. I lived in central Berlin on Hirten Strasse near the Alexanderplatz, where my house and the entire block were destroyed by a bomb raid one night." I thought of my prayer and looked down in shame as she continued. "I lost both of my parents in that attack, and my home. The fire was so intense that I passed out in the basement. I am only alive because Herr Zimmer, our sixty-five-year old neighbor, came down to the basement to look for us." She lifted her head to the sky to try and stop the flow of tears, and then carefully began to button her shirt back up. "So you ask if the bombers terrify me?" she said, looking me squarely in the face. "You cannot imagine what I see and feel when I hear the sound of them overhead, night after night; it all comes back to me like a recurring nightmare. I can feel and smell my skin burning, and I see the remains of my parents' charred bodies as Herr Zimmer carries me up the basement steps. I see the apartment across the street on fire as he carries me through the huge hole blown into the side of our house, and I hear myself say 'No, don't leave them. They're not dead! They can't be dead!' And I hear him respond, 'Hush, child. They are gone.' And then I hear my wails like the sound of a wounded animal as he carries me to the street crowded with women and children and old men, all crying and wailing like I am. My mind seems to float outside of my body as I watch Herr Zimmer and I watch myself crying, great streams of tears streaking down my face, and I am trying to get free to save my parents, who are still inside what remains of our house. I see soot-covered faces and hear cries of terror as whole sides of buildings collapse on top of people who thought they had escaped the attack of the bombs only to lose their lives to the fires and the crashing walls that follow after the bombs are finished. And then I pass out and wake up in a hospital, where I remain for two months with no visitors other than Herr Zimmer because all my family is dead." She paused for a moment, catching her breath. "I live this each time I hear the bombers, Jutta."

I realized that I had been crying and shaking my head in disbelief. I dropped my book bag and hugged her to me as hard as I could, our tears mixing together as our cheeks pressed against each other's face.

"I am so sorry, Carla." I felt her tears on my neck. "I am so sorry!" I said again.

"You didn't know." She pulled away and wiped her eyes with her sleeve.

We said nothing for a moment, and then she whispered, "I can't tell you how often I have wished that I were dead."

"No! You can't talk like that!" I shouted, pulling away and grabbing her face in my hands.

She jerked free from me, and I dropped my hands to her shoulders. "Of course I can talk like that. What is there left for me? Why was I the one left behind?"

"When did this happen?" I asked, my arm still across her shoulder while my other hand stroked her hair.

"About six months ago. I stayed in the hospital for two months, and then Herr Zimmer took care of me until we could get the paperwork and the money to bring me to my aunt's house here in Halberstadt." She wiped her eyes with the end of her shirt before she tucked it back into her skirt. I fumbled through my book bag for the handkerchief Omi always shoved in it for me. I handed it to her.

"No; you use it first. I need it for my nose," she said, making a face of disgust.

I wiped my eyes with it and then handed it to her. She blew her nose loudly several times, the sound abruptly cutting into the morning air. After wiping her nose with care to make sure there was nothing left on it, she put the handkerchief in her book bag.

"I'll wash it and bring it back tomorrow."

"Oh, don't worry about it."

She took a sharp breath. "Well, we had better get going. I'm sure we're late for school." She grabbed her book bag, allowing me to see a slight grimace as she heaved it onto her wounded shoulder with her good arm. Without waiting for me, she walked back the way we had come, down the dark alley. Bits of dirt and moss stuck to the bottom of her book bag. I watched her walk. Her skinny legs, no bigger than two sticks, moved stiffly, and her shoulders, hunched over from the weight of her book bag, looked sad and vulnerable. I picked up my book bag with ease, without pain, without a grimace, and followed her out of the alley.

I was ashamed; it had never occurred to me to ask Carla why she was in Halberstadt. I just assumed her family had sent her to escape the bombs, just like mine had. In the back of my mind I had been conscious that Carla always wore long-sleeved shirts. I had thought it odd that even on warm days she wore long sleeves, and she never seemed to use her right arm for much, but I assumed it was because she was left-handed.

"Thank you for telling me, Carla."

She glanced over at me and smiled, but my face caught her attention, for her eyebrows shot high up onto her forehead. "Don't we both look a sight!" she said, looking at my red-rimmed eyes and swollen nose. We both laughed and shrugged our shoulders. The laugh felt good after the tears, and I grabbed her hand, and we walked to school in silence holding hands. So many tears were shed at school, tears for fathers lost or brothers lost, or relatives in other cities lost or left homeless, that no one would notice.

He Looks so Normal

"They say he is responsible for removing all the Jews from Halberstadt." She nodded toward a man sitting in the corner by himself, sipping his coffee and reading a newspaper. I leaned around her to have a better look. He just looked like anybody's father, sitting there in his neat uniform with his shoes shining brightly, their black, heavily polished surface reflecting the café light, and his hair clipped neatly around his ears. He wore his hair combed straight back from his forehead; I guessed he used a lot of the same pomade Opa Muller used on his mustache, for his hair stood up a good two inches above his forehead before it curved back to meet his skull.

Tante Lieschen kicked me under the table. "Stop it! He'll notice we're talking about him, and that can do us no good. It is best to act as if these types don't exist."

I drew my head back and sipped my hot chocolate. I studied its pale color. Over the past year I noticed it had become weaker and weaker, more milk than chocolate, but it was still good. "But what does he do with them? I mean, where does he send them?"

She shrugged. "*Ja,* at first he just bothered them. You know, sent his goons around terrifying them—taunting them in the street, making it difficult for them to run a business, asking people not to buy from a Jew, and that sort of thing. Many of them left on their own."

"Where did they go?"

"Who knows?" She thought for a moment, the wrinkles creasing around her blue eyes. "Well, I do know of one family that went to Holland."

"I would go to America, Tante Lieschen. That is where I want to live one day."

She set down her coffee and looked at me with one eyebrow raised. "What? And leave all your friends and family?"

"Well, I would go first and then make it possible for you all to come."

"I see," she said quietly. I leaned around her again to get another view. He looked so normal. He put down his newspaper and was examining his bill. Tante Lieschen kicked me again, and I jerked back. "What about those who didn't leave on their own?"

"Well, they began by trumping up charges against them—mostly the men at first."

"That's terrible."

"Yes, of course it is! And then they stopped bothering with the evidence and a trial at all. They just arrested them for being Jewish!" She turned at the sound of the cash register opening—the Nazi officer stood there. He was tall, at least six feet, I guessed. He was broad shouldered. His pants were tucked precisely into his boots, and he shook his leg to brush some crumbs off. He paid his bill, clicked his heels, and said, "*Danke.*" I couldn't take my eyes off him. Again, I thought he looked so normal, like a banker or accountant or lawyer, perhaps— not at all like I would have imagined. He turned to go. He smiled and nodded at Tante Lieschen, resting his eyes only briefly on me as his glance focused on her. My skin crawled. It was the eyes!

"Frau Deesen." He bowed his head slightly to say goodbye.

She returned the gesture, and he exited her establishment. I noticed that voices that had been soft and restrained before were now loud and uninhibited. My aunt turned back to me. "You noticed?"

"What?"

"People don't talk around them. The moment he left, you could feel the difference, couldn't you?"

I nodded my head, still trying to figure out what bothered me about those eyes.

"Tante Lieschen, did you see his eyes?"

"I don't know. I guess. Blue, aren't they?"

"Yes, they were blue, but there was something about them ..." I took a sip of my milk and thought for a moment. "Like there was nobody behind those eyes—just emptiness." I stirred my milk, hoping to capture those few particles of chocolate that had settled to the bottom. I raised my gaze to meet hers. She studied me, her head tipped to one side, but she said nothing. "Well, where did he send them?" I asked after a moment.

"You mean the Jews?"

I nodded.

"Sent off to camps somewhere in the east. I don't know that much about it. The ones they charged with crimes were sent to camps outside of Berlin."

"Are they still in those camps?"

"Yes, I think so." She looked out the window again, her mood suddenly depressed. This was not the usual cheerful Tante Lieschen. I said nothing, not wanting to interrupt her thoughts. She took off her glasses and rubbed her eyes with one hand, using her thumb and middle finger.

"Opa says they live like kings in these camps. It's like the German people have to pay for the Jews to go to a resort and live a better life than we have."

Tante Lieschen snorted and rolled her eyes. "If your Opa could be any more ignorant he would be a toad." I laughed at this image. "God forgive me, but what my sister ever saw in that man!"

"Well, that's what he tells me."

"He believes all their propaganda; he never questions a word of it. But one day he will be in for a rude shock, poor man." She shook her head and stirred her coffee. Leaning across the table, she whispered, "Nobody talks about these things, Jutta. It is against the law to do so. So don't discuss it, *ja?*"

I nodded.

"It is very difficult to know what is really going on because people can't write these things in letters, or the censors will find out, and they can't say these things on the telephone, or the censors will find out. So unless you go and visit someone who lives around these places, it's hard to know what is really going on."

She thought for a moment, her expression softening. "He is not a bad man, your Opa; he just never reaches below the surface, so he is perfect for them. But you know what they say ... " She looked at me with a twinkle in her eye, and I shrugged my shoulders. "If you live with your head always in the sand, your backside will always be exposed." And then she made a gesture with her hand. I burst out laughing, and several people turned to look at us. Tante Lieschen patted my hand as she pushed her chair back and rose wearily from the table. I was weary, too. She had burdened me, and for once I wished she had refused to answer my question.

Bombs

The first year I lived with my grandmother, I saw my mother at Christmas and Easter and for a few weeks in the summer. Vati came only for Christmas and one weekend. Mutti wanted to come every month, but this was impossible, as the bombs continued to disrupt the train lines. She often had to cancel her trip or could not get the papers to travel. Increasingly the Nazis limited travel to essential personnel only. By 1944, the bombs rained down so consistently my mother could only come twice, and there was no possibility of my coming home for Christmas. I missed her terribly, even though Omi tried to make up for her absence. She was so kind and loving that sometimes I felt guilty for missing my mother and father.

Frau Grabber was in the middle of discussing the unification of Germany when it came again. She stopped mid-sentence and listened, her head cocked to the side and her right ear turned up toward the ceiling, her eyes cast down to the floor in concentration. We held our breath, and then we heard it, too. Frau Grabber said nothing. She simply listened to the sound as it grew more and more distinct.

"There must be thousands of them this time," I whispered to the girl next to me.

She nodded her head in silence. We knew death awaited our fellow Germans somewhere, most likely in Berlin. As the first wave flew directly over us, the intensity of the sound drew us out of our seats and to the window. Fascinated and at the same time horrified, we stood by the window in a single row, searching. At first we saw nothing; we only heard the sound, constant, low, and unending. And then in the distance I saw them, hundreds of them flying in formation in their tight little clusters, slowly growing larger and larger until they created macabre shadows that flitted about the schoolyard, blocking the cleansing power of the sun. They were flying very high, and I knew that meant they were Americans and they were heading to Berlin.

I stood on my tiptoes and craned my neck to look over all the heads next to me and find Carla's brown head. She was a few feet down from me. Our eyes met in understanding. The sound intensified, a low, eerie rumbling that gained strength as the density of the planes overhead grew to full force. Our windows began to vibrate, at first subtly, only my cheek pressed against the glass detecting it, but then with increasing force, and I pulled away so the sound did not hurt my ears. I raised my eyes to the blue sky and saw them streaking across the sky, their propellers turning in perfect rhythm, and so many!

"My God, there must be thousands this time!" I said again. Poor Berlin! I prayed for my parents' safety. Thank God they live on the outskirts of Berlin. My mind flashed on Carla even as I thought it. I put my hands to my ears and pressed my eyes shut; somewhere in Berlin, someone I knew, or had passed on the street, would die in a matter of minutes. How long would it take them? Please stop them!

I opened my eyes, and the room began to spin. I staggered back to my seat and sat with my head on my desk. My heart was pounding; I felt it in my chest, in my ears. My hands dripped from sweat, and my wet armpits made my shirt cling to my skin, and suddenly the smell of smoke and the sound of fire accosted me. I heard women scream, and I looked up in alarm, but Frau Grabber still stood in the front of the classroom, her eyes closed now and her lips moving as she mumbled a prayer over and over again. I took several deep breaths, as my mother had taught me, but still the sound kept coming. Although they flew high, their numbers created a sound so deafening they silenced us, and I knew all of Halberstadt heard them. I pictured the patrons of Café Deesen standing outside, looking up in muted horror, and my grandparents looking out of the living room window, my grandfather struggling to get up out of his chair to see his beautiful mountains and fields marred by the shadows of these vessels of death. My grandmother praying for her child, her only child. My grandfather racked with worry for his only child but hiding it in bombastic statements about the great German defense system.

After the first wave passed, Frau Grabber's voice broke through my thoughts.

"Ladies, sit back down, please." Only half the class responded and retuned to their seats. The rest remained at the windows, fixed on the sight overhead.

"Ladies, I said sit down!" she called again, louder than before. This time everyone sat down except for Carla. Carla remained at the window, her face glued to it, her eyes closed. Frau Grabber began to say something but changed her mind.

"Now let us pray. Let us pray for Berlin, for loved ones we may know…" Her voice cracked with emotion, and she had to pause for a moment. "For a just end to this war." Several of the girls added their own prayers, and then the sound grew dimmer. We all listened as the sound of the last of the planes grew more and more distant in the bright, sunny sky. But none of us sighed with relief. We knew they were just that much closer to their target. I prayed again and again, and then I prayed that they would not return the same way. I ran home saying this prayer, desperate for the peace of Omi's house.

Get Through to Berlin!

Omi was in bed resting, Opa said with a casualness I knew he did not feel, his face betraying his concern. I stood looking at him for a moment, trying to process what he had just said. Omi was never in bed when I came home from school. He shooed me away, saying, "She made lunch for you, my dear. Go on in the kitchen; it's sitting out."

I did as he said and, like a robot, walked through the kitchen doors. I saw my lunch sitting on the table and knew immediately that Omi had not prepared it. A plate sat there without a place mat or napkin, and the silverware had been tossed down casually, as if Opa was uncertain where it should go. On the plate were leftovers from the day before, chicken, potatoes, and green beans, but it looked as if he had shoved the full plate into the oven. I sat down and tried to eat but could only manage a few bites. I covered the plate with a napkin and placed it back in the icebox. I heard Opa lumbering across the wood floor toward the kitchen. He opened the door, propping it open with his shoulder, his cane in the other hand. "So, how was school today?"

"Fine." We both avoided talking about what we feared most.

"Well, good. Did you eat?"

"I'm sorry; I couldn't." He nodded his head. Unable to think of anything else to say, he began to retreat.

"Opa, can I go see how Omi is doing?"

He looked up at me, noted my anxiety, and nodded his head. "*Ja*, go ahead. But don't wake her if she is asleep."

"No, I wouldn't. I will just peek in quietly."

The curtains were pulled tight in Omi's room, and it took my eyes a moment to adjust to the darkness. I stepped softly into her room, leaving the door open just slightly to allow in some light. She lay on her back on the bed, propped up against three pillows. Her hands were crossed on her chest, and that made me fear the worst. I ran to her bedside and saw with relief that her hands were rising and descending slowly.

"Thank you, God! She is breathing," I whispered.

"I'm awake, Juttalein," she said, her voice barely audible. Her eyes remained closed. I reached for her hand; it felt cold, lifeless.

"Omi, are you all right?"

"Yes, my dear, but Dr. Krauss is coming to check." She said this with effort, between breaths, as a runner does who tries to talk while running.

"Don't try to talk."

She ignored me and forced herself to say, "Don't be frightened, my dear. I may need to go to the hospital."

I rested my head on the bed next to her, still holding her hand, and tried not to let her feel the tears that were pouring silently from my eyes. After a while I could not contain the sobs, and they escaped from my throat in huge, loud burst. She freed her hand from mine and placed it on my head, stroking my hair lightly. We stayed like that for a long time, neither of us speaking.

I heard Opa get up in the living room and make his way to open the door, and then I heard his voice and the sound of another. It must be Dr. Krauss. The voices came closer and they seemed to push open the door, filling the room with light from the living room.

"Jutta, Dr. Krauss is here. You need to let him examine Omi." I heard my grandfather say, but his voice seemed miles away. I pulled away from the bed and rose from my knees, vaguely aware of the two old men looking at me with concern.

"Fräulein Jutta, go wait in the living room with your Opa," the doctor said. I met his kind eyes, surrounded by hundreds of lines etched into his skin. Omi's eyes were still closed, and her pale face looked so lifeless against the pillow. I crossed my arms to protect myself from the sudden chill and walked wordlessly out to the living room.

It seemed to take Dr. Krauss forever to complete his examination, during which time Opa and I sat staring out of the window saying nothing. He sat in his chair and I sat on the edge of it, silent, observing the afternoon sky: grim, and threatening rain. The tiny stalks of wheat in the field bending right, then left against the weight of the wind, gathering force from the east. At the sound of the door opening, I leaped up. Opa struggled to stand, and we both waited anxiously as Dr. Krauss came down the hallway.

"It is the stress of the current predicament we find ourselves in that has brought on what I believe may have been a mild heart attack." I drew in my breath, and he held up his hand. "I am not certain it was a heart attack, but at any rate, if it was, it is unlikely to be fatal. However, I would like to take her into the hospital for more tests."

My grandfather stared at his shoes, nodding his head, moisture glimmering around the corners of his eyes. He said, "Shall I bring her, or will you send for her?"

"No, no. I will send for her. She must not be moved at the moment. I will send someone in the morning. In the meantime, if you can get through to Berlin, try." He paused for a moment before he added, "Only tell her if it is good news." A chill ran up my spine, and I felt goose bumps popping out all over my arms and legs. Opa saw me shudder and put his arm around my shoulder. "She needs to rest above all else. I have given her a sedative so she can rest without any pain."

After Dr. Krauss left, I busied myself around the house, picking up and cleaning up the kitchen, as I knew my grandmother would do. I was grateful for the work, for it kept my mind off of her illness. I heard my grandfather trying to call my parents in Dahlem.

He cursed the telephone. "Damn modern invention!" It clattered to the floor.

I popped my head out. "Opa, do you want me to try?"

"If you want," he said, as if it would do no good. But he obviously wanted me to try. I picked the phone handle up from the floor where it had fallen next to the umbrella stand and placed it back on the receiver.

"I can never get this damn thing to work for me!" he said irritably as he sat down, overwhelming the small side chair that stood by the telephone table in the entryway.

"I know. It is complicated." I tried to sooth his frustration. "But I think I will just call the operator and see if the lines are up."

I dialed the operator and waited a long time as the phone rang and rang. I counted twenty-five rings before a woman's harassed voice came on. "Yes, may I help you?"

"Oh yes, I am trying to call Berlin at ..."

The woman interrupted me. "You cannot get through now, young lady. All the lines are down. Try tomorrow morning; they think they may have them fixed by then. Thank you." She hung up before I could utter another word. I stood there with the phone to my ear for a few seconds, listening to the dead sound of the disconnected telephone line before I replaced it slowly in the receiver. Opa looked at me, his eyebrows raised.

"The lines are down and they say to try again tomorrow morning."

"Damn!" he said, placing his hand on the arm of the chair to slowly push himself up. I grabbed his other arm and pulled, fearing the worst for the delicate chair as it teetered under the force of his hand. "I was hoping to tell Omi everything was all right with your mother. It would help, I think." He shook his head. "Well, let's try again before you go to school." I knew that meant he wanted me to try again, and I did, but the lines were still down, so we spent another day not knowing.

I tiptoed into Omi's room before I left for school to kiss her goodbye, knowing they would come for her while I was at school. She was asleep and breathing more easily than she had been the day before. I didn't want to disturb her, so I blew her a kiss and whispered, "I'm off to school, but I will visit you as soon as I can."

———

Through the narrow window that lined the front door, I saw Opa's jacketed arm. He was waiting for me. The door flew open even before I arrived on the top step. His eyes sparkled and his mustache moved up and down as he smiled and tried to control his emotions. I set my book bag down and waited. "They are all fine!" he said, smiling, the relief evident on his face as he clapped me on the back. Frau Pechstein, from downstairs, had called through to Berlin for him, and he had waited all day to tell me.

"Oh, thank God!" I hugged him as tears welled in my eyes.

"*Ja, ja.* I spoke to your mother this morning. I told her about the Omi, and she is coming as soon as she can get a train." Relief swept over me; my shoulders relaxed, and I smiled. Opa wiped his eyes quickly and moved aside to let me in. "Jutta, I need you to tell the Omi. They took her to the hospital before I spoke to your mother." I tossed my book bag by the front door before he could finish his sentence and was already heading down the stairs when he shouted, "Wait! First you need to eat. Then you go see her."

I held up my hand. "No thanks. There's no time." I took a few more steps before turning back. "If I get hungry, I'll stop at Café Deesen on the way back."

He nodded and said nothing. I turned abruptly and clattered violently down the stairs. I almost collided with Frau Pechstein at the corner of Mozartstrasse and Speigelsbergen Weg as I headed full speed for the hospital.

"Good heavens, Jutta!" was all I heard as I veered to the left to avoid her.

"Sorry, Frau Pechstein, but I have to go tell Omi."

" Well, be careful you don't kill yourself along the way," I heard her call from behind me, but I was already too far past her to respond.

About halfway into town I had to stop to catch my breath. People stared at me. I paid no attention to them. Every moment counted. What if Omi died five minutes before I told her the good news? The thought spurred me on to even greater speed. I came to believe my news was like some magical elixir that would save her life, and I had to get it to her as soon as possible.

I threw open the heavy hospital door, startling the man on the other side who was, at that exact moment, about to exit the same door. I overestimated the door's weight and flung it with all my might, causing it to crash into the wall behind it as I rushed into the hospital lobby. "Sorry!" I called out, running through the lobby.

A woman's voice called, "Fräulein, slow down." I ignored her.

"Fräulein, you must sign in! Fräulein, come back here immediately!" But I was gone, and she had too many other people around her desk to bother chasing after me.

I followed the signs that read "Patients," only then realizing I had no idea which room was Omi's. I ran from door to door, peeking through the small rectangular glass windows of each. As I turned the corner, I spotted a nurse helping an old lady walk down the corridor. Their backs were to me. The old lady's nightgown hung on her as she shuffled along, leaning on the nurse for support. I slowed down and tried to look like I belonged. When I caught up to them I asked, "Excuse me. Where are the cardiac patients' rooms, please?"

"Third floor, north wing," responded the nurse without even looking at me.

"Thank you!" I turned back and quickened my pace, heading for the stairs.

By the time I got to the third floor, I was so disheveled and out of breath a nurse coming out of a room stopped me. She blocked the door, her broad shoulders wrapped in a white uniform. No amount of jumping up or dodging got me even a glimpse to see if Omi was in there. "Who are you looking for?" she asked, her eyebrows raised above her bifocals.

"Frau Muller."

"Your Oma?"

I nodded.

She smiled. "Three doors down."

I saw her through the glass pane, my breath fogging over the glass. I turned the handle and rushed to her bedside. She sat propped up in the metal hospital bed, light streaming through an enormous window, reading a book with her bifocals perched low on her nose. She lowered the book at the sound of the door and looked at me in surprise over the top edge of her glasses. A smile immediately lit her face.

"Why, Jutta, what a nice surprise," she said, taking in my disheveled look.

"Omi, Mutti and Vati are all right. No bombs hit Dahlem."

"That is wonderful news!" she said, but she didn't seem surprised at all.

"Did you already know?" I asked in bewilderment.

"I felt it, my dear," she said simply, and patted the bed for me to sit down.

"Vati's factory is also safe. They bombed central Berlin again, hitting factories and government buildings, and the fires are everywhere. Mutti says the refugees are pouring out from downtown all along the Kurfürstendamm, heading anywhere away from Berlin." Omi shook her head, her eyes filled with concern. I continued, "Mutti overheard one woman say she didn't care if she had to sleep in a wheat field for the rest of her life, she just wanted out of that 'damn city with its walls of fire.'" I looked down at my feet for a moment and added, "Opa told me."

Omi brought her hand to my forehead to move a stray strand of hair. "My goodness, Jutta, did you run the whole way here? You are covered with sweat!" I nodded my head and she chuckled, patting my hand. "You poor thing. Omi is just fine! I don't know why they even have me in here!"

"What are they saying, Omi?"

"Oh, they say I had a heart attack, but what do they know? I don't believe them. I think I just had an anxiety attack."

I looked at her doubtfully but said nothing.

"How is your Opa doing?"

"Fine."

"Are you two eating?"

"Yes, don't worry. I will stop by Café Deesen on my way back and see if I can't get something for us to eat!"

Omi chuckled, but pain stopped her almost immediately; she grimaced slightly. "Good idea! Opa in the kitchen is a disaster. When I get back to the house, I will show you a few simple things that you can …"

Her voice trailed off. I looked at her, alarmed.

"You'll be fine, Omi!" I said fiercely, as if willing it to be true.

"Oh, of course I will, dear" she said quickly. "I just meant—well, I made sure your mother knew how to cook, and even though she has Luise, I daresay if she had to, she could put a meal together fit for the kaiser."

"Mutti is coming down as soon as she can get a train," I said suddenly.

"Oh, dear. I wish she wouldn't risk it!" responded my grandmother.

I ignored this. "It could take a while," I warned. "They say all the tracks are bombed out from here to Berlin."

"Well, if I know your mother, she will manage somehow."

I nodded. "I miss her," I said simply. Omi patted my hand again, covering it with hers. It was warm and soft now.

"I know, dear, and I pray for an end to this dreadful war so you can go home to be with her."

I looked up quickly, "But I love being with you, Omi."

"I know. But she is your mother, and that is your home. It is natural to miss it."

"I miss Vati, too."

She nodded her head.

"I even miss *Vögelein* and Harold," I said, smiling as I began to talk about *Vögelein* and her antics outside my window, and about the time I found Harold looking confused in the middle of the street, and about how I would slip out to the garden when Luise would go back in the kitchen for something and feed my brussels sprouts to Harold. She laughed as she listened to my stories, stories of home she had heard many times before, but she always acted like this was her first time hearing them. After a while, a nurse came in to check on Omi. She told me to go before I wore my Omi out. I kissed Omi goodbye and promised to come again the next day after school. Waving to her from the door, I skipped to the end of the hall before hurrying down the stairs to the first floor.

Mutti

It took Mutti five days to get to Halberstadt from Berlin. Not five days of travel; the actual train travel took ten hours. But there were four days of waiting for them to repair enough of the train lines for her to even attempt the trip. Normally, I thought wistfully, it took only two hours to get here, but nothing was normal anymore. She arrived one day, late in the afternoon. I was sitting by my bedroom window, sketching a dress I had seen in the *Vogue* magazine my mother had somehow gotten her hands on in Berlin and sent to me. I looked up to see a small figure, elegantly dressed in a beige and blue pantsuit, walking purposefully up the street, carrying a suitcase on one side and her handbag on the other. She wore a hat with a broad brim that shielded her face. At first I did not recognize her. But as she drew closer, I caught my breath, threw down my sketchpad, and leaned out the window, screaming with excitement, "Mutti! Hello! Mutti!"

She stopped walking and looked up, raising her handbag in greeting. I leaped back from the window and raced through my bedroom to the living room, startling Opa in his chair. "Mutti is here! Mutti is here!" I shouted as I ran out the front door without waiting for his response. By the time I got down-stairs, she was almost to the corner of our street. She saw me coming and again stopped, this time setting her suitcase down on the pavement. She opened her arms and smiled as I ran at breakneck speed into them, practically toppling both of us onto the sidewalk.

"Jutta!" she whispered, holding me tight to her. We said nothing for a few moments. She pulled away and held my face in her hands. To my surprise, tears were streaming down her face, but she was laughing. We were both laughing.

She grabbed my hand, "Jutta! You are a crazy child! You almost killed us!"

"Sorry," I said, shrugging. "Oh, Mutti! I miss you so much!" I covered my eyes with my hands to hide the tears hovering ready to spill over onto my cheeks. The effort failed, and I burst into tears.

She hugged me to her again. "Let's sit down for a moment." She guided me to the edge of the street and we sat on the curb, me with my face buried in her shoulder and she comforting me and holding me to her.

"I miss you too, *mein Herz*! But soon it will all be over."

"When, Mutti? When?" I cried. "It will never end! Not until they kill every last one of us! It will never end!" I wailed, letting out all the fear that I had held bottled up inside me like a festering wound slowly sapping my strength.

"Jutta, there is nothing you or I or your Vati can do to stop this terrible war. So we just must be brave and try to get through each day. Meanwhile, you are safe here in Halberstadt. I know," she said, stopping me before I could say anything, "they will not bomb Halberstadt, and you have Omi to look after you. So try to think of these things."

"But Omi is sick, and what if she dies?" I sobbed.

"Omi won't die just yet, and besides, you can call us whenever she is sick. You are only a train ride away."

"But what if you are dead? What if a bomb hits our house and you and Vati die, and then Omi and Opa die? And then I will be in this world all alone."

"That won't happen."

"Well, it could. It happened to Carla! So don't say it can't happen. It hap-pens all over Germany every day, every night, as they drop bombs all over this country." I screamed these fears at my mother. I loved her so much and missed her so much, but somehow at that moment I was very angry. All the pent-up anger flowed out of me: anger at the world, at the idiots who had started this war and the idiots who continued it; anger at the unfairness that my friend

Carla was without a family, and that I had to live far away from my parents, not just for a few weeks but for years; anger that all my friends had been sent off to distant parts of Germany, either to live in dormitories or to live with relatives who lived in safer parts where they were free from the reach of the giant flying assassins with their horrible monotonous sound growing louder and louder.

Mutti listened in silence, holding my head and stroking my hair. She continued to hold me tight as we sat on the cold, hard stone of the curb. Finally she said, "Jutta, we cannot destroy ourselves worrying about the things we cannot change. Your worrying about a bomb hitting us will not change whether one actually does. All you do when you worry is make yourself ill."

I nodded my head and took a deep breath. I knew she was right.

"Just as worrying about Omi dying will not change when she dies. I know it is easier to say than to do, but you must take each day as it comes. You must try and think positively—tell yourself that because we live in Dahlem it is not likely we will be hit by a bomb. They won't waste one on us."

"But Vati's factory—what if they hit the factory? They target factories, and what if he is there when they hit it? They bomb all day long now, not just at night, and they know that the workers are in the factories and they don't care! They don't care how many people they kill! Carla's aunt says the British will never accept a surrender from Germany; they want to kill every last one of us."

"Well, I don't think Carla or her aunt really know what they are planning to do, and neither do we. We don't know how it will all end."

"I just want things to be normal; I just want my old life back."

"I know you do, and so do I, and one day it will be. But the fastest way for that to happen is for us to lose this war and get rid of that horrible man!" She had whispered it.

"Do you really think we will lose the war, Mutti?"

"Of course we will, Jutta." She was staring straight ahead, out into the street. "We are losing right now as we speak. Why do you think they can fly right through here in broad daylight and attack us? Because Herr Goring's defense system is working so well?" She snorted dismissively. "No, my dear, we are definitely losing this war, and the longer it drags on, the worse it will be for Germany. I pray for a swift end. It will be hard for Germany, for all of us at first, but then hopefully and with God's help, things will return to normal."

I am not sure how long we sat there in the street, but the shadows fell across the houses and the sounds of the town began to die down as people headed home to their families. Suddenly, I remembered that I had alerted Opa to Mutti's arrival. They must be anxious about us. I wonder why Opa had not come outside on the landing to interrupt us.

"Omi will be wondering about us," I said to Mutti.

"Is she already home?" asked Mutti, surprised.

"*Ja*! Yesterday."

"*Ja,* then we should go in." She patted my knee and added, "Are you all right now?"

"*Ja,*" I said, smiling, knowing my red and puffy eyes looked awful.

"You're sure?" she checked again.

I nodded. She hugged me; our cheeks pressed together, her Chanel No. 5 wafting up through her blouse.

"Now help your old tired mother get up." I stood up and pulled her up by the arm. She got up stiffly, rubbing her tailbone. "This was probably not the best place to sit after ten hours on a train!"

Poor Mutti! I had forgotten that my poor mother had been sitting on a train and then had had to walk from the station carrying her own bag because taxis were almost impossible to find now. "Mutti, I'm so sorry."

"Oh, no. This was more important, but now I could stand some of the Omi's good cooking. Come on." She grinned at me as she laced her arm through mine, and I bent down to grab her suitcase. We walked arm in arm to the stairs and ascended them, still arm in arm, laughing as we tipped from side to side, nearly losing our balance several times. Omi heard us. She opened the door when we reached the top of the landing, and with her warm smile and an arm outstretched for each of us, suddenly my worries evaporated. Three generations wrapped in each other's arms, a cocoon against the world. The smell of freshly baked cake hit my nostrils, and I knew Omi had been busy in the kitchen while I let my emotions pour out to my mother outside on the cold stone curb.

"Mutti, you should be in bed!" exclaimed my mother, pulling back.

Omi waved her hand. "I've done that for five days now! Enough!"

"You need your rest!" chided my mother.

"Oh, I did that all morning! Didn't I, Jutta?"

I nodded.

"Now come on! Put your things down! For heaven's sake, Heidchen!"

Mutti stepped in, and I followed. The door closed protectively behind us.

Certainty embraced me. With the comfort of Omi's home and my mother's presence, the anxiety drifted away, and for the first time in a long time I did not worry. She shared my bedroom—even my bed—a huge, old-fashioned four-poster double bed that you had take a step and bounce yourself up onto as it was so high off the ground. Omi had embroidered all of the sheets and the canopy that hung overhead with the most beautiful, delicate, hand-stitched designs: cornflowers, daisies, and tulips. It must have taken her years to do all of the work, and she had embroidered her initials on the pillows and sheets as well. I always felt like a princess sleeping on those sheets. I slept well next to my mother, the regularity of her breathing blocking out the night sounds.

She walked into town with me, telling me stories of her life in Halberstadt with Vati. She helped me with my homework, and she helped Omi in the kitchen with dinner. She hired a girl not much older than I was, named Ilsa, to help Omi with the cleaning and cooking, and spent most of the day while I was at school training her for Omi. Ilsa was a tall, strong girl who turned nineteen years old two days after my mother hired her. She was a willing student, grateful for the job. A refugee from Hamburg, having lost her family and home to the war, she lived with her father's sister in Halberstadt with no money and no job. Ilsa came to my grandmother's house every morning at six thirty and stayed to clean up after supper until seven o'clock. She was off from two thirty until five in the afternoon.

I liked Ilsa. She had a freshness about her, and although she had suffered much, she was an optimistic person, believing that the war would soon end and that her boyfriend, Frederick, would soon come home. It never seemed to occur to Ilsa that Frederick could easily die at any moment; or if it did, she never allowed it to take control of her. My mother said, "Ilsa is right to think that way. She can't protect Fredrick, so she must not worry about it." Sometimes Ilsa would read me Frederick's letters, editing out the personal parts. Only once did her voice catch, and then she had to put the letter away. At that moment I realized Ilsa did think about these things, but she had developed the discipline not to give in to fear.

Mutti spent every moment she could with me. We met after school every day and walked home. Often Carla walked with us, but sometimes she let us walk alone, respecting our time together. My mother fascinated the girls with her clothes, her hats, and her elegant sense of style. Suddenly I was popular at school. When I met my mother outside the school gates, I would arrive with a pack of five or even ten girls, all curious to know what she was wearing and where she had bought it. At first they were shy and only came out to look at her and whisper among themselves, but by the end of the week they boldly asked her questions.

I saw her leaning against an old linden tree that had just begun to bud; its tiny, lime green leaves contrasted against the beige of my mother's pantsuit. Her pants came up high around her waist and the jacket was long, resting around her hips with a single clasp at the waist and wide, elegant lapels that draped down slightly. She wore a beige and navy blue striped silk blouse under the jacket. The stripes ran in a diagonal design, adding to the uniqueness of the outfit. I thought she was a bit overdressed for our simple walk home, but then my mother always looked elegant, so it was not that unusual. I heard one of the girls behind me catch her breath. "Look at that!" she whispered to her friend. "Have you ever seen anything so beautiful?"

"Only in the magazines," whispered her friend. They ran ahead of me, surrounding my mother.

"Frau Bolle, is that chiffon?"

"No, it must be silk." said another.

"Is it the latest style out of Paris?"

"No," someone else said. "It must be Italian."

"It's actually not that new. It's from a few years ago. The fabric is Georgette."

"Georgette!" exclaimed one girl. "I've never heard of that before!"

"Georgette," murmured another. "That sounds like a girl's name."

"I love your clothes, Frau Bolle!" gushed another who never gave me the time of day at school.

My mother smiled and said, "Thank you, girls. Oh, hello, Jutta. Are you back there somewhere?" she asked, lifting up on her tiptoes to look over the heads of the girls to find me. I waved to her.

"I'm sorry, girls, but we have an appointment in town. I really appreciate all the attention, although you better stop it or it will go to my head, and I will never want to return to Herr Bolle in Berlin!" The girls parted reluctantly to let me through to my mother, who kissed me on the cheek and reached for my hand as we began to move away.

"*Guten Nachmittag*," called Mutti over her shoulder, waving with her free hand.

"Bye, Frau Bolle. Bye, Jutta," they all sang in unison.

How odd! I'm invisible to them when my mother is not here. They rarely even speak to me. But I smiled and waved anyway, enjoying the attention and the feeling that I was finally welcome, though I knew it was temporary and transparent.

"Where are we going?" I asked my mother after we were out of earshot.

"To the cathedral," she responded without looking at me.

I stopped walking and let go of her hand. My face scrunched up quizzically. "The cathedral? But why? Are we meeting Omi there?" My mother never went to the cathedral. Indeed, I don't recall my mother ever going to church except for special occasions, like weddings or Christmas or Easter.

"No, we are not meeting Omi," chuckled my mother. "Can't we go to church without you acting like it is the strangest thing you've ever heard?"

"I guess," I said shrugging. "But it's just that you never do it." We walked on in silence for a moment, until I couldn't stand it any more. "So why are we going to the cathedral, Mutti?"

"We are meeting with Reverend Heimuller because Omi and I think it is time that you are confirmed."

"But I've never attended that church, and I've never taken those classes you're supposed to take. Aren't there classes that you have to take?" I added uncertainly.

"I know," said my mother, waving her hands. "But in these times rules are more flexible than normal."

I looked at her skeptically.

"Jutta, it would give your Omi peace, which is why there is some urgency, and I think Reverend Heimuller will understand and maybe accelerate your classes."

It bothered Omi that I was not yet confirmed. Vati had said, "When she is ready and shows an interest, we will speak to the church."

"You mean I have to take a crash course in Lutheranism?" I said, laughing.

"Something like that, yes." She hugged me and let go. "Now, when we get there, you just let me do the talking."

I nodded my head obediently.

"Good! After we're done we'll stop by Tante Lieschen's. What do you say?" I nodded my head enthusiastically. She laughed, and we walked on to town, chatting about the girls at my school and their sudden interest in me.

I was confirmed on a beautiful Sunday in May 1944 at the *Dom* in Halberstadt with my mother and grandmother attending. My father was unable to get away from Berlin; all the rail lines had been bombed again, making it extremely difficult to travel.

It was a warm, sunny, and vibrant day—one of those days that pop out at you, that clear your head and make you feel free, a day where the blue of the sky and the green of the trees seems twice as vibrant. The birds outside my window woke me, singing loudly to each other, the warmth of the day erasing the sounds of war and encouraging them to believe they were safe. I reached over for Mutti and found only bedcovers. Alarmed, I sat up. The bed, empty where my mother slept, the bright sunlight in the room, and the intensity of the birds' songs all suggested I had slept later than I intended. I pushed back the sheets and stretched lazily before slipping into my slippers and robe. I headed for the window. I flung open the curtains and, anticipating an assault by the sun's rays, I squinted my eyes. I pushed the window all the way up, leaning out onto the windowsill as I did so. The world seemed to have been up for hours without me. I wondered if Opa Muller had already made his rounds. I ran downstairs to find Omi and Mutti. They had already finished their breakfast, and Mutti was busily cleaning up the dishes. My place setting was the only one remaining on the table. Omi and Opa sipped their coffee and looked at me with amusement as I slipped into my chair.

"Well, she has finally risen!" said my mother mockingly.

"Why didn't anybody wake me?" I moaned.

"Wake you! Bombs dropped on Halberstadt itself couldn't have woken you!"

"You must have needed the sleep, my darling," said Omi, patting my hand.

"But I need to wash my hair and my dress isn't pressed and I wanted to pick some flowers for a corsage..."

"Your dress is pressed," said Omi gently. "I pressed it this morning."

"Thank you, Omi!" I said, the relief evident in my voice.

"And I'll pick you a corsage."

I kissed her on the cheek.

It was a lovely confirmation that obviously pleased Omi, who sat smiling the entire time. After the ceremony, we had a delicious lunch at Tante Lieschen's house. At the time, I did not know it would be the last time I would see my mother until I returned to Berlin in those frightening early days of April 1945, a full year after my confirmation.

9

Home to Berlin

April 8, 1945

I said goodbye to Carla at the corner of Spiegelsbergenweg and Westen-häuser Strasse and walked slowly home to Omi's house. It was a beautiful April day, warm and sunny, and it was a Sunday, my favorite day —the day when Carla and I would walk around town swapping stories and pretending to ignore the boys.

The chestnut trees diverted my attention as a breeze softly moved their branches, creating tiny, spider-like shadows along the path. I glanced up and noticed the delicate green buds trying desperately to uncurl from their hard brown captors. A pale green shone translucent in the late morning light. I loved this green, the green of spring; it always spoke to me of new life, a fresh start. "Every year God gives us a fresh start," Omi would say. "Maybe this will be a fresh start for Germany." Then she would smile and look up to the sky, the rest of her thoughts unspoken.

I looked down the street and saw the same pale green leaves hanging from long, twisted branches all along the Spiegelsbergenweg. The branches seemed oversized compared to the tiny leaves. The trees were further along on Omi's street than they were in the middle of town. I smiled. Omi deserved better, greener trees than anyone else. I made a mental note to remember to tell her the trees on her street were especially advanced in their quest for new life. Along the walkways and fences, daffodils and crocuses popped up, and I breathed this fresh new presence, spring, deeply into my lungs, trying to get enough spring for Omi as well as for myself. Poor Omi, confined to a hospital bed for the third time this year already. I wished she could be well, still greeting me in the kitchen with her warm smile and simple way when I came home from school.

I will go visit Omi as soon as Opa will let me out of the house, I thought. I knew he would make me eat first, and I resolved to try and keep him company for a bit before I made it too obvious that I wanted to run off and be with Omi. I knew he was lonely, but it was difficult to talk to him. Once we exhausted the summary of my day at school, we sat in the awkward silence, nothing more to say now that Omi was no longer there to ease the conversation along.

I looked both ways before crossing to our side of the street. I chuckled. The habit was ingrained in me, even though cars had long since stopped coming down our street. Travel bans and gas rationing had made driving a car virtually impossible for anyone who was not either very essential to industry or very important in the government. I glanced to the end of the street and beyond, to the hills in the background past the little tourist train station, silent now for many months. The hills shimmered in the spring light, their leaves a condensed blanket of green, vibrant and beautiful, and I stood in front of my Omi's house, taking in the view for a moment before turning to climb the stairs to face the silence it now held for me.

A crack in the bottom step slithered from the middle to the outer edge. Each winter it grew worse as the ice and snow expanded it. I knew until the war was over it would not get fixed. I bent down and tore a blade of grass struggling to find a way through the concrete maze of the steps. I brushed it softly on my lips, letting it gently tickle me. How could such a tiny, delicate plant push its way through the same concrete man needed a jackhammer to get through? I thought of Opa Bolle, who said you *can* find God in a single blade of grass or a single bulb pushing its way through rock and ice in the spring.

I let the blade fall to the ground and climbed up the steps. I looked up and stopped short, my foot resting on the fourth step. I knew whose it was, but it made no sense for it to be there. My mind stumbled over its black cloth, closed neatly as it rested against the door to my grandparents' house. The handle, made from ebony, was leaning against the doorframe to keep it from falling—grooves where fingers should hold it a darker color from years of use. Vati carried that umbrella everywhere he went. It was longer than most umbrellas, and he used it like a walking stick.

I tore up the remaining steps two at a time, screaming, "Vati! Vati!"

He must have heard me coming, for by the time I flung the front door open he was already there, hand poised to open the door.

I threw myself in his arms. "Vati! You're here! I don't believe you're here!" He said nothing and simply held me, smiling with my joy. I pulled away, tears threatening to spill down my cheeks. He took his handkerchief from his front jacket pocket just in case. I glanced over his shoulder, my eyes resting briefly on the chair; it stood empty. I scanned the room until I found Opa. He sat staring at the dinner table without even looking in our direction. I frowned. "But how did you get through? Why are you here?"

"Jutta, I've come to take you home to Berlin," he said quietly.

"But I don't want to go back!" I blurted out.

"I know, but it is time," he said, holding my shoulders firmly with his hands.

"Time? What do you mean it's time?" I jerked free from his grip and sat down heavily in the chair by the door.

He crouched down next to me and held my hand. "Jutta, the Russians are at the Oder. They could be in Berlin by the end of April..."

"Never!" shouted my grandfather angrily.

My father turned to look at him but did not respond. "I want us to be together. I have heard too many horror stories of families separated in the East. They can't find each other again, and when one of them wanders about trying to find the rest, horrible things happen to them. Do you understand me, Jutta?"

I stared at him. I didn't want to understand him. I didn't want to leave my Omi, and I didn't want to go back to Berlin with its daily bombings and black fires. Goose bumps popped up on my arms, and I shivered. Vati took his jacket off and put it around my shoulders.

"Jutta, we don't have much time. The trains are running right now, but who knows if they will be later this evening?" He didn't say it, but I knew he meant that they could be hit, bombed in the middle of the night and left a twisted mass of metal. The idea terrified me. I began to cry in earnest now. I heard the Americans and British were not just bombing the lines but deliberately targeting the trains, especially those they could see were filled with people, old and young spilling out of the windows, the older boys riding on top.

"But I can't leave Omi. She's sick, and who will visit her? Opa can't visit her! I have to be here to visit her, Vati! She will die if she has no visitors." I knew even as I said these things that his mind was made up, but I couldn't help myself.

"Jutta, get your things packed. We can't take everything, just what we can carry." His voice was steady but firm.

"No! I must say goodbye to Omi." I covered my face with my hands in disbelief; this couldn't be happening. Not now, not so suddenly. Somehow I had thought that when Vati came for me there would be a warning or at least time to say goodbye. What about Carla? I couldn't just disappear on Carla.

"Let her go, Hans. What is an extra hour to you?" I looked over to Opa gratefully. He was looking at me for the first time. I smiled. His eyes softened, and he said again, "Let her say goodbye to her Omi."

My father said nothing. I threw my bag down and ran into the kitchen.

I heard my father say, "What is she doing?"

"She brings the Omi something to eat, always. The hospital food is not good these days."

I scurried around the kitchen grabbing whatever I could find. There wasn't much. Ilsa was having a harder and harder time finding food. I grabbed a hard-boiled egg and a *Brötchen* left over from the morning and shoved them into a cloth napkin, tying the ends together to form a sack.

I hurried out to join Vati in the living room. I headed for the door and then turned, suddenly remembering that I had not even greeted poor Opa. Handing my father the food package, I walked back to the dining room table and bent down to kiss Opa on the cheek.

"I'll say hello from you, Opa." He patted my hand in response, and I thought I saw moisture around his eyes. I brushed it off as the rheumy eyes of old age. I could not take on the burden of Opa's sorrow.

"We'll be back shortly."

He nodded and continued to stare at the table. I looked down at the fine, concentric, circular grains of the wooden table that seemed determined to hold his attention.

"Jutta, come," called my father, holding the door open. I kissed Opa again on top of his head and ran to join my father.

We did not speak until we reached the center of town. I saw nothing as we walked to the end of the Spiegelsbergenweg and caught the streetcar at Süd-strasse that would deliver us to the hospital. Absorbed with trying to process what lay ahead, I could not talk. The streetcar driver turned sharply to the right at Hauptmann-Loeper Strasse, jolting me; I fell against Vati. He stiffened, his body keeping me from falling further to the side. I righted myself again and looked out the window over to the *Domplatz* and the *Holzmarktplatz*. This would be the last time for a long time I would see this view. The *Martinikirche*, with its uneven towers, peeked out over the building tops in the distance. The street was crowded on this fine day with people riding bicycles and walking to town to window shop. It was a joke, window shopping; so few supplies re-mained available at the shops that the empty shelves looked sad to me now—a lonely sweater here, a pair of glasses there, a single dress in a hideous fabric hanging from an otherwise empty rack. But people still went through the ritual of window shopping on a Sunday afternoon.

I glanced down the Breiteweg, trying to catch a glimpse of Café Deesen to see if it was crowded. The Breiteweg was packed with people. A lady carried an umbrella to protect herself from the sun. Germans never seemed to tire of car-rying umbrellas. I glanced over at Vati's "walking stick." The umbrella should become the symbol of Germany, not that ugly black broken cross, I thought. A child waved at us from her stroller. I forced myself to smile back. A wurst vendor sold sausages, a long line wrapping around his cart as he placed the sausages on buns as fast as he could and his wife dealt with ration cards. I saw Frau Oberman's shop. At one time, she sold the finest soaps and perfumes in town. I was just there the other day, trying to find Omi's lavender perfume from France. Frau Oberman had laughed at me—she said she had not been able to get anything from France for over a year now. In fact, she had no soap, and the only perfume she had left was very expensive, sitting on the shelf since last year because nobody could afford Chanel No. 5 or Joy right now. She led me to a few lone bottles that resided on an otherwise empty shelf. She barely managed to stay alive, she told me, sighing heavily, by selling essentials: toothpaste and toilet paper and hairbrushes. But now even some of these things were becoming impossible to stock.

"Jutta, I know you don't want to go to Berlin, but it is for the best," said Vati, grabbing my hand as he spoke. "Really," he added.

"I know." I looked down at our hands, united on the seat.

"I understand that you don't want to leave your Omi."

"She is sick. And Opa can't take care of her. He can't walk to visit her, and they won't be able to talk to each other without me."

My father thought for a moment. "Well, maybe we can get Ilsa to carry notes back and forth and visit the Omi," said Vati.

"You think so?" I hadn't thought of this possibility. "Yes, and Ilsa could bring her food."

"Absolutely."

I smiled, and some of my sadness lifted. I looked over at my father; his eyes were creased with new lines I did not remember. I noticed gray around his temples and behind his ears. It had been almost a year since I had seen him. And now here he was, in Halberstadt at last, but not the way I wanted him to be and not the way I remembered him; he looked much older than before.

"Vati, I want to see you and Mutti. I miss you both horribly."

"I know, dear. You don't have to explain."

"But I want you to know it's just the Omi; that's why I don't want to leave."

"I know." He patted my hand. I looked out the window again; we were almost at Gleimstrasse, where the hospital faced onto the street and took up a substantial part of the block.

"Well, also the bombs." I had said it so softly, really more to myself; I didn't think he had heard it.

"I know," he said again.

I turned and looked at him anxiously. "They terrify me." Chills ran up my spine as I thought about that sound, that horrible, horrible whining sound.

He put his arm around me and hugged me to him. My head fell on his shoulder and he rested his cheek on top of my head. "It's almost over, Jutta. Really. It will all be over in a matter of months or even weeks." I was unable to process this. I didn't know if I should be happy or even more terrified. Unspoken between us was the threat of the Russians.

I waited, the question hanging in the air. "Will it be the Russians?" I finally asked.

"I don't know. Quite likely."

"No, Vati! It can't be! I have heard horrible things about what they have done in the East, and I…"

"Shhh! Jutta, please be quiet." My father looked around anxiously. I peeked past him. The lady across the aisle stared at us. My eyes held hers, and she looked away.

"You must not talk so loud," whispered my father. "We are supposed to pretend we can win this war still." I looked at Vati, and he rolled his eyes. "You know, Göebbels' 'total war' effort." My father sighed. "How many more lives will be wasted because of it?" he muttered under his breath.

As the streetcar turned a bend, the hospital became visible ahead.

"This is our stop," I said. We stood up, and the lady across the aisle looked at us again. I smiled, but she did not return the favor. I walked to the front of the streetcar with my father. I was glad to be off the thing. I hated the loud scraping noise it made as its wheels ran along the lines overhead. We walked quickly along the street. Nobody was around at this end of town. They must all be on the Breiteweg today, I thought. As we approached the hospital I ran ahead, taking the steps two at a time. I stopped suddenly, realizing that Vati would not know where her room was.

"Fourth floor, room 410," I called back to him.

He nodded. "Go on ahead. I'll catch up."

I knew he was giving me time to be alone with her, and I thanked him silently.

I ran into her room, breathless as usual. She sat up in her bed, pillows supporting her back, her bifocals perched on her nose as she read a book. The noise of my entrance startled her, and she looked up in surprise.

"Jutta!" She put down her book and smiled. "I swear, child, you are going to kill yourself with these breakneck entrances!"

I sat on her bed and grabbed her hand.

She glanced at her watch. "You're early today, my dear. I wasn't expecting you for another thirty minutes or so."

I nodded. She frowned and looked closely at me. Those piercing blue eyes, still alert despite her age, bore into mine. "What? What is it, child?" she asked quietly.

I leaned forward and put my head on her chest as gently as I could. "I have to go, Omi." Tears sprang to my eyes. At first she did not understand.

"Go? But why? You just got here!"

"No. I have to go. I have to go home to Berlin." I sobbed quietly into her nightgown.

She stroked my hair. "Oh," was all she said. We stayed that way for a few minutes, silently drinking in each other's warmth for as long as we could.

"Is Vati here, then?" she asked finally.

I nodded my head.

"I see." Her chest rose as she took a deep breath. I knew she was upset. She knew what this meant.

"I don't want to leave you, Omi." I lifted my head to look in her face. She brushed away my tears.

"I know my dear, and I don't want you to go. But your father is right in bringing you home."

"But why? Why can't I stay here?" I pleaded.

"You should be with your Mutti and Vati when it ends." She looked toward the window. "And it must be almost over, or Vati would not have come." She made the sign of the cross over her chest. That single movement of her hand frightened me more than anything.

"Omi, will it be all right?"

"I think so, my dear. The good Lord will take care of his flock."

I frowned. "But he hasn't so far, Omi. Look at all the people who have died! Look at all the horrible things happening to Germany, and it will get worse, and ..."

She silenced me with her finger pressed to my lips. "I know it seems so to you now, but he will take care of you, Jutta. I have prayed for that, and I will continue to pray for that."

The certainty with which she said it gave me comfort. I hugged her, and for a moment peace quieted my frantic thoughts.

"Now listen to me. Don't you worry about the Opa or me. We will be fine."

"I know," I said, trying to convince myself.

"I will be out of here in no time, and everything will be right again. You will see."

"Vati says that he will have Ilsa come back and forth and bring you food." I suddenly remember the little package I had brought. I still clutched it in my right hand.

"Here," I said lifting it up for her to see. "I almost forgot."

"You are so good to your Omi. What did you bring me today?" She took the package from my hand and opened it carefully, peeking inside.

"It was all we had." I said, upset I hadn't had time to bring more.

"An egg! Lovely! And you know I love Frau Burdick's *Brötchen*!" She put the package on her bedside table. I could have brought Omi stale bread and she still would have acted pleased.

"Thank you, dear." She stroked my cheek. I heard the door open and knew that it was time. Omi looked past me and smiled at my father. "Hello, Hans. I hear you have come to collect our girl."

"Hello, Mutti. How are you?" he asked. He walked to the side of the bed and bent down to kiss her on the cheek.

"Oh, I'm all right for an old lady." She chuckled.

"I'm sorry, Mutti, to take her from you, but ..."

Omi held up her hand. "You must do what you think is best, Hans."

He nodded.

"*Ja*. Jutta, now you must go, and you must hurry. The train lines may not last long." I looked at her, astonished that she knew about these things. I thought she lived in the same isolated world as Opa. She winked at me, seeing my expression.

"I will miss you!" I sobbed, hugging her again.

"I know. And I will miss you. But you must go now, Jutta. Go with your father and as soon as we can, when this is all over, I will come to Berlin to visit." I nodded. "Vati will send the car for me, won't you, Hans?"

"Of course. As soon as they let me." It sounded so strange to hear them talk of sending the car. For years now the authorities had not allowed Vati to take the car outside of Berlin, let alone to Halberstadt.

Omi pushed me up gently with both of her hands. "Jutta, you must be strong for your Omi and for Vati. *Ja?*"

I took in a deep breath and drew my lips into a straight line and nodded.

"Now go. And remember," she raised her eyebrows and pointed up to the ceiling, "He will be there." She grabbed me to her and hugged me hard for a long time. Vati took my hand and pulled me gently away.

"Goodbye, Omi," I said through tears.

Her eyes became watery. "Goodbye, my dear. Now go." She waved me away with her hand. I stopped at the door and turned around; a tear had spilled onto her cheek. She wiped it away quickly.

"I love you."

"I love you too, Jutta." She saw that I hesitated at the doorway. I wanted to come back to her.

"No. You must go with your father now, my dear!"

Vati pulled me through the door and rushed me as fast as he could down the stairs. I stopped crying out of the sheer need to concentrate on the stairs so that I did not fall. As we ran into the street, the sunlight hit my face and its heat dried my tears.

"Let's walk back," said my father. "We don't have time to wait for the street-car. It could be fifteen minutes before it comes again." Before I could say anything he grabbed my hand and walked at a speed I had never seen from him before.

We turned onto Georgenstrasse, walking quickly past the ancient water tower with its rickety wooden stairs and platform. I never understood how these sorts of things worked. How did the water collect in them? I let my mind wander to keep it from fixating on our departure. Three boys had climbed up the wooden stairs of the tower and were throwing rocks at two more down below. Their knee-length socks had large holes in them, and even from a distance I could see that their clothes were worn. One of the boys saw us and shoved his hands in his pockets so we would not see the rocks. But Vati had not even noticed them. He stared at the ground, looking up only to check on a street sign here and there. At Gerberstrasse he turned us to the right and I saw the steeple of Saint Catharine's Church ahead of us. The steeple, much smaller than those of the other churches, looked out of place sitting up on that large church, just a tiny, narrow point.

"Doesn't the steeple look funny up there, Vati?"

He glanced up and shrugged his shoulders. "I guess."

"It looks like it doesn't belong."

He smiled but said nothing. Behind his smile there was a meaning.

"Saint Catharine's is Catholic, I think," I said, more for conversation than anything.

"It must be pretty empty now," he said. "They had a large youth program and a big congregation when I lived here. I always wanted to attend their youth program."

"Really?"

"Yes! They had dances and they went hiking. I had a friend who was Catholic and he always seemed to have much more fun than the rest of us. But my father would not let me. 'We are Protestant, not Catholic! Out of the question!' And that was the end of the discussion."

"Opa Bolle was so strict with you, but with me he was so easy," I said, hooking my arm through my father's arm.

"We soften with age."

We passed the church on the south side of its nave. Colored glass windows sparkled brilliant shades of red, green, and blue in the sunlight.

"Well, Hitler ended all the fun anyway."

"Did he?"

"Of course! He banned all the Catholic youth programs. They competed with his Hitler Youth," he said his voice low.

I shook my head. We had turned onto the Hoher Weg, and I took in the scene ahead of us. I loved this street with its carved facades and many shops, but today it looked dreary to me. The streetcar ran down the center; we heard it coming behind us. Vati disengaged his arm and waved for the streetcar driver to stop, but the driver stared straight ahead. Ignoring Vati's outstretched arm, he kept on going.

"Thank you!" shouted my father.

I looked around, embarrassed that Vati had drawn attention to us. A woman stood in front of the bank watching us. Her dress hung loose around her waist. "They won't stop except where there is an actual stop."

"They used to, didn't they?" muttered my father.

She shrugged. "I think so."

"Perhaps it will be good for us to walk." He shrugged. "Who knows how long the train will take to get us back to Berlin?"

I nodded and stepped onto the street, nearly twisting my ankle on the cobblestones in my effort to avoid a woman and her baby stroller.

"Sorry," she said over her shoulder.

Vati grabbed my hand and helped me back up onto the sidewalk. A bicycle came from behind us and rang its bell to warn us, passing to the left of us. Vati shook his head. "All of Halberstadt seems to be on the sidewalk today!"

We passed an empty jewelry store and a clothing store with a few lonely dresses hanging in the window. Only the bank and the bakery were busy.

"The stores are deserted, aren't they?" said Vati, more to himself than to me.

"Yes. Since December it's gotten worse. You can hardly find anything to buy!"

"I hope you and the Omi have been able to find everything you need."

"Oh, Omi manages. We've been fine."

"She never wrote me that she needed anything," he added.

"Vati, it's been fine. Don't worry." As I said it I heard them—far off in the distance. Vati heard them a few seconds after I did. He stopped in his tracks. His fingers locked around my arm, tightening as he listened, his eyes staring down to the ground. Everyone on the street stood still, listening. It was as if for a few seconds nobody in the town moved. I could not see them yet because the towers of the *Dom* and the *Martinikirche* blocked the sky. The sound grew louder and louder. Vati grabbed my arm up by the shoulder and ran, half dragging me. The air raid siren began to wail. People who had been in their homes spilled out onto the street, running for the nearest air raid shelter.

"Don't worry, Vati," I shouted between breaths. "All those dirty things ever do is fly over Halberstadt on their way to Berlin."

But as I said it, I noticed women running into buildings, and those with children called to them to come immediately. One lady ran in front of a car, her hat flying off her head, to get to her small son who had been looking into the window of the bakery on the other side of the street. He saw his mother's panicked face and ran to meet her; she scooped him up in her arms in one motion and kept on running. Vati grabbed my arm harder, and it hurt where his fingers dug in.

"Come, we must find a shelter fast," he shouted. As he ran, he looked from one side of the street to the other, scanning for a bomb shelter.

"Vati, I'm telling you they won't bomb us," I said through short bursts of air, panting now as we ran.

We had turned the bend at the backside of the *Martinikirche*, and suddenly they emerged into view. I frowned. They were flying awfully low. They never flew this low! They weren't over us yet, but it would be only a matter of seconds before the sound, which had already begun to drown out all else, would be unbearable as it crossed directly overhead.

And then I stopped dead in my tracks, pulling my father backward in surprise. My mouth flew open as I watched what looked like little black beans falling out of the bottoms of the planes. They were bombing! They were bombing Halberstadt! This could not be! Why would they do that? Vati yanked me forward. My mind raced back to the map that the *Luftschutz* warden had passed out in school showing all the bomb shelters. I saw that map in front me. There was one by the *Martinikirche*, but where? I raced along next to Vati and saw men and women pushing through an open door. The ground began to shake, and the sound of the explosions pierced my ears. We headed for the door. My father pushed me through the same door that everyone else had gone through. I felt my shoulder bruise on the hard wood, but it gave and we pushed through, the doorway briefly casting sunlight across the frightened faces within.

It was the cellar to a grocery store. Already, within those few seconds, at least fifty people huddled together in the dark, moist cellar. The smell of old vegetables hit my nostrils. A man shouted, "Where is the light?" Another shouted, "Don't let any more in! We will be crushed back here!"

I heard a woman behind me praying, but it was so dark I could not see any faces. I only heard voices and sounds muffled in the darkness. People shifting, moving, fabric touching fabric, throats clearing, and children quietly sobbing in terror as their mothers tried to comfort them. A woman cried out suddenly, hysterically; then came a slap, and the crying stopped. Vati held my arm in the same viselike grip. I felt my arm go numb. I held my breath and closed my eyes as the deafening sound continued overhead. The ground shook from the assault, and the building above us swayed back and forth. The wood beams strained, the sound reminding me of the old door to our cellar back in Berlin. Bits of dirt and plaster rained down on us, and the dank smell of earth became stronger.

Vati's lips were on my ears so I could hear above the deafening sound of the explosions above. "Jutta, we must try and get out of here when the first wave finishes. We must get to the outskirts of town, where it is safer." I nodded my head, forgetting he could not see me. The door to the cellar let in a small amount of light, and I could tell we had been pushed about ten feet back from the entrance. Above us the sound lessened a little, and Vati began to push me forward.

"What do you think you are doing?" cried a woman whose foot I stepped on.

"Sorry."

Vati pushed harder, and we managed to squeeze forward another few feet.

"Hey. What are you trying to do, you idiots?" shouted a man in my ear.

"Excuse us," said my father.

"You can't leave. Are you crazy?"

"Are you trying to kill your daughter?" shouted another man. The light from the cracks around the door cast an eerie beam, cutting through the crowd, illuminating only a few of the people. It spotlighted us like a theater light as we came up to the door.

"Herr Führer! Where is the *Luftschutzwart?*" called someone. "Don't allow this fool to kill his daughter!"

Vati ignored him and pushed harder. Someone's elbow hit me in the chest. I ignored the pain and pressed on. Something told me not to question my father. I became as determined as he to get out of the shelter. The bombing stopped, the planes faded into the distance, and Vati pressed forward with renewed effort, faster now, almost losing me to the elbows and shoulders still between us and the door.

"What is going on back there?" came a voice that was used to authority.

"This idiot is trying to push his way out of here," called a voice behind us. We were nearly there; only a matter of two or three feet now and we would be to the door. The few people who stood between us and the door stepped back inches to let us pass, our urgency communicated in an unspoken language. As we reached the door, an arm came down to block our way.

"You are not allowed out of here. I have my orders." The voice was the same one I had heard asking what was going on. I recognized the man as a Nazi official of some sort I had seen on parade days marching proudly in his uniform. Today he was the *Luftschutzwart*; he wore a simple brown shirt.

"Please let us pass," said my father. His voice sounded foreign to me.

"No. You know the rules. You stay until the all clear sounds!"

"Let me out, now!"

"I will not! You may want to kill yourself, but I can't let you kill the girl."

"I come from Berlin, where we live this every day. Everyone in here will be killed!" shouted my father. A murmur rose behind us.

The man began to say something else, but Vati shoved him hard against the wall; his head hit the plaster with such force I heard bits of plaster patter to the ground; he lost his balance, his feet becoming entangled with the person next to him. With his free hand, Vati slammed me against the door. We spilled into the street. I fell, my knee scraping on the hard, cold cobblestones. Pain shot through my knee, followed by the warmth of blood running down my leg. Vati's arm was immediately under my shoulder, lifting me. He pulled me forward, and we ran as fast as we could down the Hoher Weg toward Spiegelstrasse.

The stench of fire hit my nostrils. Everywhere I looked I saw smoke coming from the tops of buildings. Women screamed and men shouted as people ran in different directions, all of them having only survival as their goal.

"Pull your shirt up over your mouth and nose," commanded my father. I did as I was told. He had taken his handkerchief out of his pocket and held it up to his mouth and nose with his right hand. With his left hand he grabbed my wrist and pulled me forward. I struggled to keep my balance with the awkwardness of holding the top of my shirt over my nose. Water ran down the side of the street, and we jumped over its rivers as we leaped onto the sidewalk on the opposite side of the street.

"They've hit a water main," shouted Vati.

The windows of all of the shops had been blown out by the force of the bombs. The glass crunched under our feet as we ran along what used to be a pristine sidewalk. Where the sidewalk was especially smooth, the glass made it like skating on ice. If you caught a piece of it wrong, your foot slid out from under you to the side. The once-blue sky, now black with smoke, looked menacing, when just moments ago it had held the promise of peace. Out of all the smells of war my nose detected a new smell, a smell that was vaguely familiar, but I could not place it.

Suddenly my father grabbed my hair with his handkerchief and began beating and pulling at it. I stopped running. I thought he had gone mad.

He pulled me forward. "Your hair! Your hair was on fire!"

The curling iron! The connection was made.

"Oh my God!" I shouted. "Did you get it all?" I grabbed at my hair. A section by my face was burned. Where my once-beautiful, long auburn hair had been, only brittle stubs remained.

"My hair!" I wailed, slowing my pace.

"Don't worry about that now! Keep moving!" Vati once again pulled me forward by the wrist. I had no choice but to keep up with him. There was an edge to his voice. As we passed Lindenweg I could smell gas in the air. Vati smelled it, too. "Run! They've hit a gas line! Hurry up, before the whole town blows!" He put his arm around me to guide me through the rubble that had come crashing down on the streets and sidewalks in our paths. I saw a *Käthe Kruse* doll, grotesquely twisted, outside the downstairs window of a house where it had been thrown by the force of a blast. It lay impaled on a rose bush outside what I presumed used to be a child's room; black soot marks covered the doll's once-perfect pale face.

"Jutta, you have to run faster!"

In response I shook off his arm and picked up my pace and ran so that he no longer had to pull me. He grabbed my wrist again, as if he were afraid that if he did not have hold of me, he would lose me. A red glowing cinder floated peacefully down from a house to my right. I glanced up, fearful for my hair.

"Oh my God! Vati!" I screamed.

There, ahead of us, I saw them, the next wave of bombers, small, dark dots flying in formation. We had run fast and come far, but we were only at the intersection of Hauptmann-Loeper Strasse and Spiegelstrasse, still too near the center of town for comfort and still at least a half mile from Omi's house.

A row of houses stood on the opposite side of the street. I knew Vati was heading for them. Strangely, I thought to admire the beautiful pink facade of one house with carved molding around the top. My eyes wandered over the exterior and then back up to the sky. Please don't let a bomb hit such a perfect house, I prayed. We dashed down the steps at the side of the front door and pushed through. The basement was already full of people. The smell of fear hit me immediately.

"Are they coming again?" asked an old man by the door.

"Yes."

"How many?"

"Hundreds."

A woman wailed. Another held a set of rosary beds and kept repeating, "Hail Mary, full of grace..."

My father glanced at her, his expression blank; he turned to me, and our eyes met. He hugged me to him. I saw him close his eyes, and his lips moved quickly and silently for a moment. He hugged me harder. And then he said, "As soon as the sound subsides a bit, we will run for the Omi's house as fast as we can. Don't stop for anything."

I nodded my head into his chest. I could see his hand as it hung empty by his side. Where was his umbrella? I lifted my head and looked to the other side. His other hand was around me, so I felt for it with my hand. Empty. Vati had lost his umbrella. Tears sprang to my eyes. I couldn't believe Vati had lost his umbrella. Opa Bolle had given it to him. The wood came from Africa, and now it was gone, lying in the street burning, or under a pile of rubble from some collapsed building. I began to cry.

"Not now, Jutta! Later! Now we must focus only on the Omi's house," whispered my father, thinking I was crying from fear.

"Where do you think our great leaders are?" called out a woman.

"In a cement bunker in Bavaria" replied a man. "They don't face this war in the basement of some house."

"And our great Führer?" asked another sarcastically.

"Stop with this talk of disrespect to our Führer," replied a woman from the other side of the basement. "He has done all he can. Is he not still in Berlin? Unlike the rest of the crowd."

"If it weren't for his ego, we would not be in this mess!"

"Stop it now, I say, or I will have you denounced."

The woman snorted, "To whom?" she asked sarcastically. "Everybody is dead!"

Heads nodded in the crowd. The woman looked away, unable to respond. The old man at the door looked at the ground, shaking his head. My father and I said nothing. Our ears were trained on the sound of the bombs, waiting for the intensity to lessen.

As the sound began to diminish, my father dropped his arms from around me. Grabbing me again by the wrist, he nodded to the door.

"Let's go," he said.

This time nobody tried to stop us. But I felt their uncertain stares burn into my back as we hurried out the door of the shelter.

"Good luck," my father called over his shoulders as we climbed the steps. And then we were in the street again. I heard the crackle of fire before I even saw it. The entire block across the street from us was in flames. They must have suffered a direct hit. My mind went numb. What if it had been this side? Women and children streamed out of the basement, coughing and gasping for air as they emerged. My father urged me forward. Smoke burned my lungs, and I pulled my shirt back up over my nose. The sky was dark. Live cinders floated by us, and I batted at them with my hand. Vati let go of my other hand to pull his jacket off as we ran from one corner to the next.

"Here," he said, placing the jacket over my head like the habit of a nun. I accepted it and only worried briefly about a cinder burning through his shirt. We ran forever. It was awkward running with one hand on my head holding Vati's jacket and the other holding my shirt over my nose. Vati kept pushing me closer to the buildings, under the overhangs, which made it even more difficult to run. A rat-a-tat sound, over and over again, shattered my ears. I couldn't connect the sound. I concentrated on running, running as fast as I could towards Omi's house.

We ran south on Spiegelstrasse. A huge crater now ripped through the center of the intersection of Harmoniestrasse and Spiegelstrasse, but up ahead I could see the air was still clear and the houses intact, except for a chestnut tree that stood alone, its dark branches now black and licked by red and orange flames. We passed by on the opposite side of the street to avoid its flames. Tears fell from my eyes as I ran by, and my nose began to run, making breathing all the more difficult. Why did they have to hit the tree? It had always marked where I turned down Bernh-Thierschstrasse to go to school. I dropped my hand from my shirt and wiped my eyes. In doing so I slowed my pace, and Vati pulled me forward again.

"There still could be more coming. They haven't sounded the all clear yet."

We were almost to Omi's house now, and the air was not as bad as a few blocks back. I could see Omi's apartment house ahead. I gave Vati back his jacket.

"Nothing has been hit, Vati!" I called in between breaths.

He nodded.

We entered the house, and the stillness of the house struck me immediately; compared to the chaos outside, there was not a sound in the house other than the cuckoo clock ticking away methodically. I looked around for Opa and didn't see him at first, and then I saw the top of his head, barely visible over the brown leather back of his chair. Like the house, he was still; he didn't move at all. He didn't get up. He didn't greet us or ask us what was going on in town. He just sat staring out at his view of the fields. I walked over to his chair. He still didn't look up or move. I followed his gaze out the window to the fields and the mountains beyond, and I realized he could see the bombers coming from his chair. He must have sat in his chair alone, watching as wave after wave of bombers flew toward his beloved city on their mission of death and destruction.

I shuddered. "Opa?" He did not move. But for the steady rise and fall of his chest, I would have thought he was dead. In the distance I heard the all clear. "Opa," I said again. "It's all right. It's over." He continued to stare.

My father had come up next to me. Gently he pulled me away by the shoulder. "Jutta, go collect your things, quickly. I'll talk to Opa."

I walked away, not sure what to think. Was Opa dead? I thought again. He was alive, I knew; I saw his chest rising and falling with his breath. I ran to my room and grabbed my hairbrush, my toothbrush, and a lipstick that Omi had somehow found and snuck to me without Opa knowing. For a second I wondered if Vati would approve.

"Jutta, hurry!" called my father. "Only take what you can fit in your book bag."

I grabbed my photos of Mutti and Vati and one I had from my confirmation of me with the Omi on the *Domplatz*. Omi! Oh my God! I hadn't even thought about Omi. Was she all right? Had they hit the hospital? Guilt crawled over me; I didn't have time to find out. I grabbed a pair of underwear and socks and my jacket and ran back to the living room with my book bag. Vati was in the kitchen; he had packed Omi's shopping bag with a few *Brötchen* and two more hard-boiled eggs he found in the icebox. He grabbed an empty bottle and filled it with water from the bottle Omi kept in the icebox. Placing this in the bag as well, he said, "Get a drink before we go." I obeyed without question.

We walked back into the living room. Opa had still not moved.

"He is in shock," said my father. "Ilsa will take care of him when she gets here."

I nodded. I ran over to Opa and kissed him on the forehead. He blinked his eyes but otherwise did not respond.

"Goodbye, Opa," I said softly.

"Jutta, come on. We must go."

We stepped out onto the front stoop and saw hundreds of people streaming out of the city, their faces covered in soot. Some of them carried small children. Some of them were burned—their skin falling off in sheets, the smell sickening. One lady carried a small boy whose arm was completely burned. He was unconscious in her arms. She looked up at my father, her eyes pleading.

"Dear God in heaven," said my father. "Go in and get some water!" I dropped my book bag and ran in the house to get towels and water for the boy. I watched through the window as my father helped the woman carry her burden up the stairs to our stoop.

I handed the glass to the woman, but she didn't take it. She was moaning and rocking the child, who did not move in her arms. I tried to give it to the boy, but my father put his hand out to stop me. It was only then that I realized the boy was dead. I looked away. My eyes fell on a girl of maybe ten years old standing in the street. She called out, "Could I have some water?" Her hair was covered with ashes, and some of it had burned, and her face looked like a character in a Charlie Chaplin movie, the whites of her eyes were so exaggerated against the black soot on her face. No one was with her. I ran down the steps and handed the glass to her. She grabbed it with both hands and drank it down in two gulps. I waited for the glass. A man had come up behind the girl. I thought it might be her father, but he stopped and stared at me, his face and hair covered with black and his shirt in tatters at the shoulder, exposing an arm streaked with blood. I grew uncomfortable and looked away.

He walked closer. "Weren't you and your father in the bomb shelter at the *Martinikirche*?" he asked suddenly.

"Yes."

"You were the ones who fought your way out. I remember you."

I nodded and looked back at him in alarm. It was then I realized he was the

Luftschutzwarden in the brown shirt who tried to stop us. Is it possible he will cite us in all this madness? The thought so bizarre it was almost amusing.

"Well, I am the only survivor." He said it without emotion, his blank eyes staring out from his soot-encrusted face.

A shiver ran up me and I felt my skin prickle.

"I was by the door. A bomb hit the building directly, and the force blew the door open, throwing me out of the shelter. The entire building collapsed." He snapped his fingers. "In seconds it was gone. No one had time to get out."

My father handed the man a glass of water. Vati had somehow found a bucket and filled it with water.

The man laughed a hollow laugh. How odd it sounded! "You must have a guardian angel!" He shook his head and added, "Thanks for the water," before he moved on. As he walked on, he looked over his shoulder at us and shook his head again and again. I spun around searching for the little girl but she was gone, lost in the stream of refugees.

We gave out water for the next thirty minutes, my father and I taking turns running up and down the stairs to fill the bucket. I avoided the faces of these refugees from the city. Some looked in shock like Opa; they walked by with no expression at all, as if they had died in their living bodies. Some were crying silently, the tears forming long black streaks down their sooty black faces. Some looked grim but alive and determined to arrive at some unknown destination. Nobody talked. They just walked or ran in silence out to the fields or maybe the Spiegelsbergen. Who knew?

"Jutta, I am going to get one last bucket, and then we must go. Get your bag."

I nodded and followed Vati up the steps.

———

We joined the others walking toward the little tourist train station at the corner of Beethovenstrasse. What once would have been a nice family outing was now an aimless trek for survival. We walked south for a long time, trying to put as much distance between us and the heat of the fire wall that was now Halberstadt. The main train station for Halberstadt was to the east, but the town was a solid sheet of fire and the heat was intense, felt even this far out into the fields.

"The station is this way," I said, pointing to the east.

"I know, but there is no way to walk through town. It's too dangerous."

I remembered hearing about how in Berlin entire city blocks that had one wall still standing would come crashing down without warning, killing hundreds who had thought they had survived the bomb attack.

We walked further south instead and decided that we would then turn east, making a big arc around the town, in the remote chance the train station was still standing. We trudged on with the others out to the fields, the mud from the recent rains sticking to our shoes, weighing them down with a layer of clay. As we got further away from the town, people began to talk more. And then suddenly we heard it again—the sound.

"Oh, my God. They're coming again," screamed a woman.

"They're coming back to survey how well they did," said a man bitterly.

"Those aren't bombers. Don't worry," said another.

They came closer and closer, and my father grabbed me again, and again we ran for our lives, trying to cross the field before they arrived, heading for the stand of trees on the other side. The mud, thickening on our shoes, made running almost impossible. The planes cast dark shadows over the people ahead of us, and I heard the same sound I had heard in town. Like the sound of popcorn popping, rat-a-tat. It took us a second to realize they were shooting. They were machine-gunning everyone in the field! Flying very low, they released deafening blasts of bullets down on the people ahead of us. My father shoved me face-first into a furrow of the field. I felt the mud ooze through my blouse. He threw himself on top of me and covered my head with his arms.

"It will be all right," he said over and over. I wasn't sure if he was saying it to himself or to me. I heard the bullets hitting all around in hollow thuds as they drove into the dirt of the fields. Bits of dirt flew everywhere. Terror swept over me, and my legs began to shake under the weight of Vati's body. I couldn't breathe from the mud that oozed into my nose. I turned my face up. I looked through Vati's arms and saw the face of a pilot—expressionless. He looked down, and for a brief moment I thought his eyes met mine before he released more bullets onto the shivering bodies in the field. They were Americans; I could tell by the planes. And then they were gone. It was a matter of seconds. I looked up to see if they were going to turn around and fly back over us. But they didn't. Vati and I watched as their planes grew smaller and smaller in the distance. Vati grabbed my arm and pulled me up and once again we ran, not certain if there were more following behind the first group.

We ran to the stand of trees at the edge of the field. Hundreds of others followed us to the stand, as if it were the only island in a raging sea. Others remained in the field, face-first in the black mud. They looked asleep, as if exhaustion had overtaken them, but I knew they were dead. I wanted to rest. My legs ached from the running, and for a brief moment I envied them. Vati's breath came hard and loud from behind me, penetrating my thoughts. He needed to catch his breath. I was out of breath, but not like Vati. The years of Hitler-required *Völkerball* and running finally paying off. That's why he was so keen on sports, I thought bitterly. So that when our enemies came, as he knew they would, we could run faster than anyone else.

"We should follow this road to the east, Jutta," shouted Vati over the sounds of the people around us. "I'm sure the train station has been hit, but maybe in the next town we can catch a train."

"*Ja,* the station is totally gone," offered a woman standing near us.

"And the tracks?" asked my father.

"Bombed, too. Twisted like pretzels."

"Where are you going?" asked a boy of about thirteen. Bits of mud decorated his face.

"Berlin," said my father.

The woman raised her eyebrows but said nothing.

"Try Gross Quenstedt," said the boy, pointing to the east. "Or if not there, Nienhagen is after that." He shook his head. "But Berlin will be difficult."

"How far is Gross Quenstedt?" asked my father

"Maybe five kilometers," said the woman.

"I wouldn't go to Berlin if I were you. I hear they are drafting anything male that can walk for the *Volksstorm*," said a white-haired man of about sixty. He had thoughtful, kind eyes. He laughed. "You look like a prize compared to what they are used to: wheezing old men and young boys that wet their pants at the first shots."

The woman shook her head. "They came to try and get Wolfgang." She nodded toward the boy. "Some cocky eighteen-year-old little *Scharführer*, but I threw him out. The boy is only twelve and they want him to tote a gun!" Several people shook their heads in sympathy. "If this is all the Führer can offer to protect us, then he and his fat *Reichsmarschall* should be strung up!" People shuffled their feet uncomfortably, and some moved away from the woman. The boy said nothing. He was apparently used to his mother's tirades, and besides, what was anyone going to do to her now?

"Well, thank you. We will try Gross Quenstedt," said my father, nodding to the boy. "We need to hurry before it gets dark."

"Yes, hurry. You might be just in time for the nightly bomb attack on Berlin," said another old man sarcastically as we left the group and headed up the road toward the east. Vati ignored him, and we fell in with the hundreds of others who were now all walking to get as far away as possible from the inferno that lay across the field to the north. I could hear the sirens of the fire trucks trying to fight the impossible. The entire town was engulfed in black smoke, out of which great sheets of fire licked the sky. Guilt hit me again. Omi! I hadn't even thought about Omi! I had only thought of escape from the burning flames and smoke that had engulfed us.

"Vati! Do you think Omi is all right?" I asked anxiously.

"I hope so. I'm sure they evacuated the hospital if the fire headed that way. It's far enough away from the center of town that I doubt that it was hit. And they have staff there to help evacuate."

"But only nurses are there now. No one who can carry Omi downstairs."

"Jutta, she's fine. When we get to the house we'll try and call. It may take a few days before lines are back up, but the hospital will be one of the first places they fix." He put his hand on the back of my head. "So don't worry about the Omi."

I kicked a stone in the road. "What will happen to her and to Opa?"

"I can't say," said my father softly.

I knew that practically every building in Halberstadt was made of wood. I looked over at the wall of fire that once was Halberstadt and shuddered. We walked on in silence for a long time.

"I didn't even think about her or Opa," I said after a while. The guilt had to be let out; I couldn't bear it in silence.

"Jutta, there was no time to think. There was only time to react. Nobody thinks about anything except what is immediately around them during a something like that. Now stop it. You love them and you are thinking of them now, but you could not have thought of them back there." He looked at me to see if his words were sinking in. "Besides, what could you have done for them?"

"I know, but I just can't believe I didn't even think about them."

"Stop it!" He hugged me to him as we walked, causing me to fall into him.

We stopped for a moment in the road, the people streaming past us paying no attention. I looked past him at the wall of fire behind him. The wind had picked up, and the smoke had blown free of the town. I could feel the heat on my face. I shuddered.

"Come, Jutta. Let's find a train," said my father, looking straight ahead.

I don't know how long we walked. I paid no attention. My mind numb, I placed one foot in front of the other. My father decided we should walk along the track—he guessed it led to Berlin. I hoped he was right and we weren't walking towards Hamburg instead. We walked and walked, passing empty, bombed-out stations along the way. My feet ached and my head pounded. My nostrils, cracked and dry from smoke and bits of plaster and cement, hurt when I breathed. I was grateful for the water Vati had thought to pack.

It was early evening before a train found us. It came from behind very, very slowly. It could only have come from the junction we had seen in the last town we passed through. As in a dream, it seemed to take forever to reach us in the early evening light. We stood in the middle of the tracks and waved our arms overhead, hoping the conductor would take pity and stop. I heard the shrieking of the huge iron wheels as he applied the brakes. The train labored to a standstill, stopping several meters in front of us. Swollen with people and belongings, it looked like photos I had seen of trains in India. People leaned out of its windows and doors, and young boys sat on top, holding worn belongings. Nobody said anything; they just stared at us, anxiety stretched across their faces, forcing their lips into taut straight lines. The conductor leaned out of his compartment, waiting. He too said nothing.

My father walked up to him. "Are you heading to Berlin?"

The man nodded.

"Can we get a ride?"

The man did not respond. He took off his hat, revealing a pale white skull that contrasted sharply with the black soot on his face. He scratched his head.

"Please, sir. My daughter and I have just come from Halberstadt. My wife is in Berlin. We can't walk all the way there before the Russians arrive."

The man studied us in the silence that stretched forever, then he put his cap back on his head. "Get in. But you'll have to stand in between cars; maybe your daughter can find room inside."

"Thank you. Bless you."

We ran along the side of the train, slipping on the gravel, searching for a platform in between the cars that had room. I began to fear there was none. Even the areas between the cars were completely packed with people, explaining why the train had been moving so slowly. At the seventh car we found space. My father put his hand on my elbow and helped me up. An old man reached down at the same time and grabbed my arm to pull. I was thrown into a group of people, all males from opposite ends of the age spectrum, either young or old. Nobody spoke.

"Thank you," said my father as he hoisted himself on board. Heads nodded and eyes looked at us from expressionless faces. The train pulled forward with a jerk, and I fell back against the glass of the car.

"Jutta, maybe you can step inside."

I shook my head. "No. I want to stay with you."

But my father looked into the car and opened the door. The smell of onions, urine, and fear hit my nose. I shook my head again. "We're better off out here."

He nodded and closed the door quickly.

The ground moved past quickly through the cracks where one car connected with the other, and it hypnotized me as I watched. I pulled my eyes away after a while and looked out onto fields, plowed neatly and meticulously, ready for planting. The fields intersected with other fields, their rich, red soil turned sharply, exposed. An old man stood motionless by his cows at the side of a field, watching us go by. The cows, too, watched, chewing slowly and rhythmically, not understanding what this chain of metal and humanity amounted to; the old man not grasping what passed before him, either.

Even at its slow speed, the noise of the train passing on the tracks made it impossible to talk. Once we reached Magdeburg the train stopped, and we stood still for hours. Word reached us, passing down from one car to the next, that only one line continued on to Berlin, and we had to wait our turn. I leaned out of the side and noted there were at least five trains ahead. The track curved, so I was not sure if there were more or not. We all stood in silence. I let my back slide down the car until I was sitting. Several of the boys, taking my cue, did the same. I leaned my head against my father's leg, and I must have fallen asleep. The jerk of the train moving woke me. I stood up again; the train began to push forward in the early evening light.

My father stroked my hair. "It won't be long now, Jutta."

I nodded.

The land was so flat. So dull and flat, was all I could think of, watching as it slid slowly past us. The soil, here a chocolate brown, lay stiffly turned up in rows, field after field ready for the potatoes and sugar beets that grew in the area. Periodically the fields were broken by a row of poplar trees, their leaves just barely out. An old woman leaned on her broom handle in the courtyard of her red brick house, watching as the train made its laborious way past her. She stared at us. I could see no expression on her face at that distance.

I looked inside the compartment and found the same odd silence as outside, the only movement the rocking of a woman back and forth from front to back, obviously in shock. Nobody paid any attention to her.

I turned around and leaned out the side of the train, hoping to see what lay ahead. In the distance, slightly ahead to the right, I saw a stand of trees by a small country road. Something shiny caught my eye. I couldn't make out what it was. I inched my way closer to the edge to get a better look.

"Watch out, Jutta, or you'll fall off the train!" said Vati, reaching for my arm.

I grabbed the railing. Something was hanging from one of the trees, perhaps a giant sack of potatoes or a duffel bag of clothes. How strange, I thought. Who would forget a bag in the trees during these times? As we approached and the thing came closer and closer it suddenly hit me. It was not a bag. It was a man hanging from the tree, a thick noose around his neck. My mouth fell open. His head hung limp to the side; his hands tied behind his back. He looked like a doll, not real, and at first I thought my eyes were playing tricks on me. A metal sign, like those used to name streets, hung from his neck. And then we were close enough I could read it. Someone had painted, "Traitor and coward" on it. I put my hand to my mouth. My father leaned out to follow my gaze.

"My God," he murmured. He turned me away.

"What did he do?" I asked quietly.

"Nothing."

"But then who did this? The Russians?"

"No. Herr Himmler and his thugs."

"Gudrun's father?"

"Yes." My father's voice was filled with bitterness.

I had heard rumors that Gudrun's father had committed atrocities all over Germany, but I couldn't come to terms with it. I thought of the man who looked like most of the fathers of the girls in my class: boring, middle-aged, and nondescript. Except this father wore the black uniform of the Gestapo.

"But he is a father!" I couldn't grasp how a father could order these things. Somehow I envisioned an evil man to be like the characters in the movies: identifiable, with evil eyes and a sneering smile, but certainly never a man with a family.

My father did not respond.

"But why kill him? I thought they needed every last man for the 'total war?'"

"He probably ran away from the army to see his family. Poor soul."

We did not speak again. I sat back down, looking out at nothing. I remember nothing else. I must have fallen asleep, for it was daylight when the train finally stopped and we got off. How I could have slept out on that noisy train platform, sitting up against Vati, wedged between him and the train compartment, I don't know. But I must have, for not only was it daylight, but the sun had risen high in the sky. Stately buildings peeked through the tops of the kiefer trees in the distance, and I realized we were near Potsdam. The train could not go on, the conductor told us; the tracks no longer existed. We had no choice but to walk the rest of the way to Dahlem.

The street looked familiar, but at the same time it looked odd. It struck me how empty it was. Nothing stirred, the street lifeless, dark. Of course I had expected that, but not the stillness. I knew they would have turned off all the streetlights and house lights because of the air raids. We walked in the dark, concentrating on avoiding the holes and loose stones that littered the cobblestoned street, the moon our only light. It took a moment before I realized we had finally turned onto the Föhrenweg. I peered at the corner house to see if it was Liesel's, but with its windows boarded up, I was uncertain. I checked the number to make sure this really was the Föhrenweg. Number ten! Liesel's house. We were here. I was finally home!

A numbness crept up my back. It was all wrong, not at all how I remembered it. Acacia trees that once stood glorious in the fall light with their leaves a golden amber now stretched across the street sporting blackened stumps for branches, reaching bare and grotesque toward the black sky. Some were burned to the ground. My mother's complaints echoed in my mind: "How messy those damn acacia trees are—always something, leaves in the fall, pollen and buds in the spring, and the risk of branches falling in the summer storms." I imagined her sadness now that so many were gone.

Erica's house, too, was boarded up. From what I could tell in the dark, at least half the houses had wood in their windows instead of glass. They looked out of place, neglected, as if they belonged somewhere else. Not on this street, my street, the Föhrenweg. Gardens that were once impeccable were now overrun with weeds and brambles; no daffodils or tulips had been planted this year. The roses that always graced Erica's front yard and were the pride and joy of her mother were still covered with their leaves from the fall, all brown and dirty, a few shriveled up brown blossoms wedged between their thorny branches. I looked away quickly, my eyes landing on our gate with its crossed, moss-covered wood. Number twelve was unchanged, still standing. I ran.

She must have been watching from the kitchen window—the kitchen that she had insisted be in the front of the house so she could watch me from its huge window as a child playing in the yard. Within seconds of the squeak of the gate she was running down the steps of the house and then the path toward us.

Tears streaming down her face, she ran to me first, hurling herself at me, grabbing me around the neck. Holding my face with both hands, she kissed me over and over again. With her arm still around me, she reached for Vati. It had been over a year since I had seen both of my parents together, and relief swept over me. Vati wrapped himself around both of us and held us tight before saying, "Let's go inside."

"Thank God, Hans! I heard the news!" She covered her face with her hands and wept. My father put his arm around her to guide her back to the house. He nodded for me to bring the bag he had dropped on the flagstone walk. I followed behind them. I had never seen my mother helpless. She looked so small walking next to Vati; her shoulders bent forward, shaking from the force of her crying.

The warmth of the house struck me as I walked through the door. Luise stood in the doorway of the kitchen, hands on her hips, shaking her head. "My, but you are a mess, Fräulein Jutta!" I could see tears rimming her eyes, in danger of spilling over. I ran to her and hugged her.

"My God, but your mother and I thought you were all dead!"

"It was..." I sobbed.

"I know. But we are not going to talk about it now." She laced her fingers through mine. "*Meine Güte*! Your hands are freezing! Come! You're taking a bath before we do anything else!" She pulled the bag off my shoulder and guided me up the stairs as if I had never been to the house before.

She made me undress in the empty tub so the mud from my clothes would not get on the scrubbed white tile floor. Shaking her head, she said, as if I were still a child and she was scolding me for getting too much mud on my clothes from the garden, "How could you have gotten so dirty? How am I ever going to get this mud out of your clothes?" She rinsed me off with hot water to remove the mud on my feet and legs. Handing me a towel to keep me warm, she rinsed the mud out of the tub before starting my bath.

I lay in the bathtub, in my bathroom, until the water grew tepid, trying to make sense of the past day's events. I couldn't fathom it all. I tried to block the images of the wall of fire that had once been a beautiful city. And that face, the stone-cold face of the American pilot looking down at me before he fired on us... Luise's voice thankfully cut off the image.

"Do you hear me, Jutta?" her voice cut in. "I said we spent all day fixing up your room."

"I'm sorry, Luise."

"You must try not to think about it."

"I know, but it is just so odd to have been there and... and then here I am in this beautiful bathroom, in this wonderful bath."

Luise nodded her head. "Of course your window is blown out," she continued, "but we can't do anything about that. There is no glass in all of Germany, it seems. So it is a bit dark, but otherwise just as you remember it." She patted my arm and continued to talk, but I was not listening.

"I just can't make sense out of it." I squeezed my eyes shut and hummed loudly to block the sound of children screaming in terror and the crackle of fire. When I opened my eyes, Luise was gone. I looked around the bathroom for her. Moments later, I heard a light knock on the door as it opened. My mother stepped in. She smiled at me. Her face was still blotchy from her tears, but she had regained her composure.

"Let's wash you, my *Liebling*." She reached for a new bar of her rose soap from the cabinet and, kneeling by the tub, began to scrub my neck. "Scoot under the water so I can wash your hair."

I obeyed. We didn't talk. As she worked on me, she hummed "*Für Elise*." She remembered it was my favorite piano piece. The evil of the past two days washed away. I stopped thinking and remembering and heard only the sound of the water running in my ears as my mother rinsed my hair.

Suddenly I was starving. I realized I hadn't eaten since the day before. Had it really taken us two days to get to Berlin?

"What time is it, Mutti?"

"Almost nine o'clock."

"I'm starving."

"Well, good!" she said, rinsing my hair one last time. "Because Luise has made a positive feast!"

The feast turned out to be a stew filled with a lot of potatoes and carrots and turnips with a disappointingly small amount of meat, but the brown sauce was delicious. I knew it was more meat than most German families had, but still I longed for the big hunks of soft brown meat in Luise's stews of the past. I ate hungrily. Luise had poured the stew over pasta, the kind with the little twists that always looked like corkscrews to me—my favorite type of pasta.

"Mutti?" I asked suddenly. "Is this still the pasta from Italy?"

She laughed. "Yes, it is."

"Wow, that's amazing!" I smiled.

"Thank God for your mother. She planned ahead better than any of the zoo we have running the place," said my father. "I think we are the only family on the Föhrenweg that still has plenty of soap and plenty of pasta!"

"Well, not plenty, but I think we have enough." She took another bite of stew. "As soon as possible," she added, waving her hand vaguely, "once all this bombing stops, I am going to have Gustav come and plant a garden for me."

The conversation continued; we talked about anything other than the horrors of the day. I wondered if Vati had told Mutti about our visit to the Omi.

"Mutti, we said goodbye to Omi," I blurted out.

They stopped talking and looked at me.

"Vati says she will be fine. The hospital is on the north side of town, pretty far out."

"Yes, and they have a good bomb shelter in it," added my father. I could tell he was concerned that I had raised the subject. He looked from my mother to me.

"We said goodbye to Opa, too. The house is fine, but he just sat there staring out the window. It was the strangest thing, like he was not alive." My mother's eyes were filling with tears again. "But he was alive," I added quickly.

"He was in shock. But Ilsa will take good care of him." Vati grabbed my mother's hand. She struggled with her tears. "And as soon as the telephone lines work, we will call."

"Tante Lieschen!" I shouted out, dropping my spoon. My parents looked up, alarmed.

It hit me; she was the one in the most danger. Yes, of course. Café Deesen sat right on the *Fischmarkt* by the *Martinikirche*, and that whole area suffered direct hits. The man in the brown shirt had told us. I knew every building in the *Fischmarkt* dated back to the Middle Ages and was made of wood. My nostrils flared as I tried to keep the tears from coming. The effort was pointless. I knew intuitively that my beloved Tante Lieschen was dead. I closed my eyes, pinching them shut, and prayed out loud. And what about Carla? I had said goodbye to her and then not thought of her again. She had suffered so much already. Oh my God, what happened to Carla and Tante Lieschen?

I prayed feverishly. "Dear God, please let Tante Lieschen live. Even if the café was hit, please let her be safe. And please let Carla and her aunt be safe also. Make sure the bombs didn't hit their home, Lord. "

My father's voice broke through my prayer. "Jutta, we will call. There is no point in worrying about something we can do nothing about right now."

When I opened my eyes, my mother had left the table and was standing by the window staring into the garden, her arms crossed in front of her. I pushed my chair back and went to her.

"Mutti, I'm sorry," I said awkwardly.

"You're sorry! Oh my God, Jutta, I am so sorry!" She laced her arm through mine and continued to stare out into the darkness. "I am so sorry to bring you into this awful world. I am so sorry that you have to see all of this at your age. I am so sorry that we didn't do more when maybe we could have to stop it all." She shook her head. "I don't even know how it happened!"

"You did your best," I said, trying to comfort her.

"No! Nothing we did was enough to make up for this..." she searched for words, her hand in front of her, waving at nothing in the darkness. "...this hell we are putting our children through. Robbing you of your childhood. The things you've seen, and boys your age being sent out to face tanks on their bicycles with bazookas strapped to them, and now with the Russians coming... Madness, utter madness." She wrapped her arms around me and began to cry. "God only knows what..."

"Heidchen, stop! Come, let's have a drink," Vati broke in, guiding us to the living room and calling for Luise. "And then I think Jutta must be tired."

I nodded.

Luise came in the room. "Can I bring you something, Herr Bolle?"

"Please. Bring Frau Bolle a schnapps, and I think I'll take one, too." He turned to me. "Jutta, would you like a wine?"

"No, thank you."

"What about hot chocolate?" asked Luise.

I looked up, astonished. "You still have some?"

"I think so, left over from your mother's famous Italian trip." She winked at me.

"Yes, I'd love some."

Luise left to get our drinks, and silence surrounded us. I looked over at my mother. She sat staring at her hands, entwined on her lap. It must have been awful for her these past two days, knowing that her mother and father and husband and daughter could all be lying dead in the burning flames of the town of her childhood. I had never seen my mother so distraught, and it disturbed me. She was always strong, always composed, and now she was in danger of falling apart. I wanted my old life back: the life where Mutti smiled and everything was certain.

My father got up to put a record on. He chose Louis Armstrong. She looked up from her hands and met his eyes, and then mine. "I can't believe how selfish I am being. You two are the ones who have been through so much today, and I am the one needing comfort!" She shook her head in irritation at herself.

———

I prayed in my bed that night. I prayed we would be spared from air raids that night. I didn't think my mother or I could stand it.

God answered my prayer that night.

We never called my grandparents' house until many months later, and when we finally did the war was over. The telephone lines out of Berlin were never fixed because night after night the bombers came, boldly and without fear, the German defense system dead. And then the Russians came and our lives changed radically.

10

Berlin: The End

April 20, 1945

The sun hit my face in a tiny sliver that penetrated a crack in the wood covering my window. I felt the heat on my cheek in my sleep, but when it climbed to my eyes it woke me. I sat up straight in bed. It must be late! The room was warm. I placed my eye against the crack in the wood and saw that the sun was already well on its way to dominating the morning sky. I ran to my mother's room, where the windows were not broken. Luise had already made the beds, and the windows were wide open to let the morning air into the room. A breeze rustled the trees, and the smell of lilac hit my nostrils. There must not be so much smoke in the air today, I thought as I walked to the window and leaned out. Mutti's small back looked up at me. Her hands pulled and flicked small weeds to the side of the neat rows of the vegetable garden she and Gustav had planted only ten days ago. Because of the warm weather, tiny seedlings had already begun to spring up.

"Mutti!"

She stopped thinning the seedlings, looked up, and smiled. "So, my sleepy head finally woke up?"

"Yes. What time is it?" I asked, stretching lazily in the bright sun.

"Ten o'clock!"

"My goodness! I didn't realize I was so tired!"

What a luxury to sleep through the night without interruption! It had been a long time since I had managed that! No sirens, no bombs, no walls rattling, none of the sounds of war to disturb my sleep. Since I had been home there had been one bomb raid after another. Almost every night we retreated to the basement, escaping the sky, bright from fires and flares all over the city, my heart racing at the whistling sounds that haunted the night.

"Run along to the kitchen. Luise has been waiting for you for breakfast."

I blew Mutti a kiss and skipped to the stairs by her bedroom.

Luise's back was to me as I walked into the kitchen. She was busy boiling water and putting it into huge jars that my mother had gotten from one of the neighbors, Herr Kittel, I think.

"More water!" I exclaimed.

"What happened to '*Guten Morgen*, Luise?'"

I stopped in front of her before sitting down at the kitchen table and gave her a peck on the cheek. "I'm sorry. *Guten Morgen!*"

She nodded, "*Guten Morgen*, Fräulein Jutta! And yes, more water! Your mother wants me to fill all of the jars. Some are for hiding here and some are for us to take to the Wollecks' when the time comes."

"Oh," I raised my eyebrows. My parents and the Wollecks had decided that when the Russians marched in and overwhelmed us, as they inevitably would—no one in his right mind doubted this—we should all congregate at one house. "Strength in numbers," said my father. They chose the Wollecks' house because their basement was better reinforced against bomb damage than our basement. Mutti and Luise had been preparing for the inevitable for weeks. Mutti had hidden her canned goods and dried foods and special herbs in the attic in rat-proof containers. Vati just shook his head when he saw Gustav climb up on the roof. Where tiles had blown off, she had Gustav hollow out a hidden space, and she tied baskets on the end of long ropes that he pulled up, hid, and covered over with a wood panel. I don't know what all she put up there, but I suspect money and jewelry were among the items as well. And weeks ago, Gustav had dug deep holes in the garden and placed crates filled with Mutti's precious Meissen china and Vati's wine and liquors down their cavernous insides, careful to cover them and plant seedlings over the top. Luise said Heinz had come from the factory to help lower the crates, using ropes and boards, and it was quite the production!

"*Ja*. And for breakfast? What will you have, my sleeping princess?"

I shrugged. I was tired of the cereal that was our usual fare lately for breakfast.

"Well, Herr Kittel brought us fresh *Brötchen*. Who knows where he found them!"

"*Ja, bitte*! With an egg, please," I said enthusiastically. I hadn't tasted real *Brötchen* in weeks. What a beautiful day this was turning out to be. Almost as if the war were over.

Luise scurried around the kitchen to make my breakfast. I sat down at the table and leaned on my elbow. The garden looked beautiful in its wild state with the new grass and wildflowers just coming up. The hyacinths and daffodils edged the walk to the gate with yellow and blue blossoms. Mutti's flowers had somehow survived the war.

"What a beautiful day!"

"No doubt Goebbels will tell us that it is a sign from above ordered special since it's *that one's* birthday today."

"Is it? Is today the twentieth?"

"It is indeed."

"Well, we've had four beautiful days in a row, so they can't lay claim to this one, can they?"

"They'll try!" Luise laughed, shaking her head.

I heard thunder rumbling in the distance.

"How strange. Bright sunshine, but a thunderstorm is coming?"

"It's the guns. The Russians are only seven miles away, the radio said." My mother answered me as if she were discussing the weather. She had overheard me as she came through the kitchen door to wash her hands at the sink. She wiped them dry on the towel Luise handed her. "They anticipate an extra-heavy air raid tonight for *his* birthday."

"But I didn't hear the siren."

"I don't think they sounded it. Or perhaps there is no one left to sound it," suggested Mutti. She sat down across from me at the table to keep me company as I ate breakfast. After a moment she said, "Today I want you to pack a small suitcase to take to the Wollecks'."

I nodded my head without looking up, my mood no longer so light.

"Only what you really need, Juttalein, *ja*!" She touched my arm gently as she said it. "Toothbrush, hairbrush, underwear, sweaters, and a few books, but none of your magazines and pictures and things…"

"I know Mutti. I know," I said impatiently.

She ignored me. "Oh, and a few female things—you know."

I rolled my eyes. "I know all that."

"Well, good. You know so much for your age!" she said lightly.

Luise chuckled at the stove.

"Luise, how is the water boiling coming along?"

"Good. I think I have about twenty jars from this morning alone!"

"Wonderful. I was thinking we should also…" Her voice broke off suddenly. I looked up. Her face was frozen with her mouth still open from speaking. Her eyes were locked on something in the garden, but it was the intensity of her stare and the fear that suddenly covered her face that caused me to turn quickly and follow her stare out to the street. And then I saw them: two of them in black uniforms, polished black boots up to their knees, making their way up the path to our front door. They saw us, too, but did not acknowledge us. Their faces impassive, they continued up our flagstone path. My stomach fell, and I stopped eating. I was no longer hungry. Luise, aware that my mother had stopped talking, turned to see why. She saw them through the window.

"*Gott im Himmel*! What do they want?"

My mother got up silently, straightened her shoulders, and walked to the front door. I stayed frozen to my seat in the kitchen. I heard her open the door.

"Heil Hitler!" said a male voice. And then, "Frau Bolle?"

My mother did not respond.

After a moment he said, "Is Herr Bolle here?"

"No, I'm sorry. He is out," said my mother. Her voice was strong, masking what I knew she felt inside.

"We have orders for him from the *Wehrmacht*! He is to report for duty to the *Volkssturm* this afternoon."

"But he is essential personnel!" said my mother quickly. "His factory! We have the papers exempting him from service!"

"Not anymore. They have reconfigured the categories. Only those in food and fuel distribution are considered essential."

My mother was silent.

"As I said, we have orders that he is to report this afternoon to the *Volkssturm*."

I heard papers being handed over. "It says where to go. He will be assigned a battalion commander, and then he will begin training tomorrow morning."

My mother still said nothing. Luise had moved behind my chair to stand. She put her hands on my shoulders. I grabbed her left hand with my right. Her fingers were ice-cold.

"See that he gets the papers," said the one who had been talking.

"I will," said my mother quietly.

"Good day then, Frau Bolle."

"Heil Hitler!" announced the other one. I heard the door close with a quiet click. I stayed by the window, watching them leave through the front gate with their stiff, efficient walk. They glanced on a clipboard and spoke to one another, pointing to the house diagonally across from us. Vati was obviously not their only recruit for the defense of Berlin. But I knew that the Zeismanns had fled to Bavaria months ago, and they would find no male in that household.

As soon as they were out of sight I leaped up and ran to the front door. My mother had made her way into the living room. She sat in her elegant, overstuffed chair with the beige and pale pink roses and stared straight ahead. The hand that held the papers hung limply over the arm of the chair. I ran to her.

"Vati can't go! He can't go!"

"I know."

"But what will he do? They'll kill him if he doesn't go! I saw what they do, Mutti! I saw it! They'll string him up like that man!" I began to shake. I was suddenly very cold.

"It's all right. Let me worry about this, Jutta, please!" Luise stood behind me and stroked my hair with her hand.

Mutti nodded her head toward the kitchen. "Luise, bring a cup of tea laced with schnapps for both of us, please."

Luise hurried off, happy to have something to do.

"Come here and sit beside me." Mutti scooted over and I squeezed in next to her. It was a tight fit, but the warmth of her body calmed me down. She put her arms around me.

"Jutta, you have to trust in your parents. We will figure this out. Vati will not fight in this suicidal mission. You can be certain of that." She laughed, a forced laugh. "Your father wouldn't even know what to do with a gun. He's liable to shoot himself!"

I couldn't even smile.

The schnapps calmed me down, and by the time my father came home for lunch I was back to normal. There was once again no power at the factory, so he had sent everyone home. Everyone who had not already had a visit from the men in the black uniforms, that is. The *Volkssturm* was taking a heavy toll on the work force of Berlin.

My mother had gone next door to consult with Werner Kittel and to see if he too had gotten a visit. He had not. He was still deemed essential personnel because of his position as a bakery wholesale supplier. Herr Kittel returned to our house with my mother, and we all sat in the living room trying to figure out what my father should do. I was pleased that they no longer hid things from me and I was allowed to sit and listen.

Everybody agreed that my father had to report to the *Volkssturm* headquarters in the afternoon, but he should not return the next day. He should disappear. Herr Kittel agreed to hide Vati in his house when the SS came looking for him.

"But Hans, I think I should go down there in the morning. I will announce that you have disappeared and that I am appalled at what a coward I have for a husband."

"I am not sure I want you to go down there. What if they arrest you?"

"Hans has a point," broke in Herr Kittel.

"Oh, don't be silly. Besides, if they come back to the neighborhood they will search everybody's house. No. We must already make it clear you are not here, and maybe they will not take the time to come searching."

"What time are you supposed to report?" asked Herr Kittel.

My father checked the papers. "It says three o'clock."

"What time is it now?"

"One thirty."

Herr Kittel grunted. "You better get going; God only knows what is working and what isn't! It could take you a while to get there. I'll help Jutta and Heti bring your things over. In the morning, come around the back so nobody sees you from the street. Come before it gets light , maybe around five o'clock."

"Yes. Then it is settled." My father slapped his hand on the side of the chair. He glanced down at the papers. There was a second paper under the orders, a flyer of some sort. He pulled it out, read it, and handed it to Herr Kittel. "Here have you seen this latest joke?"

Herr Kittel took the paper and read it, shaking his head in disbelief.

"Berliners, hang on! The Führer in his wisdom has recalled the troops fighting the Americans to Berlin to defend the city against the Russian hordes," he paraphrased the flyer. He looked at my parents. "Do they really expect us to believe this rot?"

"Apparently some do," said my mother.

"Just last night the BBC reported German troops surrendering en masse to the Americans at the Elbe. There are no German troops left to save Berlin!"

"And yet they let little boys go out and be killed!" added my mother softly, her eyes red and watery. "It's murder!"

The men said nothing. The silence fell heavily on the room. In the background we heard the constant drumbeat of guns, and with every shot they were getting closer and closer. Veins stood out on Herr Kittel's forehead and neck, and he worked his jaw continuously. He seemed distant, preoccupied. I glanced at my father, but his face told me nothing. Only the drumming of his fingers on the arm of the sofa suggested his concern.

"It appears the Russians are already here."

"Yes. I heard today at the factory they have surrounded the city on all sides. A tank division is heading up from Zossen and will reach the Teltow Canal by tomorrow night!"

"Happy birthday, Herr Hitler!" threw in Herr Kittel as he got up to go. "Heti, I'll be back in an hour to help you carry things."

Again I thought that Herr Kittel seemed glum and short-tempered, so different from his usual jolly and fun-loving personality. He grabbed a white paper lying on the coffee table, read it, and then shredded it violently. I knew it was the one from Himmler the Hitler Youth had papered the neighborhood with yesterday, saying any males caught with white flags on their homes would be shot, and all the members of their family as well.

I woke suddenly, the sound uncomfortably familiar. The whine was the worst part. I sat up and looked around the basement. My mother too was awake. Always that whine before the explosion. I hated how it gave me enough time to wonder who it would kill. A few seconds for my mind to imagine a family asleep in their beds, waking just in time to hear but not in time to run. Stop it, Jutta. I threw my hands to my ears.

"Jutta, take these." My mother reached over from the chaise lounge next to mine and handed me earplugs.

I took them and put them in my ears. My nightgown was wet across the chest, and I began to shiver. I hadn't even noticed that I was crying. Mutti climbed into my bed, turning me on my side so she could hold me. She placed the pillow over my ear. I could still hear it, but not so bad. It went on for hours, and so close to us. Were they going to bomb Dahlem? Nothing would surprise me anymore. I shut my eyes tight to block out the red lights that burst into the sky and flashed across the basement walls. They came in waves, over and over, again and again. It seemed they would never stop. And then suddenly it did, and I waited; we all held our breath and waited for the all clear to wail its mournful sound. When it did I relaxed a little, but sleep was out of the question. Mutti and I knew that we had to get up in a few hours and face the *Volkssturm* commander.

Earlier that evening, my father had decided we should sleep in the basement rather than get up in the middle of the night, as we so frequently did. So we had gathered our clothes, gone to our basement quarters, and began the night there. We lay silently, each aware the other was also not asleep, and we listened. I was terrified there in the pitch dark, never certain how far off the bombs were. Their explosions amplified by the night. The all clear had sounded, but bombs still exploded in the distance. Now that the explosions had lessened, I could tell the sounds came from the south, somewhere around Potsdam, and then the hum of the bombers retreating was all we heard. It sounded peaceful, almost soothing, next to the constant sounds of the explosions just minutes before.

"Can I turn on the radio?" I asked.

"Yes. We should hear what they're saying."

I reached up to the table where the radio stood next to my makeshift bed and turned it on. I had to strain to hear the announcer over the buzzing in my ears, barely making out that he was saying the RAF had bombed Berlin a record six times, flying one thousand sorties in one night. They had bombed Potsdam especially heavily.

"That's why it sounded so close!" I said to Mutti.

She nodded. "That must mean the Russians are coming in from the south—soon—from Potsdam. They are paving the way for them."

I nodded glumly.

"Why won't the Americans just march in?" I asked in exasperation. "They're only sixty some miles away!"

"Who knows, Jutta? There is nothing we can do about it. We just have to prepare ourselves for the worst."

Vati came through the door before I could answer. I hadn't even realized he was not with us. He had gone out to the bomb shelter out front. My parents thought we should split up in case of a direct hit. That way there would always be someone who could get help.

"My God, if there is anything left after that, it would be amazing!" he said.

"It was too awful this time!" responded my mother.

"Are you all right, Jutta?" asked Vati.

I did not reply. Was I all right? I didn't even know. I thought of Carla and her arm. I shuddered. Stop thinking, Jutta. Stop it!

Luise stirred in her bed, lifting one corner of the pillow she had clamped over her head. She had taken to covering herself with a duvet and pillow when the bombing started, as if these fluffy comforts would protect her if a bomb hit.

"It's over, Luise," I called.

But it wasn't, for we knew it would come again, maybe in a few hours, maybe that night, maybe the next. Who knew? The buzzing in my ears would not stop, and I watched my father telling my mother something on the other side of the room but I could not hear what they said. Only their lips moved, like in a silent movie.

We pushed the heavy door open, and an old gentleman stepped aside to let us pass. He held a rifle and a helmet in his hand. His hair, a snowy white, swept straight back without a part from a forehead covered with age spots. The lines that ran across his forehead and surrounded his eyes suggested intelligence and education.

"What? Are they now drafting women and girls, too?" he asked, half joking.

"*Guten Morgen*," said my mother in response.

He looked closely at my mother's face. "Frau Bolle, isn't it?"

"Yes," said my mother, surprised.

"Herr Wederman. I own the bookstore Herr Bolle used to frequent." He smiled. "That was back when I had books to sell."

"Oh, yes! Geselius! He loves your store!" replied my mother, smiling.

"Thank you." He inclined his head in a half bow. "Your husband, he only bought the best!"

"Herr Wederman, this is my daughter, Jutta," said my mother, turning to include me in the conversation.

"Ah, yes! Jutta! Of course! Eric Kastner and Carl May, and later," he bent down to whisper, "Hemingway, Fitzgerald, and Steinbeck, and I seem to remember *Gone with the Wind* was in there, too."

My mother looked at me and raised her eyebrows. I grinned. He remembered the books that Vati bought for me.

"What an extraordinary memory you have!"

We stood for a second, not sure what else to say.

"How could I forget Herr Bolle? He bought only the best. Always first editions." For a moment, lost in his thoughts, he said nothing. "He was a collector, a true collector." He looked down at his feet and shrugged, remembering. He raised his eyebrows before adding suddenly, "What brings you down here today?"

"I am sorry to say that Herr Bolle has disappeared and will not report for duty today," said my mother curtly.

Herr Wederman stroked his chin with his hand thoughtfully. "What a clever man Herr Bolle is! I wish I had thought to disappear! Well, it doesn't matter. I am old anyway; I will die soon one way or the other. But these poor boys!" He shook his head and indicated the lines inside with a wave of his hand. "God will be the judge," he muttered almost to himself. He laughed a dry laugh. "Well, I had better be off to defend the Reich!" He held his rifle up in mock enthusiasm. And on that note, he tipped his head in the same half bow he had done earlier and let the door close behind him.

I watched it close and heard the decisive click. Left standing facing the door where Herr Wederman had stood, we were suddenly aware of the silence in the room. We turned and faced them, hundreds of pairs of eyes. We looked at them for a moment and they at us, not quite sure what to think. They stood in long lines waiting to go up to talk to one of the officers seated at the rectangular tables. Sheets of white paper pasted on the front indicated which letters of the alphabet were to report to that table. There were old men and young boys, and the only ones in between wore uniforms and were in charge. The old men looked resigned. The young boys looked frightened. Not for the first time I thanked God I was born a girl. The silence in the room was unnerving.

My mother took a deep breath and approached a young officer. Her heels echoed loudly on the concrete floor in the silence of the room. The young officer stood beside the last table, watching us with his green blue eyes from under a perfect shock of auburn hair slicked straight back to highlight his tall forehead and straight nose. He stood up straight seeing my mother approaching him and pulled his uniform jacket into place. I looked from his face to his uniform and remembered what he stood for and went cold.

"I need to speak to the person in charge here."

"I can help you," replied the young officer politely.

As he said it, our attention was diverted suddenly to a heavyset officer who had just entered from a back room somewhere and called out to everyone, "Let's get going. Stop staring and come up when you've been called. We've got a war to fight!"

The officers behind the table looked quickly down to their sheets of paper and began to call out names, "Schmidt, Mertel, Brechtel . . ." and the room filled again with the buzz of male voices.

My mother turned back to the young officer, looked him directly in the eye, and said, "I have come to say that my husband will not be reporting for duty today because he has disappeared."

The young man frowned and didn't seem to know what to do. My mother said nothing, and for a moment he simply stared at her, trying to comprehend what she had just said. Then he turned away from us and walked quickly over to the heavyset one with the bull neck.

"What is the problem?" asked the heavyset one in the supercilious voice of a bureaucrat impressed with his own authority. The young man whispered something in his ear.

"But that is not possible!" said the heavyset one, startled. They stood back from the table and exchanged whispers. The heavyset one held up a hand to stop the young officer from speaking, as if bored with the conversation, and walked over to us with a great show of authority.

He cleared his throat, and without introducing himself he said, "Your husband must report to the *Volkssturm* or there will be very serious consequences!"

"Unfortunately, I cannot find my husband to give him this message," said my mother, unruffled.

"But these orders come from the *Reichsführer* SS himself."

"Yes, so I understand. Herr Himmler is a neighbor, and if you would like I will tell him myself that my husband has gone missing."

"I am sure Herr Himmler is in the field, Madam, and not available at his house."

Did this idiot really think my mother was serious? She simply stared at the man. It was a standoff, and I marveled at my mother's calm.

"What is your husband's name?" he asked after a moment.

"Johannes Bolle."

The officer paused for a moment. "As in Bimmel Bolle?"

"Yes."

"Frau Bolle, you do understand that if your husband is found he will be shot as a traitor and a deserter of the Reich!"

My mother nodded her head.

"The name Bolle will not help him."

My mother shrugged her shoulders. "I am disgusted with him myself, but what can I do?"

"Yes. I see."

"I didn't want to waste the *Volkssturm's* time, so I came down this morning right away to tell you."

"We appreciate that, Frau Bolle. And you will let us know if he shows up again?"

My mother smiled. "Of course I will, Herr…?"

He straightened to his full height and looked down his nose at my mother, his eyebrows raised. "*Hauptmann* Richter!" he said curtly.

"*Hauptmann* Richter, I will let you know immediately if I have any sign of him."

"Thank you, Frau Bolle. But I must warn you, there will be an investigation, and if they find him? Well, I cannot say! *Ja,* and now I must hurry. These men *have* come to defend Berlin!" he said with a sweep of his arm as he turned on his heels, and I heard them click against the floor all the way to the other end of the line, where another problem awaited him.

My mother and I were left standing there. I hadn't realized until that moment that my hands were sweating and my heart was racing. As we turned to walk out, several of the men by the door gave us the thumbs-up sign. A few said, "Well done." One whispered, "I wish I'd sent my wife down to tell them I'd disappeared." My mother permitted herself a smile but continued walking, her back to the officers. Otherwise, she did not acknowledge the men in the room. I shuddered to think that in a few weeks, or maybe days, every one of them would be dead.

Once outside, she exhaled a huge breath. "Oh, *Gott im Himmel!* I thought my nerves would give me away!"

"Mutti, you were brilliant!"

"I was nervous. He came over with his chest all puffed out like a cock."

"I know," I laughed.

"Don't laugh, Jutta! They could still be watching us from the window."

We walked purposefully without talking for ten minutes before we relaxed again. The birds accompanied us on our walk down the Kronprinzenallee. The

Grunewald seemed filled with their melody as they sunned themselves on the branches of the trees that held the beginning buds of spring. Today the freshness and sunlight only depressed me. I knew something terrible lay ahead for us, but I wasn't sure what. Poor little birds, I thought, you have no idea what awaits you. You think today is a spring day like every other one. I envy you your ignorance.

"Do you think he believed you?" I whispered.

"Yes! Definitely."

"Do you think they will send someone to search for Vati?"

"I don't know, but we will think about that when it happens, not before."

As we turned the corner off Kronprinzenallee onto Auf dem Grat, the air raid siren sounded, cutting the melody of the birds silent. Its nerve-racking, up-and-down wail made every hair on my skin stand upright. Mutti reached for my arm and we sprinted for the house, our shoulders bumping as she held me close. The beautiful, clear spring day meant perfect visibility for their death vessels. They could attack freely now in the middle of a bright sunlit day, no longer hindered by the need to hide behind cloud cover or the dark of night—there were no anti-aircraft guns left; there was nothing left. Poor Berlin, my poor city, lay naked and completely vulnerable, and we in the middle of it.

April 24, 1945

(The following dialogue is in Russian.)

"Nothing here. How about on your side?"

"No. Only bushes."

"Shit! There's a big fence. We'll have to go around."

"Back on the street?"

"Of course. You can't be afraid of those little boys!"

The other one snorted.

The Russians! I was wide awake now. *Those were Russians! Russian voices, speaking Russian!* Deep, thick voices, rough and full of hate. Heavy boots crunched the gravel and twigs as they walked back out to the street. I heard the gate squeak in the distance. I wasn't sure if they had closed it behind them or opened it wider to get out of the garden. The sound stood still in my mind. One time, not twice. They had moved the gate only once. Had they left it open to come back in?

I sat up quickly. The beginnings of light cast shadows across the basement floor, and I could just make out Mutti and Vati on the far side of the basement, crouched by the corner of the window and peering out, whispering to each other. The sound of gunfire thundered in the street. I could not tell if the sound came from our street, or maybe Auf dem Grat, or the Kronprinzenallee. My mother looked around and saw that I was awake.

"Jutta, get dressed," she whispered forcefully.

I had not noticed at first that both she and my father were already dressed. I got up quickly and dressed in the shadows, lacing my shoes from memory. I walked to the basement sink to wash my face and rinse my mouth. Placing a tiny dot of the baking soda that Mutti had scrounged from the baker on my finger, I scrubbed as best I could—a habit not even broken by fear. I couldn't find my toothbrush in the darkness of the basement, and toothpaste was a luxury that had long since disappeared from pharmacy shelves.

"I have to use the bathroom," I whispered.

"Are they gone, do you think, Hans?"

"Yes. But there may be others. We must be very careful."

"Go on. Luise is up there somewhere. But hurry, for God's sake!"

"I'll go with her and check on things," said Vati.

We walked quietly up the stairs, trying not to make too much noise, just in case. Just in case what? I wondered. In case a Russian was sitting in our living room sipping his morning coffee? As we got to the top of the stairs, Luise appeared in the door, shaking.

"Oh, Herr Bolle! I was so frightened. I saw them come through the gate and I just fell on the kitchen floor," she whispered urgently.

"Did they see you?"

"No. I don't think so."

"You didn't have the light on, did you?"

"Good heavens, no!"

"Good."

"But I was so afraid I couldn't move, even after they left."

"It doesn't matter, Luise. Did you get the food made?"

"Oh my God, the food!" She turned quickly and made her way back to the kitchen. Vati and I followed. I looked around the dark house, anxiously imagining Russian eyes watching us. But all was still.

"Go on, Jutta. Use the bathroom quickly. I thought you had to go?"

I nodded and stepped quietly into the guest bathroom by the kitchen, too afraid to wander up to my own bathroom upstairs. I heard Vati and Luise whispering in the kitchen. He told her to collect as much food as possible, and the jugs of water. And then suddenly they stopped talking. A light but firm knock broke the hushed quiet. I heard my father's shoes as he walked cautiously to the front door.

"Walter?" he asked quietly. I could not hear the response. But I knew it was Herr Wolleck when I heard the bolt slide back.

"They're here!" whispered Herr Wolleck urgently. "I saw them at the corner with their tanks. They'll be down our street at any moment."

"We're coming. Can you grab two of the baskets for Luise while I get the others?"

"*Ja!* But come through the back way."

The sound of artillery fire and shouts of men in the street silenced them. I heard my father clatter down the basement steps, the urgency echoing in each step. Silence was no longer the top priority. I hurried as fast as I could but

I couldn't stop. I must have drunk gallons last night! For God's sake, finish quickly, I mumbled. I pulled my pants up and jerked the door open, forgetting to wash my hands.

"Jutta, your father has gone downstairs to get your things. You carry these jugs of water." Luise practically threw one of them at me as she ran to the door, her plump figure barely squeezing past Herr Wolleck's back as he bent to lift all four baskets of food at once in his huge hands. "I have to help with the bedding!"

I let her pass to go down to the basement, and I walked into the kitchen. Without a word I grabbed two more jugs of water, trying to balance the middle one on my chest. I hoped I could apply enough pressure to keep the center one from falling through my arms—Mutti would kill me if I broke a jug of water.

"Come on, Jutta. Let's you and I go ahead," commanded Herr Wolleck. He was an imposing figure at six feet four, as tall and broad as the doorway. He was much more imposing than Vati, even though at sixty-five he was twenty years senior to Vati. But I didn't want to leave without telling Vati.

"I must tell Vati."

"There's not time. Luise will tell him." He tipped his head toward the front door, indicating that I should go first. "We are going around the back, through the hole your father and I made in the fence."

I walked out of our home and down the steps without arguing. The early morning air felt cool against the perspiration that had formed on my neck and upper lip, but the air was dank and heavy with smoke and the birds eerily silent in the pale morning light. I had to hurry to keep up with him. I peered over the top of the jugs, trying to see the steps to keep from falling. At the bottom he turned left toward the back garden and climbed the embankment to the hole in the fence behind one of Mutti's giant pink rhododendrons. The buds were just beginning to open, pink blossoms poking through their protective shield of green.

The artillery fire intensified. My ears ached from the deep sounds of the huge guns firing into the forest across the Kronprinzenallee. That's where, Vati said, what remained of the poor German Army, mostly boys and old men, perhaps the same ones I saw at the *Volkssturm* office, were desperately trying to hold off the Russian Army. Some said the Germans were outnumbered ten to one, and from the sounds of the gunfire all heading in one direction, I decided it must be true. I tucked my head down deep, my nose touching the lid of the middle jar, and hurried to catch up with Herr Wolleck. He held the branches back to let me pass. I ducked and tripped on the roots of the rhododendron, my knees falling into the moist, mossy soil. Herr Wolleck let the branch fall back and used his free hand to help me up. I lost one of the water jugs. It rolled aimlessly down the small embankment and out into the grass.

"Forget about it! Run, Jutta! As fast as you can, to the back steps!"

I did not hesitate. I headed for the back steps that led to the basement of the Wolleck's house. A whistling sound overhead caused me to run even faster. I could hear Herr Wolleck's heavy steps right behind me. I hope Muti and Vati hurry, I thought, desperately worried my mother would think of yet one more thing to bring and end up trapped in the house. A tree crackled as it fell, hitting the ground somewhere. The crackling continued—fire. And then suddenly I heard shots, but this time they came from the right, from the other side of my parent's house! Could the Russians be coming in from that side of the street as well? Both Herr Wolleck and I stopped and stood still for a moment. And then we heard it again. One more shot. I looked back at my parent's house to see if they were coming. There was no sign of them.

Following my eyes, Herr Wolleck said, "Go on. I'll go back and check on them." He set the baskets down at the top of the stairs and headed back to the fence. I took the steps two at a time and burst through the door at the bottom. Frau Wolleck was sitting in the dark basement on a lawn chair. She had her ear glued to the wireless radio that stood on the little table beside her. She looked up at my arrival but said nothing. Her hair, usually so well groomed, was wrapped under a bright green scarf like the *Putzfraus* at Vati's factory. I almost didn't recognize her. I only heard parts of the announcer's speech: "*Soldaten der Armee Wenck!*" and then, "*Durchgebrochen!*" The static blocked out the rest of what he was saying, and I couldn't tell if he meant Wenck's army broke through or the Russians broke through. From the urgency in his voice I feared it must be the Russians.

"The shots are coming from both sides now!" I announced.

"Oh my God, they're surrounding us!"

At first, I could not see who had spoken in the dark basement; it was just a voice coming out of the dark. But as my eyes adjusted I saw another couple, a man and a woman in their sixties. I recognized them as the neighbors from behind the Wolleck's house. I did not know them well.

"Hello, Jutta," said the woman. "Where are your parents?"

"They're coming," I said, breathless. I shivered. It was cold in the dark cellar, and in my rush I had run out of the house without my jacket.

Frau Wolleck motioned for me to sit in the vacant chair next to her. She patted my leg as I sat listening. She was trying to listen to the BBC, but it was fading in and out badly.

I sat there, uncomfortable in the dark basement with Frau Wolleck and the neighbors I hardly knew. Nobody said a word. The BBC announcer spoke in that clipped accent of theirs of the imminent fall of Berlin. "The Russians will soon have surrounded the city from all sides," he said. "They are pushing north from the southwest. The Americans continue to mass troops on the Elbe, and thousands of refugees are fleeing to the Elbe in the hopes of crossing the river to the American side."

I stared at my hands and prayed that my parents would hurry up. I wanted them here with me, now. The house shook from the guns that pounded on and on in the early morning light. The guns paused for a moment, and a lone bird called out to her family in the temporary silence. Had she called as the guns fired and I just couldn't hear? Or was she silent all along, knowing she wouldn't be heard over the pounding? Then, like us, in between the bursts of fighting and the explosions of the guns, she called out, desperate to find her family and safety. I thought of *Vögelein*. Was she safe? Was she alive? How afraid she must be of these sounds—loud, booming, disturbing sounds that interrupted and intruded everywhere, leaving no place to escape.

It seemed I sat forever listening to the assault of the guns and waiting, my eyes glued to the basement door handle, watching for it to turn. Finally I heard them on the stairs, making their way down with clumsy footsteps under their burdens. Luise came through first, carrying enough bedding to make ten beds. She could not even see over the top of the blankets and sheets flung over her shoulders and stacked up in her arms. My mother followed with two more baskets—filled with what, I couldn't tell, but I was thankful to see my jacket draped across the top of one of them. My eyes flitted to my father and then Herr Wolleck, the last one through the door, who carried the baskets he had left on the steps. I noticed he had added two bottles of cognac. His wife noticed, too.

"Walter! Why did you bring that stuff! The last thing we need is for the Russians to find that!"

"They won't," he said as he pulled wood off of the top of the woodpile and placed the bottles underneath.

My mother set her basket down and looked at me, her face emotionless but determined. She motioned for me to follow her.

"Hans, give me the scissors, please."

Vati set down his bags and dug in the pocket of his jacket, handing the scissors to my mother as if she were a surgeon.

I hesitated in my chair. "What are you going to do?"

"Make you look like a boy!" responded my mother.

"That's what took so long! Your mother insisted on going back upstairs for the scissors and the pants and shirt." My father shook his head, exasperated.

"Well, I should have done this last week like I planned, instead of listening to your silly complaints," said my mother, waving her hand impatiently for me to follow.

"No! Mutti, please! I'll wear the pants and tuck my hair up, but please don't cut my hair!"

"Stop it! Get over here right now, and not another word. Don't be a fool! Your hair will grow back, for God's sake!"

I sighed and got up to follow her. I knew it was pointless to argue. She had me sit on a low brick wall that hid the coal furnace and began snipping my hair, letting it fall into a bucket behind me. I shut my eyes tight.

My mother stood in front of me, cutting my bangs. I peeked through my hair to see my father and Herr Wolleck stand up.

"Heti?" My mother froze. She did not turn around. "We are going to go to the Kittels' house now to check on things."

Worry tore across her face. But she only nodded her head and began to cut again. I knew something was very wrong at the Kittels'. Rumors surged all over Berlin, horrible rumors of mass rape, murder, and stealing by the Russians everywhere they went. But I could not seem to imagine it. I was fearless, protected by my mind's inability to think of these things. Mutti's face told me she knew or had seen something.

"What is it, Mutti?"

She did not respond. Instead she stood back like a hairdresser, brushing my hair to the side with her hand.

"Which side do you want the part on?" she asked.

"I don't care! But you can't hide everything from me! What is it?" I insisted.

She sighed and sat down next to me on the wall. "When I was upstairs getting the scissors, I heard a woman scream. Shortly after that I heard men shouting, and then I heard a gun fire once, and then twice, and then a third time."

I gasped and held my hand to my mouth. "From the Kittel's house?"

She nodded.

"They must have been the gunshots that Herr Wolleck and I heard on our way over."

She said nothing. I knew my mother was very close to the Kittels, especially Herr Kittel. They had always been very fond of each other. It was Herr Kittel who had provided Mutti with all of the fat for her soap making. It had been the Kittels that Mutti and Vati had traveled to Yugoslavia with so long ago, when I stayed with Opa Bolle and Tante Ebi. I didn't dare say anything; I knew Mutti did not want to break down in front of the neighbors. The radio continued its crackling, the voice of the BBC announcer periodically breaking through, and I sat motionless, staring at my feet.

My mother stood up suddenly. "Well, let's finish this up," she said determinedly.

She trimmed the back of my neck again and smoothed the hair down where she had parted it. In her rush she had forgotten a comb, so she used her fingers instead.

"I think you missed your true career, Frau Bolle," called the Wolleck's neighbor.

My mother turned around. "Herr Kleinfeld! I didn't even notice you and your wife! I am so sorry. I was so intent on my project here!"

"Completely understandable, Frau Bolle," said Herr Kleinfeld, waving his hand.

"*Guten Morgen*, Frau Bolle," said his wife.

"*Guten Morgen*, Frau Kleinfeld, Herr Kleinfeld," said my mother politely, nodding her head in their direction.

The formality of the greeting seemed out of place down in the dingy cellar under these circumstances.

"Carry on. Don't mind us," said Herr Kleinfeld.

My mother nodded as she bent down and rummaged through her basket to pull out a pillowcase. I looked at her quizzically.

"Now, let's put this on you."

She stood behind me, flung the pillowcase around the front of my chest, and began to pull it as tight as she could.

"Hey! What are you doing?" I demanded.

"Getting rid of your breasts," she announced.

I blushed and looked to see if Herr Kleinfeld was listening, but he had sat down by Frau Wolleck to try and catch some scraps of news from the fuzzy sounds that emanated from the radio.

"Here, let me help," said Frau Kleinfeld.

Together they tugged and pulled and safety-pinned the pillowcase around my back. My lungs felt constricted, but I could still breathe. God help me, though, if I had to run very fast! I don't think I could have expanded my lungs enough to get any air.

"Brings back memories from when I had my babies..." said Frau Kleinfeld; her voice drifted off, and I remembered that they had lost both of their youngest sons to the war. Tears formed at the corners of the old lady's eyes.

My mother took Frau Kleinfeld's hand in hers and smiled gently. "Thank you for your help." She held her hand and squeezed it for a moment before she said, "Now, Jutta, put this shirt on and let's see what Frau Kleinfeld thinks."

I put the shirt on. It looked odd to see a flat surface down my front. I felt the back of my neck with my hand, brushing away bits of hair that scratched me. I could feel the damp coolness of the cellar on the back of my neck.

Frau Kleinfeld admired me. "Frau Bolle, you are an artist. She has been transformed into a very handsome son. Shall we call her Johannes?"

My mother smiled. "Yes, I think that would be appropriate. The only son, named after the father."

I smirked at them, not at all amused.

My mother bent down again and looked through her basket. "Now for the last touch." She handed me a pair of Vati's old trousers. They were hideous and made of wool that scratched my legs. I stepped behind the brick wall for privacy to put them on.

"But these are awful, Mutti! Couldn't you have found a different pair?"

"We are not trying to make a fashion statement, Jutta. And besides, I was in a slight hurry. I had to find an old pair from your father's youth that were small enough."

She eyed me for a moment. "Even so, you'll have to roll up the legs and pull the belt as tight as possible."

My father was not a tall man. In fact, he was only four inches taller than

I, so the length was not too bad, but the waist was impossible. The pants hung from my waist like the pants of a circus clown, except my mother had not thought to bring the suspenders clowns wore.

She busied herself tucking in my shirt and the edge of the pillowcase that hung down just below my shirt. "Let's see if it helps to tuck everything in."

It helped a little, but not quite enough. She turned me around and removed one of the safety pins from the bottom of the pillowcase that she had used to secure it. My ribs immediately took advantage of the freedom, and I took a deep breath. She grabbed my pants at the waist and took a tuck. That did the trick. Although I was mortified at how I looked, at least I could walk without my pants falling off. My mother looked pleased with the end result of my transformation into a young boy. I, on the other hand, walked to the chair in the furthest corner of the basement, overwhelmed by how miserable life had become.

After an hour, Mutti began to pace—her way of worrying. The gunfire did not stop. It seemed to travel through the very earth to penetrate the walls and rattle the windows of the basement. The sound of glass shattering in the street broke the monotony of the guns, like a cymbal in the orchestra that suddenly breaks through the steady drumbeat. I didn't think there was that much glass left to be broken. And all about we heard voices, voices that we could not understand, and then sometimes we heard German voices, and then the guns would start again. And then the Russian voices again, shouting things at each other , things I could not understand. I prayed Vati and Herr Wolleck would return soon.

When we finally heard their footsteps on the stairs, it was late afternoon. The sun had risen high in the sky.

"How are they?"

"Dead," said my father.

My mother sat down heavily.

"Kittel must have found the Russian with his wife … ," he coughed, "well, you know, bothering her." He looked over at me.

"You mean trying to rape her?" I asked. "Stop pretending I don't know about these things!" I shook my head in disgust.

"Jutta, watch how you talk to adults!" My father frowned at me. He turned to Mutti. "He must have shot the Russian." My father hesitated before adding, "Then he apparently shot Margaret and his sister-in-law, and, well …"

My mother broke in. "Well what? Is he dead?"

"Yes. He set the house on fire and then shot himself downstairs by the fireplace."

"Oh my God!" cried Frau Wolleck.

Frau Kleinfeld shook her head in disbelief.

My mother was amazingly calm. She looked at my father. "He always said he would." She wrung her hands. "Hans, Werner always said, 'If the Russians take Berlin, I will shoot Margaret first, and then destroy the house so they can't have the pleasure of destroying it. And then I will kill myself.'" She got up and began to pace again. "He always said he would!"

My father said nothing, and the silence hung heavily about us.

"Why were you so long?" asked Frau Wolleck suddenly.

Herr Wolleck cleared his throat. "We had to get rid of the Russian somehow, so we took off his uniform and burned it in the flames. Then we dressed him in Werner's clothes."

"No!"

"We had to. And we tried to get the fire under control. It was burning pretty hot upstairs. We were afraid it would spread to the other houses, especially Hans's house."

"He always said he would," mumbled my mother again and again as she paced back and forth on the far side of the cellar.

My father went to her. He held her to stop her pacing. Herr Wolleck brought a lawn chair over to her. She sat down quickly. As she sat, the tears came pouring down her face. My father tried to comfort her, but he was awkward in front of the others. She wept as he patted her hand, as if she were a distraught neighbor. "Let's give her a shot of that cognac," he said after a few minutes. Herr Wolleck stood up quickly and walked to the woodpile. The others stood back uncomfortably, not sure where to look or what to do. I felt nothing. The Kittels were dead— neighbors I had known all my life, and yet I could not imagine it. I could feel nothing, only the vibrations that tore through my body as the guns thundered on, never ceasing.

We heard them upstairs in the Wollecks' living room, their boots scraping the floor as they walked. Voices shouted things to each other in Russian—things that I could not understand. What were they saying? The fear of not understanding was the worst. The sound of broken glass shattered my nerves. I glanced at Frau Wolleck and saw tears in her eyes as she heard her possessions, her life, destroyed by the senseless actions of the angry group of men who roamed about her house like wild beasts. She placed her hand on Herr Wolleck's arm, sensing that he was about to go upstairs even though he had not yet moved.

"What good will it do?"

"How dare they!"

"They are only things. We can buy new later."

"*Schwein!*"

Their drunken laughter pierced the evening silence. Then we suddenly heard the front door open, and other voices mixed in with their drunken ones. One was a voice of authority, louder than the rest, a stern voice, a voice not pleased with what it saw. Silence fell upstairs; no more laughter and shouting.

Again the voice of authority, angry and asking questions, the boots pacing now, heavy boots; a big man, it would seem, pacing in the Wolleck's living room. The same voice shouting now, and many boots leaving in silence. Their scraping sound becoming more and more distant, they spilled out into the night. I looked up through the basement windows and saw the boots in the moonlight, thick and black and dirty, crude boots walking in twos out to the street. Some had coats on that met the boots at the top, and some had pants that tucked into the boots. I could see nothing above their knees from the basement window. I heard the twigs and leaves crunch as they walked out to the street. And then the same voice in Russian, calmer now, talking to only a few men left in the house. A chair scraped the floor, and the boots moved across the floor, heading for the stairs that led to the basement—that led to us.

They kicked the door open and stood with their rifles aimed at us, two of them with others behind them. I could not tell how many; they formed a single mass silhouetted in the doorway, a single mass of danger. My heart beat violently, even in my ears, the sound deafening, and my hands turned to ice. The two with the guns, big guns cradled in their arms, came down the steps first, slowly flashing their lights about the basement, blinding us. They flashed into every corner and every pile in the room, carefully examining them. And then came two more, followed by a tall man, the man with the voice of authority. He shouted out orders in Russian. The men responded by frisking my father and Herr Wolleck first, and then Herr Kleinfeld. The Russians prodded them in the armpits with their guns to get them to raise their arms over their heads.

The other soldier flashed his light behind every column and into every cupboard, looking for guns, I guessed. The tall man spotted me and came over and frisked me. When he hit my waist he frowned and let his hand rest on my waist for a moment while he examined my face. A flash of recognition crossed his face, but he said nothing. Oh my God, he knows! He knows I am a girl. Wild thoughts raced through my mind. He turned to my father. "*Woinna Kaputt,*" he said. "*Woinna Kaputt!*"

My father nodded.

He looked at my mother and smiled at the white handkerchief she had tied to her wrist. My father had tried to grab it from her, but the Russian seemed to like it. He barked something out to the men and they all turned to go back up the stairs. Their boots echoed in the basement, hard and unforgiving, as they climbed the steps. One of them passed by the woodpile on his way and glanced at it. My breath caught in my throat. What if they found the cognac? He hung back for a moment, letting the others climb the stairs, and then he turned abruptly to my father, who was standing closest to him.

"*Uri, uri,*" he barked in that guttural way that they all spoke. It was the voice of a heavy smoker and drinker. "*Du! Uri!*"

My father quickly unbuttoned his shirt cuff and lifted his sleeve to slide the watch off. The Russian snatched it out of his hand. He held it up to the light of his torch and nodded his head in approval. Next he went to Herr Wolleck who, as my father had done, quickly removed his watch and handed it to the Russian. His watch was not as impressive as my father's, but the Russian was not displeased. He went to Herr Kleinfeld and said, "*Uri!*"

Herr Kleinfeld said apologetically, "I am sorry, but I don't have a watch. It broke, and I ..."

The Russian butted him in the stomach with the end of his rifle, knocking the wind out of him and sending him flying backwards at an angle. The side of his head hit a chair next to him on the way down. Herr Wolleck and my father instinctively moved forward, and the Russian turned on them, pointing his gun at each one in turn; his eyes, like two black marbles, flicked back and forth between them. The silence was terrifying. Nobody breathed. Sweat had formed on my upper lip, and I felt my heart race.

Herr Kleinfeld lay moaning on the floor. A voice called back in the house from somewhere outside. The Russian eased toward the stairs, his back to the stairs. He never took his eyes off my father and Herr Wolleck. He climbed the stairs backwards. The voice called again, this time closer—from inside the house somewhere. The Russian called back. And then at the top of the stairs he glanced back at us all cowering in the basement and smirked at us.

"*Gitler Kaputt.*"

We said nothing. He turned to catch up with the rest.

We sat in silence until their voices faded in the distance. I let my breath out slowly, not even realizing that I had been holding it, taking only shallow little breaths for air. My legs began to tremble in Vati's thick wool pants, and I had to sit down. My father and Herr Wolleck rushed over to Herr Kleinfeld to help him up.

"Are you all right?" asked my father urgently.

They stood him up and sat him on the chair he had knocked over on the way down. He groaned. In the dark I could not see him, but I heard him.

"*Ja,*" came out between heavy breaths, as if he were running a marathon.

"Someone turn on the light. We need light, for God's sake," cried Herr Wolleck.

It must have been Luise who found the torch. Suddenly it came on, shining right into my father's eyes before she lowered it quickly to the floor and brought it over.

Vati took it from her and aimed it at Herr Kleinfeld's face. Blood ran down his forehead and the bridge of his nose in big streaks. He shut his eyes against the light. He had wiped the blood to keep it out of his eye, and it had smeared across his temple. Frau Kleinfled caught her breath when she saw him. It was the first sound that had come out of her. He looked macabre there in the bright spotlight, as if he were on stage: everything black around him and just that single light on his face, casting shadows that mixed with the streaks of blood.

My mother had sprung into action. She rummaged around in her bag for the first-aid kit she always brought with her.

"Hans, bring the light over here so I can find my gauze."

He flashed the light over to the corner where she stood.

"Here it is!" she said, mostly to herself. She hurried over to Herr Kleinfeld and began to clean and bandage his head.

"It's all right, Lotte. Head wounds always bleed more than anywhere else," said my mother, trying to reassure Frau Kleinfeld.

"I'm fine," added Herr Kleinfeld, but his voice did not build confidence.

After my mother was finished he tried to stand, but he cried out in pain as he did so. My mother felt around where the rifle had butted him. He groaned and bit his lip.

"I think he broke some ribs."

We all stood staring, not sure what to do.

"Luise, strip one of the pillowcases off and cut it into strips," commanded my mother as she continued to examine Herr Kleinfeld. Luise hurried off. I heard the sound of sheets tearing, but in the dim light I could only see a vague outline of movement in the corner. The sounds made me shiver. Sheets tearing—the threads ripped from one another and left jagged and exposed—explosions vibrating the rafters and the windows, and glass shattering shrilly in the streets above us, all forming a horrible chorus in the gloomy light of the basement. I put my hands over my ears. Suddenly the ripping stopped and Luise brought the strips to Mutti.

"Hold him up and keep his arms out of the way."

Vati and Herr Wolleck obeyed, watching closely as Mutti bound him up. When she was satisfied with her work, she had the men help him to the chaise lounge.

"Better than any hospital bed! Look how it can be tilted up. Now you just stay there and try not to move too much."

"Thank you, Frau Bolle."

She smiled and patted his hand, but the look she gave Vati exposed her concern.

Frau Kleinfeld had not said a word, and suddenly we noticed her, in shock, shaking uncontrollably in the darkness of a corner.

———

I listened carefully, trying to hear through the chaos of sound if they were coming again. I was listening for boots, the sound of hard-soled boots crunching gravel and twigs, or the floorboards above our heads, but those sounds didn't come. Instead, always the same sounds: shouting, sometimes in German but then more and more in Russian, from the forest and from the street—our street, where I had once played ball with Erica; our street, where Max Schmeling had played soccer with us. It all seemed so long ago. And then the sound of the huge guns, those long-nosed guns, in the distance mostly, but sometimes suddenly close, startling us, raining plaster on us, causing the windows to shake. We heard the glass break and waited—one second, sometimes two seconds—and then, from somewhere upstairs, it shattered to the ground outside. Was it a window or a roof tile? One second for a window, two seconds for a roof tile, and sometimes one of each, but always the same destructive sound—and then more guns, shouts, and glass shattering. I pulled the pillow over my head and willed it all to go away, but the sounds would not stop. I slept and woke, and slept again, but still the sounds, the endless sounds.

The guns were the worst—so jolting and penetrating; disrupting my thoughts, my sleep, vibrating in my stomach and always firing, every one of them at different intervals, firing their explosive sounds so there was no rest, no silence, no peace. And at what? What were they firing at?

"What could be left?" asked my mother.

"Boys, old men, and pine trees," announced Vati.

"But why doesn't it stop?" I asked.

"They say the fighting will stop when Goring can fit into Göebbels trousers!" Herr Kleinfeld meant to lighten the mood, but it fell flat. I had heard it before—it seemed funny then, but not now. Now it just seemed so senseless.

And then suddenly a new sound filled the air, a crackling sound, a sound like when the radio does not transmit properly. I listened intently for a moment before I recognized it as the sound of many things burning—houses burning somewhere on our street and trees burning in the Grunewald.

"They are setting the Grunewald on fire to flush them out!" whispered my mother in horror.

I shivered. It was not cold.

"What if the fire spreads?" I asked.

The adults did not speak.

I shouted, "What if the fire spreads and we all die here in the basement fried up like..."

"Jutta, stop! That will not happen!" said my father firmly over my shouts.

"But how do you know?" I stared at the adults who were standing silent, watching me.

"How do you know? You don't! And you wouldn't be able to stop it, and we would all die! And who would know? Nobody! Where are Uncle Kurt and Tante Hilde? Dead! Probably all dead! And Peti and Ingrid and Dieter? Where are they? What has happened to them?"

My mother came toward me and put her arm around my shoulder to guide me over to my makeshift bed in the corner of the dark basement. It was the same chaise lounge I had lain on for many a glorious sunny summer day, letting the sun's heat bake into my skin until it turned pink and I had to go in. I let her lead me to it, but I continued. "You can't do anything! Nothing!"

"Shhh. This doesn't help."

"Well he can't! And you can't. Not the Bolle name. Not the Bolle money! None of that matters to them. To them we are all the same—just rats that they want to kill and flush out!" I began to sob. "And there is nothing you can do."

I fell onto the bed and sobbed into my pillow. Mutti tried to hold me, but my shoulders shook violently. I heard my father come over, my father who could always fix things. My father who kept me out of the BDM, who told the SS I could not work for them when everybody else had to follow their orders. My father who sent money and food coupons when others had none. My father who got through to Halberstadt when most could not travel even a few kilometers—even he could not do anything to stop this insanity. I could not look at him. Why couldn't he do something? Even as I thought it I knew it was not rational, but I couldn't help it. I sat up suddenly, jolting my mother, who was leaning on me.

My eyes met his. "Why? Why can't you do something?" I saw the pain on his face, but I somehow could not stop. He handed a glass of something to my mother to give me. "Why? Why can't you?"

"Because I am not God," he said finally, and turned to walk to the window where he could only see ground level. He stood there in the dim light with his back to us, hands clasped behind his back in that manner he had.

I had cried so much I couldn't breathe through my nose, and my mouth hung open slightly because of it. Mutti tipped the glass to my lips and poured some of the liquid into my mouth. It burned my lips as it ran into the cracks that had formed at the corners from dehydration. I choked and spit it out across the floor.

"Drink it!" commanded Mutti. My outburst had left me weak, too weak to object, so I drank. It was cognac, and after the initial shock of it, it calmed me down. I fell asleep with my mother stroking my back.

———

I woke up to the sound of the radio. I wanted to go back to sleep. To pretend this was all a dream, a nightmare. To wake up and find Mutti sitting in the chair by my bed in my room, my beautiful room with its rose-dotted wallpaper, handing me a cup of hot chocolate to sooth my nerves.

Day and night faded together in the dark basement; I was not certain if it was morning or evening. The adults were on the far side of the room, bent over Herr Wolleck's wireless radio, listening carefully. The reception was poor, and the volume was up loud so they could hear the announcer's voice over the crackling.

The outside air, stale and smoke-filled, smelled dirty, and it had begun to penetrate the house and now the basement. It seeped in imperceptibly, finding the tiniest crack. It wasn't air anymore. It had a texture to it now, small little particles in it. My mother had put a scarf around her head to keep the dirt off her hair and also because she could not wash it. To protect what hair I had left, I kept on the hat she had shoved on my head to make me a boy. But my skin felt gritty, and bits of plaster and dirt got into my mouth. It was as if half of Berlin floated around in that air. I imagined the homes and office buildings that lay crumpled on the ground, the wind lifting tiny particles and carrying them from Berlin out here to Dahlem. I covered my mouth with a handkerchief and tried to breathe. But still I thought I could feel the dirt in my nose burrowing down into my lungs. I thought of my lungs slowly filling with dirt and bits of cement; the lining of my lungs, instead of grabbing oxygen, grabbed dirt and cement and soot as I slowly drowned. My heart raced! Stop it! I shifted my thoughts to the field of daisies—the daisies that soothed me to sleep at night, white and yellow and alert on their pale green stems, swaying in the cool summer breeze. But the acrid smell was constant. I gave up. And then, slowly, a new smell hit my consciousness, a rotten smell I could not place. It was not just sewage—that too, but this was something else, something I had never smelled before, a horrible smell, a smell that would not leave.

"Can't we open a window?" I asked.

"No. The smoke is too heavy outside," said my father.

I heard the soldiers in the street shouting, calling to each other. How could they even breathe with that air and that smell? And the guns, still the guns, but this time in the distance, not on our street. From our street came the short, sharp rap of the small guns, not the deep, throaty sounds that shook the house, not anymore. That was earlier. Now it only sounded in the forest, or maybe on other streets.

The day was dark from the smoke, like big thunderclouds, only it didn't rain. Occasionally the sun would try to peak through, not quite managing and instead casting an eerie translucent light on the street and houses of our neighborhood.

My mother had the only watch left. It wasn't really a watch. It was a tiny clock that Opa Bolle had given her, the kind that hangs around your neck. She had taken it off and put it under her pillow. It was the only one the soldier had not taken. I knew she had planned for this and hid it on purpose. We heard about the Russian mania for watches before they even arrived in Berlin, when the rumors swept the city of Russian looting and raping in the East.

April 26, 1945

The others, still in their beds, half-asleep, did not stir, but the sound had woken me—the guns firing in the distance, once again shaking the foundation of the Wollecks' house. There must be hundreds of them, I thought. They formed a low rumbling sound, like the kettledrums in Beethoven's Fifth Symphony. I put my hands to my ears to block the sound. An especially loud vibration shook the house, and the walls rattled and plaster fell on us and woke the others. Vati stood up slowly and went over to the window. I had thought he was asleep. He looked up at the sky and then walked to the door, opening it slightly. Herr Wolleck stood up and joined Vati at the door. And then I saw the lightning—bold flashes that seemed to hit the ground.

It was thunder! Thank God!

I got up and walked over to the door. The sky broke open just as I approached the door, and the rain fell all about us. I followed Vati up the steps, lifting my face, letting the rain wash the grit away. No one was in the garden. I looked out toward the street, but it was still too dark to see. There appeared to be no sign of anyone: no soldiers, no guns, no war. How odd!

The sky dumped rain on us all day. It poured and poured. Crying for Berlin.

"The rain will save the forest!" announced my mother.

And, indeed, the smell of fire subsided. But the other smells stayed: the smell of smoke, and that horrible stench—the rain could not wash that away. The rain came down so hard and long it flushed sewage from burst pipes into the street, and the smell of sewage became unbearable. Herr Wolleck came down from upstairs and announced that we could no longer use the toilets. The sewers must be backed up, he said.

In the distance we heard men calling to each other in Russian, always in Russian now. No more German voices. And then suddenly they were very close to the house. The rain poured down, and I could see water rush by the basement windows above our heads at ground level—soon it would leak into the basement. The sky was dark from the thunderclouds, and I could not tell if it was afternoon or evening. Time no longer mattered; what mattered was that they left us alone.

The voices were shouting now in Russian. Boots splashing through the rivers created by the rain caused muddy water to splatter all over the basement window, and then the door banged on its hinges. Then boots, lots of boots, scraped at the floor, and I heard more shouts in Russian. They're trying to get out of the rain, I thought. The guns pounded on and on in the distance, combining with the thunder. And then a cloud must have blocked what little light was left, and we were plunged into darkness. The men swore and the women were silent. I heard my father ask Luise for the torch.

"No, Hans. Don't turn it on, or they will know we are here." It was my mother's voice, but it was as if she were in another room, not here right by me.

"I just want to hold it, in case we need it."

"Here, Herr Bolle," came Luise's voice in a whisper.

They couldn't have heard us. They were shouting and laughing upstairs, but still we whispered. They must have found some bottles of beer or schnapps; we heard them toasting each other and drinking, and then bottles smashing.

"I thought we got rid of all the liquor," said Frau Wolleck.

"We did, but they must have found some in another house. Probably courtesy of one of our big Nazi saviors!"

All night the sounds of celebrating continued. I shook in my bed. Celebrating what? The death of hundreds, the destruction of a city, the looting of homes—what were they celebrating? We did not sleep. Fear held us together—the fear that they would come down to the basement and find us. For my father and Herr Wolleck, the humiliation of vulnerability showed in their silence. Powerless against this force that had taken over our lives, they could no longer look us in the eye. Vati stared at the floor looking at nothing, or stood facing the wall looking at nothing. When my mother spoke to him, he looked over her head, past her, his eyes skimming the wall behind her.

April 27, 1945

It began as a dull ache, and it woke me. I ignored it at first, but as the days dragged on it developed into a sharp pain.

"Mutti, I think I have an ulcer. My stomach hurts." I showed her where it hurt.

She did not reply. Instead she went over to the pot that held what was left of Luisa's stew and dished up a small serving for me. She motioned for me to follow her. She handed me the bowl.

"But I think it will make it worse. Doesn't food make ulcers worse?"

"You don't have an ulcer. You're hungry. Now eat this quietly."

I looked at her, puzzled. I had been hungry before, but not like this. I ate the stew and felt the pain subside a little. I realized we had only eaten an egg and a roll the day before. And the day before that I could not even recall what we ate. In fact, I realized that I did not know how many days we had spent in the Wollecks' basement. I knew my mother was trying to stretch the food as far as possible. But there were a lot of us in the basement, and the Kleinfelds had brought very little. The stew was meant for later. I ate slowly, trying to make my body think it was more than it really was.

We heard him before we saw him: only one set of footsteps, thank God! Unsteady footsteps above us. Footsteps that told of a body dragging and stumbling across the floor. We held our breath. He stopped by the cellar door. Tense moments passed, and then the door crashed open and he stood there, his boot still extended in the air. It was dark, and we could barely make out his silhouette. He put his foot down heavily and bent down to peer into the basement. He flashed his torch spastically around the basement, bouncing it off the walls as he descended the steps slowly and deliberately so he would not fall. I felt my mother stiffen next to me. He took the back of his hand and wiped his mouth, stretching as he did so. His rifle jerked up as he stretched and pointed wildly around the basement. I pressed my eyes shut instinctively. The other Russians must have been asleep, for no other sound came from upstairs. We stayed in our beds and did not move. There were no officers upstairs, no angry voices of authority to help us. We knew what he wanted.

He stood there for a moment, focusing.

Then he shouted, "Frau!"

Nobody moved. He walked toward the beds in the corner and said again, "Frau!"

My mother turned sideways to hide me behind her, and as she did so she reached down for my cap that was on the floor beside her. She passed it to me silently under the covers. I shoved it on my head with shaking fingers and tried not to cry; I was a boy, and boys did not cry. He flashed his light on Frau Wolleck and then Frau Kleinfeld and sniffed to himself. His flashlight illuminated his face from below; his nostrils seemed enormous in the strange light. He looked almost Asian, but with high cheekbones and small, beady eyes. I remembered those eyes, like black marbles, so black you could not see their centers, the corners pinched tight as he looked from one face to another. I knew his face; he had been here before; he had taken Vati's watch and butted poor Herr Kleinfeld.

He took another step closer to us. My father began to get up. In an instant, the Russian aimed his gun at him and said, "*Nein!*" My father froze. The Russian spotlighted Luise with his flashlight, shining it into her chubby face, white with fear. He snorted and turned to our bed. I felt the heat of the flashlight on my face. My eyes were pressed closed, and the inside of my lids shone bright red from the light. My mother grabbed my hand.

He chuckled to himself. "*Du, Frau, komme!*" he barked out.

I heard my father rising from his cot. "No!" he screamed. The light suddenly swung away from my face, leaving yellow images where the light had been. The crack of a gun shattered the silence in the basement, and plaster fell from the wall above my father's cot. The ringing in my ears deafened me, and I did not want to look to see if he had hit Vati. My mother cried out and rose from the bed; his light flashed back on us, and he grabbed her by the arm, dragging her toward the stairs. I opened my eyes and saw my father rise up, and I knew he would die if he tried to stop the Russian. I was helpless, but worse, I was paralyzed by fear. I did nothing. I could do nothing to help either of my parents.

The Russian held my mother by the arm with one hand; with the other he aimed his rifle on my father as he backed toward the stairs. In that moment, my mother pushed him with all her strength. At the same time Herr Wolleck emerged, like a guardian angel, from somewhere behind the stairs, and he raised his arm high over the Russian's head and smashed a bottle down on the soldier's head with such force I was certain he must have killed him. The glass shattered on the floor but we barely heard it, our ears still ringing from the sound of the Russian's gun. The Russian crumpled to the ground in a helpless pile. His gun clattered as it hit the basement floor and bounced over to the steps. Vati sprang into action. He grabbed the Russian's gun, handed it to Herr Wolleck, and took off his belt to bind the soldier's hands behind his back. Mutti ran back to me; she sat by me, shaking. I put my arms around her, and the other women came over, too. We all stood there shaking watching as the men turned the Russian over and tied his hands behind his back.

"They will be moving out soon. We must get rid of him before they find him."

"Is he dead?"

My father felt his pulse. "No."

"We need to find a vacant house. Let's just put him in there with the bottle and hope that he thinks he got in a fight. We'll untie his hands before we dump him. He's so drunk, he won't remember."

"It has to be fairly far from here." My father thought for a moment. "What about the Beckers' house, over there on Am Schülerheim? They vacated weeks ago, but can we carry him that far?"

"We'll have to."

They lifted him. My father took his legs, and Herr Wolleck grabbed his upper body. Slowly they made their way to the back stairs.

"Somebody open the door for us," commanded my father urgently. Frau Wolleck leaped up and ran to open the door. Up until then, the women had all stood encircling my mother protectively. The men rested the Russian's body on the top of the stairs and waited for the door. My father had his back to the door as he had maneuvered the stairs backwards.

"What do we do with his gun?" asked Herr Wolleck suddenly.

"We have to take it with us. If they find a gun down here, they will shoot all of us," said my father. "Besides, he'll wonder what happened to it."

"Can someone bring us the gun?" called Herr Wolleck in a loud whisper over his shoulder, turning his head stiffly to the side so we could hear him.

"Wait!" cried my mother, next to me. They stood unsteadily on the stairs, waiting. She walked quickly over to the gun. Before they could stop her, she took a hammer and hit the trigger as hard as she could. It took four blows before she was satisfied with her work. I heard a small piece of metal hit the floor— the trigger, perhaps. She handed it up to Herr Wolleck, who stood on the third step of the stairs; he nearly dropped the Russian as he grabbed it with one hand and laid it on the Russian's stomach. No one spoke. They continued up the steps and out the door. Frau Wolleck closed the door behind them. Mutti walked back to the bed and shoved the hammer back underneath it. I had not seen her get it out.

"Maybe I have saved one German boy! I hope so, anyway!"

We stood there shivering, unable to talk, holding each other and praying that the men would not run into any Russians as they disposed of their heavy and dangerous burden.

"Why the cognac? Couldn't you have used a bottle of schnapps instead?" joked my father.

We could laugh about it now that Vati and Herr Wolleck were safely back in the house. Vati looked at his watch, which he had retrieved off the Russian's arm. The soldier, in love with watches, had ten on his arm even without Vati's or Herr Wolleck's. They had taken the watches and tossed them into a flower bed on the way back to the basement, hoping the Russian would think another soldier had robbed him.

The Russian had no doubt been busy in our neighborhood, helping himself to the vast stores of wine and cognac left by the Nazis as they hurriedly scattered out of town, leaving the German people to face the Russian Army alone. "The rats have left the ship!" Vati joked. Rumors had spread all over Berlin that the SS and Nazi high officials had signed over two thousand passes allowing their own to flee, while we were all told to fight to the death. "No sign of our illustrious neighbor!" added Vati. I knew he was referring to Field Marshal Keitel.

"Herr Wolleck, you were incredible, standing right behind him!" exclaimed Luise, interrupting the laughter. "Where did you come from? I didn't even see you get up."

"No. And neither did he, thank God! He was so focused on Hans over there, he didn't even notice me. When Heti pushed him, I knew I had to make my move."

"It was smart to have your bed over there, opposite from ours!" said Mutti, her composure regained.

"And you, Heti. Where did you get the hammer?" Herr Wolleck shook his head.

"You would be surprised at all the things my wife has hidden in her bed, under her bed, and in her baskets!" laughed my father.

"Actually, I took it off your wall the other day, thinking we might need it. And at any rate, I thought they might take it from you. I also have your ax!"

"You're joking!" laughed Herr Wolleck.

My father shook his head. "Heti, do you know the kind of trouble we could have if they found those things under your bed?"

My mother shrugged. "Well, put them somewhere else then, but I don't think we should leave them lying around. Think of the damage they could do with them."

"Thank God the others did not hear!" said Frau Wolleck, referring to the other soldiers upstairs.

"But how could they not hear? That gunshot was so loud!" I said.

"Too drunk, I suppose."

"And their ears are so used to the sounds of gunshots. They probably didn't even think about it."

"Did you hear the guns they set off this morning to get them moving?"

"The word is that they are heading for Charlottenburg today," said Herr Kleinfeld.

Frau Wolleck nodded her head. "Yes. While you were gone, the BBC reported they have captured Dahlem and Lichterfelde."

"But still not Tempelhof."

"I don't think it will take them long to secure the airport, and then they will push to the center of Berlin," said my father.

"And then it will be over." Frau Wolleck wrapped her arms around herself protectively as she said it.

"Yes, and who knows what awaits us?" replied my father. He looked out the window, his face a mask, but I knew he was worried, desperately worried about us. How would we eat? Would they let us live in our homes? Would they kill us or harm us in other ways, other unspeakable ways? These questions hung in the air. Silence covered us, our mood again heavy with worry.

The knock was so slight that at first we didn't know what it was, but it persisted.

Herr Wolleck held up his hand. "Shhh."

We listened. And again the knocking sounded, on the heavy basement door that led out to the garden; a little louder this time, but light—not a man, certainly not a soldier.

"It's not a Russian," said my mother. "They don't knock!"

Herr Wolleck walked to the back door of the basement and cracked it open. He lowered his gaze and opened it wider. I couldn't see, but I heard a child's voice outside, a boy.

"Well, come in," said Herr Wolleck.

The child stepped into the basement and handed Herr Wolleck a note.

After glancing at it, he said, "Hans, it's for you." He handed it down to my father, who stood at the bottom of the steps.

Vati unfolded the note carefully and read it. Nobody spoke. He looked up from the note and then back down at it. He read it again.

"What?" asked my mother. "Hans, what is it?" she demanded.

"It's from Kurt. He says to come with him. He found a vacant apartment that is safe in Zehlendorf." My father looked at the boy. "Is he outside?" he asked.

The boy nodded. "On the Kronprinzenallee." He jerked his head toward the street. "Too many Russians lying around, and too many tanks. He didn't want to come into your street."

"How did you get through?"

"They don't bother children. Besides, it's too early. They are all either fighting again in the woods or too drunk to get up." The rain sounded on the metal pipes and gutters that surrounded the house. I had no idea what time of day it was. It seemed dark outside, completely dark. Was it nighttime still? It had been dark for days from the rain and smoke. We took short naps day and night, when the sounds of war ceased for a moment and let us. I glanced at Mutti's watch: five o'clock, but was that morning or evening?

"Well, come in, child. Come on down the stairs before all the rain floods in here," said Herr Wolleck.

The boy walked cautiously down the stairs. His clothes were soaked from the heavy rain that spilled from the sky and washed away the dirt of war.

"Thank you for bringing this to me," said my father.

"He said he would take care of me. He said he would give me food for my mother and sister. He will, won't he?" asked the boy, concerned.

"Yes, of course he will. I will see to it," added my father, patting the boy's head.

"Good. We need food. They are hiding, my mother and sister, because of the Russians. They don't even want to wait in the bread lines because … well, you know." He looked at my mother, embarrassed. He was thin, maybe eight or nine years old. His cheeks sunk into his face, emphasizing the large front teeth protruding above his lower lip. His legs and thin little ankles stuck out below his pant cuffs, pants that had fit him maybe two years ago. The fact they fit around the waist but were a good six inches too short told the story.

"But the man, he says you must come now! He is waiting, and it is not safe."

My father nodded. "Come, sit. You must eat something quickly while we pack."

The boy did not object, and my mother told Luise to bring him what was left of the stew. There was only a small serving left, but the boy could not believe his good fortune. He ate hungrily, shoving the food in his mouth with the quick movements of one who expects his bowl to be taken away.

"I haven't had meat in two weeks!" he exclaimed, licking the bowl clean. When he finished, I saw the look on his face—the look of guilt. He had eaten while his mother and sister were still hungry. My mother saw it, too.

"Don't worry. We will send food for them, too," she said gently.

He smiled. "Thank you."

We packed hurriedly, leaving much of the bedding behind as too cumbersome to carry, taking instead only what we really needed. While Luise and I packed, Mutti and Vati talked intensely in the corner, and then my mother walked away from my father.

"I don't care," she said. "I'm going to get it myself. You won't be able to find it."

"Heti, wait!"

Without turning, she ran up the stairs and out the door to the garden. My father followed her. At the top of the stairs, he turned and said to me, "Your mother is insisting on getting something from the house. Be ready when we get back."

We all stood speechless. It was insanity to go into the house. It was surely full of Russians, probably drunk Russians! But she was determined to get whatever it was, so all my father could do was accompany her. If the Russians decided to do something to her, there was really nothing he would be able to do, but to let her go alone would have been unthinkable.

I stood by the door and watched the bushes to see if they were coming. They had been gone only moments, but it seemed like an eternity. "Oh, come on!" I begged. Light had begun to emerge from its sleep, casting shadows on the damp grass of the garden. The birds called to each other tentatively, testing their voices, it seemed. It was still too early for them to open their daily ritual of song. Would they be heard today? Or would the guns shatter their song? It seemed so still outside this morning, so peaceful. Yet I knew that soon they would fire the guns to rouse the men, and then Berlin would once again face an assault from thousands and thousands of men. The radio had said millions, but I did not believe it. "Oh hurry, Mutti! Please!" What on earth could she have wanted? I searched the bushes again for movement. Nothing. I could barely see the roof of our house over the hedge. Some of the tiles had blown off from the explosions. Out of the corner of my eye, I caught a slight movement on the other side of the hedge, and then I saw the bushes move. My mother came through first, followed by my father. Oh, thank God! I clenched my fists.

I turned and bent to pop my head back in the basement. "They're coming!" I called excitedly.

I raced down the stairs to put my coat on so I would be ready when they got here. As I straightened my collar, my mother burst through the door. Her clothes were streaked with wet where the rain had hit them, and droplets fell off her nose and chin. They were only gone a few minutes, but it had seemed like forever. She must have known exactly where it was.

"You wouldn't believe it! Asleep like puppies, one on top of the other in a corner of the bedroom!" She shook her head. "With two perfectly good beds right there for them? Unbelievable! All huddled in a corner." Her words sounded breathless and nervous, t he adrenaline still pumping through her veins from sneaking into her own house to retrieve—what? I looked at her hand and saw a sliver of black. She put whatever it was quickly in her pocket, and I saw that it was a black velvet strap. Omi's cameo necklace? Is that what she had gone back for? There was a bulge in her other pocket as well. She reached in and pulled something out and threw it into the basket. I caught a glimpse of what I thought was a bar of soap! We may not have showers or baths, but she would see to it that our hands and faces were kept clean. I marveled at my mother. She would risk her life and that of my father's to get a bar of soap!

"Did you get what you wanted?" asked Frau Wolleck.

"Yes, I did."

"Now we must go!" Vati seemed nervous as he stooped to pick up a suitcase and a basket. "Do you have everything?" he asked me and Luise.

It was more a demand that we get moving than a real question. We both nodded. Vati asked Herr Wolleck if he should send for him. But Herr Wolleck wanted to stay in his house, to defend it somehow, I suppose. My mother hugged Frau Wolleck and said goodbye to the Kleinfelds, and then we left quickly and quietly, following the boy up the stairs and out into the street. It had been maybe ten or fifteen minutes since the boy's arrival at our door, but I'm sure to Uncle Kurt, standing by himself on the Kronprinzenallee surrounded by Russians, it must have seemed like hours.

The rain poured down on us, soaking my hair and sending tiny rivulets down my cheeks. It was hard to see through the steadiness of the rain, and I had to blink constantly to see the path to the gate. Rivers of water ran down the Wollecks' driveway and out into the street. My father cringed at the loud squeak of the garden gate hinges as he carefully pushed it open. I was the last one out and I left it open, afraid of the sound. I stepped off the walk into the street. My foot hit a puddle of water, and the cold wet seeped into my leather shoes. Irked with myself, I muttered, "Idiot!" We hadn't even left our street and my feet were already wet!

"Holy mother of God!" It was Luise's voice, and my attention shifted instantly to her. I followed her gaze and, like my parents, stopped walking and stared at the remarkable sight all around us. My quiet neighborhood street was unrecognizable, replaced by an alien landscape littered with Russian tanks—not just a few, but hundreds of them, and not the bright, shiny tanks one saw in Nazi propaganda photos. These tanks, covered with mud and tree branches and grasses that stuck out from their undersides, were dented, with huge scratches clawed deep into their sides. Their paint, faded and chipped, spoke of years of hard use. They were everywhere! Parked at angles in every direction—on the sidewalks, in the driveways—one had driven through Erica's front fence and straight through her mother's rose bushes almost to the front door.

I didn't see how they could back them out of the street if they had to, certainly not in a hurry. But there was no longer a need for that. Pictures of traffic jams in Rome with vehicles of every type driving haphazardly in every direction came to mind. I had seen such pictures in my father's books on Italy, only these vehicles with their bold single stars were deadly.

Military vehicles of every size and type added to the chaos: jeeps, trucks, and even carts and wheelbarrows were shoved in between the tanks wherever there was enough room, and there were soldiers everywhere. So many soldiers! Mostly asleep, thank God! Men were asleep under the trucks; men were asleep in the trucks and leaning against the trucks. They were asleep in the jeeps. Those under the trucks had placed wooden crates on the ground and slept on top of them to keep themselves dry. None of them moved—it was obvious they would sleep for some time still. It could not have been more than 5:30 in the morning, as the light still struggled with the darkness.

The walk was treacherous. The tanks had chewed up the cobblestones, forcing them up at different angles, and we had to maneuver carefully in the near dark to keep from tripping. Broken bottles littered the street and combined with broken glass from elegant windows and chunks of cement and plaster where artillery shells had dug deep holes into the walls of our neighbors' homes. The glass sparkled when it caught a sliver of pale light; from the moon, I guessed. We walked on gingerly to avoid sliding, but still staring uncomprehending, hypnotized by the sight.

As we turned onto Auf dem Grat my jaw dropped, but only for a second, the acrid taste of the rain immediately forcing it closed again. There in the middle of the grassy center, amongst the charred remains of acacia trees, slept shaggy ponies and donkeys! Donkeys! In Dahlem! They had formed a circle and slept on the outer edge. Inside the circle, campfires smoldered from the night before, and everywhere were sleeping men in big, heavy boots, so harmless in their sleep. And on the outside, parked in the street, were artillery guns—dozens of them, their long noses jutting into front yards where I had played.

Berlin had been destroyed, smashed into a pile of rubble. I knew this with certainty. Seeing these men, these tanks, these guns, and their work—huge holes gaping wide with ragged edges, exposing a table with chairs or a sofa in what once was a home but was now just a shell cracked bare—and seeing the smoldering trees along the road and across the street in the Grunewald, there was no doubt. The city, as I knew it, no longer existed. We had been spared most of the bombs, but even so, the tank and artillery fire alone had caused this much damage. I could not begin to image the horror that had consumed the center of town, where chronic bombings unleashed fierce tongues of fire and brutally split families from each other and their belongings—old photos, pressed flowers from a wedding, and award ribbons, all sent scattered into the street and covered with filth. There were millions without homes, without food, without clothes, and without all the things that define a life. I thought of the men and women stripped of dignity, forced to watch, helpless, guns pressed to their temples as mothers, sisters, and daughters endured one Russian after another as they unleashed their brutal hatred on those least responsible. And then to sit quietly as these same men looted the few belongings that remained to them. I studied them, these men who lay all about me, and I thought of their brothers fighting in the city. I hated them, these men that God had allowed to declare victory over my family, my city, my people. I did not understand. Why had the Americans stopped? Why? Why these men, God? Why the Russians? Despite the rain, a fire smoldered from the night before in the center of the street; it must have been a huge bonfire, no doubt to celebrate their victory, this destruction of my neighborhood and my city! What would my grandfather have thought? What would my great-grandfather have thought of the streets that his milk wagons had always run down, now full of the evidence of war and Russians with tanks and dilapidated carts pulled by ponies and donkeys and campfires in the middle of the street? My stomach lurched, and I vomited in the street.

"Come on, Jutta," whispered my father urgently.

I wiped my mouth and stared at this bizarre scene spread out before me—a deadly circus that had come to town, asleep and quiet before its next performance. I could not move. Even as he pulled me forward, I looked over my shoulder at the scene that had taken over my neighborhood. Only when we turned the corner onto Kronprinzenallee did I turn around to face front, willing myself not to look again. As I turned, my eyes fell upon them, hundreds of them, all up and down the Kronprinzenallee—the people, the refugees from Berlin—the ones over whom those sleeping men with their heavy boots had declared victory. We stood back. We did not join the stream of hundreds—women and children of all ages and old men and women to weak to walk quickly—all traveling in silence. The silence unsettled me.

I had expected the street to be empty. But it was full. They walked with their heads down. Mothers carried children far too heavy for them, and children carried bundles of clothes and food that bent them over at the waist. Nobody spoke, and the children did not cry or complain, even the very small ones. They all knew, even the youngest knew, their only hope lay in trying to reach the west, trying to reach the Americans. And so they fled to the west from their burning city filled with Russians. They fled in one continuous stream, as if they were all moving together like a giant school of fish swimming upriver. We stood to the side, searching for Uncle Kurt, not sure where to step in.

"He's up ahead," said the boy, pointing with his thin finger.

We walked on the outer edge of the flow of refugees. As we approached a house with its front stoop blown off, a man stepped out from the shadows and waved us over to him. It took a moment for me to understand. The man was Uncle Kurt. His face, covered with stubble from at least a week's worth of beard, looked drawn and tired, and his normally impeccably combed hair jutted out every which way. As if reading my mind, he smoothed down his hair with his hand before greeting my father.

"Thank God you got my message!"

Vati hugged his brother in reply. They stood there embracing for a moment, the rest of us silent witnesses. I had never seen them exhibit any sort of affection toward one another, and I studied them with keen interest, ignoring for a moment the chaos that surrounded us. When they parted, Uncle Kurt had tears in his eyes. My father's back was to me, so I couldn't tell if he too had tears.

"Thanks to this brave fellow, yes, we got your message." My father put his arm around the boy.

"Yes. Thank you, son. Here." Uncle Kurt grabbed inside his coat and pulled out a small loaf of bread. Where could he have gotten it? "This is for you."

Mutti stepped forward. "Here. Take this also." She handed the boy three hard-boiled eggs. Instinctively I wanted the eggs! Not so much! Surely a loaf of bread was enough for his efforts? What would we eat? Ashamed of my thoughts, I turned away from my mother, afraid she could read them on my face.

The boy shoved the eggs into his pockets and hid the bread under his shirt.

"Now hurry home before someone takes that from you," said Vati.

The boy nodded gravely. "Thank you, sir! I won't forget you." He placed his free hand over his heart, but he did not leave. Instead, he stood listening. My father and Uncle Kurt, immersed in conversation, did not notice him anymore.

"Where are we going?" asked Vati.

"To Zehlendorf, across from the old *Rathaus*. There is a vacant apartment. The family must have fled recently; they left everything behind. The Russians have taken over the *Rathaus* as their *Kommandantura*, and it is safe there."

"Right across from the Russians?" I exclaimed in horror.

"The closer we are to the officers, the less chaos there is. Trust me; it is safe," said Uncle Kurt, looking around Vati to find me.

I was skeptical, and it showed in my expression, for he continued, "Officially they are not supposed to bother us, so if you are near the officers they try to control the men."

"Not very successfully!" remarked my mother.

Uncle Kurt turned to her, concerned. "Nothing happened to you, did it?"

"No, nothing happened," my father broke in. He stared down at a loose cobblestone and kicked at it. "Well, nothing disastrous anyway … at least not to us." He looked up suddenly. "But we must hurry. They'll wake up soon."

Uncle Kurt nodded his head. "We should be as close to Zehlendorf as possible when they do. Luckily, the worst of the lot won't be mobile for quite some time." He paused before adding wryly, "Still recuperating from last night's activities, I imagine."

My mother looked away and put her arm around me.

"We'll walk on the Kronprinzenallee. The side streets are a death sentence. But here, where lots of people can see things, it is relatively safe." With that, Uncle Kurt turned to lead the way. Vati fell in next to him, Uncle Kurt grabbing one of the suitcases he carried, and Mutti and I walked side by side, sharing the weight of a huge basket of supplies between us, each of us grabbing a handle. Luise took up the rear with her jugs of water. I turned and saw that the boy followed behind Luise. It was awkward walking with one side tipped toward the weight of the basket, and my shoulder and forearm soon began to ache. We fell in step with the stream of refugees, trying not to disrupt them too much.

The rain poured down on us; it seemed it would never stop. Women held blankets over their heads and tried to shelter the smaller children under them as they walked along in the rain. Older children struggled to push prams filled to overflowing with pots and pans and bedding and anything else they could grab that was not destroyed, all tied down with bedding or ropes or even, in some cases, clothes. One family had used a garden hose to keep their possessions in place. My father and Uncle Kurt periodically stopped to help a young boy or girl disengage their mother's pram when the front wheel had fallen into a pothole carved in the road by the tank traffic that had been through here only a short time before. Babies, in some cases as old as three, that in other times, on another day, would have enjoyed a ride in the pram, were tied onto their mother's backs with blankets and sheets strapped tight, their thin legs dangling around their mother's hips but out of the way, freeing their mothers' hands to carry a suitcase or a basket. I remembered similar scenes from the picture books of Africa I found in Opa Bolle's elegant, wood-paneled library. Beside the mothers, young boys and girls struggled to push babies' prams stacked high with all that was left of the family's life.

Next to me, a young boy labored to pull a contraption made out of two poles with a blanket stretched across. Tied to the point of each pole was its precious cargo—a frail old man with pure white hair. Piled beside him and on top of him were blankets and pots that he tried to hold in place with his hands. He could not have weighed more than eighty pounds, but the weight was obviously too much for the boy. His older sister grabbed the poles and pushed him out of the way. She had needed a break. The mother walked ahead of them carrying two suitcases and a bag tied on her back. She stared at the ground. The ends of the poles lodged into a pothole, and the boy had to push from behind to help his sister dislodge them. The mother paused for them to catch up, sensing they were not behind her. She didn't turn around; she stared silently at the road in front of her. The human traffic flowed around them like water in a stream around a pile of rocks. Nobody spoke.

We slipped and slid on the churned-up road. The tanks had left huge track marks and in some places cut up the road to where it was almost impassable. The few able-bodied men among us helped the children and women lift the prams and wheelbarrows and improvised vessels over these sections of the road. Uncle Kurt and my father took turns handing their own burdens to each other to lend a helping hand.

I caught glimpses through legs and feet of the horribly disfigured road ahead—hundreds of tanks having churned through the day before. All about us, buildings sported huge pockmarks from the bullets that assaulted them. With black, gaping holes in their facades where windows had been blown out, they leered back at me like gap-toothed imbeciles.

Periodically, piles of rubble lay on the side roads where someone had tried to make room for more vehicles, presumably to allow more Russian tanks and jeeps through. To our right, the trees stood smoldering in the Grunewald despite the rain pouring down on them as if desperately trying to save them. They left a stench of smoke that combined with other unspeakable odors to make the air unbearable. With my free hand, I pulled my shirt up to cover my mouth and nose, as I had done in Halberstadt when Vati and I had fled.

Soldiers were everywhere—some were even propped against trees with their legs sticking out into the flow of people. They did not move, and people stepped silently over them. I looked more closely to the right, where the Grunewald bordered the road, and my mother moved forward. I tried to look around her and she moved again. Most of the soldiers wore German uniforms. Why would they let German soldiers just lie there asleep? I leaned forward again, this time avoiding my mother. The motionless soldiers had holes in their uniforms out of which spilled what looked like dark brown dirt, but I knew it was blood. The smell I had first noticed yesterday intensified, and suddenly I knew what it was.

"Don't look," said my mother. Then she was silent, focusing on the shoes and legs just ahead of her.

I could not stop looking at the bodies. Back and forth, I traded glances of the street and feet and legs ahead of me for glances of the bodies that passed by in bits and pieces, as the human picket fence between allowed only for staccato views. They meant nothing to me, these bodies, until I saw a boy no more than my age—blond like the boy in Halberstadt, with his pale skin and delicate hands. His head was thrown back against a tree and seemed attached to the tree. His mouth hung open, and a six-inch hole through the middle of his chest exposed the tree behind him. His image passed in an instant. I shuddered. I prayed for him and for all the boys my age and even younger, drafted to die senselessly when no possible hope for victory existed. And then I could not look anymore. Like the others I stared straight ahead, hypnotized by legs and feet treading slowly, deliberately, to unknown destinations.

We crossed Argentinischeallee. Afraid, I forced myself to look toward my friend Christa's apartment, wondering if she was alive. The boulevard was overrun with trucks and tanks, and my eyes could not make out the houses and apartments that I knew lined it. One truck, parked in front of what I thought might be Christa's apartment, was overflowing with dark sacks—dead soldiers—the realization only striking me after I had passed.

I didn't have time to think about them. The ache in my shoulder and forearm and the rain stinging my eyes kept my mind occupied. Ahead of us the stream of people suddenly began forming a fork around something in the road. As we got closer I saw that it was the carcass of a horse, stripped to the bone. The blood, still fresh on the ground, combined with the rain and pooled in the cracks of the road. I stepped over the deep maroon puddles, feeling nauseous.

And still the rain poured down on us—great buckets of it. It stung my face and eyes. I rubbed my eyes with my free hand and tried to shield them as one does from the sun so I could see the road ahead of me. My feet felt numb. My shoes were now soaked through, and the cuffs of Vati's old pants began to drag down into the street as they filled with water. The weight of the basket tore at my arm, worrying me that it would pull out of its socket. I wanted to stop and rest, but I knew we could not risk it. We had to keep walking, hoping and praying they would not wake up until we got to the *Kommandantura*. I turned quickly to look over my shoulder. The boy had gone. I wondered when. Where had he turned away from us? Had he made it home unharmed? We walked on, and it seemed forever.

Suddenly, up ahead of us in the distance, shouts broke the silence.

"Stop."

And then another shout. "Stop! The Russians are coming through."

A murmur rose from the crowd, beginning in front somewhere and washing over us like a great wave, and then panic took hold and the crowd began to scatter into the side streets and alleys along the Kronprinzenallee. I noticed we were at the corner of Potsdamer Strasse and Kronprinzenallee. To the right was Potsdam. People began to turn back, pushing the crowd back. A child was trampled in the chaos. Its screams, loud and shrill even in the chaos of noise, added to the panic.

I heard a loudspeaker with a deep Russian voice shouting something at us from some unknown distance in front. It could not be too far; the voice was loud and clear, commanding.

"What's happening?" asked a boy next to me.

I shrugged my shoulders. I couldn't see over Vati and Uncle Kurt and the others in front of me. And then suddenly I could. I saw a tank battalion coming toward us, parting the people ahead of me like a snowplow. Women screamed, and children shrieked in terror. A truck drove in front of the battalion, the man and the loudspeaker suddenly emerging; he was trying to tell people to step back off the road, but his German pronunciation was so heavily accented with Russian, nobody understood. I could only make out "*zooruckdreden.*" He meant *zurücktreten!* Stand back!

The crowd fell away and we ended up at the edge of the street with the tanks splashing through the muddy road only two feet in front of us. If the crowd pushed forward, we would die. Thankfully they did not; instead, they ran to the side streets in panic, the sound of the Russian voice now deafening. Some stayed, like us, watching the scene before us as if we were spectators at a military parade. I spotted the old man in the pole sling. He tried to sit up and twist around to see what was going on.

Tank after tank drove past us. I was too tired to count them with their roofs flung open and the men hanging out of them or onto the side of them staring at us, their faces blank. A few waved and smiled at us. Some of the children waved back, an automatic gesture, but most stared, uncomprehending. The rest of us watched speechless, not able to digest the numbers and the power of this military giant that had taken over our city. They kept coming, hundreds and hundreds of them. I heard the loudspeaker grow more and more distant as it continued down the road in the direction we had come from, and I imagined the resulting panic as the sound of the voice grew louder down the Kronprinzenallee toward our area of Dahlem. And then on to where? Charlottenburg? Wilmersdorf? How could they smile at us?

The rain would not stop, and it mixed with the dirt the tanks churned up to form brown rivers at our feet. Vati, usually so fastidious, had not noticed his shoes were covered in sludge. Mutti's mouth hung open as she stared at the display of military might before us. Her face betrayed her awe at the immensity. None of us had realized the vastness of the Russian Army. We had heard the numbers on the BBC, but we had thought them to be exaggerated—the bravado of a conqueror trying to encourage the enemy to surrender. We never imagined the numbers to be true—not like this, anyway. Not like what was passing before my very eyes. How odd that only an hour or so ago we had been ignorant like the Wollecks and the Kleinfelds still were right now, isolated down in the basement with no understanding of the size and might of this force that had come to conquer us.

Anger welled up inside me. The faces of old men and young boys loomed before me. The ones my mother and I had seen at the *Volksstrum* office with their pathetic rifles, sent out to fight this colossus! All that was left of them was brown dirt flowing from giant holes in their chests, and for what? For leaders who didn't care what happened to those German lives—lives that were viewed as expendable; numbers and statistics maybe, but not real flesh and blood to them. They knew the numbers; they knew the odds. Ruled by their egos, unable to admit they had lost, they sent them out to die in a hopeless war! Their war! Not our war! We didn't want this war! The single tear sliding down Vati's face merged in my mind with the rivers of brown sludge at my feet. And where were they now? I looked around at the careworn, hungry faces all about me. Where were our leaders now? Holed up with Herr Hitler, no doubt, in that fancy concrete bunker my mother ranted about.

I knew Keitel was there, and Dönitz. They always scurried off during a bad air raid. Two weeks ago my father looked on horrified while my mother shouted at Keitel's chauffeur-driven car as it flew past our front garden that she too could survive the war if she could spend it in a cement bunker under the Reichstag with wine and caviar. Keitel had studied her over the bridge of his nose with that arrogant stare of his through the tinted windows of his black sedan. If he heard her, he did not show it.

We stood under a giant oak tree that offered some protection from the rain. Its branches bent under the weight of the rain and its trunk, at least two feet in width, stood firm, untouched by the war. No bombs had struck it. I examined it—not even artillery fire had grazed it! This tree, which had already rooted when the troops of Frederic the Great had marched up this same street, escorting the kaiser from Sanssouci to Berlin, now a witness to the Russians with their tanks and loudspeaker truck pushing their way up from Potsdam to the center of Berlin. What had it seen these many years? Leaflets littered the base of its trunk—the only sign the war had touched it. I cocked my head to read the primitive, bold block print that screamed: *Glauben! Kämpfen! Gewinnen!* "Believe! Fight! Win! The Führer's call is our sacred order!" I jumped back when an old man spat on the pamphlet. He turned to me. His rheumy eyes swam in their sockets, and his breath stank of rotten teeth: "Vampires! All of them, from the top down, nothing but vampires!" He turned abruptly and walked away, seesawing up and down on a cane that supported his bad hip.

"*Woinna Kaputt!*" shouted a Russian voice. I edged back to the street. Troops and jeeps had now replaced the tanks, all heading for central Berlin down the Kronprinzenallee, just as the kaiser had done so many times before during Carl Bolle's lifetime. My father shoved me behind him, and my mother too stepped back. They marched in no order—not like Hitler's Waffen SS with their perfect unison and their immaculate uniforms, tall and ramrod straight. These men were weathered, their uniforms dirty and torn, and their faces hard, unshaven, and sleep-deprived from war. They wore dark wool tunics like Russian peasants wore, cinched in at the waist with thick leather belts. Their pants were tucked into their boots—thick, crude, and filthy. These men were not used to the showmanship of war, or the discipline of marching in unison on a parade ground, twirling their weapons in a showy display of militarism. No, these were men who knew how to use their weapons, men who got to the point without showmanship, killers who would not hesitate; men who were used to the rain, the snow, and the bitter cold. I imagined them sleeping in hammocks under snowy skies, oblivious to the cold, oblivious to death. These were men trained to win at all costs.

What did our army look like now, I wondered? Certainly not the fine show-piece it was when put on display for the Führer. Ramrod-straight men, their stiff legs thrown waist-high, marching down the Kaiserdamm, sunlight sparkling off medals and polished buttons. I thought again of the frightened, fragile faces in the *Volkssturm* office. How could they possibly be a match for this massive presence?

"*Uri! Uri!*" shouted a soldier who had fallen out of line with the rest. He was pointing his gun at my father and then at Uncle Kurt. The other soldiers laughed at him and called to him in Russian.

"*Uri!*" he said again.

My father shook his head.

"*Du,* Nazi!"

My father shook his head again. The soldier curled his lip and butted Vati in the stomach. Vati fell back, landing in the basket my mother and I carried. It ripped out of our grasp and struck the ground. Pain shot through my arm. Nobody moved. One of the soldier's comrades grabbed him and pulled him back into line. The first soldier yanked his arm free, sputtering Russian exple-tives, his eyes dark with anger. The other soldier shouted at him in Russian, and he looked behind him and then fell back into line, but not before he ran his finger across his throat, looking directly at my father as he did it. Chills ran up my spine.

The sound of muddy water splashing against tires drew my attention to a jeep making its way up our side of the street. The well-groomed uniformed officer in the back frowned as he approached and glanced at Vati still on the ground, not pleased that the soldier had fallen out of line. Uncle Kurt offered his hand to Vati and pulled him up.

"Why didn't you give him your watch?" I asked.

"Not twice," was all he said.

"Opa Bolle gave that watch to Vati on his twenty-first birthday," whispered Mutti. "It's not just a watch."

Next came the trucks, so many I could not imagine there were any trucks left in all of Germany. In their beds, soldiers stood swaying back and forth to the rhythm of the trucks' movements as they edged their way up the crowded street. The more curious leaned out or sat on the hard metal rim of the truck's bed, dangling their legs casually over the edge as if headed to a picnic. What entitled them to ride on the trucks while the soldiers just ahead trudged through the sludge? Some bizarre military hierarchy?

Finally came the supply carts, slowly pulled by jeeps, or in some cases by horses or donkeys or shaggy ponies. This was a motley group with no uniform color or symbol on them, many no doubt pilfered from German farms. Some carts had sides made out of boards. Others were just flatbeds, and still others had makeshift sides made from doors painted in shades of blue and green taken from German farm houses. The carts struggled on the torn-up road. Men shouted orders to each other and to the animals, and all about was chaos.

We watched, hunger grabbing our stomachs as the food carts toppled past us, hoping something would fall off when the cart leaned precariously over a big pothole. A soldier sitting on the back of one threw a loaf of bread into the crowd and laughed as he watched the mayhem he had caused. Mothers fought each other for the bread like pigeons in the park, each getting a fistful, the bread torn into shreds. The soldiers laughed and tried it again on the other side of the street. I hated them from deep inside, and the force of it disturbed me.

"*Schwein!*" screamed my mother, spitting into the street.

"Stop it!" shouted my father, turning on her. "Do you want to get us killed?"

"She is right," said the woman next to me, who had commented before. She too screamed, "Pigs!" An officer riding a horse, sensing the disruption, rode up to the vehicle and called out a sharp reprimand to the two on top.

Eventually, the last pony cart passed and people began, once again, to fill the scarred boulevard, making their way out of the city. Some headed toward Potsdam down the Potsdamer Strasse, but many followed our route to Zehlendorf. We crossed Potsdamer Strasse, hundreds of us, and continued on to the center of Zehlendorf, where the Kronprinzenallee became Teltower Damm. The *Rathaus* caught my eye up ahead; only a few more blocks before we would be there. My arms ached to where I thought the muscles would snap. Resting was impossible; it would disrupt the flow of human traffic, and I was afraid we would lose sight of Uncle Kurt and Vati.

The door flew open and she came flying down the stairs, her children just behind her. Uncle Kurt had to grab hold of the banister to keep from being knocked down the stairs as she threw herself at him.

"Oh! Thank God you are back! We didn't know if you would make it! We were so worried! Weren't we, children?" She kept her back to them, but they all nodded their heads in agreement. Tante Hilde hugged Uncle Kurt so hard his face turned red. Then she hugged Vati, and then she pushed past the two men to my mother. The women clung to each other, neither one of them speaking; tears touched their eyes and swam around the lids as they pulled away. Suddenly her eyes locked onto mine, and she stepped past Mutti.

"Jutta, come give me your side of this monster basket! My God, Heti, what did you pack in here? Your entire pharmacy and kitchen, no doubt!" She drew me to her chest with her free hand and then quickly pushed me ahead of her. "Go on! " She shooed me ahead of her as I stood staring in disbelief that we had made it, that we were all together, all of us, alive in this narrow stairwell that led to an apartment that did not belong to us.

My legs shook as I climbed the last few steps up to the apartment door. My arm, so light and detached, felt like it did not belong to me; I had to touch my shoulder to make sure it was still attached. Ingrid, Peti, and Dieter surrounded Uncle Kurt and Vati. Ingrid in particular looked relieved to see her father again. Peti and Dieter jumped up and ran up to me as soon as I came through the door.

"Jutta, come! You must see our bedroom!" They grabbed my hand, and pain shot through my arm. I followed, numb with disbelief. For them this was a grand adventure, a big family sleepover.

"Look! Mutti says that we can take the mattresses off the beds and make one giant bed in here! And we are all going to sleep together in the same bed. Won't that be magnificent?"

I nodded my head automatically, not really listening.

Peti grabbed my hand again, but this time I held out my good hand. "And this is going to be your parents' room." She pulled me into a room filled with pink lace curtains and a dressing table covered with empty perfume bottles that before the war must have been the owner's pride and joy. The room must have belonged to the daughter of the apartment's owners. I wondered what had happened to her. Where was she now? Why had she left everything? Was she dead? Hit in the street by artillery fire?

"Look, you can see the *Kommandantura* out of this window. Look at all the Russians!" It was Dieter who had spoken. He walked to the window and pretended to have a gun, shooting at the Russian soldiers.

"Dieter! Stop it! Mutti told you if you did that again she would string you up by your ears!"

Dieter put his arms down and instead stuck his tongue out at the soldiers across the street. I looked down in the street; they had no idea he was even at the window.

"Come on, Jutta. Let's look at Mutti and Vati's room." We walked directly across the hall to the third bedroom.

It too was a big room with everything left behind. A book stood open on the nightstand; a pair of reading glass lay across the top. A man's shirt hung over the back of a chair, and a pair of shoes stood neatly by the wardrobe.

What happened to these people? Had they fled to relatives in the west? Or had they been hit, huddled together, frightened, clutching each other in an unfamiliar bomb shelter with the walls crashing in on them and no hope for escape? I shuddered. It occurred to me that Pompeii must have looked like this, people and their activities frozen in time. I felt uncomfortable, like a voyeur intruding in someone else's life. We did not belong in this house, with these beds, these books, and these photos telling someone else's story.

We went back out to the sitting room where our parents sat close, talking intensely. The conversation stopped abruptly when we walked in the room. I felt detached, like I was observing them through a filter. Too young for the adult's world and too old for the children's world, I did not fit in. I glanced over at Ingrid; she sat off by herself, and I wondered if she too noticed the divide.

"Well, Jutta, what do you think of the accommodations?" asked Tante Hilde with her usual joviality, but it sounded forced.

"They're fine," I said quietly.

"Come join us," said Mutti.

I sat next to Mutti on a dark blue sofa with huge beige pansies on it. What odd fabric, I thought, as I lowered myself next to her.

"Well, they're safer than Dahlem, that's for sure!" said Tante Hilde, letting out her breath as she said it.

"My God, the Russians were everywhere! But I mean everywhere! It was unbelievable!"

"Yes. I know. Heti, we only got here last night. They weren't marching around yet, but the tanks! *Gott im Himmel!* I have never seen so much military hardware! Where did they get them all? The tanks, I mean. I didn't think that Russians could make tanks!"

"The Amis, I'm sure," said Uncle Kurt.

"Don't fool yourself. The Russians are not as incompetent as you think," said my father.

"It's hard to imagine that those soldiers out there come from the same country as Tchaikovsky and Tolstoy!"

"These men don't! For God's sake, Heti! These men come from the gulag, half of them!"

My mother smiled.

"No, really," continued Tante Hilde. "I heard a report about it! Or they come from some tribe in the mountains of Uzbekistan! I mean they just took everybody that walked on two limbs and wore pants!"

I had to smile. Tante Hilde made you smile even when she wasn't trying to be funny. She lightened the mood in the room, and somehow we could bear the events of the day better because of her.

"So, how did you find this place? Why Zehlendorf?" asked my mother.

"One of the Russian officers told me to leave and go away from the city," replied Uncle Kurt.

"No! He said, '*Woinna Kapputt. Alls Dutche Kaputt*,' in that way that they all have," interrupted Tante Hilde, rolling her eyes. "And then he said, '*Berlin nein. Zehlendorf, Zehlendorf.*'"

"Well, it was good of him to tell us Zehlendorf."

Tante Hilde shrugged. "And the other one, the short one, kept saying, '*Kommandantura, Zehlendorf*'. So Kurt figured it had to be in the *Rathaus* that they were setting up their headquarters. Didn't you?"

Uncle Kurt nodded his head. "Where else is there a building in Zehlendorf big enough?"

"We walked right past Auf dem Grat, but the place was swarming with Russians and Kurt didn't want to leave us alone on the street. So he decided to find us a place and then come back for you."

"I can't believe you got through to us!" My father shook his head.

"And I can't believe nothing happened to us on the way here!" added my mother.

"It was a bit uncertain there for a moment, when Hans refused to give up the watch from Vati!" said Uncle Kurt.

"They had already tried to steal it once!"

"Hans! Are you crazy?" cried Tante Hilde. "They might have shot you!"

My father shrugged.

"Mutti cried!" announced Peti suddenly. Everybody turned to look at her. We had assumed she and Dieter were busy with their tic-tac-toe game. She looked up at us.

"Well, she did! She cried the whole way from our house to your neighborhood."

I looked across to Tante Hilde. She studied her middle child, annoyed.

"Thank you, Peti!"

"You're welcome," responded Peti mischievously.

"Well, I don't blame her. What we saw on the way here is enough to make you weep for weeks!" And then, seeing that Peti had upset Hilde, my mother whispered, "A child seeing her mother cry makes a big impression, Hilde. It's just her way to let her fears out."

Tante Hilde sat back and relaxed a bit. "I'm sure you're right."

Silence surrounded our small group in this living room that belonged to another family. A family that had fled. I hoped for their sakes they had headed west or southwest to Bavaria. The sounds of the troops and tanks outside formed a distant background music, but inside no one spoke. The grandfather clock in the corner ticked away undisturbed, and we watched Peti and Dieter entertain each other with sticks and bottle caps and whatever else they had been able to collect.

————

"What are we doing for a toilet?" asked my mother.

"Well, that is a bit of a problem. We have a pot, and I am afraid we are dumping it in the alley behind the apartments. I don't know what else to do."

"The plumbing is broken here, too?" I asked, dejected.

"All over Berlin, my dear!" responded Tante Hilde.

"But hopefully, since the *Kommandantura* is directly across the street, they'll restore the plumbing to this area more quickly than elsewhere," said Uncle Kurt.

"I wouldn't hold my breath. From what I could see in our house, the Russians don't understand the concept of a toilet!" said my mother.

"You went into the house after they had occupied it?" exclaimed Uncle Kurt, astonished. "Hans! That's insanity!"

"Heti just had to get something —" He shrugged his shoulders to complete the thought. His brother frowned at him in disapproval.

"Hilde, would you believe they had gone to the bathroom in one corner, and in the other they all slept piled up on top of each other!" exclaimed my mother to shift the focus of the conversation. Uncle Kurt shook his head again.

"That's what I'm telling you, Heti. These men come from the gulag or some godforsaken part of Russia where they have never even heard of a toilet," she snorted. "So let's just see if they fix the plumbing any time soon."

"But Hilde, it's the officers that are living across the street, and they will want plumbing," objected her husband.

"I hope you're right!" she replied, rising from her chair. "Now Heti and I need to figure out how much food we have for these children. And you two need to figure out how to get more food!"

"And water!" added my mother. She accompanied Hilde into the kitchen, where we had left our baskets and cases and Luise, who was trying to organize things as best she could.

Uncle Kurt and Vati followed the women to the kitchen, leaving Ingrid and me alone on the sofa. Ingrid glanced across at me, raised her eyebrows, and pulled one side of her mouth up as if to say, "Good luck!" I smiled briefly in reply.

————

We stayed in the apartment for ten days. By far the worst part was using the bathroom. The bucket remained our toilet. The thing made me nauseous, its metal sides echoing throughout the small apartment whenever anyone used it. I drank as little water as possible so I would have to use it as little as possible. Uncle Kurt and Vati took turns carrying it down the four flights of stairs to the garden, where they had dug a large hole to dump its disgusting contents. On warm days when we had the windows open, the stench rose up the four stories and entered the apartment.

There was no running water at all. Vati and Uncle Kurt both grew full beards from the stubble already underway in the days before we reached the apartment, not willing to waste precious water on the luxury of shaving. They made fun of each other, saying they looked like the bearded old accordion players on the streets of Berlin with their monkeys. Vati's beard was silver.

Nobody took a bath for those ten days. The only one not troubled by this was Dieter. The rest of us dreamed of a hot bath and shampoo. We took sponge baths instead. Each family had their own bucket. Mutti and I would bathe first, and then Vati would have to use the already dirty water for his bath. Our skin suffered from the lack of clean water and lotion. Mine itched unbearably, and when I scratched too hard, I bled. Mutti reprimanded me, horrified, and convinced I would create a staph infection from the scratching. I didn't care. Vati's eczema came back. I noticed the big, red, wrinkled patches of skin on his hands and arms.

But the worst was my hair! I longed to wash it! It stuck to my head in stiff sheets like the Masaii warriors I had seen in Opa Bolle's books, who painted their hair with cow dung. I begged my mother to let me wash my hair, but water was far too scarce for hair washing and, she said, if I washed my hair, then Ingrid and Peti would also want to wash theirs. Nobody died from dirty hair, she added, but people have died from thirst. And so we survived in this apartment together, as a family. My father and Uncle Kurt foraged for food every day—like great hunters, Tante Hilde joked. And we, the women and children, stayed in the relative safety of the apartment, afraid to go outside except for on the balcony, where I spent hours watching the Russians moving about below, always careful not to let *them* see me.

———

"Mississippi," I said, bored.

"There is no such river!"

"Yes there is! In America!" I sang out impatiently.

"Oh! You and America this, and America that!" shrieked Peti.

"Well, you asked for rivers that begin with *M*."

"Well how about the Main? Or the Mosel?"

We had been in this apartment for over a week now, and I was growing tired of Ingrid's geography games. She would pick a letter of the alphabet and then a category like rivers, countries, or mountains, and we would name as many as we could that began with that letter. It was fun at first, but not now, not after a week!

"Did you say it had to be a German river?" I asked irritably.

Before she could respond, my mother held up her hand to silence us. Someone was climbing the stairs. Vati and Uncle Kurt had gone out a short time ago to wait in the bread lines, but we did not expect them back for several hours. The lines were long, and they moved slowly. So who could this be? My mother motioned silently for us to go back into the bedroom. We got up quietly and tiptoed down the hallway.

There was a tap on the door.

"It's us!" came my father's voice through the locked door.

"Well for God's sake!" cried my mother, throwing the bolt back to let them in.

"You scared us to death!" called Tante Hilde from the kitchen doorway.

"Sorry!" He stepped inside quickly, Uncle Kurt right behind him. "Listen. We just heard across the street that yesterday they ordered all the soldiers out of the houses and into some sort of makeshift barracks! They rounded them up yesterday all over Dahlem."

"And this means?" asked Hilde tentatively.

"This means that we will be able to go back to our home," replied Uncle Kurt patiently.

"Really? You think it will be safe?" asked my mother, looking from one to the other.

"We don't know. Kurt and I will walk to the houses and see how it looks, see if it's safe."

"That is fantastic news!" cried my mother, clasping her hands in excitement.   "You and Hilde can wait in the bread line today. It's safe now. The lines are full of women," said Vati.

"Besides, these ones are all right," added Kurt, jerking his head in the direction of the *Kommandantura*.

"Of course we will stand in line. Jutta and Ingrid can stay with Peti and Dieter."

"No," said Tante Hilde, looking at her son. "Let's take Dieter with us. They love children, these Russians, and I see them give extra to the children." She nodded toward the window.

"Well, let's take Peti then, too."

"Yes! We want to go!" cried Dieter, as if this was an outing to get ice cream.

"Jutta, you and Ingrid stay here. I just am not sure yet if it is safe for you," said my father. "Luise should be back soon, anyway." Luise had gone to fill the water jugs at the pump down the street. She would then begin the boiling process my mother insisted on to sterilize the water. We both nodded at Vati. We knew he was right to be cautious. But I was disappointed, and it showed on my face.

"Soon you can go out. Soon, my love," soothed my mother.

An excitement stirred in the others that had not been present before as my mother and Tante Hilde took the baskets from Vati and Uncle Kurt. Peti and Dieter ran to get their sweaters.

Vati kissed Mutti as she grabbed the lapel of his sweater. "Be careful, Hans!"

He nodded, placing her hand on his cheek for a moment before he came over to me.

"Will you be all right here?"

"I guess," I said moodily. "I'm so bored here is all."

"I know, but it will not be long." He patted my cheek as he said it. "How about I bring you something from the house"

"Yes! Can you bring my sketching pad?" I asked, my mood lifting.

He smiled. "I'll try."

He hugged me and moved to the door. He stopped halfway and turned back to the two of us. "Make sure you keep this door locked at all times," he said. "And let no one in!"

We nodded again and they all hurried out, the excited voices of Dieter and Peti echoing in the stairwell. My mother laughed at something Tante Hilde said. Their voices floated up to me, amplifying my loneliness. But even so, I was pleased to hear Mutti laugh again.

I watched for them at the window as they emerged from the building to the street. The women and the children crossed the street, dodging jeeps and carts that hurried past, and the two men turned sharply onto Teltower Damm, heading in the direction of Dahlem and our homes, their hands thrust into their pockets and their strides determined. They looked down, avoiding eye contact with the many soldiers that still lined the streets.

The apartment was directly across from the *Rathaus* on Teltower Damm. I watched the soldiers standing guard in front of its big, boxy exterior. Stiff and unforgiving, they moved with precision, saluting officers who entered and exited the building. These were not the soldiers that had come into our neighborhood with their filthy boots and tunics and their odor, like they had rutted around with pigs all day. From this distance, I couldn't smell them, but they didn't look like they smelled. They wore clean uniforms with the creases pressed and boots polished, and they stood ramrod straight and stared straight ahead, oblivious of the women that passed by on the street. They guarded both sides of the long steps that led into the *Rathaus*, and one soldier manned each corner of the building. The *Rathaus* was on the corner of Teltower Damm and Kirchstrasse. Across the street, on the side of the *Rathaus* that bordered Kirchstrasse, was a small park. I watched other soldiers linger and relax under the huge cherry tree that graced the park, smoking cigarettes down to the butts and tossing them into the street. Young boys hovered, hoping to collect the cigarette butts that had a bit left to them. Cigarettes were money, and even a butt could be traded. As I watched, two of them fought over a butt recently tossed on the ground. The bigger one pushed the younger one off his bicycle, and as he clattered into the street a soldier looked up. The soldier came over and spoke roughly to the older boy, shooing him away. He helped the younger boy back on his bicycle and gave him the half-smoked cigarette he held in his hand. This one act of kindness softened me for a moment, but then I saw that these men did notice the women who passed by, and I shuddered.

I looked back at the *Rathaus* with its narrow windows that ran up half the length of the building. I wondered when it had been built. It was certainly ugly enough, with its concrete facade, to have been built by the Nazis, but I doubted that they built it. At any rate, it now housed the Russian command center. I shook my head. Ten years ago, who would have envisioned such a thing?

I turned around, suddenly bored with the scene before me. "No more geography games!" I told Ingrid firmly.

She laughed, gathering up the papers in acquiescence.

"I am going to draw a dress. In fact, I am going to design a ball gown."

"On what paper and for what possible ball?" asked Ingrid.

Ignoring her, I searched the house for something to draw on. I found an old piece of newspaper shoved in the back of a drawer in the bedroom. It was dated, August 1, 1936, the opening day of the Olympics. Someone who lived in this apartment, someone who belonged here, must have been there or known one of the athletes. I looked at the smiling faces all turned in seeming adoration toward Hitler with Nazi flags flying everywhere as teams of athletes paraded past his podium. The master race! What a joke! Who could even come up with such an idea? And yet I knew many had believed in them, including many of the girls at my school. Liesel popped into my mind. Where was she now? I shook my head, and an image of Opa Bolle came to mind, sitting in his elegant leather chair, his strong hands holding his black-bound Bible, reading Galatians 3:28 to us: "There is neither Jew nor Greek, there is neither slave nor free, there is neither male nor female; for you are all one in Christ Jesus." I heard his deep, melodious voice even as I stood in this apartment surrounded by things that belonged to someone else, a world so far removed from his. Now I understood.

I stared at the paper in my hand. Where were these people now? The men were almost certainly dead, but the women? Hiding in bombed-out homes, haggard and thin from too many years of no sleep and no food? Their smiling faces stared back at me, unreal, plastic—as if they had never lived.

"Ingrid, I found some paper!" I called out.

"Great. Now what about a pen?"

"I have one in my bag," I responded.

She did not answer. I rummaged around in my bag and found the fountain pen Vati had given me for my fifteenth birthday. I hoped it would not run out of ink.

I walked out triumphantly holding my prizes, one in each hand.

Ingrid looked up from the book she was reading.

"You still have not told me what ball you plan to wear it to."

"Oh, shut up!" I snapped, and threw myself onto the sofa and began to draw.

Vati and Uncle Kurt returned late that evening, so late that my mother had begun to pace, fearing the worst. It had taken longer than expected because they had to clean up the filth the Russians had left. They wouldn't say much except that it appeared the Russians had never heard of a bathroom and that shovels were required to clean the excrement out of the corners of every room.

"But not your bedroom," my father added quickly, seeing my look of disgust.

The Russians had broken as many plates and glasses and empty bottles of liquor as possible, and the place was covered with shards of glass. The other Bolles' house was in a little better shape. Apparently our street had been the worst hit because of its proximity to the forest, where so much fighting had taken place. The Wollecks had survived, but Herr Wolleck was sick and Frau Wolleck could not find a doctor for him. She had been afraid to go out to the hospital with him.

Vati said he left our windows open to let the smell out of the house, but we may want to wait a day before we go back. But my mother insisted that she wanted to go home first thing in the morning. Tante Hilde backed her, and the two women stood firm on this. And so the adults decided we would leave early in the morning, in case they were moving troops later in the day.

At the first light of dawn, before any soldiers were up, we left the apartment with just enough light to make out the road below. We carried our baskets—lighter than when we arrived—and when we closed the door of this apartment that had sheltered us for these ten days, I was astonished to feel a pang of sadness. As the door clicked behind my father, the last one out, a surge of anticipation coursed through me. We were going home, but to what?

*Jutta at Berlin Zoo
with baby lion*

Jutta's room

The living room

The goldfish pond

Vati's factory

Carl Bolle's milk empire

Mutti with pearls

Vati

Vati giving a speech

Opa Bolle

*Opa Bolle with grandchildren; Jutta is
the baby on the right*

Luise with Jutta as a baby

*Tante Lieschen, Omi, and Jutta
in the Grunewald*

Mutti and Jutta

*Jutta with Gustav and Sisi in
Opa Bolle's apple orchard*

First day of school with Schüle Tute and friends

Going to school on the streetcar

Mutti with Jutta and Tante Hilde and Ingrid in Berchtesgaden

Jutta with Mutti on an outing

Mutti and Omi in Halberstadt

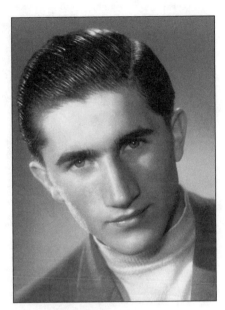

Fritz

Jutta with Fritz on the Kurfürstendamm

Jutta with Teddy

Mutti after the war

Jutta before she leaves for America

Kaiser Wilhelm Gedächtnis Kirche before the war

Kaiser Wilhelm Gedächtnis Kirche after the war

Berlin: The Americans Arrive

Soldiers and Chocolate

July 4, 1945

"But we have to go! Vati, please!"

"Absolutely not!" said my father, looking up from his paper, frowning.

"But Christa says they have passed her apartment already and are heading this way on the Kronprinzenallee. And," I paused, "they are handing out chocolates!"

He raised an eyebrow but otherwise did not respond.

"She says they are ever so nice and handsome, and they smile." I looked at him hopefully. "And they are even clean! You know, with nice uniforms and boots," I added, as if that would somehow change my father's mind.

"I don't care what they are handing out or what they look like, you are not going down there to watch an invading army enter this city!" He was angry now. "This is not a game! This is not a sport! These are armed soldiers, for God's sake!" he bellowed. He let his paper fall to the ground and yanked his reading glasses off. I looked at him for a moment, and he at me. I said nothing. Then, grabbing Peti's hand, I turned and stomped back out to the garden.

Peti and I had been sitting outside catching what there was of the sun's rays as it flicked in and out of the cloud cover. It was cool for July, but we didn't mind. We were happy just to be outside relaxing, gossiping about school and friends. The authorities had kept us home from school again because the last of the Russian regiments were moving out today as the Americans and British marched in. I threw myself down in my chair, angry. I glanced inside. My father had buried his nose in his paper again. Mutti was upstairs napping, trying to ease the fatigue that had plagued her lately. Peti had spent the night with us simply because she was bored at her house now that all of her neighborhood friends were scattered by the war to distant parts of western Germany.

I sat silently, moping. My arms crossed, I stared at nothing. Why couldn't we go? It was just around the corner! It wasn't fair! Why had I told him? Why hadn't we just gone? He probably would not have even noticed we were gone. If only we had just slipped out of the garden without asking.

Peti sat with her legs crossed on the ledge of the goldfish pond, bent over, her chest touching her legs; she pushed the moss and algae around absentmindedly with a stick. The giant goldfish were gone. Mutti would not say what had happened to them, and I did not want to know. I lay back on my mother's striped chaise lounge, my legs, covered with freckles, crossed at the ankles and extended out in front of me. I stared over my feet at the bushes that lined the fence to the Wollecks' house. I wished again that I could find some nail polish to paint on my toenails like the pictures of the smiling models in my magazines—maybe a deep red, like the color of Frau Wolleck's roses. But of course there was no nail polish to be had in Berlin—and probably none in all of Germany. I sighed.

Peti looked up suddenly, cocking her head. "Listen," she whispered.

I turned my ear in the direction she indicated, and then I heard it—a faint rumbling in the distance. We looked at each other, frowning. It took us a second to realize it was them. It was the sound of trucks and marching men—hundreds of them. I put my finger to my mouth and peeked in at my father again. He sat in his reading chair, his paper held up in front of him. He could not hear them. I got up quietly, remaining bent at the waist so he would not see me over the paper. Peti uncrossed her legs.

"Come," I whispered urgently. We tiptoed past the living room window, and as soon as we reached the corner where the brick wall hid us from his view, we ran. I opened the gate carefully, Peti so close to me I felt her breath on my neck. The gate squeaked slightly, causing us both to cringe. I didn't dare open it more, so I squeezed past it and Peti followed. We didn't look behind us, and with our hearts racing, we left it open and ran as fast as we could to Auf dem Grat. As we turned the corner we saw hundreds of people, mostly children, lining our side of the Kronprinzenallee. Some of them were classmates of mine. I noticed a girl from my English class, Maria. With her red hair held back in a thick braid, she was hard to miss. She talked excitedly to a girl next to her.

"Come on," I said to Peti.

"Uncle Hans is going to be so mad at us!"

I shrugged in response and ran ahead of her.

We squeezed in between Maria and an elderly gentleman wearing a faded blue sweater. Maria turned.

"Oh, hi!" I said, as if I had seen her for the first time.

"Hi, Jutta! Isn't this exciting?" she said, smiling and stepping into the street to look around me to see if they were coming.

"Yes! Christa called and said they were throwing chocolates!"

"Really?" She grinned from ear to ear and turned to her friend to tell her what I had said. The friend bent her neck to look over at me, smiling, and she jumped up and down like an excited child.

Leaning forward, her friend said, "I hear they are very handsome!"

"Yes. Tall and well dressed, with no rips in their uniforms," added Maria.

"Maybe one will see me and have to come back and find me and whisk me off to America," said Maria's friend, giggling. We all laughed. Peti rolled her eyes. At thirteen, her interest in boys was minimal.

"They're far more likely to take advantage of you and leave you stranded here!" said Peti.

"What do you mean, take advantage of us?" I asked.

"I don't know," countered Peti. "That's what my mother tells Ingrid all the time."

The crowd began to pull forward. Some of the boys had climbed the charred tree stumps across the street in the Grunewald to see better.

"They're coming!" shouted one.

"Get down!" called the mother of one boy. "I don't want you over there cut off from us when they come through."

"Yes. All of you get down from there! Who knows what they will be like?" shouted the elderly gentleman next to me.

"I heard they're very friendly!" called a girl with pigtails and a pale blue jumper faded from many washings.

"Says who?" responded the man.

"Everybody!"

He snorted, "Let us see what happens with them."

"Well, they can't be as bad as that Russian lot," said a woman next to him.

He did not respond.

Peti, Maria, and I talked excitedly, periodically glancing down the street as the rumbling sound grew steadily louder. We could feel the earth vibrate and hear the loudspeaker as the American shouted in his accented German, "Stand back. Everybody please clear the way."

I couldn't see them yet because of all the people next to me, but I heard the crowd down the road intermittently cheer and clap.

"They must be throwing the chocolate," I guessed.

Peti nodded her head. "Jutta, I have big pockets in my sweater, so we can bring some back for everyone."

"If they throw enough!"

My heart raced with excitement as the noise grew steadily louder.

Suddenly a cheer went out from the crowd just ahead of us and traveled down the row of onlookers until it reached us. Peti, Maria, and I began to cheer; Maria's friend started her hopping again. We weren't sure why we were cheering, but it was infectious. Curiosity forced me forward, and I stepped into the street. And then I saw them—hundreds of them coming our way, some of them walking alongside their open vehicles, others riding in them, but all of them smiling and waving. Huge American flags with their bright red, white, and blue designs fluttered from the tops of jeeps and trucks.

The younger children, lined up along the edge of the street, cheered and smiled and shouted, "*Schokolade*," and, "*Bitte, Schokolade*." The soldiers obliged them with big smiles, and reaching into the jeep seats, they threw fistfuls of brightly wrapped chocolates at the children, the gold and silver wrappers catching the pale sunlight and casting bright streaks of iridescent color as they fell to the ground. The adults looked on with crossed arms; a few smiled, but most just stood and watched. As they drew near, I heeded the command of the loud-speaker and stepped back to the edge of the street. The first of the trucks and jeeps drove quickly past—vague splashes of brown and green passing quickly by. And then came the soldiers, tall and handsome and smiling with perfect white teeth. Their uniforms were crisp and pressed, and they wore funny little hats that reminded me of the paper sailboats we used to make to sail on the lake in the park before the war. Their boots were new, not like Russian boots. These boots were polished and without cuts or cracks in the leather. But they were also not the frightening, obsessively polished black boots of the Nazis. These were friendly boots, comfortable and new.

I realized we looked shabby next to these soldiers in our darned socks and leather shoes full of holes, the boys in shorts and pants that exposed their knob-by knees and skinny legs and the girls in dresses that were worn and far too tight. Our sweaters, either way too small or way too big or full of holes, suddenly embarrassed me. What must they think of us? They, with their washed hair and clean-scrubbed faces. Self-conscious of my hair, I covered it with my hands. Mutti only let me wash it once a week, and it was toward the end of the week. Could they see my dirty hair, or were they far enough away? My hand pushed a straggling strand behind my ear. It had grown out some, but not enough to hide the awful haircut Mutti had given me that day in the Wollecks' basement. Ashamed of my appearance, and of the appearance of all of us, I longed to tell them we had not always been like this. Once we were an elegant people, a people whose clothes were new and well tailored and bought from elegant shops along the Kurfürstendamm: a people who drank coffee and ate cake at Café Kranzler after listening to the greatest symphony in the world, the Berlin Phil-harmonic. But what would they know of that now? I had heard that downtown Berlin looked like a rock quarry in Italy, with rubble and dust where buildings once stood and grotesque, twisted strips of metal jutting out in all directions. A city stripped of all identity. The Russians had neither fixed the sewer system nor disposed of all the dead bodies, and it smelled so bad downtown that people took bouquets of flowers from their gardens, holding them tight to their noses if they had to venture into the city. Christa told me her brother said dead bodies still floated in the Havel and the Spree.

Now it would be different. The Americans would fix things; I was certain of it. I studied them again. Some of them could actually pass for Germans with their blond hair and blue eyes, but they moved with an easy confidence that no German bore. They laughed and waved at us, hands held high above their heads. A soldier with dark, curly hair and a friendly smile winked at me. I felt my face grow hot, and he laughed and tossed a chocolate bar right to me. As I reached out for it I held my breath, self-conscious I might drop it. But I didn't. I caught it and, holding up my prize, I smiled a thank-you back at the soldier just before he moved on. He blew me a kiss, receiving a smack on the shoulder from his companion for the gesture. He laughed easily and continued down the road, not thinking of me again. But I held his face in my mind for a very long time.

Peti held out her pockets to show me that she had already grabbed three chocolate bars.

"Look at you, grabbing all the chocolates!"

"Well, while you were making eyes at your lover boy, I was getting chocolates!"

"I wasn't making eyes!"

Peti raised her eyebrows in response. I shrugged and turned back to watch the Americans. So many of them, and they came, more and more, not with fear and intimidation, but there were so many I thought they would need all of Berlin to house them. Some of them drove jeeps and wore sunglasses, and you could not see their eyes, but they all smiled and looked friendly. Some of them waved to us, especially to the girls and the children. I looked down the line and saw the next group coming; this group threw yellow and green packs at the crowd. I remembered the stuff from so long ago, when we had stood in this same spot during the Olympics to watch the American and British tourists driving out to Potsdam. "Gum," my mother had called it then, regarding it as some hideous American invention whose purpose was to make us all resemble cows. But I had thought it was wonderful. I remembered the woman and the man, two Americans, confident, happy, and smiling—so full of life, just like these young men. They were certain and easy about their role in the world. I envied them their confidence, their certainty that they were on the right side of God.

And here they were again, these Americans, throwing their chocolates and gum at willing German children whose tentative smiles conflicted with the urgent scramble of their bodies for the treasures. The adults, too, stooped to pick up the chocolates that had fallen, shoving them in their pockets with stealth. Between us, Peti and I ended up with at least ten chocolate bars. I took one out and looked at it. It was wrapped in brown paper over foil and had the word "Hershey" written on it.

"Herrshee," I said to myself and bit in. It melted on my tongue, and I thought I had never tasted anything so good. I thought back. It had been at least two years since I had tasted pure chocolate, not the watered-down variety served at Tante Lieschen's after the rationing.

"Oh my God! Peti, here! Try a bite." I held out the chocolate, and she willingly bit into it.

Her face lit up with a smile that exposed chocolate-stained teeth. "Delicious!" she said, licking her lips and fingers.

A murmur rose in the crowd ahead of us. We stepped forward to see what was going on, but the crowd was too thick. Eventually word passed down the line that the soldiers were stopping just ahead and setting up camp. My heart bounced wildly. Maybe I would see my soldier again.

"Where are they stopping?" I asked no one in particular.

"It looks like the Königin Luise Strasse, where it dead ends into the forest," replied the elderly gentleman next to me. He was tall and could see over the crowd.

I looked up at him and smiled at the small chocolate stain holding on to the corner of his mouth. The crowd began to close in behind the last of the jeeps and trucks and move with them toward the Königin Luise Strasse.

A hand gripped my shoulder. My heart stopped. Even before I turned, I knew it was Vati.

"It is time for you girls to come home," he said quietly.

Peti and I looked at each other and then at the ground. We did not meet his eyes. He guided us by the shoulders, one of us on either side of him, through the crowd to the Föhrenweg. We walked in silence together, my father never lifting his hand from our shoulders as the sounds of the crowd grew more and more distant. He released his grip only when we arrived at our gate. I looked up and saw my mother watching us from the kitchen window.

My father did not speak until we were in the house, and then it was only to say, "Peti, I think it is time you go home. Go get your things, and I will walk you home."

She nodded, relieved to get away from him, and ran up the stairs with me right behind her.

Her eyes big, she asked, "What will happen to you?"

"I don't know, but it was worth it!" I said stubbornly. I thought of my soldier with his beautiful smile and ready wink. I fell onto my bed, hugging my pillow.

"Jutta! Uncle Hans looks like he could murder you with his own hands."

"Well, I am hoping that the walk to your house will calm him down. Maybe you could give him a chocolate."

She giggled.

I looked at the ceiling and sighed. "I don't care if I am in big trouble. I would not have missed that for the world!"

Peti nodded in agreement.

At that moment he called upstairs, "Come on, Peti. I have called your mother."

She kissed me on the cheek and ran down the stairs. I did not envy her the silent and long walk to her house.

"But Hans, there's so little for them to do right now!" said my mother. "They're teenagers, and there are no dances, no restaurants to go to, no theater, no movies. Nothing!"

My father had returned from his walk to Peti's house. I heard the front gate and crept to the top of the stairs that led to the living room, anticipating that they would sit together in the living room and discuss my fate. My mother had not come up to see me—too busy in the kitchen, I guessed—and I had not dared go down to see her.

"But she deliberately disobeyed me!"

"I know, and she was wrong. Let her know you are disappointed in her, but leave it at that." I felt a slight twinge of guilt. I had never deliberately disobeyed him before. She continued, "It was such a thrill for them to see those handsome boys marching in here throwing chocolates and smiles about."

"They have rules against fraternization, and they may seem nice, but we don't know what they are really like!"

"I know. I know. But it is not the nature of a teenager to be cautious and wait and see."

"I don't want her to get it into her head that she can run around with these American soldiers."

"She won't. Don't worry. I will talk to her. She is a responsible girl," soothed my mother.

My father sighed. "Was a responsible girl. She is now a teenager, and they are like space aliens from Mars! They lose their common sense and only have it returned to them when they turn twenty-one."

I heard my mother chuckle. This was a good sign; they were joking.

I lay flat on my stomach on the landing, lowered my head to the level of the first step, and peeked through the railing. Vati was sitting on the sofa next to my mother. His hair had turned as white as snow from the war. I didn't remember exactly when it happened, but it was within the past four months. They both looked so tired, so frail, and so old to me. I had never thought of my parents as old. My mother still had on her apron from the kitchen. How unusual! She never wore her apron into the living room. Her hair, twisted into a simple French knot at the back of her head, was dull and without body. A pang of guilt washed over me. She looked so thin and pale. I had not even noticed how thin she had become. Her arms, usually tending toward plump that she complained about them, were now two sticks, and her hollow cheeks left shadows on her face. How could I not have noticed? I looked more closely at my father; he too looked thin. His belt was cinched in so much that it hung down at least seven inches by his pant pockets. His cheeks, too, were hollow, and they emphasized the sharp curve of his nose.

What was wrong with me? How could I not have noticed? I looked at my own arms, normal and firm. I lifted my hand to my face, running my fingers across my cheeks. They were filled out as always, and I suddenly realized that I was not hungry because my parents were sacrificing their food for me. Of what little we had, my parents always gave me more. I thought back to dinner last night, to the schnitzel my mother had cooked. My mother had managed two small pieces of pork by bartering with the butcher—the thin meat for some of her plums and cherries. What would in other times have fed two of us now fed all four. Peti and I had shared the largest piece, and Mutti and Vati shared the small one, literally three or four bites of meat at the most for both of them. Peti and I each had a wedge of rye bread and a serving of carrots. My parents only had the carrots on their plate. I had not thought about it, but now it registered. And when they weren't giving the food to me, they gave it to my mother's many charity cases: there was the piano teacher, Frau Brille, who came once a week for a package, and Gustav, and, of course, Luise. Mutti had not been able to keep her full-time; money was worthless, and we didn't have enough food to support her. She had found her a job with a Russian commander in Zehlendorf where she worked unhappily full-time, but she still came to our house once a week for a few hours to help with the wash and heavy cleaning, mostly because Mutti wanted to supplement her food allotment from the Russians. Now that the Americans were here, perhaps she could work for them.

"And with her English!" My father's voice broke into my thoughts.

"What about her English?" asked my mother, puzzled.

"What about it? She is fifteen, attractive, and she speaks their language very well. What do you not understand?" My father was agitated again. "These aren't boys! They're soldiers who've seen war and willing women. These aren't like some teenage boys at the local dance recital, for God's sake!"

My mother was silent. They both stared ahead of them. Then my father grabbed her hand.

"I'm sorry." He held her hand, lacing his fingers through hers. "I am just so worried about her. What will happen next with these Americans? First the Russians and now the Americans, so much I can't..." He shook his head and fell silent.

"So much you can't control," finished my mother for him. He nodded. She took her free hand and patted his hand that held hers. "I will talk to her. It will be all right."

"I hope so. We made it through all of this..." He searched for the word. "Horror... Hitler, the war, the Russians, and I don't want to lose her now. Not to some smiling American boy promising her things and then leaving her to go home to his fiancée in Oklahoma!"

"I know." And then after a moment she said with amusement, "Oklahoma? Where is that?"

"I don't know. Somewhere in the middle of their country. I read about the musical."

My mother laughed. "What an odd name!" She pronounced it "O-kala-ho-ma."

They sat silently in the late-evening light as it cast shadows across the living room floor, making the furniture seem larger than it was and dwarfing them—the two of them together trying to protect me from a world they could not control. My stomach turned and, ashamed I had caused them so much worry, I banged my head quietly on the carpeted floor.

"And Heti, you must get her to help you more. She does almost nothing to help you, and you do so much right now without Luise. You will get sick if you don't rest sometimes."

It was true. When she asked me to help I ignored her, more interested in my drawings and magazines than in doing the mundane business of housework, and with all the shortages and with Luise gone, there was a lot of it. For many weeks we had no water, and she had to walk to the end of our road up toward Am Schülerheim to collect all of our water, carrying the heavy bucket back slowly and carefully so as not to spill the precious water. I never once helped her.

I vowed to help her more, and to help her willingly. I promised silently I would wash the dishes every night and help her wash down the floors. I would do my own laundry, too. We still only had electricity a few hours a day, so we washed a lot by hand.

"I will talk to her," she said again simply. She patted his hand and added, "How about a Campari?"

"Yes. Please."

We had little food, but we still had all the alcohol we could possibly want. My parents had buried the good wines and schnapps, as well as the few bottles of Campari my father had left from Italy, along with their china and silver and other valuables. Miraculously, the Russians had never found it, although the deep saber marks all over our garden suggested they had clearly tried. Fortunately, the crate that my mother had Gustav bury was tall and narrow, so that to our amazement one saber had gone in on one side of it and another on the other, both just missing the top of the box. An inch on either side and they would have found it.

My mother left it in the ground, still not trusting the Russians—never certain whether or not the looting soldier would come back and demand something else. But Vati had insisted that they dig out the soil on top and retrieve a few precious bottles of wine, schnapps, and, of course, his beloved Campari. Mutti immediately had Gustav rebury it and plant seedlings over it to look like the soil was only loosened so the seeds could grow.

———

That evening after dinner I told Mutti to sit in the living room and said I would wash up the dishes. She looked at me, astonished, but did not object. I cleaned the kitchen for her and even washed down the floor. Unable to bear the thought of her surprised face, I snuck up the stairs by the kitchen to retreat to my bedroom. I took a small cup of water from the bottle by the refrigerator to use to brush my teeth. The Russians finally had fixed the water supply, but my mother did not trust their efforts enough to let us drink the water from the tap. She still boiled our drinking water.

I was tired, and I wanted to go to bed and read. The Russian teachers only allowed us to read certain select American and English books at school, and I had chosen Pearl S. Buck's *The Good Earth*. It was a depressing book, but the only other choices were Dickens or Upton Sinclair's *The Jungle*. Reading about China sounded much more interesting to me than reading about the poorhouse in London or meatpacking plants. I sat in my room, my chair pulled close to the window, reading by the last of the summer evening light. Soon the light would fade and reading would have to wait until the morning light returned—electricity too precious to waste on the luxury of reading.

My mother had allowed me to remove the wood from my windows so long as I did not damage it. It had made me tense and depressed, and I was all too happy to carry it to the basement, where it remained leaning against the wall by the giant cookstove in case we still could not find glass to cover the windows by the time winter's cold arrived again. At least the summer air could come in now, and although sometimes it got cold at night and the mosquitoes drove me crazy, it improved my mood to have the light and air coming through my room.

A warm breeze tickled my skin, fluttering over me and causing goose bumps to rise up and down my legs. I heard the stairs creak and wondered if it was my mother or my father coming up. Judging by the lightness of the footsteps, I decided it was my mother. She tapped lightly on the closed door.

"Come in," I said quietly.

I saw the handle turn before she pushed the door open. She came over to my bed, leaving the door open behind her.

"What are you reading?" she asked, pulling a chair up next to my bed.

"*The Good Earth*."

She nodded. "I read it long ago. Thank God we are not women in China."

I nodded, not looking up from the book.

"That was a beautiful job you did in the kitchen, Jutta."

"Thank you." I still did not want to meet her eyes.

She reached over and grabbed my chin gently so that I had to meet her eyes.

"Thank you. And you even did the floor!" Her eyes looked watery, and this caused my own to go watery. She smiled at me.

"Mutti, I will try to do it every night."

"Oh. Well, if possible, just the dishes would be lovely."

I put my book down.

"Scoot over." She stood from her chair and sat next to me, putting her arm around me and hugging me to her.

I waited. I knew it was coming. I dreaded the guilt her words would evoke.

"Jutta, listen. You should not disobey your father so."

I nodded.

"He only wants the best for you. He thought it would not be safe down there with those soldiers."

"But nothing happened! They were so friendly!" I thought of my soldier's wink and knew Vati would disapprove.

"I know. But something could have happened. They are soldiers and they are here to occupy our area. They are not schoolboys."

I stared silently at my hands, laced together on my lap, the thumbs moving in circles around each other.

"You must stay away from these men," she added.

My soldier flashed again into my mind, lips curled over perfect teeth that lit up his olive face. Maybe he was Italian. I had heard there were lots of Italians in America.

"But they are so friendly, Mutti!" I turned to face her, trying to make her understand. "They smile and wave and hand out chocolates. Here, look." I reached for a chocolate bar by the side of my bed. I had not had a chance to show them to her. "This is for you," I said, handing the brown-wrapped chocolate to her. She took it from my hand and examined it.

"Thank you."

"And they handed out the gum stuff. I know you don't like it, but lots of people do. And they just seem so nice." I stretched out the *o* in so to emphasize my point.

Mutti unwrapped the chocolate and bit into it.

"This is pretty good! Hershee," she read. "Must have been a German immigrant."

I laughed. "Half of them did look German, Mutti. You should have seen them!" I added excitedly. "Except these were clean, well-fed 'Germans' in new clothes!"

"Such a thing I can't envision right now!" She chuckled at my enthusiasm and let me carry on, enjoying all the details I gave her about how they looked, what they did, and what the people in the crowd did and said. I knew I had her at her weakest point. My mother had a keen curiosity about people.

After I finished she grabbed my hand, rubbing it with her thumb. "Jutta, I know how difficult it has been for you."

I shrugged. I didn't want her to feel bad. It was not her fault. I knew she held herself and Vati responsible in some deeply illogical way for all that had happened in Germany.

"I know you are at a time in your life where you only want to think about boys, and parties, and what to wear, and how to do your hair. And here you are having to help your mother scrub floors and scrub dishes and scrub clothes."

"I don't mind, Mutti. Really!"

She patted my hand. "What I am trying to say is that these soldiers provide something new and exciting. They are handsome, these boys; I know. But they are men. You must remember that, and men only have one thing on their mind."

"Mutti, please." I rolled my eyes.

"No. Your father is right to be worried. It is true. If you get too friendly, they will take advantage of you, and then you will end up hurt or with a little extra mouth to feed, and then they will go home to their girlfriends in *Okalahoma*."

I laughed, and she did, too. "It's pronounced *Oklahoma*, Mutti."

She tried again, "*Okalahoma*," but couldn't quite get it.

"Have you and Tante Hilde been talking? You talk just like Peti says Tante Hilde talks to Ingrid."

She ignored my question. "You can admire them from afar, but you must keep your distance so that nothing happens. You know what I mean ... so that your father's fears don't come true."

"He thinks I would do that?" I looked at her, horrified.

"Well, no," she corrected herself quickly. "He doesn't think that you would do that willingly, but he thinks that one of these handsome boys might pressure you ... you know." She paused awkwardly. "Well, anyway, Jutta, sometimes it can happen that you get carried away in the moment, and then you have regrets."

I looked at her curiously, wondering what it had been like for her at my age. I couldn't imagine her at my age. I knew she had already met my father at the high school they both attended, but I couldn't imagine the two of them young, and shy, and holding hands. I saw them now as they had been moments ago, the two of them on the sofa, hands entwined, heads pressed together, Vati white-haired and worried and Mutti tired and fragile.

I looked out the window to see the last of the summer light disappear. The birds called to each other to settle in for the night, and the summer crickets began to warm up for their nightly chorus. How normal it all seemed, except that we were now home to four different occupying armies, and none of us really knew what would happen from one day to the next. I knew my parents were right; they were soldiers, and not particularly interested in my personal welfare. But I needed something, something to cling to that said things would change, and those smiling, confident, American faces were that something. They spoke to me of a future that would be different, of a war that was now over, and of a life that would again be normal. But I also knew I had to keep my distance, and so I promised my mother.

"I will be careful and only smile and wave to them," I said, looking into her eyes, which were creased with worry. The tiny lines that surrounded the delicate skin below her eyes had multiplied in the past months to where they crisscrossed each other and made her look vulnerable. "I promise," I added solemnly. She looked relieved, and her eyes lifted, lifting the tiny lines with them, converting them to laugh lines. Her eyes smiled at me as she hugged me.

"Now go and apologize to your father."

12

August 1945

"It's terrible. It's ... it's inhumane!" cried my mother.

"But Mutti, they need places to stay," I reasoned.

"But to not allow them to take anything! Well, except a few clothes and what food they can carry! It's horrible!"

She began to pace the kitchen, her face red with agitation. I sat at the table, trying to do my homework. I had made the mistake of telling her how they had come to get Liesel from math class to tell her to rush home and help her mother pack. They gave them two hours to get out of their home. The Americans had been here only a few weeks, but already five girls, in my class alone, had had to vacate their homes for American officers.

"And what are they supposed to do? They can't take anything with them. They can't buy anything, and most of them have no family left here, and who knows where their family is now! Are they supposed to walk to distant parts of Germany to find them?" She shook her head as she passed back and forth in front of the kitchen table. "No! Jutta, it could be done another way. This is not right."

I shrugged. I knew she was right, but I was not willing to let her know that I agreed.

"If they take our house, we will have to move in with the other Bolles. And if they take their house, I don't know what we will do!"

I looked up sharply. Somehow it had never occurred to me it might happen to us. Others yes, but not us. I don't know why it hadn't occurred to me. Why wouldn't we be as susceptible as the rest? But somehow I believed it would not happen to us. My friends worried constantly. Would they be called away from school suddenly, a sharp, cruel knock on the door their only warning, never to return to the classroom? They would have two, maybe three hours, to move out of their home. In a home that held a lifetime of memories, how did one choose what to take in two hours? Would they have to find refuge in some remote part of Berlin, where a relative could take them in, or, worse yet, in a distant part of Germany? We spoke of these things, but the uncertainty that bothered them had never entered my thoughts until now.

And then one day I came home from school to find Frau Wolleck at our kitchen table in tears, my mother holding her hand across the table. Frau Wolleck's back was to the kitchen door, and she did not see me standing just outside.

Mutti glanced up when I walked in and motioned with her head for me to leave. I took my school bag and headed upstairs. I knew without asking why Frau Wolleck was there. The door to my bedroom was closed, and I pushed it open with my book bag. I froze, my feet glued to the floor, my bag still in mid-air. There, in my bed, was Herr Wolleck, his nose pointed to the ceiling. His breath spluttered out, loud and heavy and uneven, and his feet hung over the edge of the bed. I could not tell if he was awake or asleep. He did not turn when I came in. I dropped my book bag and ran downstairs. My mother met me at the bottom of the stairs.

"Mutti? What is going on?"

She held her finger to her lips and raised her eyebrows to warn me to shut up.

"The Americans have taken the Wollecks' house. They are moving in with us for the moment. I have moved your things into the guest bedroom." She said it all quickly and flatly, without emotion.

I stared at her, not comprehending what she had just said.

"But what about my bathroom?" I asked, dazed.

"You will have to share our bathroom, and we will let the Wollecks use yours."

"But Mutti!" I moaned. I turned abruptly and started back up the stairs.

She followed me to the landing. "Come, I will show you where I have put your things."

We entered the guest bedroom, and she shut the door quickly behind her.

"Jutta, I expect you to cooperate willingly! This is hard enough for Frau Wolleck!" she whispered with such fierceness she almost hissed the words at me.

"But why can't I keep my bedroom and they move in here?"

"Because I want them to have some privacy, and from your bedroom you'd have to walk by them all the time to use the bathroom or to come downstairs. From here you can go out the secret door and use the stairs to the living room or to come through to use our bathroom."

"So I basically have to come and go through the closet?" I rolled my eyes as I said it.

"Yes. Basically, that is correct." She answered, imitating my tone. "And I will thank you to do it willingly and remember that at least we still have a house with bathrooms that function, unlike some who are living on the street, or two and three to a single room."

"Okay, okay," I said impatiently. I knew I should be grateful, but I was irritated about the arrangement.

"And Jutta," she added, whispering very low now, "Herr Wolleck is dying. He should not have been moved. She tried to tell them, but they did not listen. I don't know how long he will live." Tears filled her eyes. "We must be very kind to Frau Wolleck."

I sat down heavily on the bed, letting my book bag fall to the floor, and stared at my shoes. "I'm sorry, Mutti. I will." I looked up at her. "Be kind, I mean."

She nodded her head. "Give me a few more minutes with her and then come down for lunch." Her voice had softened, and I was relieved. I could not bear the weight of my mother's anger.

The room was smaller than my room, but it was a nice room. I looked around. I would have to remove the wood from these windows, too. At the moment, only a small block of light came through at the bottom, where the wood was too short to cover the entire window. It was warm in the room, the breeze unable to penetrate the dense wood on this warm day—warm enough that I had noticed sweat forming under my arms and on my upper lip as I walked home from school. The room closed in on me, and I needed to get out. I rushed to the door and down the stairs heading to the garden. I did not pause by the kitchen door. I sat in a chair by the fishpond and breathed deeply. The dizziness left, and I felt steady again.

"Jutta?" called my mother. "Come on in for soup."

It was too hot for soup! I didn't want more hot vegetable soup! So I pretended not to hear. Leaning back instead and letting the sun's warmth touch me, I closed my eyes.

My mother came out carrying a tray with a bowl and glass on it.

"I'm not hungry," I said. "It's too hot to eat soup anyway."

"I agree, which is why I made a cold soup."

I looked up and watched her maneuver the uneven flagstone while carrying the bright floral tray. She set the tray down next to me, standing back for a moment to let me admire the bowl of beautiful orange-colored soup resting between a blue and white flowered napkin on one side and a silver spoon on the other. A purple pansy peeked silently back at me from the center of the soup, its black middle looking soulful against the purple and orange that surrounded it.

"Mutti! It's beautiful!" I looked at it and up at her. "How did you make it?"

"I can't give away my secrets. Try it and see if it tastes as good as it looks," she urged. She was obviously excited about the soup and the pleasure that it gave me.

I took a small amount of the orange liquid on the silver spoon with the HB engraved on its handle and lifted it to my lips. It was cool and smooth and surprisingly sweet.

"Carrots?" I asked, guessing.

"Do you like it?" was her reply.

"Yes!" I took another spoonful. A little dribbled down my spoon, and I caught it with my finger before it hit my shirt. "It is delicious."

"Then I will tell you. Yes, carrots and milk, and a few secret ingredients." My mother knew I hated cooked carrots, but for some reason they tasted delicious to me in this soup. She must have been trying to figure out a way to use up the last of the carrots from the winter that were not crisp enough to eat raw.

"Next I am going to make a beet soup to use up the rest of the beets!"

I nodded my head enthusiastically. "The color would be beautiful! How do you come up with these ideas?"

She shrugged. "I just thought the French make a soup out of potatoes and leeks, so why not try to make the same sort of thing from other roots?"

"Can I eat the flower?" I asked, picking it up carefully between my thumb and forefinger. The orange soup dripped off its delicate petals and plopped back into the bowl, forming a vague circle that instantly vanished.

"Yes. Of course. I would not have put it in there if you couldn't."

I plunked it into my mouth and noted the nutlike flavor of the petals. My mother loved to surprise us with various plants from the garden that we would find hidden in our salads or buried in a casserole of one sort or another.

"That reminds me, Jutta. We need to go back to the lake to see if the raspberries are ready." She held up her hand, anticipating my objection. "I know that you don't like to do this sort of thing, but the dandelions should be ready now too, and we need them for the vitamins."

"I don't mind." I took my finger and scraped the side of the bowl to get every last drop left behind by the spoon. I saw her disapproving look. "Sorry, but I need the vitamins."

She laughed. "Did you want to bring a friend with us to make it more fun?"

"No. They'll just think you're odd, Mutti, and start rumors about witchcraft or something."

"Oh, for God's sake! Witchcraft?" She looked at me in disbelief, her hands on her hips. "These are things that have been known since the Middle Ages. If people just read books, they would learn how much food there is out there in our forest naturally, and then they wouldn't be as malnourished right now." She threw her hands in the air in a gesture of frustration. "All of them standing around waiting for the stores to stock plums and peaches again! Well they have them; the trees still grow them, but how can we get them? How can they ship to us here in the city, with the train lines still a disaster? And the ..."

I held up my spoon. "Mutti, Mutti. I know. It makes perfect sense. I just don't want to take a friend."

She sat down next to me and watched the breeze move the branches of the kiefer trees, casting lace like shadows across the garden.

"Do they really talk about witchcraft?"

Clearly the idea bothered her.

"No. But they do talk about 'your mother's gypsy medicine.'"

"Well, they could learn a thing or two from the gypsies." She looked around the garden. "Jutta, all about you, God has placed what we need, if we would only look for it." She patted my arm and got up. "Let me go check on Frau Wolleck." She rose and walked back through the open French doors.

I smiled as I watched her walk away. A "remarkable woman" my father would say of her, and she was indeed. What some considered her crazy ideas—

her intimate knowledge of plants—kept us healthier and better fed than most Germans right now. After all, her Italian pasta still fed us, and we all thought she was insane when she brought those huge trunks with her from Italy.

A buttercup peeked through the bricks of the patio near the fishpond. My mother had placed rocks around it so we would not crush it walking. I laughed. It had always driven me and my father crazy that ours was the only lawn in the neighborhood with spotted areas that jutted out of the smooth, clipped grass like unruly patches of facial hair on a teenage boy, because she would not allow Gustav to cut the wildflowers when he mowed the lawn. These massive islands of wildflowers, sporadically scattered about our front lawn, disturbed my sense of visual order. But now I was glad of her eccentric ways, for they kept us alive and, better yet, they kept us relatively well. Those wildflowers held medicinal powers, she would say mysteriously.

She made me help her collect the linden flowers from the trees in the park for tea and gather chamomile leaves and dandelion leaves, also for tea. I had dug roots with her and picked berries in the forest. She already warned me that in the fall we would go to the Grunewaldsee and collect rose hips from the wild roses that graced its banks. They were full of vitamin C, she informed me, and she would dry them and preserve them in jars for the winter ahead. When I asked why we couldn't just use the ones from Erica's roses, she responded, "They are man's roses. Only the wild ones hold nutrition." And anywhere my mother walked she scanned the ground and bushes and trees for edible varieties of flowers, berries, and wild herbs. You could be talking to her one moment and suddenly she would dart off to the side of the road and bend over, only to right herself with some prized plant that had found a patch of dirt along the road in which to anchor itself. This is a such and such plant, she would say triumphantly, good for the nervous system, or good for the stomach, or full of vitamins. I couldn't keep their names and uses straight. About the only things that she refused to collect were mushrooms, and she was adamant that I was not to eat anything at someone else's house that had mushrooms in it collected from the forest. She knew enough to know that her expertise was too limited, and that the differences were so subtle between a mushroom that was edible and one that was lethal that she did not want to take the risk.

She stored all of her herbs and dried flowers in a medicinal-looking white metal cabinet in a cool area of the basement. It was full of glass jars and envelopes containing one odd-looking dried-out herb after another. Things hung on strings to dry inside the cabinet, and others were suspended in water. No one was allowed to open the cabinet except for my mother and, in what I considered an extreme level of precaution, she even kept the cabinet locked.

"I have dried digitalis in there, and if you grab it by accident instead of the linden flowers, let us say, you could kill us."

"But why would I do that, Mutti?" I asked. Sometimes I really thought she was crazy. "Only you are allowed to go into your cabinet anyway, so why lock it?"

"Just in case!" she would say.

———

Herr Wolleck died three days after the Wollecks moved into our house—whether it was the move that did it or a loss of will, who knew. The fact remained they made him move from his house of forty years, and now he was dead. Frau Wolleck was in shock. She sat in the chair by his dead body and refused to move. My father took care of the details of his burial, and my mother tried to console Frau Wolleck as best she could. I stayed out of sight and only occasionally saw her when my mother sent me upstairs to deliver her food. I would return hours later and find the water glass empty and the food untouched. So I carried the tray back downstairs to my mother, who looked at it, concerned.

"Will she die if she doesn't eat?" I asked after the second day.

"She will eat when her body tells her it is time. She is drinking at least."

"But she is already so thin."

"She will be fine."

———

The rapid knock on the windowpane of the door interrupted our algebra calculations, and we looked up from our math test in surprise. Susi Reich stood at the door. I could only see the top of her wavy blond head around the teacher's back, but it was all I needed to know it was her. The teacher thanked her and closed the door before reading the note. She looked up, and her eyes met mine. My heart stopped, and my hands went clammy.

"Jutta, you must hurry home. The Americans are at your house."

I began to close my book and pick up my papers.

"Leave it. I will clean up your things. Hurry! It's marked urgent," she said, handing the note to me.

I looked at it long enough to see that it was my mother's handwriting, but I didn't read it. I ran from the classroom, my movements automatic. In my rush I left all my things at school, my book bag, my pencil box, even my favorite blue sweater. I vaguely thought of them as I ran across Im Gehege, scattering the sparrows that had settled onto the grass to eat seeds and worms, their wings flapping above my head as I sprinted toward Königin Luise Strasse. The long, terrifying screech of a jeep's tires immediately caught my attention; I looked up, astonished to see the white face of a young American soldier, his arms locked with both hands on the steering wheel. I hadn't even looked when I ran to cross the boulevard. The soldier's pale face a statement—he thought he was going to hit me—and it was a miracle he did not. I waved a distracted apology and kept on running down Am Schülerheim, slowing only when I turned left onto the Föhrenweg.

I saw them up ahead of me, three of them with their infernal clipboards cradled in their arms. They wore the broad hats of the officer corps in the American Army, and I knew what they wanted. They were standing in front of our house, pointing up at something. The windows? The roof? One of them tested the gate, opening and closing it several times. They spoke to each other, and the tallest pointed across to the Schwering's house. The two shorter ones nodded and headed to the Schwering's front gate, opening it carefully to make sure it didn't fall off its hinges. The tall one looked up and saw me coming down the street. I recognized him. He had been through our house once before. He waited for me at my own front gate, obviously expecting me.

As I approached, he took off the sunglasses they all seemed to wear. He did not look unkind; his eyes sported deep laugh lines that were white in the center until he smiled and the white parts disappeared, folding back into his skin. He nodded to me and held the gate open for me.

"Hello, there," he said. "We've been waiting for you." He held out his hand. "Major Franklin," he said simply.

I cleared my throat; I was nervous. "Jutta Bolle," I answered, taking his hand briefly. "We've met before." I was not in the mood to be friendly to this smiling man who stood there ready with the stroke of his pen to kick me out of my home.

"Well, nice to see you again, Fräulein Bolle," he said, still smiling in that friendly way of all Americans. He had perfect teeth—in fact, as I thought about it, they all seemed to have perfect teeth, perfect smiles, and sunglasses.

I did not respond to him. Instead I walked past him through the gate and the garden to our front door. My mother stood at the door waiting for me.

"Jutta, thank God you are here! They want to take the house, and I am trying to tell them that Herr Wolleck died and Frau Wolleck just could not take another move." She was obviously upset.

The American major had come up beside me at the door. He could not understand what my mother said, but he clearly caught her agitation because he looked uncomfortable.

"*Ja, ja*. Mutti, I will tell him," I said to her in German.

"Shall we go in?" he asked.

I looked at him with irritation. How dare he invite himself into our home!

Understanding him, my mother responded in her heavily accented English. "Come in, please." And to me she added in German, "Jutta, don't look like you would like to cut his throat! We have to be nice. Charm him and convince him to let us stay. Anger will not accomplish this."

We walked in silence to the living room. The American looked up at the high ceiling of the room. Taking it all in, he noted the stairs that led to the bedrooms upstairs. He had been through the house several times before, taking careful notes and looking into closets and bathrooms and the kitchen. Mutti and I sat down on the sofa and he sat down in an armchair directly across from us.

"I know this is difficult for everyone, but we need housing for the officers, as I was trying to explain to your mother." He said the words softly and without pleasure. "We need your house because it has such a big living room and a modern kitchen. Well, compared to most of these houses, anyway."

"My mother wants me to speech to you about the Wollecks." I realized my mistake immediately and started again. "I'm sorry. My mother wants me to *speak* to you about the Wollecks."

"The Wollecks are the people who lived next door?"

"Yes. They moved in with us."

He shifted in his seat, uncomfortable. He obviously had not understood that they were living with us.

"Herr Wolleck died last week."

"I'm sorry." He looked down at his clipboard and wrote something.

"Frau Wolleck told you—*told* you," I corrected, "he would die if you moved him. And now he is dead!" I wanted him to know. "It was you who she told."

He did not respond; instead he looked at me and then at my mother and then at his clipboard.

"Yes. I see," he said thoughtfully.

"My mother says that Frau Wolleck is in, how do you say? She can't talk or sleep or eat?"

"Shock?" he offered, not looking up as he wrote on his papers.

"Yes," I said presuming that was the correct word. "And if she has to move again, I think she will also die. That is certain."

My mother nodded her head to add emphasis. She understood English very well, but her speaking ability was more limited than mine.

"Yes. I see," he said again.

A silence fell upon the room; my mother and I barely breathed as we watched this man who held our future in the stroke of his pen.

He looked around the room thoughtfully, tapping the pen on his clipboard. His eyes rested on the shattered window by the door that Gustav had covered with wood.

"Please don't make us move," I said, choking on the last word, tears welling up in my eyes.

He glanced up at me, hearing the emotion, and held my eyes for a moment. Then he stood up to walk around the room. He sat back down and wrote again on his clipboard. My mother sat with her hands folded on her lap, quietly waiting for this man to tell us his decision. He stood up again and walked to the window. He turned around abruptly and said to me, "I have decided that we can't use this house. There are too many windows to replace, and the cost will be too high."

I caught my breath. "Oh, thank you. Thank you."

"Tell your mother she does not have to move," he said, walking swiftly back to the sofa to pick up the clipboard he had set down on the coffee table.

But my mother had understood. She leaped up and grabbed his hand. "Thank you so much." And then, forgetting she added, "*Danke. Danke. Gott sei Dank!*"

He smiled at her, the lines around his eyes shooting out toward his cheeks, filling in the white parts again.

I looked up and held his eyes for a moment, grateful for his kindness, and then I stood up and walked with him to the door. His business done, he did not want to linger. He turned back to me. "And you, young lady, speak very good English! Where did you learn it?"

"In school."

"Well," he said looking impressed, "may we ask you to help us if we need a translator?"

"Of course," I said, flattered.

"Great! It was nice to see you again, Fräulein Bolle." Turning to my mother, he nodded his head. "Frau Bolle."

My mother nodded back.

He opened the door and was about to leave when my mother added, "Coffee?"

He smiled. "Oh no, thank you. I have to meet the other fellows and tell them we need to find a new house."

I translated for my mother, guessing at the meaning of fellows. We both smiled and said goodbye.

And then he was gone. Together, we breathed a sigh of relief and jumped up and down, hugging each other.

"Oh, thank God! *Gott sei Dank!*" said my mother again and again. And then we both looked at each other as it sank in to both of us that our home was spared only for another family to lose theirs.

As if reading my mind, my mother said, "No. Jutta, don't even think like that. They have plenty of empty houses they can use, like the Jahnkes' at the corner. Let them take that house. Why take a house where people are living? Or why not the Zimmerman house? They left a year ago."

"Yes, but those people moved in from downtown."

"I know, but that isn't their house, Jutta. It's not the same."

———

As it turned out, Frau Wolleck only stayed with us for a little over a month. She had a daughter who lived in Bavaria. One day the daughter telephoned looking for her parents. Frau Wolleck had been so distraught she had not even called her own daughter to tell her about her father's death. My mother had to tell her, and shortly thereafter the daughter sent a train ticket for her mother to join her in Bavaria. I felt very sorry for Frau Wolleck as she left for the train station. She was a broken woman who could have been going to Siberia for all she cared. I hoped that time and living in her daughter's house would heal her.

I helped my mother ready my room for my return to it, and a guilty relief that Frau Wolleck was gone crept into my thoughts.

The Apple Tree

A pale patchwork of blue peeked through the mantle of rich green leaves, the pattern shifting as the wind blew the tree's branches. I sat with my mother under the tree, eating potato salad and cherries—the cherries came from our front yard and the potatoes from our basement. My mother had been working in the "farmyard" all morning, breaking only to come ask me to bring lunch for the two of us.

We called what used to be the Kittels' yard the farmyard, for that is what it had become. My mother and Gustav had planted the entire yard with potatoes and a smaller section of beets, turnips, and carrots. Her root garden, she called it. Here her chickens roamed freely, stopped only by the makeshift fence Gustav had erected. I tossed one a cherry pit to see if it would take it.

"Don't! You'll have the whole flock over here in a moment."

The flock consisted of five hens and a rooster, as well as several baby chicks that followed their mothers around the yard. To my father's horror, she put the hens and their babies in our basement at night. Only the rooster stayed outside. Gustav built him a special house with chicken wire across the door so he could not get out. His house stood directly under my parent's window so that my mother could hear if anyone was trying to steal him in the middle of the night. Needless to say, we no longer needed an alarm clock. I called him Douglas. It was a good American name, and he strutted around confidently, not unlike the American soldiers that saturated Dahlem at the moment.

She had a surprise to show me, she had said. So I brought lunch on a tray, walking carefully through the makeshift gate—more of Gustav's handiwork—and climbed the small embankment between the two yards.

I saw her at the far end of her potato field bent over, weeding, thinning, and tending to the tender plants. My mother's always perfectly manicured hands now sported calluses and chipped fingernails. When I commiserated with her, she only said food is more important. She would hold them up to eye-level, her arms outstretched, and say, "The day we can buy food at the stores again, I will grow these back."

"Mutti," I called to her.

She stood up too quickly and had to put her hand to her head to steady herself. "Under the apple tree." She waved her hand toward the tree. "Oh my goodness, I am seeing stars," she added.

I walked to the apple tree at the right in the back of the garden, peeking over the edge of the tray I carried to make sure I did not trip on a newly dug furrow. The tree's branches hung heavily to the ground, and as I approached my mouth fell open. Tiny green apples covered its branches from top to bottom. A smile crept across my face as I turned to look at my mother approaching me from the other side of the garden.

She smiled. "*Ja.* Can you believe it?"

"No! It's incredible, Mutti!" I set the tray down on the grass under the tree and climbed under myself. I had to bend all the way down to the ground, practically crawling on my knees, so heavy were the branches with the weight of hundreds and hundreds of apples. "But it has never borne fruit before!"

My mother nodded her head in reply. She had scooted under the branch on her bottom to join me. "My knees are too old," she said simply, explaining.

We sat there for a moment looking up, taking in the fact that for ten years this same tree had never once borne fruit. We had all thought it was simply ornamental. Every year it flowered in the spring, but when the flowers blew off, no fruit followed. In fact, years ago, before the war, Herr Kittel had threatened at a dinner party to "cut the damn thing down" because all it did was create messes in his yard. My mother had convinced him to let it live, calling it a sin against nature to cut down a tree. And now, in this year of all years, it bore so much fruit its branches touched the ground, in danger of breaking off.

"We will need to prop up its branches."

"We could maybe use the garden chairs."

"That's a great idea! That way we don't have to waste any wood!"

I studied the height of the branches, heavy with fruit. "Yes, if we put the tall ones under the branch, right here," I said, standing up and placing my hand where I thought the chair back would reach, "and anchor their legs into the ground somehow, it should work well."

"You're a genius, Jutta! Let's do it after lunch. I think we can carry them between to the two of us. That way we don't have to wait for Gustav."

They were made of solid wrought iron, but we could manage.

I tilted my head back again, observing the intricate patterns of the branches. She followed my gaze. The tiny green apples bobbed in rhythm to the wind.

"It is amazing, our fruit trees this year!"

"Um." I answered, popping a cherry into my mouth. And it was amazing! Our plum tree had more plums on it than ever before, and our cherry tree had more cherries, and now this apple tree that had never in its life borne fruit was covered with apples. "I don't know what to think," I mumbled.

"Just be grateful," she said, patting my knee.

"Do you think God did this?" I asked uncomfortably.

"I don't know." She looked up again. "There are so many others with nothing that one does not want to presume that one is somehow special. You know what I mean?"

"Yes."

"Look at the fig tree, and all the trees. When they are budding you know that summer is near. So you also know that the kingdom of God is near."

"Is that from the Bible?"

"Luke 21:29. My mother used to quote that to me when the first buds of spring came. But maybe it is true. Maybe all these perfect apples are a sign that there is hope." She paused, fingering a dirt clod by her side. She let the powdery dirt fall through her fingers to the ground. "Why us? Why are the Kittels dead, and their tree now bears us fruit? We don't need to understand. We just need to be thankful."

I thought of the bomb shelter and all the people who died that day in Halberstadt. Was it God that had protected us, or Vati's good judgment? Who knew? Was it my mother's foresight and knowledge of plants and gardening that made ours a better life than most? Probably, I decided. But this tree—how does one explain this tree?

I looked over to the burned-out shell that used to be the Kittels' house. Its brick walls stood black and lonely in the bright sun. Nothing remained of the once-beautiful living room. What hadn't burned in the fire, the Russians had taken. My mother and Gustav had retrieved every scrap of wood they could pry off the place and loaded our basement full of it. It was for the winter, my mother said. What didn't fit into the basement, my mother and Gustav piled in the back garden of our house, stacked high to the level of the back fence. Gustav built a stockade-like structure to keep the large pieces of wood from rolling. My mother assumed that anything not in our backyard would be stolen. Every day, strangers—refugees from downtown or from the East—wandered through our neighborhood looking for anything that was not anchored down to take with them. Winter was not that far ahead and we all knew that coal would be in short supply.

"Those walls fill me with loneliness, Mutti," I said softly.

Without looking up, she said, "I know." She sipped her water and looked up into the branches of the tree.

"I can't help this feeling in the pit of my stomach."

She reached over and grabbed my hand. "Emptiness, like you are about to fall off a building and there is no net?"

I turned to face her. "Yes. And then I try to think of something else quickly to push it down, deep down, and I do succeed at that for a while, but then I see something." I paused. "Like those lonely black walls, and then it comes back."

"I know." She patted my hand again.

We were silent for a moment, taking comfort in our mutual understanding.

"But then you must look at this tree, this incredible apple tree with its hundreds of apples." She lifted her face again, and a smile played on her lips. "And think of the miracles of life, Jutta." She put her arm around my shoulder and drew me to her. I fell against her, anxious for the comfort. "Take one day at a time, and marvel that there is so much that man can never destroy."

Tears fell from her eyes onto my head, and I felt them soak through my hair. Without thinking, suddenly my own tears fell down my cheeks. We wept quietly together under the tree, shadows playing across us in the bright sunlight.

The Americans Take Charge

There was a chill in the air when I walked to school in the morning now, and I knew that the hot days of summer were fading. Vati and Uncle Kurt spent their days at the factory, trying to salvage what remained of their business. Demand was high, but their ability to deliver was limited both by a shortage of wood and the fact that the Americans had taken over their gasoline tanks at the factory. They had to walk to the factory, a distance of five kilometers or so, finding their way through piles of rubble and bombed-out buildings that had not yet been cleared away. The roads were in most cases still impassable, so the streetcars could not run. The streetcars stood in the streets at odd angles where a conductor fleeing for cover had abandoned them in the months before—some lay on their sides, bullet holes decorating their once-shiny exteriors; some had been moved to the side or to the end of the street. They looked like the cars in a child's sandbox, where the child, distracted by a more urgent interest, had left them to fend for themselves: on their sides and on their backs, discarded in the sand, their wheels extended to the sky.

The travel difficulties did not end with the streetcars. The S-Bahn had not been fixed; sewage and groundwater still leaked into the tunnels of the U-Bahn; and there was no gas to run the buses or cars that might have been able to travel on the few major sections of road that the Russians had managed to clear and fix. And anyway, any gas to be found in Berlin went to fuel the vehicles of our occupying armies.

Now that the Americans were here, we had high hopes that the roads would be fixed soon. They loved their cars, and we knew they would not leave the transportation system of Berlin in chaos for long. The problem was they only controlled a portion of Berlin, and it soon became clear the French and Russians intended to expend only the minimum amount of energy and capital, and then only to serve their own purposes. The British tried, but they lacked the resources of the Americans.

The Americans remained our best hope. For being such an easygoing, good-natured group of people, they were very efficient about it all. The first thing they did was put stop signs at every corner in Dahlem and a traffic light at the corners of Königin Luise Strasse and Kronprinzenallee, and another at Kronprinzenallee and Hüttenweg. Several jeep accidents a day at those particular corners alone had convinced them this was a necessary first step. We could hear the tires squealing in our classroom, and Hannelore would mark another *x* in her notebook on the page where she kept track of Ami accidents. There had never been any stop signs or traffic lights in Dahlem and some of the older people objected to them, considering them ugly and modern. But, as Vati pointed out, Dahlem was no longer a sleepy suburban village. It now housed an occupying army with hundreds of jeeps and trucks a day traveling its once-quiet streets.

The Amis fixed the main roads quickly. They had brought along an entire corps of engineers, an army in and of itself, to help with the reconstruction of our section of Berlin. Luckily, since we lived where the officers lived, the roads in our area received the closest attention—this meant even the small neighborhood roads were eventually fixed. But even once the roads were fixed, we had no vehicles and no gas to use on them, and anyway, once you left Dahlem, the roads became impassable again. So we walked; anywhere we wanted to go, we had to walk. This meant that Mutti did not see Tante Ite, her mother's sister who lived in Charlottenburg, for several months because the eight-kilometer walk, sixteen round-trip, made it all but impossible. The streets in town were still not free of the danger of collapsing walls, and every day we read another story about people, often children, buried alive under these crumbling piles of concrete and brick. The phones worked, but during the Russian occupation this was only true in our section of town, so calling other parts of Berlin was a problem. Families who once saw each other every Sunday now had no contact for months, and only if a death or wedding or birth occurred did they expend the energy to contact one anther.

The Americans had requisitioned the gas station that occupied the central courtyard of Vati and Uncle Kurt's factory. It made it difficult for the factory to operate except at the most minimal level. Slowly, Vati had the trucks converted to run on wood that burned in special engines developed by German engineers. It took time and money, though, to convert each truck. They were huge, ungainly looking affairs that spewed out smoke, but it allowed the factory to continue its business.

Much of my father's day was spent getting to and from the factory and, once there, trying to deal with the overwhelming problem of running a business with a disabled infrastructure and a collapsed economy. There were times where I could tell he was so frustrated he was ready to give up, so I would accompany him to the office if I didn't have school. I tried to help out where I could, but mostly I wanted to cheer him up. I think he enjoyed taking me to the office—he introduced me to the office staff as "my daughter, Jutta." I had never met most of them, since I had been away in Halberstadt for the past three years. And they would say things like, "Oh, so this is the one who speaks English so well!" or, "Oh, this is the daughter who went to live with her grandmother!" It was the first indication I had that Vati ever talked about me at the office.

He also introduced me to the American captain, Captain Barrett, who had been put in charge of supervising the gas station at the factory. Trucks barreled in and out of the courtyard all day long, easing their way down the steep driveway, tires and brakes squealing on the cobblestones. American soldiers, their caps on backwards or the bills of their caps turned up toward the sky, ran to fill them with the precious golden liquid held in the tall metal tanks of the factory courtyard. Then the drivers, with ugly black exhaust spewing from the tailpipes, would turn the wheels sharply, engaging the gears back and forth to maneuver their huge vehicles around the gas tanks and back up the ramp, on their way again to who knew where, but I imagined it was a very important assignment.

I liked the American captain. He had a casual, friendly smile, and he tried very hard to pronounce my name correctly. But Vati warned me not to get too friendly with the Americans. Still, I looked forward to it when Captain Barrett would stop us on our way up the factory steps to say hello. He made me feel good. His friendly confidence infected me with the belief that as long as these Americans stayed, our world would one day be normal again. Occasionally he asked me to act as a translator when one of the German workers did not understand what he wanted. He always had a pack of Juicy Fruit gum or a Hershey's bar in his pocket for me at those times. Eventually, my father decided Captain Barrett's friendliness was innocent, but he made sure that the captain knew I was fifteen.

I enjoyed the attention I got from the American soldiers, who would smile and whip off their caps when I arrived in the morning with my father. They would call out, "Well, hello, young lady," or use the American phrases "Hi" or "Hi, there." The first time they did this, I looked up when they said "Hi," confusing it with the English word "high." They loved this and roared with laughter at my confusion. One of them, a tall, lanky soldier with red hair and freckles, came over and explained in broken German that it was a greeting. I colored, but their laughter was friendly, and I smiled back at them and said, "Hi!" They all clapped at this, and from then on that was our standard greeting.

They didn't seem at all like the German soldiers I had seen marching through villages like Halberstadt or on parade in Berlin. They did not stand at attention and salute each other or look stern and serious, staring straight ahead at nothing. Instead they sat on crates in the courtyard of my father's factory, American Armed Forces Radio, or AFN, as I learned it was called, blaring from the small boxlike radio they parked on top of one of the gas tanks. They smoked and joked around until a truck came through, and then they tossed down their cigarettes and hustled into action, defying their casualness of a moment ago. They were very efficient, these Americans, but not in the stiff, dour way of Germans. These Americans laughed and told jokes and greeted each other in that warm, informal way they all had; they had fun. And again, I noticed their confidence—they seemed unafraid of the world in a way that Germans could not understand. It was as if they truly believed the world was on their side, and it certainly seemed to me to be true.

I was amazed that they tossed to the ground half-smoked cigarettes or sometimes, if they had just lit one up when a truck came rumbling through, even completely un-smoked cigarettes. Germans coveted cigarettes, and I had seen them smoke them to the very end, almost letting their fingers burn, hungrily inhaling the tobacco until they simply had to let the thing fall to the ground, ashes flying in the wind. On their way home, some of the factory workers scoured the courtyard for the butts—*stummeling*, we called it. More often than not there were none left, as the neighborhood boys rode through our gates on their bicycles to search the courtyard for treasures left by the Americans in the late evening light. Vati had given orders to the guard to let them come through until 6:30, when the gates had to be locked. The gas tank had a lock on it that only Captain Barrett could access. There was no worry that they would steal the gasoline, Vati said, so why not let them come through? Cigarettes were money, *Zigarettenwärung*— up to $15 per pack depending on the brand, and, if they found one barely smoked, they could cut the top off and sell it for something to eat. Boys followed soldiers for blocks, waiting for them to drop the cigarette butts, and then a scuffle would ensue as the boys fought each other for the prize. The soldiers, oblivious, walked on, talking to one another as if they had tossed some crumbs down for the birds.

13

Berlin Gone

October 1945

For months, each time I accompanied Vati to the factory, I pestered him to take me to see what was left of the city center.

He would tell me, "It is not safe." Or, "You don't want to see it."

But I did. I needed to see it. I needed to see what had happened to my city. I saw the bombed-out buildings along the Martin Luther Strasse as Vati and I walked to the factory, but I knew that it was so much worse in the center of town. I needed closure—verification of the death of my city. For me it was like seeing the body of someone you love actually dead rather than just receiving word that he or she had died. So many mothers throughout Berlin, throughout Germany, had simply received word their sons were dead, but no confirmation—no hard, cold body. I shuddered; it must be horrible not to bury them, not to be able to visit their graves. To wonder, always, where they had been when they died, leaving a vague and unrealistic hope they had not. The worst was to picture them alone in a mud-filled field, or tossed carelessly to the bottom of a common grave, hundreds of other bodies falling on top of them, arms and legs flopping heavily, weighted like dummies. It was like losing a piece of your soul, and somehow the body lying in its coffin erased the horror of the death. It was, for me, the same with the death of Berlin. I had to see it. I didn't want to go to town one day years from now and find new buildings where once there were old and familiar ones, buildings from my childhood filled with memories replaced by the cold metal-and-glass structures of modern architecture. I had to see them, the palaces and homes built by kaisers and wealthy families, smashed to the ground. I could come to terms with it, with the war, with all of it if I saw it as it was now, stranded and bare, stripped of its ego—a giant crumpled to the ground and left to face the elements. I explained all of this to Vati. He stared down at his desk for a long time. I couldn't tell if he was reading the papers that lay about on his desk or just staring at nothing. Finally, he looked up.

"I understand," he pushed his chair back from the desk. He looked at me for a moment before saying, "Go get your coat and bring your scarf."

———

Leaves crunched under our feet in the morning chill as we walked down

Belziger Strasse. Fall had definitely arrived. The sun shone through the leaves of the chestnut trees with a brilliance that defied the morning chill, and the sky was a clear blue, dotted occasionally with tiny white clouds. The sky was always brighter in the fall for some reason. Mutti said it was to highlight the beauty of the colors held in the trees—their warm reds and oranges, the colors of a fire against the blue of the sky. With my auburn hair and November birthday, I should have been a child of the fall. But I wasn't. Fall filled me with gloom as I watched the leaves drop from the trees above our heads and float gracefully to the ground. It reminded me that winter, with its deathlike stillness and cold, was around the corner...

Vati spoke very little as we walked quickly along the edge of the road. I had to concentrate to keep from falling into the deep ditch that ran along the road. I saw the *Rathaus* ahead of us when we reached the corner, just before we turned right to head up Martin Luther Strasse toward Tauentzien Strasse and the Kurfürstendamm. Somehow, miraculously, the Schöneberg *Rathaus* had survived, its nineteenth-century red-brick facade barely damaged by the constant barrage of artillery guns it must have faced. The street had been cleared and we could walk without difficulty, stepping to the side when a truck or army jeep passed by to avoid being splashed with the black mud that stood in puddles along the road. We had to walk in the street because the sidewalks were impassable. Huge bulldozers had pushed the rubble from fallen buildings out of the street to the side of the road. For the most part, the damage along this section of the street was limited to blown-out windows and the ubiquitous artillery holes that had left the same pockmarks on most of the buildings in the city. Bombs had been a rarity in this particular neighborhood.

"Vati, this doesn't look too bad."

He did not look up but continued to walk in silence.

"Are we going to Alexanderplatz?"

"No."

"What about the Brandenburger Tor and Pariser Platz?"

"No."

"Hotel Adlon?"

"It's gone."

"Potsdamer Platz?"

He stopped and turned. I stopped because he had. He leaned forward. "Jutta, I don't think you understand. They are all gone. All of them, gone. Café Kranzler, the Adlon, the Excelsior, all of it. Potsdamer Platz doesn't even exist anymore. Leveled." His hand cut through, the air palm facing down. "To the ground. Nothing!"

I stared at him, not comprehending. How could this be? How could it all have disappeared?

He frowned at me. "And second, all those places you ask about?" He paused. "Yes?"

"They are in the Russian zone, and I will not set foot in the Russian zone!" He turned quickly back around and continued up the street.

I stood still for a moment, watching him walk up the street, his heels hitting the pavement decisively in that clipped walk he had. I kicked into gear and ran to catch him. "But Vati, what is left?"

"Kurfürstendamm, Wittenberg Platz. That is where we are going."

"And Unter den Linden and the Pergamon, and the Altes Museum?"

"All either gone or Russian," he said without emotion.

"But how could they let that happen?" I cried.

"I suppose it was the practical way to draw the lines, Jutta. I don't really think they care much about the cultural heritage of Berlin, dear," he said over his shoulder.

"But that's horrible."

He stopped again, and I nearly ran into him as he whirled around to face me. "Jutta, be grateful that the Americans and British took our areas of Berlin— life is more important than these cultural treasures!" He continued to hold my gaze for a moment.

I looked away and nodded. I knew he was right, but it seemed such a waste. I thought of the many weekend outings with Opa Bolle to see the treasures of the ancient world discovered and brought to Berlin by Herr Schliemann. I thought of the art exhibits we saw with Opa Bolle at the Altes Museum, of the ice cream we ate at Café Kranzler on the corner of Unter den Linden and Fried-richstrasse, of Opa Bolle cursing the Nazis under his breath for having paved over the grassy expanse of the *Lustgarten* for their "ridiculous, showy" parades. I couldn't believe they were all gone, bombed, destroyed by fire, or controlled by the Russians—either way, gone, out of reach for us.

We continued up the street, crossing Grunewald Strasse, and then suddenly the landscape changed. Empty shells that once were buildings dotted the land-scape, where in the past there had been city blocks teeming with life. Between the shells lay crumbled piles—huge heaps of broken brick and mortar and pipes and metal beams jutting out sporadically in odd directions—the only remnant of what once was an apartment building or bank or restaurant. A handful of buildings still stood, their roofs blown off and their fronts collapsed to the ground in piles of dusty mortar that blocked the sidewalk. They looked like my old doll house. You could see where the rooms had been, but there were no floors, no furniture, no walls; only the metal and in some places the brick parti-tions still stood, blackened with soot from the fires that had ravaged the wood that had once graced their floors. It was too awful. My hand flew to my mouth, and I uttered an involuntary cry. Vati put his arm around me. I had not realized that I had stopped and he had walked back to me.

"Are you sure you want to continue? It only gets worse," he said gently.

I nodded a quick yes in reply, looking up to keep the tears from spilling. He took my hand and we walked on in silence, observing the destruction that had rained down on our poor city. It was gone. Berlin was no more. An unspoken bond of grief held us in its grip, words unthinkable. I thanked God again that Opa Bolle was not alive to see the city that had loved my family so deeply gone—but not just gone, savagely destroyed, and our name, so tied to it, somehow soiled as well.

I glanced to the right, down what I thought must be Barbarossa Strasse, but the street sign lay toppled on the ground, illegible, covered with dirt. Up the street, mountains of rubble met my eyes. A path wound through the rubble, climbing over it and disappearing on the other side, like the paths that meandered around the rocky bends of the Watzmann in Berchtesgaden. To the left, the same scene greeted me. On the outer wall of a first-floor apartment someone had written in chalk, "*Wir Leben*" (we're alive) and then simply, "Hanover." Some of the chalk had washed down from the rain, forming long white streaks against the black wall.

I was not prepared for the complete and utter destruction of Berlin.

"Nobody is," Vati said.

An old woman came our way, her hair tied up in a scarf, knotted in front in what my mother referred to as "the Berlin look." Vati stood to the side to let her pass. She carried a basket filled with bits of wood and pieces of metal, anything to sell for a few pennies.

"*Guten Morgen*," said Vati, tipping his hat.

She nodded her head but otherwise did not acknowledge us, her eyes glued to the road so she didn't trip on the many obstacles that lay on the ground.

Other than the three of us, the street was deserted. I glanced at my watch: nine o'clock. At nine o'clock in the morning, Martin Luther Strasse should have been teeming with life, men and women going to work, shopkeepers preparing for the day, and children already filling the school yard for their morning break. Instead, a silence hung over the city—no people, no cars, no buses, and no streetcars traveled the once-busy streets. Only the occasional military vehicle splashed loudly past us.

Out of all this chaos, a blue awning held its ground. It belonged to Schlichter's. Schlichter's still stood! Its awning hung down in the front, propped up by a metal pipe, and its facade sported the pervasive pockmarks of the war, but otherwise it still stood.

"Vati, Schlichter's is still open!"

"Not yet. But they are trying to reopen soon, they said."

"That's at least something."

Vati squeezed my hand. "Soon" had become a relative word in Germany. We both knew that "soon" in this case did not have the old meaning. The streetlights will be fixed soon, the bridges will be fixed soon, and the telephones will be fixed soon. Soon could now mean a month, or six months, or a year.

Not until we turned onto the Tauentzienstrasse as we approached Wittenberg Platz did we see any other signs of human life. I searched ahead anxiously.

Yes! I could see people milling about the once-busy station, and I deluded myself for a moment into thinking that the Kurfürstendamm would be as I remembered it. It was not. We turned onto the Kurfürstendamm. I froze. All up and down the street, stores I had visited with my mother lay shattered. The Kaiser Wilhelm *Kirche* looked decapitated, its top portion simply gone, jagged edges jutting toward heaven where once a glorious steeple had been. Huge piles of scrap metal in all sizes, from giant twenty-foot beams to thin strips, lay in unorganized piles along the Wittenberg Platz. On the other side of the street, piles of smashed bricks and mortar formed hills on which a handful of boys searched for treasures.

Vati pulled me forward, and we walked up the Kurfürstendamm toward the Kaiser Wilhelm *Kirche*. People passed us on both sides. Women and children—refugees from the East—pushed carts. Old men hobbled along with canes, pulling wagons filled with wood or bricks that had not been crushed. Boys, some not much older than I was but with the war etched in the lines of their faces, moved about the Wittenberg Platz. Some had an arm or a leg missing—one had both legs missing. He heaved himself expertly along on his crutches as if he had done it all his life. Nobody noticed us. Engrossed in the acts of survival, they had no time to notice faces or clothes or other people.

To our left, the *KadeWe* still stood, gutted by fire, its roof blown off. Metal jutted out of its top floor like an ugly, old straw hat. Every one of its windows blown out, it clung to life with its outer walls intact. Workers had reinforced the front entrance with bricks and metal from some fallen building nearby, but otherwise the old department store stood empty and without any sign of life.

A restaurant was open, miraculously saved from the bombs that had destroyed everything around it, including most of the building that housed it. The top of the building was blown away; only the ground floor remained intact. The facade of the second floor clung for support to the single column of bricks that ran up each side, but nothing remained behind it. Only the front wall stood, windows blown away, jagged edges exposed where the building next door had once connected to it. Someone had painted by hand in English, "We're open for business" on the front by the door. The restaurant was doing a brisk business catering to British and American soldiers. They drank coffee and smoked and ate breakfast, laughing at each others' jokes. Two well-fed German women in their twenties sat with the men, also smoking and laughing. I wondered what they had done for their food. One looked up as we passed by. She held my eyes for a moment and then tossed her head defiantly, blowing smoke out of her nostrils. She turned back to the American next to her. He stroked her hair and spoke to her quietly. Thin, dirty boys hovered around, watching and waiting to retrieve whatever was left in the ashtrays. Vati had not noticed the scene. I looked away and concentrated on the church ahead.

Filth covered everything with black ash and dirt, like a fine dusting of snow in the winter. Instead of trees, black sticks stuck up into the air along this once-elegant boulevard, their branches hacked away by ambitious wood scavengers. The black gave everything a bleak and surreal air, and for a second I thought I was in an old black-and-white horror movie. I wrapped my scarf around my hair and held the ends to my mouth and nose to keep from breathing in the clouds of soot stirred by gusts of wind or by trucks driving by at high speeds. It got into everything, this soot combined with death, the way spilled flour gets on your hands, your face, and your hair. I coughed and tried not to think about the horrible-smelling air.

A young German soldier, the soles of his boots torn in many places, sat on the edge of the wall in front of the Kaiser Wilhelm *Kirche*. He leaned his head on his backpack, his hands in front of him. Perhaps he had just arrived "home," finding no family, no home, and no city left where he had left them. Perhaps he had lived in one of the magnificent apartments along the Kurfürstendamm that now stood empty, like skeletons with their flesh and skin burned and torn away. I felt sorry for him.

Every once in a while a streetlight or statue still stood—a bizarre contrast to the destruction that lay at its feet. No life, no grass, no flower, no bush, no tree broke the monotony of the dismal landscape all around us.

We passed the church. Ahead lay the ruins of more expensive, elegant apartment buildings. I never knew so much metal lived within a building—piles of it lay twisted, forming grotesque figures on the ash-covered ground. An old woman sat on a second-floor balcony of one of the buildings, stubbornly refusing to leave what was left of her apartment. A mending basket sat on her lap, and she darned a sock. The ornate iron railing of the balcony with its flower-shaped swirls stood beautiful against the blackened shell of the building. Above her hung another balcony just like hers, but I could see the sky through the door-frame: the top of the building was completely blown away; only her apartment had a roof. Behind her, through the open door, I saw more sky, and I realized that the back of her apartment had no wall.

A group of children scurried up the piles of rubble, playing king of the mountain. They stopped and watched us as we walked by, their filthy faces alert and anxious above tattered clothes. One little girl had on only one sock, and her hand-knit sweater came only just under her armpits to cover the top of her dress, filthy with the black soot all about us. But on her head she sported a tiny piece of red ribbon. It was not enough to tie into a bow, so she had stuck it into her barrette. I smiled. She pushed a strand of blond hair away from her face. I waved. She did not respond.

"I have seen enough," I said to Vati, amazed that this wasteland held these few signs of stubborn life. We turned down Joachimsthaler Strasse to cut back to Martin Luther Strasse, walking almost to Grunewaldstrasse before we found a street cleaned up enough that we could cut through to Martin Luther Strasse. A heavy metal sheet covered a hole in the street, and it buckled as we crossed it. I heard water rushing underneath, and the stench of sewage hit my nostrils.

"I'm sorry, Jutta."

"No, Vati," I responded taking his arm. "I had to see it, to remember."

"It will get better," he assured me. "It is already better than it was three months ago."

I couldn't imagine.

Worn Out

My winter coat was too small; the sleeves were too short, and it came only just to my knees. It had been too small in Halberstadt, but Omi thought we should wait until fall to get a new one. Mutti was going to have Frau Schultz convert the coat into a jacket to go over my navy blue wool skirt, but she and Frau Schultz decided the fabric was too heavy for a jacket, so Mutti gave it to Frau Schultz for her granddaughter. Her daughter's husband had been killed in Stalingrad, and they had very little. They lived with Frau Schultz, all together in one room, somewhere on Schöneberger Strasse in Tempelhof. They had food, said Frau Schultz, but only just enough, and they had no money for anything extra. I was just as happy because the coat scratched me, and I could only stand it because I always wore a scarf inside the neck—I hated wool, even though I knew it was a necessity of life in Berlin.

Winter came early this year. It was only November, November fourteenth, to be exact, and my birthday, but a light snow had already come, and the ground was frozen in many places, hard and brittle. I sat in front of the fireplace, warming my toes and sipping a cup of tea, wondering how long it had been since I had felt so full. Mutti had made a birthday dinner for me—a challenge with no meat, no butter, and little milk to be had. She made spaghetti and tomato sauce and an apple tart with a crumble on top, made from some lard she "found" somewhere, she said.

I had not expected a present, but when she stood holding the coat high above her head, her arm stretched to its full length, a surge of excitement fluttered through me. The light from the fire bounced off it, highlighting the red and blond tones in the fur—it was exquisite!

I caught my breath. "For me?"

She grinned from one side of her face to the other, her eyes involved in the act as well. "Happy birthday, *meine Liebe.*"

Vati smiled at me. "Well, don't just sit there. Take it from your mother before she pulls a muscle in her shoulder!"

I leaped up and grabbed the coat, hugging Mutti as I did so. The fur brushed against my arm like a light breeze, soft, so soft that it was barely noticeable. I held it out in front of me. I recognized the fur but not the cut. I thought it must be one of Mutti's minks, the deep brown one I had always admired for the different shades that caught even the winter light and embraced its surface with sparkling tones, making me think diamonds were buried under its long hairs.

"I had Frau Schultz make it over for you in the new style, the cape look they like so much in the magazines, with a big button at the neck. That's what she assured me was *the look* out of New York!"

"Really?" I hugged it to me and twirled around the room. "Oh, Mutti, it is so beautiful. Thank you!"

"And me?" asked Vati from the sofa. "I bought the thing for your mother as an original matter."

I laughed. "Yes. Thank you, Vati, for having such foresight."

Mutti sat down next to Vati. "They're saying this is going to be such a cold winter, and you needed a new coat. So I thought, why not? She is going to be sixteen years old. She can carry it off!"

I stopped twirling. I thought of Hannelore. "I hate to hear what Hannelore has to say about my coat."

"Well, don't worry about what Hannelore has to say. You'll be warm and in style!" She was pleased I liked the coat so much. "What a struggle we had finding a large brown button!" She looked at me from the corner of her eyes. "Do you know where I finally found one?"

I looked at it. It did look vaguely familiar, but I could not place it. "Where?"

"The back of the chase lounge in the basement!" she announced with great flair.

"No you didn't!" exclaimed Vati.

"Yes!" she was obviously pleased with herself. "Well, Hans, where else would I find one? There are no buttons to be had in all of Germany."

———

The theater was cold, so cold they handed out military blankets as we walked in. Vati took my arm and guided me to our seats; despite the cold he had taken his jacket off and placed it on the back of his seat. I frowned. I could feel the chill through my new coat, and he sat in his sweater, without a jacket, sweating! Vati had gotten the tickets last week, three of them, but Mutti felt a cold coming on and decided not to risk it. We were four rows from the stage, a little to the right. The hall was packed, and the excited whispers of the audience created a constant murmur, almost a humming sound. The faces that surrounded me were tired, pale, and gaunt, but their eyes could not mask the excitement of being here, to drop their worries for a few hours and watch the opening performance in this theater that had not seen life for many years. With only four hundred or so seats in the tiny Schlosspark Theater in Steglitz, there were no bad seats in the house, and I was excited to see this new, up-and-coming talent Vati spoke about, Hildegard Knef. The sign out front had read "Hildegard Knef in *Hokuspocus* by Curt Goetz." I had never heard of either of them, and the title made me think it must be a comedy. What a funny word, *hokuspocus*.

There was no curtain hiding the stage, and I wondered how they would end scenes or change sets without the curtain obscuring their activity. I looked up and thought I saw a star twinkling through the ceiling of the theater. The front facade still sported the scars of the war, I had noted as I walked in past the American soldiers that stood like sentries at the entrance to the theater. I wondered how many were in here making sure we didn't suddenly rise up again, as if any of these tired, worn-out people had the energy for that! Vati looked pale. He took out his handkerchief and wiped the sweat beads off his upper lip and forehead.

"Are you all right, Vati?" I asked.

"I'm fine. Just a little warm, that's all." He patted my hand.

"But it's not at all warm."

He shrugged.

The woman next to me wrapped her blanket around her legs, tucking it in at the sides. It looked horribly itchy and was made out of a rough fabric, like the fabric they use for blankets. Maybe it *was* a horse blanket. The theater smelled of people and damp plaster.

Then the lights dimmed, and a hush fell over the audience. A single white light remained focused on the stage, and for the next two hours, I forgot all the sights and smells around me, letting the actors draw me into their world.

Sorrow Settles Deep

We huddled anxiously around Mutti as she used the phone on Vati's desk. It had taken many months, but finally the phone lines outside Berlin had been repaired. We waited for what seemed like an eternity for someone, anyone, to answer. My mother tapped her fingers impatiently on the wooden desk. Suddenly she stopped, and her back stiffened. She leaned forward in the heavy black chair and said, "*Hallo?*" She frowned. "*Hallo?*" she asked again.

She paused and looked at us, confused and shaking her head. "Is Herr Muller there, please?"

My heart stopped; she had asked it in English.

"They are going to get someone who speaks German," she whispered to us, placing her hand over the phone.

"*Ja. Hallo.* This is Frau Bolle. I am looking for Herr or Frau Muller, please?" She spoke in German, but it was said formally, not to someone she knew.

A pause, and then a smile of recognition. "My God! Is this Ilsa?"

I let out a sigh of relief. Ilsa was there, so that meant Opa was there, too.

"Oh thank God, Ilsa! You are alive!"

I could hear a woman's voice at the other end, but I couldn't make out what she was saying. Suddenly my mother's rigid posture went limp; she slumped into the chair and held the phone away from her ear, not even listening to what was being said on the other end of the line. My heart raced. Something was wrong. What had happened to Omi and Opa? She let the phone fall from her hand.

Vati bent quickly and picked it up. "Herr Bolle here, Ilsa."

I stood frozen, unsure of what to do. I watched Vati's face, trying to read what was being said on the phone. He looked grave and said only, "Yes. Yes, I see."

Another long pause before he added, "No, of course. You must do what you have to, Ilsa." And then, "That would be very kind. I am sure that Frau Bolle would very much appreciate it." He held the phone up, his face tilted toward the ceiling. "Yes. I will tell her. Thank you. Goodbye."

Vati replaced the receiver slowly into its black cradle, so quietly I did not hear it as it fell into place. He turned slowly to me. "Jutta, go get your mother some water, please."

I stood for a moment looking at my parents' faces, the one devastated, pale, and unseeing, the other serious and full of concern, and then I ran to the kitchen. There was no need to explain. I already knew.

When I returned, Mutti had moved to her beige chair in the living room, her head leaned back against the stuffed curve, her eyes closed. She did not speak.

Vati cleared his throat. "Opa is dead." It was directed to me, but he stared at his hands, laced together between his knees, his elbows resting on his thighs. "He died of a heart attack the day the Americans marched in."

"That was the day after we left," I mumbled.

"Yes."

"And Omi?"

He paused. "Also dead," he said quietly. "She died this week in the hospital. Ilsa said they no longer could get her heart medicine. It's amazing she lived as long as she did without it."

I couldn't move. I stared at him without speaking. He looked up to see my reaction.

"Jutta, I'm so sorry. I know how much you loved your grandmother."

"And Ilsa? Why is she still there? And why are they speaking English in Omi's house?"

"The Americans have taken the house, and they have asked Ilsa to stay on as housekeeper."

My skin crawled. Strangers. Strangers were walking through Omi's house. Strangers sat in Opa's big leather chair looking out to the fields, and strangers slept in Omi's huge four-poster bed. Strangers leaned out of the sashed windows and looked into the street below, listening for the train along Beethoven Strasse.

"Don't be upset with Ilsa. It is good for her, and at least she can eat."

"I'm not."

"Jutta, Halberstadt will be Russian. I am not sure why the Americans are still there, but they won't be for long, and then it will be the Russians. Omi and Opa could never have lived under the Russians. I know it is hard to understand, but I believe it is for the best this way."

"I just wish I could have said goodbye one more time."

"I know."

"And we can't even go for a funeral? Where will she be buried? All alone with nobody there to say goodbye?"

"Jutta, now is not the time!" Vati glanced over at Mutti.

I fought back the tears and stood up to go to my bedroom. I wanted to be alone. The enormity of this world and our helplessness in it overwhelmed me. I thought I might be sick. I stood up quickly and ran.

As I passed by Mutti's chair I laid my hand on her shoulder and said, "I am so sorry, Mutti."

She patted my hand and held it for a moment before I moved on, but she said nothing. I hurried up the stairs to the bathroom.

A sorrow settled deep into our house, reclaiming the hope we had gained from the arrival of the Americans. It seemed in Germany that peace would never find us. My mother bore the loss of her parents very hard, especially the loss of her mother. She would not speak of it and I did not press her, but I knew that it scarred her not to have been able to visit, to say goodbye. I knew my mother had spoken of taking the freeway from Berlin to Magdeburg now that the Americans had been given access to it by the Russians. But because the road to Halberstadt was not only through Russian territory but the roads were still controlled by the Russians, my father had begged her to wait. So she waited, unable to control the events around her, and now Omi was dead. She must have died a lonely death in her hospital bed with no family to comfort her—only a Russian doctor or nurse there, speaking a language she did not understand. I closed my eyes and pinched back the tears. It would do no good to cry.

As for my mother, she simply stopped talking. I never saw her cry or show any other outward sign of her sorrow. She simply ceased to communicate. This was far worse. She was there, in the house, and she still cooked and tended to the garden and did all the things she always did, but she barely spoke, and worse, she never smiled. Her blue eyes looked out hauntingly from their sunken sockets, and I noticed that she lost more weight. We thought it would pass, my father and I. But as the days grew colder and the leaves fell from the trees in orange and brown swirls, she continued her silence. My father was worried about her; she weighed only ninety pounds, and I feared she would starve herself to death. I helped as much as I could when I was not in school, and I tried to talk to her and make her smile, but she would only tell me to hush and continue with her work. And then Vati got sick, and I feared that I would lose both of them.

Typhus Fever

December 1945

That Vati was sick, very sick, I had known for a while. My mother tried to hide it. At first, I don't think she realized it; she was so wrapped up in her grief that she was not aware of him or anything else, really. It came on slowly. He had lost thirty pounds from a frame that needed to gain, not lose. I thought it was war worry and lack of food, but then the fever came. At first the high fever, aching muscles, and cough just made us think he had a bad case of the flu. It was a very cold fall, and as November turned to December and the pale, rose-colored rash appeared across his chest and stomach, my mother knew that Vati had again fallen victim to typhus fever. He had picked it up as a teenager after World War I, picking cabbages in the fields with the Polish workers.

"Conditions were not sanitary in those camps where the workers lived," Tante Hilde told me. "Just like the refugee camps and prisoner of war camps all over Germany today, and again you see the reports that typhus and cholera are commonplace." She threw her hands in the air. "My God! You would think we live in Africa!"

She told me that after the first war, most of the men were either dead or injured, so they turned to the schools for help. Vati's high school class had been requisitioned by the government to help harvest the cabbages that grew in the fields surrounding Halberstadt. I don't think that Opa Bolle, busy with the factory in Berlin, even knew that his city-born son was sent to pick cabbages in soggy fields. And now, thirty years later, after months of not eating properly and not sleeping regularly, it had stirred in him, finding the weakest point to take hold and work its sordid evil through his body.

Please don't let him die, I prayed. Mutti couldn't take it—first her parents and then Vati. I bounced between hope and anguish. He won't die, will he? He can't die! No, of course he won't die. But he might! No, he won't. Dear Lord, please make sure Vati doesn't die. I watched helplessly as the fever made him delirious, and then my mother sent me away, fearing the disease would find its way to me. She didn't think he was contagious on this second round, but to be certain, she packed me off to the other Bolles' for two weeks to live in the chaos that ruled their household. It was a long way to walk to my school from their house, and I hated the awful rice-milk gruel Tante Hilde fed us in the evening— the only thing she seemed to know how to cook. Although I loved Tante Hilde dearly and considered her a lot of fun, I was relieved when my mother came to get me after a few weeks and returned me to the calm of our quiet house.

Vati still looked sick, his face waxy and pale, but he opened his eyes and he smiled at me when I came to the door. Still not allowed in the room, I waved to him from the doorway, and he lifted his hand only inches in reply. It was Sunday, and I had been home for two days. It was the first time my mother had even let me stand by the door of his room.

"He won't die, will he?" I asked my mother in a whisper as we walked down the dark hallway. He looked so fragile against the huge pillows and white sheets of the bed, his pure white hair blending into the white of the pillow and his substantial nose and high cheekbones standing out starkly against his sunken cheeks. He was forty-three years old, but he looked as old as Opa Bolle had looked to me when he died.

"Well, he's not dead, is he?" she demanded, her face suddenly red.

I looked down. I had not expected her to take my question as placing blame, but she was under a lot of pressure, and her usual soothing demeanor had been replaced with irritation.

"And he won't die, either! Do you hear me? " She grabbed my chin and lifted my head so I had to look at her. "I can't keep the typhus in him from flaring up. But I can try to keep it from killing him. That is what I am doing, and I will succeed!"

"He will be all right, then?" I asked anxiously.

She looked at me for a moment, taking in my concern, and then she softened, placing her arm around my shoulder. "Yes, Jutta. He will be fine. He is over the worst. Slowly he will get better, but we need to fill him with everything I can think of to build his strength, and that is hard right now!"

We walked into my bedroom and sat down together on my bed. I stared in silence at the wood that Gustav had used to cover my window as soon as the weather had turned cold. I willed it to be glass. Specks of light crept through around the edges, and I knew that the sun shone brightly outside, but in my room all was dark. We couldn't even turn the lights on for fear it would use too much electricity—electricity that was needed for cooking, washing, and heating, not brightening a room. We sat together in the gloom, holding hands in silence. After a long time she spoke.

"Jutta, I am sorry," she began, shaking her head. "I have not been much of a mother to you these past few weeks."

"Mutti, it's fine. You had so much to overcome."

She shook her head. "It was not fair of me," she paused, searching for the right words, "to not think of you." She stroked my head and hugged me to her.

Tears began to fall down my cheeks, and I wasn't sure if they were my mother's or mine. We sat clinging to each other and crying until all the sorrow of the past few weeks and months purged itself from our bodies. I pulled away to wipe my nose, and then we laughed at each other, our hair a mess, our eyes red and runny, and for the first time in months we let go—our bodies falling together onto the bed as we laughed and hugged each other. The sound of my mother's laughter was like hearing a beautiful symphony. And then my father stood in the doorway.

My mother looked up, astonished. "Hans! You're up!"

"I heard laughter," he said simply.

"But you're up! That is magnificent!" she clapped her hands in pleasure and stood up to go to him. They hugged, and then I joined them. She did not object as I wrapped my arms around both of them, feeling the bones of Vati's back through his nightshirt as I did so. But it didn't matter; he was alive. I smiled. I had my family back.

Fresh Oranges and Butter

"Oh my God, but they are huge!" cried Tante Hilde.

"Aren't they?" responded my mother. "And look, Hilde. Two pounds of butter!"

"But where did you get all this?" Tante Hilde held two of the largest navel oranges I had ever seen in my life, one in each hand.

"Well, I didn't want to tell you on the phone. That's why I had you come over. But Heinz brought them here."

"Heinz?" asked Hilde, looking up sharply. "From the factory?"

"Yes. He got them from the Americans at the factory, and butter, too."

"Butter? No! You can't be serious!"

Mutti opened the refrigerator and took out two large blocks of butter wrapped in wax paper. Hilde took the butter from Mutti, her eyes darting from the butter to Mutti's face and back to the butter.

"What? They just gave him this stuff?"

"Don't be ridiculous! He bought it from them," my mother lowered her voice, "on the black market."

Tante Hilde's eyes bulged from her face as she stared at my mother.

"And he says there is a lot more where this came from, if you have the money!" continued my mother. They were standing by the counter with their backs to the kitchen door and to me. I could see their profiles, but they were so busy talking they did not even notice me as I stood in the doorway to the kitchen.

"Does Hans know?"

"Of course not."

"Are you going to ask Heinz to get more where this came from?"

"Of course!"

Hilde nodded. "Tell me what to do and count me in."

"Heinz says if we give him the money he will take care of the rest. It's all very illegal, and they have complicated ways of dealing that I don't even want to know about." She shrugged her shoulders and raised her hands in the air. "They have different places in the city where they meet, and they trade in cigarettes and coffee and I don't know what all. But he will do it for us in exchange for some of the food."

Tante Hilde sucked in her breath. "*Meine Gute*! Hans and Kurt will have a fit!"

"It is more important that we eat. And I can't have Hans sick again."

My mother turned around to lean her back against the counter, crossing her arms in front of her. She looked up and saw me.

"Jutta! How long have you been standing there?" she demanded.

Tante Hilde spun around in surprise.

"You should announce yourself, you know."

"Sorry, Mutti."

"Listen. You didn't hear any of this, *ja?*" she said quickly, walking toward me and pulling me into the kitchen.

I nodded.

"I mean it, Jutta! It is very illegal to buy on the black market!"

I took my thumb and index finger and drew a line across my lips.

My mother nodded her head, indicating the conversation was over.

Hilde continued to watch me as if she wanted to say something, but decided against it.

"Here, let's try one." Mutti grabbed an orange from the basket. She took a paring knife out of the drawer and reached in the cabinet above her head for a plate. We all sat at the kitchen table and watched as she peeled the thick, orange, pockmarked skin off the fruit. It squirted across the table, and the delicate smell of fresh orange hit my nostrils. We inhaled. The fresh fragrance filled the kitchen, and we held it in our noses for a moment. I picked up a piece of the peel and rubbed it between my hands, holding them up to my nostrils.

My mother divided the orange into three sections, giving each of us a section. I bit into mine and felt the juice drip down my chin. It was delicate and sweet, and the small membranes of the orange broke apart in my mouth, delivering their exquisite flavor to every corner of it. I pressed the tiny membranes against my teeth with my tongue, making them burst open.

"*Du, lieber Gott im Himmel!* Oh my God in heaven! This is good!" cried Tante Hilde in her dramatic manner. She rolled her eyes to the ceiling before taking another bite. "When is the last time we ate an orange? Do you even remember?"

"Probably the Christmas of 1942 at the factory Christmas party, I would guess?"

"Did we have oranges?"

"Yes. Don't you remember that huge tower of fruit in the center of the table?"

"I remember," I said, "because one of us pulled an orange from the bottom and they all rolled around on the floor."

"Oh my God! Yes! How could I forget that?" said Tante Hilde, laughing. "And of course the boys decided to turn them into soccer balls."

"Heinz says he can get just about anything from the Americans."

"Can he get *gummi* bears?" I asked.

"Don't be silly. We will not waste money on *gummi* bears right now," said my mother.

"I just want butter and fruit and meat."

"We'll talk to him tomorrow."

"Yes. I'll come with you. How do we find him?"

"He's at the factory every day. Sometimes he works for the Americans, though, when they need an extra truck driver. He says his shift starts at 6:00, so if we get there by 5:30 we can catch him."

"Oh, my God! What I don't do to feed my children!" said Hilde, raising her hands above her head. "God, Heti, who would ever have thought we would be up at 5:30 AM, let alone down at the factory hustling for food at that unspeakable hour!"

My mother chuckled. She reached over and pinched my cheek. "Yes, what we won't do to feed our children!"

I batted her hand away playfully and pushed my chair back to get up.

"Say, did they ever come back to look at the house again?" I asked, suddenly remembering that British officers had come to inspect the Bolles' house three times during the two weeks while I was living there.

"Yes. And they have rejected it once and for all." Hilde clapped her hands and looked towards heaven.

My mother clenched her fists. "Yes! *Gott seit Dank!*"

"They hate the upstairs bedrooms in our house. That little twitty British colonel told me so. He said, 'All these tiny bedrooms upstairs,' and then turned up his nose the way they do. You know, those little, skinny, straight noses they all have. Thank God, Heti, I never let Kurt enlarge those upstairs bedrooms like he wanted."

"Did he really say he hated the house?"

"Oh yes! I don't know if he thought I would be insulted or what, but it was music to my ears." She pushed a stray strand of hair back into the bun at her neck. She pursed her lips. "Well, these Tommies are not quite as nice as the Amis!"

"But they're not as bad as the French!"

"No. They are better than the French," agreed Tante Hilde. "They don't try to harm us, but they just think they are better."

"Poor Tante Hildegard up in Tegel says it is a nightmare dealing with the French. They think everybody was a Nazi and treat everybody equally bad."

"At least they're egalitarians!"

"Yes, they are that, I guess," laughed my mother.

"Well, you have it the best here with the Amis."

My mother agreed. "I guess none of us should complain. We could be over in the East zone."

"Oh my God! Those poor bastards!"

"Hilde!"

Tante Hilde laughed. Covering her mouth in mock shame, she said, "Sorry. I forgot Juttalein was here."

I shrugged. "I hear worse out on the street from all of these soldiers. They can't speak much German, but they know all of the curse words! Anyway, I am leaving." I bent and kissed them both on the cheek.

As I left the kitchen I heard Tante Hilde's expressive voice continue, "If I never see another Russian for as long as I live, I will die a happy woman!"

And they talked on, comparing notes on the Amis and Tommies and all the various authorities that governed Berlin upon whom we were all now dependent. Watching them chatting excitedly and laughing, it almost seemed like old times—until I remembered they had been talking about buying food on the black market.

Later, I learned how the American soldiers who ran the gas station bartered for cigarettes and coffee with the desperate workers, even though it would have landed them in a great deal of trouble had the military government gotten wind of their activities. I never understood why the Americans took the risk. What was a little more money against the risk? But for the Germans it was different. Vati and Uncle Kurt paid their workers well, but they paid them in *Reichsmarks*, the only legal currency. Mutti told me it was illegal to pay them in coffee or cigarettes, the only "real" currency in Germany. But everybody knew if you wanted to live, you had to trade in the real currency. *Schieben*, they called it—when someone sells goods on the black market—and the Americans were the ones you went to, mostly because they had so much.

A Tattered Piece of Cloth

"Well, I don't believe it," said Hannelore, kicking a stone as we walked along Am Schülerheim on our way home from school.

"Well, I believe it," I responded.

"Oh, please! It's just Russian propaganda!"

"I don't know, Hannelore. Those pictures looked pretty real!" Maria shivered as she said it and pulled her jacket tighter across her ample chest.

The images of mangled bodies, limbs and arms as thin as the bones themselves, sprang into my mind. I tried to push the pictures out, but those haunting faces with the dark, sunken eyes that looked out from skulls covered only with a thin layer of skin would not release me. I shivered and, like Maria, pulled my sweater closed and crossed my arms in front of my chest.

"How could they stage those photos, Hannelore? It doesn't make sense," I added.

"Soldiers. Dead soldiers in some mass grave or something."

"Oh, come on! There were pictures of women and children, too!"

"Well then it must be something that the Russians themselves did. We would never have done anything like that, anything so awful."

"I don't think 'we' did do anything like that. It was the Nazis who did it!"

"If you are right, which I don't think you are, the Führer had nothing to do with it! Of that I am certain!" She turned abruptly to face me, her blue eyes flashing and her braids swinging in a wide arc from the force of her movement. We had reached the corner of the Föhrenweg, so I decided to answer her. If we had further to walk I would not have bothered. I hated confrontation with Hannelore—she held very strong opinions, passionately expressed—and I did not like to excite her.

"Hannelore. Please! Everything the Nazis did came directly on the orders of Hitler!"

She pressed toward me, fire in her eyes, a deep crease forming between them on the bridge of her nose. "That is not true," she said slowly and deliberately. "If the Nazis did this, and I repeat that I don't believe they did, it was Himmler's or Goering's doing, not Hitler's."

"You are naïve!" I shouted, not willing to be bullied.

Her face turned red despite the chill in the air, and she pointed her finger in my face and said, "You are wrong, Jutta Bolle. The Führer was a good man. He may have deported the Jews for the good of the German people, but he would not have ordered their massacre!"

And with that, she spun around and walked so fast it was practically a run down Am Schülerheim toward her house.

Maria and I stood for a moment, dumbfounded, and watched her back grow smaller and smaller, her long braids swinging back and forth as she marched along.

"I don't think we should discuss it with her anymore!" said Maria, turning to face me.

"No! Definitely not."

We continued down the Föhrenweg in silence, both of us upset by the afternoon's events—the photos the Russian teacher had passed around the classroom, and now this confrontation with Hannelore. I knew that Hannelore's parents had been members of the Nazi Party. They weren't big in the party or anything, but they were definitely believers, and Hannelore herself had immersed herself in the BDM, rising quickly in rank.

"I hope for her sake she is right," I said, stopping in front of my gate. "But I am afraid she is not."

Maria pursed her lips. "Well, I will wait until I see what the Americans say about it all."

I nodded, and we said goodbye. That was in June.

I catch Maria's eye as the American MP walks through the door of our classroom and Frau Jacob stands and calls the class to order. Frau Jacob clears her throat before she announces why the American MP is here in the front of our classroom. She is nervous. I lean forward to look around Maria, who sits next to me, and my eyes find Hannelore. She does not raise her eyes; instead, she studies the paper in front of her, drawing circles, one inside the other. I think back to our conversation in early June. Since then, none of us have discussed it again.

"This is Major Nelson of the American Military Government. He has been sent here by General Clay himself to talk to you about a very terrible subject." Frau Jacob pauses before continuing. She tucks a strand of hair behind her ear. Her hands flutter as they pass over her hair. "But one that you must hear about. I want all of you to listen very carefully. Nobody, I repeat, nobody is allowed to leave the room for any reason or to ask any questions until Major Nelson is finished." With that she nods to Major Nelson and sits down heavily at her desk, staring straight ahead at nothing in particular.

"Thank you, Frau Jacob," says the major as he places his briefcase on the podium. "As Frau Jacob has told you, I am here on behalf of the American Military Government." He fishes a huge manila envelope out of his brown leather briefcase as he speaks. "I have some pictures to show you and some things to say that will be very disturbing to you, I am afraid. I am sorry. We realize that you are too young to have any direct involvement with what you are about to hear, but we believe you must be aware of it, for it is your generation that will stop such horrors in the future."

He snaps his briefcase shut, and I jump. A deathly silence falls on the room. We all know what the envelope contains. I stare at it. My heart races and my hands grow sweaty. I know the pictures are coming. And they come. Twenty-five in all; I count them for some reason. Pictures so horrible my mind shuts down, and I stare in morbid fascination. A boy stares back at me. His eyes, sunk deep into their sockets, look huge in his skull, his nose and mouth oddly large against the deep hollows of his cheeks. His clothes in tatters, he pleads to me with those eyes, encircled by dark rings. I guess he is Dieter's age, and I try to image what it must be like for him. He holds a tattered piece of cloth in his right hand—a comforter of some sort in a world that holds no comfort. Behind him, away from the barbed wire fence, stand the adults, not as curious as he to be photographed. They stand behind him like a forest of human limbs. I have to look away. Tears fill my eyes, and one splashes onto the photograph, staining the shiny surface. I see that it is not the first.

I cannot look at Hannelore. I know her anguish. These are not pictures from the Russian propaganda machine—these pictures came from General Clay's office, and they must speak the truth, the brutal, horrible truth. My heart goes out to her, for she among my friends has been the most active participant in their world. I wonder where Erica is at this moment. Is she in another part of Germany, also at this very moment looking at the same pictures? Have the Americans chosen today all across Germany to show us the pictures, or is it just in Berlin, or maybe just my school?

When he finishes, nobody speaks. Nobody has a question. We are all too stunned. My ears echo and fill with the sound of rushing air; I can barely hear Frau Jacob dismissing the class. We stand and, like robots, collect our things. I vaguely realize that Frau Jacob and Major Nelson are talking quietly at her desk in the front of the classroom. I walk out of the classroom, down the hall, and out into the cold winter air. A breeze blows my hair into my face, and I take my free hand to remove a strand from my mouth. I see the dead, brown leaves of the trees falling to the ground, the breeze wresting them from their branches. I see a squirrel watching me from the center of the grassy section, brown with winter, that separates the two sides of Im Gehege Strasse. He stands on his hind legs, rubbing his front paws together before scurrying up a tree as I approach. A bird flies overhead and circles; it lands suddenly on a branch, and again I see the faces, the eyes, the pictures. I don't want to, but my mind plays them over and over again. None of us waits after school for the others; we all walk home in silence and separation. I don't want to talk to them, nor they to me. Nobody does, and the silence falls all around us and covers us like a blanket on wet spring grass, crushing and smothering.

14

Survival

Winter 1946

The winter of 1945–46 was cold, bitterly cold—colder than I had ever remembered! My father had found a wood-burning stove at the factory and had it brought to the house. It stood in our living room with a big pipe that ran up to the bedrooms upstairs. Her "Rodin," my mother had called it. It kept us alive that first winter after the war. There was coal in Germany, but not for the Germans, my mother had told me. Stories abounded of huge loads of coal, piled high on the trains that ran through German towns, never stopping, heading either west to France or east to the Soviet Union. We get only the scraps that fall off, people said. We were like the pigeons at the park following behind people eating crispy pretzels, gathering the crumbs as they fell along the path. I had heard rumors that boys stood along the tracks and on the overpasses with long poles, trying to knock what coal they could off the trains as they went by, until they posted armed police and soldiers on them. The Amis often looked the other way, but the French arrested them, and the Russians shot them!

Most parts of Berlin had electricity, but only for two hours a day. In Dahlem it was on all day—the Americans made sure of that—but we could only use it the equivalent of two hours per day. They regulated our use carefully, and if you went over your allotted use they fined you substantially. The Americans sent meter readers around to check up on the use: they caused nearly as much fear as the SS troops that used to walk casually around our neighborhood, everyone breathing a little easier after they had left without the dreaded knock on the door, a knock that could mean a week's worth of food taken away from the household. We soon learned that heating and cooling required the most electricity, so every household that could acquired a new electricity-saving device—the cook box—an ugly, insulated affair that sat on a chair in our kitchen. Mutti would put our dinner in, usually a stew or soup after boiling it first, and let it sit in there all day and finish cooking. When we were lucky enough to have a larger piece of meat, she would boil it briefly and then take the pot, hot off the burner, and wrap it in several blankets before wedging it between the duvets in her beautiful Italian carved mahogany chest in the hallway. Vati once was astonished to find a ham cooking in this fashion when looking for a throw to cover his legs while reading in the study.

The American "top brass," as they called them in the paper, lived in our area, but they did not live like us—without electricity, without heat, and without food. In the morning, my mother would fume about how she had gotten up to go to the bathroom in the dark and saw, through the trees in the backyard, lights shining brightly from the two-story yellow house that used to belong to Admiral Schniewind on Gelfertstrasse, where we knew a number of American officers stayed. "We have no electricity, and they don't even have the decency to remember to turn out the lights." When I suggested that maybe they were still up working in the middle of the night, she dismissed me. "More likely partying," she would say.

Germans heated their homes that winter with wood, whatever wood they could find. The trees on our block were protected from the assault of the wood gatherer's ax by their size. But some of the smaller trees in the park disappeared, and certainly our trees, usually so messy, were always pruned, their smaller branches stripped from them. I hadn't seen it, but Vati had told us that the *Tiergarten* had been completely denuded of trees and resembled a scene from a science fiction movie—bare stumps jutting out of the ground, black with soot. Old furniture, vegetable crates, and even garden gates—nothing was safe from the ax. The hunters were mostly women and young boys. They looked anywhere for a scrap of wood to provide the heat that their families needed to survive the winter.

It was only December, and already we had had several major snows, and our own wood supply had grown dangerously low at one point. My mother had sent Gustav to Tante Ite's house for a week to make sure she had enough wood, and then it had grown so cold that Gustav could not come the many miles that he had to travel by foot from his house to ours.

On Wednesday the temperature hit forty degrees, and we were all sent to school, the administration acting as if it was positively balmy. It had been weeks since it was warm enough to send us to the unheated classrooms. After school, I arrived home for lunch at my usual time. I closed the gate, waiting for the familiar creak of the hinges. The wind had picked up while I was at school and blew so strong it whipped my hair around, stinging me when the strands hit my face. I wondered if it would ever be warm again. As I walked up the path to the door I heard a pounding sound, as if someone were taking a hammer and breaking down the walls in our house. I quickened my pace, hurrying toward the front door. I stood in the entryway for a moment, unsure where the pounding sound came from.

"Mutti?" I called.

There was no response. The pounding filled the house, shaking the walls and the floors so that I could not tell where it came from. I threw my book bag down and ran to the dining room. The room was empty. Usually Mutti set my lunch out on one of the embroidered place mats she had bought from a refugee woman who had come through Dahlem with her three small children, each one knocking on a different door. Today the only thing on its polished surface was a pale reflection from the faded outdoor light. How strange! My ears adjusted to the pounding, and I realized it came from the basement. I cautiously descended the stairs to the basement.

"Mutti?" I called again. Again, no response. I lowered my head to see under the stairs as I came around the curve, and then I spotted her. She was dressed in an old pair of riding breeches with her hair tied up in a scarf. Gustav's ax hung dangerously over her head as she brought it forward on the wood beams that supported the floor above her head. Bits of wood and plaster rained down on her as the ax made contact with the beams.

"Mutti?" I called for the third time.

She spun around, ax midway between her hand and the beam. "Jutta! You're home already?" She lowered the ax as she said it. She was covered with filth. Her dark eyebrows, blond now from the fine dust of the ceiling, looked strange above her blue eyes, washing out her face.

"Mutti? What are you doing?" I asked, bewildered.

She lowered the ax, rubbing her shoulder and stretching her neck from side to side as she did so.

"What does it look like?" she asked between breaths, her chest heaving with the effort. "I am taking out these beams that Gustav put in here so that we can make use of them." Noting my look of dismay, she added, "I will not have my family freeze to death. It is just that simple!"

"But why don't you wait for Gustav?"

"It's too cold for him to walk here, and we are very low on wood."

"But why don't you let Vati help you? Or you can ask him to bring wood from the factory. Mutti, you are going to kill yourself using that ax! And look at the size of those beams! How can you possibly think you can get them out yourself?"

She smiled and pointed to the far corner of the basement, where, as my eyes adjusted to the light, I now saw three beams just like the one she had been working on, piled one atop the other.

"I don't want Vati to help. He has enough to do with the factory. He doesn't need to worry about this sort of thing." She paused for a moment, still trying to catch her breath. "Jutta, I don't want you telling your father what I am doing down here!"

"But won't the basement collapse?" I asked, looking up nervously.

"I don't think so. I'm not taking out the original supports." Then she added, just to worry me, "At least I don't think I am." She laughed as I stared at her.

"Come. I need a break, and you need some lunch. Did I lose track of time, or are you here early?"

"I'm home at the usual time."

She nodded her head and motioned me to head for the steps.

Over the next several days, my mother single-handedly tore out the sturdy wooden beams that had served to reinforce the ceiling and walls of our basement against the bombs of the war. She would not allow me into the basement when she was tearing out the beams, just in case the floor above her collapsed and trapped us both. At least with me above, she said, I could go and get help—a statement that served to expand my lack of confidence in the project. After she tore them out, she said I could help her split them. And I did. Over the next week, together we split enough wood off the sturdy beams to keep us warm for the next few weeks. Huge blisters leaped out all over her hands, and I too sported a few by the end of the week. She only stopped when my father appeared at the top of basement stairs, wondering who was trying to tear apart his house. He had come home to surprise us for lunch that day and found the two of us in the basement. He helped us finish splitting the beam we had started on, and then he made her promise to leave the rest for Gustav.

The next morning, the rumbling of a truck in the driveway woke me. I heard a fourth male voice, not Uncle Kurt's or Heinz's or Vati's. I pressed my ear against the crack where the wood didn't quite meet the window and strained to hear the soft, guttural, voice of an old man; it was Gustav's voice. Vati had sent a factory truck to pick up Gustav, and from that day on, Gustav never missed a day because of the weather.

We, as well as the rest of the neighborhood, could hear that truck coming as soon as it turned onto Auf dem Grat, sputtering and burping as Heinz ground it into first gear after making the turn. It ran on wood, not gas. German engineers had converted its engine to run on wood. Someone had nailed wooden planks on to its flat bed to form a sidewall. The black cab in front sported a dent in the fender, and the doors let out a terrible wail when opened. Its worn leather seat only allowed for Vati and Uncle Kurt to sit, and, of course, Heinz. The truck came to our house first, since we lived furthest from the factory, and it dropped Vati off last, so he always sat in the middle with his shoulders hunched in and his legs pressed to the side so that Heinz could work the truck's massive gearshift.

Vati joked, "One never stops being the youngest brother!" The truck was not quiet, and it was a far cry from the elegant, chauffeur-driven Daimler that used to pick up Vati, but still, it had wheels, and it meant Vati no longer had to walk to the factory.

I shut one eye and pressed the other to the crack. Gustav sat in the back, on the open bed, and I was glad that the makeshift walls had been put in place so that he would not fall off when Heinz made one of his spectacular sharp turns. Gustav eased himself to the ground. I watched as Heinz backed the truck down our driveway. Vati, in the front, waved farewell to Gustav as the old man hurried across the garden to the basement door.

I thought it must bother Vati to ride around town in this old wood-burning truck while the American generals and colonels passed by in chauffeur-driven Cadillacs, flags flying from shiny black polished grilles. But Vati said he didn't really think about it; he was just glad he did not have to walk anymore. He said the truck bothered Heinz more than it bothered him or Kurt, and in fact it amused him enormously that Heinz insisted on wearing his chauffeur's uniform to drive the truck. But it had to irk Vati, I thought, to see the factory gas station used to fill the very cars that had displaced him from the road. His Daimler was neglected at the factory, parked like an ancient ship waiting for its time, out of place, not realizing that its usefulness had passed. I guessed it would be a long time before there would be gas to run German cars.

Skirting the Edge of Death

From the headlines in Vati's newspapers and by word of mouth, I learned of the hundreds of thousands of Germans who died that winter of either starvation or exposure to the cold. Many of them died alone, separated by war and desperate circumstances from their families, and they died because they had no shelter. Some lived among the rubble of a building that had blown up during the war, sheltered, perhaps, by a cement doorway that somehow had survived the chaos and leaned precariously against its former foundations. But many also died in their beds as the snow and the rain and the bitter cold hurled a fierce assault on Berlin. A house was no certainty against death if it had no heat and no windows, leaving many vulnerable to the brutal power of that winter. I often slept with Mutti to stay warm on those nights when the temperature went down into the teens. Like so many, I had no glass in my windows, and the wood that Gustav had nailed into place let the air seep through around its edges. When the wind howled I could see it move my curtains. On those cold nights, my mother would come and get me, and I would sleepwalk to her bed, my feet frozen so that they hurt. I curled up gratefully in her bed and let the warmth of her body wrap around me, melting away the cold.

Everybody knew somebody who had died that winter. For us, it was Tante Ite. Whether she died of the cold, or lack of food, or just old age, I don't know, and it wasn't discussed. The fact is, she died that winter, and every one of my friends had a similar story of an aunt or grandparent or cousin who died that same winter. But nobody spoke about it other than to state that someone they knew had died. Nobody asked why they died, and nobody told. My father said we didn't want to acknowledge how closely we were skirting the edge of death. The occupiers tried to feed us; at least the Americans did. But the small rations they gave us were not enough to fight off death, especially for the weak, the old, or the very young. The papers reported that infant mortality had reached 65 percent! Those cold, starkly lettered words exposed none of the tragedy behind them. They read like an interest rate, a statistic with no meaning.

The earth lay parched and cracked from the ice that covered everything; it crept onto sidewalks and hung off fences and tree branches, and walking became a treacherous activity. It was far too cold to go to school that winter. We had no heat at all in our school, and our breath came out in bursts of steam as we talked to each other in the classroom, hopping up and down to keep our feet from freezing. On the days when the temperature rose above freezing, we walked to school, collected our assignments, and went immediately home again to do the work at the kitchen table, only to return the next day, the assignment completed for the teacher to grade and our next lesson waiting for us to collect. Sometimes, when it was not too cold in the classroom, the teacher took a few minutes to explain a math problem or a grammar assignment as we sat shivering and stomping our feet, trying to concentrate on the complex algebra equation scribbled rapidly on the board. We had no textbooks. Instead, we worked from large tablets the size of a magazine. The text was printed on the same paper used for newspapers, and the edges were bound with the staples used in magazines. I hated the feel and smell of that paper. If you were not careful, the ink would smear on your hands, and it would soil your clothes if you pressed it up against you.

Between the Russians and the Americans, all of our regular textbooks had been thrown away, with the exception of our math books. All the other books had been tossed out because they contained Nazi propaganda. As a result, history was not taught at all, and science was taught only minimally. I learned only the basics that winter—math, grammar, and English. But to my delight, I could read American and English novels again. I decided to take American literature as my extra honors class and, fortunately for me, most of the novels I needed for class already graced my father's bookshelves. So while I was reading from his fine, leather-bound collection of first editions, most of the students in my class had to read from the horrible "newspaper texts" that the authorities printed in massive quantities. When the other girls looked enviously at my books, I soon learned to keep Vati's books at home and use the school's newspaper text in class.

My education during that school year of 1945–46 was spotty at best, and my poor mother, along with being lead cook and housekeeper, had now become my primary teacher as well. The one exception was mathematics, which was, as she said, at this point in her life, locked too firmly in the recesses of her mind for her to find it.

———

Spring came late, as if it didn't want to arrive. The cold and gloom of winter continued well into April, and just when we thought it was all over, another storm hit us, bringing freezing rains and winds that tore through my clothes. But now, finally, it was May, and spring had come. The mornings grew light earlier and earlier, and I could tell the chill had left the air. Sparrows and red-breasted robins greeted me each morning, singing their songs of life, and the trees once again held the promise of hope in their buds. Hardy shoots of daffodils and crocuses forced their way out of the hard, cold earth, and we all breathed a collective sigh of relief that we had survived that winter. We looked much like the daffodils from last season; we were there, just a little more bent and a little less brilliant than in years past.

Mutti appeared less exhausted, the strain slowly easing. It was a subtle change, but the dark shadows below her eyes lessened with each week of spring, and color came back to her cheeks. She was still too thin, far too thin, but I hoped with the arrival of summer our food ration would grow. Vati said General Clay had promised at his last press conference to increase it to the pre-winter level of 1,500 calories. Everybody silently understood that most Germans were on a slow starvation diet. As for us, we weren't starving, but we had nothing to spare. Thankfully, once Vati was again well, he had agreed that feeding us was more important than standing on principle. So through Heinz's purchases on the black market, we were some of the fortunate ones able to supplement our diets. But we were still very thin. Nobody was fat, and if you were, people whispered about what your mother did at night.

In the distance I hear the sounds of morning: American jeeps, their engines gunning, heading to Army Headquarters on the Hüttenweg. I stretch my arms over my head and quickly lower them as my stomach somersaults, an ache grabbing at my side—I hope we have eggs this morning. I hurry to throw my clothes on before the morning air can assault me.

The sun bounced off the tiles of Erica's roof, forming long, thin sheets of light, and the sparrows held noisy conversations in the delicate branches of the acacia trees as I walked toward the park. I really should have been heading for school, but I stood in the park instead and breathed in the fresh, crisp morning spring air. For the first time in months we had school regularly, and I needed to hurry, but it seemed more important to linger in front of the lake, for a few more minutes taking in the noises of life. A rustle in the long grass caught my attention. I bent down low and waited. It came from my right, down by the water, where the cattails and grasses merged their thickness to form a protective cover for all sorts of life. Time ticked away, and I knew I really should head back the other way, but I had to see. After a moment, a little brown- and black-flecked head peeked out cautiously from the underbrush. She checked each way, like a mother crossing the street, slid elegantly out into the water, swam a small circle, and returned to her sheltered spot. A smile crept across my face. Five tiny, fluffy, gray little ducklings came single file out of the grass, plopping into the water behind their mother to go on what had to be their first swim in the lake. They had been born within the week, I guessed. I watched mesmerized as they followed their mother, except for the one daredevil, already assuming a path of independence. It swam off at an angle to the right, away from the others.

This spring would be better than the last one, of this I was certain. I stood up slowly and caught my book bag before it fell off my shoulder and hit the ground. I blew the ducks a kiss and turned back toward my house and Am Schülerheim to head for school. The bombed-out houses that lined the park, their windows gaping, their rooms empty, devoid of life, stood out starkly against the lake. God could renew much faster than man; that was obvious. The small trees were gone, pulled down or hacked up by desperate mothers and sons, but already much of the park looked as it had always looked, and the weeping willows that lined the tiny lake's banks paid no attention to the actions of man.

I drew strength from the steadiness and certainty of the buds on the trees and flowers that formed in the cracked and unforgiving soil. No matter how hungry I am right now, I thought, nothing can compare to the fear that gripped us last spring—fear of rape and death, and fear of not knowing when it might come, or if it might come—that was the worst. And then, the new fear that they would ship those of us who were of use to them back to Russia. I had heard rumors of families whose fathers were scientists or engineers who, in the middle of the night, had been quietly forced onto trains and sent to…Who knew? Moscow? Siberia? I shuddered.

This spring would be different. I could feel it. And each spring from here on, I told myself. Yes, each one would be better and better until we lived again. I hurried to school, a new bounce in my step.

Angel Food Cake

Maria had an aunt in America—Philadelphia, she said—who sent her family packages filled with coffee or cigarettes and sometimes a canned or smoked ham and, even better, a tin of cookies that Maria would share with us. These packages made the rest of us long for relatives in America. Sometimes the aunt sent a magazine like *Mademoiselle* or *McCall's*, with the latest American advice on homemaking and fashions. And she would bring them to my house, where Christa, Maria, and I would sit on the floor of the music room, AFN purring on the radio in the background, bent over the thing, examining every inch of the smiling, well-fed faces of the women they featured, and we would try to imagine what it must be like to live in a world filled with so much. We presumed that included happiness.

The Christmas issue showed us tables spread with hams and giant chickens (labeled a "turkey dinner" in the caption), and enormous bowls of mashed potatoes and corn and vegetables, and something called "angel food" cake. It was beyond our grasp, and it made our stomachs growl with hunger. We laughed, pointing to each other and saying, "You have a symphony going on in there!"

We envied how the American girls we saw in the pictures filled out their dresses. Our pathetic stick arms and flat chests made us long for the voluptuous look of the models that smiled back at us. Sometimes they ran an article about one of the American movie stars, Olivia de Haviland or Rita Hayworth or Elizabeth Taylor, whom we could not believe was our age! We looked back at ourselves from the full-length mirror on the back of my door, crowding each other to try and mimic her doe-eyed, full-lipped look, only to burst out laughing.

"Even if I gained fifty pounds, I don't think I would ever have her chest!" giggled Christa.

" Me neither. I think Katherine Hepburn is the most I can strive for. What do you think?" I asked, striking what I thought was a Hepburn-like pose.

"Well, you do have the red hair and freckles, but I think it ends there, Jutta!"

Christa flipped the page, and the three models posing in what the magazine called "fresh and pretty for spring" captured our imagination.

"Their dresses!" cooed Maria. "Their dresses are made of so much fabric!" It was fabric that came down midway between the knee and ankle, just enough to show off the elegance of their long legs. It was fabric that we did not have and never would have, or so we thought at that time. The dresses were tight at the waist and sported large, wide belts made from matching fabric. There was fabric everywhere—yards and yards of it—fabric that had never been used for anything else.

"I bet every woman in America has five or six of these dresses!" cried Maria, hugging the magazine to her chest.

Christa said ten, but I agreed with Maria.

I thought of the dress that Frau Schultz was working on for me for my dance classes that would start soon—made from one of the curtains in my mother's bedroom, it had a beige background with large circles of brown and pink and orange on it. I longed to have a dress made from fabric that I had picked out special, just for that dress, rather than fabric that we found we could do without from somewhere around the house.

The advertisements, exquisite with their glossy colors, captured our imagination, especially the ones for fabrics: Shirley's Fabrics, Farmsworth Woolens, and my favorite, Verney's Fabrics of New York. I stared at the tall, dark-haired woman in the ad. Her dress, made of an elegant pastel pink and blue fabric, hand-painted with flowers and angels, wrapped around her body embracing her with color. A fabric bolt lay at her feet; the fabric unwound from the bolt and lay on the ground in waves, framing the picture all the way to the top. I had never seen anything so beautiful!

We turned the page, our eyes devouring the scenes of families eating dinner together, the children looking happy and clean in their crisply ironed new clothes, their plates full of meat and vegetables and potatoes, a new bicycle waiting for them outside the window. The mother stood holding a freshly baked cake, smiling at her children, her bright red nails peeking out from the corners of the plate. It was an advertisement for General Mills Flour. A slice of yellow cake, with chocolate icing between the layers and rich chocolate icing forming perfect little precise swirls on top, stared back at us from the glossy surface of the page. Involuntarily, my taste buds sent saliva into my mouth, and I swallowed.

"It must be amazing in America!" Christa said, looking up.

"They are so lucky!" added Maria.

"I am going to live there one day," I said quietly, not looking at either of them.

"Oh sure! How are you going to do that?"

"I don't know, but watch me."

"*Du,* Jutta. *Meine Gute*! Herr Bolle would have a fit if you married one of these soldier boys like one of these common girls that parade around the Kudam."

"Who said I was going to do that? I have no intention of marrying one of them."

A very blond model with a new hairstyle caught our eyes. Next was a page advertising Revlon's new spring nail colors. And then an ad for what seemed like hundreds of nylon stockings, and we longed to have blond hair and to paint our nails red or bright pink from bottles that read "Raven Red" or "Chrysanthemum Red" or "Blistering Pink" and to wear those beautiful, delicate stockings from Berkshire Stockings, or Townwear Stockings, or Gold Mark Hosiery, that made your legs look so elegant, instead of our thick wool stockings.

Christa and Maria forgot about what I had said about moving to America. But I never forgot it.

15

Mrs. Vockel

April 1946

I knew she was coming because Major Franklin had told me that we would be getting some new neighbors soon—a colonel and his wife from Arlington, Virginia. When I asked where Arlington was, he said it was right next to Washington DC, like Dahlem is to Berlin. I was very impressed that our neighbors would be coming from the Washington DC area. Mutti had me ask him if the "new Americans" would need a housekeeper.

Luise had grown increasingly unhappy with the Tommy commander and his staff for whom she worked in Wilmersdorf. "Barbarians!" she complained to Mutti. "They smoke, dropping their cigarette butts on the carpet, and they drink! Oh my God, Frau Bolle! I have never seen such a group! Until all hours of the night!"

To everyone's satisfaction, Major Franklin had said yes and arranged it so she worked five days a week for the new Americans, giving her Sunday and Tuesday off. Once she started with them, she would spend Monday night at our house and work for Mutti the following day. The Americans didn't like live-in help, and they didn't seem to comprehend how difficult it was for Germans to commute from their homes to their work. So Mutti let her spend Tuesday night with us as well. She even offered for her to stay on the other nights, but she declined. Luise had a solid character and much too much pride for her own good.

Major Franklin had warned me sometime earlier that many of the Americans were bringing their wives and children and that it could mean further disruption to our lives, but he would give no specifics. Rumors swirled around school, and my friends and I all feared that they would take more of our homes and also our school for their children.

"Of course they won't take Jutta's home because she is so in with Major White Teeth!" said Hannelore. Her sarcasm irritated me.

"*Ja*, that brilliant smile is the kiss of death if it comes to your house!" agreed Maria.

"I am not in with anybody," I bristled.

"Oh really, Miss Ami Translator!"

"So what if I can speak English better than most?"

"Do you really think they're going to take your house after all the help you've given them?" asked Maria.

"*Ja*, help kicking Germans out of their homes," added Hannelore.

Tears sprang to my eyes, and I whirled around to face Hannelore. "Is that really what you think I do? Because if that is really what you think of me, don't ever speak to me again!" My face felt hot, and the tears were in danger of escaping.

"Jutta, I'm sorry. I didn't mean it. "

"Because actually I help Germans explain their situations, like if they have sick relatives or if they have absolutely no place to go. Or I tell him how poor Frau Dietrich lost her husband and her two sons on the Eastern Front and has no relatives to help her. Do you know about that, Hannelore? Do you?"

Maria touched my arm. "Jutta, please. She said she was sorry."

But I wouldn't stop. I couldn't stop. "Is she still in her house? Is she, Hannelore? Yes. Thanks to me. Because otherwise she would have been given three hours." I was screaming, and I could tell I had lost control, but her words stung me. I had seen them whisper when I went with the major to someone's home, and I suspected they thought like this, but only suspected.

Maria looped her arm through mine, turning me toward home. But I yanked it away. "And he listens to me. He hears their stories, and he is not some animal who doesn't care. If someone has no place to go, he will pass over their house and go to the next house. Do you notice that?"

Maria grabbed my arm again and pulled me away in earnest now. A few girls had stopped to listen.

"I try to make him understand what it is like for us. That we have no place else to go. That we can't buy anything." Maria guided me away from the crowd and we headed home, my face still hot. Sweat droplets had formed on my forehead.

"Do you know about that, Hannelore? No!" I shouted over my shoulder, trying to jerk free of Maria's grasp.

Hannelore did not respond, and Maria pulled me so fast that I had to concentrate on the uneven cobblestones to keep from falling. My breathing did not regulate itself until we got to Am Schülerheim.

Major Franklin did listen to me as I conveyed the tragedy that had visited every family in Dahlem. My job was to translate the information. But, I did not have influence over his decisions. In fact, he never said anything in front of me. He would write things down and nod his head. Sometimes, later, I would walk by and see one of their huge cars parked in front, and I knew that an American officer had moved into the house anyway. Other times a German child in the yard throwing chestnuts or playing jump rope told me that he had heard. These moments filled me with joy, lightening my step, a skip even escaping as I continued on my way. He never discussed with me why he chose the houses he chose and why he did not choose others. For all I knew it was because of a defect in the home, not my stories of hunger and death and illness. But I think I made his job much harder. I put a human face to it. It was easier before, when he didn't really understand their stories. But now he knew, and I believed he did care, for he still asked me to translate.

I remember the day she arrived. It was one of those spring days, neither warm nor cold, neither sunny nor rainy; one of those plain days that I hate, where nature didn't seem to be able to make up its mind. I had been keeping a daily lookout for the new American lady who was supposed to join her husband and live across the street, and then one day she suddenly arrived. I actually heard them before I saw them. I was reading *The Old Man and the Sea* for my American literature class when a car horn startled me. At least I guessed it was a car horn. It was a loud, deep, throaty horn—not at all like our beepy little German horns—so for a moment I was not sure if it was a horn at all, and then I heard it again. This was a definite get-out-of-my-way horn, a serious-sounding horn—a horn that came from a large car, like the voice of a very big man, a baritone horn. It resonated down the quiet of our street. I leaped up from my chair and ran to the kitchen window to look out, but the trees blocked my view. In a second I was out the front door and down the path to the gate, and I leaned over and saw them. An enormous blue and white American car stood in the middle of the street, defeated by a cat that apparently stood frozen in terror. The driver honked again, and I jumped—surely that horn could be heard in downtown Berlin! The cat stood there on all fours, her back arched, gray hair standing straight up. Obviously, she had never heard such a horn, either. The door on the driver's side opened, and a tall army officer stepped into the street. Before he could even get around the door, the cat sprinted to the side of the street, climbing with graceful speed to the lowest branch of one of the acacia trees that still lined our street. The officer shook his head and got back in the car to maneuver it the rest of the way down the narrow street.

I knew they were going to Erica's house. They had been fixing it up all week. I had watched enviously as painters and window repairmen went in and out of the house, and as gardeners trimmed the trees and bushes that had grown wild from neglect. Then one day a cleaning lady came and spent the entire day hanging carpets from the windows and banging pillows together out front.

The car pulled into the short, narrow drive, and the driver brought it to a stop only inches from the house. Even so, the back end hung out over the sidewalk a good bit. The front door on the passenger side opened, and a crisp-looking older gentleman stepped out and opened the door directly behind him. He stood there for a moment in his military uniform with his gray hair neatly trimmed and looked up at the house before he glanced down to see if his wife had emerged from the car yet. I waited expectantly; it seemed to take her forever to get out of the backseat. I leaned out further and then, finally, a foot emerged, encased in nylons and sporting pumps like I had only seen in the magazines—black-and-white spectators with a heel that was high but not too high. Slowly, the rest of her unfolded from the backseat of the car, and I caught my breath. At first I didn't see her. I just saw the dress; the most beautiful dress I had ever seen. It came down nearly to her ankles in loose folds of cream-colored fabric with large black polka dots and was cinched in at the waist by a large black patent leather belt. I had never seen so much fabric used on one dress—Frau Schultz could have made me three dresses out of the fabric in this one dress. She wore a tiny cream-colored jacket that came down only to her belt. Her brown hair, swept up perfectly in that style I had seen in *McCall's*, not a hair out of place, glistened in the vague light, and as she turned I caught a glimpse of very red lips. She was immaculately and stylishly groomed, and I was in awe.

She stood up very straight, and with the hand that did not hold her shiny black patent leather purse, she smoothed out her dress, mumbling something to her husband as she did so. Then she turned and looked at the house for a moment. He shut the door to the car and stood with her, and together they looked at the house that the American military machine had provided them. He said something else to her, pointing down the street toward the park and then turning in my direction and pointing.

I leaped back from the gate, my heart pounding. I heard another door slam, and after a moment I slowly moved my head forward again just enough to see if they were still looking. They had moved to the front of Erica's yard, heading up the walk to the front door. She pointed to the top of the house where the roof showed through from between the tiles that had blown off during the war and had not been replaced. Her fingers sported bright red nails, and several gold bracelets jangled on her thin white arms. Her husband nodded his head but did not comment as he opened the front door for her. And then they disappeared inside. My attention turned to the military driver, who busied himself with removing the luggage from the trunk. He had already taken four enormous suitcases out, and I could not imagine how the trunk of one car could possibly hold more. But it did; a fifth one came out, and then he retrieved a sixth, smaller case from the backseat next to where she had been sitting. I turned abruptly and ran up the walkway to tell Mutti.

"Voluminous amounts of fabric! Just like in the magazines! There must have been five meters of fabric in the bottom skirt alone!"

My mother shook her head and smiled in amazement. She was embarrassed I had spied on them, but I could tell that secretly, she too was curious about the new lady next door.

"How old is she?"

"Older than you. I would say about forty-five, maybe."

"And children?" asked my mother.

I shook my head. "No. Only the two of them."

"That must be why they gave them the Küpper's house," said my mother. "I was wondering because it is not very large, and these Americans seem to like the larger houses."

"And she is very tall, just like in the magazines! But thin!" I added.

"Well, I guess she wants to fit in with the rest of us!" laughed Mutti.

Mutti sat across from me, her elbow resting on the table as she lifted a cup of chamomile tea to her lips. The sleeve of her housedress looked worn where Frau Schultz had repaired it and taken it in so that it did not hang like a sack on her thin figure. She smiled at me, amused by my excitement.

"Oh! I almost forgot. You should have seen the luggage—five huge suitcases and one small one, and the car! Oh my God! It is so big that it hangs over the sidewalk!"

"Really? Where do they propose to get the gasoline to feed it?"

I did not respond. I knew my mother thought it was terrible that the Americans brought over their huge cars that ate gasoline like no German car ever could, and then they drove them to the store in Dahlem to shop! It seemed Americans had an aversion to walking. They even drove their cars to the military command center only two blocks away! And of course, we had no gasoline for cars or for anything else, and Vati and Uncle Kurt still arrived at the factory in the wood-burning monster.

"Never mind, Mutti," I soothed. "At least it is not the Russians."

"Good God! Of course," she said quickly. "No, it will be fine." She paused and took another sip of her tea before saying, "The only problem will be school for you."

"What do you mean?" I asked, startled.

Mutti sipped her tea before replying. "They have sent out a letter saying that they will need your school for the American children when they all arrive. They are proposing that you go to school way over in Lichterfelde. They will blend the two schools together or some such thing." She waved her hand the way she always did when she couldn't remember the exact wording. "Anyway, Vati and I think that is too far."

"Then where will I go?"

"Vati is checking on the Königin Luise Stiftung."

"Oh," I said, my stomach suddenly uncomfortable. "But what about my friends?"

"Jutta, their parents will decide what they do for their own children, but Vati and I think this is the best choice for you." I looked down at the table and twisted my mouth up. She took my hand. "Besides, I'm sure some of your friends will go to Königin Luise, and even if they don't, you'll make new friends." She looked out the window, suddenly serious. "We are worried about how spotty your education has been, and we think Königin Luise will be better than throwing you into classes of fifty or more over in Lichterfelde, where they are trying to combine two schools full of children into one."

"I know, Mutti. It's just that I have had to make new friends so often." I thought of Erica and how she had left and disappeared, and of Carla, and now Maria and Christa.

"I understand, dear." She reached across and grabbed my hand. We fell silent. I stared out the window, my excitement over the American lady's arrival evaporated now.

My mother followed my gaze out the front window. Her eyes drifted over the trees in the garden. She turned back to me suddenly. "I know! Maybe shortly after you start there, we could have a party here at the house, and you could invite the girls in your class!" She smiled at me encouragingly, the corners of her small mouth turned up slightly, just enough to show a glimpse of her perfect teeth. "Would you like that? To help make new friends?"

I shrugged. "That would be nice." I really didn't want a party for a bunch of girls I did not know, but I knew it would make her feel better if we had a party.

"And of course the other Bolles are going there as well, so you will know somebody."

"Really?"

She nodded her head. "Well, I mean Ingrid and Peti. Not Dieter, of course."

Soon after our conversation at the kitchen table, a letter arrived announcing the exact date when we would have to give up our school and go elsewhere. Most of the girls accepted this like I did, without comment, but some were shaken, visibly angry, and sad that our lives, it seemed, would never be settled. I kept very quiet about the fact I was going to Königin Luise Stiftung. Not many could afford this exclusive school that had been around forever, since Fredrick the Great it seemed, and had even been kept open by Hitler for the Nazi elite's children while the rest of us, including me, had been forced to go to public school.

———

She spotted me as she came out the front door dressed in a pale pink dress in the same style as the one in which she had arrived. I stared as she swung around to lock her door, her skirt still in motion, the fabric swirling as if it were separated from the bodice. I concentrated on the road, pretending I had no idea she was there ahead of me, focusing instead on the blades of grass at my feet. Desperate to live, they had forced their way through the hard concrete, only to be trampled by the many feet that came down the sidewalk. Earthworms lay dead, the life flattened out of them where they had dared to leave the soil and explore the sidewalk, a more expedient route toward some destination, but a perilous one. When I glanced up again, she stood by her car watching me, one hand resting on the roof. In the other she held her purse and keys.

"Hi there!" she called to me.

I couldn't avoid her, so I raised my hand to wave and said hello.

She moved to the end of the car, and I knew she wanted to talk to me, so I paused by my gate for a moment before turning the handle.

"Wait," she called walking towards me. "We are neighbors, I see."

I nodded my head.

She held out her hand. I couldn't help it; I stared at the perfectly manicured white hand with bright red nails for a minute. It reminded me of my mother's hand, delicate and elegant, back before all of this when she, too, had the time for pampering. She shook her hand slightly and I grabbed it quickly, realizing I was being rude.

"Oh, good! For a moment I thought Germans didn't shake hands," she said goodnaturedly. "I'm Mrs. Vockel. My husband, Colonel Vockel, and I just moved in last week." She said colonel in a way that made me realize she was very proud of his title and rank.

"Oh, hello. I'm Jutta Bolle." I smiled. Pointing with my free hand, I added, "I live right there."

"Yes. I see that." She dropped my hand. "Is it Utah?" she asked.

I shook my head. "No. Jutta."

She tried again, pronouncing the *J* all wrong. I laughed and said it again for her.

"We Americans have the worst time with this language of yours! Let me try your last name. What was it again?"

"Bolle," I said.

"How is that spelled?"

I told her.

"Oh," she smiled. "Like the store in the village."

"Yes."

"Is that your family?"

"Yes. My great-grandfather started the company."

"Really?" she looked impressed. "So your family owns grocery stores?"

"Well, actually no. My grandfather sold the company years ago and bought a factory that my father and uncle run."

"Oh, I see." She shoved a tiny loose strand of hair back into place. "What sort of a factory?"

This woman certainly asked a lot of questions, like all Americans, it seemed. The major was the same way, always asking about my family and whether we did this or that like they did in America. A German would have waited to see if the other person volunteered the information. It was rude to be too curious about another person's livelihood, especially if you had just met them. But for Americans it seemed it was impolite not to ask.

"They make coffins." I mumbled the word "coffins," hoping she would not hear and would not really want to know.

"They make what?" she asked, turning her head so her ear faced me.

"Coffins," I said again.

She pulled back, surprised. "Oh! " She put her hand to her neck. "Well, that certainly must be a big business right now."

I just stared at her.

Her hand fluttered to her side. " I am so sorry. I didn't really mean it to sound like that."

I nodded.

She studied me for a moment. "I'm going to the PX right now. Is there anything I can bring you or your mother?"

I frowned at her in disbelief. "We aren't allowed to buy PX goods."

"Oh!" she genuinely did not seem to know this.

A breeze blew my hair across my face, and I reached to remove it from my mouth.

"My goodness, you have the most beautiful golden red hair!"

"Thank you," I said, pleased that she had noticed it.

"Well, it was very nice to meet you, Utah, and I hope to see you again soon."

"Thank you. It was nice to met you, too."

"Meet, dear. Not met."

I blushed. "Oh, yes. I meant meet."

She smiled. We shook hands again.

She turned to walk back to her side of the street, saying over her shoulder, "Say hello to your mother for me, and tell her I'll stop by to say hello."

I turned the handle of the gate and wondered how it was that she just assumed that I spoke English. She probably thought my mother spoke English as well. She did not seem to realize that Germans and Americans were not supposed to socialize. I chuckled, thinking about my mother's reaction to this friendly but naive woman.

"Where did all of this come from?" I asked, astonished at the display laid out on the kitchen table. A paper bag stood empty on the chair. On the table above it stood a bottle of something; I tipped my head to the side to read Ajax and another called Lysol. I studied the label and told my mother they were for cleaning the kitchen or the bathroom. There was a bottle of green liquid called Palmolive and a bottle of blue liquid called Windex. And next to them were three bars of Lux soap and a box of Arm and Hammer laundry detergent, two boxes of cookies, a box of Ritz crackers, and, best of all, a bottle of shampoo. I read the label out loud: "Enhance your natural golden highlights with Clairol." I smiled, setting the bottle down and grabbing another. This one, also from Clairol, was a conditioner. "Mutti, this is one of the brands from the magazine. You put this on after you shampoo and then you have no tangles!" I hugged it to me in excitement. "Did she bring this here?" I asked, lifting my head in the direction of Erica's house.

"Yes."

"But I didn't hear the door."

"You were in the music room with your records blasting! How can you hear anything?"

I smiled.

"Yes," she said again. "The American lady from across the street, Mrs. Vockel, I think she said, brought this to 'say hello.'" My mother raised her eyebrows and shrugged. She seemed slightly embarrassed. "I gave her a jar of plum preserves to say thank you," she added quickly.

She stood there for a moment, pondering the items on the table. "She must not think we are very clean."

"I'm sure she meant it in kindness, Mutti."

"Oh, yes, I am sure. And it was very nice of her." She studied them again. "I will need you to read some of these labels for me, though." She laughed, glancing at me before adding, "She seems very nice, and she had on a lovely pink dress."

"Yes. I saw it earlier. Did you see how much fabric was in it?" My eyes grew wide as I remembered fold after fold of pink fabric falling from her belt.

"I did indeed," said my mother. "They call that the 'New Look,' I believe!"*

"Wow. Mutti, how do you know what they call it?"

"Frau Schultz has the fashion magazines, too, you know. Christian Dior launched it out of Paris. I have even seen the latest *Vogue*, I will have you know!" She winked at me. "She may not have the fabric, but she has the magazines!"

I laughed. "Mutti, can I take a bath and wash my hair with this wonderful-smelling stuff before dinner?" I unscrewed the cap and let the scent drift up to my nose.

Mutti laughed. "Sure. But then I think you better read these labels to me so that I don't kill us with this stuff!"

I grabbed the shampoo and conditioner and the Lux soap and ran for the stairs.

I quickly became friends with Mrs. Vockel. She was a very lonely woman. With no children and no friends in Berlin and with her husband working long hours, she spent most of the day by herself. I began to stop in after school for a chat, mostly so I could practice my English and listen to her talk about America. She spoke of how everybody had a vacuum cleaner, and how all the ladies wore the same style dresses she wore, and how you could find any color nail polish or lipstick you wanted—in fact, the hardest part was to pick the best color from all the rows and rows of choices. She told me that the girls my age liked to go to something called a "soda fountain" after school to buy a Coke or an ice cream. They had this ice cream dish, she said, a "banana split," and if you ate too many of those you would soon be as big as a house. I couldn't believe a dessert had three flavors of ice cream and three syrups on it.

She talked about how the boys loved to play baseball and ride their bicycles

---

* The New Look actually came into style in Paris in February 1947, but because Jutta remembered "all the fabric" so vividly, I decided to describe it at her first meeting with Mrs. Vockel.

on streets wide enough for a car to make a complete turn without backing up. Maria and Christa didn't believe me when I told them about the streets. But I knew it was true. If there was one thing Mrs. Vockel impressed upon me about America, it was a sense of how big the place was, and she made it clear that she found our narrow streets and tall apartment buildings very confining. It seemed in America space was unlimited—open space, fields that went on until the eye could not see as they curved around the horizon; highways that wrapped around the earth forever, and out West, thousands of miles of desert known only to the snakes and coyotes that inhabited it.

The streets were wide, she said, because everybody drove a car. Most people lived in their own homes, so the cities spread for miles and miles. Nobody lived in apartments like those found in Berlin, except for New York and maybe Miami, she said. She didn't understand why anyone would live in an apartment, and she left me with the distinct impression that apartments were bad things, not only unsightly but a bit distasteful as well, with people living on top of each other. "Only the Jews like to live like that," she said. I never questioned what she told me about America; I figured she was American, so that made her an expert on all things American.

Mrs. Vockel often talked about Arlington, Virginia, where she and Colonel Vockel had a grand old house covered with ivy and surrounded by magnolia trees. I had read about magnolia trees in *Gone with the Wind*, I told her. She said in that case I had to see the movie with Vivian Leigh and Clark Gable, and that maybe when the military government established a theater for us in Dahlem it would be one of the films. That was the first I heard of plans to establish a theater for Germans—I found out a lot of information that I am not sure the military government would have been pleased to know Mrs. Vockel shared with me.

She gave me all of her old magazines and rarely wanted them back. Once she read them, she said, she was done with them. I became the envy of my friends as I acquired a complete library of *Vogue, Life, Mademoiselle*, and the *Saturday Evening Post*. The last I would find in Vati's study sometimes. And Mutti was forever borrowing my *Vogue* magazines to take to Frau Schultz.

She told me about the "coming out" parties, as she called them, of the daughters of her friends at places that sounded elegant and important to me, like the Chevy Chase Country Club, or about balls held at the Army Navy Club. When she spoke of these things, her eyes would drift to the bay window in Erica's living room, and she was no longer in Berlin. She made it all sound so wonderful, beautiful, clean, safe, and certain. America sounded to me like a land without problems, where food was plentiful and anyone could do and become anything they pleased, so long as they worked hard at it. But most important, everybody in America seemed happy. The magazine pictures and Mrs. Vockel confirmed this belief, and I became convinced that America was the promised land, or as close to it as I would ever find here on earth.

Often Mrs. Vockel offered me a Coca-Cola. I thought I had never drunk anything so wonderful as Coca-Cola before in my life. I loved the way the bubbles fizzed and bounced off my throat; a few drifted up my nose as I brought the glass to my lips.

I didn't stop in every day, but I did stop in about twice a week. Many days I would arrive to find her in bed. She especially seemed to want to talk on those days. She had asthma—a bad case of it, in fact, and the Berlin air, still dirty from the bomb damage, did not help her condition. The air, it seemed, didn't want to be clean. The summer breezes stirred up the ashes and dust from the charred carcasses of the buildings that still lined Berlin's streets, and when that happened a dim haze would form over the city and Mrs. Vockel could not breathe. It frightened me when she had an "episode," as she called them. She gasped for air, her shoulders heaving and her face pale, and I was uncertain what to do for her. I soon learned to hand her the black device that lay on the side table. She sucked at it hungrily until her breathing regulated itself again.

Sometimes she would stop me in the street and ask me to come in and help her with a phone call or to translate something she had gotten in the mail. As the months went on, she got to know more and more of the other military wives and she began to go to clubs. They loved clubs, these American women. She told me not to stop in on Tuesdays because she had bridge club, and on Fridays she had social club, and on the first Monday of every month she had book club. And so I became very familiar with Mrs. Vockel's schedule and her life, and the life of the other American wives.

It was only after several months that it began to occur to me that in all the conversations I had with Mrs. Vockel, she never once asked me anything about Germany or our lives, or what it was like during the war. It was as if the only life that mattered was hers.

16

They Are Only Things

My mother was ambivalent about Mrs. Vockel. She never said anything about her, but I knew my mother, and I could tell by her silence that she was not fond of the American woman across the street. She appreciated the food that we received from her through trades, but a piece of her resented the fact that her beautiful things now resided in this woman's house and, one day, that they would move with her across the Atlantic to America. And in my heart I knew that my mother could never have done what Mrs. Vockel and so many other American women did—she could never have accepted a Meissen tea set in exchange for three pounds of coffee. She would have simply given the coffee away without taking the china. To be fair, Mrs. Vockel probably figured my mother would trade the goods with some other American, so why shouldn't it be her?

At the same time I knew my mother would never have accepted charity even if Mrs. Vockel were to offer it. The few times that Mrs. Vockel sent over a cake of Lux soap or a bottle of Palmolive detergent as a gift, my mother had immediately sent me back with a bouquet of roses or a fistful of herbs. But this was not a matter of logic for my mother; it was a question of the heart. It was the humiliation of it all that was difficult for her—to have to barter her fine things for food was an embarrassment that she did only for survival. She never went to the barter store at the U.S. headquarters on Hüttenweg. She would never have suffered the indignity of standing in line waiting for some bureaucrat to appraise her item and then hand her a ticket to take to another bureaucrat who would pay her. No. She wouldn't even deal with Mrs. Vockel directly. She sent me.

When I came home from school, I would find a Meissen tea set or figurine sitting on the table by the front door with a note written in my mother's sharp hand: "Jutta, please take these to Mrs. Vockel." That is all it would say. It was up to Mrs. Vockel's conscience to determine the value of the goods and send me back with coffee or sometimes cigarettes. She never turned down my mother's offerings. Why would she? They were exquisite pieces of china from Meissen, Rosenthal, and *Königliche Porzellan Manufactur*, some from Opa Bolle's collection and some that Vati and Mutti had bought throughout their marriage. At one point I found my favorite plate, with its pale blue and gold trim and delicate pink roses, among the offerings. I held it in my hand for a moment and then tiptoed to the dining room and slipped it back into the china cabinet. I could not let this favorite little plate that had held my cake on it for so many birthdays end up across the street. My mother never asked me about it, even though I know she must have seen it back in the cabinet in its usual place next to the blue and white Rosenthal teacups.

Only once did my mother ever send me back to Mrs. Vockel's. It involved a pure white Meissen polar bear. He walked on all fours, his left hind leg raised at the heel. He looked up, as if he had heard something in the distance. His muscles and fur, intricately delineated by the artist, rippled when the light hit them. His place had always been on the bookshelf in my mother's study, next to his friend, an equally exquisite all-white Scottish terrier.

I knew not to ask my mother how much was enough, so I simply went back to the Vockels' and told Mrs. Vockel that my mother did not want to sell the bear for two pounds of coffee.

"Well, for how much then?" she asked me.

I shrugged.

She walked in her kitchen and came back with two more pounds of coffee.

When I came back home I set the four pounds of coffee on the kitchen counter. My mother, peeling potatoes at the sink, did not turn around, so I said, "She sent four pounds instead."

"Good!"

I waited for her to say more or to turn around and look at the coffee. But she did not. So I left her to her potato peels and wandered into the living room. I glanced on the shelves above the fireplace. How much was left to barter? The shelves were empty but for a few vases that came from her mother and an exquisite blue bird, a pelican, with a young boy in pale beige riding his back. The bird held its beak down to its chest the way a horse would on a short reign. It had been a wedding gift from my father. I hoped that she would never have to barter it or the vases from her mother.

"They are only things, Jutta."

I turned, her voice startling me. She leaned against the door. I hadn't heard her come in.

"Oh, I know," I said quickly, moving away from the shelf.

"And if they buy us life and health, it is a good thing."

I nodded. "But he was so beautiful."

"One day when this is all over, we will have more beautiful things." She tried to smile at me, but her eyes gave away her sadness. I went to her and hugged her.

"I hope it will be soon."

She did not respond. We both knew it would not be soon. But for that moment we wanted to believe it.

From that day on, Mrs. Vockel always sent either three or four pounds of coffee back across the Föhrenweg with me—never again two. We never mentioned these transactions to my father. He never said if he noticed that things were missing, but he must have noticed. Occasionally he would ask how she had gotten such a nice piece of pork or where the butter came from. But she would just say that the butcher had felt generous or that the store had suddenly found a few sticks of butter.

It was a difficult arrangement for everybody. Colonel Vockel, embarrassed by his wife's bartering, would look away when my eyes fell upon one of my mother's figurines sitting on their mantle. I knew it was against the military government's direct orders for Americans to barter with Germans for coffee and cigarettes, and I wondered how he reconciled his wife's actions with those orders. But all military wives did it, so he was not alone, and Mrs. Vockel was a force in her own household. I couldn't imagine that he had much to say about it.

17

Königin Luise Stifftung

The Königin Luise Stifftung was an imposing-looking school, and I was intimidated when I climbed up the wide stairs that led to the double-doored entrance. The name of the school with its coat of arms and the date of its establishment stood above the door carved into stone, its majestic script leaping out and greeting all who passed under. I glanced up as I ascended the stairs. Those girls who brushed past me quickly, I knew, had attended the school for years; they were probably the children of former Nazis. But Mutti was right. Many girls were like me, climbing the stairs uncertain of what lay ahead in this venerable old school. They, like me, took the stairs carefully, looking around as they did so, trying to take in the school, the girls, and all the new sights and sounds that accosted them that morning.

I had missed Maria at the streetcar stop where we had arranged to meet and travel the ten-minute ride together. I had been delighted when the week before she had asked if I was going to attend Königin Luise. I answered, hesitantly, yes. Maria's, "Thank God! I will have at least one friend!" was music to my ears. But she hadn't been at the station, and I couldn't wait for her or I would be late for school. So I went ahead alone, my stomach queasy.

I got off at the Königin Luise Platz, directly diagonal from the school. The streetcar that carried me had standing room only. It was stuffed with workers and businessmen and housewives alike, reminding me Germans no longer drove cars in Berlin. Pushing my way to the door, I was only too happy to exit the hot, smelly streetcar and cross Königin Luise Strasse. I waited a long time for a break in the army jeeps and American cars that were the only vehicles on the road that morning. As I crossed the street toward the school, I glanced over my shoulder to see if the entrance to Opa Bolle's beloved Botanical Gardens had survived. A smile momentarily escaped my otherwise serious face as I glimpsed the enormous redbrick facade, so out of place with the rest of the buildings on the street. The arched openings that lined the top of the building had always made me think of it as a poor cousin to the marble-built Roman Coliseum.

The school actually faced Podbielski Allee, but a corner of the schoolyard began at Königin Luise Strasse, forming a triangle where it met the street. I walked along the enormous gold-tipped iron fence that enclosed the school-yard—a yard unlike any other I had ever seen. The ones I had experienced before were basically large, bricked-in courtyards, but this? This was a garden.

No, this was a park, I thought, as I walked down the Podbielski Allee to the school's entrance. Somehow the trees that had been there for years still stood, escaping first the bombs and fires and then the axes that had taken the lives of so many that winter. I supposed the ten-foot fence that surrounded the school proved too much of an obstacle for all but the most intrepid wood hunter. Only the smallest branches could be lifted over its gold-covered iron tips. I stopped and pressed my face between the iron bars for a moment, taking in the dense spring air. It would rain today, I decided. The heavy bars cooled my face with moisture held from the night before. The grass stood green and fresh, a new carpet laid out by nature only just last month, and the lilac bushes still bloomed, their sweet scent wafting toward me. The trees did sport that now all-too-common trimmed look. I smiled and envisioned young boys scaling the iron fence with their saws, trying not to be impaled by those gold tips and handing the branches they managed to cut over to an older brother who waited on the other side.

The heavy wood door nearly knocked me down the stairs as it swung back to close behind the girl who had entered just ahead of me. I pressed all my weight against it and pushed it open. Inside, the hall rang with the excited voices of young girls as they ran and greeted friends. Many, though, were like me, not certain where to go or what to do. A woman about my mother's age stood near the door; a teacher, I presumed.

"Are you new?" she asked me.

"Yes."

"To the right. Follow the signs."

I nodded and did as I was told. I heard her ask a girl behind me the same, and then another and another. I guess we all had that lost look. I walked into a large room and saw a long line of girls at the other end; a table stood before them where another woman with glasses at the end of her nose handed them each a packet as they approached.

"Jutta!" called a familiar voice.

Several heads turned.

"Jutta Bolle! Over here."

I recognized Maria's voice, but I couldn't spot her right away. She waved to me from the middle of the line. I ran over to her and hugged her, excited to see a familiar face.

"You made it!"

"Of course I made it. But where were you?"

"I'm sorry. My mother made me leave thirty minutes early today!" She rolled her eyes.

"Oh! I waited for you at the stop."

"I was afraid that would happen, but I couldn't call you because it was too early. I'm sorry," she said again.

"Don't worry about it. I'm here now, and I'm so glad to see you."

"Come get in line here with me."

"No. I should go in the back," I said, glancing at the girl behind Maria.

"I don't mind." The girl shrugged her shoulders.

"Are you sure?"

"Go ahead."

"Well, thank you." I reached my hand to her. "I'm Jutta."

"So I gather," she said, taking my hand smiling. "I'm Hilde."

It turned out that Maria and Hilde were in most of my core classes, and in my American literature class I sat next to a small blond-haired girl named Carola, who shared her book with me on that first day. We were friends from that day forward.

My teachers were all old; very old, in fact, it seemed to me. They were all "from before," Hilde said when I commented on it several days later in the schoolyard.

"They were all fired by Hitler or they quit under him," announced Hilde.

"Really?"

Hilde nodded her head knowingly.

"But how do you know?"

"I don't for sure. But look at them. Don't you think there are younger teachers than this crew?"

We shrugged collectively. None of us had really thought about it as Hilde seemed to have done.

"Well, of course there are. But they're all Nazi-trained so," she threw her hands over her shoulders, "out they go, and back in with the old ones. We have a few younger ones who have proven they never bought into the program, if you will, and they have been 'de-Nazified' now." She put her fingers up to form quotation marks. "Stamped with a seal of approval, like in that magazine. What is it, the 'Good Housekeeping' seal of approval?"

We giggled at her joke. The traffic on Königin Luise Strasse roared behind us, the trucks and jeeps at times drowning out the laughter and talking in the schoolyard.

The German-American Club

May 1946

The first time I went to the German-American Club, I was afraid. News of its opening swirled around the Königin Luise Stiftung in a matter of minutes. I couldn't go to the opening because we had to visit one of Mutti's aunts in Wilmersdorf since the streets had finally become passable enough that we could take the streetcar to see her. But the next Saturday Mutti encouraged me to go and see what it was about. Maria couldn't go that Saturday, but Christa said she would meet me at the club. She lived along Argentinische Allee, only a half a kilometer or so from the club. I didn't want to walk the two kilometers to Zehlendorf alone, so Mutti walked with me.

I glanced at the paper; scribbled across it in Christa's hand was "corner of Schützallee and Riemeisterstrasse."

"This must be it," I said, looking up uncertainly.

"The teenagers heading up the stairs would strongly suggest that you're right," said Mutti, laughing at me. I glared at her; I was nervous and not in a mood for frivolity. I hated going places alone, making small talk and trying not to look self-conscious. And what if I couldn't find Christa?

The house was enormous, made from huge blocks of cement that had been sanded to look like stone; it stood two stories tall with a front garden that wrapped all the way around its perimeter. An American flag fluttered in the wind next to a set of stairs at least five feet wide that led to the front door, where I could see young people about my age talking to an American MP.

"The American flag hanging over the entrance is no small hint, either!"

"Okay, Mutti. I know this is the right place," I said, smoothing out my dress.

"Well, that doesn't look too scary, Jutta," said my mother. "No fingerprinting seems to be going on in there, and no mug shots, either."

I nodded, but this time I smiled. One of the rumors swirling around school was that the Americans wanted to fingerprint every German youth and that was why they started the club. My mother had been amused by that one.

I saw a girl I knew and I turned to kiss Mutti quickly on the cheek. "Thank you, Mutti. I'll see you later."

I was halfway up the garden walk before Mutti could respond. "Don't you want me to come in with you?"

I knew she was teasing me, but still I wouldn't put it past her, so I kept on walking, calling over my shoulder, "No thank you! Bye!"

"Bye," she responded, laughing at me.

The MP saw me through the glass of the front door; he held the door for me.

"Welcome, young lady. Glad to have you join us."

"Thank you," I said shyly.

"Now the only rule is that you have fun!"

I smiled at him, unsure what to say.

"We have a game room upstairs." He pointed to the stairs and then turned suddenly and frowned. "I'm sorry. You do speak English, don't you?"

"Yes," I said.

"Oh, good! We have a guy who speaks German if you need any help." He ran his hand through his sandy brown hair. He was in his thirties, I guessed. And judging by all the paraphernalia on his front lapel, he must have been an officer of some sort. "As I was saying, we have the game room upstairs, ping-pong in the basement, and music and snacks on this floor. So enjoy."

"Thank you." He smiled at me and shooed me in with his hand, ready to greet the next arrival. I moved into the front room of someone's house, someone who never would have guessed that one day a bunch of skinny, hungry German youths would be here, milling about with the Americans running a club in the middle of their living room. AFN blared from the stereo—a nice one, I noted—that stood at the far side of the room in a large wooden buffet. I recognized the DJ; Teddy, he called himself. I had become a regular AFN listener, driving Mutti crazy. It dominated the music room with its loud ads and rapid interplay between announcers. "They must drink a lot of coffee to talk that fast!" she would say, shaking her head as she passed by on her way to completing some household chore. Ours was the best stereo, so my friends often crowded into our music room after school, huddled around our stereo, listening to this lifeline to all things American—all things amazing and interesting.

A woman dressed in a maid's uniform placed plates of cookies in the center of a table that stood by the window. She was tall and attractive. She seemed out of place in her uniform. Her blond hair, swept up into a knot at the top of her head, contrasted with the dark color of her uniform. She felt my eyes on her back and turned to look at me.

"*Guten Tag*," I said, walking over to the table.

She nodded in reply and then, noting how I eyed the plates, she said in German, "Help yourself. They are for everybody."

"Really?"

"Yes. They have many more trays in the back." She smiled again. "Try the sandy-colored ones with the brown flecks. They call them 'snickerdoodles,'" she whispered.

We both laughed at how silly the name sounded. She picked up her empty tray and left for the kitchen. I watched her as she left the room. What was her story? Her accent was educated. I learned many weeks later that she had lost both of her sons, ages eighteen and seventeen at the time, and her husband to the Eastern Front. Her husband had been a banker, and they had had a nice home in Lichterfelde before a bomb, dropped in the dead of night, and the raging fire that followed had destroyed the entire block. She now lived with her sister and daughter in Zehlendorf, sharing one room that they rented from a friend of her sisters. Her daughter wanted to go to the university to become a teacher, but at the moment that was impossible. So she took care of children for an American colonel and his wife in Dahlem, only two blocks from our house.

I noticed that the American MP who had greeted me at the door—Captain Haft, she called him—was always in the room when she came to change out a tray of cookies or to bring in more punch. Often he helped her carry the heavy glass pitchers back to the kitchen, and I began to wonder if he had other intentions. She smiled and declined his help, but he always insisted. Well, I hoped he was not of the "love them and leave them" type that Tante Hilde and Mutti spoke of so regularly.

The word had circulated that there were cookies, and boys and girls crowded around the table, reaching over each other to grab a cookie as if they would all disappear. I moved away to the other side of the room, searching the heads in the room for Christa's familiar mop of blond curls. Some pamphlets lay in a pile on a small side table by the door. I studied the bold print advertising a list of classes with the dates and the times for each. They held my attention, a focal point to lessen my self-consciousness. They offered classes in every conceivable topic, including U.S. history and even hygiene, the latter broken down into two classes, dental care and body care. I could hear my mother: "They think we aren't clean? Don't they know that we have no soap, no toothpaste?"

I studied the sheet again. In small print it said: "Free soap and toothpaste samples." I slipped the paper into my purse. Free samples from American companies! I would not miss that one! Whatever they were offering would taste better than that nasty stuff Mutti concocted from baking soda and mint, and if it meant sitting through a lecture on how to brush your teeth, something I had learned at the age of three, it was well worth it for a tube of shiny white and green toothpaste.

"Jutta!"

I whirled around to face Christa. "There you are!"

"Hi. What are you doing over here in the corner?"

"Look at these classes they offer," I glanced down again, "every Thursday at 4:00."

Christa picked up a sheet and studied it.

"I'm going to the hygiene one to get the free samples."

"They are giving away samples?"

"Yes. Look." I pointed to the fine print.

"I'm with you! The soap my mother has burns my skin! Oh, I hate it." She hugged the flyer to her. "Do you think they have that Palmolive stuff we saw advertised in the magazine?"

"Maybe. Or Ivory." We giggled.

"Come on. Let's explore this place." She grabbed my hand and pulled me into the crowd.

I saw Hannelore on the other side of the room, laughing and talking to a boy that came up to her shoulder. I was surprised she was there; she hated the Americans. I shrugged. I guess the music, the food, and the boys helped her overcome her dislike. I looked around. Most of the boys were young; under fifteen I guessed. I shuddered, knowing the reason why. The older girls stood in groups, talking to each other glancing flirtatiously at the American soldiers. The soldiers, busy acting as DJs and organizing activities—like the ping-pong tournament going on downstairs amongst the boys—did their best not to notice. The MP said something to a tall soldier with black hair, and he immediately went to the windows by the table and opened them. It was hot in the room, and I welcomed the breeze from the windows. I studied the room. The walls were covered with pictures of America. Two in particular stood out; huge posters of the Redwood National Park and the California coastline, or so the plaque next to them stated. A smaller one caught my eye as well —the reds, pinks and oranges of the sheer rock walls couldn't be real, I thought—a photographer's trick. "The Grand Canyon" was written in script across the bottom.

"Jutta, let's go in the garden. I see Peter out there."

Peter was Christa's neighbor. She had a huge crush on him, and she was not going to lose this opportunity to talk to him. I followed her outside, noting the other posters of American movie stars: Gregory Peck, Jimmy Stewart, Rita Hayworth, and Elizabeth Taylor. I shook my head. I couldn't believe we had just fought a war with these people, these Americans, pitting our men against theirs, stopping at nothing to kill them and they us, and yet here they were throwing parties and providing a refuge for German youths! These were a remarkable people. Later, when I spoke to Vati about it, even he, who usually took a cautious approach to the Americans and their activities, was very impressed. On our way out, Captain Haft handed us another flyer announcing that starting next week, the club would hold dances every Saturday evening from 6:30 until 9:30, giving us plenty of time to get home before the curfew.

Christa and I agreed to go together, and we departed, tripping lightly down the stairs, filled with anticipation about next Saturday.

18

Bacon and Surprise Visitors

I stood in front of Erica's door with eight fresh eggs in my basket. We traded eggs, one of our fresh eggs for two of Mrs. Vockel's cold-storage eggs. She had phoned to ask me to bring them for Sunday because, she said, she was having guests over for brunch. My mother shook her head as she put down the receiver—the woman lived across the street, but she always phoned over to our house.

I stared at the wooden door inches from my face. I didn't like its green color. "Hunter green," Mrs. Vockel had called it. She had had it painted last week, and the smell still lingered. It was shiny and clean, but the color was too serious and formal for the rest of the house, and the color didn't belong—not here, not in Berlin. I lifted the huge brass pineapple knocker, also installed last week, and let it fall against its base. The sound echoed for a moment in my ears. Mrs. Vockel had told me that the pineapple was the symbol of hospitality in the south of the United States.

Mrs. Vockel answered the door. "Utah, my dear. Come in. Colonel Vockel and I have some friends over for coffee. Come in, dear, and meet them."

Before I could protest, she escorted me to the living room and introduced me to her friends, also military wives. Their husbands stood up when I came in as Mrs. Vockel, smiling her bright, lipsticked smile, pushed me forward from behind with her hands on my shoulders. I glimpsed the bright red of her polished nails from the corner of my eye as she lifted her hands to point to each person in the room.

"This is my dear little friend from across the street, Utah Bolle."

They all nodded in my direction. "Hello, I'm Jutta," I said, trying to correct Mrs. Vockel's pronunciation. "Pleased to meet you."

"Oh, she speaks English!" said the blonde lady sitting on the sofa. Her skirt, gathered tightly at the waist, spread out on the sofa in folds. I envied her the crisp white fabric with its pale green and pink stripes, and my free hand involuntarily smoothed my own dress, self-conscious of its simplicity.

"Yes. Utah speaks perfect English." She bent forward and whispered loudly, "She comes from one of the finest families in Berlin."

I colored and thought my mother would be horrified.

"Oh yes, the store on Königen Louise Strasse. Bolle!" exclaimed the lady on the sofa in the dress. She so distorted Königen it took me a moment to realize what she was saying. "Of course! What was your first name again, dear?"

"Jutta," I said, and spelled it. "But the *J* is pronounced like a *Y* in English."

"Well, we are going to have to get you a different name so that we Americans can pronounce it," interjected Mrs. Vockel quickly. "Judy. I think we should try Judy."

"But that's not her name, dear," chided Colonel Vockel.

"I know, but it's a name we can pronounce!" She laughed.

"Well surely we can all practice a little and learn to say Jutta," he objected. His pronunciation wasn't half bad, though it sounded a bit like the cactus I read about that grew in Mexico: yucca.

"Very good, Woody!" said the lady on the sofa.

My eyes traveled from the woman and her skirt to the coffee table, where my mother's lovely demitasse cups sat around the coffeepot etched in cobalt and gold. Each cup had gold trim on its handle and around the top rim, and the bottom of the cup was a different color—blue, green, or turquoise—with delicate wildflowers hand-painted above the solid color. I recognized it as one of the first offerings I had brought over when we were particularly desperate. I looked up quickly and caught Colonel Vockel's eye; his frown told me he felt uncomfortable. Mrs. Vockel had not noticed; instead, she carried on about my family for a few moments before saying, " Come, Utah, or Judy." She grinned at me. "Let's bring those lovely eggs in the kitchen and see what we have for you."

I forced a smile and told everyone it was nice to meet them. I followed Mrs. Vockel to the kitchen. I heard the Americans murmuring about what a nice and polite young lady I was. Erica's kitchen had one of those swinging doors. Mrs. Vockel held it open for me to pass through with my basket of eggs. She pulled the handle of the refrigerator door. The door stuck slightly and she had to pull it again to get it open.

"Oh, how I hate this refrigerator! I long for my Westinghouse back home!" She removed the eight brown eggs I had brought her from the basket, placing them on a dish with six other brown eggs that I had brought over several days before.

"Vestinghouse?" I asked.

"*W,* dear, not a *V.* Westinghouse," she corrected. "It's a brand, a type of refrigerator."

I remembered Erica's mother complaining about the refrigerator, and now this woman from across the Atlantic stood here doing the same. Where were Erica and her family? I wondered.

"Did you remember to ask Luise if she could come tomorrow to help serve and clean up?"

"Yes. I asked her, and she said she would be happy to, but she wants food, not *Reichsmarks.*"

"Oh good!" She filled my basket with sixteen pristine white eggs from a second plate that sat on the shelf below the brown eggs in the refrigerator. She handed me the basket.

"Thank you very much," I said politely.

"You're welcome, my dear." She shut the refrigerator. As I turned to go, she suddenly said, "Wait." I turned back around. She opened the refrigerator again. She took out a large package wrapped in white butcher paper. "I bought all of this bacon yesterday at the PX for brunch tomorrow. Why don't you take a few slices?" She held out the white paper package, spread open to reveal dozens of thick slices of bacon.

My mouth watered, but I thought of my mother. "Oh, no. I couldn't," I said, shaking my head.

"Don't be ridiculous, Utah. I have over four pounds of bacon here." My eyes widened. Was it really possible that someone in Berlin could buy that much bacon?

"Here. Take four slices. Your mother can chop it up into some scrambled eggs, or she can also put it on those potatoes she seems so fond of."

We walked back out to the living room. Mrs. Vockel never quite seemed to comprehend that we ate potatoes for the calories and because it was all we had, and not because we necessarily liked them. But I saw no point in commenting, so I followed her out silently. We passed by the living room unnoticed as the Americans chatted loudly about the latest movie they had seen, something with Cary Grant and Olivia de Haviland that was showing at the theater the Americans had requisitioned for their soldiers and their families.

———

Sunday came, and my mother used the precious fat from the bacon to flavor the potato salad for our lunch and saved the drippings to be used in a sauce on another day. Fat was a rare commodity, and her jaw dropped when I told her how much bacon Mrs. Vockel had bought for brunch the next day. Mutti always made a little extra for Sunday lunch, and today she had served a thin slice of ham to go with the potato salad. My stomach content for a change, I decided to walk into the garden and peek over at the Vockels' to catch a glimpse of their guests. I was too late. Only the cars stood out front—those massive, swollen American cars, all chrome and hoods glistening in the warm sun, the light blinding as it bounced off their bright blue, red, or orange exteriors, so unlike the few old German cars that one saw struggling down the road all boxy and black. The Nazis had confiscated all of the luxury cars in Germany, "for the war effort," they claimed. "Common thieves," my mother had called them when they took Vati's racy blue convertible BMW sports car. And she swore she saw Keitel driving it one day. The Americans had in turn confiscated the cars from the Nazis, so who knew where Vati's pride and joy had ended up?

I stepped out of the gate and immediately stepped back in. Coming down the street were two American soldiers, the same two that often stood sentry in front of the Hüttenweg headquarters when I walked by on my way to the German-American Club. In fact, they bore a striking resemblance to the same two I fell down in front of last March, when I slipped on an unanticipated patch of ice. I colored, remembering my embarrassment as I fell face-first, my purse flying into the street and the books and papers I carried catapulting into the street as well. One of them had left his post and headed my way to help me, but I leaped up, snatching my things as I did so, and hurried on, my face warm with embarrassment. I had felt their eyes burning holes into my sweater, and I was certain they had watched me walk all the way down Kronprinzenallee.

I peeked through the bushes again. Yes! I recognized the red hair of the one. It was almost orange, and his pale skin was covered with freckles. The other was very tall and skinny. They had to be the same two! Thank God they were talking and didn't notice me. I ducked back behind the bushes and ran up to the house. I rushed into the kitchen and, to my horror, seconds later they were in front of our gate, looking at our house. One of them saw me in the front window and waved. My face burned and my heart raced; what could they possibly want? Mutti had heard me come in. Entering the kitchen, she crossed over to the window to see what held my interest.

"Well, what on earth do they want?" she asked. She glanced at me and laughed. "You look like you just stepped out of a sauna, Jutta. Do you know them?"

I shook my head. "But I think they guard the American headquarters over on Hüttenweg."

I had not returned their wave, and they hesitated at the gate. I could tell they were trying to decide if they should come in or not. Then the tall one motioned with his head, urging the redhead to go in. They looked up and saw the two of us staring at them. The redhead shrugged and smiled at us. I cringed as the gate shrieked its welcome.

Mutti answered the door. I did not budge from the kitchen. I heard them talking at the door, and then I couldn't believe it when Mutti invited them in. How could she? I didn't want to talk to them! What would we talk about? I heard Mutti call me. I straightened my dress and hair, took a deep breath, and walked casually into the room.

"Jutta, this is Mr. Muller," she said, pointing to the tall one. "And this is Mr. Richter."

"Please call me Dan."

"Yes. And call me Jimmy," offered the redhead.

"*Ja,* Jimmy *und* Dan. This is my daughter, Jutta."

They both nodded together and said it was nice to meet me and held out their right hands, leaving their left hands to clutch the funny little boat hat they all wore. I noticed they did not try to pronounce my name. They seemed harmless enough with their simple, friendly smiles. They had that usual American casualness about them. They both held a can of something. Simultaneously, they handed the cans to my mother.

"Here. We brought these for you," said the tall one, Dan. He seemed to be the leader of the two, I decided.

"Well, thank you. Shall I cook them for you?"

"No. They are a present for your family."

I looked at the cans that Mutti now held. They were cans of meat—ham, I guessed, but the picture on the front looked like some sort of ground-up meat. I read "Swift's," and above that it said "Prem." The can was blue and white. I had seen the advertisements in *Life* magazine at Mrs. Vockel's house, and my mouth watered, remembering the picture of the slices spread out on a plate with tomatoes and lettuce.

"Well, you go on into the garden and make yourselves comfortable, and I will cook one of them for you."

I caught her eye, mine widening to say "No!" But she ignored me. Great! I thought. And just what does she propose I talk to these boys about?

They had not understood my mother; she had forgotten and spoken in German so, as I stared at her back heading into the kitchen, I translated for them.

"*Ja*, is good?" asked my mother as she reached the kitchen door, sensing we were all staring after her.

"Yes, ma'am. Thank you very much."

"*Du*, Jutta, take them out into the garden, and I will bring tea."

"Maybe they would like something else? A wine or something," I said in German.

My mother looked at me in horror. "They are nice, but they are still soldiers, and I don't offer soldiers, or any other strange men for that matter, alcohol in my house!"

I glanced at them quickly, nervous that they had understood, but it was clear from their blank faces they had not. They both stood smiling. They still held their hats in their hands, and the redhead twisted his nervously. I took them to the garden, and the tall one broke the silence and began to talk, asking me hundreds of questions about my life and Germany. They were really very nice, and I enjoyed the attention. It turned out they were both from Illinois, some place called Lena—northwest of Chicago, they said, as if that would help me locate the town. They said it was a small town of farmers and their families were farm families, and they claimed to be of German descent. I didn't know why any American would claim that heritage, but it was one of the strange things I would learn about Americans, they were proud of their country but also proud of their heritage. They would announce with great importance that they were Italian-American or Irish-American and now, as I found out, German-American. I had to admit they looked German. They spoke lovingly of the cornfields in Illinois that swayed in the summer breezes, and the tall one spoke of the pigs that his father tended. I asked if they feed the corn to the pigs.

They laughed. "Heck, no! We eat it. We feed garbage to the pigs. Slop."

I looked at them in surprise.

"Don't tell me you've never had corn on the cob, dripping with butter and salt?"

I shook my head and swallowed at the thought of butter.

"Well, Jimmy, we will have to bring this young lady some corn."

We chatted on about America and Germany, and then my mother came in with a tray. Jimmy leaped up to help her, grabbing the tray while Dan moved the garden table into place. She had sliced the meat into thin slices and made a brown sauce with onions to go on top. It looked delicious.

Jimmy laughed. "Ma'am, I don't believe I have ever seen simple old Prem turned into a gourmet treat."

I translated, and Mutti smiled at their compliment. And it was delicious. They came around several more times over the next few weeks, but I noticed that they came less after Vati made a point of announcing repeatedly that I was only sixteen.

19

Fritz

June 1946

He leaned against the wall next to the record player, his head moving rhythmically to the beat of the music while everybody around him laughed and danced. He was completely oblivious to their revelry, engrossed instead in the sounds of the music of Frank Sinatra. He tapped his fingers lightly against the wall behind him. I noticed him because he was tall, like an American, and because he stood apart from the rest—unconcerned about fitting in. He had crossed one long leg in front of the other as he leaned casually on the wall. I looked around and noted the stiff, upright, awkward stance of the other boys in the room as they gazed about, looking from one girl to the other, not sure who to ask to dance or who would accept them. My eyes again returned to the tall boy against the wall. I noticed the light as it bounced off his long, wavy dark brown hair; it was almost black, and it could have used a trim, I thought. He felt my gaze and looked over at me, nodding his head in greeting. I colored and quickly shifted my eyes to the other side of the room. But I couldn't help looking back, and to my horror I saw that he was coming over to me. A smile played on his lips as he approached. I turned away, desperate to find Maria or Christa or Peti, but they were all dancing.

"Hello," said a deep voice behind me.

I turned quickly and found myself staring at his chest. My eyes had to travel up quite a distance to meet his.

"Oh, hello," I said nervously, and then looked back at the dancers.

"Do you like dancing?" he asked.

"Yes," I said without looking at him.

"Well then, why aren't we?"

I turned now to look up at him and said, "Because no one has asked me."

He held his arm out in reply; I hesitated but then took it, and we walked onto the dance floor.

He was without question the worst dancer I had ever danced with—his large feet stepped on mine, he had no idea about the proper dance steps, and he held my hand up in the air so high I felt like I was being stretched. He was not the least bit embarrassed by his awkwardness. He was actually amused by it. The song finally ended, and I hurried us gratefully over to the side.

"I'm Fritz Mertel," he said before I could run off.

I took his extended hand and replied, "I'm Jutta Bolle."

"Well, thank you for the dance, Jutta Bolle. You are a very good dancer, by the way."

"Thank you."

He held up his hand. "Don't flatter me about my dancing. I know all the girls long to dance with me."

I laughed. "You're a terrible dancer!"

"I know, and you're a very honest person. But they said if you want to really learn to dance, you need to dance with Jutta Bolle." He nodded his head sagely. "She is the one to teach you."

I laughed again. "Fritz Mertel, I think you are beyond my poor abilities. You need to see Frau Sommer at the *Tanzschule Sommer*."

He pretended to be crestfallen. "So you will not teach me?"

"I will reinforce what she teaches you."

He laughed, an easy laugh that came from deep down in his chest.

"Well, will you at least listen to music, and maybe consider talking to me until I achieve ..." He paused. "What would I need in your eyes, a basic understanding of dance steps, or a good understanding?"

"A good one."

He nodded, pretending to be very serious. "It is a lofty goal for feet this big." We both looked down at his feet. "But together I think we can do it, feet! What do you say we give it a try?" He tapped his foot up and down.

"She holds classes on Tuesdays and Thursday."

"Is that when you go?"

"Yes. But I don't think we will be in the same class, Fritz Mertel!"

"Well, Jutta Bolle, I thank God for that! What makes you think I want to be in the same class?"

My cheeks grew hot and I looked away, embarrassed. Had I misread him?

He took my hand in his. "I don't want you to see me dance again until I have achieved the proper level of expertise."

I smiled at him. Everything about him was big, not just his feet. His hand engulfed mine, and his large blue eyes looked at me from under long eyelashes. His nose was large too, but it fit his face. He was very handsome in a complicated way—not in the usual pretty-boy way of a Heinz Schmidt with his small, straight nose and closely cropped blond hair.

"In the meantime, would you do me the honor of having a glass of punch on the terrace?" He said it as if he were offering me a glass of champagne. "I believe it is an interesting American variety, a pink punch of some sort."

"I'd love to," I found myself saying with a smile, and then immediately regretted my enthusiasm, not wanting him to think I was too interested. "Well, for a minute anyway, and then I need to get going," I added more nonchalantly.

We walked outside together, each holding our glass of punch, and I was horrified to see out of the corner of my eye Peti giving me a thumbs-up sign over the shoulder of some boy with whom she was dancing. I glared back at her, and she giggled.

The German-American Youth Club had a small balcony on the second floor that looked out over the green lawn of the garden. The rhododendrons were still in bloom, and the bulbs peeked out from the dark, wet soil that held them in place. It had rained while we were inside, and everything looked fresh and clean. The neighborhood had been undisturbed by the war—amazing, really, when one thought about how close it was to Kronprinzenallee. None of the homes even sported a blown-out window.

"It's beautiful, isn't it?" He breathed in the summer air.

I looked at him, astonished. He was the first boy I had met who noticed the trees and flowers. "Yes, it's amazing that everything is perfect here."

He knew what I meant. "Was your home destroyed?"

"No. Only some of the windows knocked out, and many tiles knocked off the roof. How about yours?"

"Yes. I'm afraid the entire upper floor is gone. So we all live crowded into one level, sharing space with the flour and the butter and the equipment."

I looked at him, puzzled. "Oh, my father is a baker. He owns a *Konditorei* in Lichterfelde."

"Oh!" I said, not knowing what else to say. I thought for a moment. I vaguely remembered a *Konditorei* Opa Bolle would visit on occasion. "I know where it is!" I said suddenly. "On the corner of Ring Strasse and Drake Strasse! Right?"

"Yes! Have you been there?"

"Yes. Years ago, when I spent the night at my grandfather's. He lived in Lichterfelde, and he would go there sometimes."

A light seemed to go off in Fritz's mind, and his mouth opened, but for a moment he did not speak. I was pleased that this self-assured boy also had moments of embarrassment. "Of course! Herr Bolle of the Bolles. I didn't know you were..." His voice trailed off.

"It's okay, isn't it? To be a Bolle, I mean?"

"Well yes, of course!" He looked down at the garden for a moment. "It's just I remember when Herr Bolle would come—what a fuss my mother would make over him, and the way all the customers would whisper after he had left. And now here you are with me on this balcony!" He chuckled.

"We are all the same, you know. We're all just people."

"I know, but don't tell my mother that—to her, Herr Bolle was very special."

"He was to me, too," I said quietly.

He looked at me, and the corners of his eyes spoke of kindness. "I've made you sad. I'm sorry. I meant to flatter you."

"Don't worry." I crossed my arms against the chill of the late afternoon. "I just miss him."

We fell silent again and watched the birds and the clouds overhead and the movement of the teenagers below us in the garden, some acting silly, shouting and throwing things at each other, and others talking earnestly in the shadows of the bushes. And then I began to talk. Something about this boy made me want to talk and tell him everything. I told him about *Vögelein*, and he listened. I told him about how Sasha had disappeared during a bomb raid, and he listened. I told him about living in Halberstadt with my grandparents and the last day when Vati came to get me. He listened to it all, not politely but actively, asking questions and making comments of his own.

"Did you have to fight? In the end, I mean?" I asked.

"No. Thank God I had intelligent parents! We were in Bavaria, in my father's hometown, and one of these little *Scharführers* came to the house and knocked, saying to my mother, 'I hear there are boys here from Berlin. Is this true?' And she said, 'Yes, they are my sons.' 'We need them to fight for the Führer,' he said. And my mother said, 'The Führer will have to get his cannon fodder somewhere else. My sons are only fourteen and thirteen, and they won't be fighting.'" He chuckled. "My mother is and was a force. One look from her can send the bravest soul running. The young man left, and he did not bother us again."

"You were lucky! Some of the boys from my neighborhood had to fight, and they too were only fourteen!"

"They didn't have my mother answering the door."

"She sounds like my mother!" And I told him about Vati being called up to fight.

We laughed together, both impressed with the strength of our mothers. He admired his mother, and I liked that about him.

"But it was bad for us there in that village after that, because all of the people ostracized us and talked about how it was all right for Bavarian boys to die, but the Berlin boys were too good to die." He shrugged. "My mother said, 'Let them talk. My sons won't be dead; theirs will.'" He chuckled, remembering.

"When did you come back to Berlin?"

"Last June."

"But how did you get here? I remember how hard it was just to get here from Halberstadt!"

"I walked."

"No!"

"Yes!"

"But that is over five hundred kilometers!"

"I know, and believe me, these feet know," he said, lifting one of them up for me to inspect.

"And your mother and brothers?"

"Oh, no! I came back alone. I wanted to find my father. I had to know if my father was alive. He had stayed in Berlin to run the bakery." He put his fingers up to form quotation marks. "He was an essential worker, so he stayed and sent us to Bavaria by ourselves, my mother and the rest of us. I was the oldest, and I told my mother that I would go to Berlin to see if Vati was alive. She didn't stop me. She needed to know too, I think."

"But that is amazing that you made it alive, by yourself!"

"Well, I was with a soldier. He had come through my father's village on his way to Berlin, and he agreed to take me with him. I think that is the only reason my mother let me go."

"But how old was he?"

"Oh, maybe twenty. My mother gave him a set of my clothes. I was actually already a little taller than he, but they fit well enough. We burned his uniform, and my mother gave us what food she could spare, and then we set off. We had to walk through farms and stay off of the main roads so that we would not be arrested."

"They would have put you in one of those horrible prisoner of war camps, wouldn't they?"

"Yes, especially since I didn't look fourteen. We tried to stay within the American zone, just in case we were caught, but it was hard to know what was what. We were certain once we crossed the Elbe that we were in Russian territory, and then we were extra careful. But we did get arrested by the Russians."

"Oh my God! And you lived to tell it!"

"It was actually funny, looking back at it. They arrested us and put us in a big barn; it was on a big pig farm. They asked us a few questions, and then the next day they let us go. They had exactly the same number of people arrested to take our place."

"But why?"

"Who knows? They're Russians! How can you explain Russians?"

I nodded in understanding. "But how did you eat?"

"The farmers fed us and let us stay overnight with them."

"That was nice of them."

He shrugged. "They all had sons, too. Sons that they prayed were still alive to walk home across Germany from somewhere, staying with other farmers who they hoped would feed them."

"There are good people in this world," I said, lifting my face to watch a breeze move the new green leaves of the maple tree at the bottom of the garden. The sun had come out from behind a cloud, casting new light, the last of the day, across the tops of the trees in the gardens all around us, making their color a bright pale green mixed with yellow.

Fritz nodded. "But when we crossed the Elbe, it was very difficult. All the bridges had been bombed, and we had to climb across the cement and metal pieces that jutted out over the river. And everything was bombed out—destroyed. It was impossible to look at, and after a while your mind just went numb." He shook his head and looked out over the garden, trying to mask the sadness in his face.

I said nothing, sensing that he didn't want sympathy.

He grabbed the rail of the balcony. "And then when I got to Berlin, well, what words can describe it? It was unbelievable. I had trouble finding my way home because the streets were so destroyed. Buildings were completely gone or so destroyed I did not recognize them, and the street signs were all missing. It was very strange. You think in your mind, at the bank I take a right, and then the bank is not there. So you say is that where the bank was, or was it the next corner? And then maybe you see something, the butcher shop or something, that tells you yes, that must have been where the bank was; that must be the right street, but it all looks so different, so surreal."

"I know what you mean."

"And even Lichterfelde was bombed!" He shook his head. He stood up straight. "Well, we are all together again, and it is over, and amazingly none of us died!"

"Yes. We too were very lucky."

"I can't help but think it was a combination of luck and the intelligence of our parents." He paused again and added, "My father would say that He had something to do with it, too." He pointed to the sky.

I nodded. "That's what Opa Bolle and my Omi would have said, too."

He turned toward me and bowed. "Well, Jutta Bolle, I am glad that we both made it through to meet here on this beautiful summer day. Now may I walk you home?"

"I would like that very much."

———

We had talked out there on that balcony for over an hour, and then we talked all the way home. I had never met a boy like Fritz Mertel. We talked about everything, and it seemed as if I had known him forever.

My parents loved Fritz, especially my father. He and Fritz spent long hours in Vati's library discussing all sorts of subjects: politics, philosophy, religion, history, theater, and literature—no subject was safe. Vati shared his vast collection of books with Fritz, and in him he found the kernels of an intellect as keenly curious as his own.

Mutti loved Fritz because he took me away from Heinz Schmidt. Actually, both Mutti and Vati were only too pleased that I had dumped "the riding teacher's son," as they referred to him; they never called him by his name. Heinz was one of those boys who had to be in charge. It was his way or no way. My parents had not been fond of him and his aggressive way of talking. He happened to come over the day after I met Fritz, and I simply told him I did not want to see him anymore. His surprise turned into anger, and my mother had to come into the living room to tell him she thought it was time for him to leave. Thankfully he did not argue, and that was the last I saw of him.

How could I possibly have gone out with him? I was appalled that I had been even vaguely interested in him. He was handsome in that "perfect German" sort of way the Nazis loved: blue eyes and blond hair and a perfectly straight nose (a distinct contrast to my own), but as I got to know him better, he became less and less attractive. I found that's how it was with people who are attractive on the outside but have ugly personalities. I was angry with myself for not reading him better early on.

I watched Fritz listening to my father, leaning forward intently, his sensitive face creased with thought. I tried to imagine Fritz in the Hitler Youth. I knew he had to participate; everyone did. I could easily imagine Heinz marching around in his Hitler Youth uniform with a zeal unmatched by his comrades. A little power under his belt, and he would happily lord it over the younger boys. But Fritz? I could not see him in that uniform. How had he survived? How awful it must have been for him! My mind flashed back to Halberstadt and the three boys leaning against the building, waiting for me. All of them dead now. Of this I was certain.

———

Fritz was a few months younger than I, a fact that embarrassed me, but only slightly. I had always been proud of the fact that the boys who were interested in me were a bit older. The reality, though, was that with so many of them dead between the ages of sixteen and thirty, older boys were a rare commodity snatched up by women sometimes ten or more years older. Frau Sommer, the dance teacher, certainly had no reluctance about going after a younger boy. I colored remembering how I had stood there alone, the only one on the dance floor without a partner, watching the others awkwardly. It was the end-of-the-season ball, and I had arrived with Freddy Decker, my partner for the semester. Freddy and I were just friends, but we had always planned to go to the dance together. Both of us were very good dancers, and we were expected to win the grand prize for dance because of our intricate footwork and graceful movement—at least that is what Frau Sommer always said when she watched us dance. The dance school ball was a big event for us, and Mutti had a special dress made for me out of her navy blue bathrobe. It had a huge white circle on the front that Frau Schultz had expertly cut in half and sewed in such a way that half of the circle was in front and the other half in back, but on the opposite side of the dress. I thought it was quite modern and chic-looking, and I bubbled with excitement when Freddy picked me up and we walked in the warm June sun down to the old mansion on the corner of Kronprinzenallee and Schützallee, where we had been attending dance classes since February. She must have been planning her move for some time. I didn't even have a moment to think. The instant we walked in, she swept down on us. Grabbing Freddy by the arm, she said, "Freddy, why don't you and I start the dancing, and then everybody can fall in."

That was the last time Freddy was anywhere near me. I just stood there sipping punch and watching everybody else dance. Frau Sommer laughed at something Freddy said, throwing her head back as they spun around the dance floor. Her dress swirled around her legs as she placed her feet in the intricate patterns of the dance with a pizzazz that the other dance couples lacked. Freddy was a good dancer too, and they danced with surprising intensity. It vaguely occurred to me that Frau Sommer had other plans for Freddy. Every once in a while, Freddy looked my way and raised the hand that held her back as if to say sorry. I don't know why I just stood there! Why didn't I leave and walk home? I guess I thought they would stop, and then I would have my turn, but they never did. Peti and Maria kept looking over at me, concern writ large across their faces. I wanted to melt into the pale white stuccoed walls. Instead I just stood there, frozen in mortification, a smile glued to my face.

Mutti was furious. "A woman nearly thirty going after a sixteen-year-old boy! Ridiculous! What a fool!"

Vati's, "Lucky Freddy," said under his breath, did not amuse Mutti. But Vati said that the woman's behavior was so outrageous that you could only make a joke about it.

Vati's voice brought me back to the pleasant scene in our living room. I smiled. What Fritz lacked in age, he made up for in maturity. He had a wisdom about him that transcended age. As I got to know him better, I realized he understood instinctively that happiness is internal.

He came for dinner often, and he always brought a much-welcomed box of cakes or a loaf of bread from his father's bakery. We would take walks in the park after dinner in the late summer evening light and talk, sitting on the little bench that looked out over our small lake, with the ducks dodging in and out of the cattails looking for their babies. I would tell him stories about my life, about Freddy and Heinz, and he would listen as if they were the most interesting things he had ever heard. And so we spent the summer of 1946, Fritz and I, learning about each other's past and desires for the future. We became close friends.

He stared at the etching on the narrow strip of wall between the door and the window in Vati's study, turning slightly as I entered.

"This is amazing!" he said, pointing to the etching.

"You like it?"

"It's fantastic!"

"I think Vati found it in a gallery on the Kudam, back before the war."

Fritz put his arm around my shoulder and pulled me close, and we studied the etching together. I was so used to it. Sometimes it took a fresh pair of eyes to show you the things in your own house, I reflected. The etching, an elaborate maze with a cross in the center, had always puzzled me.

"Do you think it means how complicated it is to find our way to God? Or do you think it means how we complicate the journey by taking irrelevant twists and turns when really the path is quite simple?"

"Both," he answered.

20

Always the Eyes

His eyes, always it was those eyes, staring at me, following me from their sunken sockets. In his right hand he clutched his tattered piece of cloth, and with his left he grabbed the barbed wire fence, the barbs not seeming to bother his tiny, bony hand. His filthy fingers pressed tight around the metal prongs. His shaved head looked huge on the tiny neck and shoulders, their blades jutting out to the heavens. His mother stood behind him and mouthed the word "please" at me. I covered my face with my hands, but when I took my hands away they were still there: the boy, his eyes, and the mother.

"Hurry, Heinz. Can't you hurry?"

"We'll be to Berchtesgaden soon enough, Jutta. What's your hurry?" answered Vati from the passenger seat of the Daimler.

"Can't you see them? Can't you see their faces?"

But Vati did not respond. He was gone, and only Heinz was there, driving the car. And still they came as the car passed by the ugly, twisted metal fence, hundreds of them in gray-and-black-striped pajamas. To the fence they came, and always with the boy and his mother in the front.

"Hurry. I can't take it," I shouted at Heinz. He turned, his chauffeur's hat turning my way slowly, like the lid of a jar. I looked at the icy blue eyes under the brim, and Gudren's father stared at me from the front seat.

"No!" I screamed at him. He laughed, a horrible, cackling laugh.

I grabbed the door handle to jump out, but it was locked. Still the icy blue eyes held my gaze, his head turned completely around, like a doll's. I screamed again, turning to the window, and now the boy's face was pressed on the window, his hollow eyes begging me, beseeching me. I screamed again and woke with a start. Panting, I sat up and tried to catch my breath as my mother ran in the room, her pale nightgown billowing behind her like the sail of a ship.

"Jutta, what is it?"

I looked at her, not recognizing her at first.

"I heard you scream. What is it?" she asked again.

"I can't get those pictures out of my mind. Their faces! Mutti, you should have seen their faces! They look out at you from bones covered with a thin layer of skin. And one was a little boy's, maybe nine or ten, and his mother, and they stood naked, all clinging to each other before the guards..." I bit my lip. I couldn't continue.

My mother said nothing. She only hugged me to her.

"Did we know?"

"No."

She held me, rocking me as if I were a baby.

"But we must have known!"

She did not answer at first, and then after a minute she said, "The last year we heard rumors, but it is a crime…" She stopped, searching for words. "It is a crime so large it is hard to believe such rumors. I am sure some knew. Of course the ones ordering it and the ones carrying it out, and they, I am sure, talked to someone." She stood up before continuing and walked to the window to look up at the star-filled night. "We knew they were taking trains full of Jews to the East to work in camps. The official line was that they were a war threat, that they might form resistance groups from within. That act alone was a big enough crime, but this? What sort of human being can do this? And so it never occurred to us."

"The Americans sent the Japanese to camps, too. I read about it in one of Mrs. Vockel's magazines. *Life,* I think."

"Really? A lot, or just those they suspected of collaboration?" She asked still facing the window.

" All of them, I think. All of the Japanese that lived on the west coast of America were sent."

"I didn't know." She was silent for a moment. "I am surprised. But they did not harm them? Physically, I mean?"

"No."

"They did not kill them." It was a statement, not a question.

I nodded my head in agreement, even though she still had her back to me. "What must the Americans and the rest of the world think of us?"

As she turned and came back to my bed, she shook her head slowly. "They will hate us. For many generations to come, they will hate Germany. They will blame all of us for the crimes of these animals, especially those who don't know us, who have never lived among us."

"But if you didn't know, and most people didn't know?" I prompted.

"Maybe we should have known. Maybe we should have asked more questions."

"Fritz says he knew. He saw the trains heading east when he was at the dormitory in Pomerania, and they knew."

"How could they know?"

"I don't know, but he says they knew."

"Just from the trains going by?"

"He says his uncle told his parents about it."

She turned to face me for the first time. "Really? How did his uncle know?"

"Because he is a doctor, and he attended a conference where other doctors spoke about the experiments that the Nazi doctors were performing on the Jews at the camps."

"No! You mean they had a conference about it?"

"No, no! The doctors spoke privately about it. You know, quietly to each other. They had heard from other doctors that this was going on. Like that. Not that they themselves had performed the experiments."

"Oh, I see. And I am sure some believed it and some didn't."

I shrugged.

"For me it is like reading a story about a mother who has killed her own child. I find I can't believe it. I always think they must have that wrong— there must be a mistake; something else happened to the child. Because it is so incomprehensible to me that a mother could do that." She looked up to the ceiling to stop the tears that rimmed her eyes from spilling. "And then I think the mother must have been crazy. One of these delusional people who saw the devil instead of her own child in front of her, and that is how I think of these men. They must have been crazy, delusional, to kill the way they did, to so separate their own humanity and just kill like it was a job at a factory. I just can't..." She stopped and looked down at her feet, encased in her night slippers.

I reached out and grabbed her hand. "Mutti, you didn't know." I was comforting her now.

Her face was grave, and it bore the weight of Germany's crime on it in the turn of her mouth and eyes. She sighed. "I only hope that God will forgive those good Germans who had nothing to do with it."

"He will," I said firmly.

"I thank God my parents and Opa Bolle did not live to see this. To see Germany stripped naked, and this depravity exposed to the world." She turned to the window again, to the dark of the night, and she whispered so that I barely heard her. "It will be many generations before Germans can hold up their heads again and say proudly, 'I am German.'"

I said nothing. I knew she was right.

She turned to me and held my gaze. Her eyes spoke of her pain. "What a legacy to leave one's children and grandchildren."

"It wasn't you and Vati, or even most of the people we know." I thought for a moment. "It was people like Gudrun's father."

She stood up suddenly, the folds of her pale silk nightgown falling to the floor gracefully. "And now we will not speak of this again. It is the sort of thing that we must push down." She took the palm of her hand, her fingers splayed, and motioned down, toward the bottom of her stomach.

I nodded.

She bent to kiss me, pulling the blanket up as I fell back into my bed. Her lips brushed my forehead, and then she was gone. I couldn't fall back to sleep.

Mutti's words haunted me until the early hours of the day, when I finally fell asleep. I was so exhausted I slept until ten the next morning.

I never spoke of it again. I learned, as did every child of my generation, not to talk about the Jews or the war or Adolph Hitler or the Nazis. These were topics that one didn't bring up, and if children were so ignorant as to violate that unspoken ban, the answers were curt and chilly, and they quickly learned.

21

August to September 1946

I hated the squeak of the wheels of the *Bollerwagen* with its wood side slats and red metal underside. My mother insisted we drag it behind us everywhere we went, hoping to fill it with scraps of wood or a piece of meat the butcher had by special arrangement set aside for her.

Often we would run into neighbors or acquaintances on the way to the store and they would say, "I see, Frau Bolle, you have the *Bollerwagen* out again. Lucky for you. I hope you find enough to fill it." I looked away, embarrassed, only to be chastised after we had walked on for being unfriendly.

We would go to the back door of an establishment, usually midafternoon, and knock on the door. My mother carried a bag—filled with what, I did not know. She never opened it in front of me. It had snaps across the top so that I could not look in, but I knew it could only contain coffee or cigarettes. Nothing else would have bought us the meat the butcher handed to her, wrapped in newspaper and tied off with bits of string that had been knotted together to form a long enough piece to wrap around the package.

Mutti walked ahead of me, and I pulled the cart over the flagstones of our walk, sometimes having to jerk it to prevent it from sticking on the bits of grass that jutted out between the flagstones. It was a Friday afternoon, warm and humid, one of those days Mrs. Vockel referred to as "close." Fritz was coming to pick me up later that evening to go to the movies, a Fred Astaire dance number, he said. All I wanted to do was sit in the sun with my book and get a little color, but instead here I was pulling this ugly wagon to butcher shops.

She held the gate for me. As I passed through with the wagon, to my horror I heard her say, "Good afternoon, Frau Vockel."

"Oh, Frau Bolle. How nice to see you." And then, seeing me come through with the wagon, "And Utah. Hello, dear."

"Hello, Mrs. Vockel," I said, coloring as I saw her glance down at the wagon. She had been talking to another American lady. I noted the lady's elegant shoes and hat and felt ashamed about our appearance. The summer dress that Frau Schultz had so miraculously cut out of one of my mother's old dresses scratched at my skin as my body grew hot with embarrassment.

"This is Mrs. Denton, a friend of mine, who has just come out from Washington DC to live with her husband over on Gelfert Strasse."

"I'm very pleased to meet you," said my mother, smiling at the woman.

Mrs. Denton returned the greeting in that slow way that I now recognized as the way Americans from the southern part of the United States spoke.

"I'm trying to show her the ropes here," said Mrs. Vockel, laughing. I did not understand what Mrs. Vockel meant, and I'm sure Mutti didn't either. We all stood there smiling at each other for a moment, not sure what else to say.

"Listen," said Mrs. Vockel, turning to me. "Mrs. Denton and I were just commenting on how nobody seems to have fixed the windows around here! It just drives us crazy, especially at the stores—they are all boarded up except for that little tiny square they cut out so you can see they are open. Surely you people aren't still afraid of the bombs, are you? I mean, I know there was no point in it before, but why don't you fix them now?"

My mother's smile had frozen on her face, and her face held that blank expression that meant she was really angry. In German, she said out of the corner of her mouth, "Tell this woman that there is no glass to be found in all of Germany, and any glass that comes from outside of Germany is pounced on by the Americans like a pack of hungry wolves to fix their own houses! Houses they stole from us."

I looked from my mother's icy smile to the genuine smile of Mrs. Vockel, whose head was cocked to the side trying to comprehend what my mother had said, and I tried to soften the message as best I could.

"Well," I stammered, "it is because there is no glass to be found in all of Germany."

"Oh, don't be silly! The Americans find glass all the time to fix the windows."

"Exactly!" said my mother, the smile still frozen to her face. "And now if you will excuse us, we have to go and find food, a thing we find more important at the moment than windows. Good day, ladies."

Before Mrs. Vockel could say anything else, my mother turned abruptly and walked hurriedly ahead. Mrs. Vockel looked confused, and her smile faded to a vague upturn of her bright red lips as she watched the back of my mother disappearing down the Föhrenweg. I nodded to Mrs. Denton and Mrs. Vockel and ran to catch up with Mutti, the wagon clattering over the cobblestones noisily behind me.

"Well, bye," called Mrs. Vockel.

"Nice to meet you both," called Mrs. Denton.

My mother did not hear. She was halfway to Auf dem Grat already, but I turned and waved quickly as I ran. I saw the two ladies turn toward each other to continue their conversation.

I reflected on a person who had lived here for five months but still was so ignorant that she did not understand how desperate we were for food and other essentials, and that we had no time or money to worry about luxuries like windows. She wasn't a bad person. She was simply a person incapable of dwelling outside her limited world, the world of the American officer's wife with its dinner parties and social club events. But when I expressed these views to my mother, she rebuffed me.

"I don't want to talk about Mrs. Vockel and her views."

So we never discussed her; another subject off-limits.

Fritz opened the gate for me, laughing at me as I danced my way up the walk, trying to make my skirt twirl like the beautiful woman in the movie. My poor dress, the one Mutti had made for me from one of her curtains, would not cooperate; it twirled, but only momentarily. The fabric was too heavy, nothing like those magnificent spins with folds and folds of chiffon floating through the air as they danced their way through the garden in the movie.

"Fritz, we have to try that move they did!" I said, grabbing his hand and forcing him to dance me the rest of the way up to the house. I led because Fritz's dancing still left a lot to be desired. He tried, he really did, but he wasn't going to replace Fred Astaire any time soon. He gave up on his serious attempt and grabbed me jokingly, exaggerating Fred Astaire's moves and almost sending us flying into the wisteria by Mutti's kitchen window. As it was, we knocked the little garden elf Gustav had given her off the rock he sat on and sent him flying into the flower bed.

"Oh my God! Stop!"

We both collapsed laughing on the steps.

The door flew open and Mutti looked down at us, eyebrows raised.

"What is going on? *Um Himmels willen*, they could hear you down at Army Headquarters with all this racket!" But she was smiling. She held her book, and her reading glasses were perched on the end of her nose.

Fritz leaped up and bowed slightly. "Good evening, Frau Bolle. I'm sorry if we woke you."

"Oh, heavens no. You didn't wake me. I was just reading. Now, Herr Bolle…" She looked up to the bedroom window. "You might well have woken him! And that is like facing a bear!"

I laughed. "Mutti! You should have seen it! They danced through gardens; they danced through kitchens and living rooms! Everywhere!"

"Well, come in you two! Dance your way into the house. It's chilly out here." She pulled her thin sweater tightly around her chest.

"Come, let's go in the kitchen."

"Fritz, would you like some tea?" asked Mutti.

I knew Fritz hated Mutti's homemade mint and chamomile tea. "Actually, Mutti, I was wondering if we could have a little glass of something?" I smiled at her innocently. "Maybe a wine or a port?"

"Oh! Yes, of course!" She closed the kitchen cabinet quickly and hurried into the living room. We followed her single file. "You know, I forget you two are young adults! I still think of Jutta as my baby that I have to put to sleep with tea, Fritz!"

Fritz smiled. He helped her open the bottle of white wine.

"Mutti, they were dripping in yards and yards of silk and chiffon and furs! And I can't believe that houses really exist like those, with all the beautiful furniture and these staircases that wrap around and around!"

"*Ja*, but Jutta! It's a movie!" objected Fritz. "I don't think most people in America live like that!"

"Well, *prost*!" said Mutti, handing us each a glass of wine. "To the day we will have yards of fabric again so my daughter will be happy and design the most beautiful evening gown in all of Germany!"

"I don't think that day will ever come!" I shook my head sadly.

"Oh, don't be silly. Of course it will." Mutti dismissed me with a wave of her hand. "Now tell me about the rest of the film. Besides yards of fabric, what did you like? Maybe I should ask Fritz?"

"The music was wonderful. It was by Gershwin, the American composer." Fritz began to sing:

They may take you from me.
I'll miss your fond caress.
But though they take you from me,
I'll still possess,
The way you wear your hat.
The way you sip your tea.
The memory of all that oh, no.
They can't take that away from me.

He stopped suddenly, watched me closely, and sipped his wine. And then he shifted his gaze to Mutti again. "And the cinematography? Fantastic!" He continued turning his body to face her. "The camera angles were very interesting—shooting from the floor and sometimes the ceiling!"

"Who would notice a thing like that except for you?" I said, rolling my eyes. Fritz wanted to be a movie director, and he was always talking about camera angles. He would shape his thumb and forefinger to form a camera and then say, "Imagine if you could just take a picture of this rose and you could edit out all the rest"—referring to the soot-encrusted rubble that lay all around the rose bush, the sole survivor of many bomb raids around the Roseneck. "Look, Jutta. Isn't it magnificent what you can do with a camera? You can tell the truth, but you can also lie!"

He was right. You could use the camera to show what you wanted people to see.

"But I know this movie!" exclaimed Mutti. "This is from the thirties, I think. *Shall We Dance*? Right? They must be showing you old movies at that little theater!"

"I don't care! It was just gorgeous! The whole movie was gorgeous, and they danced so beautifully and the dresses were so wonderful, and the houses! Oh my God!" I said dreamily.

Mutti and Fritz looked at each other and laughed over my enthusiasm. We talked for a few more minutes, and then Mutti went upstairs, leaving us to ourselves. Fritz did not stay long. The streetcars would stop running soon, and he had to make it home before the curfew. We kissed good night on the steps and made plans to see each other the next day. He turned and waved from the front gate and I waved back, twirling dramatically, trying to get my skirt to co-operate. He laughed, and then he was gone, disappearing down the darkness of the Föhrenweg. I heard his footsteps echoing in the night. I stood on the step, engulfed in the silence of the night.

I shut the door and leaned against it for a moment, imagining that our brick staircase with its wrought iron rail was that opulent mahogany rail that curved into infinity, and that Fred Astaire waited there at the bottom to dance me step by step to my room. An owl hooted its melancholy song from high up in the acacia tree, and I shivered. I ran upstairs to go to bed.

Cornmeal and Chickens

Fall 1946

These hunger pains come often. I rarely notice them. It's like when your hair grows too long but you don't notice it until one day you suddenly realize your hair is much too long. My stomach turned a somersault. These will be hard to ignore today, I thought. I don't want to let Mutti know, or she will give me extra from her plate, and she is already too thin. She is so thin that her clothes hang from her and her face is hollow, making her delicate nose and lips seem even more so. I can't stand seeing her like this, and it frustrates me that she gives so much food away. I know it frustrates Vati too, but he says nothing. It would do no good to say anything; she still would give it away, and Vati and I would just appear greedy in her eyes, so we say nothing. But she gives too much away—food boxes for Frau Schultz and for Frau Seeman, the piano teacher, even though I haven't taken lessons in years, and, as always, Luise and Gustav. Sometimes I wonder if there will be enough left for us. She always tells me, "There will always be plenty for those who share." And then I feel guilty for asking the question, so I don't anymore.

I might need to visit Mrs. Vockel today. Sometimes when I visit her, she gives me a treat. She bakes well and often. One time she sent me home with a piece of sweet cake cut into squares made from cornmeal. Mutti smelled it curiously. It was still warm. Mrs. Vockel had just taken it out of the oven.

"She said you eat it hot, with butter," I said. "She called it corn bread."

"Corn bread? But it's like a cake!" She took a bite, cupping her hand under her chin to keep the cake from crumbling all over the floor. "Good heavens! It falls apart!"

"She said they make it in the South out of cornmeal." I fished into my pocket and brought out a piece of paper with Mrs. Vockel's looped handwriting. "I brought the recipe so we can try it."

"Oh! I just went to the store, and the Americans have sent cornmeal again!" She walked to the cabinet and opened it to show me a two-pound bag of cornmeal. "I worried you and Vati might be sick of my polenta!"

"I love your polenta, Mutti. But this is good, too." Mutti's polenta was delicious served with fresh tomatoes and herbs from her garden. We were lucky my mother loved Italian food and had remembered so many dishes from her trips to Italy. Most Germans had no idea how to use cornmeal, except to feed it to the chickens.

"Well anyway, I thought we could try it, or I will give the recipe to Christa for her mother. She said her mother doesn't know what to do with the cornmeal, so she just makes this awful mush."

Mutti made a face. "*Ach*. No!" She took the recipe from my hand, holding it at arm's length to read. "Let's try it, but write down the recipe for poor Christa!"

I nodded. "Mrs. Vockel says that we will be getting a lot more cornmeal."

Mutti shrugged. "It's better than nothing."

She grabbed her bag of cornmeal. "And now let us try to make this South American thing!"

"Not South American, Mutti! That means *Sud* America. This is southern American cooking, Mutti. You know, from the South, as in *Gone with the Wind*."

"Well, you knew what I meant! Now go get me some eggs and stop correcting my English!"

I laughed and headed for the stairs to the basement.

———

"But that is simply ridiculous!" scoffed my father.

They were in the kitchen, my mother leaning against the sink, her arms crossed in front of her.

"I don't care what you think. I can't eat them. Period!" She shook her head and looked at the floor, pushing a crumb around with the tip of her shoe. "I just can't!"

"But you must, Heti," pleaded my father. "You need the protein."

"What's going on?" I asked as I emerged from the shadows of the doorway.

My father looked at me and then at my mother. He raised his hands in frustration and strode past me and out the kitchen door. "You tell her. It is just too ridiculous."

She turned to stir the soup she had been making for lunch. It was Saturday, and my father was home for lunch.

I walked over and stood next to her at the stove.

"What is it, Mutti?"

She stopped stirring and looked at me. A smile played around the corners of her lips. "Oh, nothing. Your father is upset because I won't eat the chickens Gustav butchered this morning."

"Oh. I see." And I could see. She had raised those chickens from birth, naming them and calling to them each day. It would be like me eating *Vögelein*.

My father burst back into the kitchen, startling us. His voice caused us both to turn around and face him simultaneously. "Well, then you get all of the other meats. Ham, or whatever I can find. We will eat the chickens and you eat the other meats."

"We'll see," said my mother simply.

"No. We will not see. That is the deal! If you don't want the chicken, then you eat the other stuff."

"It depends on how much other stuff you find." She held up two fingers on each hand to form quotation marks. "And I need a point of clarification. Do you mean I eat the equivalent amount?"

My father paused for a moment. He let out a breath. "Yes. Fine!"

"Then you have a deal!" she said.

"You realize what an impossible woman you are, don't you?" But he was smiling.

"Yes, I do!" she said, winking at me as she turned back to her pot.

He threw his hands in the air as he turned to retreat to his study. "Why didn't you go to law school instead of me?"

Mutti smiled and winked again.

———

Vati brought a salami home on Monday. Mutti and I were sitting in the music room chatting about Maria and Carola, both of whom now had American soldier friends. Most of the soldiers were between the ages of twenty and twenty-three, I explained to Mutti, so it was not so terrible that they were interested in sixteen-year-old girls. My mother remained unconvinced. Just in time to save me from the "they will ask for favors and then leave you to deal with the leftovers" lecture, I heard the truck pull up, its gears grinding to make the tight turn into the driveway. I ran to the window and knelt on the windowsill. Vati emerged from the black monster, reached back in, and hoisted something long and narrow onto his shoulders—it was a two-foot-long salami! He slammed the car door shut with his free hand, bent to pick up the briefcase he had set down moments before, and walked toward the house. Heinz backed the ungainly black truck carefully out of the driveway, scraping the sides on the rhododendrons and junipers that ran the length of the driveway.

"Mutti! He has a salami!" I called excitedly as I pushed myself up off my knees and ran to the front door.

"He has a what?" asked my mother, startled.

"A salami!" I called back over my shoulder.

I met him halfway down the path.

He grinned at me. "My God! I can't even get in the house to surprise you before you accost me in the driveway."

"Vati! Where did you get..."

"Shhh." He jerked his head toward the house.

"Sorry," I whispered, putting my hand over my mouth.

My mother stood at the door waiting for us.

"Hans Bolle! What have you been up to?"

"Foraging food for my family!" he answered, joking.

"But where did you get it?"

"Now, Jutta, it doesn't matter where I got it. *Das geht dich nichts an!* You just need to enjoy it."

He set down his briefcase in the hall closet and lifted the salami off his shoulder, handing it to my mother as if it were a bouquet of red roses. "For you, the lady of the house who will not eat perfectly good, fat chickens." He shrugged. "So I must instead go out and forage in the streets for you, my lovely lady."

My mother laughed. It was good to hear them laugh and joke, and I let the thought slip through my mind that maybe things would come out all right one day.

Mutti took the salami to the kitchen, Vati and I at her heels.

"What is that delicious smell?" he asked.

"It is called *zuppe di pane!*" she said. "The humblest of Italian soups. Bread, chicken broth, and tomatoes and onions."

"So, basically, bread soup?" I said doubtfully.

"No! It is *zuppe di pane,*" she responded. "Say it. *Zuppe di pane.*"

I did not want to eat soggy bread steeped with tomatoes and onions no matter what she called it. But I went along with her, knowing that it made her feel better to serve us *zuppe di pane* rather than bread soaked in broth.

I didn't quite get how she could eat the chicken broth but not the chicken meat, but I did not point this inconsistency out to her. Instead I said, "But now we have some salami to go with it."

Whatever we had, no matter how little, my mother managed to make everything taste wonderful. She would take our bread, toast it, and sprinkle tomatoes and dill from her garden on it, and a tiny amount of bacon fat, when she had it, and call it *Bruchetta ala Mutti.* So while my friends ate plain bread or, at best, perhaps French toast when their mothers could find the eggs, we ate Italian-style bruchettas and soups. Vati said Mutti was one of the truly great chefs in Germany. "A great chef can make something out of nothing."

Jürgen Returns

September 1946

I love Sundays, even though Fritz can't come for midday dinner. His mother and father insist that he spend Sunday dinner with his family, preceded by a church service that lasts "interminably," Fritz complains. But he would come later for a walk or a drink. So I am alone, with only Mutti and Vati for conversation this late-summer afternoon, the sun streaming through the window in great wide bands of light, reflecting off the shine of the flagstone floors, causing rainbows to catch the glass of the front windows. I sink into Mutti's beige and pink chair, its cushions embracing me, my right hand holding Fitzgerald's *The Great Gatsby*, my index finger marking the page where I left off. I listen to the Berlin Philharmonic play "Beethoven's Overture to Egmont." The music is loud and rich and deep, and the sound climbs into my ears and I reflect on how music is the only art form that truly enters your body. The sound travels into your ears, echoing around, sending signals of pleasure through to the brain. The birds sing companionably to each other in the garden, their shrill sounds muffled by the rich texture of the music. I have just begun this book that I had longed to read for many years. *"Whenever you feel like criticizing anyone," he told me, "just remember that all the people in this world haven't had the advantages that you've had."*

I look up, frowning. It's barely audible, but still I think I hear a tapping sound. And then again. I strain to hear it above the music, cocking my ear toward the door, and then again. The knock on the door startles me this time. I look at my watch; it is only one o'clock in the afternoon. I clutch my book, my index finger still marking my place, and run to answer the door, secretly hoping that Fritz somehow has escaped and come to visit early. But it is not Fritz.

I don't recognize him at first. He stands, staring at me from eyes that seem to have receded into his skull. He tries to speak. His lips move, but the words do not come out, and then tears form at the corners of his eyes and begin to spill over as his mouth continues to try to work. Without thinking, I cover my nose and mouth with my hand to avoid his smell. A reaction. His clothes hang on him in sheets and are tattered and filthy; a large hole in his gray shirt exposes his shoulder—a shoulder that is all bone. I look down and see that he has used a rope to tie his pants on in place of a belt, and the leather of his shoes has separated from the soles.

I don't hear Mutti come up behind me. Her gasp startles me. "Jürgen. Oh my God, it is Jürgen. Jutta, let him in for God's sake!" She grabs him by the elbow and guides him into the entryway, the tears now staining his shirt and his mouth still moving in his gaunt face, no sound coming out.

"Hans. Come quick! It's Jürgen!"

My father comes from his study and stops dead in his tracks.

"My God, what have they done with you, boy?" He stares for a moment, not comprehending that this skeleton in front of us is really Jürgen Koch, the boy who lived across the street, the boy who used to play with me on my swing set, the boy I had hated in the way that children do, because he spied on me and threw hard red berries at me from behind the hedge. Vati grabs Jürgen from my mother; he looks so fragile it is as if they think he will fall over if one of them does not hold on to him. Vati seats him in the living room before hurrying to get him schnapps.

He accepts the clear liquid from my father with shaking hands. I notice how large his joints seem, his knuckles and wrists huge. It takes me a moment to realize that they only appear huge because he has no flesh on his bones to balance them out. I look away as he struggles to maneuver the glass to his lips, hands still shaking. He spills half of it on his shirt to join the tear stains that already have formed a pattern on the torn, filthy fabric. We sit waiting for the schnapps to take effect.

Finally he speaks. "I'm so sorry," he begins, but my father waves his hand to silence him.

"Don't be ridiculous. Nothing to be sorry about. Now you just take your time."

He looks at me and then at his hands. "It was just seeing your house still here, and then seeing Jutta standing there just like before..." His voice trails off. That he remembers my name and recognizes who I am makes me feel small and guilty. I could have passed him on the street without stopping, never realizing this was the boy I grew up with. "I just... It overwhelmed me."

"Of course it did," says my mother.

"I came to find my parents, and they are not here anymore," he says simply. He turns to my mother. "Frau Bolle, do you know where they are?" And then, before she can speak, "They are alive? Please tell me my mother is alive?"

"Yes! Yes!" she says quickly. "Your mother is alive. They are all alive."

"Oh, thank you, God!" He says it to the ceiling, as if we are not in the room, and suddenly I feel uncomfortable, as if I shouldn't be here, intruding on his privacy. My mother lets him pray for a moment, saying nothing. Frau Koch had given her a letter for her only son, her "Jürgenlein."

He finishes his prayer and looks at my mother again. "Do you know where they have gone?"

She nods her head. "Yes. They left for Frankfurt before the Russians came."

"Frankfurt am Oder?"

"No. No. Frankfurt in the West."

He relaxes immediately. "Then they are all safe? My father?"

"Yes. They are all safe, and your mother left me a letter for you telling you where they went. To her sister's, I think she said." Mutti gets up and goes to her writing room to find the letter.

"Tante Anna," he mutters to himself.

She comes back and hands him the letter. To my surprise, he puts it inside his shirt, tucked into the rope of his pants. We sit in silence for a moment, none of us sure what to say next.

"Jürgen, would you like to stay for dinner?"

"Thank you, Herr Bolle," he says gratefully. "But I am so dirty. I can't sit at the table with your family."

"Come upstairs with me and we will fix you a hot bath."

Jürgen looks at Vati and nods his head, the tears in danger of falling again.

"Or if you need to spend the night and rest up before you set off, you're welcome," adds my mother.

"No. Thank you. I have come so far, and I want to find my family."

Mutti nods. "But you must stay for dinner. I cannot let you go on without eating. I could never face your mother again."

He smiles and nods his consent. He needs to eat! It seems to me he needs to stay for a whole month of dinners before he presents himself to his mother or he will worry the poor woman to death.

When I walk into the dining room to set the table I see a new man, washed and scrubbed, his hair too long but combed back with some of Vati's pomade on it. I recognize the smell. He has shaved and splashed on Vati's 4711—its clean, fresh citrus fragrance greets my nostrils. I notice that Vati has given him a new shirt and one of his belts. He looks almost respectable, and I think it is good his mother will not receive the same shock as I. Vati has a map of Germany laid out on the table and they are studying it intently, heads bent to read the small print.

"When you cross the Elbe, it won't be far until the American Zone. The American Zone starts in Helmstedt."

"The autobahn to Magdeburg is all right, isn't it?"

"Well, yes. You could get stopped by the Russians. They patrol it, but they seem to be letting people travel. The best is the train. They check your papers when you get on, but then they leave you alone. They do not stop the trains. The only problem is you may need to change trains."

My father looked at Jürgen for a moment. The young man kept his head bent over the map, studying it. Vati folded it up suddenly. Jürgen looked up, surprised, but said nothing.

"We will buy you a train ticket," said my father, as if there was nothing further to discuss.

"No. Herr Bolle, I could not accept that. A train ticket costs too ..."

Again Vati waved his hand to silence the boy. "You have walked across half of Germany already. You do not need to walk across the other half!"

"But I couldn't ..."

"I will take you to the train station after we eat, and you can probably be in Frankfurt in the morning if the night train is running."

Jürgen's eyes lit up, and I saw that he would give up his objections, both because there was no point—Vati would buy him a train ticket whether he wanted it or not—and because the thought of seeing his family the next day was too tempting.

"Thank you, sir," he said quietly as he fingered the silverware I had set out for dinner.

Mutti stood over her pot of potato dumplings, the steam rising all about her. She looked over her shoulder as the door banged closed.

"Jutta, hand me the sieve, please."

I brought it to her. "Vati is buying Jürgen a train ticket," I whispered to her over the boiling sound of the pot.

She stopped stirring for a moment and looked at me and smiled. "That is good. He is so thin, and if he walks much more, no matter how much food I give him, he will arrive thinner than he is already!" She shook her head. "His poor mother, to see her boy like this!"

"I know! Do you think they starved him?"

"Almost. Not quite, and they probably fattened him up before they let him go."

"I hate the Russians! They are horrible, just horrible."

"Well, let's not talk about it. He is lucky they let him go, you know. They still have hundreds of thousands of German soldiers that they are using for labor and refusing to let go." She stirred the pot again, letting the steam hit her face. "I think because he is so young, they let him go."

I nodded.

She moved to the side to check on her plum sauce. It was beginning to thicken.

"It smells delicious, Mutti."

"Thank you. Here, Jutta, stand in front of the dumplings. The steam is good for your skin."

I laughed.

"It is. Really!" she said.

Mutti was always worried about her skin and mine. She even burned the inside of her nose once because she held her face too long over a pot of boiling water to "purify her pores." I could only take its warmth for a moment before I had to pull away.

"Are we not having any meat?" I asked.

"He shouldn't eat meat."

"Why not?"

"Because it is very hard to digest and he probably hasn't had any in a long time. He needs to ease back into meat, and I don't want him to get sick. I want something that will stay inside him and stick on his ribs." She pointed to the potatoes as she said it. "Besides, I don't have any today."

We had finished the chickens the week before, and I knew the salami was all but gone.

I had placed the sieve in the sink and it took the two of us, one on each side, to lift the enormous pot and pour the water through the sieve into the sink. The dumplings fell on top of each other, only a few of them splitting open from the force of their fall. Mutti placed them gently in an enormous crystal bowl and then poured the bubbling plum sauce on top of them. Its rich, purple red color seeped around the sides of the bowl and reflected through the cuts in the glass.

"Mutti, it is beautiful."

"It will cheer him, don't you think?"

"Yes!"

My mother amazed me with what she could do with food, not only making it taste good but look good, too!

She walked ahead of me, carrying her bowl in front of her as if it were a prized trophy. The smell drifted to my nostrils, and my stomach lurched in hunger. I looked at Jürgen and looked away quickly, guilt quieting my stomach.

Vati and Jürgen looked up, surprised at the incredible sight before them.

"Heti, what is this?" asked my father, smiling.

"Potato dumplings with plum sauce, all fresh from the Bolle garden!"

"It looks magnificent!"

"It is beautiful. Thank…" Jürgen again had to choke back tears that now threatened to spill onto the clean shirt Vati had given him.

Vati stood up quickly—I think more to divert Jürgen than anything else—and said, "What do you think? A red or white with this, Heitchen?"

"I think a red!"

He nodded and went to the cabinet.

Mutti served Jürgen first, and I marveled at his restraint as he waited for Vati to come back to the table with the wine and then waited for Mutti to serve all of us and then for Vati to give a toast.

Vati held up his glass. "To Jürgen's safe arrival."

"*Prost,*" we said in unison, the glasses clinking loudly in the silence of the dining room.

I watched a smile play faintly across Jürgen's lips as he took in the scene before him. He ate one dumpling and then a second one, and then he paused. Again, I was astonished at his restraint; I would have thought he would wolf down each dumpling in about two bites. Mutti told him he must be careful about meat and to begin to eat it only slowly when he got home. She said she had some cheese for dessert but that he could only eat it after he ate something simple like potatoes or bread, and she would give him some cheese to take with him to start him on protein again. He listened carefully, mumbling his gratitude.

"Jürgen, how did you get here?" I asked. "Did you walk along the roads or the farms?"

He took a third dumpling but put down his fork before he could take a bite and began to talk. He talked for at least five minutes before he took another bite. He told us of the kindness of the farmers who helped him along the way, and of the joy but also fear he felt the day the Russians released him. He told us there were many more like him still in camps all along the Eastern Front, and that the Russians worked them to death. He told us that the younger you were, the better they treated you, and that they were only releasing the young ones. He said nothing about the war and the horrors he must have seen, and we were careful not to ask. By the time he had finished talking he had eaten five dumplings and drunk two glasses of red wine. I brought the cheese out, and we talked some more.

Vati looked at his watch and said, "Jürgen, unless you are spending the night, we need to get you to the train station."

He nodded and pushed his chair back from the table. "Frau Bolle, thank you so much for this wonderful meal."

"Oh, you are more than welcome! Now, let me pack you some food for the train," she said, standing up and heading for the kitchen. I followed her, carrying the plates. Vati and Jürgen came behind me, carrying the empty bowl that had held the dumplings and the empty wine bottles and glasses.

"Jürgen, I will make you cheese *Brötchen* to take along. They are easy to carry."

"Thank you so much, Frau Bolle," he turned to my father, "and Herr Bolle, for everything."

"It is nothing more than what we should do," said my father.

After Mutti had made the cheese *Brötchen*, she told Vati to wait a moment and ran into her study to write a quick note for Jürgen's mother. We stood in silence, waiting for her in the entryway. Vati began to tap his foot impatiently, but he waited. She handed it to Jürgen and he put it with the letter from his mother tucked behind Vati's leather belt. As he shoved it in I saw that the letter from his mother had been opened. He must have read it in the bathtub. I smiled at the thought.

"You write me that you have arrived safely." She put her hand to his cheek for a moment. The softness of her hand contrasted starkly against the angular shape of his cheekbones jutting out from below his eyes. "You hear me?"

"Yes. I promise."

We said our goodbyes quickly, and then he left with Vati. I stood with Mutti in front of the house. A breeze gently stirred the leaves of the acacias, and a seedpod left over from spring floated to the ground as we watched them walk up the path to the front gate. Jürgen paused for a moment, looking across to what was once his home but now housed refugees from the city, a Herr Braun and his family, who had simply found the house and moved in. My father put his arm around the boy's shoulder and pulled him along—the train was waiting.

Jürgen never returned. His family did not want to live in a city surrounded by Russians and they simply stayed in Frankfurt; the Americans eventually confiscated their house, and I never saw them again.

22

A Party to Warm the Soul

January–March 1947

It was cold again that winter of 1947, so cold that it sucked the air out of you with a deathlike grip. Mornings were the worst, walking to school through the park to Thiel Platz in the dark cold or along Kronprinzenallee if the streetcars were running. Electricity was still rationed, and it didn't become light until halfway through the morning. Often we had no school because we still had very little coal to heat the huge furnaces that stood in the basement of the Königin Luise Stiftung, waiting to be fed so they could belch forth heat that became more and more vague the further the classroom was from the basement. On those days I would stay home and help Mutti or go to the office with Vati. But when we had school, I had to brace myself for the walk.

It was the first minutes that I hated the most. Leaving the warmth of Mutti's kitchen, the warmest room in our house, to step into the frigid air always seemed to me the cruelest way to greet the day. I gingerly stepped out onto the icy flagstone stairs, gripping the rail so as not to slip as I eased my way into the garden. The grass crunched under my feet, frozen into small swirls, and the black left from night surrounded me. There were streetlights in Dahlem, probably the only ones that functioned in Berlin, but only on the main roads; not on the Föhrenweg and not in the park. The cold surrounded me, seeping through my clothes and climbing down my throat when I breathed. It seemed as if it froze every hair on my body, just like the grass below my feet. Ice stood everywhere, making the short walk treacherous.

I waited for Maria at the corner of Auf dem Grat and Föhrenweg. I refused to walk by the forest that ran the length of Kronprinzenallee in the dark, alone. I stomped my feet to keep the cold out and peered anxiously into the dark, hoping she would come. There was an unnerving stillness about these cold, dark mornings. I imagined it was what it must be like to be locked in a meat locker. Did that happen to butchers? Or were there safety locks on the other side? I shuddered. In the vague light, the homes looked back at me, their fronts still pitted and scarred with bits of plaster dug out, reminders of the war. The moon cast shadows off the blackened sticks in the center of Auf dem Grat, where we once played and watched cars pass under the cool canopy of the leaves that would never live again. My eyes began to water from the cold, and I hopped up and down to keep my blood moving. I heard her shoes clicking on the frozen street before she emerged from the darkness.

"Hello," she called when she got close enough. The word shattered the silence, like a doorbell does when you're reading a book in a quiet corner. Her breath formed a halo around her face.

She was next to me now, and we hugged and rubbed each other's arms to stay warm.

"My God, it is cold this morning!"

"Oh! My feet are already frozen!" she said, stomping them. I looked down at her boots and at mine and thought how lucky we were to have boots. So many didn't have any—even girls at my school.

"Well, come on. We'd better hurry before they find us frozen together out here like a statue!"

We walked, half running to stay warm, toward the streetcar stop. Lights appeared in some of the windows. A single light meant Germans lived there. Where the whole house was lit up, I knew only Americans could live. We walked with arms linked to keep each other from falling on the ice. There were only the sounds of the ice and gravel crunching under our feet; no birds, no ducks—they were too smart to stay in Germany for the winter, Mutti always said.

It was not my imagination, Vati said. This was again one of the coldest winters on record, and we wondered if God's wrath cast upon Germany would ever end. Many continued to starve to death or freeze to death or both. We still had no heating fuel, and my mother joked that if this cold didn't stop there would be no furniture left in Germany! My mother's "Rodin" kept our own house relatively warm in the kitchen and living room, but the bedrooms were freezing, and the worst was undressing to take a bath. You couldn't bathe in the morning, only in the evening, after the house had had the entire day to heat up, which meant the difference between forty degrees and fifty degrees. Hot water was not regulated like electricity, as it was heated by wood or coal, so I made the water as hot as my skin could stand. My skin turned red and burned from the heat of the water as I stepped in, and the contrast between the cold room and the water always shocked me at first. I eased my way into the steaming tub, forcing myself into the uncomfortably hot water, knowing it would be only a matter of minutes before the temperature of the room brought the water temperature down to tepid.

Some days it seemed I never warmed up, and once the chill set in it never stopped no matter how many clothes I put on. I vowed to live in a warm climate one day. Why Germans had ever settled this land was beyond me. They must have arrived in the spring and thought it lovely with spring flowers dotting the green grassy meadows, unaware of the winter that lay ahead for them. Pictures of Italy or the pictures of California or some place called Arizona in magazines like *Life*, or *Vogue*, or *McCall's*—places that never had winters—filled me with envy. I wanted to live there and swim in a pool in the middle of winter! A gloom settled over me after looking at these pictures that Mutti tried to lift.

"It won't be long, Jutta, and the cold will be a distant memory."

"But it comes back. Every year it comes back."

She raised her eyebrows and nodded her head. "Yes. It does come back."

"Exactly," I said, as if there was nothing more to say.

"Well, maybe you can have a winter home in Italy one day," she said, smiling.

"I want a home in California."

Her smile faded and she rose wearily from the table.

"What we need is a party!"

"What for?"

"It will cheer us up! We need cheering up."

"I need this economy to turn around and the communists to leave, is what I need," remarked my father.

"Well that's a bit out of your control, but a party we could manage."

"You and your parties for everything! What's a party going to do?"

"Take everybody's mind off all this worry and give them an evening where they can pretend that they have no problems."

"Everybody will think we're crazy, having a party when half of Germany is starving."

"No they won't. We can have a welcome-in-the-spring party. You could invite your business council members, and I will invite our friends, and we can relax for an evening."

"Oh come on, Vati. Mutti's right. It will be fun."

My father looked from her to me as if we were both crazy.

"Besides," I added, "the Americans have parties all the time, and nobody thinks they're crazy!"

"See, Hans! There you have it. That does it. We are going to have a party next Saturday night. And Jutta, you can invite some of your friends, too."

"Yes. I haven't had a party since I began at Königin Luise."

My mother flicked her hand. "Oh, that wasn't a party; that was a small gathering. We are going to have a party. A real party with music, and lots of alcohol, and food..."

"And maybe I can talk to Fritz and have his father make a special cake!" I interrupted, the excitement bubbling out of me.

"Sure, but, *du*, Jutta, you make sure he charges us for it!"

I nodded, knowing he wouldn't.

Vati rolled his eyes at us. "And where do you plan to get all of the food for this soiree that you are insisting on?"

"Oh, you just leave all of that to me! I have many, many ideas," she said in her best Marlene Dietrich voice, tapping her head.

My father laughed. But he recognized defeat when it stared him in the face. "All right! All right!"

I jumped up from the table and hugged him. My arms still wrapped around his neck, he pointed at my mother. "But you let me take care of the alcohol!"

My father needed a party more than any of us. The German economy continued to stagnate, and the communists were an ever-present threat, waiting patiently like a lion for someone to stray from the pack. His election as president of the *Verein der Berliner Kaufleute* (Berlin Businessmen's Association) brought him in direct contact with the bickering, self-interested business leadership of the city—none of whom could agree on a plan for Berlin.

"If this is how it is here, how can they possibly devise a plan for all of Germany?" he lamented to my mother. The failure of the military government to reunite Germany and implement what he considered "the vitally needed" currency reform depressed him. Most Germans still lacked sufficient food. Starvation and child malnutrition for the city of Berlin had increased, regressing to 1945 levels, and the refugee problem continued as Germans fled from the East and from the Russians in record numbers, passing through Berlin in the hundreds of thousands each month and placing further strain on the already fragile economy. Fuel continued to be rationed, and the harsh winter had again left thousands—some news reports stated as many as twelve thousand in Berlin alone—frozen to death in their beds at night. Meanwhile, huge trains full of coal headed east to Russia or west to France. Vati did not understand the American policy toward France. It frustrated him that a nation that had contributed so little to stopping Hitler was allowed so much power. He could not for the life of him figure out why France was not forced to join the British and Americans in their efforts to unite Germany.

"They have established a bizonal economic unit between the American and British zones, but they allow France to remain king of their own zone. Why they can't force France to join so that Russia is isolated is beyond me. Just beyond me," he ranted to my mother, pacing back and forth in the living room one evening. "All the French have to do is raise an eyebrow in concern, and the Americans back off. France wants to destroy us. They want the Ruhr and the Saar and the Rhineland. Every bit of our industrial and economic heart!" And then he turned on me, pointing his finger. "And don't think all of the Americans are our friends, either!" I shrugged at him. "There are many people in important positions that would like to see us turned into a pastureland, and they love France. They would happily give the Ruhr to France. Just like that!" He snapped his fingers. "I can't understand it!" He took a sip of his wine before adding, "But thank God for General Clay. I don't know if this Marshall is going to be good for Germany or bad. Rumor has it that he loves France, too! I liked Byrnes. He gave that wonderful speech in Stuttgart in forty-six. But Marshall? I don't know." He ran his hand through his hair in frustration. "It is so shortsighted of the French! If Germany fails, the communists will take over, and do they think France will remain immune? The communists are everywhere, Heti. It is unbelievable how they have infiltrated everywhere, and they are starting to make sense to people who are still starving and cold after almost two years of occupation."

"General Clay pledged not to allow them to spread," she said simply.

"Let's just hope that he can stand firm. But Poland, and now Czechoslovakia? And Greece is in danger. And Turkey?" He threw his hands in the air. "They are like a cancer; they just spread everywhere, silently and deviously." He paused for a moment. "And sometimes not so silently—how can the British let them broadcast propaganda from the *Rundfunkhaus*? Right in the middle of British sector! Unbelievable!"

"General Clay will stand firm, Hans. And the British won't let us slip under, either. It just takes time."

"I know, but we have got to be self-sufficient." He had set his wine down and was pounding his fist into the palm of his hand. I had really never seen Vati this worked up, and I looked at my mother, concerned. But she simply continued to sip her wine and listen. "We can't live off handouts; they are like Band Aids when you're hemorrhaging. But how can we be self-sufficient when Germany is divided into four—correction, now three—sections, with differing policies in each and cigarettes are the main currency and they have price controls so severe that no German in their right mind would place their goods up for sale because they can get ten times as much on the black market. And on top of all of that, our factories are only allowed to produce at a minimum level because the French are afraid of a reindustrialized Germany!"

"I wish Vati were in charge of Germany," I said. "He would straighten things out!"

My mother smiled. But Vati had not heard.

He grabbed his wineglass. "And have you seen the refugees? My God! They are flooding in from the East. All needing food and shelter! Soon there won't be anyone left for the Russians to have to feed. It will be a land of nothing but Russian occupiers."

All of these things weighed heavily on his mind, and Mutti was right to think he needed a diversion.

———

We scheduled the party for the next Saturday, only six days away. I invited twenty friends and Mutti invited double that, so we had a full house. It was a beautiful, unusually warm spring day, and we set up some of the tables outside on the garden terrace so we could leave room inside for dancing.

"Jutta, does Frau Bolle want the tablecloths turned like this, do you think?" Luise asked as she angled the second, smaller tablecloth diagonally across the table.

I glanced up from the daffodils I was arranging in the small brandy glasses that served as vases for each table.

"I don't know! You know better than I do," I said, wondering why Luise was asking me this; she had arranged many tables for my mother. But it was almost as if she did not remember anything from those events so far removed before the end of the war. "But that looks great," I added, seeing her look of concern. "I'm sure she'll love it."

She smiled.

My mother had asked Luise to work that evening, serving food and helping to set up and wash up. She had begun working full-time for my mother again a few weeks before. She had not liked working for Mrs. Vockel, she told us, because she was too demanding. "Luise can you this, and Luise can you that! I just about went crazy over there," she would say. Now that my mother could pay her both in cash and food, she had asked if she could come back. Mutti was thrilled, but told her to find a replacement for Mrs. Vockel before she quit. I was thrilled because it meant I could stop doing dishes at night and cleaning my bathroom, and Vati was thrilled because it meant that Mutti would rest a little more. And indeed, she looked less and less tired and, most importantly, I thought anyway, her hands regained their elegant, manicured look from before. She now sported nail polish in the same shades that I favored—reds and pinks from Revlon.

Luise grinned at me from her chubby face. She had lost considerable weight over the past few difficult years, thirty or forty pounds, I estimated, but her face still retained its cherubic look. "Oh, how I missed my little girl!" she said suddenly, rushing to me and hugging me so hard that I dropped the flowers on the table and felt like the wind was being squeezed out of me.

"I missed you, too," I squeaked. Thankfully she let go to wipe a tear from her face as she turned to go to the kitchen.

———

The buffet table stood just inside the door in the dining room, and all the doors had been thrown open to the patio so people would be able to flow freely from inside to outdoors until the cold of the evening would drive them indoors. The table looked magnificent, covered with one of Omi's lace tablecloths and an enormous vase of pink and purple rhododendrons from the garden. Crystal bowls that caught the evening light and sent little sharp beams of light across the room waited empty, ready for Luise to fill with the potato, noodle, and beet salads Mutti had prepared in the kitchen.

I made my way to the music room, where Mutti had told me I could set up a separate table for my friends. We could also eat from the main table, she said. But maybe we would want a few of our things on a separate table where the music played, she thought. I had requested *Americaners,* the cookies that were frosted with one half chocolate and the other half white, vanilla frosting. I didn't know why they were called *Americaners,* but as I stared at the plate of two dozen cookies, it struck me that they reflected black and white Americans. I had noticed the big trucks filled with black soldiers speeding along Kronprinzenallee. Black and white soldiers did not seem to mix. They lived in separate facilities and didn't even travel together in the same jeeps and trucks! One day I asked Mrs. Vockel about it. She confirmed that it was no different than in America, where blacks and whites lived separately, attending separate schools and churches.

"But why?" I had asked, puzzled.

She looked at me as if I was simpleminded. "It just wouldn't work, dear," she responded. "They are not like us, you know. They are very different."

"Really?"

"Oh yes! They aren't intelligent like us. There is very little point in educating them, and the men only think of sex and alcohol!" She shook her head and shuddered. "Oh no! In the South, where I come from, you just can't allow that at all."

"Can blacks and whites marry?" I asked, curious.

She almost dropped her teacup. "Good God, no! What a thought! It is against the law."

"That is how it was with Hitler and Jews. By law, Germans couldn't marry Jews or associate with them."

"Yes. Well, that is different," she said quickly.

I didn't see how, but I let it go. Mrs. Vockel ended the conversation and instead directed my attention to the latest *Vogue* she tossed over to me. She was sick again from her asthma and propped up in bed, reading.

"Here. You can have it, dear. I don't see anything that interests me in it," she announced, picking up the *Saturday Evening Post* instead. I flipped through the magazine absentmindedly, thinking about our conversation.

When I walked along Kronprinzenallee it nagged at me, bothering me whenever I saw a truck full of black soldiers drive by, and more and more it struck me that blacks were treated just like Jews under the Nazis—except that they weren't sent away to concentration camps. It seemed to contradict everything else that I knew about America. I thought of the phrase, "all men are created equal." They had taught it to us during one of the history classes at the German-American Club. It was one of the basic foundations of American philosophy, they had said. I thought of the Old Bolle and his sponsorship of Africans to the university in Berlin—what would Mrs. Vockel think of the fact that they had lived in his house while they studied here? I decided one day I would tell her and see how she reacted. I grabbed a cookie and with my finger mixed the icing together, smearing the dark chocolate into the white frosting. I chuckled.

I examined the table again. It wasn't filled with platters of oysters on the half shell or the salmon or venison of early times, but it looked gorgeous. An enormous wooden bowl held the potato chips Mrs. Vockel had given me when she heard I was having friends over for a party. Mutti's sour cream and chive dip in the small fluted silver bowl looked tiny next to it. Mrs. Vockel had also given me six bottles of Coca-Cola that came in a distinctive red and white cardboard carrying case with the Coca-Cola logo on it. The case made an interesting divider on my desk for pencils and pens and other small things I collected, like feathers and dried grasses. I wasn't sure what she expected me to do with the Coke. There were only six bottles—not enough for everybody, and I knew everybody would want one. Maybe she thought I could buy more? Even if I could, Mutti would never waste precious food coupons on Coca-Cola! So instead, Mutti and I had a bottle each in the afternoon to perk us up from the exhaustion of getting ready for the party, and I decided to save the rest for something special.

At the opposite end of the table, Luise had placed Mutti's beautiful cut crystal punch bowl filled with *Himbeer Saft* (raspberry juice). We would mix in the soda water "to stretch it" once the guests arrived. Mutti floated four little pansies on the top of its rich purple surface. I smiled; they floated like lily pads on a dark lake. I wondered if Mutti's lace tablecloth would survive the punch. In the center stood my tray of *Americaners*, and next to them a platter with Luise's *Apfelstrudel*, using the last of the cold-stored apples from the Kittels' tree that my mother said were too soft to eat. Luise had made two, one for our table and one for the larger table. Another crystal bowl stood next to the desserts with my favorite noodle salad or, as Mrs. Vockel informed me it was called in America, macaroni salad. Mutti had put some carrots and red beets into it to give it beautiful highlights of purple and orange. A large vase filled with purple lilacs from the bush by the driveway completed the look of the table, their sweet fragrance perfuming the room.

Luise bustled in with a stack of plates and forks for the table.

"Do we have a cloth that is not too nice that we can put under the punch bowl?"

"Yes! I told Frau Bolle we shouldn't put that bowl on her nice lace cloth. Young people spill and drip, and *meine Güte*!" She put the plates down, shaking her head. "But you know how she wants everything to look perfect!"

"Well, maybe we should find something. Omi made this tablecloth and Mutti would be sad if my friends gave it purple spots!"

"I know what we have," said Luise, arranging the silverware in a half-moon shape. "That small, square cloth that Frau Bolle bought from the refugee lady!"

"Perfect!" I said. She hurried off to retrieve it. I gave the table one more glance before turning to head for the stairs.

Fritz would be here soon to help organize the music. He had said he had a surprise for me. Not only would we use my parents' extensive record collection, but he had more, he said—the absolute latest from America. He had already been over once before. He had delivered two cakes earlier in the day. One for the adults, he said—filled with "liquor and other adult flavors," and one for us—"a little bit on the sweet side." He winked at me, acknowledging my weakness. He refused money for either, and my mother did not press him when he looked insulted at the suggestion. I glanced at the clock above the fireplace—already six o'clock! I ran upstairs to get ready.

"Good evening, Frau Bolle." It was Fritz's deep, melodious voice. I hurried. I was dressed but not made up yet! I powdered my nose with the Max Factor powder Mrs. Vockel had brought me, and hurriedly penciled my eyebrows and applied mascara. I stood back and took in the effect. It was startling what a little dark color did to my face by hiding my blond eyelashes and eyebrows behind charcoal brown. I found a red lipstick and applied just enough so that Vati would not have a fit, pinching my lips together over a piece of toilet tissue and then applying a little more. Perfect! I thought, studying the reflection in the mirror. I smoothed my dress and headed for the door, taking one last look in the mirror above my dresser as I did so. Oh my God, my hair! I still had it up in a ponytail from my bath! I tore the ribbon out of it and grabbed my brush. With a few strokes it fell in place, smooth around my neck, its color a golden red in the early evening light. "*Ja.* Now I think I am really ready," I said out loud to myself. My heart beat quickly, and I took a little skip as I headed for the stairs.

Vati met me at the bottom of the stairs, having just come up from the cellar, a bottle of red wine in each hand. He bowed as I came down the last step.

"*Durch Eleganz entstellt.*"

I giggled and kissed him on the cheek. "I think you're exaggerating my elegance!" I glanced past him to the living room. "Where's Fritz?"

"He's in the music room."

I hurried past him to the music room, grateful he had not noticed my lipstick.

Fritz sat on the floor next to a large box, from the depths of which he pulled one record after the other. He studied their covers carefully before sorting them into two piles, their jacket covers shiny in the bright room.

He looked up when I came through the door, and his admiring up-and-down glance told me I had achieved the look I wanted. He leaped to his feet.

"You look amazing!"

"Thank you," I said in mock formality as I curtsied. I came over to him and he stole a kiss before my father could see.

I smiled and rubbed the red lipstick off his lips.

"But what is all of this?" I asked, astonished at the number of records on the floor. There must have been at least fifty.

"Herbie, my friend at the station, said they were throwing these out!"

"But why?" I asked, retrieving one from the pile on Fritz's left. "Oh, *du,* Fritz! Look, this is Frank Sinatra!"

"Yes. I know." Fritz bent down in excitement and grabbed a record jacket from the floor, holding it out to me like a prize. It was Bing Crosby. "He says they have scratches on them or they are duplicates. The station was going to throw them away, so he saved them for me."

"Throw them away! How could they?"

Fritz shrugged. "Americans. They do that."

"How nice of him to save them for you."

"Yes. The scratches aren't necessarily on the hit songs, he says. So we just have to play them and see. I was going to organize them and test as many as I could before everybody gets here."

"Are you the DJ for the evening?"

"At your service, ma'am."

We busied ourselves testing the records.

"Do you like your surprise?" Fritz asked, glancing up anxiously as he sorted.

"I love it."

He smiled, pleased.

"I love you!" he said, looking me in the eye over the cover of a Frank Sinatra recording in that disconcerting way he had.

I blushed and looked down. "Oh look, this is Bing Crosby," I said, my heart pounding. I held it up to the light to read the title. "*How Deep is the Ocean?*" I read slowly in English.

He grabbed my hand. "I don't care how deep the ocean is! I said I love you!" His intensity made me uncomfortable. "Do you feel anything for me?" he asked quietly.

I nodded my head yes in reply. I felt the heat radiate off of my neck and cheeks.

"There you two are!" said my mother. Fritz dropped my hand, and with relief I looked up at her. She stood in the doorway looking like I hadn't seen her look in years. Her hair, gently curled, fell around her face, and her silk dress shimmered in the light. She had applied a pale pink lipstick that made her blue eyes sparkle. I smiled.

Teddy

"What's that?" I asked. I could barely hear it, but I could swear it sounded like a whimper.

Mutti frowned and looked up from the paper she had been reading. It was Monday, and Saturday's party still weighed heavily on us. It had been a late night, some of the most determined guests not leaving until 1:30 AM , when the candles we used for light finally gave out. I had not been able to sleep until the early morning hours, only to be awoken by a car horn at 7:00 on Sunday morning. Vati had pronounced the horn and its blower "completely uncivilized!" We knew it had to be one of our American neighbors.

There was only silence, and we both shrugged and continued our breakfast. Mutti snapped her newspaper to remove the crease that had formed in it.

"Shhh! Listen!" Again I heard it; an almost imperceptible whimper, but this time it was followed by a sharp, staccato bark.

"Sasha!" I cried, leaping up from my chair.

My mother shook her head. I pushed my chair back and ran to the door.

There on the stoop was a small dog, but certainly not Sasha!

"Oh! Who are you?" I bent down to pet the little thing, but before I could do so the dog bolted into our house and headed straight for the kitchen.

"Hey, what do you think you're doing?" I cried. Mutti burst out laughing. We both followed him into the kitchen. He had leaped up onto one of the chairs and sat there looking at us, as if to say, "Well, where's my breakfast?"

Mutti and I looked at each other and giggled.

"You're a bold little thing!" I exclaimed.

He wagged his tail and barked at us.

"He must be an American dog, brash but friendly!"

"Now, Mutti," I remonstrated.

"I said friendly!"

"Can we feed him?"

"I have some potatoes and carrots from last night."

I scrunched up my mouth.

"Jutta, if we have to eat potatoes, he will have to eat potatoes."

I shrugged and got the potatoes. He gulped them down in a matter of seconds.

"See, I told you he was American. No table manners!" Mutti joked.

"He was hungry, poor little thing!" I sat down and put him on my lap; he licked my neck and hands and snuggled into a comfortable position.

"*Du*! Jutta, you need to get to school," said Mutti, suddenly glancing at her wristwatch and picking the dog up off my lap.

"Can we keep him, Mutti? Please?"

"I'll check around the neighborhood today and see if he belongs to anybody."

"But can we keep him if he doesn't? He'll starve to death or freeze to death if we don't!"

Mutti held him up to eye level. "Somehow, I don't think this little fellow will ever starve to death or freeze to death. Scrappy! That's what he is, scrappy! Aren't you? " He licked Mutti's nose and wagged his tail. She put him down, and he immediately jumped back into my lap.

"No. You must go." She grabbed the dog and waved me up. "Go on, now."

I did not move and continued to pet the dog in her arms now.

"If he has nowhere else to go, Jutta, we will keep him."

I leaped up. "Thanks, Mutti! See you later, Teddy!" I called over my shoulder.

"Teddy?" Mutti asked.

"Yes. He's my favorite DJ on AFN."

I heard her murmur, "Teddy. It suits you."

Teddy was the opposite of Sasha in every way. Like Sasha, he was a long hair dachshund, but his hair covered his face as well as his body, and it didn't fall in perfect lines like Sasha's. Instead, Teddy's grew every which way, forming small circles of wiry hair that struck out on their own independent paths. He had a tiny, pitch-black button nose and eyes to match, and his ears fell forward, almost covering his eyes and giving him a cocky air. Carefree about his appearance, like a boy who doesn't tuck his shirt in or comb his hair, he was unkempt but sure of himself. Teddy had guts; he was afraid of nothing and certainly kept the rodents out of my mother's garden. He also sometimes dug up her garden, having developed a fondness for carrots, cooked or raw. My father was not too fond of Teddy, and the feeling was mutual. Teddy knew that he could woo the ladies much more readily than the men, and he practiced his charms on us, while with Vati he would bark and sometimes show his teeth. On those occasions we could hear Vati shouting, "*Raus! Hinaus mit dir!*" and then the newspaper hitting furniture and the floor as Vati chased Teddy out of his study, calling, "*Mistvieh*" after him. Mutti and I would giggle quietly together before she would retrieve Teddy from the outdoors, where my father had banished him, making sure he stayed in the kitchen with her.

Mrs. Vockel put a notice up at the PX for me, but nobody came to claim Teddy.

"Too smart!" announced my father. He insisted that Teddy must have belonged to Americans who departed for the States, wisely deciding Teddy should stay behind. And indeed, there may have been some truth to Vati's theory, for if Teddy responded to any command, it seemed he understood English better than German. So Teddy stayed and added a colorful dimension to our small household.

23

Summer 1947

A Bully's Paradise

"I always liked that house," commented Fritz.

I glanced up. "Which house?"

"That one across Auf dem Grat."

I let go of his hand for a moment and slowed my pace to point to the gray stucco house, overgrown with weeds, that stood on the opposite side of Auf dem Grat, where the street ended and the park began.

"The flat-roofed house?" I asked, pulling my eyebrows together in surprise.

"Yes."

"I think it's hideous!"

Fritz laughed. "That's what I like about you, Jutta. You always 'tell it like it is.'" He said the phrase in English, and I knew it must be a bit of Ami talk he learned from his friend Herbie at the radio station.

We turned down the gravel path and walked past the *Hexihutte* to find our favorite bench. Hidden by the branches of a weeping willow, it overlooked the entire park. It was just above the path on a tiny hill. The tree encircled us with its branches, giving us just enough privacy. Fritz brushed the bits and pieces of tree droppings from the bench, and we sat down.

"I always liked that house because it stood there defying Hitler!"

"And just how did it do that?"

"Well, you know he banned all flat roofs."

I nodded.

"And he had to have seen it from Kronprinzenallee every time he drove to the *Luftwaffe*, not to mention that Keitel must have seen it too, every morning and every evening as he drove by. It stood there all these years silently reminding them that they couldn't control everything."

"I remember when the Stiens moved out. They had a hard time selling that house because everybody knew Hitler didn't approve of the style. I never understood why."

"Degenerate, my innocent darling. Don't you realize such architecture, developed by Jews, could lead to degeneracy and the immediate downfall of Germany?" he said, mimicking Goebbel's self-important tone, the tone that used to accost us regularly through the radio.

"The apartments on Argentinische Allee were the same way. The ones where your friend Christa lives? He wanted to blow them up!"

We fell silent. I leaned my head back against his shoulder. A breeze stirred the elegant, thin branches of the willow tree above our heads. The sun beat down hot rays on my feet, and I could feel them burn. I pulled them back, tucking them under the bench and away from the heat.

"But it's very interesting. Of all the homes over there on Auf dem Grat," Fritz tipped his head toward the street, "every one of them suffered damage from the Russians except for that one."

I sat up, smiling. "You know, that's true. And the same with those apartments."

He smiled back and pulled me back toward him. We sat listening to the sounds of the park. Young children called to each other, playing hide-and-seek somewhere up by the *Findling*, I guessed, judging by the distance of their high-pitched, excited voices. The big rock had landed there sometime during the ice age, and not even British and American bombs, or even Russian guns, could move or destroy it.

"Fritz? What was it like for you back then? I mean as a child, like them?" I tipped my head in the direction of the voices.

"This is Wednesday afternoon, so I would not have been playing in the park, would I?"

"No. I guess not," I said.

"They used to collect us right after school, and we had to march to the headquarters in these single file columns." He shook his head. "I hated those songs."

"It must have been hard for you in the Hitler Youth."

"Not so much when we were starting out, when I was a *Pimpf*, but when we all turned about twelve..." He looked up at the sky. "They would make us fight each other until one of us did not get up from the ground!"

"No!" my hand flew to my mouth.

"I heard rumors of boys being killed, but nobody in my group was killed."

"Poor Fritz!" I stroked his hand.

He shrugged. "I survived. They always paired me up with this other tall boy, so he and I developed a pact. We would fight for a while, and then one of us would punch the other in the stomach, but not as hard as it looked like, and he would collapse on the ground and not move." He laughed. "We took turns each week being the loser."

I shook my head. "I didn't even go to the Hitler Youth. I was the only one in my school, I think, who didn't. Mutti would threaten it as a punishment. 'If you don't behave, I'll send you down for that Hitler Youth meeting!'" We both laughed.

"You were lucky your father could get you out of those things."

I nodded. Guilt needled me.

"It was the small, slight ones and the bad athletes that had it the worst," continued Fritz. "I remember this one boy. Dieter Meyers was his name. I will never forget him. They made a sport of picking on him—to toughen him up, the *Scharführer* would say. They would take him in the forest when we played war games, and two of the bigger boys would throw him on the ground and sit on him, hitting him and stuffing grass in his mouth. Then they would leave him there by himself while we all marched back."

I stared in front of me. I had nothing to say. What could one say to such things?

"Until one time, the *Gefolgschaftsführer* was along to see how we were progressing with our 'military skills.' That's what all this was, you know—training, so later we could be served up to the war when we were old enough." Fritz shifted on the bench. "He was the next level up in their little bureaucracy, older than our regular leader, maybe nineteen or twenty, I would guess. He seemed very old to me at the time. We were all on our best behavior, and the *Scharführer* ordered the boys to attack Dieter, like he always did. At first the *Gefolgschaftsführer* didn't see it because he was helping the rest of us with target practice. But then a group of boys ran over to watch, and so it caught his attention. He hurried over to see what was happening, and we followed him. Two big boys were on top of Dieter. One of them—Horst was his name—I'll never forget his face with his small, deep-set eyes and thick neck. His muscles bulged as he choked Dieter, and I could see he was enjoying himself. At that moment... It was really strange, but I felt sorry for Horst." Fritz shook his head.

"I couldn't imagine what sort of scum could enjoy something like that." Fritz paused, remembering. "Dieter's face began to turn purple, and the *Gefolgschaftsführer* came up from behind them. He never stopped moving. In one motion he picked Horst and the other boy up by the collars and threw them off. He was a big boy, the *Gefolgschaftsführer*, almost a man. He was very imposing, and he just tossed them to the side, maybe three meters. I will never forget the look of rage in his eyes. Dieter lay rolling around on the ground, choking and crying, curled up. And the *Gefolgschaftsführer* turned on the boys who had done it, and on the *Scharführer*, and he said in this very controlled way, almost too calm, 'I never want to hear that anyone has touched this boy again!' And then he turned to our *Scharführer* and said, again in that very controlled way, 'You, come with me.' I have no idea what he said to him, but things got a little better for us after that, and certainly for poor Dieter!"

Fritz shook his head. "Most of us were relieved. We hated the way they treated Dieter." He stretched his long legs out in front of him and laughed. "*Ja*, the Hitler Youth! A bully's paradise! Luckily, Horst was drafted six months later. He was seventeen. I feel bad about it, but we all celebrated the day he was drafted." Fritz fingered a seedpod that had blown down from the tree. "I'm sure he is dead now. He was sent to the Eastern Front."

I waited silently. We both stared straight ahead at the lake—the breeze had formed tiny ripples on its surface. I could tell he was not done. So I waited. He shifted in his seat and sat up straight.

"When I turned fourteen I had to join the upper division of the Hitler Youth. We had to pick a branch that we wanted to be in, like the Hitler Youth riding or the Hitler Youth *Luftwaffee*. I picked the *Luftwaffee*."

"Why? Wouldn't that mean you would end up fighting in the *Luftwaffee*?"

"Maybe. But my father and I discussed it. I was tall, and we knew that if I didn't volunteer for something important, they would select me for the Waffen SS. Hitler liked to pick the boys 1.9 meters or more for the Waffen SS. I had seen this happen to older boys from our school. So we decided it was safer if I volunteered for something. And it got me out of the military exercises in the forest. We learned hang gliding!"

"Oh my God! I would have been terrified."

Fritz chuckled. "They pulled us up with a plane to three hundred or four hundred meters, and then they would let us go, and you had to glide down!"

"Four hundred meters! At fourteen years old!"

"They didn't care about our safety. I never told my mother what I was doing, though."

"No. I can imagine you didn't." I thought of Frau Mertel, her stout figure swaying from side to side as she marched down to the headquarters to tell the Hitler Youth leader what she thought of all this.

"My mother!" He shook his head, smiling. "You know they always held their meetings on Sunday morning so the boys could not go to church. The Nazis did not want competition from God."

"True. They took down the crosses from our classroom. I remember that."

Fritz paused as a group of noisy ducks flew overhead and then dove for the lake. "Mutti and Vati insisted we go to church on Sunday. It was embarrassing for us because all the other boys from school and in the neighborhood attended. We were the only ones who never did. They would harass us about it. So one day this little *Scharführer* came to the house. He was maybe two or three years older than we were, and he spoke to my mother, all self-important and assured, saying he had to have a written excuse from her about why her boys could never attend his meetings. Well, she lit into him!" Fritz shook his head, chuckling. "Oh my goodness! She told him, if I tell you he is in church, that is good enough! Now get out of here! But with a bit more colorful language! And he did, and that was the end of it. He never came back. But I was so worried they would come and get Mutti and take her down for questioning."

"So you never had to go to the meetings?"

"Not those, but we had to go after school to the practices, and in the evenings they held meetings, too. Veterans came and told war stories—all propaganda—about how Germany was winning the war, and always for the Führer this and for the Führer that, and for the motherland, and I hated it! I had no interest in their stupid talk. But many boys believed all of this."

"Really?"

"Oh, yes. Don't you remember Hitler made a speech about the German youth and how they would save Germany? *'Zäh wie Leder; schnell wie ein Windhund: und stark wie Krupp Stahl'* (Tough as leather; fast like a greyhound; and strong like Krupp steel). And the boys? Most of them really believed him—that we were better than our parents: smarter, tougher." Another silence fell, and then he continued. "Many of the boys liked it. Maybe because many of their parents didn't want them involved, so it was a rebellion."

"That's true! I know Hannelore told me her group leader told her not to listen to her parents or grandparents because they were too old to understand what Germany really needed. And Hannelore believed them!"

"*Ja.* And of course they liked the music and the marching. Oh, I almost forgot!" Fritz sat up and pulled his shoulders back. "I was also in the *Fanfarenzug* (marching band), and I looked very impressive in my uniform with the bars on the arm!" He took his fingers away from mine to show me. "And that got me out of all of the military training also, because we had to practice so much!"

"But then you had to march at all of those awful rallies, didn't you?"

"Mostly sports festivals. It wasn't so bad."

Fritz slumped back down on the bench. "A lot of boys loved it," he said again. "All the activities, riding and gliding." He paused for a moment, pushing a stone with his foot. I watched as he drew lines in the dirt with the stone under his shoe. "The first place I went when the *Kinderlandverschickung* started was unbelievable! We had state-of-the-art facilities! Riding and boating, everything you can imagine. It was built specially by Hitler as an elite training center to educate only the top members of the Hitler Youth, like a military center, almost." He drew another line. "Those who had been trained there before us were all drafted." He said this last bit quietly. Then suddenly he looked up and stretched. "By the time I was sent there, it was for everybody."

I said nothing.

"But the facilities were, like I said, fantastic. For many boys this was a paradise compared to hard labor on the farm."

"I guess that's true."

"No, really," continued Fritz. "These were not all city boys from Berlin. Many came from the provinces, and we were all herded together and sent away to school together." Fritz laughed. "Some of these country boys would send letters home marked 'Heil Hitler.'" He shook his head. "They bought the whole Nazi story. But we Berliner boys were a bit too bright for all of that!"

I shook my finger. "No. But in the small towns they kept closer track. I can remember in Halberstadt, if you didn't say 'Heil Hitler' to greet people, they looked at you and talked. It's not like in Berlin, Fritz, where there are too many people to keep close tabs."

"That's true."

"I'm sure they or their family members could have gotten in trouble if they didn't sign off, 'Heil Hitler.' They had censors that read all the letters in those little towns."

"Really?"

"Yes! Mutti and Vati had to be very careful what they wrote me, and the telephone! Oh my gosh, you could hear them breathing into the phone! It made Vati furious, and he developed a signal for me to hold the phone away from my ear. Then he would bang something into the phone and say, 'Good heavens, what was that? Jutta, dear, are you all right?'" Fritz chuckled.

"Yes. If you were a little clever, you could work your way around it. Help yourself a bit. Like I volunteered to be the starter for the glider team, so I sat on the ground and gave the signals and kept track of the signals." He laughed, but then a frown passed over his face. "Well, at least until the *Kinderlandverschickung* began. After that there was no way out. At school you had the Nazi teachers, and in the dorms you had the Hitler Youth." He looked up to the sky. "Some terrible things happened there." And he fell silent. I pressed his hand but did not speak. The children's voices had drifted away, and only the sounds of the breeze through the tree provided steady music in our ears, broken occasionally by the sounds of jeeps and trucks accelerating on Kronprinzenallee.

After a moment I said, "I went away too, somewhere in the Baltic. But I got sick, and the doctors couldn't figure out what was wrong with me."

"Me too! The first place I went I got sick. The doctors told my parents they had no idea what was wrong, but my parents said I had to stay." He spread his shoulders wide. "You know, 'The boy must be tough.' They wanted me safe, away from Berlin and the bombs."

"My mother was not so strict. She sent for me to come home."

"After a while we all came home anyway, because no bombs were dropped on Berlin."

"That must have been very early on."

"Yes. Maybe forty-one?"

I nodded. "Yes. That's about the time we went to Berchtesgaden, but then we too came home."

"I was home for maybe two years, I think. And then the second *Kinderlandverschickung* started. First we went to Rügen on the Baltic, and then in the fall of forty-three to a monastery in Poland."

"Oh, good God!"

"Yes. All of these places were in the East, I think so they would have ready replacements for the war against the Russians." Fritz bent to take a pebble and toss it into the lake.

"And when the Russians started to come?"

"They wouldn't evacuate us, and my parents were very concerned. The head of school said we had nothing to fear; the Führer loved the children of Germany and would let nothing happen to them." He put his arm out, tracing an outline in the air. "I can still see him standing there, up behind the podium where a priest should have been standing, and all of us clean-faced and innocent, listening, depending on him for the truth." He lowered his hand and tossed another stone at the lake. "They waited and waited to get the proper documents from Berlin. Then they told us the Russians were not near; that those were lies, and that the Führer's soldiers would protect us, but the locals told us a different story. Some of the boys cried at night and wet their beds." His voice caught, remembering, and he cleared his throat before he continued. "Finally they gave the order, and we were all put on a train and sent to Berlin. The Russians marched into the town three days after we were evacuated."

"Thank God you got out!"

Fritz nodded his head. "As we traveled through East Germany, you should have seen the train stations! People everywhere, overflowing off the platforms, all trying to head west. They had to stop the train before it entered the station to ask everybody to step back!" He bent and tossed another pebble into the lake. It skipped, causing ring after ring of ripples before falling into the middle of the lake. A duck flapped its wings, startled. "All of them desperate to get away from the Russians. One woman's face still haunts me. She stood there on the platform, arguing with the attendant, her arm stretched out to him, desperately pleading with him. I think she didn't have the right paperwork; he kept shaking his head. Tears streamed down her face. She held a baby in her arms and a little boy, about two, maybe three years old, dressed in his best clothes, held onto her skirt. The whistle blew, and the attendant stepped onto the first step of the train. She tried to get on too, but the attendant yelled at her and pushed her off, and then the train began to move. I leaned out the window and saw that as the next steps came by, she lifted the boy onto them and pressed his hands around the rail. He screamed. His tiny hands clung to the bar, and then I saw a man grab him and pull him in as the train picked up speed. Whether she ever made it on or not, I don't know. The train track curved, and I lost sight of the platform." He fell silent for a moment and then, more softly, he said, "I pray that she did. What sort of desperation leads a mother to separate herself from her child like that?"

I closed my eyes and leaned my head back onto Fritz's arm. My mind saw the child, the desperate mother, and then images raced through me—fire engulfing me and Vati as we ran; the smell of burst gas lines; the small, innocent-looking, dark beans falling from the sky; the orange and red flames that licked the sky, already black with smoke where Halberstadt once stood; the cold, mask-like face of the man as he shot at us from the sky; the smell of mud oozing into my nose; and always the boy at the fence with his mother. My head began to pound. I sat up as the blood rushed to my ears and the back of my neck, the heat seeming to take over my head and upper body in a wave.

Fritz squeezed my hand. "Are you all right?"

I nodded yes and brushed the sweat off my brow. I thought of the children and their tiny, innocent voices, silent now, but who only moments ago had played contentedly in the park. Was it better to be born when they were? Or during this time of hunger and poverty but with no war, no bombs, no air raid sirens, and no Russians? The war! Definitely the war! That was the worst. The horrible, brutal war! So many lives lost. Their bodies piled in huge, mangled mountains somewhere, unidentified, a bulldozer waiting patiently to push them into a mass grave, their mothers' uncertainty haunting all of us.

A Well Stocked Pantry

"What movie did you and Fritz see?" asked Maria. Her big, lanky body had always been heavy, but in the past few years it had become slim and lean. She sat, leaning back casually on the striped cushions of the sofa, her long, muscular legs stretched out in front of her and crossed at the ankles. I noticed she had removed the hair from them and raised my eyebrows at her.

"American style!" she said, and then giggled, running her hand over her smooth brown calf.

I laughed. Extending my arm and pointing to my armpit, I cocked my head questioningly.

"Of course!" She giggled again.

I gave her the thumbs-up and flounced down on the sofa next to her.

"*Song of Love*," I said, adjusting my skirt to keep it from wrinkling. "And it was really, really good!"

"With Katherine Hepburn?" asked Christa.

I nodded.

A ping-pong ball came flying at us. "*Du!* Watch out!" shouted Hilde. The boy ran over, stooped to pick it up, and hurriedly apologized over his shoulder as he ran back, flushed from the heat of battle. Sweat glistened on his forehead and neck despite the coolness in the basement.

"Maybe we should move upstairs, where it is less dangerous," suggested Maria, her big brown eyes large with mock concern.

The others had wanted to watch the table tennis tournament, or ping-pong, as Captain Haft informed us they called it in America. The Americans really did have some funny words, I reflected: snickerdoodle and ping-pong. But as the tournament reached its final stages the boys were becoming more and more aggressive, so to avoid the sting of a flying ping-pong ball, we made our way upstairs, past the photos of American movie stars.

"Well, I think *Gentlemen's Agreement* is the best movie ever!" said Hilde.

"Everything has to have a meaning for you, Hilde. Sometimes we just want fun entertainment," I announced, even though I actually thought *Gentlemen's Agreement* was a great movie.

"Yes! *Like Blue Skies!*" Maria hugged herself. "Oh my gosh! I loved that movie!"

The light bounced off Hilda's pale forehead, creased in thought. "What value is there to those movies? I think *Gentlemen's Agreement* is an important movie because it exposes the prejudice against the Jews in America." She sniffed. "They aren't free of guilt, these Americans," she added, directing her comments to me.

I straightened my back and leaned forward. "Yes. But you notice they make movies about their weaknesses. They don't cover up or hide them, and they don't punish people for exposing them, either!"

"They are very self-critical, these Americans!" said Frau Richter, coming over from the table where she had been arranging napkins to join our conversation.

Hilde rolled her eyes but said nothing.

"I just think Gregory Peck is absolutely gorgeous!" announced Maria from across the room, helping herself to punch. Maria was bent on having a good time. She hated for any controversy or deep thinking to interfere with her pursuit of happiness.

Frau Richter fanned her hand as if she were going to faint. "If he walked in here today and asked me to go with him, I would drop everything and run out that door with him without a moment's hesitation!"

We all giggled at her enthusiasm.

"What are you ladies talking about?" asked Captain Haft, ascending from the basement, where the table tennis tournament still raged.

"Oh, nothing!" blushed Frau Richter, but she winked at us before walking back toward the kitchen doors.

Captain Haft watched her go, and we watched him. He shrugged. "I guess it must have been girl talk." He headed to the front room to see why the record player was not working.

We burst out giggling as he walked away, and I saw him stiffen slightly.

"I think Frau Richter and Captain Haft have something going on," whispered Christa. She was always prim and proper, and I thought I noted a hint of disapproval.

I nodded. "Do you see how he watches her?"

We giggled together—a giggle bonding us in a conspiracy that excluded the rest of the world—in that way only teenage girls have of giggling.

"It's funny. She doesn't really seem to belong here in this job."

"No. Her husband was a banker, you know," I said.

" Really? High up in the bank, or just a clerk?" asked Maria.

" He was president!"

Their jaws fell open. "No wonder she speaks and carries herself the way she does."

"Jutta, what are you and Fritz doing tomorrow?" asked Maria suddenly.

"The symphony!"

"You're so lucky! You always go to the symphony." Christa sat up to grab a magazine from the side table. "You have the best life, Jutta Bolle!"

I shrugged, uncertain how to respond.

Christa flipped the pages of the magazine absently. She looked tiny sitting next to Maria. Her pretty, thin legs crossed neatly at the ankles, and her skirt pressed and clean. I had never seen Christa look anything but impeccable, her short blond hair always perfect and her eyes never sporting the mascara smudges that so often lurked under Maria's eyes. Christa had lost her father early in the war, and her mother did not have much money, and more than anything Christa wanted to live in Dahlem and never have to worry about money again.

"I love the *Titania Palast* with its black-and-white tower out front!" added Maria.

"What are they playing?"

"I'm not sure. I think Beethoven."

And the conversation continued around the magazine as we flipped from page to page and saw the movies and books and new styles coming out of America.

"Frau Vockel has all those things they advertise in her pantry," I said.

"No!"

"Oh, yes! She asked me once to go and get the 'ketchup.' That's what they call it, not 'tomato sauce' like the Tommies, and she has Hunt's, just like in the picture!" I pointed.

"What is it?"

"Tomato sauce with a bit of vinegar for hamburgers and hotdogs."

I heard the loud and frenetic speech of a DJ, the style favored by AFN. Captain Haft, clearly unable to master the record player, had turned on the radio.

"Listen!" Maria clapped her hands for silence as the Andrews Sisters broke through our conversation, singing their "boogie woogies" and their "a-toot, a-toot, a-toot, diddle-ee-ada-toots." I grinned at Maria bopping her head rhythmically to the music. I didn't really like the Andrews Sisters, preferring the smooth, rich voices of either Frank Sinatra or Bing Crosby, but this was one song of theirs I liked.

"And does she have Nabisco crackers?" asked Maria, suspending her bopping for a moment to point to an ad for Ritz crackers.

"Oh, yes. And Kellogg's cereal." I flipped to another ad. "And Prem canned meat, and Campbell's tomato soup." I turned the page again. "And Eagle brand condensed milk. Now that is heaven—it's canned milk that's thickened with sugar!"

All three looked at me, astonished. "No, really!" I insisted. "She puts it in her coffee."

"What does she need all that food for?" asked Maria. "Isn't it just the two of them?"

I shrugged. "She says it's important to keep a well-stocked pantry." I mimicked her voice, and they giggled.

"I wish we could. But anything that goes in the pantry comes out the same day in our house," said Maria

"Isn't that the truth!" giggled Christa.

We prattled on and on about the ads and movies and our favorite movie stars until the light began to dim and we knew we had better hurry if we were to beat the dark of night home.

Sunday Dinner

I enjoyed going to the Vockels' house for Sunday dinner. It wasn't that Mrs. Vockel was such a great cook; in fact, my mother's cooking, when she had access to the same ingredients, was far superior. It's just that there was so much food on the table, and it was American-style food, and it was such a relief to be able to eat until I was too full to eat anymore. I could have seconds or even thirds and not feel guilty or worry that the food I took was calories taken away from my mother or father. I always hoped that Mutti would eat my portion when I was at the Vockels', but instead she set it aside, and inevitably on Monday my plate held an extra portion of everything.

Mrs. Vockel had been inviting me for dinner every other Sunday for about six months now. They were a lonely couple with no children of their own, and I was a surrogate child for Mrs. Vockel. She could mold me, correcting my English and teaching me about the wonders of America, and I, a willing participant, listened carefully to all she had to say, absorbing everything she shared with me about America. When she corrected my English, I copied her pronunciation, desperate to rid myself of my German accent. I never corrected how she pronounced my name or any other pronunciation of hers in German—I knew it was hopeless to try.

She served simple food, chicken-fried steak or something she called "Salisbury" steak, with overcooked vegetables and corn or macaroni, or sometimes mashed potatoes. She always served milk with dinner. I thought it was funny that she and Colonel Vockel both drank milk with dinner. For us it was a children's drink, not something adults drank. The Vockels never drank alcohol with dinner. They always had their "cocktail hour" before dinner at five o'clock. When I was invited, I came at six o'clock, and I learned that she did not like it if I was late or early.

"Well, what do you think?" she asked proudly, setting the tray down before us on the white linen tablecloth.

"They look lovely, my dear," said Colonel Vockel.

"They're wonderful! What are they?" I asked.

"Tomato tulips stuffed with chicken . And wait until you see what I have to go with it!"

She hurried back into the kitchen, emerging a few seconds later with an enormous casserole dish of macaroni and cheese held between huge, bright green oven mitts.

"Your favorite, Jutta. Macaroni and cheese!"

My mouth watered and my eyes grew huge. "This is wonderful! Thank you."

"It looks great, dear. Now sit down so we can eat."

"I am. Let me just take my apron off and get rid of these." She held up the mitts. Moments later she joined us, and Colonel Vockel stood up as she sat down.

"I made these for the book club last week and everybody loved them, so I thought, why not make them for my two favorite people?"

"We appreciate it, don't we, Jutta?"

I nodded my head, but my mouth was too full of chicken to respond.

Moments later Eva, Luise's replacement, brought in a platter covered with a green substance that jiggled with every step she took. I had no idea what it was. It danced on the platter, sending off bright green slivers of light, as shredded bits of cucumber and something else green peeked out like tiny bits of grass emerging from the soil. She had made it in a mold, and it was shaped like a Bundt cake. The center of the mold held a white substance that reminded me of the curd from the yogurt my mother sometimes made, but the small little white bits were more uniform than yogurt curd.

"My goodness! What is it?" I asked, and then grew red, thinking maybe I should know. I didn't want Mrs. Vockel to think we Germans didn't know anything.

"It is a lime Jell-O mold with cucumber and celery. It's made from gelatin!" She reached for my plate and cut a large section of the Jell-O with a cake knife. It jiggled dangerously on the end of the cake server and threatened to slide off, but she managed to get it on my plate. "And you have to have cottage cheese to go with it."

"Cottage cheese? I thought that was yogurt."

"No. Don't you have cottage cheese over here?" she asked, surprised.

"No."

"Well, we are introducing you to the finest in gourmet dining then, aren't we, Vera?" threw in Colonel Vockel, chuckling.

"I'll have you know this is the latest rage in America instead of regular salads!"

"I'm sure it is. Why else would we serve it?" he added. I couldn't tell by his blank face whether he was being sarcastic or sincere. Mrs. Vockel looked at him for a moment, not sure either, before spooning a large serving of cottage cheese onto my plate.

It tasted delicious; the cool, sweet Jell-O combined with the creamy cottage cheese—mild and sweet, unlike the sour taste of our yogurt. It went down well, and I accepted seconds when Mrs. Vockel offered. "This is amazing! Vati would love this instead of salad. He is not big on the 'green stuff,' as he calls it."

"Well, you have to tell your mother about it."

"But I don't know where we would buy Jell-O."

"Oh, I can get it for you."

Colonel Vockel raised his eyebrows.

But she just shrugged and winked at me. "I'll get you some."

———

Teddy lay curled in a little bundle of fuzz at the end of my bed, snoring.

"If he keeps that up, I'll have to put him in his basket in the hall."

"Don't bother," I shrugged. "He'll just come back in here. Besides, I'll put my earplugs in and I won't hear a thing."

Teddy hated the cold and always slept at the end of the bed. I actually welcomed him as a foot warmer, but Mutti thought it was disgusting having a dog sleep in bed with me—though she had given up on me and Teddy.

"Well, don't let him crawl under the covers, Jutta. *Gott im Himmel*, he is probably full of fleas from his wanderings all over the neighborhood."

"I doubt it—as much as you bathe him with that herbal concoction of yours."

Mutti sat on the edge of the bed and tucked a loose strand of hair behind my ear. I told her about the dinner. She always wanted to hear about my dinners with the Vockels, and the Jell-O especially intrigued her. She listened and asked question after question. She nodded her head a lot, saying, "Interesting." I don't think she was as impressed with Mrs. Vockel's culinary skills as I was—but in my permanently underfed state, the plentitude of the food at the Vockels' influenced my palate enormously.

She patted my hand. "Well, I'm glad they filled you up and you had a nice time."

"Mutti, I hope you ate my portion from tonight's dinner."

She smiled. "Oh, don't worry about me, dear. You better get some sleep. Don't you have a big exam tomorrow in American Literature?"

"Yes." I grabbed her arm before she could straighten up all the way. "Please, Mutti, eat my share."

She looked at me for a moment, the smile still playing on her lips. She nodded her head, "*Ja*, Jutta. I will. Now go to sleep."

I fell back on my pillow, embracing its soft depths, enjoying the happiness that had settled over me. Comfortable, full, and warm, I fell asleep before she reached the stairs.

24

Cold and Hungry

Fall 1947

The light faded and a handful of leaves fell to the dark brown ground, dislodged by the slight breeze that rustled the branches that housed them. We were heading into winter—cold and gray—and I thanked God that the trees in the Grunewald were pines and kiefers to provide a spot of green in the drab winter ahead. I breathed in the moist air as we walked arm in arm down the Kronprinzenallee. I liked the walk from the German-American Club along the edge of the forest and past the American headquarters—the red, white, and blue of their flag comforting as it fluttered in the breeze. The red flags of the Nazis and then the Russians no longer dominated the roofs above the concrete buildings at the corner of Hüttenweg and Kronprinzenallee. Red, the color of blood, the color of power, never fluttered gracefully in the wind: it overpowered the wind, shrill and loud. Red made me nervous, and I made a mental note to never wear it.

Bang!

I lowered my head, covering it with my free hand.

And again. Bang!

The sound shattered the stillness of the afternoon. Instinctively I ducked lower, my chest practically touching my knees. Fritz tightened his grip on my arm, pulling me closer. Both of us turned in the direction of the sound, like two dancers hunched over, Fritz above me protectively. But it was just an old woman rummaging through the garbage at the American headquarters. Dressed in a housedress and enormous shoes that must have been her husband's or perhaps a son's, she threw open the lids to the garbage bins, oblivious to the clattering noise of metal banging on metal. The Americans threw so much away it was well worth her while to look for half-eaten apples, or the ends of carrots deemed to hard to use in the Ami cafeteria, or bits of bread, deemed too stale. Even whole loaves of bread were thrown out because of a spot of mold. Stale bread didn't exist in German households anymore, let alone moldy bread; it was eaten so fast it could barely get from the bakery to the table.

We straightened together, still in our dance routine, neither of us speaking, unsettled by the sound and our own automatic reactions. Despite the cold, perspiration moistened my sweater along my chest and armpits. Our footsteps echoed along the hard gray cement. Jeeps gunned their way along Kronprinze-nallee, and the lid of the garbage can banged down one final time—she had retrieved all she could.

"But you have to admit, Jutta, it is ironic that they are telling us that Jews should be treated like we treat all Germans, while at the same time as they treat an entire category of Americans as something less than everyone else!" Fritz's voice broke into my thoughts.

"But what does that have to do with the killings?" I asked, turning my gaze toward him. He was concentrating on the sidewalk and frowning, his heavy black brows drawn together in thought.

"Nothing!" Letting go of my arm, Fritz quickened his pace so he could walk in front of me; he turned to face me for emphasis. I pulled my sweater tighter and crossed my arms in front of my chest to keep the growing cold from penetrating through to my moist skin. "Don't misunderstand me. I'm not saying the American government is equivalent to the Nazis. No!" He raised his hands in exasperation. "That would be ridiculous! I'm just saying that the self-righteousness of the American de-Nazification effort is amusing. Surely you have to see that, at least in the sense that they are not just telling us about the killings; they are also teaching us that people should be treated equally."

"Well, shouldn't they?" I asked innocently.

"Yes! That's my point. Are you deliberately trying to miss the point?"

"No. I just don't see the point of your point," I said, shrugging.

"They have these concepts they teach us." Fritz threw his arms wide. "You just heard them. You know what I'm talking about: all men are created equal, and equal protection, and freedom of this and freedom of that. And yet they don't let black soldiers live in the same barracks as white soldiers, or even fight in the same combat units, or hold the same jobs, or even eat at the same mess!"

I had to admit it was strange. We had just left a lecture on the American Revolution and the Declaration of Independence. The MP teaching the class emphasized these words, reading the first sentence of the Declaration of Independence to us carefully and slowly. He spoke eloquently of their importance in America. His face beaming with pride, he told us that all Americans, no matter what their religion or economic background, had an equal opportunity. If you worked hard enough, anyone in America could get ahead and make a better life. None of us had thought to challenge him—none of us except Fritz. The MP had cleared his throat and frowned at Fritz. "That is a discussion for another day."

The American attitude toward black people was strange indeed, if Mrs. Vockel was any example. I remembered her horrified face when I decided to tell her about Carl Bolle's sponsoring African scholars to come to the university in Berlin and how he had let them stay in his house while they were here. She looked at me aghast, and then snapped her mouth shut suddenly before saying, "Well, that's different. They were probably the sons of kings or something. Not the same type as we have in the United States."

Fritz slowed until he was next to me again. He grabbed my hand, his face inches from mine. "Be honest, Jutta. Don't you see an irony in all this?" His need to make me understand infected me. His eyes, deep and intelligent, pleaded with me.

"Yes. It is ironic," I relented.

He relaxed and squeezed my hand as if to thank me.

We stepped around a boy sleeping in his *Bollerwagen,* his cap lowered over his face, one leg and one arm draped over the side. He wore no shoes, and his toenails were soiled black, chipped and broken. He was dirty. Streaks of dirt formed rivers on his arms and face where rain or sweat or saliva had mixed with it. I worried he would not wake when the night cold fell all around, but Fritz said, "Let him rest. Who knows where he sleeps normally, and the cold will wake him." I reached into my pocket and slipped the snickerdoodle I had brought for Mutti from the German-American Club into the pocket of his coat. The flap lifted periodically with the rhythm of the wind. Fritz nodded his approval. The boy stirred but didn't wake. We passed on.

"But why is this so important to you?" I asked after a moment.

"Because it is wrong, just as wrong as the Nuremberg Laws." He threw his hands in the air again. "I mean to not allow human beings to interact with each other, and to make it a law!" He saw me frown. "Yes, it is by law. In some states, Herbie says, there are laws that don't allow blacks to go to the same schools or restaurants or to sit on the bus with white people!"

"Really?"

"Yes. Not in every state; mostly in the South. And Herbie says that President Truman is trying to change things, but he is meeting resistance."

"But Fritz, it's not the same!"

"Oh, I know." He held his hand up. "But it's only one step removed."

I did not respond.

We passed several old ladies, their bags heavy from collecting. They came out onto Kronprinzenallee from the forest path and stared for a moment in wonder at the excited young man before continuing on their way home.

"I mean, it is like the old Nazi propaganda about the Jews: the coarse Jew, the greedy Jew, the lustful Jew." He shook his head. "Hate is the same no matter how you package it."

"I know. But I like them, these Americans. There is something about them, some quality..." I couldn't find the words for it. I shook my head in frustration. "I know they have faults, but somehow I think they will fix them. You said yourself that President Truman is trying to fix it!"

Fritz slowed his pace again. He was never going to turn me against Americans, and he really didn't want to. I think he just wanted me to see that they too were flawed. Somehow it made him feel better about being German.

Winter Again

The days grew shorter, and the chill of fall brought the dread of winter firmly before us. Everywhere I turned I was assaulted by images of death and disease, and Mutti's "*Gott im Himmels,*" followed by a quick folding of the newspaper, always told me that more had died. The question hovered over all of us: how many would starve this winter?

"Eight million refugees flood Berlin to the breaking point," screamed the headline of the *Life* magazine I had picked up from the pile on the table. AFN played in the background. It was a tune I didn't recognize with an uplifting, happy beat. Images of the ruins and poverty of my people were splashed across the magazine's pages—pictures of families living in rubble and boys fighting over cigarette butts: a people's humiliation laid bare for the world to see. I shook my head in disbelief that something so personal had found its way across the ocean from one continent to another so distant, and then back again to accost me in the overstuffed armchair of the German-American Club. It was like watching a scene from your own life. I shook my head again.

The sound of nylons rubbing together caused me to look up. Frau Richter stood in front of me. She had taken off her uniform, and she seemed out of place in her plain navy dress, her blond hair tied back in a loose bun at the base of her skull. I had never noticed how thin she was, her white, starched apron hiding the narrowness of her hips and the flatness of her chest. But still, she had a small waist, and I could see with ten or even twenty pounds added to her present weight she would probably have a nice figure. She wanted to talk, but for some reason a new shyness had overcome her.

" Hello, Frau Richter. How are you?" I said to encourage her.

She held her purse in her hands, clutching it with all ten of her fingers.

"I'm very well. How are you?"

I tossed the magazine back on the table. "Well, I could do without all the problems in Berlin thrown in my face, that's for sure!"

She nodded. "Yes. Too much knowledge can sometimes be a bad thing, I think."

I looked out the window. The trees had lost most of their leaves; only a few tenacious ones clung to the branches. She cleared her throat, and I shifted my gaze back to her face.

"I just wanted to tell you that this is my last day here."

My eyes bulged. Nobody who had a job quit it, especially a job working for the Americans. "What happened?" I asked.

"I'm leaving for America next week."

I was speechless. A part of me filled with envy, and my skin grew warm under my sweater—and then almost instantly my better side felt pleased for this poor woman who had lost so much.

"With Captain Haft." She looked down shyly. "We were married last week."

I leaped up from the chair and hugged her. "That is wonderful news! Congratulations!" I kissed her on both cheeks.

Tears formed around her eyes, and she quickly wiped them away. Smiling, she said, "Thank you. We have received permission to transfer back to the United States, somewhere in Texas." She shrugged.

"Well, you better learn to speak English very slowly and through your nose, because that's how they talk there!"

She giggled, and suddenly she was a schoolgirl, grabbing my hand and talking quickly about how it had all happened so fast, and the Captain had wanted to get married in the States but he had married her now so she could go with him, and they were planning another wedding in Texas with his family, a big one, and how she planed to eat a steak as soon as she gets there—he says they have sixteen-ounce steaks in Texas, she said—and how they will have a large house with citrus trees—can you imagine, Jutta, living where citrus trees can grow in the winter?

I was happy for her, but after she left to go home—"so much to organize before next week"—I sat in the chair staring out the window, watching as the snow began to fall in little swirls. It was only November, and already snow flurries fell. An overwhelming sadness seized me, gripping my chest. And with my heart pounding in my ears, I knew with a clarity that comes only occasionally that I did not belong here.

"My God! You look like someone has died!"

I jumped. Peti stood over me, peering at me. Lost in my own thoughts, I hadn't heard Peti and Maria come up from the basement, where they had been learning how to develop photographs in the newly built darkroom. My lecture on the American West had ended a half-hour before, and we were to walk home together.

I waved away their concern. "I'm just looking at this horrible weather," I lied.

They both looked out the window simultaneously.

"*Du*, we should hurry up and go before it really gets going," said Maria.

"It's starting to get dark. Maria is right; we probably should go." I looked at my watch: 4:15, and it was already getting dark. They followed me to the long brass rack adjacent to the front door where our coats hung side by side in a neat row, scarves and hats as well.

"Ladies," said the MP who monitored the door, "are you leaving us already?"

"Yes. It's starting to snow," I said sadly.

He looked through the glass panels of the door. "By golly, it is! How do you people stand these winters?" He shook his head.

I screwed up my lips, buttoned the top button of my coat, and stepped into the cold Berlin air. "Exactly," I muttered.

"Frau Richter is leaving next week."

"Really?" Mutti looked up from her book, surprised. "She's the nice lady you like at the German-American Club?"

"Yes. She married Captain Haft and is leaving for the States." I paused. "Texas, she said." I waited for a reaction.

Mutti said nothing. She did not approve of relationships between the American military men and German women—I knew this only too well. After a moment she put down her book. "Well, I hope it is all that she expects it to be. Now I must go to the kitchen and see what we have for dinner."

I watched her leave the room. Her gray wool dress hung in loose folds around her knees and clung to her a little more than it did last year, I noticed. She didn't want to talk about it—about America—about Germans leaving for America. I sighed and lifted Teddy onto my lap.

For us, 1947 closed much as 1946 had: we were cold, hungry, and filled with uncertainty. As the days grew darker, my mood seemed to parallel the gloom. Currency reform was still a distant prayer, and Germans continued to starve in mass numbers, reported with a macabre attention to detail in the now thirteen newspapers that had sprouted up all over Berlin. And still the Russians waited.

25

1948

"What an idiot!" Vati folded the paper back up and showed us the headlines on the front page of *Die Neue Zeitung*.

I only caught the word *Hühnerfutter* before he slammed it down on the table. "What is it? Something about chicken feed?"

Vati stirred his tea. "This idiot, Semler, said the Americans were only sending us chicken feed to eat!"

"Because of the corn," explained Mutti, looking in my direction.

"Who is Semler?"

"Jutta, you know who he is! The economics minister, Johannes Semler."

"Oh, him." I thought for a moment. "He's the one Mrs. Vockel says General Clay is not happy with over his comments. That's right; now I remember the name. Herr Semler." I paused for effect before casually announcing, "He will probably be fired."

Vati and Mutti exchanged a glance. "When did she tell you this?" asked Vati.

"Yesterday afternoon. I went over to see her. She's sick again."

"Frau Vockel should not tell you such things," said my mother.

I nodded and became very busy with my bread and egg, dipping the bread carefully into the yolk. I could feel the stares of both of my parents.

"Herr Semler is not a wise man!" added my mother.

I looked up in surprise.

"When a country feeds you for free, you don't criticize the quality; you accept what they send over with gratitude."

Vati grunted his agreement. "And the sad part is he's one of the better ministers. A lot of his criticism of the military government is accurate. He's right; we have got to be allowed to become self-sufficient! But why did he have to add this silly chicken feed comment?"

Mutti shrugged. "He got caught up in the moment, Hans. You know how that is, and then the press takes off with it."

Vati sipped his tea and picked the newspaper up again. He set it down seconds later. "If what Frau Vockel says is true, I wonder who will replace him."

"Does it really matter?" asked my mother, getting up from the table.

"It could. We need a strong advocate, but one with good judgment, too."

"Well, I think it should be you!" I offered.

Mutti laughed. "Your father has his hands full with the *Verein der Berliner Kaufleute*!* I don't think his nerves could handle dealing with the economic problems of all Germany!"

March 1948

The mornings were no longer cold, and the air began to hold a vague promise of warmth. I knew spring was really around the corner.

"Hurry up, Jutta! Maria is waiting for you," called my mother from the kitchen. It seemed my mother was always in the kitchen. She never was in the kitchen before—before the war. Back then, if she was at home, I would find her in the music room or her study or her bedroom, but now she was either in the kitchen or the garden. It suddenly occurred to me that she had not played the piano since the war ended. I made a mental note to ask her to play something when I came home from school today.

"I'm coming," I answered, grabbing my books from the dresser and shoving them under my arm American style. I clattered down the stairs. "See you this afternoon, Mutti," I called as I rushed to the front door before she had a chance to see me.

"Hold it!"

I stopped dead in my tracks. "Yes?"

She emerged from the kitchen, wiping her hands on a towel. She shook her head adamantly. "I don't think so, young lady! You head right back up there and put on some proper stockings!"

"But Mutti, Maria is waiting for me!"

"I will talk to her."

"Oh, come on! It's spring. I'll be warm enough."

"Absolutely not. Now march. I don't want another word about it!"

"But all the American girls wear bobby socks, and they don't even wear coats!" I protested.

"Yes. And they have buses that take them to school and heated schools. German girls walk to school and sit in unheated classrooms, and I will not let you catch pneumonia! Now go!" And she shooed me upstairs, fluttering her hands at me.

Angrily I took off my bobby socks. They weren't even real bobby socks. They were an old pair of white knee socks, too short for me, that I had rolled down to imitate the American look. I reflected sadly that being in style would always be out of reach for German girls. Never could we wear those fluffy pink sweaters that I so longed for, or those cute black-and-white shoes that Mrs. Vockel had called "saddle shoes" that were all the rage among the American girls. I jerked open my dresser drawer and pulled out the ugly navy blue tights.

---

*   Berlin Businessman's Association.

"Yuck!" I said, sticking out my tongue at them as I pulled and tugged them over my bottom, dancing a bit to fit them into place.

I hurried now, slamming the door behind me. We would be late if we didn't walk quickly. The early morning air bit me as I walked down the flagstone path, and I was secretly glad I didn't have bare legs. I looked down at my legs as they moved below me, carrying me down the path. Did these practical German stockings really have to be so ugly? I vowed to design a warm but attractive alternative to thick wool stockings.

"Sorry I'm late." I shut the gate as I said it. "My mother made me change." I rolled my eyes and pulled my mouth to the side.

"What did you have on?" asked Maria, her eyebrows raised.

Before I could answer, I heard Mrs. Vockel's voice. "Utah!" I hated how she dragged the first syllable out. "Utah, wait a moment."

I looked across the street to see Mrs. Vockel waving and hurrying down the front stoop of Erica's house. She seemed flustered, and I was surprised to see that her hair was not done and she had on no makeup.

I walked quickly across the street, leaving Maria by my gate. Whatever she wanted it seemed urgent, and it occurred to me she had been watching for me!

"Good morning, Mrs. Vockel," I said, trying to hide my surprise at her appearance, as well as the fact that I had never seen her before ten o'clock in the morning.

" I am so glad I caught you! That *Saturday Evening Post* I gave you yesterday?" She paused for a moment. "I need it back." She said the words quickly and forcefully.

"Sure," I spluttered in surprise. "But I haven't read it."

She seemed relieved to hear this. "I'm sorry, Jutta, but there is an article that Colonel Vockel needs," she paused again before adding vaguely, "for work."

I knew she was lying, but why? "I'll have to give it to you when I get home from school." I pointed to my watch and then to Maria. "We're really late already."

She did not seem pleased, but she said, "Well, I guess that would be okay. I may not be home when you come home, so just leave it by the back door if you don't mind."

"Sure."

"Thanks, Utah. Sorry to have to yank it back like this."

"That's all right. But I must go."

"Yes. Yes, of course." And suddenly she seemed self-conscious about her appearance. Her hands fluttered over her hair before waving goodbye to me.

"What was that all about?" asked Maria as we walked toward Auf dem Grat to head for the streetcar at the corner of Kronprinzenallee and Königin Luise Strasse.

"Very strange!" I said, shaking my head. "She wants me to return the *Saturday Evening Post*, which she always gives me to read and has never wanted back before. But, I mean, she seems to want it back in a bad way!"

"I wonder why?"

"I don't know, but I plan to read it from cover to cover before I give it back."

Maria giggled. "Well, you better race home from school, then. I think she'll be waiting at the door for you!"

"I know," I said, turning to Maria as we walked. "Didn't it seem like she was waiting for me to come to the gate?"

"Yes! Definitely!"

I rushed home from school. Teddy greeted me at the door, his high-pitched bark—tin meeting tin—could be heard out in the street. I opened the door and let him follow me to the bottom of the steps before petting him. His tail wagging, he threw himself on his back and squealed with excitement as a long arc of urine escaped from him, wetting the flagstone by my feet.

"That's why we say 'hi' outside, isn't it, boy? Yes! We don't want Mutti mad at us, do we?" I stood up. "Okay. Come on, Teddy. Enough." He flipped over onto his legs in one deft move and raced ahead of me up the steps and through the door. I closed the door and ran to Mutti's music room, grabbing the *Saturday Evening Post* as I walked by Vati's desk. I chose the music room just in case Mrs. Vockel decided to come by and ask for the paper. It was the only room where she could not look in from the front window. I threw myself onto Mutti's sofa and began to skim the headlines for anything that had to do with Berlin or the American occupation. Maria and I decided that whatever it was it must have something to do with the Russians, and the Americans, and Berlin.

After only a few minutes I found it, and it made my stomach fall.

"Vati, Mutti, listen to this!" I said, sitting straight up on the sofa and holding the magazine wide open as I read. Mutti and Vati had just come in from the garden. Vati had come home to bring Gustav from the factory to help my mother with the spring planting.

"Wait," he said, holding up his hands. "Let me sit down so I can concentrate." Vati's English was not the best; he understood it, but he had to concentrate, and I had to speak very slowly. We walked single file into the dining room and sat down.

"They even quote General Clay," I said in German, and then I began to read in English. My parents listened very quietly as I read the English to them, translating those words they did not understand. And then I came to this sentence, directly attributed to General Clay: "For many months, based on logical analysis, I have felt and held that war was unlikely for at least ten years. Within the last few weeks, I have felt a subtle change in Soviet attitude which I cannot define, but which now gives me a feeling that it may come with *dramatic suddenness*." I lowered the magazine onto the table, letting it crumple up under my hand and forearm, and searched their faces to see if they felt the same wave of nausea as I did.

Vati stared at the table, a frown creasing his face. Mutti stared at me, her face as pale as the beige tablecloth covering the walnut dining room table.

"What does it mean?" I asked quietly.

Vati looked up. "It means that the Americans are worried about Mr. Soko-lovsky and Mr. Stalin and the future of Berlin."

"Berlin!"

Vati nodded.

"You mean we could go communist? Go to the Soviet Union?" I practically screamed the words.

"*Gott im Himmel*, let us pray not! Surely not, Hans!" My mother placed her hands together, covering her mouth as she spoke. "They have taken Prague, and now us?"

"No," my father said, and then again more firmly, "No. It depends on the Americans and how strong they are—if they are willing to fight for us. I mean diplomatically and in the game of politics. The Soviets have been more and more difficult, making all sorts of demands threatening the access routes to Berlin."

"The access routes? Why didn't they negotiate a treaty with the Russians about access routes?" interrupted Mutti, throwing her hands in the air. "These Americans are sometimes so naïve! Imagine. A handshake about something so critical to Berlin."

Vati continued. "And demanding that their currency be the only official currency, and so far General Clay has been firm with them. I have great confidence in him. The only question is this Marshall. I am not so sure about him."

"Who is Marshall again?" I asked.

"He is the foreign secretary for the United States, remember? "

I nodded.

"But they have no troops left, Hans. The British and Americans have sent most of their troops home, but not the Russians. They have thousands and thousands! Frau Schultz says they're on every street corner in the East sector, still leering at the women."

"But the Americans and British have air power."

"Air power? What will that do?"

Vati ignored the question. "I am surprised that this statement is in the mag-azine. And according to what you read, it has caused quite a stir in the United States."

"Mrs. Vockel sure wants this back. She was anxious that I return it this morning, but I told her I was too late for school."

"Well, you better take it back. I'm sure Colonel Vockel would not be pleased that she gave it to you with this statement in it."

"How far is it to Helmstadt?" I asked.

"Oh, I don't know. One hundred fifty, two hundred kilometers or so."

"Is it that far?" I asked, incredulous. It seemed worlds away. It was the western exit point from the Russian Zone, and we were so isolated and vulnerable here on our island in the middle of the Russian Zone.

My father nodded. "But we are not going to panic about this. And Jutta, I don't want you talking to your friends about this. Talking leads to stirring," he moved his hand as if he were stirring a pot, "which leads to panic. I am sure the Americans and the British will stand by us. And so far the Russians have only played games."

I tried to feel Vati's confidence, but I was shaken. I pushed the images of leering Russian faces and the fear that my parents could not mask from me deep down. But sometimes the images came to visit, and there was no retreat from them. It was then that my stomach felt empty—not from lack of food, but just empty, like there was no point to it all, no point at all.

———

Mrs. Vockel didn't come home until almost dinnertime, and as soon as I saw her car pull in the short driveway I ran over to give her the magazine. She looked startled to see me.

"Utah, I thought you were bringing it after school."

"I was, but I didn't want to leave it outside."

She looked at the house and saw that it was dark. "Well, no matter. Colonel Vockel is not home anyway." She took the magazine from me as she stepped out of the car. "Thank you, dear."

"You're welcome. Have a good evening."

I turned and walked back to my side of the street. I could feel her eyes on my back, watching me as I crossed the street and pushed the gate open to go home. I turned to latch the gate. She waved slightly, catching my eye, and I replied with a short wave. I had the feeling she wanted to tell me something but did not know how to. Or perhaps she felt she couldn't. Instead, she turned and walked up the driveway and into Erica's house.

———

"You know they're leaving next month?" I said quietly.

"Who's leaving?" Mutti looked up from painting her nails with the polish she had had me purchase from Mrs. Vockel. I picked up the bright red dispenser. "China Red" was printed on a clear sticker across the bottom. "Jutta, you know I hate it when you start in the middle of something and expect us to figure out what you're saying! Now who is leaving, and where are they going?"

" The Vockels. They're going back to the States."

" *Really?*" She stopped painting her nails and studied my face.

"Yes. She said their tour is over. They've been here two years, and she wants him to retire so they can move to someplace out west called Phoenix, Arizona."

"Good heavens! Is there anything but cacti and cowboys and Indians out there?"

"Yes. She says it will be good for her asthma. It is very dry and warm, and lots of people are moving there who have breathing problems."

"Respiratory problems, you mean?"

"Yes."

"Goodness, have they been here two years? I guess so. It was April of forty-six, wasn't it?"

I nodded.

She screwed the top tightly back on the polish bottle. "How do you feel about their leaving? About Mrs. Vockel leaving?"

I shrugged. "It doesn't matter," I said nonchalantly. "I'll miss the dinners and our conversations about America."

"And all the magazines and the little things she gets for you from the PX," persisted Mutti, still studying my face.

"Well, I can read the magazines at the German-American Club, and she says she will send me a package every once in a while." I didn't mention that she had also encouraged me to move to the United States and said she and Colonel Vockel would sponsor me if I ever decided to come over.

"Well, that's nice of her." My mother unscrewed the polish bottle again to fix an imperfection. She was going out to dinner with Vati to Schlichter's, one of a handful of restaurants able to reopen, and then to the symphony. It almost seemed like old times. Her hands were again elegant, the nails finally long enough to warrant polish. Her fingers were splayed on top of her dressing table so she could polish them. She wore the ruby ring that Vati had given her for their tenth wedding anniversary. It was my favorite. The deep red of the main stone sparkled and matched the color of her nails perfectly. She had on a new dress, made by Frau Schultz just last week, and her hair was up in a chignon with a bit of wave around the face. It glistened in the bedroom light, almost forming a halo around her head.

" I think I'm finished," she said, holding her hands up for inspection.

"You look perfect," I said.

"And you, my dear? What are you and Fritz doing tonight?"

"We are going to the movies with some friends."

"At the Capitol? Or in Steglitz?"

"No, Steglitz at the Titania-Palast. *Hamlet*, with Sir Laurence Olivier."

"Oh, I want to see that also!" She stood and put her hand to her chest. "'The time is out of joint, O cursed spite That ever I was born to set it right.'" She dropped her hand and nodded to me. "A play for our times, don't you think?"

I looked at her, amazed. "How do you remember that stuff? I can't even remember what they made me memorize last month."

"It doesn't interest you, I guess."

I shrugged. "I would really rather see one of the dance movies, but Fritz wants to see this, and the others say Olivier is supposed to be fantastic."

"'Our indiscretion serves us well, When our deep plots do pall: and that should teach us There's a divinity that shapes our ends, Rough-hew them how we will.'"

"Do you have the whole play memorized?"

"No. Just a few favorite lines. They made us do memory work in high school."

"We weren't even allowed to read Shakespeare!"

"Well, that was ridiculous, wasn't it? But you read some at home with Vati, remember?"

"Yes. We read *Romeo and Juliet*."

"Well, you'll enjoy the movie. Who's going?"

"Christa and her friend Peter, and Peti and a friend, and Hilde, and Maria. But I'm not sure if they are bringing friends. It's always a bit dicey with those two and their boyfriends."

"Would you like to have them over after the movies?"

"Yes!" I said enthusiastically.

"I'll have Luise set a few things out."

"Including some wine?" I suggested hopefully.

"Of course! I'll have Vati set out a bottle."

"Thanks, Mutti. You're the best!"

I practically skipped off to my bedroom to finish getting ready.

Mutti stuck her head in the door. "Jutta, Fritz is here, you know."

I set the brush down and followed Mutti downstairs. The scent of Chanel No. 5 followed her, and I smiled.

"There they are, the two most beautiful women in all of Berlin!" said Vati, standing. Fritz nodded and stood as well.

"Good evening, Frau Bolle, Jutta."

"Good evening, gentlemen."

They had been sitting drinking a beer in the living room. Vati offered us a seat. "Can I get you anything, dear?"

"No. I'm fine, thank you."

His eyes fell on my face, locking onto my lips for a moment, but he said nothing. He shifted his gaze to my shoes. "*Gott im Himmel!* How are you ever going to make it to the streetcar in those things?"

I lifted my foot and examined my shoes. The heel was about two inches. "I'll manage."

"Well, why doesn't Heinz take you, and then he can come back for us." He looked at his watch. "We'll have enough time, don't you think, Heitchen?"

"Oh, yes."

"Heinz is here?" I asked. How could I not have heard the truck?

"Yes, of course. You don't think I will have your mother walking to the symphony! But maybe you should get going now." He turned to Fritz. "We'll have to finish our conversation another time."

"Thank you for the ride."

"Come. I'll go tell Heinz." Vati rose from his chair.

"I hope you have a lovely evening, Frau Bolle," said Fritz, bowing slightly.

"Why thank you, Fritz." She nodded in his direction. "Oh, I almost forgot. I told Jutta you could all come back here after the movie. Is that good?"

"Excellent. Thank you." Fritz smiled.

"Listen. Next week Frau Bolle and I cannot attend the symphony." Vati waved his hand dismissively. "There's some awful dinner with the business group we must attend, so if you and Jutta would like to go, you may have our tickets."

"Thank you. We would be thrilled to go." Fritz turned to me, an eyebrow raised in question. I nodded in reply.

"I think they are playing Mendelssohn's Fifth Symphony." We had arrived at the truck, and Heinz stepped out to greet my father. "Heinz, would it be possible to take these two to Steglitz first, and then come back for us?"

"But of course, Herr Bolle."

"Excellent! Well then, you two, we will see you later this evening."

I kissed Vati. "Have a great time tonight," he said.

"You and Mutti also! I am so glad you are going out again!"

Vati smiled and winked at me. "Now go, or you'll make us late."

———

"I told you I studied music lessons as a boy," said Fritz, his broad shoulders pressed between me and the window of the cab of the truck.

"Yes. I remember." I shifted my leg toward Fritz so Heinz could shift more easily.

"Well, one of the piano teachers loved to play this melody. It was so beautiful, and he asked me to turn the pages for him so I could practice reading music. I only found out this year that it was Mendelssohn, because he had ripped the cover off the music and he would never tell me who it was or what it was. He didn't want the trouble."

"Was Mendelssohn banned?"

"Yes. He was Jewish."

"I didn't know. Mutti always played Mendelssohn."

It was funny sitting next to Heinz in the front cab of the truck. He said nothing, trying, despite the circumstances, to maintain the chauffeur-employer relationship. We bounced and lurched along the Kronprinzenallee, our shoulders and legs touching as Heinz turned the corner onto Königin Luise Strasse.

We were silent. It was dark; a Coca-Cola sign caught my attention in the window of the Bolle store. I chuckled. I liked all the American advertising that was cropping up in store windows and along the Kurfürstendamm. We drove past the Königin Luise Stiftung and the botanical gardens toward Steglitz and Schloss Strasse, the school dark and deserted behind a canopy of trees.

"I will miss that place!" I said, turning to look at the iron fence with its gold-covered points.

"You only have a few weeks left," said Fritz. "But maybe you won't miss it."

My *Abitur* was in two weeks, and they had been drilling us like crazy, trying to make up for the past five years of bad education all in a few weeks.

"Well, these past few weeks I won't miss, but it was a nice place to go to school."

"Yes, it was."

"But maybe there will be a spot for me at the university."

"Maybe." Fritz squeezed my hand.

It would be hard. They had a pecking order for admission: veterans had priority, then young men like Fritz, then older women without husbands, and finally, girls like me. My chances were pretty slim.

We had arrived at the corner of Schloss Strasse and Königin Luise Strasse. "Heinz, you can let us out here so that you are not late for Mutti and Vati," I said.

"No. It's only a few more blocks, and Herr Bolle would not be happy with me if he knew I did not deliver you to the front door." He concentrated on turning right onto Schloss Strasse. An army jeep whizzed past us at a speed well above the limit. Heinz exhaled loudly and shook his head.

———

"Oh! It was good!" exclaimed Mutti, taking off her coat and gloves. Vati helped her and hung her coat in the front closet. She came in, and I got up so she could sit in her favorite chair.

Fritz got up to turn the radio down.

"And you, my dears? How was your movie?" asked my mother.

"Unbelievable! Honestly, this Olivier is really fantastic. He makes you think you are there with him in the same room." Fritz shook his head. "He pulls you into that screen."

"And you, Jutta?"

"Jutta fell asleep," called out Peti from the other side of the room.

Mutti laughed.

"I did not!"

Hilde and Christa crossed their arms and looked at me, eyebrows raised.

"Well, maybe during some of those extraordinarily long soliloquies I might have dozed a little. But I did not fall asleep."

"The funny part is, Jutta is the only one who could understand everything," threw in Hilde. "And we were counting on her to translate some things for our after-the-movie discussion." They all giggled at this one.

"God forbid. I'm not discussing that thing. Hamlet had a mother complex, and he was unbalanced. There, that's the end of my analysis."

"Well, Shakespeare is not for everybody," said Vati. "I find him difficult, too."

"Thank you, Vati." I looked at him gratefully.

Tante Hilde

I heard the laughter and the dramatic voice, and I knew Tante Hilde was visiting with Mutti in the kitchen.

"My God, Heti, what do you expect from the people who allow the Russians to broadcast propaganda against them from their very own sector!"

That the Americans and British had not shut down Radio Berlin, broadcast out of the British sector, long ago totally baffled all of us, but it made Tante Hilde and Mutti downright mad! Last summer the Americans had started "Radio in the American Sector," a more adult version of AFN featuring news and theater rather than popular music. I presumed it was to counter Radio Berlin, but why they didn't just shut down the propaganda pit, as Vati called it, no one could understand.

"*Ja*. They have no logic, these Americans! Look at what they do with the Russians! They shake hands with them, and all the Russians have to do is smile and slap them on the back, and then they stick the knife in, still smiling. No. They need to be hit over the head with a two-by-four to help them with their logic." Hilde waved her free hand that wasn't petting Teddy. Teddy opened his eyes and looked at me, arching his brows to do so but otherwise not moving a muscle. He loved Tante Hilde and considered her lap his personal bed, curling up on it in a tight little ball whenever she came for a visit. "Isn't that right, *Liebling*?" She scratched him under the chin. He stood on his front paws to lick her face.

"Hilde, don't let him do that. You'll get sick!"

"Oh, please! What haven't I been exposed to during all this mess? I mean please, little Teddy couldn't possibly have anything worse."

Mutti noticed me standing in the door and looked at me doubtfully. We both knew about Teddy's garden activities.

"Well, I'm glad you could make it down, Jutta."

I walked in and kissed Hilde on the cheek. "How is my *Schatzchen*?" she asked, pursing her lips for another kiss.

"I'm fine, thank you."

"She has her exams this week. So she can't be late for school," said Mutti, raising her eyebrows for emphasis as she handed me my plate with a *Brötchen* and a tiny piece of cheese.

"Oh, yes. The horrors of modern education. All those tests! I don't know how you young people do it. I don't think I could have sat still long enough for them."

I laughed. No doubt she was right.

"So what are you two doing today?" I asked.

"*Quatching!*" laughed Tante Hilde. "*Du*, Heti, let's have some real coffee today. None of that *Blümchen Kaffee*, but real, thick coffee. I'll pay you back."

"Don't be ridiculous. You don't have to pay me back." Mutti put two extra scoops of coffee into the coffee ring. "In honor of your tests, Juttalein!" She reached over and kissed me. "Now go, or you will be late."

"I expect straight 100 percents from you, Jutta Bolle, especially in that American literature section. It is American literature that she is studying, isn't it, Heti?" asked Hilde, leaning toward my mother.

"Yes," laughed Mutti.

I kissed them both again and tousled Teddy's head. He didn't even bother to look up as I hurried out the door. I was happy to see Tante Hilde; she always cheered Mutti up, and I was pleased they had started their weekly coffee tradition again. On Mondays, Heinz would pick up Uncle Kurt and Tante Hilde, depositing Tante Hilde at our house in exchange for Vati, who went to the factory with Kurt. That way she only had to walk home. Neither Mutti nor Tante Hilde had to walk to stay thin now, and in fact, the less walking and the fewer calories burned, the better. Now that the weather had begun to turn warmer, she had started to come again.

I smiled as I closed the gate and looked back toward the kitchen to see Tante Hilde at the table, mouth open wide and arm extended, sharing some interesting gossip with Mutti. She would keep a smile on Mutti's face, I thought as I swung out into the street, hurrying to catch the streetcar at Königin Luise Strasse and Kronprinzenallee.

May 1948

She was there, across the street from me with her long dresses full of fabric and her perfect shoes and manicures, and then she wasn't. Or so it seemed. She left quickly, with more bags and an extra trunk full of my mother's china, but not much more.

The car pulled up, and the sound of the driver slamming the door broke through the lonely silence of the grandfather clock ticking away in the living room. I peered out the front window and saw the driver walking up to the front door. She had asked me to come over to say goodbye. She was not sad about leaving Berlin. She had hated it. At least I had assumed so by her comments about the weather and the "dismal gray sky" and the "horrible smoky air." "So depressing!" she would say.

"Well, dear, I guess this is goodbye. I must say I will miss you." She held my hand for a moment. "You have become like a daughter to me," she added quietly.

When she lifted her face, her eyes brimmed with tears. "Here is my address in Arlington, Virginia. I don't know exactly where we will move to in Arizona, but I will write you as soon as I know." She smiled at me.

"I will miss you, too," I said. My stomach felt queasy. She was my only link to America, and now she was leaving. I had grown used to her conversation and our Sunday dinners.

"I will send you magazines and, please, if there is anything you want—well, small things that I can mail, just let me know."

"Thank you."

She held out her arms. "Give a hug, and let's be done with these goodbyes. To drag them out only makes one sad." She reached for me, and we patted each other on the back in that way I had seen her greet her friends. It was never a true hug.

Through the window, I saw that the officer had loaded the last bag into the long blue car with the American flags on the front. She opened the front door for me, and we both stepped out onto the front stoop. The sun broke through a cloud, and we squinted against its brightness.

"I'm leaving, and the sun finally breaks out!" she joked, removing her sunglasses from her purse. "I haven't needed these in two years!"

I smiled and followed her to the car in the driveway.

"Well, I must hurry. Colonel Vockel wants me to pick him up in ten minutes, and our flight leaves in an hour." She looked around and breathed in the spring air, touched with the smell of lilac. "I can't believe we are finally leaving. Now listen. I'm serious about you coming over to the States. The offer is always open."

I nodded.

"Okay, Utah. Goodbye, dear."

"Goodbye." And suddenly, inexplicably, I was crying. She grabbed me and hugged me hard, then pushed me toward my house, waving her hand as she did so. She stepped into the car. The officer slammed the door and tipped his hat to me before he too disappeared behind the door on the other side of the car. He backed the car out into the narrow street, missing our fence on the other side by inches, and carefully maneuvered it down the Föhrenweg. She waved from the back window, not turning around, and then she was gone. I waved back, knowing she could not see, and with my hand still in the air, it was as if I had fallen into a deep, dark lake. Water sealed over my head and I struggled to breathe. And for a moment the stillness overtook the street. In the distance, a car horn sounded on the Kronprinzenallee. A breeze ran through the acacias overhead, dislodging a seedpod. Wings spread, it floated elegantly down in front of me from the sky. I wrapped my arms around my chest and walked through our gate. My mother stood in the window watching me.

26

They've Done It

June 1948

The Russians began the blockade of Berlin on June 24, 1948, and did not lift their chokehold until May 12, 1949. I remember the day it began. I had just heard that I had been accepted into the Victoria *Fachschule*, and my parents had agreed to let me attend even though it meant traveling to downtown Berlin five days a week. Vati was not convinced he would let me ride the subway, however, because the Russian police had taken to coming over to the Western sector to scour the subway station magazine kiosks for newspapers and magazines that they considered anti-Russian. The western powers had yet to put a stop to it, and Vati said, "If a Russian in any kind of uniform is anywhere near, no Bolle will set foot in the vicinity." Mutti had offered to accompany me on the subway, but Vati would have none of it. So, absent the detail of getting me to and from the school, I knew I was going.

I had spent the afternoon *bummeling* in Dahlem with my friends at the *Konditorei* on the corner of Taku and Königin Luise Strasse to celebrate my acceptance. Mutti had given me a few extra coupons for *spendieren* to "buy ourselves a kingdom."

The little bakery had been there for as long as I could remember. But I hadn't been to it in a long time because Fritz always brought us wonderful treats from his father's *Konditorei*, and Mutti saved the coupons for "more worthwhile calories." The bell jingled on the door as we entered, masking the squeak of hinges badly in need of repair. I noticed the windows no longer sported the bright yellow curtains I had remembered as a child. I smiled. No doubt the baker's children were now wearing them instead. A long countertop edged in metal with two diagonal ridges ran the full length of the wall on the right. Only two chairs were available, and Maria and Hilde immediately commandeered them. Christa followed them to the table. Peti and I went to the case, as we were the only two with coupons. The selection was limited and the quantities were meager. A plate with ten *Himbeertaschen* sat in the middle of the case. Where before there would have been fifty or more, I thought ten represented a kingdom.

"They have *Himbeertaschen*!" I called to Hilde and Maria.

"You order what you like, Jutta. They're your coupons," replied Maria easily.

"No. I have my own," said Peti.

"Well, Jutta can order for us."

"Can I have three *Himbeertaschen*, please?"

"Do you have coupons?" asked the baker.

He was from the East, I guessed, judging by his accent. Old Mr. Kohn had died when the Russians marched in, and his widow had died a month later. Who this man was I didn't know, but I didn't really like him. He had a skinny little torso, and his skin was pulled tight across the features on his face. Above his head on the wall, a perfect dark blue rectangle stood out against the faded blue of the rest of the wall. A picture had obviously held that spot for years and only been removed recently. I knew whose it was.

"Of course," I responded, lowering my eyes to meet his, indignant at the question.

He shrugged. "Well, why not get all ten?"

"I only want three, thank you." I turned to Christa, who had come to join us. I knew she did not like *Himbeertaschen*. "What do you want, Christa?"

She examined the case for a long time. The baker stood impatient, my plate of *Himbeertaschen* held in his left hand. He tapped the top of the case with his right hand.

"Let's see. Maybe I'll have a *Mandelecken*," she said finally.

"And two *Mandelecken*," I said to him.

"Oh, one is fine! Do you have enough for two?" she asked, obviously hoping that I did.

"Yes. Mutti gave me plenty."

I gave the baker my coupons, and Peti's as well, and we joined Hilde and Maria.

"Gregory Peck! He is it!" I kissed my fingers and blew the kiss to the ceiling.

"Oh, Jutta. You and your Americans!"

"I agree with Jutta," shouted Maria. "It is not possible to be more handsome than Gregory Peck!"

"See?" I looked triumphant. "I grant you Will Quadflieg cuts a nice picture too, but Gregory Peck? Those eyes!"

Peti giggled. "Jutta, wipe the *Himbeere* off your teeth. I don't think Gregory would find that too attractive."

"Well, I am a realist. And I'm sticking with Will Quadflieg because I at least live in the same city as he does, and I might meet him. And then, who knows?" Christa struck her best movie star pose, sticking out her chest and pushing her hair back. "He just might fall for me."

We all laughed at Christa.

"*Gott im Himmel! Ja!* You're a realist, all right," said Hilde, rolling her eyes. "No. No." She shook her head emphatically. "Horst Casper! His perfect nose and cheekbones, and such a good actor!" said Hilde.

"*Ja*. I have to agree. He is very good looking," said Peti.

"Too cold! Too perfect!" I retorted, licking my fingers.

"Well, maybe," conceded Peti.

"This is heaven!" Maria licked her lips. "I haven't had *Himbeertaschen* in three years. Mutti won't use her coupons on them." She made a face. "Somehow she thinks eggs and meat are more important!"

"Yes. Please say many thanks to your mother, Jutta. She is so sweet!" Christa loved Mutti and thought she could do no wrong.

"Well, she's not always sweet," I said.

"Oh, stop it. Your mother is the best." Peti pushed me in the arm for emphasis. "And you know it. Try my mother!" She rolled her eyes toward heaven.

"*Guten Tag*, Frau Becker!" called the baker to the old woman entering the shop. Her bag caught in the door and she struggled with it for a moment. Her shoulders hunched over a bit, and her gray hair was held in place by a scarf that she had tied behind her head. Her bag was filled with small scraps of wood and a few bits of what looked like weeds; maybe some type of edible green. The bag was in danger of falling apart even though she had lined the bottom with newspaper.

"Have you heard the news?" she responded without greeting him.

A silence fell at our table.

"No."

"They've done it! They've blockaded the city!"

A crash rang out, causing all of us to jump. The baker had hit the case with his hand.

"Who?" asked Maria.

Frau Becker and the baker looked at her with disbelief. "The Russians, of course," they said in unison.

"Blockaded the city? How?" asked Hilde, rising from her chair to join the adults.

"Every road, every train, every boat, all of it. I just heard it. My brother works for the railroad, and he phoned me from downtown."

We looked at each other in disbelief.

"Are you sure?" asked the baker.

"*Ja. Ja.* I'm sure. You just wait they will announce it on the news."

"But why?" asked Maria.

"They want to starve us out and then swoop in and ..." Frau Becker drew an imaginary noose around her neck.

I put my second *Himbeertaschen*, only half eaten, down on my plate; suddenly it was tasteless, and the grease stuck to my teeth. "Let's go," I said, my good mood evaporated. I pushed my chair away and walked to the door. Christa and Peti followed me, while Hilde stayed to talk. We walked in silence past the kiosk that had always been open after school when I was a child and now stood boarded up, waiting for chocolates and candies to sell again. How would it ever open now? I asked myself. I hate it. I hate all of this! Tears began to rim my eyes.

"It will turn out all right, Jutta. Don't let it spoil your celebration."

I turned on Christa. "How? How will it ever be all right as long as they are near us? Tell me, how?"

Christa stopped walking, taken aback by my intensity. "Well, you just have to believe, that's all." Her words did not move me.

Peti hooked her arm through mine. "Besides, we don't know the truth of it. Let's wait until Vati and Uncle Hans come home. They'll know something more than this Frau Becker, whoever she is."

I shook my head. "Every time! Every single time I start to feel a little bit secure and happy, or I start to think that maybe everything will be all right, something happens. The God of unhappiness sits up there and says, 'We better put her in her place. She is happy again. We can't let that happen!'"

"Well, you're not the only one going through all of this, you know." It was Christa who had hooked her arm through my free arm. I stopped walking, dragging them both to a standstill with me, and looked at Christa. Of course she was right. We were all together in the same big, unending mess.

I drew them close. "I know. I'm sorry," I said quietly.

Rumors swirled all day that the Russians had blockaded the access routes to Berlin. News traveled fast in Berlin. Isolated and vulnerable, we spread truths and rumors with the zeal of teenagers, especially when they concerned the Russians. We were terrified of them; the spring of 1945 was not so long ago.

"Yes. I heard the same news," said Fritz, answering my mother's question. "My father's supplier called and said that he could only guarantee flour and butter for the next week or so, and then who knows? The Russians have cut off the *Helmstead Autobahn* and the bridge over the Elbe also, I think, to both trains and trucks."

"My God! When will we ever be free of them and all of their games?" Mutti threw her hands up in the air. "I just can't understand why the Americans would not secure the supply lines when they first took over. It is just utterly idiotic!"

"Mutti, please," I bristled.

My mother shook her head and looked at her watch. "Herr Bolle should be here any moment, and then maybe he can tell us exactly what is going on."

Fritz nodded and folded his hands in front of him in that gesture he had of waiting. He had come for dinner, bringing us a gift from the bakery, a small loaf of rye bread wrapped up in a piece of brown paper that Luise folded carefully for Fritz to return to his father. I tried to fill the time with talk about my day, giving my mother the latest news about friends and my outing to the bakery. Normally she would have listened keenly, asking questions, but today she was distracted and asked me again and again to repeat what I had just said. So I gave up.

I heard the door squeak, then the familiar heavy slam of the truck's door that always followed, and then the crisp, quick footsteps of my father's shoes as they struck the flagstone walk. I leaped up and ran to the door.

He was coming up the walk with his head down, looking at his shoes—he was thinking.

"Vati," I called out from the steps. He looked up sharply, startled.

"Jutta," he smiled.

"Hans, is it true?" called my mother from behind me before he was even halfway through the door.

"What happened to hello?" he asked, amused, and then seeing Fritz he added, "Hello, Fritz! How are you doing, young man?"

Fritz stood up and nodded his head toward my father. "I am well, sir. And you?"

"I am very well, thank you." He turned and kissed my mother on the cheek, ushering us all inside. "Is what true, my dear?"

My mother tapped her foot impatiently. "The blockade! Have they blockaded us?"

"Yes." He took his jacket off and hung it on the coat tree by the door and then loosened his necktie. "They have sealed us off!" He drew a line across his throat.

"Well, you certainly don't seem too upset about it," said my mother, her hands now folded across her chest.

He shrugged. "There is nothing I can do about it. There is nothing any of us can do about it. Only the Americans and the British can do something."

"And?" interrupted my mother.

"And the rumor is that they are planning something." He sat in his chair and stretched his legs out in front of him, crossing them at the ankles. He leaped up suddenly, heading to the cabinet to pour a brandy for himself and for Mutti.

"Heitchen, let's get the youngsters a bit of wine. Do we have any open?" he asked. I looked at Vati, grateful that he remembered we were not too young for wine.

"Yes. We have a red in the cabinet."

"I'll get it, Herr Bolle," said Fritz.

Once we all had our drinks, my mother said, "Now, why don't you tell us all that you know, please, Hans."

And he did. He told us that the rumor was that the Americans and British planned to keep the city alive. They would stand firm against the Russians one way or another, and his confidence in them bolstered our mood. He was not sure, he said, how they would bring the supplies in; there were even rumors of an armed convoy escorting supply trucks along the freeway, he said. But he was certain that they would not let the city starve, nor would they let it capitulate to the Russians. The news was comforting, and my mother and I wrapped ourselves in his certainty.

But still I was sad: sad for my parents, sad for Berlin, and especially sad for my father. Only days before, for the first time in years, Vati had been upbeat about the economy and had come home excited about the news of the currency reform. The business council, of which he was president, along with many other groups throughout Germany, had been pushing for it for months, if not years— to end the inflation that threatened to kill the German economic recovery and to end the abuses of the black market. And finally, it seemed, the military government agreed that the time had come. Herr Erhard, the economic minister, had announced it several days before on his weekly radio show on *Hessische Rundfunk*. In addition, Vati said they were planning to lift the price controls that prevented German farmers and businessmen from selling their goods at a decent price. He had said the Russians would not like the currency reform; they wanted *their* version of the currency to rule in the East and the West, which is why it had taken the West so long to decide on the timing for the reform.

But he had never expected the Russians to blockade Berlin in retaliation, to cut us off entirely. It was brutal: it was typically Russian in style. In a way it was like dealing with the Nazis—bullying and deadly—but in another way it was even more confusing. The Nazis loved rules, and they would codify all of their arbitrary, brutal decisions. The Russians just acted; they did not codify anything, so you never knew if this was a new policy or just the whim of the moment. I suppose the end result was the same. That is what Vati said, and so did Fritz, but I found it a bit like walking through the forest during a thunderstorm, uncertain whether lightning would strike.

They tried to strangle the life out of us, but instead they cemented our resolve to live—and not only to live, but to live in a free society. With one stroke they cut off every supply line to Berlin: all the roads, autobahns, and train lines that brought food, coal, and every other supply to the city. And for the second time we were completely vulnerable—at the mercy of the arbitrary Russian political machine with all of its mercurial nature. They offered no explanation. They didn't need to; they were Russians, and they simply acted without worrying about explanations. They had the troops there; the Americans did not. They controlled the territory through which all supply vehicles had to come; the Americans controlled only our small sliver of Berlin. We all continued to wonder at the naiveté of a country with the power and might of the United States that would not secure these supply lines. And so we held our breath and prayed that the United States and the British would not leave us. The French, we knew, would do whatever was best for the French, but we believed in our hearts—we had to believe—that the United States, with Britain backing her, would stand strong. And again we were not disappointed.

In fact, what happened next bound every Berliner's heart, every German's heart, to the West forever—never again would the threat of communism seriously fester within West Germany or West Berlin. The United States was our model now and forever, and our gratitude was overwhelming. I for one would not tolerate a negative word about the United States. I had always believed that they were our saviors, but now I embraced that belief with a zeal that bordered on the fanatical, and my friends learned never to even hint at anything negative about the United States.

Hundreds and Hundreds

The low buzzing sound, almost imperceptible at first, grew louder and louder, breaking the stillness of the afternoon. Chills ran up my spine. Memories poured out, even though I knew what it was—Vati had told us—American and British planes once again flying in formation over the skies of Berlin, but this time to bring food and supplies. Mayor Reuter had spoken to us, and we all stood prepared to take on whatever hardships faced us—anything to keep the Russians from taking Berlin. It was like a second war, but this war wasn't only about survival. It had a moral cause, and the anger that spilled out of Berliners could not be measured. The only question in our minds was how far the Russians were willing to go. The paper noted that American and British troops numbered only about six thousand, no match for the huge Soviet Army assembled in and around Berlin. Would they sweep back through the city one night, suddenly and with deadly precision? I shuddered, remembering. The idea that two million of us could be fed by planes flying in and dropping cargo day after day seemed fantastical. I was certain that the Americans would try, but would they succeed? Could they succeed? It seemed impossible.

———

A bicycle bell rang out at the front gate, an innocent contrast to the droning of the planes. I knew it was Fritz. He always did that, rang his bicycle bell to warn me of his arrival. A habit from deliveries, he said. The gate banged, and I set my book down on the arm of the chair and went out to greet him.

"You should have seen them, Jutta!" he called as he propped his bicycle against the house, where it was not visible from the street. He came to me and grabbed my hand in his excitement. "Hundreds and hundreds of them flying in, one after the other, just one, two, three, and then another!" He showed me with his free hand, forming the shape of an imaginary plane. He and a friend had ridden their bicycles to Tempelhof, he said, to watch as the planes landed. It was so like him, curious about everything.

I looked down at his large hand clasping mine. He shook my hand to get my attention. "You have to come and see it with me! Honestly, it brought tears to my eyes! I'm not sure why, but it did."

"I can't," I said simply. "I can't," I said again. "The sound . . . That sound is too familiar."

He did not respond; instead, he grabbed my arm. "Let's go over to the park."

I let him lead me to the gate. He squeezed my hand and put his free arm around my shoulder, kissing the top of my head. "I understand." We walked on the uneven cobblestones, and I was aware of a breeze rustling the leaves of the acacia trees and, in the distance, the constant hum of planes.

I nodded, grateful for his understanding. It is what I loved about Fritz. He never demanded explanations. The sun beat down on us, and I felt sweat begin to form on my back. We stood at the entrance to the park and watched children throwing berries at the ducks on the lake. The ducks were back—they had come before, only to be shot by someone, a speck of red brown and a few feathers the only evidence of their existence. The willow trees brushed the top of the lake with their feathery leaves, causing ripples in the water, and the children laughed at the ducks as they dove for the red berries, and the planes sounded in the background. We walked to our favorite bench in silence.

"But how can they possibly feed a city of two million?" I shook my head.

"Jutta, I'm telling you, if you could see them landing those planes, it would give you confidence." He sat up, emphasizing his point with his right hand acting as a plane, landing and then taking off and landing again and again.

"But Fritz, they have to bring in everything! And what happens in the winter when we need coal?"

"Well, let us hope it will be over by then." He ran his hand through his hair.

"And what about all the supplies we have only just begun to get, like my shampoo and Lux soap?"

"Who cares?" He was irritated. "Why are you so negative? Don't you see? This is one of those critical times in history! This is the line in the sand! And we are living through it."

I shrugged. "I just don't like the uncertainty."

He snorted. "Vati says the only thing certain in life is death."

I stood up and walked toward the *Findling* at the end of the park. I heard gravel crunch behind me. Fritz was following me. I didn't want him to. I didn't want his enthusiasm. I just wanted it all to end. I wanted things normal again. Just normal! My God, why can't everything be normal? I thought. We walked on in silence, each feeling the other's anger and our separation, exposed by a moment we could not share together. I wanted to feel his confidence, but I could not share in it. Instead I felt the empty uncertainty of the world surround me.

"It's hot today," I said to relieve the tension.

"Yes. And tomorrow, too," he said, walking next to me now that I had spoken.

We reached the *Findling* and I hoisted myself on to it, letting its warmth embrace and comfort me.

I smiled at Fritz. "I'm sorry." Tears filled my eyes. "I just hate all of this. I'm tired of living for something around the bend, something that might never come. I want to live for now—to be free from worry, to be happy now, at this moment!"

Fritz looked away across the lake.

I grabbed his arm. "I don't want to hope that it will come next year. Next month. I want everything to be normal again, like in…"

"Like in America." He finished for me. He sat down heavily next me, still looking at the lake. Neither one of us spoke for a long time. The solitary barking of a dog behind us on Bachstelzenweg broke through the silence, filling me with a loneliness I could not explain. "Jutta, things aren't so perfect in America. Happiness comes from here." He patted his chest.

"I know. But I can't be happy where there is never any certainty."

He bent to pick up a pebble and throw it across the valley; it hit the bench on the other side and fell in a clatter to the ground, the sound frightening the ducks.

"We will have certainty again soon," he said quietly.

"How? With Russians all around us? How can there be certainty?" I shook my head. "No. Since I was four years old, this country has been in turmoil."

"And in America you think you will find this certainty?" he had somehow read my thoughts.

"Yes," I said quietly, relief sweeping over me. I hadn't actually intended to tell him I wanted to move to America, but now it was out in the open. "I want to move there."

"I see. And us?"

I breathed quickly. "Why can't you come, too?"

He stood up, his arms crossed in front of his chest. He turned and studied me for a moment, his eyes filled with a sadness that hurt me so that I had to look away. Why did it have to be like this? Fritz and Germany tied together and, on the other hand, America and a future filled with certainty, light, and hope. No, I thought. I will convince him. I will have to convince him. He turned away, studying the lake and the scene before us, the silence amplifying the sounds of the afternoon, and always the buzzing sound overhead and the children's laughter in the distance.

The sun grew too hot as it pushed our shade away slowly but determinedly. We walked around the path on the opposite side of the lake before heading home. The lake lapped at its shores, pushing bits of grass and leaves up the tiny bank, the rhythm of the water soothing my nerves and erasing my emptiness. I loved this little lake by our house. It held so many memories for me—ice skating and sledding with Erica in earlier times, and now walks with Fritz. I looked back to the *Findling*: steady, firm, and unmovable, holding its place on that bit of earth for thousands of years. Children climbed on it where we had vacated it, and a group of boys pretended to shoot at the planes overhead.

I smiled, thankful for this little park with its graceful willow trees that dangled their thin, delicate branches into the water's edge. Bits of dried flowers and oak and elder leaves clung to them as they brushed the water. Birds ducked in and out of the leaves, calling to each other, and a squirrel sat on the thick branch of a tree that hung out over the water, its bark rubbed smooth by too many boys scooting out to throw stones and berries at the fish hiding among the reeds and plants that were their shelter. Jürgen was once one of those boys. I swallowed hard, emotion rising up, remembering. For a moment a silence fell over the sky. It was broken within seconds by another wave and the drone of the planes, forming background music to the activity of the park. We walked home hand in hand, and I tried not to think about what the sound meant and what the future held, and about leaving Fritz.

———

An *Elster*† tears at the flattened carcass of a squirrel in the middle of the street. The light strikes its bright green and blue tail, illuminating the feathers as it moves in its effort to rip at the fur and bits of skin and blood flattened on the road. I stand transfixed, at the same time fascinated and horrified. And then a jeep shatters the stillness of the afternoon, scattering the *Elster* to the opposite side of the street and flattening the squirrel further into the asphalt. A horn toots, and I look up to catch two smiling faces blowing me kisses as they tip their funny boat-shaped military hats at me. They pass, and the *Elster* stands on the opposite side of the street, eyeing me for a moment before hopping back to its sordid task.

September 1948

"All right, girls. Finish up your drawings. It's time to go!"

I snapped my notebook shut and made a face. I didn't like my drawing. I was having trouble visualizing the dull gray and brown fabric as a holiday dress, but it was the only fabric the school could find for us, and we all had to use the same fabric. After months of no fabric, suddenly a shipment had come in of hundreds of bolts of the same fabric—you saw it everywhere in Berlin. Pity the poor workers who had to unload bolt after bolt of the stuff from the C-54 planes at Tempelhof Airport.

It was so ugly; my mind just drew a blank. Maybe inspiration would hit me after lunch. I fluffed my hair and headed for the stairs. I hoped Fritz would already be there, waiting for me under the tall pillars that supported the entrance to the Victoria *Fachschule*. I had begun attending fashion design school in August. There had been some question because of the blockade as to whether or not the school would open for the fall semester, having at one point no pins, no needles, and no thread, let alone fabric. But the authorities decided to open on faith and a promise from the military government that fabric and the like soon would be on its way.

———

† An Elster is similar to a raven, but black and white with a bright green and blue tail.

The single classroom was long and narrow. Double-sashed windows ran the full length of the room along the Kurfürstendamm side, letting in plenty of light to make up for the minimal artificial light allowed in the room, and making it difficult sometimes for the teacher to hold our attention as clusters of girls ran to watch some activity on the Kudam, as we lovingly called the once beautiful boulevard. Long rectangular tables ran down the middle, and lamps on long wires hung down from the ceiling, almost touching our heads, but only every other one held a light bulb. The bolts of ugly fabric lay stacked at the end of each table, and sewing machines lined the low wall in front of the windows.

It was Friday, and my mouth watered with anticipation over my lunch with Fritz. Vati had offered to let us lunch at Schlichter's on his account—a rare treat. I had not been since my eleventh birthday. I wondered if the blockade would put the restaurant out of business. So far it hadn't, but who knew how long they could hang on? I hurried down the stairs with the other girls.

"So? Is your handsome friend going to be meeting you again?" asked the girl who sat next to me in class.

"Yes." I blushed.

"Lucky you!" she said and ran ahead.

Fritz usually met me on Friday afternoons to escort me home. Sometimes we took in a movie or stopped at a café before we headed home. It all depended on how much work he had to do at the bakery for his father. I saw him leaning against the pillar, watching the traffic pass by on the Kurfürstendamm. He straightened up and turned as the girls ahead of me opened the door. They smiled at him and winked, and then giggled as they continued down the street, whispering.

"Did you design something beautiful?" asked Fritz, kissing me on the cheek.

"*Ach*! Today I have no ideas!" I shook my head in disgust.

"Well, it doesn't matter. Whatever you design it will look lovely on the prettiest girl in all of Berlin!" He took my hand and we began to walk.

"Fritz! You are a *charmeur*!" I smiled.

"Here, let me carry your notebook." He grabbed the oversized notebook from my arm. I did not object.

It had been exactly three years since Vati and I had ventured that chilly fall morning up the Martin Luther Strasse to the Kurfürstendamm. Since then, the *Trümmerfrauen* had been busy clearing away the rubble and debris. The piles of twisted metal beams and the mountains of shattered brick had disappeared, along with the fine brown powder that had dusted everything. The work of many rains, I supposed. Buildings had been made safe, but nothing more. They were dirty and sad, and black soot still held to their scarred facades. In some places workers had simply put up wood scaffolding to hold the abused building in place and keep it from falling into the street until someone came up with the money to fix it. Nobody knew who owned these buildings now. Vati said it was complicated because some of the owners were dead, but not their family members, and some had fled to the West but might come back to claim their property.

I spotted a boy, no more than twelve, laying bricks with a deliberation and expertise that spoke of years of experience. A thin rope ran the length of the area where he worked, providing a guide. He concentrated on his work, scraping the muddy cement that filled the area between the bricks and then reapplying it. The bricks, uneven and chipped, had obviously once been a part of another building and added to the difficulty of his work. He wore a faded sweater over his shirt, once a navy blue but now closer to gray, and a felt cap held his hair in place. He never looked up, concentrating as he laid one brick after another in perfect rhythm: swiping the mortar and then laying the brick, and then swiping the mortar again and then again. I thought of old Carl Bolle laying bricks at the same age to earn money for his family. I wished the boy the same success in life as my great-grandfather.

I looked away to scan the venerable old boulevard that remained a shadow of its former self. Where they had rebuilt, the once-deliberate attention to detail, the carved stone and elaborate ironworks, had been replaced with utilitarian steel and cement. But still, it felt good to see there was life on the Kudam again, and it gave me hope. The movie theaters functioned, and the cafes bustled again with customers other than soldiers and their German girlfriends. I smiled. The sun bounced off a red metal Coca-Cola sign in the window of a café. I doubted they had any to sell at the moment. I knew the military government would not authorize flying in loads of heavy Coke bottles.

We walked toward the *Gedächtnis Kirche*. The severed steeple, black at the top like an ancient volcano, loomed in front of us, and Fritz told me about his day. The air was warm and humid, one of those fall days where summer tried to reassert itself, but the orange and yellow of the new trees that had been planted along the Kudam spoke of the season.

We cut through on Joachimstaler Platz to Augsburger Strasse, and Fritz glanced over at the girls, who even at this time of day stood under the clock waiting for customers, their lipstick a little too red, their dresses a little too short. They smoked cigarettes and wore nylons. He chuckled. "Do you remember the time your father almost had a heart attack because you told me to meet you under the clock tower at Joachimstaler Platz?"

"Oh my God, yes! He turned bright red and bellowed, 'Absolutely not!' I had no idea what those girls were doing."

"Jutta, couldn't you see how they were dressed and how many army guys hung around them?"

"I thought they had an exotic sense of dress and, well, fabric is in short supply."

Fritz burst out laughing. "You go beyond naïve sometimes!"

I laughed with him. "And as for the army guys, I thought they were giving away chocolate or cigarettes to the pretty girls."

Fritz shook his head. The sound of a ball bouncing echoed past me, and children's voices and a whistle followed. It made my stomach turn. "God! That sounds like they're playing that god-awful *Völkerball!*"

" I think there is a school at the next corner."

"How I hated that game!"

Fritz laughed. "We had to play a lot of team sports. Remember? Sports were writ large under Hitler, weren't they?"

I nodded. "I was always picked last to be on everybody's team."

"My poor little Jutta." Fritz put his arm around me and kissed me.

"Poor children," I said, turning from the fence where we had stopped to watch. "I was hoping the Americans with their de-Nazification would have ended that game."

"Maybe they play it in America?"

"Maybe. But in my mind, that damn horse and *Völkerball* will always be tied to the Nazis!"

We had reached Martin Luther Strasse, and I saw Schlichter's ahead of us, its blue awning looking stately and elegant but completely out of place against the broken-up facades of the buildings that lined the street.

"Good afternoon, Fräulein Bolle," said the maitre d' with a nod. "I see you have brought your friend."

"Yes. This is Fritz Mertel."

"Welcome, Herr Mertel." He extended his hand to greet Fritz. "Herr Bolle is expecting you at his table."

"Vati is here?" I asked, surprised.

"Yes. Shall I take you back?"

"Please."

Vati sat at a table by the window. He stood when he saw us approaching. I noticed he had a Campari in front of him.

"Vati, what a lovely surprise," I said, kissing him on the cheek.

"My meeting fell through, so I thought why not join you two for lunch. You don't mind, do you?"

"No. Of course not."

Actually, Fritz and I liked it when Vati joined us for a meal because he always ordered wine for us.

"How are you, Herr Fritz?"

"I am very well, sir. And you?"

"Can't complain, thank you."

He beamed at us, raising his glass. I had not seen him so relaxed in years.

"Now then, we will celebrate. What do you two say to a nice Riesling?" Before we could answer he turned to the waiter, who stood patiently by our table. "Something nice and light."

"Certainly, Herr Bolle." The waiter bowed slightly and hurried away.

"Vati, what are we celebrating?"

"The airlift, of course!"

"The airlift? But the airlift has been going on for months," I said, surprised.

"They reached a new record yesterday. Seven thousand tons in one day! And last week over two hundred fifty thousand Berliners came out to protest the communists! So we will drink to the airlift, and to democracy, and to Mayor Reuter's stirring speech. I think we should, don't you?"

"Absolutely," said Fritz enthusiastically. "It is amazing when you see them flying at night, one plane after the other. They could only be minutes apart."

"The paper said every ninety seconds."

"Really? But that barely gives them time to get out of the way."

Vati nodded. "And that is precisely why we will toast them for their bravery."

The waiter had returned, and we fell silent as he went through the wine-opening production. Vati hated all that, the smelling of the cork and all that *quatch,* as he called it. But he went along and pronounced the wine acceptable. The waiter poured us each a glass. Vati raised his. "To the Americans and the British and the foresight that they have been blessed with to recognize that Berlin is of central importance to all of Europe!" We raised our glasses, but he continued and we quickly held the glass away from our lips again. "And to the bravery and skill of the young men flying the cargo planes, and to the organizers of the whole affair, whose efficiency and skill I would love to have at the factory. And finally, to ..."

"Vati, please!" I laughed as I propped my arm up at the elbow. "My arm is getting tired."

He held up his hand to silence my protest. "The brave Germans who came out en masse last week to plead for democracy and freedom." He finished and clinked first my glass first and then Fritz's, spilling a few drops on the crisp white tablecloth. I drank the ice-cold Riesling with a small sip at first and then a larger one. It went down smooth and cool, filling my nose with the smell of an early August morning.

"Refreshing and slightly effervescent," said Fritz approvingly.

Vati nodded.

"I wanted to go down last week, but my father needed my help at the bakery," said Fritz.

"Well, it is probably a good thing you didn't, given the Russians and their zeal for arresting and shooting at everyone."

"Is there any news?

"Of course not."

"What happened to the ones they arrested?"

Vati threw his hands in the air. "Typical Russian secrecy, but I'll tell you what. If they don't let them out or give them a light sentence, all of Berlin will rise up."

Fritz nodded, and they continued to talk about the protest.

I looked around the room full of bustling waiters and tables covered with starched table linens that hung almost to the floor. Schlichter's had changed very little changed. It was a little slice of before; even the paneled walls were unharmed. Vati told me the place had been dirty from the plaster that peeled off the ceiling because of the force of the bombs that had dropped all around it, and it had some water damage from broken pipes and a few broken windows, but otherwise it was untouched by the chaos that had surrounded it. Amazing! In here, I could believe for a moment that the war had never happened.

I flashed back to my eleventh birthday—it seemed so long ago, almost a lifetime. Mutti sat across from me. Vati in the middle between us, but where? I turned in my seat. Which table? That one, over there, by the far window? Yes. That must have been it. Vati had always preferred that window, but now it was covered with wood—a victim of the war. Mutti in her soft beige and black dress, a hat perched on her head, looking well, not thin, complaining about her weight. And Vati also looking well, his hair black, not white; his face smooth, unmarked by the lines that now danced all around his eyes. The food cart covered with plates of oysters on the half shell, lobster, and salmon; the waiters happy and efficient, and the well-fed clients dressed in the latest style. Watching them parade past to the ladies' room or to talk to a guest at another table was like viewing a Paris fashion show, and they, confident and loud, enjoyed their lunch uninhibited by sorrow and death. How often had my mother said during that meal, "Jutta, stop staring. It's not polite."

I glanced around the room. Everyone looked vaguely shabby, but unlike so many Germans, they at least looked warm. Their suits, ties, dresses, and coats were out of style and tired, but they were still well dressed. If they were in style, like mine, they were made out of a fabric that could not hide the fact it had once been a tablecloth or curtain. Looking around, it was hard to believe the Berlin of the 1930s was once the fashion capital of the world. From the corner table, the table that had been Vati's favorite for years, I heard the deep guttural sound of Russian voices. Goose bumps stood up on my neck, and I turned back around quickly. Had they heard Vati's toast?

Vati's voice broke into my thoughts. "Where have you been, Jutta? Not here with us, apparently." He laughed.

"My eleventh birthday," I said simply.

"Ah, yes. It seems like only yesterday. I can't believe you will be eighteen in a few weeks! A regular adult."

I reached over and patted his hand, idle on the table next to his wineglass. He smiled and held my gaze for a moment.

Lunch was fabulous. The blockade had affected the menu. The lobster dishes and oysters and the exotic fruits and vegetables had been replaced by herring, red beets, and cauliflower. But the fresh produce came from small growers around Berlin, the waiter said—people like my mother who traded her many potatoes, apples, and plums for meat. We lunched on potato salad and *Wurst*

Salat, and Vati and Fritz had chicken breast in wine sauce. After lunch, Heinz drove Vati back to the factory and we sat in Schlichter's, just the two of us, sipping our wine. And for a moment I felt happy, and warm, and full. I could almost forget, but the reminders lurked all about me. I tried not to think of them, but always they seeped back into my mind: the items not on the menu, the smell of wet ash mixed with plaster and dirt that would greet my nostrils the moment we stepped back out into Martin Luther Strasse, the sound of Russian voices from the corner table. I tried to focus on this moment right now with Fritz. His face pressed close to mine, a smile on his lips, and he content just to be here with me. I wanted so much to feel the same. For it to be simple. I smiled, and he reached under the table for my hand.

———

We took the U-Bahn back to Dahlem before dark. We sat next to each other chatting and I tried not to notice the man across from me. The man made me nervous: staring at me, unsettling me. I scooted closer to Fritz. He grabbed my hand, thinking I was being affectionate.

The man continued to stare at me, shifting his eyes to Fritz whenever I looked up. Heavyset with thick features, he wore a beret on his head, and his hands were balled up in fists, like two sledgehammers, one on each knee. The man next to him slept, snoring loudly, causing the children next to me to giggle. The heavyset man turned his stare to them. Hard and penetrating from behind deep-set eyes, it held no emotion, and they stopped giggling and moved closer to their mother. I felt the hair on my arm rise, and my stomach twisted, sending spasms into my chest, and instinctively I knew.

"Russian!" I whispered into Fritz's ear.

Fritz looked across at the man and I colored, realizing the man would know we were talking about him. Fritz felt me tense up and let go of my hand to put his arm around me. "Don't worry; he can't do anything," he whispered back.

"Rüdesheimer Platz," called the announcer.

I shifted uncomfortably, not listening, focusing only on the man and his cold, hard stare. I wished our stop would hurry.

The man shifted in his seat, leaning forward, resting his elbows on his knees. He looked up at us from under heavy eyebrows, making his eyes seem even more deeply set. He worked the muscles of his jaw and cheeks rhythmically, as if he were chewing on something, and then glanced away to the other end of the subway car. The car shook from a bend in the track, jostling his friend, who woke up with a jolt. A small dribble of saliva ran down his chin, and he wiped it away. The heavyset man sat back up against his seat and looked at him with disgust.

The announcer called, "Podbielskiallee."

Thank God. Only two more stops. Tiny balls of sweat had formed on my forehead. The train slowed, and the men stood up together in silence. The man who had been staring reached in his pocket and pulled out a flyer. He held it in his hand as the train came to a stop, and then quickly shoved it in Fritz' free hand before he and his companion exited the train.

"What is it?" I whispered anxiously.

Fritz unfolded the paper and read. "Don't let the oppressor continue its evil drive to control you. Come hear the People's Voice at Dietrich's just off the Alexanderplatz." Soviet flags were printed on each corner of the paper.

Fritz chuckled. "A recruiting mission, I guess."

"How dare they," I bristled. "How dare they come to our side! And why did he give it to you?"

"They're everywhere," said an old man next to Fritz. "For God's sake, they broadcast their rot right out of the *Rundfunkhaus* in the British sector!"

Fritz nodded.

"Well, they wasted one on me."

The man laughed. "Good. It cost them money."

Our stop came next. "Thielplatz," sang the announcer.

We stood. "Goodbye," said Fritz, looking down at the old man, still seated. "Goodbye." He winked at Fritz.

Fritz put his arm around my shoulder. "You were really shaken in there."

"*Ja*! I don't like being in such close proximity to a Russian," I said.

"But how did you know he was a Russian? He never spoke a word."

"You can tell. Believe me, I've seen enough of them swarming all over this neighborhood! All over my house, and the Wollecks' house, too." I shuddered as we crossed the street and entered the park to head home. This park we walked through, my park, had once held hundreds of Russian tanks, guns, and soldiers. Memories flashed to the surface—their mule carts parked along Auf dem Grat under what was left of the trees, hundreds of filthy, drunken men sleeping under those carts, on the benches in the park, and even in the *Hexehütte*, curled up next to their mules for warmth. I breathed deeply, pushing the memories down with each breath, down deep, until they were gone.

The late afternoon stillness helped my nerves. The only regular sounds were a light breeze rustling the tree leaves, sending them to the ground like tiny bits of yellow and orange paper, and the constant humming of the planes overhead. We passed the *Findling*, steady and strong; the light cast pale shadows on its indented surface, darkening with every moment as the sun fell further and further in the sky, and the birds called a final good evening to each other before settling in for the evening. The sounds, so familiar, lifted me from my fears, and I relaxed a little.

"Let's get you home and pour you a stiff drink! Maybe one of your mother's brandies."

I nodded.

"Jutta, that man can't do anything to you. Why are you so afraid?"

"Because they are there. Here." I waved my hand around. "On the train. Everywhere."

Fritz did not reply.

Christmas 1948

The package came from America, arriving a few days before Christmas. I stared at it. The stamps were American flags, and it had been tied with extra string, over and over, as if the person wanted to make sure that this little slice of America did not leak out before arriving at our home. Mrs. Vockel sent packages through a contact at the military government headquarters, a young man who used to work for Colonel Vockel named Dick. He never told us his last name, but periodically he showed up on our doorstep with a package, and once I even sent him back with a package from me, a gift for Christmas: a small tablecloth I had embroidered for Mrs. Vockel. The military government had designated a special plane, he told us, to allow gifts to come through to dependent military families stationed in Berlin. It was called "Operation Sleigh Bells," and Mrs. Vockel's packages came through addressed to Dick. I was certain Colonel Vockel knew nothing of this arrangement.

The return address read Phoenix, Arizona. I mulled the name over in my mind. Phoenix, like the bird of ancient times, rising out of the ashes to live again. Phoenix. I whispered it out loud. Phoenix. It flew out from between my lips, carried along by my breath, suspended for a moment before disappearing in the silence. It sounded exotic, mysterious, and exciting; bright and sunny, unlike the grim dankness of Berlin. I had seen pictures in *Life* magazine, advertisements and articles featuring the hotels with names like the Wigwam, the Casa Blanca Inn and the Camelback Inn. One image stuck with me: a model dressed in a cowgirl shirt, turquoise with white buttons, her perfect white teeth exposed in a bright smile from behind red lips, and her red nails glistening in the sun as she cupped her hand above her forehead to protect her eyes from the sun. An enormous cactus towered over her—a saguaro, Mrs. Vockel called it when I showed her the advertisement for Elizabeth Arden nail polish and lipstick. "She has a spa in Phoenix called 'Main Chance,'" Mrs. Vockel had said, and then joked that she and her friends called it "Last Chance." Phoenix, Arizona. I read the address again.

I looked outside. Icicles hung on the pine trees that separated our garden from the Wollecks' old house, and the rhododendron I had crawled through almost four years before stood sad and drooping, its leaves an ugly dark green, almost a gray brown color.

Loneliness settled in on me, engulfing me. I swallowed; a lump had formed in my throat. Berlin was dead. Gone. No longer the city of my childhood, of Opa Bolle or of Carl Bolle, my great-grandfather. It was a city without time. As a child I loved to watch the water in the bathtub slowly fill; it crept up my legs until only the knees were not covered. Like two little white islands they stood above the water, and the water slowly rose higher and higher, and I knew it soon would close over them in one final push. I only looked away when that moment came. That was Berlin: two tiny islands, the American sector and the British sector, surrounded by treacherous water, and I knew that it was just a matter of time before the Russians would swallow us in one final push. I fingered the package and set it down on top of the piano.

"One day that will be my address, too," I whispered.

I did not look forward to Christmas as I did when a child. The past three Christmases had been bleak affairs, serving to remind me how little we had, and if *we* had so little, I shuddered to think what others had. Mutti would struggle to find a nice piece of meat, and some fruit, and she always managed to make things beautiful and festive, but without Opa Bolle and Tante Ebi there to join us, and without the colorful Christmas markets and brightly wrapped chocolates, it was not the same. Now all one saw was a few refugee women pushing carts selling straw stars and bells for the Christmas trees, and sometimes, downtown on the Kudam, I spotted a cart stationed by Wittenberg Platz with long lines in front of it, and I knew they must have *Glühwein*. But there was no *Kadewe* display with brilliant white lights and mechanical train sets and Santa's villages in the front window, no little shops with brightly wrapped chocolates set out in bowls or dangling from the branches of miniature trees.

This year Mutti had invited the other Bolles to come for dinner—it was the first year we had enough food. The irony of the blockade was that we all ate better this year than any year since the war ended. Tante Hilde was bringing some of her special *Glühwein*. She wanted to bring a dish, but Mutti politely suggested the wine. Vati and Uncle Kurt had kept poor Heinz busy all week buying butter and oranges from the Americans on the black market. And they had bought a goose from somewhere. When I asked where, Vati said, "*Das geht dich nichts an!* Just enjoy it." Uncle Kurt promised to bring the wine to go with the goose, and Vati had the after-dinner drinks covered. So it promised to be a festive occasion filled with laughter—Tante Hilde was always good for that— but still my throat clenched up when I thought of the Christmases of the past, and I glanced again at the package.

Sadly, Fritz would not be there for Christmas Eve, but he promised to come Christmas Day after church. He had to help his father deliver all the last-minute cakes and cookies. "The *Baumkuchen* were the worst!" he said. They were so tall he could only fit a few in his bicycle basket, and he had to hold them when he turned a corner. "I will never eat another one of those things for as long as I live," he announced. He promised to bring a box of my two favorites, *Himbeertaschen* and *Mandelecken*, when he came for dinner on Christmas Day.

I tore open the envelope. The card stared back at me: a gold dove flying encircled by a wreath and the words "Peace on Earth" embossed across the bottom edge. I opened it and immediately recognized Mrs. Vockel's loopy American script.

Dear Jutta,

I hope you and your family will have a wonderful Christmas filled with happiness. Colonel Vockel and I are spending our first Christmas in Phoenix, Arizona. It is a little strange to have Christmas with no snow and the sun beating down on us. Yesterday it was sixty-five degrees, amazing for the beginning of December! We have a beautiful house with three bedrooms and two baths near an enormous park called Encanto Park. You would never guess we lived in the desert if you saw all the trees and grass in our yard. I think of you often and the time we spent together in Berlin. I hope that you are continuing to practice your English. I think you would love it here in Phoenix, especially since you hate cold weather so! My offer to sponsor you still stands. If you are serious about coming over here, you must start the process right away. It can take up to a year to complete!

Fondly,
Mrs. Vockel

I clutched the letter to my chest.

"What does she say?" asked Mutti, watching me.

I blushed. "Oh, just that they have a house in Phoenix." I pushed the card back into the envelope. I looked up. Vati had stopped opening his present from Mutti and was watching me also. I smiled at them. "It has three bedrooms and two baths and is in the middle of a big park," I exaggerated.

"A park in the desert?" asked Vati.

"That's what she says." I shrugged. "She says it is amazingly green with trees and grass. Oh, and guess what the temperature is in the middle of December?" I looked from one to the other excitedly.

They shrugged.

"Sixty-five degrees Fahrenheit!"

"What is that in Celsius?" asked Mutti, frowning.

"Warm," said Vati, impressed. "That is amazing. Like a summer day here in Berlin."

Mutti looked out the window.

"*Ja.* But *du,* Jutta, how warm is it in the summer then?" shouted Tante Hilde from across the room. "*Ja.* Like the deserts of Saudi Arabia!"

Uncle Kurt nodded in agreement. "Stifling."

Mutti looked at them gratefully.

"Well, I think it would be wonderful. Can you imagine, Jutta, swimming at one of those hotels we saw in the magazine in the middle of winter?" Peti hugged herself. "What heaven."

I nodded.

"*Ach quatch*! Christmas without snow and a warm fire? *Das gibt's nicht*!" announced Tante Hilde. She carefully opened the box from Uncle Kurt and peeked inside, shrieking with delight as she pulled the exquisite beige calfskin handbag from the box. "Where did you find it?" she cried, hugging the bag to her chest and leaping up. The box fell to the ground as she ran to hug him, throwing herself on him to where we all thought she would smother the poor man. Uncle Kurt laughed and beamed. "I think she likes it? What do you think, Heti?" he joked.

"I'm not sure, Kurt. Now if she had pushed you and the chair over backwards, then we could be certain." They joked and laughed, opening presents, but my mind was not there with them. I was in Phoenix, Arizona, with its sun that beat down on the bright desert landscape, cleansing and purifying all that it touched.

———

"Did you like the garnet pin your mother gave you?" asked my father as he bent to help me clean up the remains of Christmas from the living room. Mutti was in the kitchen with Luise, and I could hear their chatter over the strands of music playing on the stereo.

"I loved it!" I answered, surprised.

"You didn't tell her."

"I didn't?" I stared at him, unbelieving. "I thought I did."

"No." He shook his head. "In fact, you said nothing at all."

"No!" I couldn't believe it.

"Listen, Jutta. I know you like the fantasy of America, and I'm sure if I were your age right now, I would feel the same way." He paused for a moment to look at me. I looked back, grateful that he understood. He sat down on the sofa and pulled me down next to him. "I'm sure I would want to leave all of this mess, too. For that I don't blame you. But handle it with care so that you don't hurt your mother."

I turned away, ashamed. Had I been that obvious? "I'm sorry."

"From the moment you read Mrs. Vockel's card and opened her gift, there was nothing left for you in this room."

"That's not true," I protested.

He held up his hand. "Well, so it seemed to your mother. I could see it on her face."

"I'm sorry, Vati. I loved the pin, and we had a wonderful Christmas. It's just that…" I paused, careful not to cause more damage. "I can't imagine how incredible it must be there. Safe, secure, warm, and all the food and clothes that one could want."

"I know," he said.

"I'll tell her how much I loved the pin," I said, standing.

"Not now. Wait for bed, and then tell her."

I nodded.

February 1949

"How do you know men are running the airlift?" asked Maria mischievously.

"I don't know. They make the bags weigh more than thirty pounds?" I threw out.

"No! They forgot to pack the sanitary napkins!" she joked, hitting her hand on her thigh.

"Isn't that the truth? My God, it's like trying to find nylons in a store," said Christa.

"No. It's like finding one pound of butter in the same store," giggled Maria. We all laughed.

"That's why I come here when I'm on my period," whispered Maria. "They always have some in the bathroom."

"They do?" I asked, astonished.

She nodded. "Yes. Under the sink."

I raised my eyebrows, wondering why she was snooping under the sink.

"Really," she insisted. "One day I was looking for toilet paper, and so I opened the cabinet and there was a whole stack of them."

"I don't believe it."

"Go check for yourself."

Christa got up and walked to the bathroom by the entrance, where an American MP stood with a clipboard checking off names for that afternoon's class. He heard us giggle and looked our way. We smiled sweetly at him. It seemed to take Christa forever in there. Finally, she walked out with her arms glued to her side, her face beaming. She approached us, her back to the MP, and pulled two sanitary napkins out of her sweater. We burst out giggling, covering our mouths with our hands. I peeked around her to see if the MP was watching. He looked back at me, raising his eyebrow and shaking his head. I motioned to Christa to hide the napkins.

"They do have them!"

"I told you!"

"I have to see this for myself." I walked over to the bathroom.

The MP looked up and shook his head again. "Did you girls drink too much punch or something?"

I blushed and shrugged at him before I slipped into the bathroom, closing the door and locking it. I opened the cabinet with two hands, trying to keep it from making noise. I could hear the MP talking to the students as they came through the entrance. It was why I never used the restroom here; it seemed like everybody could hear. There in front of me were two neat stacks of sanitary napkins. A sign above them read, take only if needed. I reached in to grab two like Christa and then pulled back. I didn't need them. I thought for another moment; I could feel my face reddening. I grabbed two quickly and stuffed them in my purse, and then on second thought I grab two more. In my haste I bumped the door, and it slammed shut. I reached over and quickly flushed the toilet to mask the sound, and then ran the water just long enough to be legitimate.

When I came out the MP was chatting with a tall blond boy about his own height but a good fifty pounds lighter. The boy ran his hand through his hair, smiling, and the MP nodded at something he had said. I hurried back to Christa and Maria. They beamed at me and held out their hands for me to show them. I maneuvered my purse in front of me and opened it to show them. Maria clapped her hands.

"You can have them. Mutti has a box at home."

Their eyes lit up. "Thanks!"

"*Ja,* I grabbed four. That's all I could fit in here, so two each, ladies."

Maria's eyes traveled above my head and I felt the warmth of another human being behind me. I snapped my purse shut.

"Two of what each, ladies?" asked the MP, towering over me.

"Um. Two cookies each," I said innocently.

" Ladies, I'm sorry, but you know the rules. One apiece until we make sure that everybody has one. Okay?"

"Okay!" We all smiled back at him.

"And we have a big class today, so are you joining us?"

"No, not today. We have to go home."

"Well, the cookies are only served after the class."

We tried to look crestfallen. He bent over so the students going into the class couldn't hear. "I tell ya what. I'll have Hanna bring you each a cookie anyway, but just eat outside so the others don't see." He winked at us before he left for the kitchen. He was a nice man. Not used to teenage girls, but still very nice in his efforts to get along with us.

"Wow! Today is our day. This is really swell!" exclaimed Maria.

I burst out laughing.

Maria had taken to using American expressions she heard from the MPs in her everyday speech, her accent almost obliterating the word to such an extent that no American could possibly have understood her.

"What?" she demanded.

"Nothing." I tried to stifle my laughter.

The MP emerged from the kitchen, Hanna right behind him. He waved. "Goodbye, ladies."

"Thank you. Goodbye," we called in unison.

"Today we have *shockolade* chip," said Hanna, Frau Richter's replacement. She too fancied herself an American speaker.

I laughed again. "Thank you. These are my favorite."

We grabbed our coats and left, spilling down the front steps in a rush of fresh giggles. We dutifully did not bite into our cookies until we turned onto Schützallee. It was February, but I could walk with my coat unbuttoned, not like the February of the past three winters when the cold tore through to your skin no matter how many layers of clothes you wore. This winter had been different. Thank God! Everybody had worried about how the Amis and Tommies could possibly fly in enough coal to protect us from the cold they had predicted would again be record-breaking. But God finally took pity on us and sent us a winter warmer than we had seen in years. A miracle, cried women in the street as they greeted one another over the heads of their children. It was still gloomy, overcast, and rainy, and the fog that settled down on the city suppressed any joy we may have felt over the mildness of our winter. But at least it wasn't cold. And then one day in January we read in the paper that they found an extra seven thousand tons of coal that nobody had spotted. How that much coal could go unnoticed puzzled us all, and many believed it too was a gift from above.

———

Brown leaves wetly clung to each other around a brick gatepost, and brown rivulets ran down the length of Schützallee from the rain that had recently fallen.

"Can you believe this weather? It's February and still in the forties!"

"I know, and we have hardly seen snow and ice this winter."

"I love it!"

One lone streetcar rattled on the track far ahead of us, steel scraping on steel as it took off down the Kronprinzenallee.

"You're so lucky you live in Dahlem!" Christa shook her head. "By our house they've shut down the electricity and the streetlights are never on. Worst of all, the streetcars only run in the early morning and late at night."

"I know. We are lucky," agreed Maria. "Can you imagine Americans doing without electricity and hot water?"

Christa let air out from between her lips. "Please! They'd have a mass rebellion on their hands. No showers? Oh my God! I really think they would die if they remotely smelled of body odor." She laughed. "Do you see how the MP's turn up their noses when some of the boys come in and maybe they don't smell perfect?"

"Try sitting with thirty of them in a classroom!" Maria winced and held her nose.

We giggled. "Remember how Captain Haft would grab them and lead them to the bathroom? Wolfgang told me he would very patiently explain that one had to wash every day, and then he would hand them a bar of soap and a washcloth and tell them to wash. He gave them all deodorant. Each time they came back to the club, they smelled again. He couldn't figure out why they didn't learn." Christa laughed. "The boys would wait to wash until they got to the club so they didn't use the precious hot water and soap at home."

"I bet he did know," I insisted. "He was just being nice letting them shower there."

"Oh my God! Remember that one boy? Frau Richter had to wash all of his clothes because they did stink!" Maria waved her hand in front of her nose. "He sat there in a towel in the kitchen, waiting for his clothes. Thank God it was summer, or they never would have dried."

Christa bent to pick up a perfectly shaped wet brown leaf, a chestnut leaf. "Do you think I can press this one?" she asked.

"Maybe, but it might go moldy on you," I answered.

She looked at Maria. "Are you still going to the airfield every Friday?" she asked.

I glanced sharply over at Maria. Her color rose.

"Well, not every Friday. But sometimes," she said sheepishly.

"What on earth for?" I sputtered.

"To thank the pilots for their efforts."

Christa guffawed, her blues eyes twinkling.

I turned, surprised to hear such a sound emitted by my usually prim and proper friend.

"It's true," insisted Maria, her voice rising, her handsome, strong features defiant. "I bring them things my mother has: pots of jam, or flowers sometimes from the garden. Well, not now I don't bring flowers, but embroidery. Just little thank-you gifts."

" And you just give these to the secretaries up front, or do you insist on handing them to the pilots personally?" asked Christa.

"Stop it, you two! I just give them to the officers in charge."

"You've never met a pilot?"

"Well, sometimes. But they don't let me back there where they have their break, and they don't come out front very often."

"But they do come out front sometimes. Right?"

Maria looked across the street, where a woman was checking her mailbox. "Sometimes," she said nonchalantly.

" Maria thinks she will overwhelm them with her gratitude and they will say, 'Please, German Fräulein, please. Will you marry me and let me take you back to America?'"

"Oh, stop it! I don't think anything of the sort."

Christa and I giggled, but Maria found nothing funny about it and marched ahead, tossing her thick red hair behind her back as if to dismiss us. And it occurred to me that she really was looking for a husband among the pilots that were Berlin's saviors. Maria, among my friends, loved the Americans second to me. She spoke fondly of her aunt in Philadelphia, and she longed to visit America. And those daring pilots who flew all those dangerous missions just to save us? They were of interest, I had to agree.

Army Headquarters

March 1949

I tucked Mrs. Vockel's card in my purse, and for the next few weeks I took it out every night to read it, again and again. I pressed my purse with both hands, feeling the crisp outline of the stiff paper inside its soft interior: a comfort, this small card; a lifeline to America and to the future I dreamed existed there among the red rocks and brown soil of the Arizona desert. I let the idea of Arizona and the desert sear itself into my mind for several weeks before I finally got the courage to go to Army Headquarters on Hüttenweg and ask about immigration papers.

———

I stand at the bottom of the steps for a long time, watching the soldiers come in and out. A few tip their hats to me; most, engrossed in their conversations, pay me no attention. I take a deep breath and grab the rail that runs along the side of the stairs, pulling myself up one step at a time. I let a soldier pass ahead of me; he holds the door and smiles back at me. Shyly, I nod and pass through the entry. "Thank you," I whisper, barely audible, but he has not heard. He hurries on.

"Jutta?" asks a familiar voice.

I whirl around in surprise to see Major Franklin standing behind me.

"What are you doing here?"

"Oh, hello, Major Franklin." I smile self-consciously. "I'm here to find out about emigrating to the United States." I fill with pride as the words finally release themselves from my lips. I hadn't allowed myself to say the words, to form the letters with my mouth and actually breathe life into them as an utterance. They had, until now, only been thoughts, dreams—visions even, but not reality.

"Oh." He cocks his head to the side and raises his eyebrows. "Well, you would certainly be an asset to the United States, but what a loss for Germany." I can't tell if he is serious or teasing. "And your parents? How do they feel?"

I look down. "I haven't asked them yet."

He shuffles the papers he holds in his hands. "Well, you will need their permission, you know."

I nod. I don't know, but I suspect as much.

"How old are you?"

"Nineteen."

He chews on his lip for a moment. "Follow me."

He leads me past the long line of people waiting to see the immigration officer at the front desk. The officer glances up and salutes Major Franklin as we walk past to a small office halfway down the hall. A young woman sits at a desk by the door, typing away with such force and rapidity that I think the typewriter will break.

"Sally, this is my friend, Jutta Bolle."

The young woman looks up from her typing and smiles brightly. She has the most startling blue eyes, and blond hair so light it is almost white. "Oh yes, the translator?"

"Yes." I blush.

"Jutta, this is Sally Humphreys."

"Very pleased to meet you, Miss Humphreys." I curtsy slightly. This seems to amuse Miss Humphreys. She giggles and extends a hand sporting bright pink nails. I wondered how they survive the daily assault they make on the typewriter.

"Nice to meet you, too."

"I need you to get Jutta the immigration papers." He reels off a list of numbers that I assume correspond to various papers I will need. Miss Humphreys nods her head and jots the numbers down efficiently on a pad of paper. She pushes her chair back, uncrossing her legs as she does so, and says, "I'll be back in a flash."

He turns to me. "You'll need a sponsor, you know."

"I have one. Colonel and Mrs. Vockel." I can't help the touch of pride that colors my words.

"Oh, well. Good for you." He nods, impressed. "So now you will have the papers, and then you just have to tackle the parents."

"*Ja.* That's the hardest part," I say, looking down. I notice the ceiling light reflects in the perfect black polish of his shoes.

He nods. "Once you get their approval, I'll see what I can do to help you."

"Oh, thank you!" I jump up a little in excitement.

He holds up his hand as if to calm me. "Just so you know, it can take up to a year for the papers to come through."

"I know. I will be patient."

Mrs. Humphreys bustles in arranging a stack of papers. She clicks off their numbers to the major as she hands them to him.

I walk out, my papers hugged to my chest. I pass the American flag that almost touches the ceiling. I pass the photo of the American president, President Truman, his eyes peering out from behind wire spectacles. The hall seems long and dark, and at the far end I can see the traffic of the Hüttenweg through the glass double doors. I swallow as I push the doors open and step into the warm spring air. I blink. Standing on the top step, I let my eyes adjust to the bright sunshine after the darkness of Army Headquarters, and for a second I wonder if this isn't all some crazy dream.

I can't believe I have finally screwed up the courage to come down here. I puzzle over the fear that paralyzed me for so long, keeping me from taking this first step. And I smile; it has been so easy, thanks to Major Franklin. Still, I leave the papers in my desk, under my journal and personal writing paper, where I know Mutti won't look. I'm not ready to fill them out yet. I'm not ready to tell Mutti. But they are never far from my mind.

The sound rattled the kitchen window, and Mutti turned from the stove to see what the racket was.

"*Gott im Himmel*! Do they want the windows to break?" Luise shook her head as she peeled a potato from the pot of potatoes on the counter in front of her.

I glanced up from the morning paper. An army truck had stopped in front of our gate. A transparent black cloud of smoke spewed into the blue sky from an exhaust pipe, erect and tall like a chimney that ran along the side of the truck's cabin. Two men got out, laughing over something the one who had been driving said. They both wore the khaki green of the U.S. military. Leaving the truck running, they lit cigarettes and talked casually, leaning against the front fender of the truck. The black smoke continued to seep out of the truck's exhaust, blurring the view of the trees across way.

"Oh no! Not in my front yard!"

And before I knew what she was doing, Mutti had ripped off her apron and headed out the front door. I saw her march down the flagstones, calling out as she walked. Teddy ran behind her, barking vigorously to let them know he too meant business. I opened the window to listen. The men did not hear her over the din of the truck's engine until she was practically at the gate. When they did, they leaped off the truck's fender and stood up straight, whipping off their funny cloth caps as they did so.

"You go on. Finally fresh air, and you leave the engine going?" She pointed to the black smoke, now only a thin stream as the engine calmed down, muttering quietly in neutral.

Luise chuckled. She put her arm around me, and we watched from the open kitchen window. "Your mother is afraid of no man!"

The men looked up and then back at her, confusion on their faces.

"We have no gasoline, and you waste," she shouted in English.

They looked down, embarrassed and threw their unfinished cigarettes to the ground. "Sorry, ma'am, but we're lost."

"Yes, ma'am. Can you help us find Bachstelzenweg?"

They pronounced it so badly I didn't think Mutti would understand. She asked them to say it again. "No. Not here. You go Kronprinzenallee," she motioned with her hand to the right, "Königin Luise Strasse," and another right hand motion, "Bachstelzenweg!"

The taller one repeated her directions, and she nodded her head. "*Ja!*"

"*Danke*," they said in unison with heavy American accents, stretching the *a* out far too long. They tipped their heads politely and turned toward the truck.

"No! Don't forget your dirt."

They turned to her again, obviously puzzled, but when she pointed to the ground they understood. The driver picked up the cigarettes. A thin stream of smoke still came from each end, and carefully took the heads off them before putting them in his pocket.

"Don't throw them away. Give them to someone!" she called after him.

They nodded. "Yes, ma'am. And you have a good day, now," said the driver.

The taller one opened the door on the passenger side, and he laughed when Teddy dove into the truck. Teddy was not disappointed; before they could stop him he grabbed the half-eaten sandwich sitting on the seat.

"Come on, fellow. Get out. Go on."

Mutti laughed. "Teddy. Come."

"Teddy?" asked the tall one.

"Yes. He is an American dog," she said simply.

The one not driving grabbed Teddy, snuggling him into his arms and petting him under the chin. "Well, Teddy, my guess is you better do what this lovely lady says!"

Mutti laughed and took Teddy out of the man's arms. Teddy wagged his tail, excited to be the center of attention. The men tipped their hats to Mutti again as they climbed into the truck, and then the driver let the clutch out and the truck lurched forward a few inches before he ground it into reverse. They carefully reversed, with Mutti waving her hand to drive away the huge plume of exhaust smoke that actually was nowhere near her. It had blown to Erica's house, covering the rose bushes with its black powder. Mutti turned and headed up the walk. She saw me in the window and shook her head. I laughed but was glad they hadn't looked toward the house and spotted me.

The Blockade Ends

"For they intended evil against thee; they imagined a mischievous device, which they are not able to perform." Psalm 21; verse II.

May 1949

"It's over!" sang Vati as he walked into the house. He flung his hat across the room and it floated through the air like a saucer, landing on the back of Mutti's favorite chair. He clapped his hands together and grabbed my mother, lifting her off the ground and spinning her around, her feet flying out behind her.

"Good heavens, Hans! Put me down!" she squeaked.

He set her down and grabbed me next, hugging me; he lifted me at the same time. "It is over! We beat them!"

"Are you sure, Hans?" doubt played across her delicate features.

"Yes! The Russians have agreed. May twelfth at midnight, the first trucks come through!"

"The Russians agree?" asked my mother skeptically. "What is that? Another handshake with Russians?"

"No, Heti. I'm telling you it is over." He said it earnestly, holding her face with both of his hands. "It is over," he said again softly.

Tears began to well up and flow down her face. She grabbed him and sobbed into his chest. I stood there, uncertain what to do. Uncomfortable. He glanced over at me and motioned me to join them. We held each other for a long time, Mutti crying and I, not sure what to do, clinging to his free arm, and Vati holding us and we him. The relief was overwhelming.

And so it was over, this blockade that had dominated our lives for over a year and had threatened to suck the very life out of us and smash our depleted will into submission. It ended much less dramatically than it started. Nobody cheered, nobody lit off sparklers, there were no parades, and we went about our business as we always did. Most of us didn't believe it was really over, and in fact we were waiting for the next Russian move. Like a master chess player, we figured they were taking their time, thinking it through. The fact the Americans and British continued to fly in supplies despite the opening of the freeways and railways added to the disbelief—maybe it was over, maybe it wasn't, maybe it would never be—echoed all around me in bits of conversation on the streetcar or at the street corners or in the shops. One thing was clear to us: the Russians continued to play power games just to remind us. One day they let in five trains and the next six or seven, but never the sixteen per day that we needed to supply the city. And from these games it seemed we would never be free. They were pointless, futile, senseless games, and I hated them.

At the Victoria *Fachschule*, the instructor made an announcement and held a moment of silence "to thank those who saved our city." Then we were told to start our machines, and the buzz of sewing machines soon drowned out the sound of the planes still flying overhead. The food supply continued to be critically low, but the power restrictions had been lifted, and we noticed it most because the lights of the city were once again on all night. Mutti could once again roast things in the oven and fry things on the stove, and, most important to me, we again had soft towels and ironed sheets and maybe even some ice now and then. When I looked out my bedroom window toward town, a pale glow fringed the top of the trees like a halo, and I prayed that all would be normal and remain normal and I tried to be happy.

All the while, the fear nagged at me that it could happen again. Berlin was a divided city now, sliced in two, one half Russian and one half Western. The rest of Germany was too, divided between a Russian Zone and a Western Zone, and we in Berlin, me and my family and all that I loved, sat in the middle of that Russian Zone, and I saw nothing to be happy about. Half my city was dominated by a force that would stop at nothing to dominate and "readjust" the thinking of all who did not comply with its dictates. A force of outsiders whose entire focus was to convert us into a giant supply shed for its war machine. To whom life, even that of its own people, was no more significant than a fly, casually swatted to death for buzzing too loudly. A force without justice, grace, or humanity; a force not unlike the Nazis, but this one a mercurial force whose unpredictable moods shifted like the uncertain weather of Berlin. Woe to those whose unlucky lot it was to reside on the wrong side of the line, the line of death that ran through the heart of Berlin and swallowed the pulse of the city—for them, it was a battle for survival. We at least lived on the right side of the line; of that I was certain, and I, as well as everyone else who lived on our side, thanked God every day for our good fortune.

I was grateful to the Americans for saving at least half of the city from the Soviet machine that threatened to eat up all things German, but for how long were we safe? I couldn't get the question out of my mind. The day Vati brought us the news of the lifting of the blockade, I determined, once and for all, never again to live in a place where I could be the victim of the whims of a government not accountable to anyone. I decided to fill out the papers that lay idle in my desk. The final decision had come to me slowly. I had toyed with the idea of living in America, dreamed of it, spoken of it, and even gotten the papers, but it was an idea, not a certainty. I held my breath during the blockade, subconsciously not wanting to give the Russians the satisfaction that their actions in part had driven me from my city, my family. But now I could leave, and I was equally certain Fritz should follow me. Even if he didn't understand that right now, I was confident one day he would. The future lay in America; of that one thing I was certain. The Nazis, the war, and now the Russians had taken the soul of my city. It lay bare, exposed, turned inside out, and I could not stand to see it. I had to go. Every picture in my mind spoke of America and converted itself into that single refrain, "Go to America". It whispered to me from the trees along the Kronprinzenallee. It spoke to me in the faces I saw along Kurfürstendamm: the faces of old women, hard and shrewd, their hair tied up in scarves; the faces of dirty children, barefoot, clothes hanging off them as off a hanger—faces that held no expectations, faces of survival. It whispered to me from the faces of the Americans: bright smiles leaping out at me, smiles that spoke of confidence and happiness and a better life. I saw it in Major Franklin's white creases around his eyes and in Captain Haft, simple but nice, solid; and in Frau Richter, her elegant features highlighted by the hair and makeup of her new life. I saw myself dressed in yards and yards of fabric, pink with bright red roses, fabric that reached to my ankles, Fritz and Mutti and Vati standing by me as we examined a dinner table filled with plates of ham and chicken and vegetables and salad and ice in every glass. The streetcar whirred past me, and I heard it in the silence and in the sound of the hammers workmen used to rebuild what man had destroyed, and I knew I had to face Mutti.

"But why?" asked my mother.

"Because I want to live among these people..." I paused. "These people who have saved us, who have risked their lives to save us."

I had found my parents in the living room having a drink, and I blurted out my decision. I knew if I waited any longer, the whole thing, the idea of America would come undone, and I would never do it. They said nothing. Instead they looked at each other, each seeming to tell the other it was up to them to say no. A breeze fluttered the sheer lace curtains that kept the flies from entering through the open window. It billowed in, forming a sail, before an invisible force sucked it back out, flattening it against the window frame. The silence hung in the room. My mother swallowed her wine, and the sound seemed to echo about the room.

"Don't you think it is incredible? Their help, I mean," I implored them, desperate to break the silence.

"Yes. But they do not do it only out of humanitarianism," said my father. "I think we are the line in the sand for them, Jutta. They are a nation with wisdom, and they understand that peace in Europe means peace in Germany, and that means freedom and democracy."

"But they didn't have to do it like this, Vati! They could have done it with half measures, like the French. They didn't have to send candy in parachutes. Those came from the American people themselves. Those came from the heart! They didn't have to send the extra pork and all the chocolates at Easter."

"Yes. I agree they have big hearts."

Still my mother said nothing. Silence filled the room again. Birds called each other home in the early evening light, and a dog barked somewhere far off in the distance. My father's selection, Mozart's Symphony no. 39, had ended moments before, and the monotonous sound of the record circling around and around dominated in the silence. He stood to turn it off.

My mother stood up. I looked up at her. "Well. I will not help you, but I will not stop you." She had walked to the far side of the room, heading for the kitchen. She stopped and turned around to face me. "You must find out about all of the paperwork yourself, and anything else. I will have nothing to do with it." With that, she walked into the kitchen to finish supervising the dinner preparations.

Vati cleared his throat. "Jutta, make sure this is really what you want, and not just based on a fear of the moment."

"I know what I want, Vati, and it is to live among a people who have hearts this big!"

He dismissed me with his hand. "Yes, well. I only hope they will not disappoint you. They are, after all, only human."

I looked out the window.

"I don't mean to make Mutti sad." Tears filled my eyes, and I looked up to keep them from spilling over. "But I can't live here, Vati. I can't live here worrying about the Russians and food and the cold all of my life!"

"But what about moving to the West? You could go to the university in Heidelberg perhaps?"

"No. It is still Germany. I can't live in this place anymore. I want to live where people smile, where there is certainty, where they do things because it is the right thing to do. Not because they can gain something from it. No such place exists in Europe! Don't you see? Only the Americans think like this."

My father said nothing. We sat in silence. And then he finally cleared his throat again. "What about Fritz?"

"He will join me later, or I will come back here after a few years. But for now I need to live in total freedom from all of this..." I stopped, unable to think of the words. "Vati, can't you see?" I pleaded.

Vati raised his eyebrows and sipped his wine but said nothing.

———

I spent the rest of the summer completing my paperwork. The many trips down to army headquarters made it a regular walk for me. Fritz and I did the usual things that summer, went to the movies and the theater, and occasionally to dinner at Schlichter's on Vati's account, but we never talked about my leaving.

Fritz grabbed the door before it swung closed and hit me. The young man exiting ahead of me was engrossed in his analysis of the play. "Magnificent. Such an impact," he muttered to his girlfriend ahead of him. Fritz chuckled. The tiny Schlosspark Theater had been warm, and I welcomed the cool night breeze that stirred all around us. I stretched my arms over my head and breathed in the air, letting it push my hair away from my face.

"Well, what did you think?"

"I think the man is brilliant! I think he used his actors to..."

"Jutta? Jutta Bolle?" interrupted a voice on the other side of me. "Is that you?"

I snapped my head around, surprised by the voice and its proximity, and found myself staring into a pair of serious blue eyes. "Oh, hello! How are you?" I said with enthusiasm. "I haven't seen you in ages."

She smiled slightly, but the smile looked uncomfortable on her face—out of place, as if it hurt her.

Turning to Fritz, I said, "Do you know Fritz?"

She peered above me and shook her head. "Hannelore," she said simply and held out her hand.

"Pleased to meet you, Hannelore. I'm Fritz."

"Did you see the play?" I asked to make conversation.

"Yes. I thought it was very good. And you?"

"I loved it!"

I hadn't spoken to Hannelore, or rather she had not spoken to me, since the American MP had shown us the pictures, and they flashed in front of me for a brief moment. I looked away. Hannelore continued to eye me in that disconcerting way she had. "Is it true? The rumors?" she asked finally.

"Good heavens, what rumors? Hopefully something exotic or daring that I am rumored to have done."

"Are you going to America?"

I felt Fritz stiffen behind me. He crossed his arms in front of him and looked across the street to some distant point of interest.

"Oh, that. Yes, I am leaving."

"When?"

"As soon as I can arrange the paperwork. Colonel and Mrs. Vockel are sponsoring me," I added, just to have something to say. The intensity of her stare was making me increasingly uncomfortable.

"So you are leaving us?"

"Well, I am not so much leaving you as going to America," I offered, rather disingenuously.

"No. You're leaving us."

I shrugged.

"Don't you feel any obligation to your country?" She hissed the words at me.

I was taken aback by the force she used to say it. Fritz grabbed my arm. "Come, Jutta. I think it is time for us to go."

He pulled me gently as I continued to stare at Hannelore, puzzled by her anger.

"Well, don't you?" she persisted.

"Jutta doesn't owe you or Germany an explanation," he said with equal force. We turned, and he maneuvered me through the traffic along Schloss Strasse to the streetcar. My heart pounded in my ears, but no words escaped from my lips. I was angry that I had not responded. As I stood frozen, a stupid smile plastered across my face, it had been Fritz who had responded.

"How dare she!" muttered Fritz as we waited for the streetcar. I looked back, hopeful that she was not taking the same streetcar. I leaned against him, grateful I had not spotted her among the crowd. Fritz hated people who thought they were the moral conscience of others—telling people what to think and how to act. "She has no right to ask you that! Who is she, anyway?"

"That's the girl I told you about. Hannelore," I repeated her name slowly. "She is the one who didn't believe the pictures and lived by the 'if only the Führer knew about this' line."

He nodded, remembering. "So that's the girl. Well, she is just the type." He turned to me. "Listen. I hate you going more than anyone. But you have to do what is right for you. Don't let people like that influence you. She's just angry because she has no choice but to stay here. If she did, she would be on the next boat, believe me."

I laughed. "No, I'm serious. I know her type: bitter and angry, and she is only nineteen! Imagine what she'll be like when she's forty."

I laughed and hugged him. "You always have exactly the right thing to say.

Do these things just sit there at the back of your mouth waiting for the right moment?"

"No. They come from here." He patted his chest and smiled at me, but his eyes exposed a gentle sadness. He bent and kissed the top of my head and held me for a moment longer than I had expected.

———

My mother's back moved in front of me, the weight of the *Bollerwagen* she pulled behind her causing the muscles of her back and shoulders to flex through her dress. Oblivious to the stares all around her, she talked to Tante Hilde, who pulled an equal load in an identical wagon next to her. They talked and laughed as if they were returning from a shopping spree at the Bolle store.

"Jutta, Peti, come help!" called Mutti, stopping at the corner of Königin Luise Strasse and Thielallee. Peti and I caught up reluctantly, and we each grabbed the end of our mother's wagon to help lift it off the curb. I turned my head to avoid the smell, my nose curling as the pungent perfume assaulted my nostrils and the flies swarmed around my head. We stayed on the curb, letting my mother and Tante Hilde get ahead of us before stepping into the street to cross. Mutti looked behind her and rolled her eyes. I couldn't hear what she said to Tante Hilde, but Tante Hilde turned and shouted, "Oh, for God's sake! As if you've never been around a little *mist* before. Come on, girls! Stop acting like you don't know us."

Horrified, Peti and I hurried after them, dodging the jeeps and trucks that hurried along the street.

"Could my mother possibly be more embarrassing?"

"Not much," I agreed.

Peti looked to the heavens for strength.

Seeing that we had crossed the street, Mutti and Tante Hilde again ignored us and continued their conversation for the short distance down Königin Luise Strasse. In a moment we would turn right onto Kuckucksweg, away from the prying eyes of strangers and American soldiers, and it couldn't come soon enough for me. A jeep sped past, honking at us, heads thrust out the window blowing kisses. We looked down, studying the ground intensely and acting like we had no relationship to the two women in front of us. Blessedly, our mothers and their wagons had already turned onto Kuckucksweg and were out of the jeep's sight. We both heaved a sigh of relief when we turned the corner.

"I can't believe we have to do this again tomorrow."

"I know. It's humiliating."

Mutti and Tante Hilde waited at the next corner for us to catch up. They chatted casually to one another, swatting at flies and laughing.

We waved for them to go on ahead, but they ignored us.

"*Gott im Himmel,* you two! Carl Bolle smelled this smell every day," shouted Tante Hilde. Mutti laughed. Peti and I saw nothing amusing about it, but rushed to catch up so Tante Hilde's voice did not penetrate all the way to the center of town for everyone to hear.

"I mean it is part of your heritage, girls." She took a deep breath. "It is in your blood, so to speak. What feeds you!"

"Mutti, stop!" cried Peti.

Tante Hilde reached over and ruffled Peti's hair. Peti pulled back quickly.

"Oh, for God's sake. I don't have it on my hands!"

Shaking her head, she turned back to Mutti, and she and Mutti pulled their wagons into the street.

"Just think of all the fresh vegetables we will have in a few months," called Mutti over her shoulder.

"But the blockade is over. Why can't we just go to the store and buy them like we used to?"

"Because you never know, do you? So we will grow ours for a bit longer."

Mutti shared the potatoes and tomatoes she grew with Tante Hilde. In exchange, Tante Hilde helped every spring with hauling the manure from the cows that had grazed for as long as I could remember in the fields of the old manor house along the Königin Luise Strasse, just across from the thatched roof of the subway station. Mutti had some sort of an arrangement with the farmer. Unlike other families that could not grow vegetables because the military government didn't airlift in fertilizer or seeds, we had both because of my mother's ingenuity. I admired her for it, but I just didn't want to participate in the collection of it. The seeds I didn't mind. We had seeds because Mutti took the seeds from the first and last crop of the season and carefully dried them in brown paper bags in our basement or in the sun, depending on the weather. Only last week she and Luise had stood at the sink, carefully seeding tomatoes and drying them in the sun before placing them in paper envelopes dated and marked "tomatoes."

But to have to collect the manure! I couldn't believe she would ask us to do it! And the worst part of it was the old skirt and sweater she made me wear for the task. Why couldn't Gustav come on these forays, rather the two of us? But Mutti insisted that Gustav's limited time away from the factory was better spent weeding and digging rows for her garden than gathering the manure. So we went, reluctantly, believing there was nothing in the world so humiliating as to be walking along the Königin Luise Strasse with our mothers, a pile of manure directly behind them and in front of us, its smell wafting back to us as we tried to dodge the attention of the American males who drove by every minute.

Farewell to General Clay

September 1949

General Clay left in May, almost immediately after the Russians lifted the blockade. It was a Sunday, and Fritz and I decided to walk down to Army Headquarters to see the Sunday parade. We walked along the Kronprinzenallee toward Hüttenweg, curious why so many people stood three- and four-deep along the road, and then we saw the car up ahead of us.

General Clay leaned forward, eager to say goodbye in his crisp uniform, was waving; his wife, with her hair up, an elegant hat placed just right on her head, waved one gloved hand. He glanced out the window, and for a moment his eyes held mine. He had the most unusually deep eyes, filled with an intensity—a frightening intensity—but he had saved my city, and Vati said he had fought hard when others in America would have let us fall. I wished I could talk to him; I nodded, and he was gone in an instant. Tears filled my eyes, and as I looked at the faces of grateful mothers and wives and sons and daughters that lined the street, I saw that I was not alone.

"They are all leaving us," I said simply.

Fritz nodded but continued to watch as the motorcade made its way slowly past the rows of women and children and old men cheering and waving at the American commander and his wife. They had lived on Im Dol, a few blocks from my house, but I rarely saw them. In fact, I had only seen them once before, walking their dog. That was it, and yet I felt an indescribable sadness about their leaving.

We turned in silence and headed down the Hüttenweg toward the Grunewaldsee for a walk along the lake, our mood somber, we did not speak.

The last plane of the airlift arrived and delivered its load on September 30, 1949. An inscription, "Positively the last load from Lubeck—73,705 tons—Psalm 21 verse II," was painted by hand on the side of its smooth, gray belly.

And then the sound stopped. The constant hum of hundreds of planes landing at Tempelhof and Gatow, and for the last year at Tegel, suddenly ended. Still and empty, the sound of the wind rushing through the pine trees of the Grunewald filled me with a loneliness I had not anticipated as I walked along the Kronprinzenallee to Army Headquarters. I had grown accustomed to the soft, droning sound of the planes, like background music unnoticed until it is suddenly gone. It had been a comfort—a blanket of security, letting us know the world had not forgotten us. But now, the sound gone, the silence crept in around us, and fewer and fewer army trucks and jeeps splashed mud, and fewer young Americans leaned and waved jauntily out the window, smiles free from worry spread across their faces. Isolated and alone, we longed for the sounds of these occupiers so many had resented. Now I was never sure from one visit to the next at Army Headquarters whether the same faces I had become familiar with would still be there. The Americans were pulling out, cutting staff everywhere. Weary, they wanted to go home. They had won the battle, and now we were left to fend for ourselves. Major Franklin had told me he would be leaving soon, and I begged him to see what he could to do to rush my paperwork. He promised to try to shepherd it through before his departure, but he warned me that when his orders came to depart he would only have a few day's notice. So I began to make daily treks down to Army Headquarters, believing my presence alone would somehow hurry the process. Maria sometimes accompanied me. She had not found her true love at the Tempelhof Airfield, or better put, he had not found her, and she clung to the vague hope that maybe he was waiting for her at Army Headquarters.

And then one day in November I received word that my paperwork was complete. I stood for a moment, not sure I had heard Major Franklin right.

"Welcome to the United States, Jutta Bolle," he said, handing me a package with all the papers signed and stamped. I stared at him, unsure. My stomach tightened, and I could find nothing to say. His eyes crinkled at the sides and he smiled quizzically. "You do still want to go, don't you?"

"*Ja*. I mean yes!" I stammered. "I just…" I looked above his head. The seal of the United States on the back wall held my gaze, the spread of the eagle's wings friendly and warm. "I just can't believe it has finally happened."

He pressed my hand, still in midair, fingers held stiff around the documents. "Well, you still have to book your boat travel, and that can be difficult, I hear."

I nodded, but I was not listening. The only thing I could see was my mother's face: motionless, stiff, like a mask; her eyes, red-rimmed and glistening, but she, determined not to cry, and Vati pragmatically discussing the details of my departure, his way of hiding his sorrow. And then I saw Fritz—his eyes, those thoughtful, expressive eyes, filled with sorrow. A sorrow that I had caused.

And I stopped. I couldn't think about him, not now. I had to go ahead, move forward. Fritz would join me. Yes. He would see that he must follow me to America.

"Jutta, are you okay?" Major Franklin peered into my face. "You've gone pale."

"I'm sorry! I'm fine." I shook my head and drew my hand back, placing the papers in my purse without looking at them.

"Here. Have something to drink before you go." He turned to Sally, sitting with perfect posture at the desk in front of me. "Sally, please get Jutta some juice or whatever we have." She rose immediately, her plaid dress swishing as it rubbed against her legs, smooth and beautifully shaped in their nylon casings.

"Sit down." He motioned me to a sofa in the waiting area.

I sat, and he sat next me. "I know it will be hard to tell your family and friends, and it is a big change for you." I stared at my shoes and did not reply. "It's hard when you've wanted something this big for so long, and then there it is."

I nodded.

"But once you get over there, it will be fine. You will forget all your doubts, and I know you will love it. And we will be proud to have you as one of us."

I looked at him and smiled.

"Besides, if I'm not right, you can always come back." He looked up. Sally had returned with a glass of orange juice.

I took the glass eagerly. I had not tasted orange juice in four years. The tang hit my taste buds, puckering my mouth. I smiled and turned quickly to Sally, realizing I hadn't said thank you. "Thank you!"

She smiled from her desk. "Oh, you're welcome."

"I'm just dreading telling Mutti and Vati," I confided to Major Franklin. I couldn't even mention Fritz by name.

"It won't be easy," he agreed.

"Major Franklin, Colonel Smith is on the phone for you," called Sally from her desk. Her manicured fingers held the receiver in the air, the other hand poised over the phone where she had hit the hold button

"I have to get that, Jutta, but good luck to you, and if you need anything, Sally will know how to find me." I stood, and we shook hands. He walked toward his office. He was halfway there before I found my voice.

"Thank you, Major Franklin!" I called. He turned and saluted me. "Thank you for everything." And then he went through the double doors and disappeared behind them.

I bent down to grab my purse and hurried out the front door. The wind had gathered the leaves together, clustering them in piles along the curb and then rearranging them with each new gust. The sky was cloudy and gray, threatening rain but not quite ready for it. I hurried along Kronprinzenallee, a million thoughts spinning around in my head, chief among them how I should act when I arrived home. The birds sang out, squabbling over the few shriveled blackberries still on the bushes. A bicycle rushed past, crushing leaves under its wheels, and I thought of Fritz. I swallowed and hurried on.

Telling Mutti and Vati was the hardest thing I ever did. I don't think Mutti ever believed I would actually get the paperwork done.

27

Departure

December 1949

I departed from Berlin. That is all I can call it. I simply left. I didn't allow myself time for nostalgia as I packed and planned and looked at the pictures of Arizona over and over again that I had cut out of *Life* magazine and hung up in my room. I always kept Mrs. Vockel's card held close in my purse. Mutti planned a farewell party for me the Saturday before I left, inviting all of my friends, and I said my goodbyes gaily and quickly at the end of the night, my spirits lifted high by wine. We danced and ate and sang, and no one mentioned the purpose of the party, but when Bing Crosby crooned, *Far away places with strange-soundin' names, Far away over the sea, Those far away places with the strange-soundin' names, Are callin', callin' me*, Fritz reached over and snapped off AFN, placing a Frank Sinatra record on the stereo instead. Maria began to tear up as the evening closed, and she tried to hug me. I pushed her away quickly. "None of that! This is a time of celebration. Besides, think of me as doing reconnaissance for you. I shall tell you all about the boys in America!" She laughed, and I added brightly, "You will be right behind me. I'm sure of it!" My thoughts were focused only on the future and the freedom I believed with all my heart lay ahead for me in America.

———

"None of us are free," Vati said. "We all have chains of one sort or another that bind us. No matter where we live."

I watched him for a moment, his head bent over several volumes of Goethe, Schiller, and Hesse, trying to decide which ones to send with me—"So I didn't forget my countrymen entirely." My eyes burned into the back of his head and he looked up, the light from the lamp bouncing off his white hair. He pushed his glasses up his nose. "It's true. You may think you are free, but there is always something. Children, responsibility, things you don't want to do." He thought for a moment. "The only true freedom is inside you, from self-respect and truth."

"Truth?"

"Yes. Truth."

"What do you mean?"

"Well now, that is a question it has taken me all my life to figure out." He smiled and turned to pull a book off the shelf behind him. He handed me a stack of three books. "Here. These might help you answer that question."

I looked at the titles and nodded. I smiled back at Vati. That was Vati: mysterious, philosophical. I hadn't really believed him; I knew I would find freedom in America. And now he sat next to me on the plane, the giant propellers humming so loud it was difficult to talk. We were flying to Hamburg because Vati did not want to take the train through the Russian Zone. In Hamburg we would stay at a hotel until Vati could book me passage on the next ship leaving for America. It was good to have him with me. The departure from Mutti and Fritz had been less final with Vati still with me.

Mutti had not cried, and neither had I, until the end. We both kept our distance so that we did not fall apart. Her face a perfect mask, she grabbed my hand and pulled me to her while Vati stood waiting by the truck with Heinz. Then she pushed me away quickly; I caught only a glimmer of moisture around her eyes. "Now go. Hurry. Your father is waiting."

Fritz walked me down the steps, holding my hand.

My father called out, "Hurry up, Jutta, or we will miss our flight."

We stopped a few feet from the truck, and Fritz hugged me, lifting me off my feet as if he would never let me go. "I love you," he said, his honest eyes filling with tears. He looked up to the sky to stop them. "Don't forget me."

Don't let the tears come! Push them down! Push them down, I shouted silently to myself. The feeling rose from my stomach and climbed to my throat. No! I won't do it! Besides, Fritz will come later. This is only temporary. Yes, this is temporary. Push them down. Don't give in. There. Now you can talk.

"Of course I won't forget you! I love you!" My voice caught as I said it, and I looked up. Push it down. No. No. Please, no tears. I breathed deeply.

"And besides, you are coming to join me," I said brightly, opening my eyes wide and willing myself the strength not to cry.

He smiled at me, his eyes normal again—all the kindness of the world seemed to rest in those eyes. And I wondered if I was a fool for leaving him. But he would join me. Yes. Push it down now! Don't let it control you! He will join you, maybe in six months or a year at the most. "Six months. One year at the most, and then we will be together again," I said out loud.

"I hope so. Now go. Hurry." He pushed me away, holding my hand for a lingering moment, our arms extended.

I turned and ran to the truck without looking back, my arm raised above my head. I waved to him, the tears blurring my vision. I hopped in next to Heinz. Vati held the door, staring at the ground, tapping his foot, and then he climbed in after me. I turned to see that my two trunks were safely secured in the back of the truck. As Heinz reversed the truck down our driveway, I looked at them and waved again. Fritz had walked back to the steps and joined Mutti, his arm draped around her shoulder, a united front, defeated; they had both tried to keep me from going. The feeling started again in my stomach, just under my rib cage, and caught in my throat. I was powerless against it, and I had to look away.

I looked up at the trees, their bare branches stark against the gray sky. A single bird, black and large, flew above them. I looked again and waved. Mutti's hand under her eye told me she was crying. Fritz waved, and then he turned her slowly to the house, pivoting on one foot, bent over talking to her, only the top of his head visible. Vati coughed, and I was brought back to the inside of the truck. Heinz ground the gears, and we lurched forward. The tears spilled onto my cheeks and down my blouse. No longer able to control them, I gave in and let them come. Vati patted my leg with his hand and handed me his finely pressed handkerchief but said nothing. His face stern, he looked straight ahead as Heinz turned onto Kronprinzenallee and we headed to the airport.

The engines roared and the clink of seatbelts tickled my ears as the plane hurried to the end of the runway. I watched the warehouses that had held our survival pass by, the fumes from the engine blurring their images slightly. Vati's hands clutched the handles of the seat, the knuckles white where they curved over the edges. He had never flown in an airplane and neither had I, but I was not nervous. I had seen them fly over my city so often that it never occurred to me that there was something to worry about. The pilot's voice came on the intercom, preparing us for takeoff, and then suddenly he hit the gas. My head snapped backwards, hitting the back of the seat, but a smile escaped my lips.

I am really leaving! A chill of excitement ran across me, and my smile grew wider. I watched as the terminal at Tempelhof whizzed past, and then I felt us rise in the air. The pressure threw our stomachs against the backs of the seats. Vati had his eyes closed; his white head leaned against the back of his seat, his knuckles still white. As soon as the plane straightened out enough that I could peel my head off the back of the seat and look forward, I pressed my face against the window to look out. I drew in my breath. There below stood Berlin—my city, my Berlin, no more. A black skeleton of a city, a blackened heap of partial walls and rubble, stared back at me in silence, like the intricate sand castles I had labored over at the North Sea beaches as a child after a single wave had come and knocked the walls down, leaving only the skeleton of what was once something beautiful. From the air, there was no pretending about it. Berlin was destroyed. Flying across the ruined city, the completeness was undeniable. On the ground I was aware of one building or one block, but not like this, the awesome reality of the view before me, an entire city decimated. I shuddered, remembering the sounds of the planes, the sounds of sirens, the smells of fire and burning flesh and gasoline and of sewage lines burst open, spewing out their disease-filled insides. I was leaving a city I no longer recognized. The place I had known—my

Berlin—bore no resemblance to what stood below. It no longer existed. I turned back to Vati and did not look out again.

"I hope you will be happy in America."

I threw my arms around his neck and buried my face in his shoulder, pinpricks of doubt forming in my mind.

"I hope you will find your hopes and dreams and all the things that you long for in America."

I looked up at him. "There will be no war, no Russians," I said simply.

He nodded. The ship's horn blasted a warning for us to board, and he pushed me away. "And now you must hurry."

I walked up the ramp backwards, facing him, tears streaming down my face. And he smiling, stood straight and waved, holding one hand behind his back in that manner of his. I turned and walked quickly up to the top of the plank, with every step steeling myself not to turn and flee back down the steep plank to where he stood and beg him to tell me not to go—to tell me there was no need to go. So easy to turn back! No. You can't. Just a moment of weakness. You must see this through. I took a deep breath and turned to face the dock. I waved again to Vati from the deck of the ship.

All about me, people bustled. Sailors called to one another, and passengers crowded along the edge of the platform. He waved back and then turned slowly, his shoulders a little more slumped than before as he walked past the newly rebuilt dock silhouetted by the shattered ruins of Hamburg—stiff peaks of black and gray anchored by wood scaffolding or simply left to crumble with the weather—ugly reminders that Hitler had destroyed Vati's country, his city, and now he had taken his only daughter.

The ship's enormous horn sounded, releasing vibrations that seemed to hang on the air, suspended in time. The waves washed against the ship, forming deep ridges as it cut through the water, slowly at first, and then faster and faster. And I thought about my city, so easily washed away—changed forever. Tears fell and met the water. A gull flew over, following us out to sea. I turned quickly, wiping the tears with the back of my hand, and watched the gull fly, wings stretched wide, calling out its song, a song for all time, a song belonging to the world.